# COMMONLY USED SYMBOLS

| SYMBOL | TERM | FIRST INTRODUCED |
|--------|------|------------------|
| $Y$ | GDP | 27 |
| $C$ | Consumption | 27 |
| $I$ | Investment | 27 |
| $G$ | Government spending | 27 |
| $X$ | Net exports | 27 |
| $F$ | Government transfers | 40 |
| $T$ | Taxes | 40 |
| $V$ | Net factor payments from abroad | 40 |
| $S_p$ | Private saving | 40 |
| $S_g$ | Government saving | 40 |
| $S_r$ | Rest of world saving | 40 |
| $N$ | Employment | 63 |
| $K$ | Capital stock | 63 |
| $A$ | Technology | 64 |
| $W$ | Wage | 66 |
| $P$ | Price level | 66 |
| $N^*$ | Full employment | 69 |
| $Y^*$ | Potential GDP | 69 |
| $n$ | Labor force growth rate | 71 |
| $s$ | Net saving rate | 74 |
| $R$ | Interest rate | 109 |
| $M$ | Money demand/supply | 111 |
| $R^*$ | Equilibrium Real Interest Rate | 111 |
| $t$ | Tax rate | 154 |
| $\pi$ | Rate of inflation | 211 |
| $\pi^e$ | Expected inflation | 211 |
| $R^K$ | Rental price of capital | 304 |
| $E$ | Exchange rate | 339 |
| CU | Currency | 389 |
| $D$ | Deposits at banks | 389 |
| $B$ | Bonds | 391 |
| RE | Reserves of the Fed | 391 |
| $M_B$ | Monetary base | 391 |
| $m$ | Money multiplier | 393 |
| $\hat{Y}$ | % deviation of $Y$ from $Y^*$ | 408 |
| $U$ | Unemployment | 439 |
| $U^*$ | Natural unemployment rate | 439 |
| $Z$ | Exogenous price shock | 450 |

# MACROECONOMICS

### FIFTH EDITION

To Accompany This Text

*STUDY GUIDE, Fifth Edition*, by David H. Papell

# ECONOMICS

## FIFTH EDITION

# ROBERT E. HALL
# JOHN B. TAYLOR

W • W • NORTON & COMPANY • NEW YORK • LONDON

## To our families

The text of this book is composed in Garamond
with the display set in Leawood
Composition by University Graphics, Inc.
Manufacturing by Von Hoffman Press, Inc.
Book design by Natasha Sylvester

Library of Congress Cataloging-in-Publication Data

Hall, Robert Ernest. 1943–
    Macroeconomics / Robert E. Hall, John B. Taylor.—5th ed.
        p.   cm.
    Includes bibliographical references and index.
    **ISBN 0-393-96835-9.**
    1. Macroeconomics.   I. Taylor, John B.   II. Title.   III. Title:
Macro economics.
HB172.5.H35   1996
339—DC20                                                96-31305

W. W. Norton & Company, Inc., 500 Fifth Avenue, New York, N.Y. 10110
http://www.wwnorton.com

W. W. Norton & Company Ltd., 10 Coptic Street, London WC1A 1PU
    3 4 5 6 7 8 9 0

# Contents

Preface    xvii

**PART**

# INTRODUCTION

**CHAPTER 1**

## Economic Growth and Fluctuations                                                    3

1.1   Macroeconomics and Its Uses                                                       4
1.2   Recent Macroeconomic Performance                                                  6
      EMPLOYMENT 9    INFLATION 10    INTEREST RATES 11
1.3   Explaining Economic Growth and Fluctuations: A Preview                            14
      THE MODEL OF LONG-RUN GROWTH 14
      Growth Rates   15
      THE MODEL OF FLUCTUATIONS 16
1.4   Currents of Thought in Macroeconomics                                             17
      How Did Today's Macroeconomists Come to Study
      Economics?   19
1.5   The Macroeconomic Model Used in This Book                                         20
Review and Practice                                                                     21
      MAJOR POINTS 21    KEY TERMS AND CONCEPTS 21
      QUESTIONS FOR DISCUSSION AND REVIEW 21    PROBLEMS 22
      MACROSOLVE EXERCISES 24

**CHAPTER 2**

## Measuring Economic Performance                                                      25

2.1   Gross Domestic Product                                                            25
2.2   Measuring GDP through Spending                                                    26
      CONSUMPTION 27    INVESTMENT 27    GOVERNMENT
      PURCHASES 29    IMPORTS AND EXPORTS 29    THE RECENT
      COMPOSITION OF SPENDING 30
      Bringing Astronomical Numbers Down to Earth   31
      WHICH SPENDING ITEMS SHOULD BE INCLUDED? 31
      REAL GDP 32
      Chain-Weighted GDP   33
2.3   Measuring GDP through Production: Value Added                                     34
2.4   Measuring GDP through Income                                                      36
2.5   Saving and Investment                                                            39
      SAVING AND INVESTMENT IN AN OPEN ECONOMY 40
2.6   Transactions with the Rest of the World: The Balance of
      Payments Accounts and the Exchange Rate                                          43
      THE EXCHANGE RATE 44

2.7   Measuring Inflation                                                        46
        PRICE INDEXES 46     DEFLATORS 48
2.8   Measuring Employment and Wages                                           49
        HOURS PER WEEK AND TOTAL HOURS 50
Review and Practice                                                            51
        MAJOR POINTS 51     KEY TERMS AND CONCEPTS 52
        QUESTIONS FOR DISCUSSION AND REVIEW 52     PROBLEMS 53
        MACROSOLVE EXERCISES 58

PART

**LONG-RUN FUNDAMENTALS**

CHAPTER
3

Economic Growth                                                               61

3.1   The Determinants of Economic Growth                                      62
        LABOR 62     CAPITAL 63     TECHNOLOGY 63
        THE PRODUCTION FUNCTION 64
3.2   Full Employment and Potential GDP                                        65
        THE DEMAND FOR LABOR 66     THE SUPPLY OF LABOR 66
        FULL EMPLOYMENT 68     POTENTIAL GDP 69
3.3   The Solow Growth Model                                                   70
        SAVING AND BALANCED GROWTH 71     THE EFFECT OF SAVING
        ON GROWTH 74
3.4   The Growth Accounting Formula                                           75
        NEW RESEARCH IN PRACTICE Convergence or Dispersion of
        Per Capita Income Around the World?   76
        HISTORICAL GROWTH ACCOUNTING 78     EXOGENOUS
        TECHNOLOGICAL CHANGE 78
3.5   Endogenous Growth Theory                                                80
        A PRODUCTION FUNCTION FOR TECHNOLOGY 80     INCREASING
        THE LONG-RUN GROWTH RATE 82
3.6   Policies to Stimulate Growth                                            84
        NEW RESEARCH IN PRACTICE Endogenous Growth Theory
        and International Trade Liberalization   85
        POLICIES TO IMPROVE TECHNOLOGICAL GROWTH AND
        PRODUCTIVITY 86
        POLICIES TO STIMULATE CAPITAL FORMATION 87     POLICIES TO
        INCREASE LABOR SUPPLY 88
3.7   Wages and the Labor Productivity Slowdown                               90
        THE LABOR PRODUCTIVITY SLOWDOWN 91

Review and Practice　　　　　　　　　　　　　　　　　　　93
　　MAJOR POINTS 93　　KEY TERMS AND CONCEPTS 94
　　QUESTIONS FOR DISCUSSION AND REVIEW 94　　PROBLEMS 95
　　MACROSOLVE EXERCISES 96
Appendix: Deriving the Growth Formula　　　　　　　　97

**CHAPTER**
**4**

## Fiscal and Monetary Policy in the Growth Model　　98

4.1　How Fiscal and Monetary Policy Affect Real GDP in the Long
　　　Run　　　　　　　　　　　　　　　　　　　　　　99
4.2　How Fiscal Policy Affects the Shares of Output　　　101
　　　INTEREST-RATE SENSITIVITY OF CONSUMPTION, INVESTMENT,
　　　AND NET EXPORTS 102　　GOVERNMENT PURCHASES 103
　　　THE BUDGET DEFICIT AND THE TRADE DEFICIT 104
　　　OTHER FISCAL POLICY CHANGES 104
　　　**NEW RESEARCH IN PRACTICE** How Should We Divide
　　　$8 Trillion in GDP?　106
　　　IMPORTANCE OF THE LONG-RUN ASSUMPTION 107
　　　**NEW RESEARCH IN PRACTICE** International Policy
　　　Coordination　108
4.3　Money and Inflation　　　　　　　　　　　　　　109
　　　THE DEMAND FOR MONEY 109　　THE SUPPLY OF MONEY 112
　　　EQUILIBRIUM IN THE MONEY MARKET 112　　INFLATION 114
4.4　Summary: The Classical Dichotomy　　　　　　　115
Review and Practice　　　　　　　　　　　　　　　　116
　　MAJOR POINTS 116　　KEY TERMS AND CONCEPTS 116
　　QUESTIONS FOR DISCUSSION AND REVIEW 117　　PROBLEMS 117
　　MACROSOLVE EXERCISES 119

**CHAPTER**
**5**

## Unemployment, Job Creation, and Job Destruction　　120

5.1　Measuring Unemployment　　　　　　　　　　121
5.2　Flows into and out of Unemployment　　　　　　123
　　　FLOWS INTO UNEMPLOYMENT 123　　FLOWS OUT OF
　　　UNEMPLOYMENT 124
5.3　The Natural Unemployment Rate　　　　　　　127
　　　DOES THE NATURAL RATE CHANGE OVER TIME? 130
5.4　Unemployment in Recessions and Booms　　　　130
　　　CHANGES IN THE UNEMPLOYMENT FLOWS 132　　OKUN'S LAW 134
5.5　Analysis of Unemployment in the Framework of Supply and
　　　Demand　　　　　　　　　　　　　　　　　134
　　　**NEW RESEARCH IN PRACTICE** A Silver Lining to the Storm
　　　Clouds of Recession?　136

Review and Practice                                                                          139
    MAJOR POINTS 139    KEY TERMS AND CONCEPTS 139
    QUESTIONS FOR DISCUSSION AND REVIEW 139    PROBLEMS 140
    MACROSOLVE EXERCISES 141

**PART**

**3**

# ECONOMIC FLUCTUATIONS

**CHAPTER**
**6**

## Short-Run Fluctuations                                                                 145

6.1    Forces that Push the Economy off Its Growth Path                          146
6.2    Aggregate Demand and the Spending Decision                               149
    THE UNRESPONSIVENESS OF THE PRICE LEVEL 150    AN EXAMPLE:
    GENERAL MOTORS 150
6.3    The Point of Balance of Income and Spending                               151
    THE INCOME IDENTITY 152    THE CONSUMPTION FUNCTION 152
    GRAPHICAL ANALYSIS OF SPENDING BALANCE 155    ALGEBRAIC
    SOLUTION 157
    Graphs, Slopes, and Intercepts versus Algebra and
    Coefficients    158
    HOW SPENDING BALANCE IS MAINTAINED 159    THE
    MULTIPLIER 160    SPENDING BALANCE WHEN NET EXPORTS
    DEPEND ON INCOME 165
    The Decline of the Multiplier    167
Review and Practice                                                                          168
    MAJOR POINTS 168    KEY TERMS AND CONCEPTS 169
    QUESTIONS FOR DISCUSSION AND REVIEW 169    PROBLEMS 169
    MACROSOLVE EXERCISES 172

**CHAPTER**
**7**

## Financial Markets and Aggregate Demand                                                  173

7.1    Investment and the Interest Rate                                          173
    THE INVESTMENT DEMAND FUNCTION 174    THE MEANING AND
    INTERPRETATION OF $R$ 175
7.2    Net Exports and the Interest Rate                                         176
7.3    The IS Curve and the LM Curve                                             177
    THE IS CURVE 179
    **NEW RESEARCH IN PRACTICE** The Stock Market    180
    THE LM CURVE 183    ALGEBRAIC DERIVATION OF THE IS AND LM
    CURVES 186    FINDING INCOME $Y$ AND THE INTEREST RATE $R$ 188
7.4    Policy Analysis with IS-LM                                                189
    MONETARY POLICY 189    FISCAL POLICY 190

IS-LM in the Business Pages   191
THE RELATIVE EFFECTIVENESS OF MONETARY AND FISCAL
POLICIES 192     THE IS-LM INTERPRETATION 193

7.5   Deriving the Aggregate Demand Curve                                        196
MONETARY AND FISCAL POLICIES 198

Review and Practice                                                             199
MAJOR POINTS 199     KEY TERMS AND CONCEPTS 200
QUESTIONS FOR DISCUSSION AND REVIEW 200     PROBLEMS 200
MACROSOLVE EXERCISES 202

CHAPTER
8         The Adjustment Process                                                 205

8.1   Price Stickiness and the Determination of Output and
      Unemployment in the Short Run                                             205
DETERMINATION OF OUTPUT 206     DETERMINATION OF
UNEMPLOYMENT 208

8.2   Price Adjustment                                                         210
WHAT DETERMINES EXPECTED INFLATION? 214

8.3   Combining Aggregate Demand and Price Adjustment                          215
RESPONSE TO MONETARY STIMULUS 215     RESPONSE TO FISCAL
STIMULUS 218
NEW RESEARCH IN PRACTICE The Other Complete
Model   220
ALGEBRAIC DERIVATION 221

Review and Practice                                                             222
MAJOR POINTS 222     KEY TERMS AND CONCEPTS 222
QUESTIONS FOR DISCUSSION AND REVIEW 222     PROBLEMS 223
MACROSOLVE EXERCISES 225

CHAPTER
9         Macroeconomic Policy                                                  227

9.1   Shocks and Disturbances to the Economy                                   228
SHOCKS TO AGGREGATE DEMAND 228     ANALYZING THE EFFECTS
OF AGGREGATE DEMAND SHOCKS 228     SHOCKS TO THE PRICE
LEVEL 231
Model Validation: Four Oil-Price Shocks   233

9.2   Responding to Aggregate Demand Shocks: Stabilization
      Policy                                                                    233
WHEN DO MACROECONOMISTS DISAGREE ABOUT STABILIZATION
POLICY? 235

9.3   Responding to Price Shocks                                                237
Okun Gaps and Harberger Triangles   240

9.4   Monetary Policy Rules                                                     240
9.5   Setting Monetary Policy to Hit a Target Level of GDP                      241

9.6  Disinflation                                                                              243
     ALTERNATIVE DISINFLATION PATHS 243
     Other Schools of Thought on Disinflation   246
Review and Practice                                                                            247
     MAJOR POINTS 247    KEY TERMS AND CONCEPTS 248
     QUESTIONS FOR DISCUSSION AND REVIEW 248    PROBLEMS 248
     MACROSOLVE EXERCISES 252

PART

**4**

# MICROFOUNDATIONS OF MACROECONOMICS

CHAPTER
**10**

## Consumption Demand                                                                          257

10.1  Fluctuations in GDP, Consumption, and Income                                             258
      GDP AND PERSONAL DISPOSABLE INCOME 260    THE RELATION
      BETWEEN REAL DISPOSABLE INCOME AND CONSUMPTION 262
10.2  Defects in the Simple Keynesian Consumption Function                                     263
      THE EFFECT OF CONSUMPTION ERRORS ON FORECASTING AND
      POLICY 265    SHORT-RUN VERSUS LONG-RUN MARGINAL
      PROPENSITY TO CONSUME 265
10.3  The Forward-Looking Theory of Consumption                                                268
      THE INTERTEMPORAL BUDGET CONSTRAINT 269    PREFERENCES:
      STEADY RATHER THAN ERRATIC CONSUMPTION 271
      PREFERENCES: HOW LARGE AN INHERITANCE FOR THE NEXT
      GENERATION? 271    THE MARGINAL PROPENSITY TO CONSUME
      OUT OF TEMPORARY VERSUS PERMANENT CHANGES IN INCOME 273
      ANTICIPATED VERSUS UNANTICIPATED CHANGES IN INCOME 275
10.4  How Well Does the Forward-Looking Theory Work?                                           276
      THE SHORT-RUN AND LONG-RUN MPC: A ROUGH CHECK OF THE
      THEORY 277
      Why Is the Saving Rate Higher in Japan Than in the United
      States?   278
      ANDO AND MODIGLIANI: DO ASSETS MATTER FOR
      CONSUMPTION? 279    FRIEDMAN: DOES PAST INCOME MATTER FOR
      CONSUMPTION? 279    WHERE DO WE STAND NOW? 280
      DEFECTS IN THE FORWARD-LOOKING MODEL 283
      **NEW RESEARCH IN PRACTICE** Locked-Up Savings   284
10.5  Real Interest Rates, Consumption, and Saving                                             286
      EFFECT OF REAL INTEREST RATES ON WORK 287
10.6  Consumption and the IS Curve                                                             288
      THE SLOPE OF THE IS CURVE 288    SHIFTS IN THE IS CURVE DUE
      TO TAX CHANGES 289

Review and Practice                                                                289
MAJOR POINTS 289    KEY TERMS AND CONCEPTS 290
QUESTIONS FOR DISCUSSION AND REVIEW 290    PROBLEMS 291
MACROSOLVE EXERCISES 294
Appendix: A Graphical Approach to Consumption Planning              295

**CHAPTER**
**11**   Investment Demand                                                        298

11.1    Fluctuations in Investment Spending                                   299
11.2    How Firms Make Investment Decisions                              302
DETERMINATION OF THE RENTAL PRICE OF CAPITAL 306    THE
RENTAL PRICE AND THE DECISION TO BUY NEW CAPITAL
GOODS 307    EXPECTED CHANGES IN THE FUTURE PRICE OF
CAPITAL 308
11.3    The Investment Function                                               309
DEPRECIATION AND GROSS INVESTMENT 311    LAGS IN THE
INVESTMENT PROCESS 312    THE AGGREGATE INVESTMENT
DEMAND FUNCTION 313
11.4    Taxes and Investment                                                  313
PERMANENT TAX CHANGES 314    ANTICIPATED TAX CHANGES 315
NEW RESEARCH IN PRACTICE The Effect of Tax Policy on
Investment    316
11.5    Residential Investment                                               317
HOUSING INVESTMENT AND MONETARY POLICY 319
11.6    Inventory Investment                                                 319
11.7    The Investment Function and the IS Curve                        322
Review and Practice                                                        323
MAJOR POINTS 323    KEY TERMS AND CONCEPTS 324
QUESTIONS FOR DISCUSSION AND REVIEW 324    PROBLEMS 325
MACROSOLVE EXERCISES 329
Appendix A: Capital Budgeting and the Rental Price of Capital        330
Appendix B: Tobin's $q$ and the Rental Price of Capital              332

**CHAPTER**
**12**   Foreign Trade and the Exchange Rate                              335

12.1    Foreign Trade and Aggregate Demand                             337
12.2    The Exchange Rate                                                  338
THE EXCHANGE RATE AND RELATIVE PRICES 340
12.3    The Determinants of Net Exports                                 342
THE EFFECT OF THE EXCHANGE RATE 342    THE EFFECT OF
INCOME 343    THE NET EXPORT FUNCTION 343
12.4    A Model of the Real Exchange Rate                              345

12.5    The IS Curve and Economic Policy in an Open Economy            347
        ALGEBRAIC DERIVATION OF THE OPEN-ECONOMY IS CURVE  348
        EFFECTS OF MONETARY AND FISCAL POLICY ON TRADE IN THE
        SHORT RUN  349      PRICE ADJUSTMENT  349
12.6    The Exchange Rate and the Price Level                          350
12.7    Protectionism versus Free Trade                               352
        MACROECONOMIC EFFECTS OF PROTECTIONISM  352
12.8    Stabilizing the Exchange Rate                                 353
Review and Practice                                                   356
        MAJOR POINTS  356      KEY TERMS AND CONCEPTS  357
        QUESTIONS FOR DISCUSSION AND REVIEW  357      PROBLEMS  358
        MACROSOLVE EXERCISES  360

**CHAPTER**
**13**

## Spending, Taxes, and the Budget Deficit            362

13.1    Government Budgets                                            363
        THE FEDERAL GOVERNMENT BUDGET AND DEFICIT  363      STATE
        AND LOCAL GOVERNMENT BUDGETS  364
13.2    Fluctuations in the Deficit: Purchases, Transfers, and Taxes   366
13.3    The Effects of the Government Deficit                         371
        CYCLICAL VERSUS STRUCTURAL DEFICITS  371      HAVE DEFICITS
        BEEN RELATED TO INTEREST RATES IN RECENT U.S. HISTORY?  372
        THE DEFICIT AND THE EXPLOSION OF GOVERNMENT DEBT  374
        ECONOMIC SIGNIFICANCE OF THE NATIONAL DEBT  376
13.4    The Government and the IS Curve                               378
Review and Practice                                                   379
        MAJOR POINTS  379      KEY TERMS AND CONCEPTS  380
        QUESTIONS FOR DISCUSSION AND REVIEW  380      PROBLEMS  380
        MACROSOLVE EXERCISES  385

**CHAPTER**
**14**

## The Monetary System and the Fed's Policy Rule         386

14.1    Elements of a Monetary System                                387
14.2    How the Fed Controls the Money Supply                        389
        EXCESS RESERVES AND BORROWED RESERVES  393
        DISTINGUISHING BETWEEN MONETARY AND FISCAL POLICIES  394
        Financing Government through the Printing Press   394
14.3    The Demand for Money: Currency and Checking Deposits          396
        WHAT ARE THE OPPORTUNITY COSTS OF HOLDING FUNDS AS
        MONEY?  396      THE TRANSACTIONS DEMAND FOR MONEY: AN
        INVENTORY THEORY  397      THE DEMAND FOR MONEY AS A STORE
        OF WEALTH  400      RECENT TRENDS IN CURRENCY AND
        DEPOSITS  400      THE DEMAND FUNCTION FOR MONEY  402

14.4  The Monetary Policy Rule                                                     404
    SETTING INTEREST RATES OR MONEY GROWTH 404    REACTING TO
    EVENTS IN THE ECONOMY 408
14.5  Interaction between Monetary and Fiscal Policy                   410
14.6  Lags in the Effect of Monetary Policy                              413
NEW RESEARCH IN PRACTICE The Depression of the 1990s in Japan  414
Review and Practice                                                         415
    MAJOR POINTS 415    KEY TERMS AND CONCEPTS 416
    QUESTIONS FOR DISCUSSION AND REVIEW 416    PROBLEMS 417
    MACROSOLVE EXERCISES 420

**CHAPTER**
**15**

## The Microeconomic Foundations of Price Rigidity      421

15.1  The Imperfect Information Theory                                   422
    DERIVATION OF THE LUCAS SUPPLY CURVE 423    THE APPEARANCE
    OF PRICE RIGIDITY 426    POLICY INEFFECTIVENESS THEOREM 427
    CRITIQUE OF IMPERFECT INFORMATION THEORY 428
15.2  Sticky Prices and Nominal Wage Contracts                       429
    STICKY PRICES 430    STICKY NOMINAL WAGES 431    THE
    RELATION OF WAGE STICKINESS TO PRICE STICKINESS 432    WAGE
    DETERMINATION IN THE UNITED STATES 433    WHY ARE WAGES
    SET FOR LONG PERIODS WITH FEW CONTINGENCIES? 435    WHY IS
    WAGE SETTING STAGGERED? 437
15.3  A Model with Staggered Wage-Setting                            438
Review and Practice                                                         441
    MAJOR POINTS 441    KEY TERMS AND CONCEPTS 442
    QUESTIONS FOR DISCUSSION AND REVIEW 442    PROBLEMS 443
    MACROSOLVE EXERCISES 446

**PART**
**5**

# MACROECONOMIC POLICY

**CHAPTER**
**16**

## Inflation and Output Fluctuations                          449

16.1  Price Adjustment                                                        449
    THE EFFECT OF WAGE INDEXING 451    LENGTH AND SEVERITY OF
    BUSINESS CYCLES 452    MODELS OF THE EXPECTED INFLATION
    TERM 452    A GRAPHICAL REPRESENTATION OF PRICE
    ADJUSTMENT 454
16.2  Summarizing the IS Curve                                           455

16.3    Combining Price Adjustment with Aggregate Demand                    457
        EXAMPLE 1: A BOOM 460    EXAMPLE 2: DISINFLATION 461
        EXAMPLES 1 AND 2 COMBINED: A BOOM FOLLOWED BY A
        DISINFLATION 462    EXAMPLE 3: AN OIL PRICE SHOCK 463
16.4    Experience with Inflation and Output in the United States           464
Review and Practice                                                        465
        MAJOR POINTS 465    KEY TERMS AND CONCEPTS 466
        QUESTIONS FOR DISCUSSION AND REVIEW 466    PROBLEMS 466
        MACROSOLVE EXERCISES 468

CHAPTER
17      Designing and Maintaining a Good Macro Policy                      469

17.1    General Principles of Macro Policy Analysis                         469
17.2    Instruments, Targets, and Uncertainty                              475
        UNCERTAINTY AND TIMING CONSIDERATIONS 476
17.3    The Benefits of Full Employment and Price Stability                477
        WHY IS INFLATION UNDESIRABLE? 479    COSTS OF OUTPUT LOSS
        AND UNEMPLOYMENT 481
17.4    The Policy Trade-off between Inflation and Output
        Fluctuations                                                       483
        What Would an Optimal Policy Have Been in
        1979 to 1995?    488
        FINDING AN OPTIMAL POLICY 489    THE MESSAGE FOR
        POLICYMAKERS 490    NOMINAL GDP TARGETING: A REASONABLE
        WAY TO EXPRESS POLICY? 491
        NEW RESEARCH IN PRACTICE Why We Should Appoint a
        Central Banker Tougher than Ourselves on
        Inflation    492
17.5    Changing the Policy Frontier                                       493
        STREAMLINE THE LABOR MARKET 494    IMPROVE INDEXATION 495
        AVOID GOVERNMENT PRICE SHOCKS 495
        NEW RESEARCH IN PRACTICE International Evidence on
        Inflation and Economic Growth    496
        USE TRADE POLICY 497
Review and Practice                                                        498
        MAJOR POINTS 498    KEY TERMS AND CONCEPTS 498
        QUESTIONS FOR DISCUSSION AND REVIEW 499    PROBLEMS 499
        MACROSOLVE EXERCISES 502

CHAPTER
18      The World Economy                                                 504

18.1    The International Financial and Monetary System                    505
        HOW A CENTRAL BANK CARRIES OUT ITS EXCHANGE-RATE
        POLICY 507    STERILIZED INTERVENTION 509    CAPITAL OR
        EXCHANGE CONTROLS 509

18.2    History of the World Financial and Monetary System                    510
        THE DEVALUATION OF THE DOLLAR AND THE COLLAPSE OF BRETTON
        WOODS 512    EXCHANGE-RATE POLICIES TODAY 513
18.3    Macroeconomic Policy, Exchange Rates, and Inflation                    514
        POLICY WITH FLOATING RATES 514    POLICY WITH A FIXED
        EXCHANGE RATE 515    ANALYSIS OF FIXED- AND FLOATING-RATE
        POLICIES 516    WORLD INFLATION WITH FLOATING EXCHANGE
        RATES 517
18.4    International Macro Policy Coordination                                519
18.5    Monetary Union                                                        520
        NEW RESEARCH IN PRACTICE Does Western Europe Need a
        Central Bank?    522
Review and Practice                                                           524
        MAJOR POINTS 524    KEY TERMS AND CONCEPTS 525
        QUESTIONS FOR DISCUSSION AND REVIEW 525    PROBLEMS 526
        MACROSOLVE EXERCISES 528

Glossary    A1

Index    A19

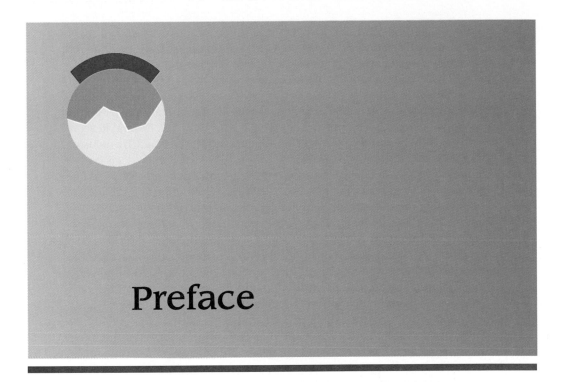

# Preface

As economic theory, facts, and policies change, so must economics textbooks. In this fifth edition, we have incorporated key new developments in
macroeconomics while keeping to the basic goal of our first edition: to capture the spirit and content of modern macroeconomics in a form that is man-
ageable at the intermediate level. Moreover, by consolidating material and
streamlining the exposition, we have shortened the book as we have mod-
ernized it.

Students and faculty have expressed enthusiasm for the book's strong
emphasis on long-term economic growth, which we first achieved in the
third edition by putting the growth chapters before the economic fluctuations
chapters. This desire for greater emphasis on economic growth reflects
changes in the field of macroeconomics and changes in the real world, as
the problem of slow growth has proved to be more and more persistent. In
this fifth edition we expand the coverage of economic growth in two ways:
first, we provide a more solid underpinning of the Solow growth model, and
second, we provide a complete explanation of a new, exciting area of growth
theory—the endogenous growth model.

The problem of unemployment has also received renewed attention in
macroeconomics in the 1990s, as corporate downsizings or the short-term
impacts of international trade have concerned both the public and policy-

makers. High long-term unemployment and low productivity growth have been of particular concern in recent years. For this reason we have added an entirely new chapter on unemployment and labor market dynamics, where the fascinating process of job creation and job destruction is explored.

Changes in the way that monetary policy is conducted have given us the opportunity to streamline greatly the analysis of monetary policy and to place greater emphasis on policy rules. During the 1990s the Federal Reserve Board and other central banks have conducted monetary policy by focusing directly on the short-term interest rate when they make their decisions. A completely rewritten chapter on monetary policy integrates the interest rate setting behavior of central banks into the complete model using the idea of a policy rule, thereby greatly simplifying the analysis of business cycle dynamics. Other areas where the book is streamlined are national income accounting and wage-price dynamics.

Weaving up-to-date, real-world policy examples into the text has proven to be a useful pedagogical feature which we have tried to preserve in each writing. In preparing this fifth edition, we reviewed all of these examples, and where we felt we could enhance readers' interest, we replaced the examples with recent events. We have also expanded our series of essays—placed at appropriate locations throughout the book—that highlight how new research has been used in practice. We portray how successful, or unsuccessful, each application has been. In highlighting applications of new research, we do not mean to denigrate old research. Indeed, much early macroeconomic research is more important than ever. It is fully embedded in the basic model used in the book.

Economic fluctuations—recessions and booms—continue to be a key theme of the book. Recessions cause serious hardship and economic loss. We continue to view them, however, as temporary departures of the economy from its full-employment long-run growth path.

We take the view that many types of shocks are responsible for departures of the economy from its long-run path. These include changes in monetary and fiscal policies, as well as sudden increases in world oil prices, a factor that was of great importance in the 1990 recession and its two direct predecessors. They also include technological shocks, which have been featured in real business cycle research as a major source of economic fluctuations.

In our view full employment is not restored immediately after a shock because the economy adjusts slowly, a sluggishness primarily due to price and wage rigidity. We study rigidities within an overall framework in which expectations and other features of people's behavior are basically rational, and we provide a microeconomic account of the way in which price and wage rigidities delay the return to full employment.

Changes in the instruments of monetary and fiscal policies have powerful effects in this kind of model. We see ourselves as part of a newly evolving consensus that recognizes the value of clearly stated, credible, and systematic monetary and fiscal policies. We examine how such policies should be designed and implemented.

As in the earlier editions, we begin by developing a *complete* macroeconomic model. The model focuses on three major ideas: the fundamental determinants of output in the long run, the determination of output and employment in the short run through the aggregate demand curve and the predetermined price, and the process of price adjustment that takes the economy back to the long-run growth path after a shock causes a recession or boom.

We then go on to provide a systematic treatment of the microfoundations of aggregate demand. Consumption, investment, imports, exports, government spending, taxes, and the monetary system are studied in detail, as are the microfoundations of price and wage setting. Finally, we look in detail at the design and implementation of monetary and fiscal policies using the fully embellished model with wage and price rigidities and rational expections, both in a national and an international setting.

## Distinctive Features at a Glance

A number of important features have made this book work well in the classroom:

- Consistent development of a *complete working macro model,* with short-run fluctuations, price adjustment, and long-run growth.
- Thorough examination of how macroeconomics is used in *practical policy applications.*
- Consistent *numerical values* of the coefficients of the complete model to give a sense of the magnitudes involved and provide a bridge between the text and the end-of-chapter problems.
- *Computer software* that displays the same complete model and permits many kinds of experiments with the model.
- Discussion of the *determinants of long-run growth* before describing fluctuations around the growth path.
- Treating the *price level as a predetermined variable* when explaining short-run departures of the economy from its growth path.
- Considering the United States as an *open economy* throughout the book, rather than adding trade and exchange rates late in the book.
- Attention to the *microeconomic foundations* of all subjects discussed.
- Careful exposition of the *empirical regularities* of the U.S. economy at the start of each chapter on microfoundations.

## Summary of Pedagogical Features

Teachers and students who have used the text have found many pedagogical features that enhance the student's understanding of the material. Here is how those features work:

- *Summary boxes.* Key ideas are drawn together at appropriate places within each chapter. The boxes serve a reinforcing function by allowing readers to check their understanding of one aspect of the analysis before tackling new material. And they also serve a review function; they help readers locate the building blocks of the analysis without reading entire chapters.
- *Topic boxes.* Special concepts that are related to the discussion in the text are introduced. These include computing growth rates, quarterly gross domestic product statistics, budget projects, indexing taxes, and the relationship between graphs and algebra. The boxes also present discussion of historical examples, current policy issues, and other illustrations of points in the text.
- *Problems and policy simulations.* At the end of each chapter there are questions for review and three types of problems: numerical, analytical, and computer simulation exercises to be used with the *MacroSolve* program. The numerical problems require the use of a hand calculator and usually take some time. We have found these useful for special projects. The analytical questions can be done with graphs or simple algebra. We have found much enthusiasm for putting *MacroSolve* exercises in the text in the third edition. In this fourth edition we have made the computer problems more interesting by simulating decisions facing policymakers in a practical setting.
- *References.* We have tried to keep footnotes to a minimum. Footnotes are used mainly to document a specific statement or reference in the text.
- *Parallel graphical and algebraic presentation.* In most cases arguments are presented in both graphical and algebraic form. We have found that some students learn better with graphs and some learn better with algebra, especially if the algebra is presented in a way that does not intimidate. Graphical arguments are not necessarily easier for all students, and the algebra is provided to help those with a preference for algebra. Of course, graphical presentation usually helps with the intuition, and we expect even the less graphically inclined students to learn basic diagrams. A special effort has been made to demonstrate that graphs and algebra are just two ways to describe the same economic concepts.
- *Multicolor figures.* All diagrams and charts of data are now shown with several colors to highlight different ideas. Shifting curves are easier to visualize with these colors. Micro relationships are generally given special colors to distinguish them from macro relationships.
- *Policy essays: New Research in Practice.* In order to highlight how new research is used in practice, a series of policy essays have been placed at appropriate spots throughout the text.
- *Real-world examples.* Seeing how economic theory works in practice is the best way to learn. Too often, however, these lessons of experience are placed at some distance from the analysis, with the result that students

often sense that a barrier exists between macroeconomic models and the real world from which they are drawn. We have chosen to make the performance of the economy an integral aspect of the exposition, with new concepts constantly illuminated by examples.

- *Teaching supplements.* An excellent *Study Guide* prepared by David H. Papell of the University of Houston is available for student purchase. The *Instructor's Manual* has been revised by David Gillette of Truman State University and we have prepared an extensive set of teaching suggestions; both may be found on the publisher's site on the World Wide Web (http:\\www.wwnorton.com). The Web page includes many teaching "tricks" to prompt students to become actively involved in the subject. These include macro-forecasting contests, policy projects on Federal Reserve monetary targeting and federal budget projections, debate formats for lectures, classroom skits to illustrate the forward-looking theory of consumption and other models, and formats for class participation in financial decision making. The printed *Instructor's Manual* includes a *Test-Item File* of roughly 800 questions, which is available in electronic format with the publisher's test-making program, *Norton TestMaker.* The publisher also provides an easy-to-use multimedia display program, *Norton Presentation Maker.* This powerful CD-ROM program contains all the art from the text and a copy of MacroSolve for display in class.
- *Highly regarded computer software.* The MacroSolve package, now available in a new Windows format, embodies the IS-LM and price-adjustment equations developed in the text. This innovative software has received rave reviews from students and teachers and is now included with each copy of the text.
- *Data sources.* Whenever possible the data in charts and tables are taken from the most recently available *Economic Report of the President.* This makes it easy for students and instructors to explore the data in more detail.

## A Guided Tour

The book starts with a short course in macroeconomic analysis in the first three parts. All the major topics are covered. In Part I we introduce the basic macroeconomic facts to be explained. We also discuss macroeconomic measurement, including the new "chain-weighted" GDP, which is now the main measure of real output in the national income and product accounts. In Part II we explain the long-run growth model and the determination of the natural rate of unemployment. A graphical analysis of the determination of the investment and other shares of GDP is used to show the long-run effects of fiscal and monetary policy.

Then in Part III we delve into the reasons for the departures of the economy from its long-run growth path. We use the aggregate demand curve to explain the determination of output in the short run when the price level is predetermined. Our approach to aggregate demand uses the IS-LM apparatus.

The path to full employment is governed by the price-adjustment process. Our analysis shuttles back and forth from price adjustment to output determination. Once the price level has adjusted, output is found at the point of the new price level on the aggregate demand curve. We do not drop the predetermined-price assumption when we trace the economy's move to its long-run path. IS-LM remains our theory of output determination in each period of the dynamic analysis.

The expositional simplification we achieve in this way is enormous. We do not feel that the empirical evidence justifies the complexity of simultaneous determination of prices and output in each period. There is certainly no contradiction to the predetermined-price assumption if the period is a quarter of a year, and the assumption is valid as a close approximation if the period is a full year.

The adaptation of price adjustment to inflation ranks high among the ideas that have evolved in macroeconomics over the past two decades. We avoid characterizing this adaptation solely as a matter of changing expectations. Even with rational expectations, price adjustment depends partly on recent inflation experience, since contracts and other rigidities prevent quick adjustments. We discuss how the adaptation of expectations to inflation depends on how prices and wages are set.

After the short course in macroeconomic analysis, we go on to develop the micro foundations of aggregate demand in Part IV. At the start of each chapter we present the key facts or puzzles that need to be explained. At the end of each chapter we look at the implications for the complete macro model. The consumption chapter (10) develops a forward-looking theory of consumption based on the life-cycle and permanent-income formulations, emphasizing the role of rational expectations. By establishing an intertemporal budget constraint, we avoid present discounted values and forbidding summations. Chapter 11, on investment, focuses on Dale Jorgensen's model. The foreign trade chapter (12) focuses on flexible exchange rates, with a rational expectations model of the exchange rate as its centerpiece. Chapter 13, on government, presents material on the deficit and government debt alongside a standard treatment of automatic stabilizers and related subjects. When the intertemporal budget constraint for the government is presented, the idea is already familiar to the student from consumption and investment. Chapter 14, on the monetary system, takes up money demand and describes the role of the Federal Reserve in determining the short-run interest rate. We emphasize the determinants of the Fed's decisions using a policy rate.

Chapter 15 considers market-clearing or equilibrium views of price rigidity, including Robert Lucas's imperfect information model of aggregate supply. Chapter 15 also considers alternative views that emphasize wage contracts or sticky prices.

Part V pulls the analysis together into a comprehensive treatment of macroeconomic policy evaluation. Chapter 16 integrates the monetary policy rule into the model. Chapter 17 takes up general policy issues such as time inconsistency, multiplier uncertainty, targets and instruments, and the rational expectations critique of policy evaluation. The inflation/unemployment trade-off appears as a policy frontier between output stability and price stability. Chapter 18 then considers macroeconomic policy in the world economy, including a review of how the international monetary system evolved from Bretton Woods and how policy works in countries with fixed exchange rates.

## Acknowledgments

We thank the students, teaching assistants, and instructors in numerous sections of intermediate macro at Stanford for their many helpful comments and corrections throughout the development of this book. We are also deeply grateful to the many teachers and students at other universities who wrote to us with comments on earlier editions. The book is immeasurably better than it would have been without their feedback. In particular, we would like to single out the following: Francis Ahking, University of Connecticut; Ugur Aker, Hiram College; Robert Barry, College of William and Mary; Dan Ben-David, University of Houston; Ernst Berndt, Massachusetts Institute of Technology; Olivier Blanchard, Massachusetts Institute of Technology; Dwight M. Blood, Brigham Young University; Ronald Bodkin, University of Ottawa; Robert K. Brown, Texas Tech University; Norman G. Clifford, University of Kansas; Gregory Crawford, Stanford University; Betty Daniel, SUNY-Albany; Wilfred J. Ethier, University of Pennsylvania; George Evans, London School of Economics; Craig Furfine, Stanford University; Rajendra Gangadean, Stanford University; David Gillette, Truman State University; Frederick Goddard, University of Florida; Peter Gomori, St. Francis College (New York); Rae-Joan B. Goodman, U.S. Naval Academy; Harvey Gram, City University of New York; Howard Gruenspecht, Carnegie-Mellon University; Joseph Guerin, St. Joseph's University; John Haltiwanger, University of Maryland; James Hamilton, University of Virginia; Daniel Himarios, University of Texas at Arlington; Brad Humphreys, University of Maryland; Takatoshi Ito, University of Minnesota; Charles I. Jones, Stanford University; Demetrius Kantarelis, Assumption College; Chulsoo Kim, Rutgers University; Stephen R. King, Chemical Bank; Michael Knetter, Dartmouth College; John Laitner, University of Michigan; Julia Lane, American University; Bennett McCallum, Carnegie-Mellon University; Basil Moore, Wesleyan University; Richard F. Muth, Emory University; Neil B. Niman, University of New Hampshire; Ian Novos, University of Southern California; Ernest H. Oksanen, McMaster University; David H. Papell, University of Houston; Edmund S. Phelps, Columbia University; Mikko Puhakka, Cornell University; Garey Ramey, University of

California, San Diego; Duane J. Rosa, West Texas State University; Michael Sattinger, SUNY-Albany; Edward Trubac, University of Notre Dame; J. Kirker Stephens, University of Oklahoma; Michael Truscott, University of Tampa; Larkin Warner, Oklahoma State University; Shinichi Watanabe, University of Kansas; John Williams, Stanford University; and Hou-Mu Wu, Tulane University.

Finally, we would like to thank Ed Parsons, Drake McFeely, Donald Lamm, and Joan Benham of W. W. Norton for outstanding editorial help and advice.

Stanford                                                                                                        R.E.H.
November 1996                                                                                         J.B.T.

PART

1

# Introduction

# Economic Growth and Fluctuations

Our economy grows irregularly. In some years, jobs and production grow rapidly. In others, the economy grows slowly. Sometimes it even shrinks. Over the past 25 years, the average growth of the economy, measured as the total production of goods and services, has been about 2.5 percent per year. Growth of jobs has been about 1.3 percent per year. But growth of the U.S. economy, along with most other economies, fluctuates widely around the long-term average from year to year. In some years, such as 1991, growth might even be slightly *negative*: production declines, workers lose jobs, and unemployment and poverty rise. In other years, the economy advances more rapidly than the average of 2.5 percent per year. In 1994 production rose by 3.5 percent, jobs grew rapidly, and unemployment fell. Brisk growth alleviated some of the hardships as unemployment declined.

The cycle of recession and recovery in the early 1990s has occurred many times in U.S. history. In the last few decades, there have been economic contractions in 1970, 1974–75, 1980, and 1982. Following each of these contractions were years of unusually high growth, similar to that of 1994, as the economy recovered. Growth was above average for the six consecutive years from 1983 through 1988, one of the longest periods of above-average growth in U.S. history. But history shows that booms and slumps are temporary. Even the long boom of the 1980s came to an end when growth dropped below its normal rate in 1989 and began to contract in the middle of 1990.

Year-to-year fluctuations in growth occur against the backdrop of persistent, long-run rates of growth, such as the 2.5 percent growth of the last 25 years. Yet, these long-run growth rates are subject to change. During the 1950s and 1960s, the U.S. economy enjoyed unusually high growth—production grew at an average rate of 3.5 percent per year. Will these higher rates return in the coming decades? If not, living standards will not rise significantly, and the country will have fewer resources to pursue higher consumption, improved education, and lower poverty.

# 1.1  MACROECONOMICS AND ITS USES

**Macroeconomics** tries to explain how and why the economy grows and fluctuates over time. The general upward path of the economy is the result of slow-moving forces—increasing population, more factories and machines, and better technology. Recessions—periods of declining total output—and other fluctuations divert the economy from a smooth growth path. Macroeconomics tries to explain growth and fluctuations using the standard principles of economic analysis.

The other branch of economics is **microeconomics**—the study of the behavior of individual consumers, firms, and markets. Microeconomics differs from macroeconomics in two ways. First, microeconomics is more concerned with how individual markets differ than with how the economy as a whole grows and fluctuates over time. Second, macroeconomics explains the determination of variables, including national income, the price level, and interest rates, that microeconomics considers given. Although it has different objectives, macroeconomics employs the basic ideas of microeconomics. When macroeconomists try to explain growth and fluctuations, they look at the behavior of consumers and firms, the organization of labor markets and industry, the workings of financial markets, and even the machinations of government. They rely on microeconomics to do so. Good microeconomics is a necessary but not sufficient condition for good macroeconomics.

Although long-run economic growth and short-term fluctuations have dominated discussions of economic performance in recent years, other important variables change as the macroeconomy grows and fluctuates. For example, inflation and interest rates in the United States rose toward the end of the 1983–88 high growth period, declined as production and employment fell in 1990 and 1991. Interest rates rose again in 1994 and 1995. Although the high inflation of the 1970s has become a faded memory, it is important to remember that it caused great harm to the economy, and ending it brought on the pain of two recessions in the early 1980s. Exchange rates and the foreign trade deficit, as well as inflation and interest rates, are all part of the natural focus of macroeconomics.

What is macroeconomics good for? One answer is that macroeconomics is essential for good economic policy. Used appropriately by policymakers, it has the potential greatly to improve economic welfare in the United States and other countries, including the less-developed economies of Africa, Asia, and Latin America and the newly emerging market economies of Eastern Europe and the former Soviet Union. Consider the following applications of macroeconomics.

Macroeconomics can help policymakers decide what to do to help avert recessions and to ensure that recessions are as short and mild as possible when they occur. Fluctuations are not unique to the last 25 years. They have been recorded for hundreds of years in the United States and other countries, and they will undoubtedly continue into the future. Hence, the possibility of another recession in the economy will remain a continual concern to policymakers. When the next recession strikes, it will have substantial effects on our welfare, just as the last one did. Unemployment and poverty rise in all recessions. Even those who don't lose their jobs may be forced into part-time jobs. The lower income throughout the nation reduces the funds available to make new investments that fuel long-term growth.

Macroeconomics can also help policymakers sort through various government spending and tax proposals to increase long-term economic growth. Production *per hour* by U.S. workers grew by only 1.2 percent per year since 1973, way down from the 2.8 percent per year from 1959 to 1973. After 1973, the labor force expanded rapidly, as the postwar baby boom generation entered the workforce and more women chose to work outside the home. Thus, the slowdown of *total* production was moderate, though total production would have increased substantially if the rate of production per hour had not fallen.

Macroeconomics can help policymakers keep inflation low and stable without making the economy unstable in the short run. Many analysts feel that low and stable inflation is essential for strong long-term economic growth. Suggestions about how government institutions can be designed to best ensure low and stable inflation are some of the more important recent contributions of macroeconomics.

Finally, macroeconomics tells us how broad policy changes affect the types of goods produced in the economy. Even when overall economic growth is relatively smooth, there are major fluctuations in the kinds of goods being produced. For example, during the early 1990s, production of defense and nondefense goods for the federal government shrank, while the production of goods for export abroad soared. During this same period of steady overall growth the production of new houses actually fell. These developments in the government, export, and housing sectors of the economy represented sharp reversals of developments in the mid-1980s. As we will see, they led to large changes in the trade deficit. The trade deficit rose in the mid-1980s and fell in the late 1980s. Explaining the trade deficit is one of the responsibilities of macroeconomics.

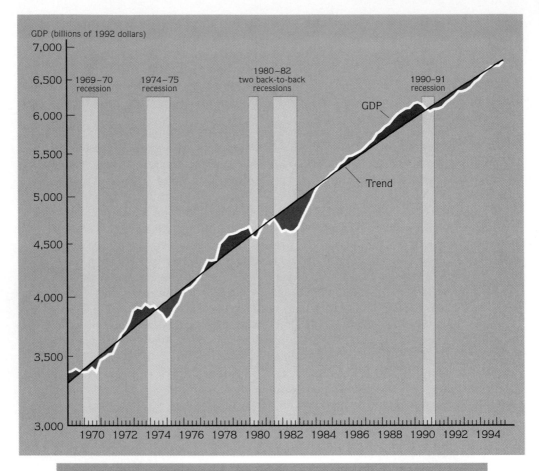

GDP (billions of 1992 dollars)

**FIGURE 1.1**   Real GDP in the United States, 1968–95

The white line shows what has happened to real GDP. The black line shows what real GDP would
have looked like if it had grown smoothly at about 2.5 percent per year during the period instead
of fluctuating as it did.
Source: *Economic Report of the President*, 1996, Table B-2.

## 1.2  RECENT MACROECONOMIC PERFORMANCE

Figure 1.1 documents the fluctuations of the U.S. economy over the last
quarter century. The white line in the figure traces **real gross domestic
product (GDP),** a concept we will examine in more detail in the next chap-

ter. Real GDP measures the actual physical production of cars, trucks, TV sets, rock concerts, Hollywood films, medical care, and every other good or service that people in the United States produce for trade with one another or with the rest of the world. We get real GDP by summing up the dollar value of production, and then adjusting for any price changes that have occurred from year to year. Frequently, real GDP is simply called real *output*, as it represents the total output of goods in the economy.

The vertical axis in Figure 1.1 shows the values of real GDP in 1992 dollars; the horizontal axis indicates the year. GDP rose fairly consistently during this period at an average growth rate of 2.5 percent. Growth in the labor force and the capital stock, the two key inputs to production, accounted for part of the total growth. The rest came from technological improvements. The black line in the chart indicates the steady upward trend that underlies the behavior of real GDP; it measures the amount of output that would have been produced had the economy been in neither boom nor recession.

During the period shown in Figure 1.1, the U.S. economy experienced five **recessions**—periods when real GDP declined. The recessions are highlighted with boxes in the figure. Recessions start just after the **peak** of the previous expansion. The end of each recession is called a **trough.**

Figure 1.2 gives a more detailed look at the deviations of real GDP from trend. The ups and downs are exactly the same as in Figure 1.1, but the **percentage** deviations of real GDP from trend are shown.

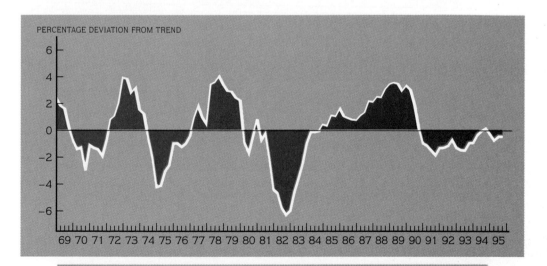

**FIGURE 1.2** Fluctuations of Real GDP around the Smooth Trend

The chart shows the *percentage* deviations of real GDP from trend. Real GDP was more than 6 percent below trend in 1982 and about 2 percent below trend at the end of 1991.

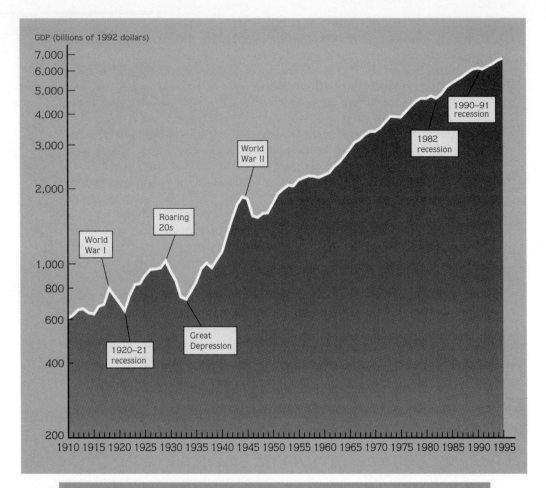

**FIGURE 1.3**    Real GDP, 1910–95

The largest decline in real GDP occurred from 1929 to 1933, the years of the Great Depression. Another important contraction occurred in the early 1920s. Both were more serious than any recession since 1950.
Source: *National Income and Product Accounts of the U.S.* (U.S. Department of Commerce) and *Economic Report of the President*, 1996, Table B-2.

Fluctuations do not occur at regular intervals. They certainly cannot be anticipated with great accuracy, and this is what makes macroeconomic forecasting both difficult and interesting. For example, the recovery that began in 1982 was very long, whereas the recovery that began in 1980 was short.

Figure 1.3 gives a longer perspective on the growth and fluctuations in economic activity, showing the ups and downs in the economy over the last

85 years. The most noticeable single fluctuation during this period was the downturn during the Great Depression of the early 1930s. Note, however, that the recession in the early 1920s and the subsequent boom in the late 1920s were also comparatively large in magnitude. Although economic fluctuations in the United States have not ceased, they appear to have diminished in magnitude compared with this earlier period.

## Employment

Fluctuations in employment follow closely the fluctuations in real GDP. Figure 1.4 shows the ratio of employed workers to the working-age population for the same period covered by Figure 1.1. Employment fell rapidly as the economy went through each of the five recessions during this period. Firms laid off workers as the economy's production fell and hired fewer new workers as well. As the economy began to recover after each downturn, employment again grew as firms called workers back to work and hired many new

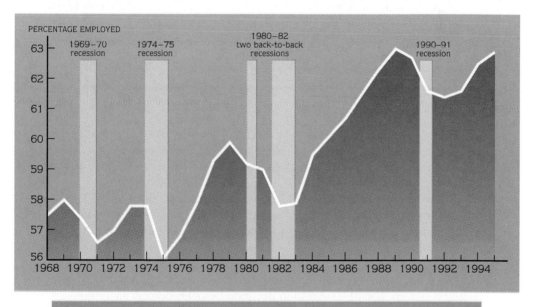

**FIGURE 1.4**   Employment as a Percentage of Working-Age Population

Recessions are periods of declining employment, measured as a fraction of the working-age population. Because of the fluctuations in employment, recessions influence a large fraction of the public. The percentage of the working-age population who are working reached an all-time high in 1989 and almost regained that level in 1994.
Source: *Economic Report of the President*, 1996, Table B-35.

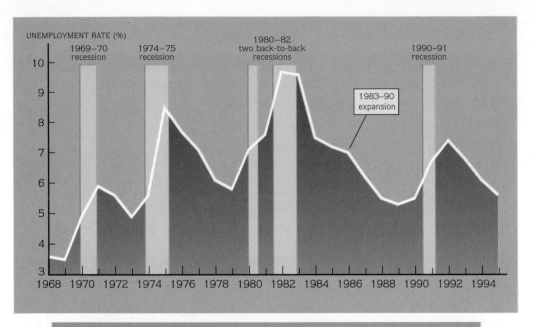

**FIGURE 1.5**   Annual Unemployment Rate, 1968–95

The unemployment rate rises during recessions and falls during recoveries.
Source: *Economic Report of the President*, 1996, Table B-38.

workers. This close association between production and employment as the economy fluctuates is one of the key facts of macroeconomics. Recurrent recessions are serious social problems, because they involve large-scale job losses.

Mirroring the fluctuations in employment are the fluctuations in the **unemployment rate,** the percentage of those in the labor force who are not working but who are looking for work. When employment falls, the unemployment rate rises as workers are laid off. Figure 1.5 shows the unemployment rate. In 1982 the unemployment rate rose to about 10 percent. In 1989 it had fallen to about 5 percent. Unemployment rose again, reaching nearly 8 percent for 1992, and then declined below 6 percent in 1995.

## Inflation

Another important fact of economic fluctuations is their correlation with the rate of *inflation*—the percentage change in the average price of all goods in the economy. In general, prices tend to rise faster when the economy is operating near its peak. Conversely, prices tend to rise less rapidly when the

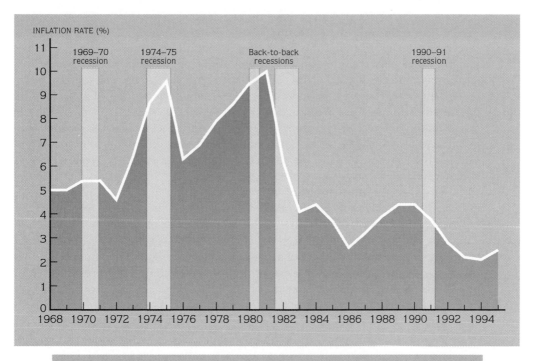

**FIGURE 1.6**   The Rate of Inflation

Inflation was high and volatile in the 1970s. In the 1980s it declined and remained relatively steady.
Bursts of inflation have preceded or accompanied recessions. Typically, inflation subsides during and
just after recessions.
Source: *Economic Report of the President*, 1996, GDP deflator in Table B-3.

economy is near a trough. These rises and falls lag behind the fluctuations
in real GDP.

Figure 1.6 shows the rate of inflation. One of the most striking aspects
of inflation is that it was much higher and much more volatile in the 1970s
than in the 1980s. This is clearly demonstrated in the chart. Almost all the
significant increases in the rate of inflation preceded recession periods. Declines in inflation usually follow recessions. Do increases in inflation cause
recessions? Are recessions a necessary part of the disinflation process? These
are two of the central concerns of this book.

## Interest Rates

**Interest rates** also tend to fluctuate over the business cycle. The interest
rate is the amount charged for a loan by a bank or other lender per dollar

per year, expressed as a percent. For instance, if you borrow $100 and repay $110 a year from now, the interest rate is 10 percent. Figure 1.7 shows one representative interest rate, the federal funds rate, during the same period that we previously considered. The federal funds rate measures how much banks pay to borrow funds from each other overnight. As we will see, the federal funds rate is a key measure of the effect of the Federal Reserve Board, the central bank of the United States. There was a general rise in interest rates starting in the 1960s as inflation rose. Interest rates usually rise with inflation to compensate lenders for the falling purchasing power of the dollar. The interest rate minus the expected rate of inflation is called the **real interest rate.**

However, the fluctuations of interest rates during recessions are most dramatic. Interest rates are **procyclical;** they rise during booms and fall during recessions. They are also one of the most volatile of macroeconomic variables, and the most difficult to predict. Nevertheless, as Figure 1.7 makes clear, these interest-rate fluctuations are intimately related to the fluctuations in production and employment. A thorough understanding of interest-rate behavior is crucial to any explanation of economic fluctuations.

A variable closely related to the interest rate is the **money supply.** The

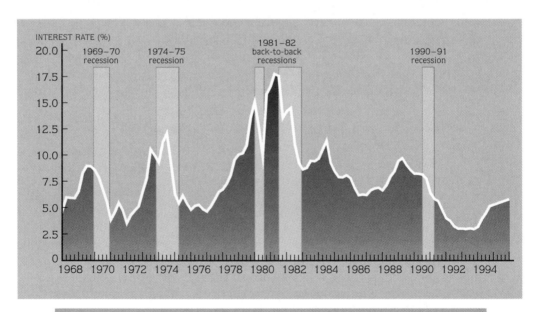

**FIGURE 1.7**   The Federal Funds Interest Rate

Like other interest rates, the federal funds rate reaches a peak just before a recession and then usually falls sharply.
Source: *Economic Report of the President*, 1996, B-69.

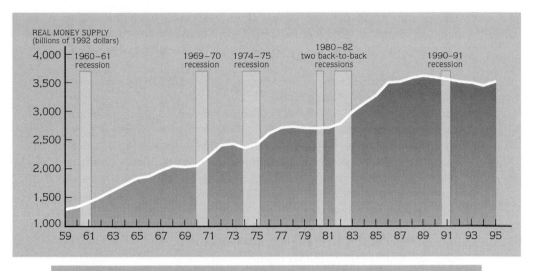

**FIGURE 1.8** The Money Supply

The money supply divided by the price level—real money—seems to decline before recessions. The general trend in real money is positive because the growth in the economy creates a need for more money to assist in buying and selling goods.
Source: *Economic Report of the President*, 1996, Tables B 3 (GDP deflator) and B-65 (M₂).

money supply consists of currency and the deposits that people have at banks and certain other financial institutions. It is controlled by the Federal Reserve Board. The behavior of the money supply is shown in Figure 1.8. The chart shows the money supply divided by the price level, or *real money*. There seems to be a relationship between money and the timing of recessions and booms. The relationship suggests that changes in the money supply may be one of the causes of the fluctuations in the economy.

The ideas, theories, and models we study in this book endeavor to explain why GDP and employment fluctuate so much. They will also try to provide reasons for the cyclical movements of inflation, interest rates, and the money supply as well as a number of other macroeconomic variables.

## GROWTH AND FLUCTUATIONS

**1.** In most years, the economy grows. The long-run growth path of the economy depends on population growth, capital accumulation, and technological progress.

2. The economy undergoes recessions, recoveries, and other fluctuations at irregular intervals. Recessions are periods of contracting economic activity; recoveries are periods of above-average economic growth following a recession.
3. The physical volume of output—measured by real GDP—contracts in a recession and expands in a recovery.
4. Employment moves closely with output. Recessions are periods of job loss, that is, rising unemployment.
5. The period between World War I and World War II saw two very large contractions. Recessions have continued since World War II. In the early 1980s the overall contraction was the worst since the Great Depression. The recession that began in 1990 was less severe.
6. Inflation generally increases before a recession and subsides in the wake of a recession.
7. Interest rates usually reach a peak just before a recession starts and then fall considerably during the recession.

# 1.3 EXPLAINING ECONOMIC GROWTH AND FLUCTUATIONS: A PREVIEW

The aim of this book is to develop a theory to explain both the short- and long-term movements of the economy. Recall that long-run growth refers to the general upward trend path of real GDP, shown in Figure 1.1, while economic fluctuations refer to the shorter-run movements of real GDP around that path.

In developing an explanation of how the economy grows and fluctuates, the macroeconomist constructs a **model.** A model is a description of the economy expressed in graphs or equations. It shows how the decisions of households and firms interact with each other in markets to determine output and other variables.

## The Model of Long-Run Growth

Macroeconomists use a long-run growth model to study the general upward path of the economy over time. The growth model focuses on the amount of labor and capital that go into the production of goods and services. Labor and capital work together to produce output. Most of the output is consumed by households; the rest is invested by businesses in new factories and equip-

## Growth Rates

Macroeconomics gives a lot of attention to growth rates. Often, the recent change in a variable is the most important aspect that macroeconomics needs to discuss. For example, real GDP grows rapidly during an expansion and has a negative growth rate during a recession. One growth rate, that of the price level, even has a special name, the *rate of inflation*.

The growth rate of a variable between two periods, in percent, is defined as *the change in the variable divided by the value of the variable in the first period multiplied by 100*. Thus, the growth rate of real GDP from 1994 to 1995 is

$100 \times$ (real GDP in 1995 − real GDP in 1994)/(real GDP in 1994)
= 100 (6739.0 − 6604.2)/(6604.2)
= 100 (134.8)/(6604.2)
= 2.5 percent.

Growth rates are usually converted to "annual rates" because everyone is used to annual rates. For a change from one year to the next, the growth rate is already at an annual rate. For the growth rate from one quarter to the next, the annual rate is approximated by multiplying the quarterly growth rate by 4.

---

ment or is used by government. In focusing on the upward path of the economy, the growth model does not dwell on how the economy adjusts to temporary shocks, such as brief wars or financial turmoil. This is an oversimplification, because such shocks are frequent and the economy is always in the process of adjusting to one shock or another. After developing the long-run growth model, we will consider the adjustment process through which the economy responds to shocks. We describe a complete model that considers temporary fluctuations, adjustment over time, and the process of growth in the long run.

One of the sources of growth is rising employment. The population grows over time, and, at least in the past three decades, a growing fraction of the population chooses to work outside the home. With more labor available, the economy produces more output. A second source is increases in the stock of plant, equipment, and other capital: workers produce more when they have more tools to work with. A third source of growth is improved technology. During recent years, the output of the economy has grown at least 1 percent per year from improved methods of production. In the 1950s and 1960s, technological improvement ran at a much higher pace of about 2.5 percent per year.

In addition to describing the sources of growth in total output, the growth model explains the division of output among alternative uses. Consumption is the main use of output. Investment in new capital—plant and equipment—is a second. The government uses output, especially for defense. Finally, the rest of the world supplies us with output, in the form of goods imported from other countries, and the United States provides output to other countries in the form of exported goods. The interest rate has the central role in dividing output among these uses. When the need for government to use output is particularly strong—for example, when military spending is high—the interest rate is high. Then the high interest rate induces businesses to limit or defer their investment. Exports fall and imports rise when the interest rate is high. And households may defer some types of consumption, such as buying new cars, when the interest rate is high.

The growth model provides a baseline for judging macroeconomic performance even in the short run. The level of **potential GDP** is the amount of GDP that the economy will produce according to the growth model. Although fluctuations not considered by the growth model cause actual GDP to depart from potential, the potential level is a baseline that actual GDP returns toward, once a temporary fluctuation subsides.

## The Model of Fluctuations

Look back at Figure 1.1. Actual GDP is the white line and potential GDP is the black line. During recessions actual GDP drops below potential, and during booms actual GDP rises above potential. These fluctuations are transitory—the smooth potential GDP line describes how GDP behaves in the longer run. The model of fluctuations explains why there are temporary movements. In particular, it considers why the economy contracts sharply during recessions, when employment falls and unemployment rises as well.

What kinds of forces cause recessions and booms? Some originate from private sources in this country. In some years there is a spontaneous decline in the amount that families spend on cars, appliances, and houses, or that businesses spend on new plant and equipment. Another source of shocks is public policy. The Federal Reserve has a powerful influence because it controls the money supply. Congress sets income taxes and these affect consumption; business taxes are an important determinant of investment spending. Some shocks reach the United States from world markets—the oil market has been the most important source of this type in the past few decades.

Certain important characteristics of the economy affect the way these shocks influence output and employment. In an ideal economy where prices and wages could adjust immediately to new conditions, many of these shocks would probably have little effect on total output (they would still affect the distribution of output, however). The fluctuations model pays particular attention to the role of slow price and wage adjustment in amplifying and extending the effects of shocks. Once the price and wage adjustment occurs, the economy moves back to potential. The factors considered in the fluctuations model do not affect the long-run trends of the economy.

### GROWTH AND FLUCTUATIONS

1. Economists use the long-run growth model to study the general upward path of the economy over time.
2. In the growth model, the level of output is determined by labor, capital, and technical know-how; the economy grows as these determinants become more plentiful.
3. The path of output from the growth model is called potential GDP.
4. The economy experiences booms and recessions, when actual GDP is above or below potential; these departures from potential are temporary.
5. An important reason for the time it takes for the economy to return to potential is slow price and wage adjustment.

## CURRENTS OF THOUGHT IN MACROECONOMICS

The story we previewed briefly in the last two sections draws from two major strands of thinking in macroeconomics. The analysis of long-run growth with the emphasis on flexible prices comes from **classical macroeconomics.** The classical model was the earliest formal statement of macroeconomics and dominated thinking before the Great Depression of the 1930s. Classical macroeconomics is basically the application of standard supply-and-demand analysis to the whole economy. The growth model builds on this analysis, showing how the growth of capital and labor determines the growth of potential GDP.

The collapse and recovery of all of the major world economies in the 1930s challenged the classical model. John Maynard Keynes and his followers created a model of fluctuations based on quite different principles in order to explain the puzzle of the Depression. For a time, Keynes's ideas replaced the classical model, and the basic economic concepts of supply and demand (especially supply) seemed to have little role in macroeconomics. But soon the importance of the classical model in explaining the behavior of the economy in the longer run became evident. Today, most macroeconomists believe that the classical model, with its emphasis on long-run economic growth, should be the starting point for understanding macroeconomics. The organization of this book reflects that belief.

The theory of economic fluctuations is more controversial. Many macroeconomists believe that some form of "price stickiness" is needed to understand recessions and depressions. Other macroeconomists believe that the standard model with flexible prices and rapid adjustment is sufficient to explain fluctuations. They view the fall in jobs and output that occurs in a recession in the same way that a microeconomist would analyze a drop in carrot production—as the result of downward shifts in supply, in demand, or in both. In the past decade the **real business cycle model** embodying this approach has received both acceptance and criticism.[1]

A related area of dispute among macroeconomists is about the effects of economic policy. Almost all macroeconomists accept the principle that changes in the money supply affect only inflation in the longer run. A related principle is that, over a decade, changes in the money supply have little effect on employment and output. In fact, most analyses of long-run economic growth put the money supply and inflation completely on the back burner. On the other hand, there is sharp disagreement about the effects of money in the short run. Many economists believe that increases in the money supply affect output in the short run. But some macroeconomists question whether a money expansion does anything more than cause inflation even in the short run. And among those who do grant that the Federal Reserve—through changing the money supply—has the power to affect employment and output over a span of a few years, there is disagreement about the mechanism. The idea that changes in the money supply affect output because prices and wages are "sticky" in the short run has many followers today. But other macroeconomists have developed models in which a money expansion raises employment solely because it confuses suppliers about the state of the economy: the firms are "fooled" into producing more.

Corresponding to different views about whether and how the money supply affects output are different recommendations about the role of the Federal Reserve. Because almost all macroeconomists agree that money affects only inflation in the longer run, there is agreement that the Federal Reserve should keep inflation low in the longer run. But there is disagreement about whether the Federal Reserve should try to offset recessions. Macroeconomists who question the effect of money-supply expansion on employment obviously don't recommend that the Federal Reserve be asked to try to mitigate recessions. Those who accept the idea of price rigidity are more likely to favor an antirecession monetary policy.

Macroeconomists also disagree over the general desirability of using government spending to solve the problems of the economy. There are advocates of activist policies and of hands-off policies. In particular, Keynes argued for the active use of policies to adjust government spending to the

---

[1]See Finn E. Kydland and Edward C. Prescott, "Time to Build and Aggregate Fluctuations," *Econometrica*, Vol. 50 (November 1982), pp. 1345–1370; and N. Gregory Mankiw, "Real Business Cycles: A New Keynesian Perspective," *Journal of Economic Perspectives*, Vol. 3 (Summer 1989), pp. 79–90.

## How Did Today's Macroeconomists Come to Study Economics?

Macroeconomists began studying economics for many different reasons. Some got interested because the hardships of the Great Depression of the 1930s touched them personally. For others it was pure chance. But whatever the reason, they all liked it and stuck with it. Here are some answers to the question "How did you come to study economics?" from some macroeconomists whose work we will study in this book.*

### Franco Modigliani

[Laughter] That's a good question. I'd say, by chance. I started my university years with the expectation that I would become a doctor, because my father was one. . . . At the last moment I realized that I wasn't cut out for that profession; I cannot stand the sight of blood. So I went into law, which is in Italy very general.

Then there was a national competition among university students to write an essay about the effect of price controls. I decided to participate. . . . I wrote my essay and won first prize. The judges said that I should pursue the study of economics and so I began.

### James Tobin

I went into economics for two reasons. One was that as a child of the Depression I was terribly concerned about the world. It seemed then that many of the problems were economic in origin. If you thought that the world should be saved, and I did, then economics looked like the decisive thing to study. The second thing was that

you could have your cake and eat it too, because it was an intellectually fascinating subject.

### Robert E. Lucas, Jr.

I have always liked to think about social problems. It may have something to do with my family. We always argued about politics and social issues. I studied history. . . . But I came around to the view that economic forces are central forces in history, and started trying some economics. It was a big shock to me to find books in English that were incomprehensible to me . . . [Like] Keynes's *General Theory*. I still can't read Keynes. [Laughter] I realized I couldn't pick it up as an amateur. So I got into economics in a professional way and got my Ph.D. at Chicago.

### Thomas J. Sargent

[Long pause and hesitation] I liked it when we studied it in college. But also I was truly curious, ever since I was a kid, about what caused depressions. The Great Depression had a big effect on me: a lot of people in my family got wiped out. My grandfather ran a quarry in the construction business, and he got wiped out. My other grandfather was in the radio business, and he got wiped out. It was the common story.

*The answers come from separate interviews published in Arjo Klamer, *Conversations with Economists* (Totowa, N.J.: Rowman and Allanheld, 1984).

condition of the economy. In fact, the phrase *Keynesian economics* is often considered to mean the advocacy of raising government spending to deal with a recession. There is no direct connection between Keynes's idea of price-wage stickiness and his policy recommendation that the government should spend the economy out of a slump. All macroeconomists agree that the economy expands when the government buys more goods and services. The disagreement is about whether the government should try to offset recessions at all, and about the choice between monetary policy and spending policy. Many macroeconomists accept some of Keynes's ideas about price-wage stickiness but reject the government spending response to recessions.

One of the areas where most macroeconomists agree is about the concept of **rational expectations.** Many parts of this book show the influence of the concept. Robert Lucas received the Nobel Prize in economics in 1995 for a research program that developed and applied rational expectations to a number of significant areas of macroeconomics. The hypothesis of rational expectations holds that firms and consumers make the most of the information that is available to them. If they know from past experience that the Federal Reserve lowers interest rates whenever there is an increase in unemployment, then they will expect the Federal Reserve to act the same in the future and will make their own plans accordingly. Consumption, investment, and price adjustment are areas where we have to deal with the issues of how people form their expectations.

# THE MACROECONOMIC MODEL USED IN THIS BOOK

Although many alternative theories are discussed, a main model appears throughout this book. The model *combines* the model of long-run economic growth with the model of short-run economic fluctuations previewed in this chapter. In other words, the model assumes that the classical principles describe the growth trend of the economy in the longer run. Supplies of labor and capital, and the process of innovation and technical progress, are important parts of the longer-run growth model. Recessions are temporary departures from the growth path. Because of price and wage stickiness, the economy does not return immediately to potential after a shock.

We call this the *complete model,* because it combines the two elements of modern macroeconomics, which we feel are essential to explaining growth and fluctuations. There are other complete models—the real business cycle model is one example of a different model that considers both growth and fluctuations—and we will compare the complete model of this book with these other models. The complete model is developed in a "no-frills" form in Chapters 3 through 9, with the important microeconomic foundations and more advanced policy analysis provided later in the book. In developing the rudimentary form of the complete model, we begin with the determinants of long-term potential growth (Chapters 3, 4, and 5) and then discuss departures from the potential growth path (Chapters 6 through 9).

## REVIEW AND PRACTICE

### Major Points

1. Output and employment expand and contract at irregular intervals.

2. Other measures of the state of the economy, like interest rates and inflation, also track fluctuations.

3. The goal of macroeconomics is to develop models that give us an understanding of the determinants of both short-term economic fluctuations and long-term economic growth. Such an understanding will permit us to design fiscal, monetary, and other government policies that promote growth and mitigate fluctuations.

4. According to the long-run growth model, output is set by supply conditions alone; output is always at its potential level. The model with flexible prices has problems explaining short-term declines in output, but describes long-term growth quite well.

5. The model of economic fluctuations with sticky prices says that output need not be equal to potential output. In the very short run, changes in spending affect output.

6. The price adjustment process describes the transition from the short run to the long run. Prices fall when output is below potential GDP and rise when it is above. The price adjustment moves the economy in the direction of potential GDP.

7. Economists disagree about how government should try to influence the economy through changes in government spending and the money supply.

### Key Terms and Concepts

| | | |
|---|---|---|
| fluctuations | potential GDP | economic fluctuations model |
| recession | rate of inflation | complete model |
| recovery | rate of interest | sticky prices |
| trough | unemployment rate | flexible prices |
| peak | price adjustment | John Maynard Keynes |
| gross domestic product | procyclical | real business cycle model |
| real GDP | long-run growth model | |

### Questions for Discussion and Review

1. Which of the following are procyclical?

   a. Interest rates    c. Inflation

   b. Employment    d. Money supply

2. Explain the difference between potential GDP and real GDP.

3. Describe a typical macroeconomic fluctuation, starting from a peak.

4. What are the determinants of potential GDP?

5. How have economic fluctuations changed during the last 80 years?

6. How does GDP respond to a change in spending when prices are perfectly flexible?

7. How does GDP respond to a change in spending when prices do not adjust?

8. What could cause a recession in the long-run growth model with flexible prices?

## Problems

### NUMERICAL

1. Real output in the United Kingdom from 1960 through 1991 is given below. All data are in billions of 1985 pounds.

| | | | | | |
|---|---|---|---|---|---|
| 1960 | 200.4 | 1971 | 271.9 | 1982 | 322.9 |
| 1961 | 206.4 | 1972 | 278.0 | 1983 | 335.4 |
| 1962 | 208.1 | 1973 | 300.1 | 1984 | 341.3 |
| 1963 | 217.4 | 1974 | 297.3 | 1985 | 354.0 |
| 1964 | 229.0 | 1975 | 295.4 | 1986 | 366.2 |
| 1965 | 234.0 | 1976 | 306.3 | 1987 | 382.0 |
| 1966 | 238.8 | 1977 | 309.5 | 1988 | 392.0 |
| 1967 | 245.3 | 1978 | 321.7 | 1989 | 401.0 |
| 1968 | 255.7 | 1979 | 328.9 | 1990 | 404.2 |
| 1969 | 259.1 | 1980 | 322.5 | 1991 | 396.5 |
| 1970 | 265.1 | 1981 | 318.9 | | |

a. Plot U.K. real output over the 32-year period. Put real output on the vertical axis of the graph and the year on the horizontal axis.

b. Estimate potential output by drawing a smooth trend line through the points on the graph. Identify any shifts in the trend of potential. By what percent did real output grow during this period?

c. Identify the fluctuations of real output around potential output. How many complete (peak-to-peak) economic fluctuations occurred during this period? How does the frequency of economic fluctuations during this period compare with that of the United States during the same period?

2. Suppose that the demand for carrots is $D = 5 - 2P + E$, where $D$ is the quantity demanded, $P$ is the price, and $E$ is a shock to the people's demand for carrots. Suppose that the supply of carrots is fixed: $S = 4$, where $S$ is the quantity supplied.

a. Assume first that $E = 0$. Set $D = S$ and find the price ($P$) and output ($S = D$) of carrots.

b. Now suppose that the demand for carrots shifts up (there is a shock raising $E$ from 0 to 1). Find the new price and *output.*

c. Again suppose, as in Part b, that $E$ rises from 0 to 1, but now suppose the price of carrots is *sticky* and remains at the value in Part a. By how much does the quantity demanded increase? Suppose that output equals the quantity demanded and compare your answer with Part b.

d. Which macroeconomic model described in the chapter is analogous to Part b? to Part c?

3. We have the following data on interest rates and the price level (in the United States) for the years 1977–95:

| Year | Price Level | Interest Rates (Percent) |
|------|-------------|--------------------------|
| 1977 | 60.6 | 5.6 |
| 1978 | 65.2 | 7.6 |
| 1979 | 72.6 | 10.0 |
| 1980 | 82.4 | 11.4 |
| 1981 | 90.9 | 13.8 |
| 1982 | 96.5 | 11.1 |
| 1983 | 99.6 | 8.8 |
| 1984 | 103.9 | 9.8 |
| 1985 | 107.6 | 7.7 |
| 1986 | 109.6 | 6.1 |
| 1987 | 113.6 | 6.1 |
| 1988 | 118.3 | 7.0 |
| 1989 | 124.0 | 8.0 |
| 1990 | 130.7 | 7.5 |
| 1991 | 136.2 | 5.5 |
| 1992 | 140.3 | 3.6 |
| 1993 | 144.5 | 3.1 |
| 1994 | 148.2 | 4.7 |
| 1995 | 152.4 | 5.6 |

a. Calculate the rate of inflation for the years 1978–95.

b. Calculate the expected rate of inflation for the years 1979–95 assuming (i) people expect the rate of inflation to be the average rate of inflation in the two previous years and (ii) people have perfect foresight and expected inflation just equals actual inflation.

c. For each of the assumptions in Part b, calculate the real interest rate for the years 1977–95.

d. In light of this example, explain why economists have such a difficult time measuring the real interest rate.

e. How do you think people forecast inflation? What information do they use? Do you think they systematically underestimate changes in the price level?

**ANALYTICAL**

1. What explains the fluctuations in output in models where prices are flexible? In models where prices are sticky?

2. Comment on the following two explanations of the large drop in output in the early 1980s in the United States:

    a. "There was a decline in potential output because the number of people available for work declined."

    b. "There was a decline in spending. With very high interest rates, consumers and firms purchased fewer goods so that production and employment declined."

Which statement seems more plausible? Which statement is consistent with the macro model with flexible prices and which with the model with sticky prices?

3. Is it reasonable to ignore departures from potential GDP in the study of change in real GDP over periods of 10 years or more? Why or why not?

4. The notion that departures from potential GDP are important is a necessary, but not sufficient, condition to warrant active use of government policy to offset recessions. Why is some belief in the importance of departures from potential GDP essential to rationalize activist policy to fight recessions? Why is it not sufficient to make activism superior to nonintervention?

## MacroSolve Exercises

1. Plot the GDP gap (the percentage deviation of real GDP from potential GDP) using annual data and the **PLOT** option. Identify the years when troughs and peaks occur. (It will be useful to tabulate the data to identify the exact years when these occur. Peaks occur in periods when the GDP gap is greater than the surrounding observations, and troughs occur when the GDP gap is more negative than the surrounding observations.)

    a. On average, how frequent are recessions? Has this frequency increased or decreased since the Second World War? Why might the frequency have changed?

    b. Are business fluctuations symmetric? In other words, is the period of decline between peaks and troughs longer or shorter then the upswing from troughs to peaks? Can you think of any reasons for this?

2. Using annual data, graph the GDP gap on the horizontal axis against the unemployment rate on the vertical axis. Is unemployment procyclical or countercyclical? In other words, when output is high relative to potential output, is the unemployment rate high (so that unemployment is procyclical) or low (countercyclical)? Explain why.

3. Plot both the real interest rate and the inflation rate on the same screen using quarterly data from 1967 to 1995. When the inflation rate changes, do the real and nominal interest rates generally move in the same direction or in opposite directions? Why?

4. Do the real interest rate and the GDP gap generally move in the same direction or in opposite directions? Can you think of any explanations for this?

5. Using the statistics option, follow up on MacroSolve Problem 1 and calculate the mean and standard deviation of the GDP gap. Are recessions more or less severe since World War II? or before? (Split the data for this question into two groups, 1930–47 and 1948–95.)

# Measuring Economic Performance

In Chapter 1 we examined the behavior of several key macroeconomic variables—production, employment, and inflation. In this chapter we'll show how these and other important variables are defined and measured.

 ## GROSS DOMESTIC PRODUCT

We begin with gross domestic product (GDP). GDP refers to production during a particular time period, which we will usually take to be a year or a quarter of a year. It is the *flow* of new products during the year or the quarter, measured in dollars. When we adjust GDP for the effects of inflation, we get real GDP, the measure of physical output discussed in Chapter 1.

There are three different ways to think about and measure GDP. First, we can measure **spending** on goods and services by different groups—households, businesses, government, and foreigners. Second, we can measure **production** in different industries—agriculture, mining, manufacturing, and so on. Last, we can measure the total wage and profit **income** earned by different groups producing GDP. Each of these measures has its own special purpose, but they all add up to the same thing. We consider each in turn in the next three sections.

How do we know that the total amount of spending is equal to the total value of production, which in turn is equal to the total amount of income? Think about an individual firm. Suppose the value of its production is $1 million. Suppose that spending by consumers on the firm's product is $900,000. For accounting purposes, we treat the remaining $100,000 as spending. It is the firm's investment in inventories of its own goods and is included as part of total investment. Both at the level of the firm and at the level of the whole economy, the equality of production and spending is the result of considering inventory investment as part of spending; that is, spending = $900,000 + $100,000 = $1,000,000 = production.

The equality of the value of production and income also derives from accounting principles. Our firm takes in $900,000 in one year. In addition, we add in the $100,000 value of its inventory accumulation as sales, for a total value of production of $1 million. The firm pays out $450,000 in wages. That amount is counted in the incomes of the workers. The firm pays $50,000 in interest, which is counted in the incomes of whoever lent money to the firm. It pays $400,000 for its raw materials, which is counted in the incomes of the sellers of materials or of their employees. The residual, $1,000,000 − $450,000 − $50,000 − $400,000 = $100,000, is the profit that is earned by the owner of the firm and that counts as part of the owner's income. All the receipts of the firm from its sales are paid out to somebody as income. The value of production and the total amount of income generated are the same.

As a result of the two accounting rules—including inventories in spending and computing profit as the residual between sales and expenses—it is always true that production, spending, and income are exactly the same. This kind of relation is called an **identity;** it is the inevitable outcome of the accounting system, not a statement about how the economy works.

The alternative measures of GDP are gathered together in the national income and product accounts (NIPA). Economists and statisticians at the Bureau of Economic Analysis (BEA), an agency of the United States government in Washington, D.C., are responsible for collecting the GDP data and publishing the NIPA. Many of the ideas behind the GDP were developed by the late Simon Kuznets of Harvard University. He won the Nobel Prize in economics in 1971 for this work.

## MEASURING GDP THROUGH SPENDING

Total spending on goods and services produced by Americans during any period can be broken down as follows:

Gross domestic product = Consumption
+ Investment
+ Government purchases
+ Net exports (or exports minus imports).

Using symbols, this key identity can be written on one line:

$$Y = C + I + G + X$$
where $Y$ = Gross domestic product
$C$ = Consumption
$I$ = Investment
$G$ = Government spending
$X$ = Net exports (exports minus imports).

## Consumption

Consumption is defined as spending by *households*. It includes purchases of (1) **durable goods,** such as washing machines, stereos, and cars, (2) **nondurable goods,** such as food, clothing, and gasoline, and (3) **services,** such as haircuts, medical care, and education. Spending on new houses is the only type of household spending that is not included in consumption. Instead it is included in fixed investment.

## Investment

Investment is the sum of spending by firms on plant, equipment, and inventories and spending by households on housing. We separate total investment into **fixed investment** and **inventory investment.** Fixed investment is the purchase of new factories, machines, and houses. Inventory investment is the change in inventories at business firms. We first discuss fixed investment.

FIXED INVESTMENT.   Fixed investment is broken down into **nonresidential** fixed investment and **residential** fixed investment. Nonresidential fixed investment is spending on structures and equipment for use in business. Steel mills, office buildings, and power plants are examples of structures. Trucks, lathes, and typewriters are examples of equipment. Residential fixed investment is spending on construction of new houses and apartment buildings. The term "fixed" connotes that these types of investment goods will be around for a long time and thus distinguishes them from inventory investment, which is much more temporary, as we will see below. The term "fixed" is conventionally dropped when the meaning is implicit from the context, and we will follow this convention.

Investment is a *flow* of new capital during the year that is added to the *stock* of capital. The **capital stock** is the total physical amount of productive capital in the economy; it includes all the buildings, equipment, and houses.

The capital stock increases from one year to the next as a result of investment. However, because the capital stock is constantly wearing out, part of the investment reported in each year's GDP is actually devoted to replacing worn-out capital, not increasing the capital stock. What is reported in GDP is *gross* investment. This accounts for the term "gross" in GDP. Statisticians have a number of ways of estimating the loss of the existing capital stock from one year to the next. This loss is called **depreciation. Net investment** is defined as follows:

$$\text{Net investment} = \text{Gross investment} - \text{Depreciation.}$$

We have the following relation:

$$
\begin{aligned}
\text{Capital stock at the end of this year} = \;&\text{Capital stock at the end} \\
&\text{of last year} \\
-\;&\text{Depreciation during} \\
&\text{this year} \\
+\;&\text{Gross investment} \\
&\text{during this year.}
\end{aligned}
$$

By rearranging this equation and putting in the definition of net investment, we have:

$$
\begin{aligned}
\text{Net investment} = \;&\text{Capital stock at the end of this year} \\
-\;&\text{Capital stock at the end of last year.}
\end{aligned}
$$

These equations hold whether we are looking at total investment or separately at nonresidential and residential investment.

**INVENTORY INVESTMENT.**   Now consider inventory investment, which is simply the change in the stock of inventories held at businesses.

$$
\begin{aligned}
\text{Inventory investment this year} = \;&\text{Stock of inventories} \\
&\text{at the end of this year} \\
-\;&\text{Stock of inventories at the} \\
&\text{end of last year.}
\end{aligned}
$$

For example, when a publisher produces and stores 10,000 copies of a newly printed book in its warehouse, the books are counted in GDP as inventory investment. Even though no one has yet purchased the books, they must be counted in GDP because they have been produced. If subsequently you purchase a book directly from the publisher, consumption is up by one book and inventory investment is down by one book; GDP does not change, nor should it since there is no new production. When the publisher sells a book to a bookstore, the publisher's inventory investment is down by one book and the bookstore's inventory investment is up by one book. Total inventory investment does not change, and neither does GDP.

Inventory investment is positive when inventories are increasing, and negative when inventories are decreasing. In 1994, a year of strong growth, inventory investment was $58 billion. In 1991, a recession year, it was −$2 billion. If inventory investment were not added to spending when computing GDP, we would underestimate production when inventory investment was positive, as in 1994, because spending would be less than production; similarly we would overestimate production when inventory investment was negative, as in 1991, because spending would be more than production.

As the data for 1991 and 1994 show, inventory investment adds to the fluctuations of GDP. **Final sales** is a measure that excludes inventory investment. Final sales is defined as GDP minus inventory investment. Final sales fluctuates less than GDP.

## Government Purchases

**Government purchases** are the sum of federal government and state and local government purchases of goods and services. In 1995, state and local government purchases were 63 percent of total government purchases. Schools, road construction, and military hardware are examples of government purchases. Government purchases are only part of the total government *outlays* that are included in the government budget. Government purchases exclude such items as welfare payments and interest payments on the public debt that are included in government outlays.

The distinction between consumption, investment, and government purchases is based primarily on the type of purchaser rather than on the type of product that is purchased. If a Chevrolet is purchased by a household it goes into consumption—as a consumer durable. If it is purchased for use by a business, it goes into investment—as business fixed investment in equipment. If it is purchased by government, it goes into government purchases. The only exception to this rule is residential investment, which includes all housing purchases whether by households, businesses, or government.

## Imports and Exports

The United States has an open economy. An *open economy* is one with substantial interaction with other countries. The United States has experienced a growing volume of transactions with the rest of the world, and GDP has to take these into account. **Exports** are deliveries of goods and services from the United States to foreigners. **Imports** are deliveries of goods and services from foreigners to the United States.

Part, but not all, of United States exports represent goods and services *produced* by Americans. The other part has been imported to the United

States and then sold abroad, perhaps as part of manufactured products. For example, General Motors might put a radio imported from Japan into a Chevrolet that is exported to Mexico. We want to subtract the radio from the exported car if we are measuring goods produced by Americans. More generally, if goods are imported from abroad and purchased by United States consumers, businesses, or governments, the goods should not be counted in a measure of U.S. production. For these reasons imports are subtracted from spending and exports are added to spending when computing GDP. In other words, only **net exports,** that is, *exports less imports*, are added to the total volume of spending when computing GDP. The total of net exports is sometimes referred to as the **trade balance.** When net exports are positive there is a **trade surplus.** When net exports are negative there is a **trade deficit.**

## The Recent Composition of Spending

Table 2.1 shows how U.S. GDP broke down in 1995. Consumption is the biggest component—about two-thirds—of GDP. Services is the biggest component of consumption—about 57 percent. Services (restaurants, utilities, housing, transportation, medical care, and the like) have been growing as a

| TABLE 2.1   Gross Domestic Product in 1995—The Spending Side (billions of dollars) | |
|---|---|
| Gross domestic product | 7247.7 |
| Consumption | 4923.4 |
| Durables | 606.5 |
| Nondurables | 1485.2 |
| Services | 2831.7 |
| Investment | 1067.5 |
| Fixed investment | 1029.3 |
| Nonresidential | 739.9 |
| Residential | 289.4 |
| Inventory investment | 38.1 |
| Government purchases | 1358.5 |
| Net exports | −101.7 |
| Exports | 804.5 |
| Imports | 906.2 |
| Final sales | 7207.6 |

*Note:* Final sales is GDP less inventory investment. Details in the table may not add to totals because of rounding.
*Source:* U.S. Department of Commerce, *Survey of Current Business*, March 1996, p. 7.

## Bringing Astronomical Numbers Down to Earth

Table 2.1 shows that GDP was $7,247.7 billion, or about $7.2 trillion, in 1995. With all the zeros this looks like $7,247,700,000,000. An astrophysicist would write it $7.2477 \times 10^{12}$ dollars. How can we make intuitive sense of such large numbers?

The best way to bring numbers like these down to size is simply to divide by the population—that is, to calculate GDP per person, or GDP per capita. The population in the United States in 1995 was 263 million. GDP per capita in the United States is thus $27,558 (7,247,700,000,000/263,000,000 = 27,557.79). U.S. consumption in 1995 was $4,923 billion. This amounts to about $18,719 per capita for food, clothing, transportation, and other consumer items. On average, every man, woman, and child in the United States consumed $18,719 of goods and services in 1995.

Government purchases of goods and services were $1,358.5 billion in 1995. This amounted to $5,165 per capita for national defense, schools, highways, police, and so on. Net exports were −$101.7 billion in 1995, or about −$387 per capita. In other words, on average every person in the United States bought $387 more goods that were made abroad than they made goods that were sold abroad.

share of consumption. In the early 1950s services accounted for less than a third of consumption. Medical services have grown most rapidly.

Fixed investment is about 15 percent of GDP. Nonresidential fixed investment is much larger than residential fixed investment. Government purchases are larger than investment, at about 19 percent of GDP. Imports are about 12 percent of GDP. Exports are 11 percent of GDP. Foreign trade is now a much bigger factor in the United States than it was 20 or 30 years ago. In the early 1950s exports and imports each were about 5 percent of GDP.

These shares fluctuate from year to year, but the two-thirds consumption share is fairly typical of recent years in the United States. Inventory investment and net exports fluctuate dramatically and can be negative as well as positive; no year is typical. Since exports were smaller than imports in 1995, net exports were negative. Final sales were less than GDP in 1995 since inventory investment was positive.

### Which Spending Items Should Be Included?

In deciding which spending items to include in computing GDP, we must be careful to avoid double counting. For example, the purchase of a 10-year-old house should not be counted; that house was counted 10 years ago when it was constructed. Similarly, the purchase of the assets of Gulf Oil by Chevron should not be counted; the Gulf building in Pittsburgh and Gulf's offshore oil rigs were included in business fixed investment when they were built.

To avoid double counting, we also do not include the purchase of **intermediate goods.** These are goods that are converted into other goods in the production process (for example, steel is an intermediate good used in the production of cars). We only include **final goods,** such as the cars themselves. The value of the steel is included in GDP as part of a car when someone buys the car. The purchases of steel by automobile manufacturers are not counted.

In computing GDP, we value different types of goods, such as apples and oranges, using the price of each good that is paid by the purchaser. The price includes sales and excise taxes. If apples cost twice as much as oranges, then each apple will contribute twice as much to GDP as will each orange.

## Real GDP

GDP is a dollar measure of production. In comparing one year with another, we run into the problem that the dollar is not a stable measure of purchasing power. In the 1970s especially, GDP rose a great deal, not because the economy was actually growing rapidly but because the dollar was inflating. For comparisons across years, we need a measure of output that adjusts for inflation. We want *GDP in constant dollars*, or, as we will generally call it, **real GDP.** In contrast, the GDP that we have looked at so far is sometimes called **nominal GDP.** From 1972 to 1995 nominal GDP grew by 486 percent, from $1,237.3 billion to $7,247.7 billion. During the same period real GDP grew by about 72 percent. The conversion from nominal to real makes a big difference.

The concept of real GDP is straightforward. We want to measure consumption, investment, government purchases, and exports in physical rather than dollar units. Further, we want to subtract imports in the same physical units, so that real GDP is a measure of production.

To compute consumption in real terms, the national income statisticians gather data on the prices of consumption goods in great detail. They take the data on the corresponding detailed flows of goods to consumers and restate them in 1992 dollars. For example, suppose the retail price of a typical shirt rose from $10.00 in 1992 to $12.00 in 1996. The flow of shirts to consumers was $3 billion in 1992 and $5 billion in 1996. Consumption of shirts in real terms was $3 billion in 1992 dollars in 1992 and $4.17 billion in 1992 dollars in 1996. The $4.17 billion is computed as

(5 billion 1996 dollars) $\times$ [(10/12) 1992 dollars per 1996 dollar]

$$= 4.17 \text{ billion 1992 dollars.}$$

## Chain-Weighted GDP

The calculation of GDP starts with data on many components of consumption, investment, and other categories. The data show the dollar flows of purchases and the prices. For each component, the real flow of purchases is the dollar flow divided by the price. How should we calculate total real consumption, total real investment, and total real GDP? In the past, the answer was to choose a base year (most recently, 1987). Real quantities in the base year are taken to be the dollar quantities in that year. The prices are set to 1 in the base year. For later years, the national income and product accounts compute real quantities by dividing the dollar amounts by the prices. Then the real totals are the sums of the real components.

The traditional procedure has the defect that, as the years go by, it gives too much weight to components whose prices have fallen. The category that has caused the most trouble is computers. The easiest way to see the problem and the solution is in an example. Suppose that investment consists of computers and dump trucks and that the basic data over a four-year period are as follows:

| | Dollar Purchases | | Prices | |
| Year | Computers | Dump Trucks | Computers | Dump Trucks |
|---|---|---|---|---|
| 1 | 100 | 106 | 1.00 | 1.00 |
| 2 | 105 | 98 | 0.80 | 1.05 |
| 3 | 103 | 104 | 0.60 | 1.10 |
| 4 | 99 | 100 | 0.40 | 1.15 |

The traditional calculations are:

| | Real Quantities | | Total Real | Investment |
| Year | Computers | Dump Trucks | Investment | Deflator |
|---|---|---|---|---|
| 1 | 100.0 | 106.0 | 206.0 | 1.000 |
| 2 | 131.3 | 93.3 | 224.6 | 0.904 |
| 3 | 171.7 | 94.5 | 266.2 | 0.778 |
| 4 | 247.5 | 87.0 | 334.5 | 0.595 |

The weighting problem is evident: Although in year 4 dollar spending on computers is slightly below spending on dump trucks, the real quantity of computers is almost three times as large.

The solution to this problem has been known for many decades. For two adjacent years, we can calculate the rate of growth of each real component. Then we can calculate the rate of growth of the aggregate as the weighted sum of the individual real growth rates, using the current dollar spending flows to derive weights. Finally, we can cumulate the growth rates to get the real aggregate. Here are the calculations for the investment example:

| Year | Weight for Computers | Growth Rate of Total Real Investment | Cumulated Total Real Investment | Investment Deflator |
|------|---------------------|--------------------------------------|--------------------------------|---------------------|
| 1 | 0.485 |       | 206.0 | 1.000 |
| 2 | 0.517 | 0.017 | 209.6 | 0.969 |
| 3 | 0.498 | 0.046 | 219.4 | 0.943 |
| 4 | 0.497 | 0.061 | 233.2 | 0.853 |

The result of keeping the weights in line with the relative dollar spending is to reduce the growth in total real investment and to raise the growth in the deflator. The use of a fixed earlier year invariably gives too optimistic a picture about real growth. For the period 1988–1994, the bias in the traditional approach is about 0.4 percent—the traditional measure of real GDP growth was 15.3 percent and the new chain-weighted measure was 14.8 percent.

The same type of adjustment for price change is applied to each detailed category of consumption, investment, government purchases, exports, and imports. Then real GDP is real consumption plus real investment plus real government purchases plus real exports less real imports.

## 2.3 MEASURING GDP THROUGH PRODUCTION: VALUE ADDED

GDP can also be computed by adding up production of goods and services in different industries. As we observed on the spending side, we must avoid counting the same items more than once. Many industries specialize in the production of intermediate goods that are used in the production of other goods. If we want each industry's production to include the contribution of those industries to total GDP, then we want to take the production of intermediate goods into account.

The concept of **value added** was developed to prevent double counting and to attribute to each industry a part of GDP. The value added by a firm is the difference between the revenue the firm earns by selling its products and the amount it pays for the products of other firms it uses as intermediate goods. It is a measure of the value that is added to each product by firms at each stage of production.

For General Motors, for example, value added is the revenue from selling cars less the amount it pays for steel, glass, and the other inputs it buys. For a car dealer, value added is the revenue from selling cars less the wholesale cost of the cars. Wages, rents, interest, and profits are what make up value added at each firm.

GDP is the sum of the value added by all the firms located in the United States. If a firm sells a final product, the sale appears in that firm's value added but does not appear anywhere else. On the other hand, if a firm sells its output as an input for another firm, that sale appears negatively in the other firm's value added. Products sold by one firm to another are called **intermediate products.** When the two firms are added together in the process of computing GDP, sales of intermediate products wash out. When a firm imports a product, the transaction appears negatively in that firm's value added, but does not appear positively in the value added of any U.S. firm.

A breakdown of real GDP in terms of the value added by various industries is given in Table 2.2 for 1977 and 1992. These figures tell some interesting stories about the modern U.S. economy. Manufacturing is the largest sector, but services is now close behind, and the wholesale and retail trade sector, whose function is to take produced goods and make them available to the public, is a close third. The finance, insurance, and real estate sector is also large.

Near the bottom of the list is a small item called **statistical discrepancy.** Although the value-added computation of GDP should give the same answer as total spending, in practice there are measurement errors that cause a slight discrepancy between the two.

**Table 2.2**   Value Added by Industry in 1977 and 1992 (billions of 1987 dollars)

|  | 1977 | Percent | 1992 | Percent |
|---|---|---|---|---|
| GDP | 3533.3 |  | 4979.3 |  |
| Agriculture | 63.7 | 1.8 | 110.3 | 2.2 |
| Mining | 83.5 | 2.4 | 89 | 1.8 |
| Construction | 190.8 | 5.4 | 201.4 | 4.0 |
| Manufacturing | 741.6 | 21.0 | 924.6 | 18.6 |
| Transportation and utilities | 314.3 | 8.9 | 494.5 | 9.9 |
| Wholesale and retail trade | 488.1 | 13.8 | 827.6 | 16.6 |
| Finance, insurance & real estate | 596.5 | 16.9 | 893.4 | 17.9 |
| Services | 538.9 | 15.3 | 889.9 | 17.9 |
| Government | 475.7 | 13.5 | 584.2 | 11.7 |
| Statistical discrepancy | 19.4 | .5 | 7.3 | .1 |

*Source: Economic Report of the President, 1995,* Table B-12.

# 2.4    MEASURING GDP THROUGH INCOME

The Americans who produce GDP receive income for their work. This income provides a third way to compute GDP. To see the relation between GDP and income, think again about the value added of a car dealer. Value added is the difference between the revenue from selling cars and the wholesale cost of cars. That difference must be somebody's income. Part of the difference is the wages the car dealer pays to salespeople and mechanics. Another part is the rent that the car dealer pays to a landlord for the use of the showroom and garage. Another part is the interest that the car dealer pays to a bank for loans to finance inventory. The rest of the difference is profit, which goes into the income of the owner of the car dealership. All of a firm's value added is either rent, interest, or profit. Since we know that the sum of all firms' value added is GDP, the sum of all incomes must also equal GDP.

Because of taxes and certain other complications, there are several concepts of income. The most comprehensive is **national income.** It is a broad measure of the incomes of Americans, including income taxes and several other items that are deducted before people receive actual payments. There are three important reasons why national income is different from GDP. First, some Americans earn at least part of their income abroad, and some have invested capital abroad and earn income on that capital. This income from work or capital is called *factor income from the rest of the world.* It must be added to GDP to get a measure of income. On the other hand, some of U.S. GDP is earned by foreigners who work in the United States or who have invested capital in the United States. This is called *factor income to the rest of the world* and must be subtracted from GDP to get a measure of income. GDP plus factor income from the rest of the world minus factor income to the rest of the world is called gross national product (GNP). It is a measure of goods and services purchased by Americans rather than in America.

A second reason that GDP is different from national income is that depreciation must be subtracted to get national income. A third is that national income is measured in terms of the prices firms receive for the products they sell, whereas GDP is measured in terms of the prices paid by purchasers. Prices received differ from prices paid by the amount of sales and excise taxes.

There are two other minor conceptual differences. Business transfer payments—such as business gifts—are deducted from national income. Subsidies paid by the government to the businesses it runs are added to national income.

**TABLE 2.3** Relation between GDP and National Income in 1995 (billions of dollars)

| | |
|---|---:|
| Gross domestic product | 7247.7 |
| plus: Net factor payments | −10.2 |
| equals: Gross national product | 7237.5 |
| less: Depreciation | 825.8 |
| equals: Net national product | 6411.7 |
| less: Sales and excise taxes | 595.9 |
| less: Business transfers | 30.5 |
| less: Statistical discrepancy | 4.2 |
| plus: Net subsidies to government business | 18.1 |
| equals: National income | 5799.2 |

Source: U.S. Department of Commerce, Survey of Current Business, March 1996, p. 9.

Finally, there is the statistical discrepancy. Conceptually, the income calculation should be numerically the same as the spending calculation of GDP. But because of measurement errors, there is a small discrepancy. (This discrepancy is identical to the discrepancy in the calculation of value added, which attributes incomes to the various industries.)

The relation between GDP and national income is shown below in Table 2.3.

Government and businesses also raise and lower the incomes of some people. The NIPA contain two concepts of income that take account of these diversions and augmentations. **Personal income** is total income received by the public before income taxes, and **disposable personal income** is total income after income taxes.

For wage income, the social security tax is one of the important differences between wages paid by businesses and wages received by workers. The aggregate amount of social security tax, called **contributions for social insurance,** is one of the items that is subtracted from national income to get personal income.

All the profits of corporations are included in national income, but only the cash payments of dividends by corporations are included in personal income. The difference between profits and dividends consists of **retained earnings** and the income taxes paid by corporations. These two items are excluded from personal income.

People have two important sources of income other than the production of goods and services. First, the government pays social security and other benefits. Second, people receive interest from the government debt and from other nonbusiness sources. Both of these are included in personal

**TABLE 2.4** National Income, Personal Income, and Personal Disposable Income in 1995 (billions of dollars)

| | |
|---|---:|
| National income | 5799.2 |
| less: Contributions for social insurance | 660.3 |
| less: Corporate retained earnings | 373.8 |
| plus: Nonbusiness interest | 313.4 |
| plus: Transfer payments from government and business | 1022.6 |
| equals: Personal income | 6101.0 |
| less: Income taxes | 794.6 |
| equals: Personal disposable income | 5306.4 |

*Note:* Wage accruals less disbursements, a trivial accounting item, is omitted from the list of adjustments to national income.
*Source:* U.S. Department of Commerce, *Survey of Current Business*, March 1996, pp. 9, 11.

income. Note that social security contributions by employers are taken out of personal income, but the benefits financed by the contributions are added back into personal income.

The relationship between the three concepts of income is shown in Table 2.4. Disposable personal income was $5,306.4 billion, or $20,176 per capita. Consumption per capita was $18,719, so all but $1,457 of income per capita was consumed.

How much of national income is earned by workers and how much is profit? Table 2.5 shows the breakdown for 1995. About 73 percent of national income was earned by labor; this includes payments to workers in wages and salaries as well as fringe benefits. The profit share includes not only corporate profits, but also rental income, proprietors' income, and net interest income. Since labor plus profits exhausts income, the profit share was 27 percent in 1995. These relative shares are fairly stable from year to year. In 1970 the labor share of national income was 74 percent.

**TABLE 2.5** Labor and Profit Shares of National Income in 1995 (billions of dollars)

| | | |
|---|---:|---|
| Compensation of employees | 4209.1 | Labor share 73 percent |
| Proprietors' income | 478.3 | |
| Rental income of persons | 122.2 | |
| Corporate profits | 588.6 | Profit share |
| Net interest | 401.0 | 27 percent |
| National income | 5799.2 | |

*Source:* U.S. Department of Commerce, *Survey of Current Business*, March 1996, p. 10.

## THE NATIONAL INCOME AND PRODUCT ACCOUNTS

1. Gross domestic product (GDP) is the production of goods and services in the United States. The spending, value added, and factor income measures of GDP are all equal.
2. Consumption, investment, government purchases, and net exports are the four basic components of spending. Consumption is the largest component and investment is the most volatile component.
3. The investment component of GDP includes the replacement of depreciating capital. It is thus gross investment. Net investment is gross investment less depreciation.
4. Real GDP is a measure of production that is adjusted for the effects of inflation. It measures the physical volume of production. Nominal GDP measures the dollar volume of production.
5. Final sales is GDP less inventory investment. It fluctuates less than GDP.
6. To avoid double counting, we measure the contribution of each industry by its value added and do not include any goods that were produced in an earlier year.
7. Disposable personal income is the amount of national income that is available for households to spend. It excludes retained earnings of corporations. It includes what is left of wage and salary income, fringe benefits, rents, dividends, interest, and small business income after all taxes are paid to governments.

## 2.5   SAVING AND INVESTMENT

Saving is defined as income minus consumption. An important principle is that *saving must equal investment.* To see this, consider first a closed economy with no government and therefore no taxes. Then,

$$\text{Spending on GDP} = \text{Consumption} + \text{Investment}.$$

Also, from the definition of saving,

$$\text{Income} = \text{Saving} + \text{Consumption}.$$

Since spending on GDP equals income, we know that

$$\text{Consumption} + \text{Investment} = \text{Saving} + \text{Consumption}$$

or

$$\text{Investment} = \text{Saving.}$$

The equality of saving and investment follows from none other than the definitions of GDP and income. As long as the statisticians adhere to these definitions, there is no possibility that investment can ever differ from saving. We don't have to say, "If our theories hold, saving and investment will be equal." No matter how investors and consumers behave, saving and invest-ment will be equal.

## Saving and Investment in an Open Economy

Some more symbols will save space in the explanation of saving and in-vestment in an open economy. Let

$F$ = Government transfers to the private sector
$N$ = Interest on the government debt
$T$ = Taxes
$V$ = Factor income and transfer payments from abroad (net)
$S_p$ = Private saving (saving of the private sector)
$S_g$ = Government saving
$S_r$ = Rest of world saving

and recall that we previously defined

$Y$ = GDP
$C$ = Consumption
$I$ = Investment
$G$ = Government spending
$X$ = Net exports.

**PRIVATE SAVING.**   From the definition of saving we know that private saving is disposable income $(Y + V + F + N - T)$ minus consumption $(C)$:

$$S_p = (Y + V + F + N - T) - C. \tag{2.1}$$

**GOVERNMENT SAVING.**   Government saving equals income (tax receipts, net of transfer payments and interest payments) minus purchases of goods and services:

$$S_g = (T - F - N) - G. \tag{2.2}$$

Government saving is also called the government **budget surplus** or **budget deficit.** The budget is in surplus when $G$ is less than $(T - F - N)$ and in deficit when $G$ is greater than $(T - F - N)$.

**REST OF THE WORLD SAVING.**   The rest of the world saving in the United States is defined as payments received from the United States less payments made to the United States. We need to keep track of three types of payments. Payments received from the United States include (1) payments for our imports, (2) factor payments to foreigners, and (3) transfer payments to foreigners. Payments made to the United States include (1) payments for our exports, (2) factor payments to Americans, and (3) transfer payments to Americans.

Rest of the world saving is the sum of the net payments for each type: (1) imports less exports, or *net* exports with the sign reversed, (2) factor payments to foreigners less factor payments from foreigners, or *net* factor income from abroad with the sign reversed, and (3) transfer payments to foreigners less transfer payments to Americans, or *net* transfer payments from abroad with the sign reversed. In terms of our notation, (1) is equal to $-X$, and (2) plus (3) is equal to $-V$. Thus

$$S_r = -X - V. \tag{2.3}$$

The sum $V + X$ is sometimes called *net foreign investment of the United States*. Recall that $X$ is sometimes called the trade deficit. As we will describe in the next section, $V + X$ is sometimes called the surplus (or deficit) on the *current account*. Hence, foreign saving is positive in the United States when the United States is running a current account deficit. The rest of the world saving is used either to buy financial assets in the United States or to reduce foreign financial liabilities. Either is called a *capital inflow*. Put another way, the United States finances any excess of imports over exports by borrowing from abroad. Then rest of the world lending is equal to U.S. borrowing.

For the three sectors as a whole, saving must equal investment. The sum of the three sectors' saving is

$$S_p + S_g + S_r = (Y + V + F + N - T)$$
$$- C + (T - F - N - G) - V - X \tag{2.4}$$

Everything cancels out on the right-hand side except $Y - C - G - X$, which from the income identity is equal to investment, $I$. Thus, private saving plus government saving plus saving from the rest of the world equals investment. This identity is of great importance in interpreting movements in investment and saving. Because of large shifts in the saving of these three sectors in recent years, the identity deserves particular emphasis, as is illustrated in Table 2.6.

Table 2.6 shows gross investment in the United States in 1995 and where the saving came from. *National saving* is the sum of private plus government saving and in 1995 equaled $963.0 billion. Investment in new factories and equipment in the United States was larger than national saving because of the willingness of foreigners to save in the United States.

| TABLE 2.6   Gross Saving and Investment, 1995 (billions of dollars) | |
| --- | --- |
| National saving ($Y - C - G$) | 963.0 |
| plus: Foreign saving ($-X$) | 102.3 |
| equals: Gross private domestic investment ($I$) | 1065.3 |

*Source:* U.S. Department of Commerce, *Survey of Current Business*, March 1996, p. 9.

   Figure 2.1 shows the trends in investment and saving since 1980. Except in the recession year 1991, investment has been greater than national saving, so that foreign saving has been positive. That foreign saving is, of course, related to the trade deficit. As the gap between investment and national saving rose and then fell in the 1980s, the trade deficit also rose and fell. Figure 2.1 shows how dramatic that pattern was. Figure 2.2 shows how the trade deficit ($X$) has the same pattern.

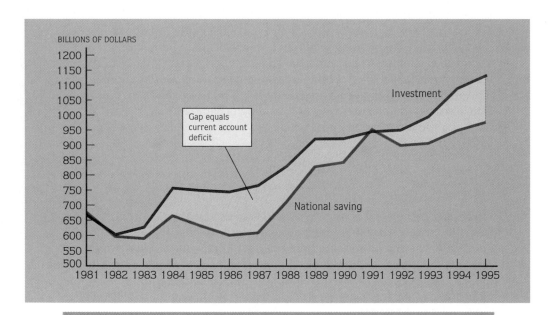

**FIGURE 2.1**   Investment and National Saving in the United States

The gap between investment and national saving (private plus government saving) rose and then fell during the 1980s. It rose again in the 1990s. The gap equals the current account deficit.
Source: *Economic Report of the President*, 1996, Table B-28.

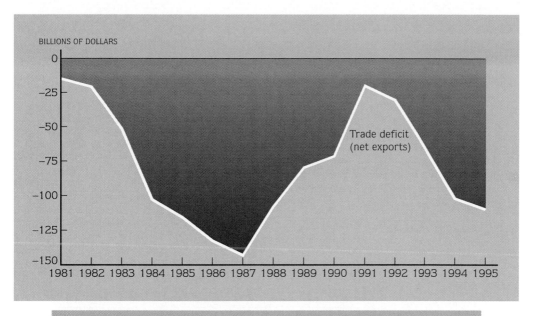

BILLIONS OF DOLLARS

Trade deficit
(net exports)

1981 1982 1983 1984 1985 1986 1987 1988 1989 1990 1991 1992 1993 1994 1995

**FIGURE 2.2**   U.S. Trade Deficit

The trade deficit is closely related to the gap between investment and national saving shown in Figure 2.1. As the gap widened, so did the trade deficit. (The gap equals $X + V$ where $X$ is the trade deficit and $V$ is other net payments to foreigners.)
Source: *Economic Report of the President*, 1996, Table B-1.

## 2.6  TRANSACTIONS WITH THE REST OF THE WORLD: THE BALANCE OF PAYMENT ACCOUNTS AND THE EXCHANGE RATE

International transactions are divided into *current account transactions* and *capital account transactions.* The current account keeps track of net exports as well as government grants and interest payments from the U.S. government abroad. The capital account keeps track of borrowing and lending. When an American lends to a foreigner, by making a loan, buying a bond, or some similar transaction, the lending appears with a negative sign in the capital account. When an American borrows by taking out a loan in another country or by selling stocks and bonds, the borrowing appears with a positive sign. The term "balance of payments" refers to both the current account and the capital account.

An important principle of the balance of payments accounts is that the current account and the capital account should sum to zero. When the United States imports more than it exports, it must be borrowing from the rest of the

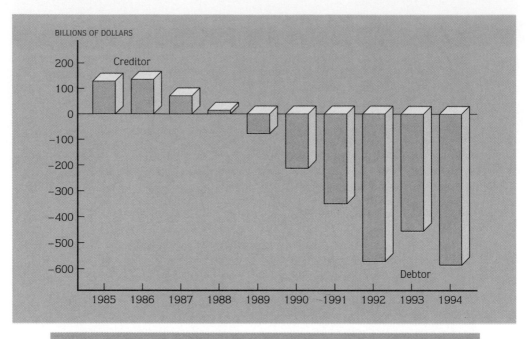

BILLIONS OF DOLLARS

**FIGURE 2.3**  Net Creditor/Debtor Position of the United States

Data series on U.S. assets at market values shows that the United States has moved from being a creditor nation to being a debtor nation in the last 10 years.
Source: *Economic Report of the President*, 1996, Table B-103.

world to finance its current account deficit. There should be a positive balance in the capital account equal in magnitude to the current account deficit. This principle is what underlies Equation 2.3. When Americans buy more than they sell, they must borrow from abroad. Figure 2.3 shows the net effect of U.S. borrowing and lending abroad in the late 1980s and early 1990s. The U.S. current account deficit meant that we were increasing our net indebtedness to foreigners. Our net asset position—assets less liabilities—went from positive to negative.

## The Exchange Rate

Transactions with other countries require that U.S. dollars be exchanged for foreign currency—Japanese yen, German marks, Italian lire, Canadian dollars, and so on. The *exchange rate* is the price at which these exchanges of dollars for foreign currencies take place. The dollar exchange rate measures the *price of dollars* in terms of foreign currencies. For example, the exchange rate between the U.S. dollar and the Japanese yen in the last quarter of 1994 was 99 yen per dollar. That is, one could go to a bank and get 99 yen with 1 dollar. The *price* of 1 dollar was 99 yen. When Americans purchase foreign goods—such as a cup of coffee in Tokyo—they must pay for these goods with foreign currency—such as yen. Hence, the exchange rate is important for international transactions. A cup of coffee that costs 198 yen in Tokyo would cost an American 2 dollars if the exchange rate is 99 yen per dollar. If the exchange rate rises to 198 yen per dollar, that same cup of coffee would cost "only" 1 dollar.

The exchange rate determines how expensive foreign goods are compared with American goods. When the exchange rate rises, foreign goods become cheaper compared with home goods. As we will see in Chapter 7, this causes Americans to buy more goods abroad and foreigners to buy fewer goods in the United States.

There is a dollar exchange rate for every foreign currency. Rather than keep track of all of these exchange rates, it is a useful simplification to consider an average of the different exchange rates. The **trade-weighted exchange rate** is an average of the exchange rates between the dollar and several different currencies, with those countries that trade more with the United States getting more weight.

Figure 2.4 shows the trade-weighted dollar exchange rate against 10

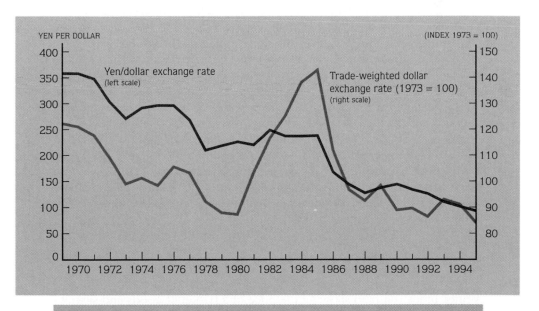

**FIGURE 2.4**  Yen-Dollar and Trade-Weighted Dollar Exchange Rates

The exchange rate has had large fluctuations during the last 16 years. Some of these fluctuations are associated with the movements in U.S. output. The dollar fell during the boom of the late 1970s and rose during the slump of the early 1980s. Other fluctuations seem unrelated to the state of the U.S. economy.
Source: *Economic Report of the President*, 1996, Table B-106.

major currencies, along with the dollar-yen exchange rate. Note that both exchange rates fluctuate by large amounts. Some of these fluctuations are associated with the fluctuations in real GDP in the United States. For example, the dollar fell during the boom in economic activity in the late 1970s and rose during the slump in economic activity in the early 1980s. But there are many other movements in the exchange rate. During the period from 1968 to 1995 the dollar was generally falling relative to the yen. As we will see, this was a result of the higher rate of inflation in the United States compared with Japan during these years.

# MEASURING INFLATION

The national income and product accounts discussed at the beginning of this chapter are important measures of economic performance. But two other measures—inflation and employment—are released to the public at more frequent intervals and form the basis of most policy initiatives. Data on inflation and employment are released every month.

Almost everybody watches the rate of inflation. It is a major indicator of how the economy is doing, and changes in inflation are related to fluctuations in real GDP. The *rate of inflation* is defined as the percentage rate of change in the general price level from one period to the next. The general price level is a measure of the purchasing power of the dollar, or the amount of goods and services the dollar can buy. For example, one measure of the price level was 152 in 1995, which means that the same basket of goods that cost $100 in 1983 cost $152 in 1994. In this example, 1983 is the base year. There are two approaches to measuring the general price level: constructing **price indexes** directly from data on the prices of thousands of goods and services, and calculating **deflators** by dividing a component of nominal GDP by the same component of real GDP.

## Price Indexes

A price index is a ratio showing the price of a basket of goods and services in various years in relation to the price of the basket in a base year. The index is 100 in the base year and correspondingly higher in later years if the prices of the things in the basket have risen. The most conspicuous price index is the **consumer price index (CPI).** This index measures the cost of living for a typical urban family. The Bureau of Labor Statistics (BLS) of the Department of Labor computes it in the following way: Once every 10 years or so, the BLS makes a survey of the buying habits of American families. The survey covers not only the products they buy in stores, but other expenditures like the purchases of houses. Then the BLS makes a long list of goods and services whose prices they can determine once a month. From the survey of buying habits, they estimate the quantities of each item bought by the average family. The list includes tomato soup, for example. However, the amount of tomato soup in the CPI basket is greater than the fraction of income that the typical family spends on tomato soup. The price of tomato soup is considered representative of the prices of similar products that are not included in the index.

Every month, the BLS sends surveyors into stores to write down the actual prices of goods and services. When discounts are available, they take them into account. The BLS is particularly careful about new car prices because cars have a large role in the price index and few people actually pay the sticker price for a new car.

Each month, the BLS computes the new level of the price index by using the detailed prices to compute the cost of the CPI basket. The basket is chosen so that its price was 100 in 1983, which means that the index had the value 100 in 1983. In 1994, the index was 148.2, so prices rose by 48 percent over 11 years. Some prices rose more than others. The 1994 level of the medical care price index was 211, while the level for energy was only 104.6. Both started at 100 in 1983.

Figure 2.5 shows the rate of inflation, the percent change in the U.S. price level as measured by the CPI, since 1968. Inflation was moderate in the early 1960s, but, as shown in Figure 2.5, gained momentum in the late 1960s and early 1970s, and reached two peaks in 1974 and 1980. Inflation moderated in the early 1980s and has been low since then.

The CPI is the most widely used measure of the purchasing power of the dollar. When people make an agreement that is set in dollars and want to protect themselves against inflation, they can write in a provision that payments rise in proportion to the increase in the CPI. This practice is called **cost-of-living adjustment (COLA)** and is used for social security payments and in many collective-bargaining agreements that spell out the terms of employment for unionized workers.

The government puts out another major price index in addition to the CPI. It is called the **producer price index (PPI).** Instead of measuring the prices actually paid by consumers, the PPI measures the prices charged by producers at various stages in the production process. There is no clear basis for the choice of weights for the PPI, comparable to the market basket that gives the weights for the CPI. As a result, there is much less interest in the monthly value of the PPI. However, the BLS reports all the detailed prices going into the PPI and these prices and the price indexes computed from them are the best source of information about prices of crude materials and intermediate goods. Some economists think that the PPI for crude

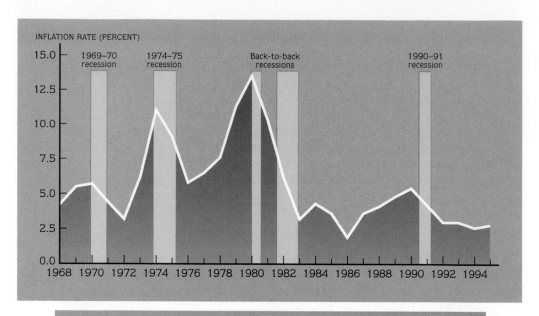

INFLATION RATE (PERCENT)

**FIGURE 2.5**   Consumer Price Inflation

The consumer price index measures the price of a bundle of goods and services representative of the purchases of a typical family. The chart shows the percent change in this index (December to December) for each year.
Source: *Economic Report of the President*, 1996, Table B-60.

materials is one of the most sensitive early warning indicators of future inflation.

## Deflators

The construction of data on nominal and real GDP results in another type of price index. The purpose of measuring real GDP is to get rid of the price effects in nominal GDP. Thus, the ratio of nominal GDP to real GDP is a measure of prices. It is called the **GDP implicit price deflator.** For example, in 1995, nominal GDP was $7,246 billion. Real GDP was $6,739 billion 1992 dollars. The GDP deflator for 1995 was $100 \times 7,246/6,739 = 108$. That is, with a base of 100 in 1992, the price level according to the GDP deflator was 108.

Each component for GDP has a deflator. For example, the ratio of nominal consumption to real consumption is the **consumption deflator.** It is widely used as an alternative to the CPI as a measure of the cost of living.

## INFLATION, PRICE INDEXES, AND DEFLATORS

1. Inflation is the rate of increase in the price level. The price level is an average of all prices in the economy.
2. There are two types of measures of the price level: price indexes and deflators. The consumer price index (CPI) and the producer price index (PPI) are the two major price indexes. The weights on the individual prices in the CPI are based on a survey of consumer buying habits. The GDP deflator is the ratio of nominal GDP to real GDP. It is a measure of the prices of all goods and services produced in America.
3. The CPI is used for cost-of-living adjustments in many union contracts and in many government programs.

 **2.8**

## MEASURING EMPLOYMENT AND WAGES

Employment falls along with production during recessions and rises again during recoveries. Over the long haul, employment grows along with potential GDP as firms hire more workers to produce the growing output. Information on employment in the United States comes from two surveys, one of *households* and the other of *establishments*—the offices, factories, stores, mines, and other places where people work.

The household survey—called the Current Population Survey—is conducted each month by the Bureau of the Census, and the data are tabulated and reported by the BLS. About 100,000 adults are interviewed each month to find out whether they are employed during the calendar week that includes the 12th of the month. Everyone who worked an hour or more during that week is counted as employed for that month. The results are blown up by multiplying by about 1,000 so that they are good estimates of the total number of workers employed that month in the whole economy (each person in the survey stands for a little over 1,000 people in the population). Some other people who did not work—notably those on vacation—are also counted as employed.

Total civilian employment by this measure was 124.9 million in 1995, up almost 2 million from its level of 123.0 million in 1994 and up by 8.1 million from its level in the recession year of 1991. In the recession of 1990–91, employment fell by a million, whereas in normal years, it rises by several million. The expansion that started in 1992 involved substantial growth in employment, as expansions generally do. On the other hand, employment falls during recessions, as it did in 1991.

The establishment survey interviews employers to find out the number of people on the payroll at each workplace. The survey excludes farm employees. Because it is based on payrolls, it also omits people who are self-employed. Total nonagricultural payroll employment was 115.1 million people in December 1994.

## Hours per Week and Total Hours

The number of hours worked each week varies among workers and over time. Some people normally work only a few hours a week and others work 60 to 70 hours. The average factory worker now puts in about 42 hours per week, while the average store worker puts in about 29 hours. Also, the number of hours per week falls during recessions and rises during expansions. When demand is booming, many workers are asked, or choose, to work overtime. Average weekly hours fell from 34.5 hours per week in July 1990 to 34.0 in April 1991 and rose back to 34.5 by 1993 in the recovery. The data also

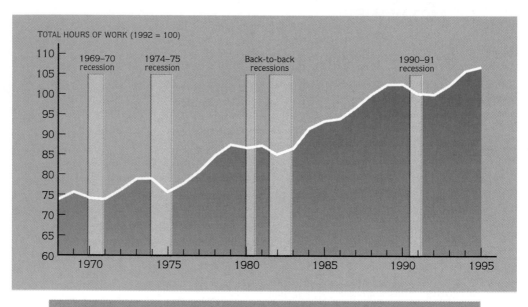

**FIGURE 2.6**   Growth and Fluctuations of Hours Worked

The total amount of work performed in the United States, measured by the hours of all workers, fluctuates along with the business cycle. In each of the five recessions shown here—1969–70, 1974–75, 1980, 1981–82, and 1990–91—total hours declined. In general, total hours have been growing. Growth was particularly strong from 1975 to 1979, from 1982 to 1988, and from 1992 to 1995.
Source: *Economic Report of the President*, 1996, Table B-45.

verify the fact that the average workweek has declined over the long term. Average weekly hours for store workers fell from about 40 hours per week in 1947 to about 29 hours per week now, and average weekly hours in manufacturing have remained steady at about 40 hours per week since 1947.

For all these reasons, employment by itself is not a complete measure of labor input to the economy. Total hours of work—the number of people working multiplied by the hours of work of the average worker—is a better measure. The BLS index of total hours for the business sector is shown in Figure 2.6 for the period from 1968 to 1995. The upward trend in hours is clear in the figure, but so are the fluctuations. When the level of real output of the economy declines, total hours of work decline. The work force feels the effects of a recession in the form of fewer hours of work per week; they feel it as well in the possibility of being laid off. In either case, their pay declines even if the wage rate does not change.

## REVIEW AND PRACTICE

### Major Points

1. There are three ways to measure and think about GDP: the spending side, the production side, and the income side. The components of spending are consumption, investment, government spending, and net exports. The components of production are the values added by each industry. The components of income are wages, profits, and interest.

2. Real GDP is the physical volume of production, after the effects of rising prices have been removed. Real GDP growth has averaged about 3 percent per year since the end of the Second World War, but there have been many fluctuations. Potential GDP is real GDP after the economic fluctuations have been removed. Nominal GDP is just GDP without adjustment for inflation or for economic fluctuations.

3. Value added by a firm is the difference between the revenue of the firm and its purchase of goods and services from other firms. It is the firm's contribution to GDP. GDP for the whole economy is the sum of value added across all producers.

4. Depreciation is the loss of capital from wear and tear. Net investment is gross investment less depreciation.

5. Conceptually, income and production are equal. All value added is somebody's income. In the national accounts, there are various measures of income. National income is GDP less depreciation and less sales and excise taxes and adjusted for net factor payments. Personal income is national income less social security taxes and corporate retained earnings plus transfer payments and interest paid by the government to consumers. Disposable personal income is personal income less income taxes.

6. The international accounts—called the balance of payments accounts—consist of a current account and a capital account. The two sum to zero. The current account is in surplus when the United States is exporting more than it is importing.

At the same time, the capital account is in deficit—capital is flowing out because the United States must be lending to the rest of the world if the United States is importing less than it exports.

7. The exchange rate is crucial for international transactions. It is the price of dollars in terms of foreign currency. When the exchange rate rises, more foreign currency can be bought with each dollar. This makes foreign goods cheaper in terms of dollars.

8. An important implication of the equality of income and product is the equality of saving and investment. It will always be the case that investment equals private saving plus the government surplus plus the capital inflow from abroad.

9. The consumer price index is the number of dollars required to purchase a market basket of goods and services typical of the consumption patterns of Americans.

10. Price indexes called deflators can be calculated by dividing a component of nominal GDP by the same component of real GDP. The consumption deflator is widely used by economists as an alternative to the CPI. The overall GDP deflator is a measure of the price of domestic production; it does not include the price of imports.

11. The best measure of total labor input to the economy is the total number of hours worked by all workers each year. That measure tends to fluctuate in the same direction as real GDP.

12. A good measure of hourly wages is total labor earnings divided by total hours worked. The real wage is the ratio of the hourly wage to the price level.

## Key Terms and Concepts

gross domestic product
value added
consumption
gross national product
fixed investment
national income
inventory investment
government purchases
imports
exports

depreciation
net investment
final sales
factor incomes
private saving
personal disposable income
intermediate goods
government saving
real GDP
nominal GDP

balance of payments
current account
capital account
exchange rate
trade-weighted exchange rate
price indexes
consumer price index
producer price index
price deflators
labor force
rate of inflation

## Questions for Discussion and Review

1. Explain why spending on GDP is equal to income earned from producing GDP.

2. Identify which of the following are flows and which are stocks: consumption; government bonds outstanding at the end of last year; government purchases; inventories; inventory investment; depreciation; factories and equipment in the United States on December 31, 1994; the budget deficit.

3. Explain how real GDP is calculated.

4. Which components of spending fluctuate the most over the cycle?

5. What is the difference between high prices and inflation?

6. What is the difference between being unemployed and not working? Give some examples of people not at work who are not unemployed.

## Problems

### NUMERICAL

1. The following are data for the U.S. economy for 1993 in billions of dollars.

| | |
|---|---:|
| Net rental income of persons[a] | 24.1 |
| Depreciation | 669.1 |
| Compensation of employees | 3,780.4 |
| Personal consumption expenditures | 4,378.2 |
| Sales and excise taxes | 525.3 |
| Business transfer payments | 28.7 |
| Statistical discrepancy | 2.3 |
| Gross private domestic investment | 882.0 |
| Exports of goods and services | 659.1 |
| Net subsidies of government business | 9.0 |
| Government purchases of goods and services | 1,148.4 |
| Imports of goods and services | 724.3 |
| Net interest | 399.5 |
| Proprietors' income | 441.6 |
| Corporate profits | 485.8 |
| Net factor income from rest of world | 5.7 |

[a]Adjusted for capital consumption.

   a. Compute GDP using the spending approach.
   b. Compute net domestic product.
   c. Compute national income two ways.

2. Fill in the blanks.

   a. If investment is $1,100 billion, private saving is $1,050 billion, and capital inflow from abroad is $100 billion, then the government budget deficit is ___ billion.
   b. If the stock of inventories in the economy is $1,000 billion at the end of 1998 and $1,050 billion at the end of 1999, then inventory investment for 1989 is ___ billion.
   c. If production by Americans and American capital abroad is $80 billion and GNP is $7,000 billion, then GDP is ___.

3. (Warning: This problem is difficult.) Data on the U.S. economy are given in the following tables (billions of dollars).
   Assume that consumer and government purchases from abroad are zero and that there is no inventory investment.

   a. Compute consumption, investment, government purchases, exports, and imports. Compute GDP from these.
   b. Compute value added for each industry. Calculate GDP by summing all value added. Is it equal to GDP from Part a? (Hints: Government value added is its wage payment. In calculating value added, do not subtract capital inputs.)

c. Compute profit for each industry as sales less purchases of current inputs (do not subtract investment). Compute national income as total profit plus total wages. Is it equal to GDP?

d. Compute net exports.

| Industry | Purchases of Intermediate Inputs from | | | | | | |
|---|---|---|---|---|---|---|---|
| | Agricul-ture | Mining | Manufac-turing | Transportation and Utilities (T&U) | Trade | Finance, Insurance, and Real Estate (FIRE) | Services |
| Agriculture | — | 1 | 19 | 14 | 7 | 7 | 18 |
| Mining | 8 | — | 21 | 4 | 18 | 18 | 8 |
| Construction | 21 | 21 | 22 | 23 | 18 | 15 | 5 |
| Manufacturing | 54 | 153 | — | 139 | 20 | 106 | 11 |
| T&U | 1 | 60 | 20 | — | 25 | 55 | 12 |
| Trade | 9 | 7 | 464 | 79 | — | 76 | 8 |
| FIRE | 0 | 13 | 24 | 36 | 14 | — | 7 |
| Services | 4 | 9 | 104 | 29 | 56 | 73 | — |

| Industry | Purchases of Capital from | | |
|---|---|---|---|
| | Construction | Manufacturing | Abroad |
| Agriculture | 2 | 3 | 1 |
| Mining | 11 | 12 | 2 |
| Construction | 0 | 8 | 1 |
| Manufacturing | 21 | 132 | 14 |
| T&U | 8 | 17 | 3 |
| Trade | 27 | 25 | 0 |
| FIRE | 143 | 6 | 0 |
| Services | 19 | 15 | 1 |

| Industry | Imports of Inputs | Sales to Government | Sales to Consumer | Exports | Wages |
|---|---|---|---|---|---|
| Agriculture | 12 | 8 | 12 | 37 | 60 |
| Mining | 90 | 9 | 1 | 21 | 88 |
| Construction | 2 | 23 | 0 | 0 | 98 |
| Manufacturing | 181 | 188 | 21 | 206 | 315 |
| T&U | 5 | 5 | 101 | 13 | 132 |
| Trade | 2 | 6 | 935 | 15 | 287 |
| FIRE | 3 | 11 | 178 | 5 | 256 |
| Services | 6 | 4 | 583 | 21 | 195 |

Government wages: 337
Earnings of U.S. factors abroad: 49

4. Consider a closed economy with the following expenditure totals for a year:

| | |
|---|---|
| Consumption | 1,300 |
| Investment | 500 |
| Government purchases | 500 |
| Government tax receipts | 400 |
| Depreciation | 200 |

Suppose that the financial assets in the economy consist of money and bonds. Assume that money equals 500 at the start of the year and that government bonds equal 700 at the start of the year.

   a. Assuming that 90 percent of government deficits are financed by bonds, calculate the new levels of bond and money holdings for the private sector and for the government.
   b. Show how the total change in government liabilities—money ($M$) + bonds ($B$)—can be computed in two ways.

5. The consumer price index for the 1978–82 period and the GDP deflator are listed below. This was a period of unusually high, but declining, inflation. (The CPI is equal to 100 in the base years, 1982–84; the GDP deflator is equal to 100 in the base year 1987.)

| | CPI | GDP Deflator |
|---|---|---|
| 1978 | 65.2 | 60.3 |
| 1979 | 72.6 | 65.5 |
| 1980 | 82.4 | 71.7 |
| 1981 | 90.9 | 78.9 |
| 1982 | 96.5 | 83.8 |

   a. Calculate the rate of inflation according to both measures from 1979 through 1982. What might explain the differences between the two?
   b. Suppose that the hourly wage rate for a group of workers that sign an employment contract for the 3-year period starting in 1979 is indexed to the CPI according to the formula

$$\Delta W/W = .03 + .5 \, \Delta \, \text{CPI/CPI}.$$

   Calculate the actual increase in the wage during each year of the contract period. If the wage is $12.00 in 1979, what was it in 1980, 1981, and 1982? What happens to the real wage measured in terms of the CPI?
   c. Repeat your calculations with .03 reduced to 0 and .5 increased to 1. What indexing formula would the workers' employer have preferred? Is there any reason for the employer to have been happy with the other formula before the actual inflation experience was known?

6. The CPI is calculated for a fixed market basket. It measures the change in the cost of the market basket from the base year until the current year. An index with the market basket fixed in the first year—like the CPI—is called a Laspeyres index. An alternative index—called the Paasche index—is based on a market basket in the end year. It measures the change in the cost of a market basket

fixed in the end year. Suppose that the base year is 1993. Suppose that the market basket contains only two items, peanut butter and gasoline, and that the quantities consumed in 1996 and 1997 are:

|        | Peanut Butter | Gasoline   |
|--------|---------------|------------|
| 1996   | 100 jars      | 50 gallons |
| 1997   | 150 jars      | 45 gallons |

Suppose that the price of peanut butter increases from $1.00 per jar in 1996 to $1.20 per jar in 1997 and the price of gasoline increases from $.50 per gallon to $2.00 per gallon.

a. Calculate the rate of inflation for the Laspeyres (CPI) index and the Paasche index.

b. Will inflation calculated using the Laspeyres index always exceed inflation calculated with the Paasche index? (Hint: Use standard indifference curve analysis.)

c. Workers often receive an adjustment in their wages equal to only a fraction of inflation as calculated using the CPI. In view of the preceding analysis, explain why workers would likely be better off than they were before if they were fully compensated for inflation. Would this also be the case if inflation was calculated using the Paasche index?

## ANALYTICAL

1. Identify which of the following purchases is counted as part of GDP: You purchase a used lawn mower at a garage sale. General Motors purchases tires from Goodyear to equip new Chevrolets. General Motors purchases tires from Goodyear to replace worn tires on executives' company cars. A neighbor hires you to baby-sit for an evening. You purchase a share of AT&T. A neighbor breaks your window with a golf ball, and you purchase a new window. You pay your tuition for the semester.

2. As part of its drive to replace welfare with workfare, the government decides to redesignate $100 billion in welfare benefits as government wages. The recipients become government employees.

   a. For each of the methods used in calculating GDP, describe the effect of this policy change.

   b. Suppose now that the workfare recipients are removed from the government payroll and are moved into the payroll of the newly incorporated Workfare, Inc. As part of its support for the workfare program, the government stands ready to subsidize Workfare, Inc., if its sales do not cover its costs. Since Workfare, Inc., has no products to sell, the subsidy ends up being the full $100 billion. How does this arrangement affect your answers to Part a?

3. Suppose that automobile purchases were to be treated like housing purchases in the national income accounts. How would that affect saving? Investment?

4. Determine whether the following statements are true or false, and explain why.

   a. The trade deficit is equal to the government budget deficit plus investment less private domestic saving.

   b. If GDP were measured at the prices firms receive for the products they sell, then sales and excise taxes would not be subtracted from GDP in computing national income.

   c. The importance of different goods in GDP is determined by their relative price: for example, the production of one ounce of gold counts much more in GDP than the production of one ounce of steel.

5. In 1987, spending by Americans on personal consumption, private investment, and government operations totaled 103 percent of GDP. How is that possible?

6. Explain how the trade deficit in the 1980s helped finance the large government budget deficit as well as the large increase in private gross investment in the United States. Should Americans care whether foreigners or other Americans hold the U.S. public debt?

7. Suppose initially that exports are zero and imports are $100 billion. Then assume that the government places a ban on imports. Assume that the spending habits of consumers, firms, and government remain the same (i.e., they spend the same amount but substitute domestic goods for imports).

   a. What happens to GDP?

   b. What happens to each category of savings (assume taxes remain unchanged)?

   c. Does total savings still equal investment?

8. Suppose that in a given year U.S. foreign trade consists of some consumer importing a single Toyota Tercel for $12,000 (1.8 million yen). Here are some possible financial transactions to accompany the purchase: (i) The consumer pays with $12,000, which Toyota puts in its American bank account. (ii) The consumer pays with 1.8 million yen that happens to be in a Japanese bank account. (iii) The consumer pays with $12,000; Toyota invests the proceeds in U.S. Treasury bills. (iv) The consumer purchases 1.8 million yen on the foreign exchange market from some anonymous American foreign exchange trader and then pays for the car.

   a. Is the United States running a current account surplus or deficit?

   b. For each of the financial transactions described above, explain the effect the transaction has on the U.S. capital account. What is the sum of the current account and capital account balances?

9. Net domestic product is considered to be a better measure of welfare than GDP, since it adjusts for the fact that part of GDP must be devoted to replacing physical capital that has worn out during the course of the year. If we took this principle of adjusting for depreciation more seriously, what other expenditures would you want to deduct from GDP to get a clearer measure of net national product?

10. With the exception of housing expenditure, consumption and investment spending are delineated by the decision-making unit responsible for each type of expenditure. An alternative accounting scheme might be based on the durability of goods. Suppose investment was equal to total expenditures on goods that last one year or more. All other expenditures count as consumption. How would this

revised scheme affect consumption, investment, depreciation, and the capital stock relative to the current accounting system? Which system do you think is more informative and why? Which system would be more costly to manage?

## MacroSolve Exercises

1. Tabulate annual data on the ratios of investment in GDP. Describe how the ratio of investment to GDP has changed since the 1930s. Why does the share of investment in GDP fall during recessions? Why do you think that the ratio investment to GDP may have fallen in the 1940s when the GDP gap was high?

2. Tabulate annual data on the ratios to GDP of saving, investment, the government deficit, and net exports.

   a. Confirm that saving equals investment plus the government deficit and net exports. Explain intuitively rather than algebraically why this must always be the case.

   b. According to the above identity, $S_p = I + \text{Deficit} + X$. Equivalently, $S_p - \text{Deficit} - X = I$. Private saving and investment should be positively related (everything else constant), the government budget deficit and investment should be negatively related (everything else constant), and net exports and investment should be negatively related (everything else constant). Graph each relationship using annual data. Historically, have these relationships existed? Do the data support the argument that government deficits crowd out investment? Are high government deficits correlated with low net exports?

3. Plot the ratio of the government deficit to GDP. Why do you think that the government deficit was such a large share of GDP in mid-1975?

4. Plot the trade-weighted exchange rate using quarterly data from 1967 to the present. Between 1981 and 1985, the exchange rate rose sharply.

   a. Does this mean that the U.S. dollar became worth more or less in terms of foreign currencies during that period?

   b. In this period, would foreign goods become relatively more expensive or cheaper for U.S. consumers to buy?

5. Plot the quarterly growth rates of the CPI and the GDP deflator ("Inflation [CPI]" and "Inflation [GDP]", respectively). Why are the two not always the same? (Hint: What exactly do the two indexes measure?)

   a. What major event helps explain why the growth of the CPI was larger than the growth in the GDP deflator in 1979–80?

   b. Why was the CPI inflation rate less than the GDP inflation rate in 1986?

6. Plot inflation (GDP) and real GDP growth using annual data. Does inflation seem to lag behind real GDP growth? Explain why this relationship may exist.

# Long-Run Fundamentals

# Economic Growth

In this chapter we assemble a model of **long-run economic growth.** The long-run economic growth model is designed to explain the general upward path of output over time.

By describing the upward trend in the economy, the long-run growth model enables us to address many crucial economic policy issues. Most importantly, it can help to explain why the trend in economic growth has declined in the United States in the past two decades and why economic growth differs greatly in different regions and countries of the world. Small differences in the economic growth rate make enormous differences in economic well-being. A growth rate difference of just 6 percent per year enabled income per capita in the U.S. South to rise from only 40 percent of the North's after the Civil War to almost the same as the North's today. If the growth rate in the United States had been the same since the 1970s as it was in the 1950s and 1960s, then production in the United States would have been about 1.7 trillion dollars more in 1995. That would be $6,600 per year for every man, woman, and child in the United States, or about six times the national defense budget. That "lost" production could have been put to use in many ways: a higher standard of living for Americans, including the poor; more investment in plant, equipment, and infrastructure; less dependence on foreign resources. But because the growth rate slowed down, those resources have not been available.

The long-run growth model does not try to explain the departures of the economy from its growth trend. Hence, it does not explain important events like the 1990–91 recession or the increase in unemployment that occurred at that time. Unlike the complete model, which is examined starting in Chapter 6, the long-run growth model abstracts from these short-run fluctuations. We use it to project economic conditions in the more distant future and to understand variations in growth rates.

The long-run growth model describes the economy in a state where supply and demand for both goods and workers are in balance. Wages and prices have moved as needed to equate supply and demand. Incentives are having their full effect in inducing an efficient level of production.

# THE DETERMINANTS OF ECONOMIC GROWTH

There are three important determinants of the long-run growth path of output:

1. *Labor*—the people available for work
2. *Capital*—equipment, structures, and other productive facilities
3. *Technology*—the knowledge about how to use labor and capital to produce goods and services

## Labor

Growth in the number of people available for work is an important source of the growth of GDP. Since the 1970s growth in the number of workers has been strong as the post–World War II baby boom generation came of working age and women entered the labor market in large numbers. Growth in the future is expected to be weaker.

Not everybody in the population is in the labor force. It is against the law for children to work; many adults are in school, working at home, or in retirement, and quite a few others are unable to work because they are disabled or sick. Some people are committed to working full-time no matter what the incentives; others will choose the level of their work effort depending on the incentives provided by the labor market. About 7 percent of the working-age population was in the labor force in 1996. This percentage—the **labor force participation rate**—has been steadily increasing during the last 20 years, primarily because of increasing participation rates for women.

Another important fact about the labor market is that at any given time not everybody who is in the labor force and available for work is actually employed. Unemployment is a feature of the economy even when supply and demand appear to be in balance. In February 1996, a good period for the economy, 5.5 percent of the labor force was unemployed during the typical week. Unemployment rises in recessions and falls in booms, but there is a certain level of unemployment called the **natural rate of unemployment.** The natural rate is the amount of unemployment when the labor market is in equilibrium. One simple measure of the natural rate is the average rate of unemployment over several decades. The natural rate appears to lie between 5 and 6 percent in the United States.

If we subtract the number of unemployed workers from the number of workers in the labor force, we get the number of workers employed. Production depends not only on the number of workers employed but also on the amount of hours they work each year. Hence, when looking at the effects of employment on production and growth, we count only the hours that workers actually work. The total number of hours worked in the economy in a given year is what we mean by *labor input*. We frequently refer to labor input simply as employment and label it $N$.

## Capital

In any given year, the volume of physical capital—aircraft factories, computers, trucks, tractors, barns, clothing stores, etc.—is determined by investment in previous years. An increase in the amount of capital in the economy will enable the economy to produce more output. For example, a farmer with a tractor can produce tons more wheat than a farmer without a tractor. Boeing couldn't produce any 747s without manufacturing plants. The capital stock increases from one year to the next as long as gross investment is greater than the depreciation of the capital stock. As long as net investment is positive, the capital stock is growing. However, any investment project undertaken this year to increase the capital stock will not add to the stock until the project is complete, a process that takes time. We use the symbol $K$ for the existing capital stock.

## Technology

The third determinant of production—technology—tells us how much output can be produced from the amount of labor and capital used in production. Technology includes anything that influences the productivity of workers or capital. It includes technology in the usual sense of the word, such as a communications technology that enables a firm to fax a supplier an order form rather than send it by regular mail. It also includes how efficiently businesses are organized and managed.

We use the symbol $A$ to represent technology. Technology is perhaps the most abstract of the three determinants of growth, and it is more difficult to measure than labor and capital. Fortunately, there are many vivid examples that can reduce the level of abstraction, such as the following automobile example.

**HENRY FORD'S ASSEMBLY LINE.**   One of the great—and most visible—technological advances of the 20th century was Henry Ford's idea of mass production through the assembly line. Mass production greatly increased the productivity of workers and capital employed in the automobile industry, and eventually other industries as well. It represents an example of an increase in technology—an increase in $A$.

Ford's innovation occurred in 1913 at his Highland Park factory in Detroit, where he arranged an assembly line in which cars moved past workers who remained in place, rather than having the workers move around the factory. Observers at the time calculated that this one technological advance reduced the time it took a group of workers to assemble the major components into a complete car from 12½ to 1½ hours! With this increase in productivity it is not surprising that Ford could double wages to $5 a day and still cut prices.

Technological change increases the productivity of both labor and capital. Labor and capital are factors of production. Technological change may increase the productivity of both factors in a neutral way such that their marginal productivities increase in the same proportion. It is then useful to define technological change as something that increases *total factor productivity.*

## The Production Function

A simple way to represent how the three determinants of production combine to produce output is through the **production function,** which shows how much output can be produced from given amounts of labor, capital, and technology. The production function can be represented using symbols as follows:

$$Y = F(N, K, A). \quad \text{The Production Function} \tag{3.1}$$

This is simply shorthand notation for saying that output $Y$ depends on employment $N$, capital $K$, and technology $A$. (Reading out loud we say "$Y$ is a function $F$ of $N$, $K$, and $A$.") The notation $F$ followed by variables listed in parentheses means a general function of those variables. With such a notation we are not specific about what the function actually looks like, whether it is linear or the square root of $N$ or whatever.

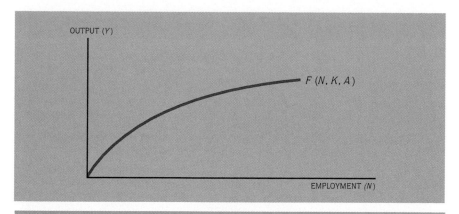

**FIGURE 3.1**   The Production Function in Terms of Labor Input

With a given capital stock and technology, the volume of output $Y$ produced from various levels of employment $N$ shows the diminishing marginal product of labor.

The production function relates output to employment, capital, and technology, whatever their levels. It tells us how much real GDP would be produced, for example, if there were a very severe depression and only half the normal number of people were at work.

Figure 3.1 shows how production depends on labor for a given capital stock and a given level of technology. The production function curves toward the horizontal axis. The **marginal product of labor** is the additional output that is produced by one additional unit of work. The marginal product of labor is the slope of the production function in Figure 3.1. Note how the production function gets less steep as more labor is employed. This means that the marginal product of labor declines as the amount of employment increases.

## 3.2  FULL EMPLOYMENT AND POTENTIAL GDP

The growth model assumes that the economy is at full employment, with the quantity of labor demanded equal to the quantity of labor supplied. We define potential GDP as the amount of production that occurs when labor is fully employed. In order to determine potential GDP, therefore, we must calculate the level of $N$ corresponding to full employment. For now, we

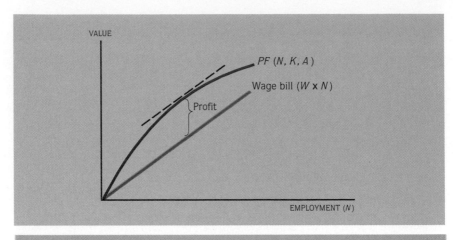

**FIGURE 3.2**   Profit Maximization

Profit is the difference between the value of output, $P$ times $F(N, K, A)$, and the wage bill, $W$ times $N$. It reaches a maximum when the slope of $P$ times $F(N, K, A)$ equals the slope of $W$ times $N$; that is, the value of the marginal product of labor equals the wage.

consider the level of technology $A$ and the level of capital $K$ as given. To find $N$, we consider the demand for, and supply of, labor.

## The Demand for Labor

A first principle of microeconomics is that a profit-maximizing firm in a competitive market will choose the level of employment where *the marginal product of labor equals the real wage*. The **real wage** is the dollar wage $W$ divided by the price level $P$, that is, $W/P$. If firms had employment below this level, the marginal product of labor would exceed the real wage and an opportunity for improved profit would exist. A firm could hire a worker for the wage $W$, produce more output in the amount given by the marginal product of labor, sell that output at price $P$, and make a profit on the deal. Firms will pursue this opportunity for profit until their additional hiring pushes the marginal product of labor down to the real wage. The point of maximum profit is shown in Figure 3.2.

The demand function for labor is a negative function of the real wage because the marginal product of labor declines with increased labor input, as shown in Figure 3.3.

## The Supply of Labor

The supply of labor is determined by the decisions of individual workers about how much of their time to spend working. The real wage measures

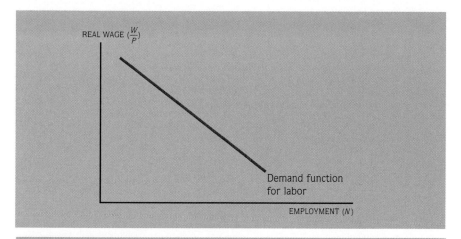

REAL WAGE $(\frac{W}{P})$

Demand function
for labor

EMPLOYMENT ($N$)

**FIGURE 3.3** The Demand Function for Labor

The demand function for labor is a downward-sloping relation between the real wage, $W/P$, and the level of employment, $N$. For each real wage, it gives the level of employment that firms will choose by equating the marginal product of labor to the real wage.

the incentive to work. At higher real wages, those already at work will want to work more. In addition, a higher real wage may draw people into the workforce who would not work at all with a lower real wage. A higher real wage has an incentive effect toward more work. For most people, however, wages are the dominant source of income. When wages rise permanently, they are better off. People who are better off choose to spend more time at home and away from the job. On this account, permanently higher real wages bring lower labor supply. Microeconomic theory labels these two contrasting influences the substitution effect and the income effect.

**SUBSTITUTION EFFECT.** As something becomes more expensive, people substitute away from it. In the case of labor supply, as time at home becomes more expensive (as its opportunity cost, the real wage, rises), people substitute away from time at home and toward time in the labor market. To put it another way, the real wage provides an incentive for work, and people substitute toward work when the real wage rises.

**INCOME EFFECT.** As income rises, people tend to consume more of most things. In this case, they consume more of their own time at home and offer less of their time in the labor market. Permanently higher real wages make people better off, and they work less on that account.

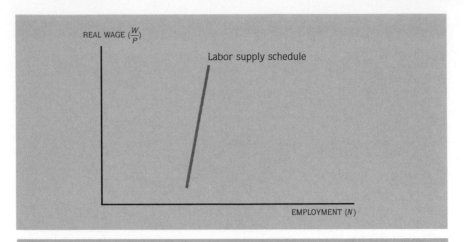

**FIGURE 3.4**   Long-Run Labor Supply Schedule

The labor supply schedule gives the amount of labor offered in the labor market for various levels of the real wage. When real wages rise permanently, the incentive to work is greater, but people have more income, and this tends to offset the incentive. The evidence suggests that the long-run labor supply schedule is almost vertical.

The long-run labor supply schedule, illustrated in Figure 3.4, shows the net effect of these two offsetting influences. Research by a number of economists has agreed rather closely that the net effect of the two influences of real wage on labor supply is roughly zero.[1] However, it is important to keep in mind that the agreement is that the *net effect* is approximately zero, not that each of its components is zero. The substitution effect, prompting people to work more when the real wage rises, has been shown to be strong in some studies. In these studies the income effect happens to be equally strong in the opposite direction.

## Full Employment

Another principle of microeconomics is that employment will be at the intersection of the labor supply and labor demand schedules. The equilibrium is shown in Figure 3.5. On the vertical axis is the real wage, which is the ratio $W/P$ of the dollar wage to the price level. In equilibrium at the real wage $W/P$, the quantity of labor $N$ chosen by firms equals the quantity supplied by the public. In Figure 3.5, the labor market is in a standard microeconomic

---

[1]The most recent econometric studies have used experimental data or panel data of the type we describe in Chapter 10 in our analysis of consumption. A useful survey of available results is found in John Pencavel, "Labor Supply of Men: A Survey," in Orley Ashenfelter, ed., *Handbook of Labor Economics* (Amsterdam: North-Holland, 1987).

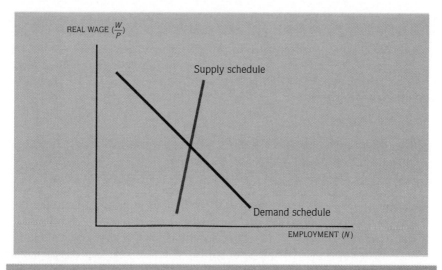

**FIGURE 3.5**   Labor Market Equilibrium

In the model with perfectly flexible wages and prices, the real wage is determined by the
intersection of the supply and demand curves for labor.

equilibrium. Every worker is able to find a job. If the real wage were too
high to provide jobs for everyone interested, the real wage would fall. The
fall would stimulate labor demand by firms and discourage work effort by
workers. The real wage would fall immediately to the point where the supply
and demand curves intersect and everybody had work.

We define **full employment,** $N^*$, as the volume of employment at the
intersection of supply and demand in Figure 3.5. It is the total amount of
work that would be done if each worker could find a job after a brief search
and earn as much as similar workers are already earning. Notice that full
employment is not the absolute maximum amount of work that the population is capable of doing. It is the amount people want to work given the
real wage that employers are willing to pay. If productivity rises, so that the
labor demand schedule shifts upward, the equilibrium level of employment
rises. Moreover, as the population grows, the labor supply schedule will shift
to the right and equilibrium employment will rise.

## Potential GDP

**Potential GDP,** denoted by $Y^*$, is the amount of output produced when the
labor market is at full employment:

$$Y^* = F(N^*, K, A). \tag{3.2}$$

The level of output, $Y^*$, is the amount of output that would be produced if everybody who wanted to work could find a job. For this reason, $Y^*$ is also frequently called the **full-employment level of output.** Recall that in Figures 1.1 and 1.2 we compared actual GDP with estimates of potential GDP. We found that potential GDP grows steadily, whereas actual GDP fluctuates around a growth trend.

## POTENTIAL GDP AND THE LABOR MARKET

1. Potential GDP is the level of real GDP when labor is fully employed. Prices and wages have moved so that markets are in balance.
2. The determinants of potential GDP are the labor force and its willingness to work as expressed by the labor supply schedule, the capital stock, and the technology of the economy.
3. In the labor market, the real wage adjusts as needed to keep the market in balance. Full employment is the common value of labor supply and labor demand after the real wage has made the two equal.
4. When the labor market is in balance, there is still some unemployment. The natural rate of unemployment is between 5 and 6 percent in the United States.

**3.3     THE SOLOW GROWTH MODEL**

Having defined the production function in the previous two sections, we are now prepared to explore the behavior of the economy as it steadily grows through time. In particular, we want to look at the relationship between labor growth, capital growth, and technological growth and to examine whether the growth process has any inherent tendencies to slow down. We focus on a particular real-world example: the growth path of the United States economy from now into the first part of the twenty-first century.

The growth of the labor force is predicted by the Bureau of Labor Statistics to average around 1 percent per year from now through the year 2010. The forecast is very reliable, because the people who will be in the labor force—which is limited to those who are 16 years of age and over—during this time have already been born. Projecting the labor force much beyond 2010 is more difficult because it requires forecasting future birthrates.

Now consider the growth of the capital stock over the same future period. Capital growth will depend on how much investment there is each year, which in turn depends on how much Americans save and how much foreigners invest in the United States. Forecasting future saving and foreign investment is much more difficult than forecasting the growth of the labor force. Saving will depend not only on what private individuals do, but also on whether the federal government succeeds in reducing the budget deficit. Instead of trying to forecast future capital growth, we consider the implications of a future in which the growth rate of capital exactly equals the growth rate of labor, so that the amount of capital available for each worker neither rises nor falls. Such a steady growth path—called a **balanced growth path** because the growth rates of capital and labor are balanced—would be a useful baseline from which to make judgments about how alternative economic policies would affect the future. But first we need to check whether the economy tends to follow a balanced growth path.

Robert Solow of M.I.T., who won the Nobel Prize in 1987, wrote a paper in 1956 on balanced growth paths such as the one hypothesized.[2] In fact, the long-run growth model was introduced for the first time in that paper. Solow's model is sometimes called the *neoclassical growth model* because it built on the classical models used by economists before Keynes. The Solow analysis makes extensive use of the production function, the identities we discussed in Chapter 2, and a simple assumption about saving.

## Saving and Balanced Growth

In the simplest version of Solow's neoclassical growth model, the economy is closed (so domestic saving equals investment) and there is no technological change (the term $A$ is constant over time). Both assumptions can be modified, but they make it easier to see what is going on. Later in this chapter we will allow $A$ to increase over time and even be determined endogenously within the growth model. Labor force growth is assumed to be at a constant rate, $n$. Each year the labor force increases by $n$ times $N$, the level at the start of the year. Currently, growth of the labor force in the United States is about 1 percent per year, so $n = .01$.

We saw in Chapter 2 that the change in the capital stock equals net investment. If capital is to grow at the rate $n$, then each year capital must rise by the amount $nK$. In order to stay on a growth path where the capital stock grows at rate $n$, net investment must be $nK$ each year. We can think of $nK$ as *balanced growth* investment. For example, if the capital stock is $10 trillion and $n$ is 1 percent, then net investment must equal $100 billion (.01 times $10,000 billion) if the capital stock is to grow at the same 1 percent

[2]R. M. Solow, "A Contribution to the Theory of Economic Growth," *Quarterly Journal of Economics*, Vol. 70 (February 1956), pp. 65–94.

rate as labor. To summarize, we have derived the first key condition for balanced growth:

$$\text{Net investment} = nK. \tag{3.3}$$

The second major element of Solow's analysis deals with saving. Saving depends on (1) the fraction of national income that is saved and (2) the level of national income. Let $s$ be the fraction of income that is saved; $s$ is called the *saving rate*. Saving in the economy is equal to $s$ times income. We know from Chapter 2 that income equals output, $Y$. Hence,

$$\text{Saving} = sY. \tag{3.4}$$

For example, if income $Y$ is \$5 trillion and the saving rate is .02, then saving would be \$100 billion. Since saving equals net investment, we see that $sY$ equals the *actual* amount of net investment in the economy.

A subsidiary assumption of Solow's growth analysis is that the production function has *constant returns to scale*. Under constant returns and with unchanging technology, if there are equal proportional changes in labor and capital, output changes by the same proportion. Recall that the production function is

$$Y = F(K,N,A). \tag{3.5}$$

We could divide $K$, $N$, and $Y$ by any number and the production function would still apply, with constant returns. We choose to divide by $N$. This has the effect of stating output as output per worker, $Y/N$, and capital as capital per worker, $K/N$:

$$Y/N = F(K/N,1,A). \tag{3.6}$$

*Example:* Suppose $Y = F(K, N, A) = K^{1/3}N^{2/3}A$. Divide by $N$ to get

$$Y = \left(\frac{K}{N}\right)^{1/3} \cdot \left(\frac{N}{N}\right)^{2/3} \cdot A = \left(\frac{K}{N}\right)^{1/3} \cdot 1 \cdot A = F(K/N,1,A);$$

in other words, we replace $K$ with $(K/N)$ and we replace $N$ with 1 in the production function. Output per worker depends just on capital per worker, since we are assuming that technology, $A$, is constant over time.

Actual investment can be either greater or less than balanced growth investment. Solow developed a famous diagram to explain what happens in the two cases. The diagram is shown in Figure 3.6.

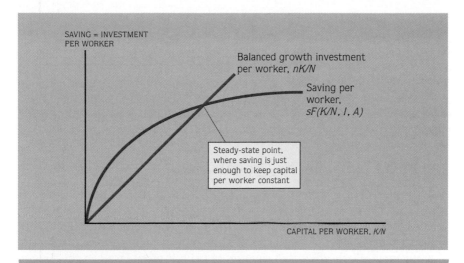

SAVING = INVESTMENT
PER WORKER

Balanced growth investment
per worker, *nK/N*

Saving per
worker,
*sF(K/N, 1, A)*

Steady-state point,
where saving is just
enough to keep capital
per worker constant

CAPITAL PER WORKER, *K/N*

**FIGURE 3.6**   Solow's Growth Analysis

Solow's growth diagram shows the amount the economy saves per worker (the curving line), and the amount of investment per worker needed to keep the capital stock growing at the same rate as the labor force (the straight line). The steady state occurs at the intersection where saving generates just the right amount of investment to stay on the balanced growth path. If capital per worker is less than the steady-state level, investment exceeds the amount needed for balanced growth, and the amount of capital per worker rises. Hence the economy tends toward its steady state.

The straight line in Figure 3.6 expresses our conclusion about the amount of net investment needed to keep capital growing at the same rate as labor grows. The total amount of net investment is $nK$, so the amount per worker is $nK/N$. Because the horizontal axis is capital per worker, $K/N$, the amount of net investment—$n$ times $(K/N)$—is a straight line with slope $n$. The curving line expresses our conclusion about saving per worker. Total saving is $sF(K,N,A)$, so saving per worker is $sF(K,N,A)/N$, which we can also write as $sF(K/N,1,A)$; the line is curved because it is a constant $(s)$ times the curved production function.

The intersection of the investment line and the saving curve in Figure 3.6 is the *steady-state point*. At this point, the actual amount of investment, determined by saving, is just the amount needed to keep the capital stock growing at the same rate as labor input is growing. If the economy starts at the steady state, it will stay there.

What happens if the economy starts with less capital per worker? This would correspond to a point to the left of the steady-state point in Figure 3.6. Saving per worker, and thus actual investment, *exceeds* the amount needed to keep capital per worker constant. Each year, capital per worker increases. The economy will gradually approach the steady-state point. Similarly, if the economy starts with more capital per worker than the steady-state amount, capital per worker will decline each year and the economy will approach the steady state.

Solow showed that the growth process is *stable*. No matter where the economy starts, it will converge over time to the same steady state, with the capital stock growing at the same rate as the labor force.

## The Effect of Saving on Growth

Another important conclusion from Solow's work is that, in the longer run, the growth rate does not depend on the saving rate. In the steady state, the capital stock and output both grow at the same rate as the labor force. The only factor that matters for the rate of growth of the economy is the growth of labor input. Economies that save more do not grow faster in the longer run.

What then is the impact of increasing the saving rate in the Solow analysis?

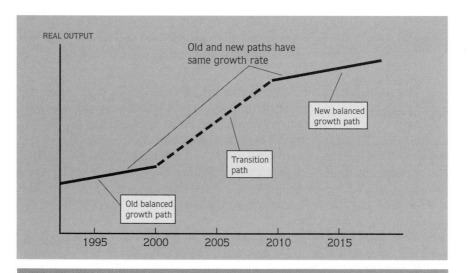

**FIGURE 3.7**   Transition between Balanced Growth Paths

A higher saving rate starting in the year 2000 leads to a higher level of real output. During a transition period growth is higher. The growth rates in the old and new balanced growth paths are the same.

Suppose that the saving rate suddenly rises from .02 to .04 and stays there. Then the balanced growth condition is violated with $K/Y = 2 < s/n = 4$. According to Solow's stability argument, capital will increase more rapidly than labor, and because of diminishing returns to capital, the capital-output ratio increases. The ratio will continue to increase until it reaches 4 and the economy returns to the balanced growth rate of 1 percent. There is a **transition period,** however, during which the growth rate of the economy is greater than the balanced growth rate. This is illustrated in Figure 3.7, which shows how the level of output rises as a result of the increase in saving, but the growth rate of the economy returns to the balanced growth rate after the transition period. Hence, greater saving benefits the economy by raising future GDP, but not by increasing the long-term growth rate, according to the Solow model.

## BALANCED GROWTH AND THE SOLOW ANALYSIS

1. Balanced growth occurs when the labor force, capital stock, and real output all grow at the same rate.
2. Along a balanced growth path, the ratio of capital to output equals the ratio of the saving rate to the labor force growth rate.
3. Solow showed that the balanced growth path is stable: if the economy is off a balanced growth path, it will naturally tend to return to that path.
4. A higher saving rate will raise GDP in Solow's analysis of the long-run growth model, but it will not permanently raise the growth rate.

## THE GROWTH ACCOUNTING FORMULA

**3.4**

Solow also developed a framework that can be used to determine the size of the contributions of labor, capital, and technical change to economic growth.[3] His formula is used by economists throughout the world to assign credit for growth. In its simplest form Solow's formula says the rate of growth

[3]Robert M. Solow, "Technical Change and the Aggregate Production Function," *Review of Economics and Statistics*, Vol. 39 (August 1957), pp. 312–320.

## NEW RESEARCH IN PRACTICE
## Convergence or Dispersion of Per Capita Income Around the World?

The neoclassical growth model has important empirical implications for the growth performance of different countries and for economic policy. These empirical implications have been the focus of extensive research in the 1990s—collectively called the "new empirical growth literature"—with scholars such as Robert Barro, currently of Harvard University, Steven Durlauf of the University of Wisconsin, Charles Jones of Stanford University, and Alwyn Young of Boston University among the key contributors. This research was made possible by the painstaking efforts of Alan Heston and Robert Summers of the University of Pennsylvania to put diverse data sets from countries around the world on a comparable basis.

The neoclassical growth model indicates that a country's long-run per capita growth rate is independent of its saving or investment rates, but that there are long "transition periods" during which growth can either be higher or lower than this long-run average value (see Figure 3.7). Countries with *low levels of physical capital per worker* are below the long-run average per capita income level; they will grow relatively fast while they "catch up" or *converge* to the average. Moreover, the further below the long-run average a country is, the higher its growth rate will be. Thus, according to the neoclassical growth model, countries with low levels of income per capita should grow faster than countries with high levels of income per capita. Is this prediction of the model borne out by the empirical research?

The two graphs on the next page summarize the research. The top graph pertains to the more advanced countries in the world—such as those in Europe, Japan, and the United States. The bottom graph pertains to all countries of the world, including countries such as China and India as well as the countries in the top graph.

On the horizontal axis of each of the graphs is a measure of per capita income in 1960; on the vertical axis is a measure of the average growth rate during the years since 1960. Note that there are differences in per capita income for the advanced countries as well as for the countries as a whole.

According to the model there should be a negative relationship between the level and the growth rate: that is, countries with low levels of income per capita should have higher growth rates. The top graph shows a strong negative correlation, just as the model predicts. The model appears to perform well. However, the lower graph shows virtually no correlation; there is very little "catch-up" behavior. Many countries with very low levels of per capita income have very low growth rates. The model does not perform very well when applied more broadly.

Empirical researchers have offered a good explanation for the difference between the top and bottom graphs. Countries in the top graph are similar in many of the characteristics other than physical capital that affect economic growth, such as education, public infrastructure, and stability of government policy. However, many developing countries do not have the same level of education, and their economic policy is less stable, with frequent bouts of high inflation or restrictive international trade practices. That is, the growth-related characteristics vary much more across the countries in the bottom graph than they do in the top graph. This explains the greater variation in the bottom graph and the lack of a clear negative correlation.

In other words, the explanation for the difference between the two graphs is that convergence of relatively poor countries to higher average per capita income levels is a *conditional convergence*: the countries will converge on condition that the characteristics of the countries that affect growth are similar. If a country has a poor educational system or an unstable or unreliable political system, for example, then low growth can persist even though income per capita is low.

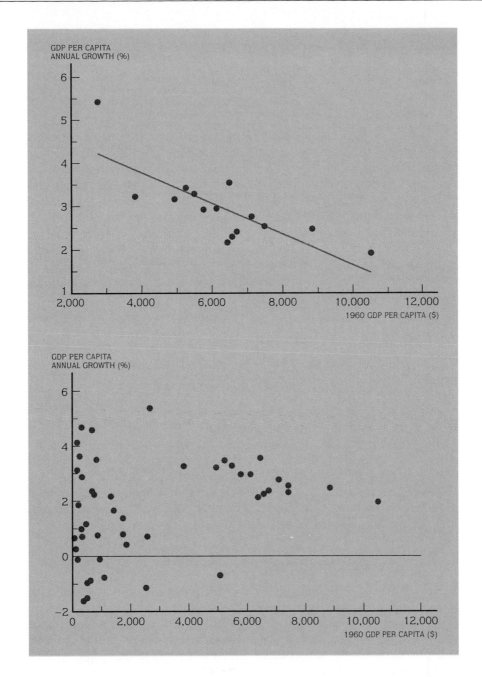

of output equals technology growth plus the weighed rates of growth of labor and capital:

$$\frac{\Delta Y}{Y} = \frac{\Delta A}{A} + \frac{.7\Delta N}{N} + \frac{.3\Delta K}{K}. \tag{3.7}$$

The derivation of this *growth accounting formula* is shown in the appendix to this chapter. The growth accounting formula shows how total growth relates to growth in the three determinants. In words, the formula says that the rate of growth of output is equal to the rate of growth of technology plus .7 times the rate of growth in labor input plus .3 times the rate of growth of capital input. What is interesting about the formula is its lack of dependence on the details of the production function. All that matters is that technology increases the productivity of both factors in a neutral way. The weight .3 and its complement .7 are derived from data on the relative shares of capital and labor in national income. In Chapter 2 we saw that these income shares are roughly .3 and .7.

## Historical Growth Accounting

The growth accounting formula can be used to determine the contributions of each factor to long-term growth in the United States during the last 30 years. In order to smooth out short-run business cycles, it helps to look at averages over longer periods, such as 10-year intervals.

The data for the United States over three 10-year periods are shown in Figure 3.8. Observe that economic growth slowed down in the mid-1970s from about 4 percent per year to about 2¼ percent per year.

According to the growth accounting formula, as shown in Figure 3.8, the most important reason for the slowdown in economic growth has been a decline in the rate of technological change. Declining growth of capital was the second most significant factor.

## Exogenous Technological Change

In our discussion of balanced growth in the previous section we made the simplifying assumption that there was no technology growth; that is, the term $A$ was a constant so that $\Delta A/A = 0$. With this assumption, along a balanced growth path with labor and capital growing by 1 percent per year ($\Delta N/N = \Delta K/K = 1$), the growth accounting formula would tell us that output growth is also 1 percent per year. That is,

$$\frac{\Delta Y}{Y} = 0 + .7(1) + .3(1) = 1.$$

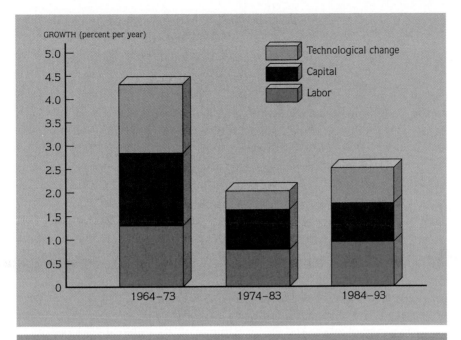

GROWTH (percent per year)

Technological change
Capital
Labor

1964–73    1974–83    1984–93

**FIGURE 3.8**   Sources of Growth

The height of each bar shows the annual growth rate of real GDP over 10-year intervals. Each bar
is broken into blocks showing the contributions from labor growth, from capital growth, and from
technological change. The contributions are calculated using Equation 3.7 in the text.
Source: Data on real output growth are from the *Economic Report of the President*, 1995, Table B-47; the labor
growth data are from Table B-44; and the capital stock data are calculated from investment data in Tables B-2
and B-116.

But the growth accounting formula also shows that technology growth
need not be zero. For example, suppose that technology growth is 1 percent
per year ($\Delta A/A = 1$); that is, the quantity of output that can be produced
with a given level of labor and capital increases by 1 percent per year. If we
maintain the assumption that capital and labor both grow by 1 percent per
year, then according to the growth accounting formula (Equation 3.7) output
grows by 2 percent per year:

$$\frac{\Delta Y}{Y} = 1 + .7(1) + .3(1) = 2.$$

Although the capital-labor ratio ($K/N$) is constant, labor productivity ($Y/N$)
increases because of the improvements in technology.

Allowing for the possibility that technology increases at a constant positive rate is an improvement over assuming that technology does not grow at all. However, we have still not explained *why* technology might increase or what factors might determine technological change. In other words, technological change—the increase in output produced with given labor and capital input—is still **exogenous** in our discussion of the neoclassical growth model. We simply assumed that technology growth was 1 percent per year. In the next section we develop an **endogenous** growth theory in which the increase in technology is not exogenous but is explained by endogenous forces within the model.

## 3.5    ENDOGENOUS GROWTH THEORY

Economists typically think of the long-run growth rate of output as being *exogenous* in the neoclassical growth model. As we have shown, if there is no technological change, then the growth rate of output depends only on the growth rate of labor. And the growth rate of labor ultimately depends on the growth rate of the population, which is essentially exogenous. If the saving rate rises, the long-run growth rate does not increase; it remains equal to the growth rate of labor. True, adding technology growth to the neoclassical growth model does allow the growth rate of output to change, but if technology growth is itself treated as exogenous, as in the last section, then the growth rate of output is still exogenous to the model.

An area of macroeconomic research that has been important since the 1980s is called **endogenous growth theory.** Paul Romer of Stanford University has been one of the major contributors to this theory. Compared with the neoclassical growth model, endogenous growth theory focuses on *explaining* technological growth rather than treating technology as exogenous. In other words, *endogenous growth theory endeavors to provide an explicit theory that determines the behavior of the technology factor* (*A*), much as we provided a theory to determine the amount of labor (*N*) in Section 3.2 above.

### A Production Function for Technology

Recall that an increase in technology (*A*) is anything that increases the quantity of output produced with the same amount of labor and capital. Thus, many things can bring about an improved technology: the assembly-line method of production discussed earlier, the replacement of a horse-drawn plow with a tractor, an increase in the skills of workers (called an *increase in human capital*), and so on. Because of the wide diversity of types of technological improvements, it is difficult to develop a single simple model that includes all of these activities.

One successful approach, suggested by Paul Romer,[4] is to imagine that the ideas or inventions that represent technology are produced with labor and capital much like any other good. To see how this works, imagine that there are "invention factories" throughout the economy in which new inventions are produced by workers. In fact, research laboratories are not uncommon in the United States and many countries; the job description of the researchers who work at these research laboratories is to produce new ideas and inventions. The managers of these laboratories measure production partly by the number of new **patents** that the lab produces. But the notion of an "invention factory" is more general and includes less formal though still purposeful methods of improving technology, whether in a laboratory or not.

Analogous to the production function for output (Equation 3.1), we can describe a **production function for technology** as

$$\Delta A = T(N_A, K_A, A), \tag{3.8}$$

which says that the increase in technology $\Delta A$ each year depends on the amount of labor producing the technology ($N_A$), the amount of capital employed in producing the technology ($K_A$), and the existing technology ($A$). The function $T$ is the production function for technology. Note that the amount of labor and capital employed in technology production (research) is only part of the total available supply of labor and capital; that is, $N_A < N$ and $K_A < K$.

Equation 3.8 readily shows how technology is endogenous. If more labor resources (i.e., researchers) are devoted to technology production, then technology increases by a larger amount. If more capital (i.e., research laboratories and equipment) is devoted to technology production, then technology production also increases by a larger amount. In the next section we consider economic policies which might bring about such changes in labor and capital resource use.

Note that technology itself ($A$) also contributes to the production of new technology ($\Delta A$). There are important spillover effects of technology. An idea developed in one laboratory can be used to help create new ideas in other laboratories. While some inventions can be patented and therefore excluded from use without permission in the production of goods, often the idea underlying the patent can be used by researchers at other laboratories. Technology as it is used in the production of new technology is an example

---

[4]Paul Romer, "Endogenous Technological Change," *Journal of Political Economy*, Vol. 98 (1990), No. 5, Pt. 2, pp. s71–s102.

of a good which is *nonexcludable*: one firm cannot exclude another firm from using it. Technology is inherently different from other economic goods because one can use the same idea over and over again.

## Increasing the Long-Run Growth Rate

It is clear from Equation 3.8 that the production of new technology can be increased by investing more resources in research. But can the growth rate of technology—and therefore the growth rate of output—be permanently increased? Or can the growth rate be increased only during a transition period, as in the neoclassical growth model?

In an interesting and important special case of the technology production function, the growth rate can be permanently increased. To see this, suppose the technology production function is

$$\Delta A = cN_A A, \tag{3.9}$$

where $c$ is a coefficient. This implies that

$$\frac{\Delta A}{A} = cN_A. \tag{3.10}$$

Equation 3.10 says that the long-run growth rate of technology depends on the number of workers in technology production; that is, the number of workers doing research. Hence, an increase in the share of workers doing research will increase the growth rate of technology $\Delta A/A$. Since $\Delta A/A$ appears in the growth accounting equation, this will increase the growth rate of output as well. In other words, for a technology production function like Equation 3.9 an increase in investment in research will cause a permanent increase in the rate of growth, as illustrated in Figure 3.9, and not only during a transition period as in Figure 3.7.

The reason for this crucial difference between Figure 3.7 and 3.9 is that technology—the stock of ideas—does not have diminishing returns in Equation 3.9. Observe that higher levels of technology increase researchers' productivity in producing more technology in Equation 3.9, much as higher levels of capital increase workers' productivity in producing more output in Equation 3.1. But each additional unit of capital increases output by a *smaller* amount, while each additional unit of technology increases the production of new technology by the *same* amount. If diminishing returns to technology did exist, for example, if rather than Equation 3.9 we had

$$A = cN_A\sqrt{A}, \tag{3.11}$$

then there would be no permanent effect on long-term growth. Figure 3.10

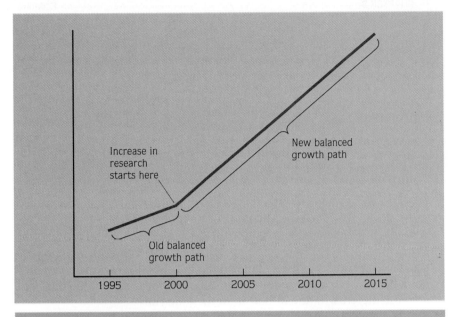

**FIGURE 3.9** An Increase in the Growth Rate

If technology does not have diminishing returns in the production of more technology, then an increase in the number of workers doing research will increase the growth rate permanently, as shown here, in contrast to Figure 3.7, which shows only a temporary increase in growth.

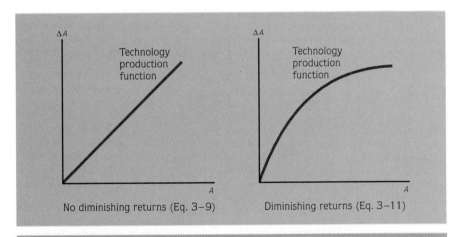

**FIGURE 3.10** Two Technology Production Functions

In both cases higher technology leads to the creation of more technology. In one case there are diminishing returns, in which case growth will not increase permanently, when more labor is devoted to research.

illustrates the difference between the technology production function in Equation 3.9 without diminishing returns and the technology production function in Equation 3.11 with diminishing returns.

## ENDOGENOUS GROWTH THEORY

1. Endogenous growth theory endeavors to provide an explicit theory of technology. A production function for technology is one simple way to describe how technology depends on labor, capital, and technology inputs.
2. If technology does not have diminishing returns in producing more technology, then devoting more resources to improving technology will increase the growth rate of output in the long run.
3. According to endogenous growth theory, economic policy may increase the growth rate permanently; within the neoclassical growth model, a permanent increase in the growth rate may occur only during a transition period.

## 3.6 POLICIES TO STIMULATE GROWTH

The government can influence all three of the determinants of growth—technological change, capital formation, and labor input. Disappointing rates of growth since the beginning of the 1970s have led to a number of federal policies to stimulate growth. Under what circumstances might a free market economy deliver an inadequate rate of growth in potential output that could be improved by government intervention? In general, government intervention is justified if a market failure exists. A *market failure* exists when there is a divergence between social and private costs or benefits of a particular activity. Many activities, such as education and research, that generate growth have social benefits that exceed private benefits. Government can encourage such activities.

## NEW RESEARCH IN PRACTICE
### Endogenous Growth Theory and International Trade Liberalization

There has been much interest in applying endogenous growth theory to economic policy. An important example is international trade policy—the policy of reducing barriers to international trade.

Trade policy has been much in the news in the 1990s. Two major initiatives to reduce trade barriers in the 1990s are the Uruguay Round of multilateral trade negotiations (under the General Agreement on Trade and Tariffs), which aims to reduce or eliminate tariffs in many sectors worldwide, and the North American Free Trade Area, which aims to eliminate tariffs among the United States, Mexico, and Canada.

Estimating the benefits of these trade liberalization efforts is important. While the classical theory of comparative advantage tells us that there are gains from trade, public debate can be influenced by the perceived magnitude of the gain, because in the short run certain interests can be harmed by trade liberalization.

How much effect does trade liberalization have on the economy? Estimates that ignore growth seem surprisingly small. In the traditional analysis, there is an increase in the level of real GDP, due to the more efficient allocation of resources among different economies. However, increased trade may raise the return to investment (in physical capital, human capital, and research and development). For example, access to a world market may increase the return to a new product or invention. If so, then investment will increase, and this will raise the economy's growth rate for a while. The total increase due to the trade liberalization equals the static gain in income plus the dynamic gain achieved over time as investment responds to the change in policy.

In a 1992 paper in the *Journal of Political Economy*, Richard Baldwin of Columbia University provided some quantitative estimates of these ef-fects. He found that if trade liberalization leads to a 1 percent increase in productivity (the *A* coefficient in the production function increases), then the long-run increase in output is 1.6 percent, with the additional .6 percent due to capital accumulation. Hence, approximately $6/16 = 3/8$ of the long-run increase in output is due to capital accumulations. Of course, output is not the sole variable of interest to policymakers. Increased capital accumulation requires an increase in saving. Thus, although capital accumulation fostered by trade liberalization leads to a large increase in output, the effect on consumption is less.

These calculations share the characteristic with the Solow model that the long-run growth rate is unaffected by policy. Other models of endogenous growth explicitly consider the implications of economic policy on the long-run rate of growth. In such models, trade liberalization may lead to greater R&D and human capital investment as firms and workers take advantage of the larger markets and the greater flow of ideas and knowledge across borders. The market return to productivity-increasing investments is increased, and this leads to an increase in the rate of growth. In this case, the long-run effect of trade liberalization is not only a higher level of output in the future, but a higher rate of growth of output. Trade liberalization thus may lead to a permanent increase in the rate of growth of output and consumption. If this type of model is more appropriate for describing the economy, the estimates of the benefits of a free trade agreement discussed above may underestimate the true values.

The estimates of the effect of trade liberalization under the Uruguay Round used by the Office of the United States Trade Representative in 1992 incorporated the increase in growth due to the increase in investment as described above.

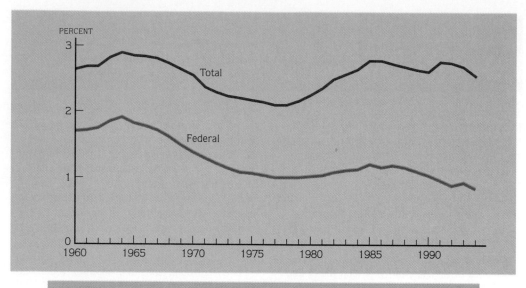

**FIGURE 3.11**    Federal Spending for R&D as a Fraction of GDP

Total R&D spending has been stable at around 2.5 percent of GDP. The federal portion has fallen and been replaced by rising private spending for R&D.
Source: *Economic Report of the President*, 1990.

## Policies to Improve Technological Growth and Productivity

Figure 3.8 shows that technological change has fallen significantly. Hence the idea of stimulating technology has been attractive to policymakers.

Perhaps the most important role that the government can play in improving technology growth is in the area of education. In the United States, state and local governments provide most of the support for primary and secondary schools and universities. A highly skilled labor force is obviously a key ingredient to successful productivity growth.

As we emphasized with the technology production function, an important source of technology growth is investment in research and development (R&D). Figure 3.11 shows the total amount of R&D spending in the United States as a fraction of GDP. The fraction has been stable at around 2.5 percent. Figure 3.11 also shows federal spending for R&D as a fraction of GDP. The federal government's contribution to the total has declined substantially—in the 1960s, the government contributed about two-thirds of the total, but by the 1990s, the fraction fell to a third.

Like education, through spillovers, discussed in the previous section, basic research may provide social benefits in excess of the private benefits that accrue to those engaged in these activities. Left to their own devices, individuals and firms will choose levels of spending on education and research that fall short of the social optimum. Government may want to encourage these activities through grants and subsidies.

The Research and Experimentation Tax Credit in the United States has provided tax incentives for research and development expenditures. This special tax credit allows firms to reduce their taxes by 20 percent of their research and development expenses. If R&D programs are an important source of technology growth, then tax incentives like these should improve growth. The use of public funds for this purpose, through the tax system, is justified if the sponsors of R&D are unable to capture the full benefits themselves.

## Policies to Stimulate Capital Formation

Until recently, government policy to stimulate growth concentrated almost entirely on capital formation. A rising capital stock will add to economic growth as the growth formula in the previous section made clear. Numerically, an extra percentage point of capital growth will add about .3 percentage point to growth in output. To get an added 1 percent of growth in output, the capital stock would have to grow 3.3 percent per year.

Consider a numerical illustration. At the end of 1993, the capital stock was about $6,560 billion, counting plants, equipment, housing, and inventories. The 3.3 percent growth in capital needed to add a point to growth of output would be

3.3 percent times $6,560 billion = $217 billion in added investment.

Total fixed investment in 1994 was about $1,000 billion. Investment would have to rise by 217/1,000 = 22 percent to add just 1 percentage point to growth in output. Of course, 1 percent more growth would take us a long way to restoring the growth path that the United States experienced in the mid-1960s and would compound itself to an impressive increase in living standards in 20 years. Moreover, it is possible that the increase in new plants and machines would bring forth additional technical innovations which could spur productivity growth.

Increased growth in the capital stock requires consistently high levels of investment spending. This can occur only if there are fewer competing demands on output from households and government purchases. To expand investment, we need to reduce consumption, government purchases, or net exports.

Under the right combination of economic conditions, a large increase in investment is possible. For example, investment was at depressed levels in 1962 when President Kennedy sponsored the first investment tax credit. The new investment incentive plus generally expansive conditions caused investment to rise from 306 billion 1987 dollars in 1962 to $401 billion in 1966, an increase of about 30 percent.

Although an increase in investment of 30 percent is feasible, it does not appear to be sustainable. Output growth can be raised by a percentage point for a few years, but then investment tends to decline to more normal levels. For example, annual growth of the capital stock reached its peak from the Kennedy stimulus at 7 percent per year in 1966, but then subsided to about 5 percent through 1974. During most of this period, the investment tax credit was in effect. Between 1975 and 1982, the growth of the capital stock fluctuated between 1 and 4 percent per year. The investment credit was in effect at a higher rate throughout these disappointing years.

## GROWTH THROUGH CAPITAL FORMATION

1. Because the coefficient of capital growth in the growth formula is about .3, it takes about 3.3 percent of growth in capital to add 1 percent to output growth.
2. In 1994, it would have taken a 22 percent increase in the amount of investment to raise the growth of the capital stock by 3.3 percent.
3. Increases of this magnitude in investment have occurred in the past, but only when special incentives were combined with other favorable conditions. Even then, the high levels of investment were sustained for only a few years.

## Policies to Increase Labor Supply

In the growth equation, employment growth has more than twice the leverage of capital growth. Each percentage point of extra growth of employment adds .7 percent to output growth. To put it the other way around, it takes 1.4 percent of added employment growth to increase output growth by 1 percent per year. Reductions in income tax rates are one way to stimulate work effort by improving incentives.

The income tax depresses the incentive to work by reducing the wage that workers receive for their work. On this account, one might expect that a cut in income taxes would stimulate work by improving incentives. A prime

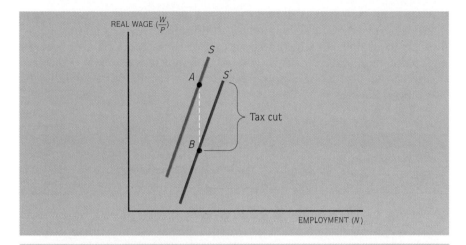

**FIGURE 3.12**  Shift in Labor Supply from a Tax Cut

A tax cut shifts the labor supply function downward in proportion to the cut. *S* is the labor supply schedule before the tax rate cut; *A* is an arbitrary point on it. *S'* is the supply schedule after the cut. *B* is a point on *S'* where the real wage after tax is the same as the real wage after tax on *S* at *A*. *B* is below *A* by the amount of the tax cut. The amount of labor supplied at *B* is the same as at *A* because the real wage received by workers is the same at *B* as at *A*. A downward shift in a schedule that is nearly vertical has almost no substantive effect on employment.

selling point of tax cuts put into place in 1981 and 1986 was precisely this incentive argument. But a cut in income taxes also makes people better off, which depresses labor supply. The net effect of a simple tax cut could therefore be quite small. This is illustrated in Figure 3.12. If the labor supply curve is steep, as statistical evidence seems to suggest, the intersection of supply and demand occurs at almost the same level of employment. A prediction of large stimulus to employment and output from tax cuts would be contrary to the evidence.

Growth policies need not take the exclusive form of tax cuts. In fact, the federal government's need for revenue makes it impossible to improve work incentives dramatically by cutting taxes. Another type of policy is *tax reform*. A tax reform keeps revenue the same although tax rates are cut. This can be done by reducing deductions and lowering tax rates on earned income. Because revenue is the same, the typical taxpayer pays the same amount of tax and there is no income effect. The cut in taxes due to the lower tax rate is offset by the increase in taxes due to the lower deductions. This type of reform necessarily involves a reduction in the progressivity of the income tax. What matters for work incentives is the *marginal* tax rate, the rate applied to the last dollar of earnings. For example, a flat tax system that puts roughly the same tax rate on all dollars of earnings above the first few thousand dollars of income could raise the same amount of revenue with lower marginal rates. This type of tax reform has no income effect to depress work. The labor supply schedule shifts by the full amount of the substitution effect.

## GROWTH THROUGH INCREASED WORK EFFORT

1. Because the labor supply schedule is nearly vertical, even a large tax cut has only a small effect on employment. The substitution effect of lower tax rates raises incentives to work, but the higher level of income depresses work.
2. If the tax change is a tax *reform*, which keeps tax receipts constant, rather than a tax *cut*, it improves incentives without changing average income. Then the substitution effects are not offset by income effects.

## 3.7 WAGES AND THE LABOR PRODUCTIVITY SLOWDOWN

Because the real wage is equal to the marginal product of labor in the growth model, we should be able to learn about growth by looking at the movements of the real wage over time. Remember that the income side of the national income and product accounts reports the total earnings of workers. Total annual earnings divided by total annual hours of work gives a measure of the average hourly wage paid to workers in the United States. The Bureau of Labor Statistics calls this *compensation per hour*. Compensation per hour includes the value of fringe benefits as well as cash wages. Wages are the most important component of the cost of production.

Wages and prices generally moved together throughout the swings in inflation in the 1970s. Dividing the hourly average wage by the cost of living gives us the real wage. From the point of view of workers, the real wage measures the purchasing power of the wage—the amount of goods and services that can be bought with one hour of work. From the point of view of employers, it measures the real costs of labor input. The real wage does

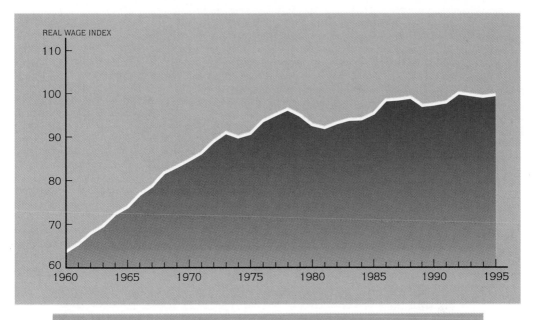

**FIGURE 3.13** The Slowdown in Real Wage Growth

The real wage is the ratio of the dollar wage (compensation per hour) to the cost of living (the consumer price index). Real wage growth slowed down significantly in the early 1970s and has not yet picked up.
Source: *Economic Report of the President*, 1996, Table B-45.

not fluctuate in any systematic way during recessions or booms. Its most noticeable property is growth over time. The real wage since 1960 is shown in Figure 3.13.

After steady growth in the 1960s, the upward path of the real wage was interrupted in the early 1970s. Since then real wage growth has been much lower. One of the most pressing problems facing the U.S. economy is the slowdown in real wage growth. The behavior of real wages mirrors the behavior of productivity.

## The Labor Productivity Slowdown

Productivity is the amount of output produced per unit of input. Because labor is the most important input, the most popular measure of productivity is **labor productivity,** or output per hour of labor. When economists talk about productivity, they usually mean labor productivity. A broader measure of productivity, called **total factor productivity,** is output per generalized

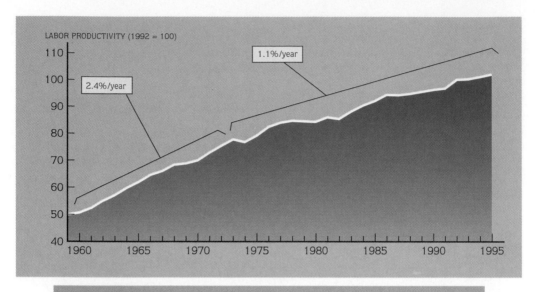

**FIGURE 3.14**   The Slowdown in Labor Productivity Growth

Productivity is the amount of output produced per hour of work. The general trend in productivity has been upward, but growth slowed down in the early 1970s. Productivity also fluctuates during recessions and booms.
Source: *Economic Report of the President*, 1996, Table B-45.

unit of input ("factor" is a general term for an input like labor or capital). The generalized unit counts capital, energy, and materials as inputs in addition to labor. However, output per unit of labor and total factor productivity for the United States as a whole tell about the same story in recent years.

The recent history of labor productivity is shown in Figure 3.14. Productivity has generally been increasing as workers have become more efficient and have had more and better machines to work with. This increase in productivity underlies the growth in real wages that we saw in the previous section. But productivity is also procyclical: it rises in booms and falls in recessions. Firms tend to keep skilled workers on the payroll and let them produce fewer items in slack times, rather than lay them off and run the risk that they will find jobs elsewhere. They make up for their low productivity in bad times with higher productivity in good times.

Productivity growth slowed down in the early 1970s, and this is the main reason that real wage growth has slowed down. Economists disagree about the reasons for the productivity slowdown. Some stress the role of the increases in oil prices, but the real price of crude oil is not much different from what it was in the 1950s and 1960s. Others point to a reduction in expenditures on research and development and say that technical innovation has slowed down as a result. Still others say that we are not investing enough in new machines and factories. Of all the puzzles about the recent performance of the U.S. economy, the slowdown in productivity growth is perhaps the most difficult for economists to solve.

## REAL WAGES AND PRODUCTIVITY

1. The real wage measures the purchasing power of the wage payment. The real wage grew steadily in the United States until the early 1970s, when its growth slowed down.
2. Labor productivity is defined as output per unit of labor input. Labor productivity has been growing for a long time, though with fluctuations during business cycles.
3. In the United States productivity growth slowed down in the early 1970s. Growth of productivity permits the real wage to grow, and the slowdown in productivity is the main reason for the slowdown in real wage growth in the United States.

## REVIEW AND PRACTICE

### Major Points

1. The long-run growth model is one in which the economy is always operating at full employment. Output is determined by the labor force, the capital stock, and technology.
2. Even when the economy is operating at potential, there is some unemployment. The rate of unemployment when the labor market is in equilibrium is called the natural rate.
3. At any one time, the capital stock and technology are predetermined. Thus, output is determined in the labor market. Employment is given by the equality of labor demand and labor supply.
4. Potential GDP is the amount of output predicted by the long-run growth model. It is the amount of output the economy would produce if it were at full employment.
5. Balanced growth occurs when labor and capital grow at the same rate.

6. GDP growth can be divided into three sources: growth in labor input, growth in capital stock, and technological change.

7. In the neoclassical growth model an increase in saving does not permanently raise the growth rate.

8. In the endogenous growth model, technology growth is endogenous and the growth rate can be permanently increased.

9. The 1970s and 1980s had reduced rates of growth in output. The slowdown is attributed primarily to slower growth in technology.

10. Government policies can improve economic growth through increased expenditures on education and basic research or through tax incentives to encourage labor supply or capital accumulation.

11. Tax reform can improve incentives without reducing the tax revenue collected by government. Such a reform usually requires flattening marginal tax rates on income.

## Key Terms and Concepts

| | | |
|---|---|---|
| long-run economic growth | production function | potential GDP |
| neoclassical growth model | labor demand | growth accounting formula |
| balanced growth capital-output ratio | labor supply | production function for technology |
| natural rate of unemployment | labor market equilibrium | endogenous growth theory |
| | full employment | |

## Questions for Discussion and Review

1. What are the three basic determinants of long-run growth?

2. What is the unemployment rate when the economy is in equilibrium?

3. Why is the demand for labor a negative function of the real wage?

4. Explain why microeconomic theory predicts that for labor supply the income effect is negative and the substitution effect is positive. What do empirical studies indicate about the sum of these two effects?

5. Explain why the long-run growth model predicts that the level of real GDP in any one year is determined solely in the labor market. What would happen to the real wage, the price level, and the nominal wage if the money supply were increased?

6. Why doesn't a higher saving rate increase growth in the neoclassical growth model?

7. Does an increase in the rate of growth of labor add more or less to the growth rate of output than the same size increase in the rate of growth of capital? Explain why.

8. Describe three different policies that could be used to increase the growth rate of potential GDP. Identify whether the policy is aimed at technology, capital formation, or labor supply.

9. Explain what is meant by endogenous growth theory.

## Problems

### NUMERICAL

1. a. The labor supply function is given by $N = 1,000 + 12\,(W/P)$ and labor demand is $N = 2,000 - 8\,(W/P)$. Draw a diagram showing these schedules. Find the equipment level of employment and the real wage.

   b. Given existing technology and the capital stock, output is given by the function $Y = 100\,\sqrt{N}$. Graph the production function. Does the production function exhibit diminishing marginal product of labor?

   c. Using the labor market from Part a and the production function from Part b, determine the equilibrium level of output for this economy.

2. Assume that over a 10-year period the growth rate of capital is 4 percent, the growth rate of employment is 2 percent, and the growth rate of real output is 5 percent. Calculate the growth rate of technology. Suppose that a permanent cut in the budget deficit increases investment, and the growth rate of capital rises by 1 percent. How much does the growth rate of output increase? Suppose that a tax reduction increases the supply of labor by 1 percent in one year. What happens to the growth rate of real output?

3. Suppose that the production function takes the special form $Y = AN^{.7}K^{.3}$. By taking logarithms and first differences of this production function, show that the growth formula is satisfied. (If you have had calculus, calculate the marginal products of labor and capital. Derive the labor demand function. Calculate the labor share and the capital share.)

4. Assume that the technology production function takes the form $\Delta A = 1 + N_A\sqrt{A}$. Trace out the effects of an increase in researchers' $N_A$ on technology growth over time.

### ANALYTICAL

1. Explain the relationship between the following terms: equilibrium employment, the natural rate of unemployment, and potential GDP.

2. Suppose you think technological change always improves from year to year. Using the neoclassical growth model, describe two ways in which it may be possible for equilibrium employment to decline in spite of positive growth in productivity.

3. Suppose the target rate of long-run equilibrium per capita GDP growth is 1 percent per year. Labor input and population are expected to grow at 1 percent.

   a. What rate of GDP growth is required to achieve the target for per capita GDP growth?

   b. Using the growth accounting formula, what is the required growth in the capital stock necessary to achieve the target assuming technology growth of .5 percent? What is the required growth in the capital stock if there is no growth in technology?

4. Can tax reform that increases labor supply permanently raise the rate of growth of GDP? Explain.

5. Suppose that the labor supply schedule is vertical. What would be the effect of a change in the tax on labor?

6. The unification of Germany created a nation with a much lower capital-to-labor ratio relative to what previously existed in West Germany. What impact do you think unification had on the level of productivity compared with what existed in West Germany alone? What impact will unification have on the growth rate of labor productivity after the initial shock? Explain.

## MacroSolve Exercises

1. Plot the unemployment rate using quarterly data. What level should the rate of unemployment approach if the labor market is in equilibrium? What does the time series indicate? How does the long-run growth model account for this discrepancy?

2. How does the long-run growth model explain fluctuations in output? Plot real GDP growth and the unemployment rate on the same screen using annual data from 1930 to 1995. How credible is the long-run growth model's explanation in light of the data? What might contribute to the high correlation in these two series that the long-run growth model overlooks?

3. Construct a series for the growth rate of the capital stock. Graph the growth rate of capital on the vertical axis against savings as a percent of GDP on the horizontal axis. How are these two variables related? What difference does it make if you use annual or quarterly data? Explain. (Hint: Calculating the statistics can shed some light on this problem.)

4. Plot real compensation per hour and output per hour. How does microeconomic theory explain your findings?

5. Using the **CREATE FORMULA** option, create series for the growth rates of real compensation and output per hour. Plot the growth rates for real compensation and output per hour and calculate statistics for each series. How do the results differ between the levels of Question 5 and the growth rates of this problem? What explains this difference?

# APPENDIX: **Deriving the Growth Formula**

Suppose that $A$, $N$, and $K$ grow by rates $\Delta A/A$, $\Delta N/N$, and $\Delta K/K$. We will derive a formula for the growth rate of output, $\Delta Y/Y$. First, with neutral technological change we can write the production function as $F(N,K,A) = Af(N,K)$. Then the growth rate of output is approximately

$$\Delta Y/Y = \Delta A/A + \Delta f(N,K)/f(N,K). \qquad (3.12)$$

In other words, the growth rate of the *product* of $A$ and $f(N,K)$ is the *sum* of the growth rates of $A$ and $f(N,K)$.

Second, the part of the change in output that comes from changes in employment and capital can be further broken down using the marginal products of the two. Let $M_N$ be the marginal product of labor and $M_K$ be the marginal product of capital. Then

$$\Delta f(N,K)/f(N,K) = M_N \Delta N/Y + M_K \Delta K/Y. \tag{3.13}$$

In words, this expression states that the proportional change in $f$ can be divided into two components that measure the contributions of the proportional changes in $N$ and $K$. (If you have had calculus, this formula can be derived by taking the total derivative of $f$ and dividing by $Y$.) Putting this into the formula for $\Delta Y/Y$, we get

$$\Delta Y/Y = \Delta A/A + M_N \Delta N/Y + M_K \Delta K/Y. \tag{3.14}$$

If firms are using labor and capital up to the points where their marginal products are equal to the real wage and real rental prices, then

$$M_N = W/P \quad \text{and} \quad M_K = R^K/P. \tag{3.15}$$

Now the formula is

$$\Delta Y/Y = \Delta A/A + (W/P)\Delta N/Y + (R^K/P)\Delta K/Y. \tag{3.16}$$

We can rewrite this as

$$\Delta Y/Y = \Delta A/A + (WN/PY)\Delta N/N + (R^K K/PY)\Delta K/K. \tag{3.17}$$

$WN/PY$ is the fraction of revenue, $PY$, paid out to labor in the form of compensation, $WN$. Similarly, $R^K K/PY$ is the fraction of revenue earned by capital. From the national income and product accounts, we find that these fractions are about .7 and .3. Thus,

$$\Delta Y/Y = \Delta A/A + .7\Delta N/N + .3\Delta K/K, \tag{3.18}$$

which is the growth formula (Equation 3.7).

Observe also that the growth accounting formula can be written simply in terms of labor productivity, or output per unit of labor ($Y/N$). The growth rate of labor productivity is $\Delta Y/Y - \Delta N/N$. Thus by subtracting $\Delta N/N$ from both sides of Equation 3.18 we get

$$\begin{pmatrix} \text{Growth rate of} \\ \text{labor productivity} \end{pmatrix} = \frac{\Delta A}{A} + .3\begin{pmatrix} \text{Growth rate of} \\ \text{capital per unit of labor} \end{pmatrix}.$$

# Fiscal and Monetary Policy in the Growth Model

We can use the long-run growth model introduced in the previous chapter to study the long-term properties of monetary and fiscal policies. The framework for evaluating these policies is simple because the long-run growth model does not deal with the complexities of departures of the economy from full employment. Although a complete treatment of the short-run effects of monetary and fiscal policies must await the development of the complete model in Chapters 6 through 9, it is useful to establish the long-run properties now. They are an integral part of the complete analysis and important principles in their own right.

The long-run growth model is useful for evaluating the effects of monetary and fiscal policies over long spans of time; 10 years or more would be ideal and in most applications a minimum of about 3 years is necessary. Fiscal policy in the United States, for example, was more expansionary from 1985 to 1994 than from 1965 to 1974. The federal deficit averaged 4.1 percent of GDP in 1984–94 and 1.1 percent of GDP in 1965–74. What was the effect of this difference on interest rates? On exchange rates? On the trade balance? The growth model can provide good answers to these important questions. Another long-term fiscal policy issue is the effect on the economy of the reduction in defense spending in the 1990s, reflecting the demise of the Soviet Union.

In our discussion of monetary policy in this chapter, again the focus is on the long term and we do not deal with the departures of the economy from potential. For example, money growth was much higher in the 1970s than in the 1980s in the United States. The long-term growth model indicates that the main effect of this change on the economy would be a higher rate of inflation in the 1970s than in the 1980s. This was, in fact, the case.

# HOW FISCAL AND MONETARY POLICY AFFECT REAL GDP IN THE LONG RUN

**Fiscal policy**, by definition, involves changes in government purchases ($G$), taxes ($T$), transfer payments to the private sector ($F$), and interest payments on the government debt ($N$). (The symbols in parentheses were introduced in Chapter 2.) Changes in any of these four items cause changes in the federal budget deficit, which is simply defined as total expenditures less taxes:

$$\text{Budget deficit} = G + F + N - T. \qquad (4.1)$$

Fiscal policy is determined by the President and the Congress. The primary focus of fiscal policy in recent years has been to find a way to reduce the federal budget deficit. One of our purposes here is to understand why this would be a good policy for the long term.

**Monetary policy** involves changes in the money supply. In the United States the money supply is controlled by the Federal Reserve System (the Fed)—the country's central bank, established by Congress in 1913. There are important interactions between monetary and fiscal policies; this means that Congress, the President, and the Fed have a joint role to play in determining the overall stance of monetary and fiscal policies, or simply macroeconomic policy.

What are the effects of monetary and fiscal policies on output in the long run? By and large, fiscal policy will have effects on total output in the long term, while monetary policy will have almost no effect. To see why, let's look at the growth model. We know that in the long-term growth model with perfectly flexible prices, GDP is always equal to potential GDP and therefore depends only on the supply of the three productive factors: labor, capital, and technology. If monetary and fiscal policies are to affect GDP in this model, they must affect one or more of these three factors.

Consider first the effects on potential GDP of government spending, a key component of fiscal policy. A change in government spending, such as a decline in defense spending, does not immediately have any substantial effect on the *supply* of the three productive factors. If the government decides to build fewer missiles, the supply of labor does not decline, according to the growth model. Nor, in the absence of a reduction in R&D spending, is there a change in technological know-how. If there is some increase in private investment in the economy to fill the gap left by the decline in defense spending, then eventually this will increase the supply of private capital; however, this increase in the supply of capital will initially be small relative to the existing size of the capital stock and will not have a noticeable effect on GDP for several years.

What about the effect of the other major components of fiscal policy? In the previous chapter we showed how changes in tax rates affect worker incentives. We noted that a tax-rate reduction improves incentives to work but also reduces the desire to work (through the income effect), so the net effect may be small unless the reduction is part of tax reform. An increase in tax revenues paid by consumers to the government will reduce income available for consumption and thereby decrease consumption. If investment increases as a result, then the capital stock will grow and real GDP will rise. But the effect on GDP will be relatively small for several years. Changes in interest payments or transfers from the government that do not affect incentives or investment will have no impact on real GDP.

Similar reasoning suggests that a change in the money supply will not affect the supply of the productive factors. There is no reason to expect an increase in the money supply—currency and deposits at banks—to change the incentive to work or to be more inventive. In the long-term growth model with perfectly flexible prices, an increase in the money supply will leave GDP unchanged. But with more money persistently chasing the same amount of goods, prices will rise. Hence, monetary policy can increase the inflation rate. Some economists feel that higher inflation reduces productivity and thereby reduces GDP—a possibility that we will pursue later in the book. If so, then monetary policy affects real GDP by affecting the rate of inflation.

## EFFECTS OF FISCAL AND MONETARY POLICY ON REAL GDP IN THE LONG RUN

1.  In the long run, GDP depends only on the supplies of the three productive factors: labor, capital, and technological know-how.
2.  Fiscal policy can raise GDP by stimulating labor supply or by inducing additional investment. For many policy changes, these supply effects are likely to be small in the short run but build up over time.
3.  A change in monetary policy will affect the price level. Inflationary monetary policies may have some adverse effect on GDP.

# HOW FISCAL POLICY AFFECTS THE SHARES OF OUTPUT

In the previous section we looked at the long-run effects of fiscal policy on the *total amount* of real GDP. In this section we look at the effects on the *components*, or *shares*, of GDP. Recall that in Chapter 2 we presented the components of GDP using the simple accounting identity

$$Y = C + \underbrace{I + X +}_{\text{Nongovernment purchases}} \underbrace{G,}_{\text{Government purchases}} \qquad \text{The Income Identity} \qquad (4.2)$$

where $Y$ is GDP, $C$ is consumption, $I$ is investment, $X$ is net exports, and $G$ is government purchases.

Many of the long-run questions about fiscal policy involve the effects of changes in government spending as a *share* of output. For example, we might want to know what will happen if government purchases in the year 2000 are 20 percent rather than 15 percent of GDP. Or what difference it makes for interest rates if the deficit as a share of GDP is 1 percent in the late 1990s instead of 4 percent as it was in the 1980s. Equation 4.2 can be rewritten and interpreted in terms of shares of GDP if we simply divide both sides of the equation by $Y$. This gives

$$1 = \frac{C}{Y} + \frac{I}{Y} + \frac{X}{Y} + \frac{G}{Y}. \qquad (4.3)$$

In other words, the shares of the different components of spending must sum to 1.

We now want to use Equation 4.3 to determine what happens to the components of output when fiscal policy changes. A quick glance at the equation shows that *a change in government purchases as a share of GDP must bring about a change in nongovernment purchases as a share of GDP by the same amount, but in the opposite direction.* For example, a decrease in government purchases of 3 percent of GDP must bring about an *increase* in nongovernment purchases of 3 percent of GDP. An increase in government purchases of 3 percent of GDP implies that nongovernment purchases must fall by 3 percent of GDP. This is straightforward arithmetic. It is also straightforward logic.

How much do consumption, investment, and net exports individually rise? Would consumption $C$, income $I$, and net exports $X$ each rise by 1 percent of GDP in the case of a cut in government purchases of 3 percent of GDP? Or would some other combination of percentages occur? The answer depends on how sensitive each of these items is to interest rates.

## Interest-Rate Sensitivity of Consumption, Investment, and Net Exports

What brings about a change in consumption, investment, and net exports in the long-term growth model? We have simply used arithmetic and logic to show that such a change must take place. The economic mechanism involves interest rates. An increase in interest rates will tend to reduce investment, net exports, and consumption. A decrease in interest rates will have the opposite effect. These changes in interest rates, which accompany changes in fiscal policy, are what bring about the changes in the nongovernment components of output.

Why do consumption, investment, and net exports depend negatively on the interest rate? Consider consumption first. Consumption is expenditure by households. Higher interest rates mean that consumers will have to pay more to finance consumption of automobiles and other durables. These higher finance costs discourage consumption. For example, higher required payments on a car loan discourage purchases of cars. Higher interest rates discourage investment for similar reasons. Recall that investment is expenditures by firms on machines and equipment. Higher interest rates mean that firms will have to pay more to finance their investments, and thus higher interest rates discourage investment.

The relationship between interest rates and net exports is more complicated, involving two steps. First, recall from Chapter 2 that the exchange rate determines how expensive foreign goods are in comparison with American goods. When the exchange rate rises, foreign goods become cheaper compared with home goods (see page 45). Hence, with a higher exchange rate, Americans want to import more and foreigners want less American exports. With American exports falling and imports rising, net exports—exports less imports—decline. In other words, a higher exchange rate reduces net exports. Now the second step: Higher interest rates in the United States make U.S. assets a more attractive financial investment and drive up the value of the dollar. Hence, a higher interest rate tends to be associated with a higher exchange rate. Now combining these two steps, we see that higher interest rates tend to reduce net exports by raising the exchange rate.

Figure 4.1 shows the three negative relationships between the interest rate and (1) consumption, (2) investment, and (3) net exports. Note that in the diagram the slope of the consumption relationship is less steep than that of investment and net exports. This reflects historical observations that the sensitivity of consumption to interest rates is smaller than that of investment and net exports. Note also that the fourth panel on the far right in Figure 4.1 is the sum of consumption, investment, and net exports shares. This illustrates how the total nongovernment share $(C + I + X)/Y$ depends negatively on the interest rate. Having derived the interest-rate sensitivities of the major

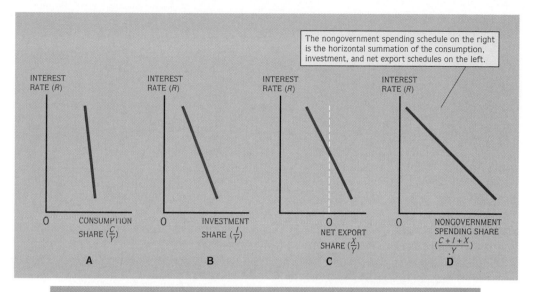

**FIGURE 4.1**  Interest-Rate Sensitivity of Consumption, Investment, and Net Exports

Consumption, investment, and net exports shares all depend negatively on the interest rate $R$. Therefore, the sum of the shares depends negatively on the interest rate. Panel D is the sum of the shares in the other panels at each interest rate.

components of output, we now can proceed to derive the impact of a change in government purchases and other fiscal actions on the composition of output.

## Government Purchases

When government purchases fall, we know that nongovernment purchases rise. Figure 4.2 shows how a decrease in interest rates brings about this increase in consumption, investment, and net exports. First look at Panel D, which shows that lower interest rates must be associated with higher spending on nongovernment purchases. This panel also tells us how much interest rates must fall. Panels A, B, and C can then be used to determine by how much consumption, investment, and net exports individually rise. According to Figure 4.2, consumption rises by a smaller amount than investment does because consumption is less sensitive to interest rates than investment is. Net exports rise because the lower interest rates cause a decline in the exchange rate.

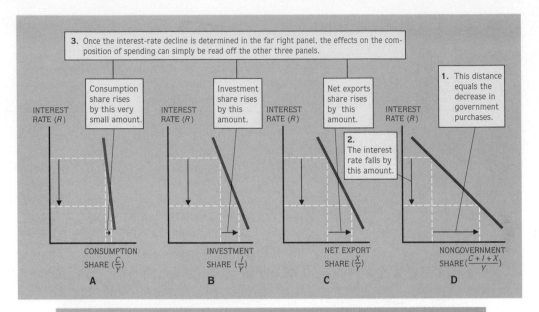

**FIGURE 4.2**  Effects of a Decrease in Government Purchases

The nongovernment share of GDP must rise by the same amount as the fall in the government share of GDP. This rise is brought about by a decline in interest rate $R$. The decline in the interest rate also causesxchange rate to fall.

## The Budget Deficit and the Trade Deficit

Note that this analysis illustrates the close connection between the budget deficit and the trade deficit. The cut in government purchases as a share of GDP will reduce the budget deficit as a share of GDP, as is clear from Equation 4.1. But as we have seen, the cut in government purchases also reduces the trade deficit (net exports rise). That is, the government's attempt to reduce the budget deficit has reduced the trade deficit.

## Other Fiscal Policy Changes

The analysis of other types of fiscal policy changes in the long run is very similar to the above analysis of a decline in government purchases. The analysis of an increase in government purchases is just the reverse of the analysis of a decline in government purchases. In this case, the interest rate rises to depress the demand for investment and net exports in order to make room for a greater government use of resources. The term **crowding out** is used to describe this process—higher government spending crowds out investment and net exports. A dollar of government purchases crowds out almost a dollar of investment and net exports and perhaps a small amount of consumption.

Changes in taxes will affect consumption. For example, higher taxes on consumption will reduce consumption because people have less to spend. But the reduction in consumption does not immediately affect potential GDP because the supply of the three productive factors does not change. Hence, the decline in consumption must result in an increase in net exports and investment. The effects can be illustrated in a diagram similar to Figure 4.2 and are left as an exercise at the end of the chapter.

Figure 4.3 illustrates how well the model works in predicting the effects of policy changes. It compares GDP shares in 1970–74 with those in 1990–

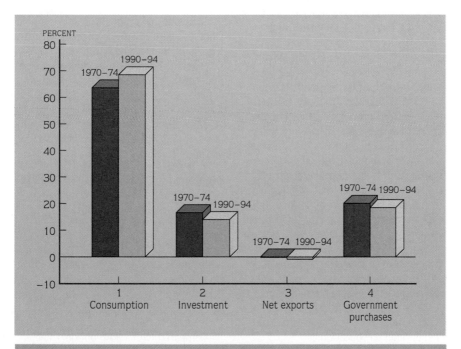

**FIGURE 4.3**  Changes in GDP Shares between 1970–74 and 1990–94

Because of tax cuts and other factors, the consumption share rose. The share of government purchases fell, but not by as much. Both the investment and net export shares fell as well.

## NEW RESEARCH IN PRACTICE
## How Should We Divide $8 Trillion in GDP?

Figures 4.1 and 4.2 may seem remarkably simple given the complexity of the policies being considered. That is the beauty of the long-run framework. It does not require an elaborate system of equations to derive results about the allocation of GDP among different uses—consumption, investment, government, and net exports. It demonstrates how, if the government uses a larger share of GDP, the private sector has to use less. Interest rates play the role of determining whether it is investment, consumption, or net exports that gets crowded out.

Herbert Stein of the American Enterprise Institute, and formerly chairman of the Council of Economic Advisers, has suggested a framework for the analysis of the federal budget which is based on this notion of allocating different components of GDP to different uses. He argues that federal budget policy should be viewed more broadly as budgeting GDP rather than simply budgeting federal expenditures. His book on the subject, *Governing the $5 Trillion Economy*, describes his proposals in detail. The theoretical framework that underlies his practical suggestions is essentially the long-fun framework described in Section 4.2.

Stein's basic point is that decisions about the federal budget should be based on two considerations: (1) an ordering of national priorities and (2) a view of the relation between the budget and the achievement of those priorities. Clearly, people will have widely different views about priorities. To some, national health insurance is a high priority. Others feel that we need more roads and bridges or fiber-optic cable lines. People have different views about defense spending in the aftermath of the Cold War. Others are concerned that we are not spending enough on education.

People also have different views on the efficacy of budget policy for achieving those objectives. Here the long-run economic analysis can be very useful in analyzing both incentives to work, save, invest, and innovate and the mechanism through which GDP is allocated to different uses.

To see how Stein's proposals would work, consider the following.

**Shares of GDP in 1984 and 1994 (percent)**

|  | 1984 | 1994 | Change |
| --- | --- | --- | --- |
| Defense | 6.2 | 4.3 | −1.8 |
| Other federal | 2.1 | 2.1 | 0.1 |
| State and local | 10.3 | 11.0 | 0.6 |
| Domestic investment | 16.3 | 13.9 | −2.4 |
| Consumption | 65.1 | 68.7 | 3.5 |

Domestic investment is total investment less the trade deficit. It is the accumulation of net wealth in the United States. The figures show three essential facts about the mid-1990s compared with the mid-1980s: (1) Defense spending was much lower, (2) consumption was much higher, and (3) investment was much lower.

Now consider two options for budgeting GDP in the year 2000 using Stein's approach. For convenience focus on a single year.

**Options for Shares of GDP in 2000 (percent)**

|  | Option 1 | Option 2 |
| --- | --- | --- |
| Defense | 4 | 2 |
| Other federal | 2 | 2 |
| State and local | 10 | 12 |
| Domestic investment | 15 | 17 |
| Consumption | 69 | 67 |

Compared with 1994, option 1 keeps expenditures on defense about constant, while option 2 cuts defense in half. Both options also have more expenditures on investment than in 1994, but option 2 adds two more percentage points. That reflects a general consensus that national saving in the United States in the 1990s was too low. Option 2 is more investment oriented. Option 2 has two more percentage points devoted to state and local purchases, which are dominated by education.

Choosing between these two options—or indeed many other possibilities—is one of the functions of our political system and government. Especially in comparison with the shares of the mid-1990s, these options represent significant differences in economic policy and would have profound effects on the evolution of the United States economy. A shift in the composition of spending from the levels in the mid-1990s to either of the two options would involve movements in interest and exchange rates. The model in Figure 4.1 can tell us how this would happen and by how much interest and exchange rates would change. It is hard to imagine a more practical application of the simple long-run model.

---

94. Two policy changes occurred during the 20 years separating the two periods. First, taxes on saving were raised, compared to consumption, through the elimination of savings incentives such as through tighter restrictions on individual retirement accounts. Families had more resources at their disposal, and they consumed more. Second, government use of resources fell, as measured by the share of government purchases in GDP. However, the rise in the consumption share was 4.9 percentage points of GDP (from 63.6 percent of GDP to 68.5), much larger than the fall in government purchases, which was only 1.6 percentage points of GDP. The net effect of policy changes was to make investment fall by 2.6 percentage points and net exports fall by 0.7 percentage points of GDP.

## Importance of the Long-Run Assumption

Where does the assumption about the long run fit into these calculations? Clearly, the shares of output add up to 1 in both the long run and the short run. The answer is that the long-run assumption makes sure that other things besides interest rates do not affect the shares of spending in GDP.

For example, as we will show in later chapters, if we cut government spending by 3 percent of GDP in one fell swoop, real GDP itself will fall in the short run, possibly by more than 3 percent. A fall in real GDP will result in an even sharper decline in investment as businesses see their sales falling. The share of investment in GDP will fall rather than rise. The results in this section would be all wrong and terribly misleading to policymakers if applied in the very short run. The long-run assumption allows us to view the economy on its long-run potential growth path. Hence, there will be no sharp movements in GDP.

The relationship between the short run and the long run will be clearer after we have studied the departures of real GDP from potential. Then we will see that the results obtained through these simple share calculations are exactly the same as long-run calculations that will be obtained with the more complete model.

## NEW RESEARCH IN PRACTICE
## International Policy Coordination

Because net exports (*X*) appear in the income identity, the long-run analysis of the composition of GDP has applications for international macroeconomic policy. For example, a reduction in government spending raises net exports (reduces the trade deficit). This analysis underlies many international discussions of fiscal policy that occur at multilateral forums such as the Organization for Economic Cooperation and Development (OECD) in Paris, the International Monetary Fund in Washington, and, more frequently, the group of finance ministers of the seven largest industrial countries (commonly called the G-7). The analysis also forms the underpinning of bilateral negotiations.

One particular application illustrates very well how this type of analysis is used in practice. The application occurred as part of a bilateral coordination effort between the United States and Japan known as the Structural Impediments Initiative (SII). One of the objectives of the SII was to reduce both the United States trade deficit and the Japanese trade surplus. Such a reduction, it was hoped, would help reduce trade friction between the two countries and ease protectionist pressures. The SII talks were always meant to be a two-way street: both the United States and the Japanese would make policy changes.

The United States government's economic analysis stressed that the U.S. trade deficit as a share of GDP would go down if the U.S. budget deficit as a share of GDP went down, assuming that no other factors that would offset this changed. The same analysis suggested that the Japanese surplus would go down if the Japanese increased the share of GDP devoted to public infrastructure investment in Japan. These are both long-run propositions that can be handled with the long-run model. Both propositions can be proved with the simple diagrams in Figure 4.2. You should try to do it. What would happen to interest rates and exchange rates?

As part of the SII, the government of Japan agreed to increase government infrastructure investment in Japan over a 10-year period. The government agreed to increase such investment by ¥430 trillion during the 1990s. That would raise the share of investment in GDP about 1 percent by the end of the 10 years compared with what it otherwise would have been. For its part, the United States offered the five-year $500 billion reduction in the U.S. budget deficit in the 1990 budget agreement.

International policy coordination seems mysterious to outsiders. How much influence does one sovereign government have on another? Some argue, for example, that coordination efforts like SII or the work of the G-7 have little effect; governments only agree to do what they would have done anyway. For example, even before SII started, many Japanese had argued that more public infrastructure investment was needed. And in the United States there was already a consensus that something should have been done to reduce the budget deficit. So maybe these and other actions would have occurred without coordination efforts. It is difficult to know for sure. Certainly, in the discussions there is a notion of making concessions, for example, increasing infrastructure investment in Japan in exchange for something else from the United States. There is also the element of diplomacy and international goodwill, the importance of which is hard to measure.

Note that there would have been other ways for the Japanese to reduce their trade surplus. Increasing consumption as a share of GDP was discussed in the preliminaries to the SII talks, but the United States government felt that it would not be good economic policy to promote antisaving in any country, especially in a decade in which there appeared to be a shortage of saving around the world. Hence, the United States position was that the gap between saving and investment in Japan would be better reduced by increasing investment rather than by reducing saving.

## FISCAL POLICY AND THE COMPOSITION OF OUTPUT

1. In the long-run growth model, an increase in government purchases will raise interest rates and reduce (crowd out) investment and net exports. The exchange rate will also rise.
2. The budget deficit and the trade deficit are closely related. A decrease in government spending which lowers the budget deficit will also lower the trade deficit.
3. The interest rate is a key factor in the analysis of fiscal policy. Consumption and especially investment and net exports are negatively affected by higher interest rates.

# MONEY AND INFLATION

In the previous section, we discussed how the real interest rate divides output among consumption, investment, government, and net exports. We showed how fiscal policy affects these variables. Now we consider the long-run behavior of another important macroeconomic variable, the inflation rate. **Inflation** is the rate of increase in the price level. In order to explain the price level, and thereby inflation, we need to consider the demand for and supply of money. In the long-run growth model, the price level is determined by equating money demand to money supply. Monetary policy determines the money supply.

## The Demand for Money

When we speak of **money**, we have a rather special meaning in mind. Money is the currency issued by the Federal Reserve—for example, coins and dollar bills—together with the checking account balances held by the public in banks. Money is used to facilitate the purchase and sale of goods. When we buy goods, we usually pay with currency or with a check. Money does not include the much larger amounts of wealth held in mutual funds, bonds, corporate stock, and other forms, even though these forms of wealth are measured in dollars, because they are not usually used to pay for goods.

Three basic propositions about the demand for money are important for macroeconomics.

1. *People will want to hold less money when the interest rate is high and, conversely, will want to hold more money when the interest rate is low.*

    This means that there is a negative relation between the demand for money and the interest rate $R$. People hold money for transactions purposes, to pay daily expenses and monthly bills. But they could obtain higher earnings by keeping their wealth in other forms, such as savings accounts or bonds. Currency pays no interest. And even though many checking deposits now pay interest, the rate is less than on other forms of wealth. Because of this, people tend to economize on the use of money for transaction purposes. A common way to do this is to go to the ATM or bank more often to withdraw money from a high-interest savings account to obtain currency, or simply to transfer funds to a lower-interest checking account. With more frequent trips, a smaller amount can be withdrawn each time from savings accounts. This means that, on average, a smaller amount of currency or checking balances will be held by the individual. For example, you could go to the ATM every week, rather than every month, to obtain currency and thereby hold a smaller amount of currency on average.

    How much economizing will occur will depend on the interest rate. The interest rate $R$ represents how much a consumer or firm could earn by holding more of their wealth in forms that pay full interest instead of in currency, which pays no interest, or checking deposits, which pay less than full interest. Clearly the more that can be earned by holding those other forms—the higher $R$ is—the less money an individual or firm will want to hold.

2. *People want to hold more money when income is higher and, conversely, less money when income is lower.*

    The more a family receives as income, the more the family will normally be spending, and the more money the family will need for transaction purposes. When income increases, the transaction demand for money increases. More money will be needed to buy and sell goods.

    This means that there is a positive relationship between income $Y$ and the demand for money. As income in the economy increases, on average each family's income increases and the demand for money in the entire economy increases.

3. *People want to hold more money when the price level is higher and, conversely, less money when the price level is lower.*

    If the price level rises, people will need more dollars to carry out their transactions, even if their real income does not increase. At a higher price level, goods and services will be more expensive; more currency will be needed to pay for them and checks will be written for larger amounts. This means that the demand for money is an increasing function of the price level.

To summarize these three basic ideas, the demand for money depends negatively on the interest rate $R$, positively on income $Y$, and positively on the price level $P$. An algebraic relationship that summarizes the effect of these three variables on the demand for money is presented in the following equation:

$$M = (kY - hR)P. \qquad (4.4)$$

Here $M$ represents the amount of money demanded by firms and consumers. The other variables in Equation 4.4 have already been defined: $P$ is the price level, $R$ is the interest rate, and $Y$ is income or GDP. The lowercase symbols $k$ and $h$ are positive coefficients: the coefficient $k$ measures how much money demand increases when income increases; the coefficient $h$ measures how much money demand declines when the interest rate increases.[1] Equation 4.4 is called the **money demand function**. It is a more complicated algebraic expression than the equation we used previously for consumption and investment demand. The money demand function shows that money demand depends on three variables (the interest rate $R$, income $Y$, and the price level $P$), whereas consumption demand and investment demand each depend on only one variable.

When studying algebraic relationships like the money demand function in macroeconomics, it is very important to distinguish between the constants and the variables. Sometimes the constants are called **coefficients**. In the money demand function the variables are $M$, $Y$, $R$, and $P$. The constants, or coefficients, are $k$ and $h$. Variables move around; constants stay fixed. To highlight this important distinction, we use lowercase letters for constants and uppercase letters for variables. This convention is used throughout this book.

**EXAMPLE.** If $k$ equals .1583 and $h$ equals 1,000, then Equation 4.4 looks like this:

$$M = (.1583Y - 1,000R)P.$$

If income $Y$ is \$6,000 billion, the interest rate is 5 percent ($R = .05$), and the price level $P$ is 1, then the demand for money is equal to \$900 billion. An increase in income of \$10 billion will increase the demand for money by \$1.583 billion. An increase in the interest rate of 1 percentage point will decrease the demand for money by \$10 billion.

---

[1]Note that the appropriate interest rate for the money demand function is the nominal rate. Most alternatives to holding currency, such as bonds, pay a nominal interest rate. In order to keep our analysis simple, we place the real interest rate $R$ in the money demand function. If inflation is low, this is a very good approximation.

## The Supply of Money

The Federal Reserve System determines the level of the **money supply**. In Chapter 14 we will study the interesting question of how the Fed goes about setting the money supply. For now, we will assume that the Fed has picked a certain level for the money supply.

We will also assume that the demand for money and the supply of money are equal. For this reason we do not introduce a new symbol to represent the money supply; the variable $M$ means both money supply and money demand. Since these are always equal, this should cause little confusion. (Recall that the symbol $Y$ also refers to two variables: income and GDP.)

How does the demand for money become equal to the supply of money? Suppose that the demand is greater than the supply. Since the supply of money is fixed by the Fed, the demand for money must fall if the two are to be equal. The demand for money can adjust down by an increase in the interest rate, a decline in the level of income, or a decline in the price level. For example, an increase in the interest rate will cause people to demand less money. In principle, all three variables could move, but in the long-run model income and the interest rate are determined outside the money market. Thus, only the price level can move to equilibrate the money market.

## MONEY AND THE INTEREST RATE

1. Money is currency plus the balances in checking accounts.
2. The demand for money falls if the interest rate rises, if income falls, or if the price level falls.
3. The Federal Reserve determines the money supply.

## Equilibrium in the Money Market

We will continue to assume that the economy is on the long-run growth path; GDP is at potential $Y^*$, and the interest rate is at the value $R^*$ determined in Figure 4.2. Money demand is

$$M = (kY^* - hR^*)P. \qquad (4.5)$$

Money demand is proportional to the price level; if $P$ rises by 10 percent, people will want to hold 10 percent more money. Money supply is fixed by the Fed. The price level equates money demand to money supply, as shown

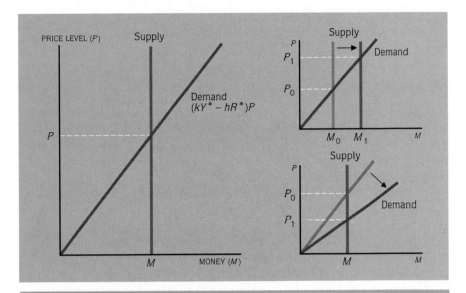

**FIGURE 4.4** Determination of the Price Level in the Money Market

On the left, the demand for money depends positively on the price level. The supply of money is fixed by the Fed. Equilibrium occurs at the intersection of supply and demand. On the top right, if the money supply rises, the price level rises in the same proportion. On the bottom right, if potential GDP is higher, the price level is lower.

in Figure 4.4. The algebraic expression for the price level that brings the amount of money demanded into equality with the amount of money supplied is

$$P = \frac{M}{kY^* - hR^*}. \tag{4.6}$$

When the Fed raises the money supply $M$ by 10 percent, the price level rises by the same 10 percent. With money more plentiful, its purchasing power falls and the price level rises. If potential GDP rises and the money stock remains the same, the price level falls; money becomes more valuable when the economy is producing a higher volume of goods and services. If government spending or some other determinant of demand falls, the equilibrium interest rate $R^*$ falls, and the price level also falls, to offset the rise in money demand.

In the long-run growth model, monetary policy is a very simple matter. The price level is proportional to the money stock. The money supply has no influence on output or the interest rate. This property is known as the **neutrality of money**. Another term for the independence of real variables like output from the money stock is the **classical dichotomy** because the real variables are determined *separately* from the money variables. We can think first about the determination of employment and output and then, separately, about the price level.

## Inflation

Recall that *inflation* is the rate of increase of the price level. In an economy where GDP doesn't change, our model of the money market implies that the price level is proportional to the money supply (see Equation 4.6). More money simply raises prices. The Fed can choose whatever rate of inflation it wants just by raising the money supply by that percentage each year. For price stability, the Fed should keep the money supply constant from one year to the next. For 5 percent inflation, it should raise $M$ by 5 percent each year.

In a growing economy, the rate of inflation will be less than the rate of money growth. If $Y^*$ is growing over time, some money growth is needed just to keep the price level from falling from one year to the next.

Figure 4.5 shows the relationship between money growth and inflation in a group of seven countries. Money growth is measured over an 18-year

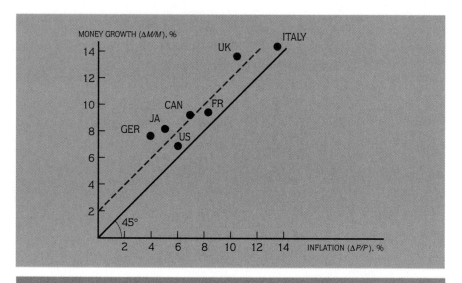

**FIGURE 4.5**  Money Growth and Inflation in Seven Countries, 1973–90

The vertical axis shows the average annual growth rate of money supply over an 18-year period. The horizontal axis shows the average annual rate of inflation. Generally, the observations appear to lie about 2 percent above the 45-degree line, clustered around the dashed line. Growth in real output absorbs about 2 percent of annual money growth, and the remaining money growth leads to inflation.

period, so the long-run analysis should apply even if recessions or booms are important over a 3- or 5-year period. If the relationship were as simple as 1 percent of inflation for each percent of money growth, all the observations would lie along the 45-degree line that equates inflation and money growth in the figure. Because growth of output also affects the relation between money growth and inflation, all the points lie above the 45-degree line. But it remains clear that money growth and inflation have a close relationship over a period of this length.

In the United States and all other economies, monetary policy and inflation are contentious issues. The United States has had episodes of inflation at rates of 10 percent and more, and some countries suffer hyperinflations, with rates of price increase of thousands of percent. Why does this happen if the central bank has direct control over inflation? There are two reasons that central banks don't deliver an inflation-free economy. In the United States, the reason is mainly that the long-run growth model does not describe the year-to-year movements of the economy. Instead, the economy can move away from potential. A monetary contraction is one of the forces that may cause a recession—a period when GDP is below potential. The fear of setting off a recession may prevent the Fed from cutting money growth, even though the reduced growth is just what the long-run growth model says is needed to end inflation.

In some smaller countries with less efficient tax systems, the second reason for inflation is important. The central bank—an arm of the government—issues large amounts of new money each year because the government is spending more than it takes in as taxes or from issuing bonds. The deliberate creation of high rates of inflation is one of the ways of financing government, though not a very good way. Severe deliberate inflation has not been part of U.S. economic policy since the Civil War.

# SUMMARY: THE CLASSICAL DICHOTOMY

The analysis of fiscal and monetary policies in this chapter illustrates an important property of the long-run growth model: Real variables like the interest rate and the composition of spending in the long-run growth model can be analyzed solely by looking at other real variables like government purchases. Nominal variables such as the money supply do not influence the level of GDP, the composition of GDP, or the level of interest rates. The diagrams in Figure 4.2 enabled us to determine the interest rate and the composition of output without considering monetary policy. In other words, to study the real economy, we could conveniently restrict ourselves to real variables in the economy. Once we know the stance of fiscal policy, we know all we need to know to determine the interest rate. Information about the money supply would not tell us anything else about the interest rate. Monetary variables such as the money supply affect only other nominal variables like the price level.

In the next chapter we begin to develop the complete model, in which this classical dichotomy does not always hold. But even in the complete model the results of this chapter are useful and important. They tell us the effects of monetary and fiscal policies that must hold in the long run in the complete model. Hence, the results derived in this chapter, with a minimum of algebra and technical detail, provide us with a benchmark from which to judge our results in the more complete model.

## REVIEW AND PRACTICE

### Major Points

1. The long-run growth model is a good guide to the effects of fiscal and monetary policy over periods of three years or more.

2. Fiscal policy involves changes in government purchases, transfers, and taxes.

3. Monetary policy involves changes in the money supply.

4. In the long-run growth model, changes in government purchases crowd out investment and thereby affect the long-run path of GDP.

5. An increase in the money supply has no effect on real GDP in the long run.

6. A decrease in government purchases as a share of GDP causes an equal increase in nongovernment purchases as a share of GDP.

7. Consumption, investment, and net exports depend negatively on the interest rate.

8. A decrease in government purchases causes a decline in the interest rate.

9. In the long run, the price level moves as necessary to equate the money demand to the money supply set by the Fed.

10. The price level is proportional to the money supply in the long run.

11. The Fed chooses the long-run rate of inflation by choosing the rate of money growth.

### Key Terms and Concepts

| | | |
|---|---|---|
| fiscal policy | money market | neutrality of money |
| monetary policy | demand for money | inflation |
| crowding out | supply of money | money growth |
| interest rate | money-market equilibrium | classical dichotomy |
| interest-rate sensitivity | | |

## Questions for Discussion and Review

1. What is the difference between fiscal and monetary policies?

2. Explain why an increase in government purchases decreases nongovernment purchases by the same amount.

3. How does monetary policy affect real GDP?

4. What determines the interest rate in the long-run growth model? In what sense does the interest rate guide resource allocation?

5. What effect does an increase in government purchases have on output and the interest rate in the long-run growth model?

6. Describe how the price level is determined in the long-run growth model. Is the price level a good indicator of economic welfare?

7. What is meant by the neutrality of money?

## Problems

### NUMERICAL

1. Consider a closed economy in which net exports $X = 0$. Suppose that consumption is insensitive to the interest rate, but that the share of investment in GDP rises by 2 percent for every 1 percent decline in the interest rate.

   a. By how much does investment rise as a share of GDP if government purchases decrease by 4 percent of GDP?
   b. By how much does the interest rate change?
   c. Using the growth accounting formula from Chapter 3, calculate how much more real GDP there would be if the capital-output ratio starts at 2.

2. Suppose that output is equal to potential at 4,000 and the equilibrium interest rate is .05. Money demand is given by

$$M = (.3Y - 4,000R)P.$$

   Money supply is set at 1,000 by the Fed.
   a. What price level is required for equilibrium in the money market?
   b. Suppose the Fed increases the money supply by 100. What is the new price level? What is the percentage change in the money supply? In the price level?
   c. Starting with a money supply of 1,000 and price level of 1.0, how does an increase in the interest rate from .05 to .10 affect the equilibrium price level? What could cause such an increase in the real interest rate?
   d. Starting again with $M = 1,000$ and $P = 1.0$, what effect does an increase in output from 4,000 to 4,500 have on the equilibrium price level?

### ANALYTICAL

1. Investment spending and net exports are negatively related to the interest rate. In the hopes of increasing output in the economy, a regulation is imposed that precludes the interest rate from exceeding 5 percent. Suppose that in the absence

of this regulation, the interest rate would be 6 percent. What effect will the regulation have on the level and allocation of output according to the long-run growth model? Explain why in the absence of such regulation the interest rate reflects the scarcity of output while preventing shortages.

2. Describe the qualitative effect of each of the following on output in the long-run growth model:

   a. An outward shift in the labor supply schedule.
   b. An improvement in technology.
   c. An increase in the money supply.
   d. A reduction in the tax rate $t$ on income.

3. In the long-run growth model, money is neutral. Changes in the supply of money influence the price level, but not the level of output. Reconcile this fact with the observation that labor supply and labor demand—which do determine output— are a function of the real wage $W/P$, which depends on the price level. How would you determine the nominal wage $W$ in the long-run model?

4. Suppose government purchases go toward refurbishing bridges and freeways in major metropolitan areas that suffer from congestion. What are the short-run (before the project is completed) and long-run (after the project is completed) effects on interest rates and investment, assuming other factors are unchanged? (Hint: Think about how potential GDP is affected in the long run.)

5. Higher real interest rates today make current income worth more in terms of future consumption. For this reason, some people argue that labor supply is positively related to interest rates.

   a. If this is true, how is the diagram that plots output against the interest rate affected?
   b. Explain why fiscal policy has more influence over output in a model where labor supply is positively related to interest rates.

6. Suppose that there is a reduction in investment incentives in the long-run growth model. Investment as a share of GDP is lower for any given interest rate.

   a. Show what happens in a diagram like Figure 4.1.
   b. Assume that neither consumption nor net exports vary with the interest rate. Does investment fall? Why or why not?
   c. Now assume that net exports vary negatively with the interest rate. What happens to investment?

7. Suppose the Fed attempted to keep the price level constant over time—a zero-inflation policy. Describe how the money supply would have to change in response to each of the following situations.

   a. An increase in potential GDP.
   b. An increase in income taxes with no change in potential GDP.
   c. A change in investment incentives that increases investment at any interest rate.
   d. An exogenous increase in foreign demand for U.S. goods.

8. In the early 1980s government purchases grew as a share of GDP. Simultaneously, the current account moved from near balance in 1980 to a large deficit in the

mid- to late 1980s. Use the long-run model to explain the behavior of net exports in relation to the growth of government purchases.

9. Describe the qualitative effect of each of the following on the price level in the long-run growth model:

   a. An increase in the labor supply.
   b. A decrease in the sensitivity of investment to the interest rate.
   c. A widespread, increased taste for consumption rather than saving.
   d. A decrease in government purchases.
   e. An increase in the average tariff rate on imports.

10. The end of the Cold War enables the United States to reduce government expenditure on national defense. Suppose the government believes it can cut defense by 2 percent of GDP. Using the long-run model, analyze the impact of this defense cut in combination with each of the following policies for allocating the "peace dividend." In each case, indicate what would happen to the real interest rate, consumption, and investment relative to the situation prior to the defense cut.

   a. The full amount of the cut in defense is applied toward a tax cut for households.
   b. The full amount of the cut is put toward government expenditure on infrastructure and education.
   c. No tax changes or other changes in government spending are combined with the defense cut.
   d. Rank the policies according to how much they will increase real GDP growth in the long run.

## MacroSolve Exercises

1. Plot the real interest rate with investment using quarterly data. What relationship do you find? What might explain this relationship?

2. Plot the rate of inflation and the rate of money growth using annual data. Comment on the strength of this relationship. Does the evidence support the implications of the long-run model? Why or why not?

3. Plot the growth rate of real GDP and the investment-GDP ratio. Are the two closely related? Does growth in the investment-GDP ratio seem to have a temporary or permanent effect on GDP?

4. Graph the money growth rate on the vertical axis against real GDP growth on the horizontal axis. Does the relationship between these two variables support or refute the principle of money neutrality? Explain.

5. Graph the money growth rate on the vertical axis against real interest rates on the horizontal axis. Does the relationship between these two variables support or refute the principle of money neutrality? Explain.

# CHAPTER 5

# Unemployment, Job Creation, and Job Destruction

Unemployment is a key variable in macroeconomics. The most significant aspect of a recession is that people are thrown out of work and become unemployed. In a bad recession, one worker out of 10 is unemployed. Even in normal times, 5 or 6 percent of the labor force is unemployed in the United States, and unemployment has been even higher in most European countries for the past 15 years. In booms, a low unemployment rate—4 or even 3 percent—is a sign of plentiful jobs for workers and recruitment problems for some employers. One of the most important questions in macroeconomics is why the economy does not provide work for the entire labor force. Even in the best of times, some people are unemployed.

In this chapter, we develop a unified view of unemployment that deals with the amount of unemployment in normal times (the natural rate of unemployment) and with the bursts of higher unemployment that occur during recessions. Our discussion of unemployment is a bridge from the long-run growth model to the short-run fluctuations model. In the growth model, the natural rate of unemployment is a limit on the amount of labor available as an input to production. In the fluctuations model—to be developed in the next three chapters—unemployment can change rapidly over time. The factors that cause production to fall in a recession also cause unemployment to rise, sometimes dramatically.

# 5.1  MEASURING UNEMPLOYMENT

The unemployed are people who are looking for work and are available for work, but who have not found jobs. One of the principal purposes of the Current Population Survey (discussed in Chapter 2 as one of the main sources of information about workers) is to determine how many people are unemployed each month. The survey counts you as unemployed if you did not work at all during the survey week and you are looking for work. In each survey, several million people are found to be unemployed. The **labor force** is defined as the number of people 16 years of age or over who are either working or unemployed. The *unemployment rate* is the percentage of the labor force that is unemployed.

There are millions of people who are not working but who are not counted as unemployed. They are considered out of the labor force because they are retired, in school, at home looking after their own children, sick, or not looking for work for some other reason. The *labor force participation rate* is the percentage of the working-age population that is in the labor force.

The survey data can also be used to tell us the reasons for unemployment—a job loss, a quit, or simply someone who just entered the labor force. Of the 7.4 million people unemployed in February 1996, 48 percent had lost their jobs, 10 percent had quit, and 42 percent had newly entered or reentered the labor force. In a year with more unemployment, 1992, 56 percent of the unemployed had lost their jobs.

## MEASURING UNEMPLOYMENT

1. The unemployed are looking for work, available for work, but have not yet found jobs.
2. Unemployment is measured in a national survey of households.

# 5.2  FLOWS INTO AND OUT OF UNEMPLOYMENT

Flows into and out of unemployment are huge—every month, almost 3 percent of the labor force becomes newly unemployed, well over 3 million people. And in most months, about the same number of people leave unemployment. With 3 percent of the labor force becoming unemployed each month, and with a normal unemployment rate of less than 6 percent, most of the unemployed don't stay that way very long. Normal spells of unemployment last for a few weeks, though a small fraction of spells last for many months.

One of the main ways that people become unemployed is by losing jobs. But flows of job seekers into the labor market from school and other nonwork activities are also important. Similarly, one of the main flows out of unemployment is by finding jobs. But many unemployed people drop out of the labor force rather than finding work. We will discuss the determinants of these flows shortly.

To understand the determination of the unemployment rate that results from these high flows into and out of unemployment, it will help to go through a simple mathematical exercise. We let

$b$ = the job-losing rate, the ratio of the number of people who become unemployed in a month to the labor force in that month.

$e$ = the job-finding rate, the fraction of the unemployed who leave unemployment in a month.

$u$ = the unemployment rate, the fraction of the labor force that is unemployed.

Then the flow into unemployment is the amount $b$, and the flow out of unemployment is the product of the unemployment rate $u$ and the departure rate $e$; the flow is $ue$. The flow of increasing unemployment is the difference between the inflow $b$ and the outflow, $ue$; the flow is $b - ue$. So, to understand why unemployment rises in a recession, we need to know why the inflow rate to unemployment, $b$, is high and why the outflow rate from unemployment, $ue$, is low.

Before we look at recessions, though, we want to consider normal conditions. Suppose that unemployment does not change from one month to the next, as we would expect to be true in normal conditions. Then the inflow must equal the outflow:

$$b = ue \qquad (5.1)$$

This can be solved for the unemployment rate:

$$u = \frac{b}{e} \qquad (5.2)$$

The unemployment rate is just the ratio of the job-losing rate, $b$, to the job-finding rate, $e$. An economy with a large job-losing rate or a small job-finding rate will have a high unemployment rate. We can break down our discussion of the determinants of the natural unemployment rate into two parts: determinants of the rate at which people lose jobs and determinants of the rate at which they find jobs. To be more precise, these are the rate at which people become unemployed (since some people become unemployed without losing jobs) and the rate at which they leave unemployment (since some people leave the labor force while they are unemployed and do not find jobs).

In Chapter 3, we learned that there is always some unemployment in the U.S. economy and that economists speak of the natural rate of unemployment as the amount that prevails in normal times. Even in normal times, there are substantial flows into and out of unemployment. One good way to measure normal conditions is to take averages over fairly long periods. For the period 1967 through 1993, average conditions were as follows:

| | |
|---|---|
| Job-losing rate, $b$ | 2.7 percent per month |
| Job-finding rate, $e$ | 43 percent per month |
| Rate of unemployment, $u$ | 6.3 percent of labor force |

By this measure, the natural rate of unemployment was 6.4 percent. An average over a longer period including the low-unemployment years of the 1950s and 1960s would be about 5.5 percent. Some economists have concluded that the natural rate may have been over 6 percent in the 1970s and 1980s, but may have fallen to around 5.5 percent in the 1990s.

## Flows into Unemployment

How do workers become unemployed? We will break down the sources of new unemployment into the following three categories:

1. Job destruction
2. Job loss without destruction
3. Personal transitions

*Job destruction* is the result of an employer's decision to terminate a position, dismissing the worker without refilling the job.[1] Job destruction often takes the form of plant closings or elimination of second shifts. Recessions generally have a burst of job destruction around the time that output is declining most rapidly. Even in normal times, rates of job destruction are high—in the average month from 1972 through 1988, almost 2 percent of all jobs in manufacturing were destroyed. Even when the economy is doing well, some industries or firms will be doing badly and will find it necessary to shut down plants or offices or to cut back their employment aggressively.

---

[1]See Steven J. Davis, John C. Haltiwanger, and Scott Schuh, *Job Creation and Destruction* (Cambridge, Mass: MIT Press, 1996).

Job destruction occurs when individual plants or firms are no longer viable and have to be shut down or scaled back. In normal times there is somewhat more job creation than destruction, so employment grows along with the labor force. Part of the source of chronic job destruction and creation is continual shifts across industries. In any year, there will be contractions in some industries and expansions in others, as the economy adjusts to changes in world markets and in consumer preferences. For example, in 1994, a year of strong overall growth in employment, more jobs were destroyed than were created in mining, nondurables manufacturing, and the federal government. Even more job destruction occurs within industries, as dynamic new firms displace the losers.

*Job loss without destruction* occurs when a worker loses a job but the employer does not reduce total employment. Either the discharged worker is replaced directly or another worker is hired and duties are reorganized. There are massive flows of this type of job loss. Over 5 percent of workers lose their jobs each month.[2] Though this figure includes job destruction and situations where workers quit jobs voluntarily, it is likely that over half of the flow is job loss without destruction. Many of these losses involve explicitly temporary work, including summer employment for students. The construction industry is a large contributor to this category—contractors hire and lay off workers with particular skills with great frequency.

*Personal transitions* cause people to quit their jobs. For example, a graduating student may quit a part-time after-school job and look for full-time work. Although flows of job quitters are large, quits are not an important flow into unemployment—only 13 percent of the newly unemployed have quit jobs. Much more important is the transition from nonwork activities. Almost half the newly unemployed were previously out of the labor force. The decision to look for work after being in school, being sick, or being involved in home activities is a major source of the flow into unemployment. In economies or markets where people frequently change their roles in the economy, flows into unemployment will be higher.

## Flows out of Unemployment

About two-thirds of the flow out of unemployment is the result of successful job search; one-third of those who stop being unemployed decide to leave the labor force.[3] Thus, the major determinant of the flow out of unemployment is the job-finding rate. That rate is the result of interaction of the avail-

---

[2]Patricia M. Anderson and Bruce D. Meyer, "The Extent and Consequences of Job Turnover," *Brookings Papers on Economic Activity, Microeconomics* (1994), pp. 177–236.
[3]Olivier J. Blanchard and Peter Diamond, "The Cyclical Behavior of the Gross Flows of U.S. Workers," *Brookings Papers on Economic Activity,* Vol. 2 (1990), pp. 85–143.

ability of jobs, on the one hand, and the strategies that job seekers use to find jobs, on the other hand.

Jobs are constantly available because of the natural flows out of jobs that we just discussed. First, in normal times, there is a flow of job creation at the same rate of almost 2 percent per month that jobs are destroyed. In the same industries where some firms are shutting plants and terminating workers, other firms are opening up new plants and hiring workers. Job creation is actually more stable over the business cycle than is job destruction.[4] Even in the most severe part of a contraction, when the job destruction rate skyrockets, job creation continues at levels not far below normal.

Just as there are job losses that occur without job destruction, there are flows of new hires that occur without job creation. Workers whose jobs ended normally, as in temporary work, or who quit to return to school or to take other jobs, need to be replaced.

Thus, at all times there are jobs available to absorb the unemployed. Though evidence is scant, it appears that the number of jobs available at any one time is far lower than the number of people looking for work. Nonetheless, in normal times, most of the unemployed find jobs in a month or two. The reason we know this is that job vacancies last only a week or two, on the average. The flow of new vacancies is huge. The typical job seeker keeps in touch with employers who might offer suitable jobs and waits until one opens up. The employer considers applicants quickly and makes a hire. Job seekers remain unemployed until they win suitable jobs.

The strategies followed by job seekers are the other important determinant of the speed at which they find work and thus of the flow out of unemployment. Economists have looked carefully at optimal strategies that workers should follow. The result has been a body of thinking called **search theory**.[5] One of the basic assumptions in search theory is that wages and working conditions vary across jobs. An optimal job-seeking strategy would not be to take the first job that comes along—it's probably one at the nearest fast-food restaurant. Instead, the job seeker should balance the benefit of starting an available job right away against the benefit of taking a better job that comes along later, net of the cost of waiting. An improvement in wages can justify a long wait. For example, if you have an offer at $350 per week for a job immediately available, but think that a job paying $400 per week (14 percent higher) will probably take six weeks to find, and you expect to hold either job until a year from now, it will be better to hold out for the better job. You will make $350 × 52 = $18,200 in the lower-paying job against $400 × 46 = $18,400 in the better job with six more weeks of unemployment.

---

[4]See Davis, Haltiwanger, and Schuh, *Job Creation and Destruction.*
[5]See Christopher A. Pissarides, *Equilibrium Unemployment Theory* (Cambridge and Oxford, England: Basil Blackwell, 1990).

Search theory portrays the activities of job seekers as economically rational, just like other household decisions. We can establish links between the economic environment of job seekers and their job-finding rates by using search theory. Then we can use Equation 5.2 to draw conclusions about how that environment affects the unemployment rate.

First, the job-finding rate will depend on the availability of jobs. If there are large numbers of job seekers and a small flow of new jobs, the probability is small that one job seeker will both find out about a particular new job *and* be offered that job. Second, the job-finding rate will depend on the amount of variation there is in the wages and working conditions for jobs. What matters is the chances of getting a really good job. If there is a small but significant chance that a job will come along that is much better than the typical one, the rational searcher will wait quite a while for that job to materialize. Job-finding rates in such markets—for example, the market for corporate executives—will be low. On the other hand, if all jobs are basically the same, the job seeker will want to take the first one that is offered. Job-finding rates are high in such markets—for example, in the market for temporary office work. Third, the job-finding rate will depend on the cost of waiting until a better job offer is made. If the cost is low, people will have a smaller incentive to find jobs, and so will have lower job-finding rates. Similarly, a program that subsidized people for looking for work would lengthen their period of search and lower their job-finding rates. Finally, the job-finding rate will be lower for jobs that are expected to last a long time. It pays to look for months for a career job, but not for a temporary job.

## UNEMPLOYMENT FLOWS

1. About 3 percent of the labor force becomes newly unemployed in the average month.
2. When the unemployment rate is neither rising nor falling, it is given by a formula: the ratio of the job-losing rate to the job-finding rate.
3. A major source of unemployment, especially in recessions, is job destruction. A job is destroyed if the worker holding it is laid off and nobody is hired to replace the worker.
4. The unemployed either find jobs or leave the labor force. About 43 percent of the unemployed depart unemployment in the average month.

# THE NATURAL UNEMPLOYMENT RATE

In normal times—when real GDP is equal to potential—unemployment is not zero. Recall from Chapter 3 that the unemployment rate equals the natural rate in normal times. When workers enter the labor force for the first time or after a spell out of the labor force, they need some time to find a job. During this period they are counted as unemployed. Similarly, when workers quit their jobs, there will frequently be a span of time before they find new jobs. Movements from one job to another are particularly common for young workers as they find out what type of job they are best suited for. This is one reason why young workers have higher unemployment rates than older workers. In addition, there are some low-skilled workers who are frequently unemployed. Additional training for such workers would reduce the unemployment rate.

Recall that the formula in Equation 5.2 applies when the unemployment rate is steady, neither rising or falling. Thus the formula describes the natural rate because in normal times the unemployment rate is holding steady. In words it is:

$$\text{Natural unemployment rate} = \frac{\text{Job-losing rate}}{\text{Job-finding rate}} = \frac{b}{e} \qquad (5.3)$$

The natural rate will be high in a labor market that has high rates of inflow and low rates of outflow. Economies with high rates of job destruction and creation will have high rates of inflow to unemployment and thus high natural rates. High rates of personal turnover contribute to the numerator and thus also raise the natural rate.

The natural rate will also be high in an economy or market with a low job-finding rate, the denominator in the equation for the natural rate. Economists have identified four special factors that may lower job-finding rates and thus raise the natural rate.

**EFFICIENCY WAGES**[6] According to the "efficiency wage" view, the employment relationship works best when workers feel that their current jobs are valuable. In this view a valuable job is one that pays well above what

---

[6]See George A. Akerlof and Janet L. Yellen, *Efficiency Wage Models of the Labor Market* (New York: Cambridge University Press, 1986), and Andrew Weiss, *Efficiency Wages: Models of Unemployment, Layoffs, and Wage Dispersion* (Princeton: Princeton University Press, 1990).

the worker could earn from looking for another job, including the cost of search. If the job is valuable, the threat to fire a worker is effective as a way to get the worker to perform. One way for an employer to make its jobs valuable is to pay higher wages than other employers do. But not every firm can pay more than other firms. As firms bid up wages in order to make their jobs valuable, they will reduce the number of jobs available (because labor demand slopes downward) and increase the number of people looking for those jobs (because labor supply slopes upward). Job-finding rates will be lower in that setting. Jobs will be valuable because fired workers face long periods of search to find new jobs. In a labor market where the efficiency wage theory applies, firms will have numerous applicants on the spot for every job opening and job seekers will find job offers few and far between. Figure 5.1 illustrates the difference between a low-unemployment labor market and a high-unemployment one where the assumptions of efficiency-wage theory apply. Only the right column, with high unemployment, can be an equilibrium in the market.

**UNION WAGE PREMIUMS**    Labor unions may also raise the natural rate. How? One of the purposes of labor unions is to improve wages and working conditions. In markets where unions are successful, the same type of asymmetry predicted by the efficiency wage theory would hold. Firms find hundreds of applicants for good union jobs and job seekers find opportunities for union jobs to be rare. As we noted in our discussion of the search model, it is worth searching longer if there is a small chance of getting a really good job. So an economy with successful unions will probably have a higher natural unemployment rate, according to this line of thought.

**MINIMUM WAGES**    The government intervenes in labor markets for low-wage workers in much the same way that unions do for more-skilled work. If there is rigorous enforcement of minimum wages at levels well above what would otherwise occur, the jobs affected by the minimum wage will be harder to find. To the extent that the legal minimum wage is low relative to wages in general and to the extent that employers simply ignore the law, the minimum wage may not raise the natural rate by very much.

**UNEMPLOYMENT INSURANCE**    Some workers receive payments from the unemployment insurance system during periods of job search—in February 1996, there were 7.4 million workers unemployed and 2.7 million of them drew benefits. Because the benefits are paid to replace lost earnings during unemployment, they are a subsidy for job search. Recall our earlier example where you would be willing to wait 6 weeks for a better job. Suppose instead that you received $200 per week in unemployment benefits. Then it would pay to search for as long as 12 weeks for the $400 per week job instead of settling for the $350 per week job right away. You would make $18,200 from

| LOW UNEMPLOYMENT | HIGH UNEMPLOYMENT |
|---|---|
| *Worker's perspective:* Wage at current job: $400 per week. Wage at next job: $400 per week. Time required to find next job: 1 week. Loss if fired from this job: $400. *Conclusion:* I don't have to work too hard at this job because I only lose $400 if I am fired and have to move to another job. | *Worker's perspective:* Wage at current job: $400 per week. Wage at next job: $400 per week. Time required to find next job: 15 weeks. Loss if fired from this job: $6,000. *Conclusion:* I better work hard at this job because I lose $6,000 if I am fired and have to move to another job. |
| *Employer's perspective:* I should raise the worker's pay because under present conditions the worker has no reason to work hard. | *Employer's perspective:* I don't need to change the worker's pay because under present conditions the worker has a good reason to work hard. |
| ***Conclusion:*** The market cannot stay like this because all employers will raise wages. | ***Conclusion:*** The market can stay like this because employers will keep wages at this level. |

**FIGURE 5.1**  Comparison of Low- and High-Unemployment Labor Markets in the Efficiency Wage Model

The left side considers a labor market where employers want to make it expensive for workers to leave their jobs. But it is easy for the workers to find new jobs because jobs are plentiful and it will only take a week to find one. Employers will then raise wages. The left side does not depict an equilibrium. On the right side, it is difficult to find new jobs and a worker sacrifices $6,000 by losing the current job. Employers feel no need to change wages. The labor market is in equilibrium with high unemployment.

the lower-wage job over the year, but $200 \times 12 + \$400 \cdot 40 = \$18,400$ from the unemployment benefits and the higher-wage job. Thus unemployment insurance makes the unemployed choosier in accepting lower-wage jobs, and encourages search strategies with lower job-finding rates. Of course, the motive for the unemployment insurance system is to help workers deal with the sudden loss of income that goes with unemployment. The lengthening of the job search and consequent increase in the natural rate are a side effect.

## Does the Natural Rate Change over Time?

The forces that determine the natural rate are not immutable. As they change, we would expect the natural rate to change. The natural rate should be high if an unusual restructuring of the economy is in progress, with high rates of job destruction in shrinking industries and job creation in expanding ones. Large changes in defense spending might be one source of this type of restructuring. The natural rate should be high if the labor force has an unusual proportion of younger workers with higher rates of personal transition. Declining unionization may lower the natural rate. Higher minimum wages and higher unemployment benefits would raise the natural rate.

   Over the past decade, most of these trends would suggest a lowering of the natural rate. The majority of the baby boom generation are now over forty, a time of low turnover. Unionization of the workforce has declined dramatically. The minimum wage has not grown as fast as wages in general. A declining fraction of the unemployed receive benefits, and benefits have not risen in relation to wages. Although there is much disagreement about change in the natural rate among economists, some evidence supports the hypothesis of a decline. Unemployment was above 6 percent in the expansion of the late 1970s, even when other conditions, such as worsening inflation, suggested that the economy was in a boom. By contrast, unemployment in the expansion years of the mid-1990s fell below 6 percent, without signs that these favorable labor market conditions were unsustainable.

---

### THE NATURAL UNEMPLOYMENT RATE

1. The natural unemployment rate is the amount of unemployment in normal times and is around 5 or 6 percent.
2. Forces tending to raise the natural rate are efficiency wage setting, union wage premiums, minimum wages, and unemployment insurance.
3. The determinants of the natural rate vary over time. Current trends are probably lowering the rate.

---

## 5.4  UNEMPLOYMENT IN RECESSIONS AND BOOMS

Figure 5.2 shows how the unemployment rate has fluctuated since 1950. Unemployment moves with the business cycle. In booms, when real GDP is

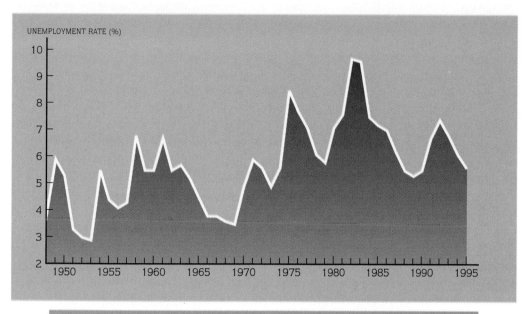

UNEMPLOYMENT RATE (%)

**FIGURE 5.2**   The Unemployment Rate

The unemployment rate has fluctuated between 3 and 10 percent since 1950. Unemployment rises during recessions and falls during expansions.
Source: *Economic Report of the President*, 1996, Table B-38.

high relative to potential, unemployment is low. In recessions, unemployment rises sharply and then declines more gradually as the recovery gets under way.

We can analyze fluctuations in unemployment in the framework developed in the first section. Recall that the number of people becoming unemployed each month in relation to the labor force is the inflow rate $b$. The number leaving unemployment, in relation to the labor force, is $ue$, the product of the unemployment rate $u$ and the rate at which people depart from unemployment $e$. The rate at which unemployment is rising, in relation to the labor force, is $b - ue$. If we know the starting unemployment rate and the inflow and outflow rates, we compute the increase in unemployment. Then we can update the unemployment rate and repeat the process. To put it differently, we can think of today's unemployment rate as the result of the history of inflows and outflows. Because most spells of unemployment last only a month or two, today's unemployment rate actually depends on the history of inflows and outflows only during the last six months or so.

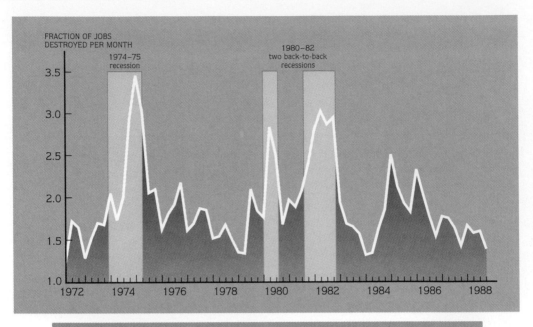

**FIGURE 5.3** Job Destruction Rate in Manufacturing

Each month, between 1.5 and 3.5 percent of jobs in manufacturing are destroyed by plant shutdowns, elimination of shifts, or other sources of reduced employment. The job-destruction rate reaches sharp peaks in recession years such as 1975, 1980, and 1982. But even in years of good conditions in the labor market, many jobs are destroyed. Job destruction is a major source of unemployment, especially in recessions.
Source: Davis, Haltiwanger, and Schuh, *Job Creation and Destruction*, 1996.

## Changes in the Unemployment Flows

By far the most important source of changes in inflows to unemployment is job destruction. Figure 5.3 shows the job destruction rate in manufacturing.[7] Occasionally, job destruction skyrockets. The peaks in 1975, 1980, and 1982 coincided with recessions. The peaks in 1985 and 1986 occurred during expansions; the one in 1986 may have been triggered by the collapse of oil prices in that year. Rates of inflow to unemployment jump up during these episodes of job destruction. As is shown in Figure 5.2, the unemployment rate jumps up as well, because inflows to unemployment exceed outflows.

Inflow rates to unemployment remain high after a burst of job destruction.[8] There are secondary effects from the displacement of workers. For example, a worker who is terminated in a plant closing may take temporary

[7]Calculation of the job-destruction rate requires processing data on individual plants. The data are available in suitable form only for manufacturing and only for the period 1972–88.
[8]See Robert E. Hall, "Lost Jobs," *Brookings Papers on Economic Activity*, Vol. 1 (1995), pp. 221–273.

work after a period of search. When the temporary job is over, the worker will once again become unemployed. The secondary effects of the job destruction from a serious recession, such as that of 1982, appear to last for several years.

Outflows from unemployment decline after a burst of job destruction, as well. When job-finding rates are high, the fraction of unemployed workers who remain unemployed for extended periods is low. When outflows from unemployment occur more slowly, the fraction of long-term unemployed rises. Figure 5.4 compares unemployment duration in a good year, 1989, and a weak year in the aftermath of a recession, 1992. In 1992, 21 percent of the unemployed had been looking for work for more than 26 weeks, compared to only 10 percent in the good year, 1989. People find jobs more rapidly in strong markets than in weak markets. Probably the main difference is that job seekers are competing with larger numbers of rivals for each job opening when unemployment is high.

The overall story of fluctuations in unemployment starts with a burst of job destruction, resulting from an oil price shock, financial crisis, or other

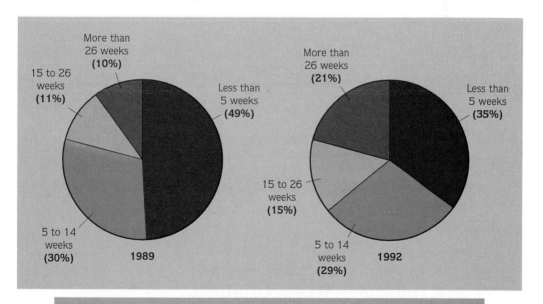

**FIGURE 5.4** Unemployment Duration in a Slump and in a Boom

The pie charts show the percentage of workers unemployed for different lengths of time in a bad year just at the end of a recession (1992) and in a good year just before the start of a recession (1989). Long-term unemployment is relatively high in a bad year. Job-finding rates are higher in good years.
Source: *Economic Report of the President*, 1995, Table B-42.

adverse development. Unemployment jumps upward. It remains at levels above the natural rate for several years after the shock. During this period, there are continuing unusually high flows into unemployment from the secondary effects of the shock, as workers have second and third spells of unemployment after their displacement in the original job destruction. Another factor holding unemployment above the natural rate is that job-finding rates are lower for several years after the shock.

## Okun's Law

There is a useful shorthand formula that closely approximates the cyclical relationship between unemployment and real GDP. Commonly called **Okun's law**, after its discoverer, Arthur Okun, the law says that for each percentage point by which the unemployment rate is above the natural rate, real GDP is 3 percent below potential GDP. The percentage departure of GDP from potential is called the **GDP gap**. For example, if unemployment is 8 percent, 2 percentage points above the natural rate of 6 percent, the real GDP is 6 percent below potential. The GDP gap is minus 6 percent. The historical accuracy of Okun's law is illustrated in Figure 5.5.

### FLUCTUATIONS IN UNEMPLOYMENT

1. Unemployment in the United States fluctuates from 3 percent of the labor force in the sharpest booms to 10 percent in the worst recessions.
2. The unemployment rate is closely related to the deviations of real GDP from potential GDP. This relation is called Okun's law.

# 5.5  ANALYSIS OF UNEMPLOYMENT IN THE FRAMEWORK OF SUPPLY AND DEMAND

Why do so many people lose their jobs in recessions? Why does unemployment linger for several years after a recession? Why doesn't the labor market adjust quickly to provide employment for everyone willing to work at the

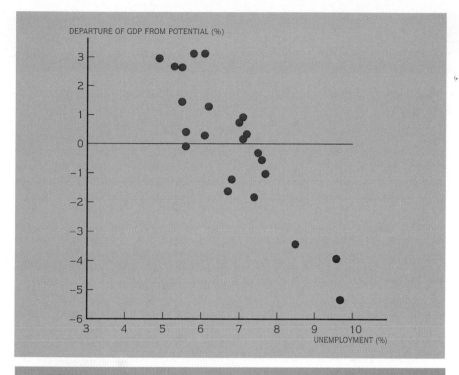

**FIGURE 5.5**  Okun's Law

The movements in unemployment are closely related to the movements in the percentage departures of real GDP from potential GDP. The slope of the relationship is roughly 3 percentage points of real GDP for each percent of unemployment.

market wage? Why is the standard model of supply and demand not an accurate model of the labor market? These are central questions of macroeconomic analysis.

The discussion earlier in this chapter showed what happens during the extended period when unemployment is high, during and after a recession, without completely answering these central questions. Instead of closing plants and destroying jobs, for example, employers could lower wages in order to keep marginal plants in business. And employers could hire aggressively during periods of high unemployment, when job seekers are numerous and jobs are easy to fill, and pay workers a little less than they would in good times. In search theory, job seekers should set their sights a little lower when jobs are hard to find.

## NEW RESEARCH IN PRACTICE
## A Silver Lining to the Storm Clouds of Recession?

Recessions are times of hardship for unemployed workers and lower average incomes for people in general. But recently economists have been looking at the benefit side as well.* The benefits arise because recessions are times when the economy has a chance to regroup and reorganize. There are two branches to this line of thought. One says that booms tend to keep outdated plants in operation and recessions are times to prune them out and expand modern plants. The other says that recessions are times when firms have less incentive to produce output and therefore a lower opportunity cost for reorganizing. In both cases, there is no claim that recessions are desirable, only that the economy is good at figuring out useful alternative activities during recessions.

In the "cleansing" view, firms wait until a recession to shut down old-fashioned plants. The market can respond to lower demand both by reducing the rate of opening of new plants and by shutting down old ones. In the cleansing model, the second effect is the more important. This property of the cleansing model is in line with the evidence that a disproportionate fraction of employment reductions in recessions take the form of increased job destruction rather than reduced job creation.

The second view has been called the "pit stop" model of recessions. In auto racing, cars are required to slow down when the yellow light is on because of an accident. Drivers often choose yellow-light periods to make pit stops to refuel and change tires. Relative to the situation when the green light is on and they can drive as fast as possible, the opportunity cost of a pit stop is lower when the yellow light is on. A recession is like a yellow-light period. It's less profitable to produce and sell output, so firms and workers have lower opportunity costs for other activities. Restructuring is an activity that is cheaper in a recession. During restructuring, firms lay off workers who are not well matched to their current jobs. These workers enter the labor market and search for new jobs that are better matches. Recessions and the periods of high unemployment that follow them are times when the economy is building better organizations, getting ready for the next burst of demand for output.†

Whatever the merit of these views, the flows through the labor market are much greater during recessions and their aftermaths than in booms. In 1982, a year of severe recession, 3.5 percent of the labor force became newly unemployed each month. In 1994, a year of favorable and improving conditions, only 2.1 percent of the labor force became newly unemployed each month. The labor market was called upon to handle about 70 percent *more* matching of job seekers to jobs in the recession year than in the good year. Even if there proves to be little support for the optimistic view that finding new jobs for so many extra workers is good for the economy, our thinking about recessions should always keep in mind how much bigger the flows are in the labor market during recessions. If the market could not handle the higher flows, recessions would be even harder on job losers than they are in today's U.S. economy.

---

*Ricardo J. Caballero and Mohamad L. Hammour, "The Cleansing Effect of Recessions," *American Economic Review* 84 (December 1994): 1350–1368.

†Robert E. Hall, "Labor Demand, Labor Supply, and Employment Volatility," *NBER Macroeconomics Annual* 1991, pp. 17–47.

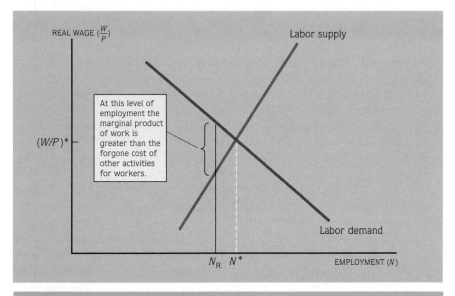

**FIGURE 5.6** Incentives When Employment Is below Equilibrium

If employment is at the recession level, employers and workers have incentives to increase the amount of work. The incentives are measured in dollars per hour on the vertical (real-wage) axis.

Standard principles of economics seem to suggest that the incentives to correct excess unemployment are strong. Figure 5.6 shows the labor supply and demand diagram, with employment $N$ on the horizontal axis and the real wage $W/P$ on the vertical axis. Recall that we first derived this diagram in Chapter 3 (see Figure 3.5). However, unlike in Chapter 3, we now consider the possibility that there is unemployment; that is, the actual level of employment in a recession ($N_R$) is less than the equilibrium level of employment ($N^*$).

One reason why employment might be at the low level $N_R$ rather than at the equilibrium level $N^*$ is that the real wage $W/P$ is above its equilibrium level. Then the quantity of labor demand by firms on their labor demand curves is $N_R$. The real wage could be above equilibrium because of government restrictions on wages or because of slow adjustment of wages. High unemployment in Germany, France, and Spain in the mid-1990s may have been the result of excess real wages, for example.

Regardless of the level of the real wage in Figure 5.6, when employment is below the equilibrium level, there are incentives facing either employers or workers or both to raise the amount of work. The difference between the marginal product of labor (the labor demand schedule) and the real wage is the incentive facing the employer. One added worker will increase the firm's revenue by the marginal product, but the worker only has to be paid the real wage. The difference is a profit opportunity for the firm; it provides an economic incentive to expand output.

The difference between the real wage and the worker's value of time (the labor supply schedule) is the incentive facing the worker. Another hour of work will earn the worker the real wage, but the cost (forgone time in other activities) is a smaller amount. The difference is an economic opportunity for the worker; it provides an economic incentive to increase hours worked.

Both firms and workers have incentives to raise employment when employment is at a recession level, below equilibrium. How long it takes for these incentives to bring about an expansion of employment back to equilibrium is a question macroeconomists debate frequently and intensely. For now, we will simply make the practical observation that employment does frequently drop below its equilibrium level, especially in recessions. It takes several years for employment to return to equilibrium. We conclude that incentives operate slowly over years, not days, weeks, or months. Until incentives do their job, the level of employment can remain below equilibrium. In the next chapter, we begin the development of a short-run model to describe the transitory departures of the economy from its long-run growth path.

## THE LABOR MARKET OUT OF EQUILIBRIUM

1. When level of employment is lower than the full-employment level, firms and workers face incentives to expand employment.
2. These incentives take time to operate. High unemployment can persist for several years.

## REVIEW AND PRACTICE

### Major Points

1. Unemployment is measured in a survey of households. A person is counted as unemployed if he or she is available for work and looking for work, but has not yet found a job.

2. There are substantial flows into and out of unemployment. The unemployment rate is the ratio of the job-losing rate to the job-finding rate.

3. The natural rate of unemployment is the amount that prevails in normal times; it is around 5 or 6 percent.

4. The flow into unemployment comes from job destruction, other job losses, and personal transitions that cause people to quit jobs and look for new ones.

5. The flow out of unemployment depends on the job-finding rate, which averages 43 percent per month.

6. The efficiency wage model offers one reason for low job-finding rates. If jobs are easy to find, employers will raise wages in order to motivate their workers.

7. Union wage premiums and the minimum wage are other reasons why jobs may be hard to find.

8. Unemployment insurance causes job seekers to be choosier and thus lowers job-finding rates.

9. Unemployment moves over the business cycle. In recessions it rises as high as 10 percent and in booms it falls as low as 3 percent.

10. Okun's law describes the relation between unemployment and real GDP. For each percentage point by which unemployment is above the natural rate, real GDP is 3 percent below potential.

11. When unemployment is high during a recession, there are incentives to put more workers to work—the marginal product of labor exceeds the real wage.

12. It takes several years for the level of employment to respond to incentives and to return to normal after a recession.

### Key Terms and Concepts

| | | |
|---|---|---|
| unemployment rate | job destruction | efficiency wage theory |
| participation rate | natural rate of | GDP gap |
| job-losing rate | unemployment | Okun's law |
| job-finding rate | | |

### Questions for Discussion and Review

1. What is the difference between being unemployed and not working? Give some examples of people not at work who are not unemployed.

2. What situations cause workers to become unemployed?

3. Explain why when the unemployment rate is steady it is equal to the ratio of the job-losing rate to the job-finding rate.

4. What factors determine the job-finding rate?

5. List four factors that tend to raise the natural unemployment rate.

6. Explain why unemployment falls when output rises. In the process, mention what happens to employment.

7. Explain the role of labor supply and labor demand in determining the incentives to return to equilibrium.

## Problems

### NUMERICAL

1. In a particular month, the labor force is 130 million, there are 9.1 million unemployed workers, the job-losing rate is 3 percent per month, and the job-finding rate is 40 percent per month. How many people will be unemployed next month? At what unemployment rate would the number of unemployed remain the same from one month to the next?

2. A firm finds the following relationship between the amount that workers lose if they are fired and workers' productivity:

| Dollars Lost by Worker as a Result of Being Fired | Improvement in Productivity Because Workers Work Harder to Avoid Losing Their Jobs (extra dollars of profit to firm) |
|---|---|
| 1000 | 1000 |
| 2000 | 3500 |
| 3000 | 5000 |
| 4000 | 5500 |

Workers are paid $500 per week at other firms and all jobs last 50 weeks.

a. If there is no unemployment, so workers can find jobs instantly at other firms, how much will this firm pay its workers?

b. How many weeks of job search are needed so that this firm will pay its workers no more than they could get at other jobs?

c. What is the natural unemployment rate in this labor market if all firms are in the same situation?

3. Suppose that Okun's law relating unemployment and GDP is given by

$$(Y - Y^*)/Y^* = -3(U - U^*),$$

where $U$ is the unemployment rate, $U^*$ is the natural rate of unemployment, $Y$ is GDP, and $Y^*$ is potential GDP. Unemployment is measured as a fraction. Suppose that the natural rate is 6 percent; that is, $U^* = .06$.

a.  Calculate the GDP gap for each of the years in 1990–95 using the following unemployment data: $U = $ 5.6, 6.8, 7.5, 6.9, 6.1 and 5.6 percent, respectively.
b.  GDP for these same years is as follows: $5,744, $5,917, $6,244, $6,550, $6,931, and $7,246 billion. Using these data and your answers to Part a, calculate potential GDP for each of these years. What is the average growth rate of potential GDP?

### ANALYTICAL

1.  Discuss briefly how each of the following changes would affect the natural rate of unemployment.

    a.  The economy enters a period of little structural change and all industries are growing at about the same rate.
    b.  Schools operate for the full year, so there are no students looking for summer work.
    c.  The Internet lists all the jobs available in the whole country, so it is easier for job seekers to locate potential jobs.
    d.  People who quit their jobs are drafted into low-wage community service jobs.
    e.  In addition to unemployment insurance, the unemployed receive a bonus for finding new jobs; the bonus is greater if the job is found in the first few weeks of search and declines with the duration of search.

2.  Okun's law suggests that over the course of the business cycle a change in the unemployment rate of 1 percentage point will be accompanied by a 3 percent change in output. Using the formula

$$Y = (Y/H)(H/N)(1 - U)L,$$

where $Y/H$ is output per hour worked, $H/N$ is hours per worker, $N$ is the number of employed workers, $U$ is the unemployment rate, and $L$ is the labor force, explain in what direction and why some of the factors other than $Y$ and $U$ might change. (Note that if $W = XYZ$, then for small changes the percentage change in $W$ is given by the sum of the percentage changes in $X$, $Y$, and $Z$. Note also that $1 - U = N/L$ and that a change in the unemployment rate of 1 percentage point corresponds to approximately a 1 percent change in $N/L$.)

## MacroSolve Exercises

1.  Okun's law states that for each percentage point by which the unemployment rate is above the natural rate, real GDP is 3 percent below potential GDP. The percentage departure of GDP from potential is called the GDP gap. Using quarterly data, graph the unemployment rate (on the horizontal axis) against the GDP gap (on the vertical axis).

    a.  You will see that the curve seems to shift outward over time. Does this imply that the natural rate of unemployment has risen over time? (Hint: If the GDP gap is zero for any length of time, then unemployment should be close to the natural rate.)

b. Compute the slope of the Okun relationship between 1933 and 1944 by tabulating the data for the GDP gap and the unemployment rate. The slope is given by the change in the GDP gap divided by the change in the unemployment rate. Make the same calculation between 1978 and 1983. Has the slope changed? What factors might account for such a change?

2. Using the **PLOT** and **STATISTICS** options, determine on average how much greater unemployment is for women than for men. What might explain this occurrence?

3. Using the **PLOT** and **STATISTICS** options, determine on average how much greater teen unemployment is than that of all civilian workers. What might explain this occurrence?

4. Using the **PLOT** and **STATISTICS** options, determine on average how much greater minority unemployment is than that of white workers. What might explain this occurrence? How similar or dissimilar is this to your explanation for Problem 3?

5. Using the **PLOT** and **STATISTICS** options, determine on which group of workers recessions have the most severe impact: males, females, teenagers, whites, or minorities. What might explain this occurrence?

# Economic
# Fluctuations

# Short-Run Fluctuations

The long-run model of Chapters 3, 4, and 5 is an important part of modern macroeconomics. But it does not explain recessions such as those that occurred in 1981–82 and in 1990–91, when the economy deviated from its long-run path. The long-run model is incomplete.

Why does it take several years for the economy to return to potential GDP after a shock? What forces push output away from its potential? In this chapter and the next two chapters, we will develop the complete model, which tries to answer these two key questions by adding a model of economic fluctuations to the long-run growth model. In the complete model, demand can affect output in a way not considered in the long-run growth model.

In this chapter, we first explain why changes in spending, or demand, can cause real GDP to depart from its potential. We then examine an important determinant of spending—people's income. The relationship between income and spending gives rise to the concept of spending balance which we derive in this chapter and use in later chapters.

# 6.1  FORCES THAT PUSH THE ECONOMY OFF ITS GROWTH PATH

In the last chapter, we concluded that the economy can deviate from full employment and that the forces pushing it back to full employment take time. What kinds of forces are responsible for departures from full employment? In order to answer this question, macroeconomists have to take a stand on which relationships in the economy hold in both the short and long run and which hold only in the long run. The view that we take is that prices are unresponsive to current developments; they move only gradually over time. On the other hand, certain key relationships involving spending hold even in the short run. Accordingly, the complete model we develop considers spending relationships. It takes prices, and therefore the average price level, as given for now from the past history of the economy. In the short run unemployment can be above the natural rate.

In the short run, we assume that firms stand ready to supply whatever output their customers want, given existing prices. When firms let their customers determine their level of output and employment, demand becomes the ruling force. If demand is strong, real GDP exceeds potential. In recession, when demand is weak, real GDP drops below potential. Firms then adjust their prices gradually to get back toward equilibrium. Price adjustment eventually takes the economy back to its long-run growth path. Chapter 8 will consider this transition process of price adjustment.

To preview how we use these ideas to explain economic fluctuations, we introduce the diagram in Figure 6.1, with the price level on the vertical axis and real GDP on the horizontal axis. This basic diagram is called the **aggregate demand (AD) curve.** This chapter and Chapters 7 and 8 develop the details of the aggregate demand curve. Figure 6.1 illustrates its basic use. Given a price level on the vertical axis, we can find the amount of output generated by the spending process by moving across, on a horizontal line, to the aggregate demand curve.

Any event that shifts the aggregate demand curve will move the economy away from potential. Figure 6.2 illustrates the effect of a leftward (inward) shift of aggregate demand. The shift leaves output below potential. In accord with our assumption that the price level does not respond immediately to this type of shift, the price level remains unchanged. In the next two chapters, we will consider the types of changes that would shift the aggregate demand curve. They include changes in the government's tax and spending policies, spontaneous changes in consumption and investment, and changes in purchases of U.S. goods by foreigners. Changes in monetary policy and in financial markets also shift the AD curve.

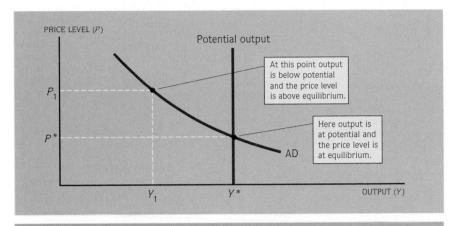

**FIGURE 6.1**   The Aggregate Demand (AD) Curve

Given a price level on the vertical axis, the AD curve tells us the amount of output demanded in the economy. A higher price level corresponds to lower output, and a lower price level corresponds to higher output.

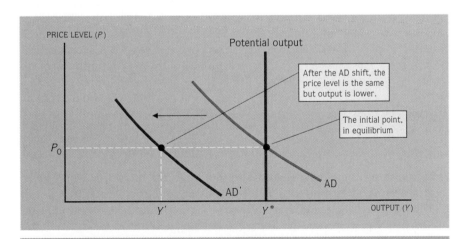

**FIGURE 6.2**   Output Declines When AD Shifts Inward

A shock moves the AD curve and pushes the economy away from potential. The economy starts in equilibrium at output $Y^*$ and price level $P_0$. Because of a negative shock, the AD curve shifts to the left, to AD'. The price level stays at $P_0$. The new level of output is $Y'$, which is below $Y^*$.

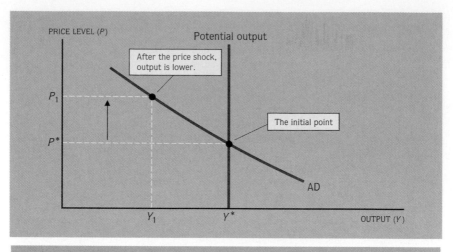

**FIGURE 6.3**   A Price Shock

A price increase moves the economy to a point on the AD curve with lower output.

A second event that could move the economy away from potential is a shift in the price level. Changes in world prices, especially oil prices, are the most common source of price shocks. Figure 6.3 shows the effect of a price increase. From an initial position, the economy moves to a lower level of output. Again, the AD schedule tells how a price increase leads to a decline in output.

## THE AGGREGATE DEMAND CURVE

1. In the short-run model, demand determines output; firms provide the level of output their customers demand at existing prices.
2. The aggregate demand curve shows the level of output corresponding to alternative price levels, including the existing price level.
3. Any event that shifts the AD curve pushes the economy away from potential. Fiscal and monetary policy, consumption, investment, and foreign purchases can all shift the AD curve.

# AGGREGATE DEMAND AND THE SPENDING DECISION

Firms produce goods because people have decided to buy them. Aggregate demand theory starts by examining people's decisions to buy goods, or their spending decisions. Many factors influence spending. If a personal tax cut occurs, then the demand for consumption goods by households will rise. If interest rates rise because of a change in monetary policy, then investment demand from firms is likely to fall. If there is a cut in defense spending, then government demand will fall. By adding up the spending demands of the various sectors of the economy we obtain an estimate of aggregate spending. But a crucial next step is to see if this aggregate spending is consistent with the income that the public is basing its spending decisions on. The explanation of how spending is consistent with income is the topic of this chapter. Because total spending is an aggregation of demand in all sectors of the economy, we refer to the total as **aggregate demand.**

Our discussion of the short run sets aside, temporarily, the question of whether the economy has the resources to produce the volume of output demanded. We make the assumption that aggregate demand determines the amount of goods produced in the economy. This assumption is central to our analysis of economic fluctuations. In Chapter 8, we bring back the resource constraints described by the long-run growth model. In the complete model developed there, fluctuations in demand have effects on output in the short run, but the growth model, with its emphasis on resources, takes over in the longer run.

To see why the assumption that aggregate demand determines output is usually a reasonable assumption, we need to consider the typical behavior of business firms at the microeconomic level. Under normal conditions most business firms operate with some excess capacity and respond to increases in demand by producing more goods. In the United States the average level of capacity utilization in manufacturing industries is about 81 percent. Some machines are left idle on standby; others are run for only two out of three shifts. Hence firms have considerable leeway to produce more by increasing capacity utilization when demand increases. If additional labor is necessary to operate the equipment more intensively, it is usually possible to have some workers increase their hours per week, to recall some workers from layoff status, or even to hire additional workers. The natural rate of unemployment is between 5 and 6 percent; this indicates that additional workers can be hired in the short run, even at full employment. Hence, for both capital and labor inputs to production, there is considerable short-run flexibility for firms to meet an increase in the demand for their products. And though we have been speaking entirely in terms of increases in demand, the same response occurs for declines in demand. A firm will produce less when the demand for its product declines.

In sum, both increases and decreases in demand for a firm's product get translated into increases and decreases in production. In the economy as a whole, short-run fluctuations in aggregate demand result in similar fluctuations in GDP. In this sense, the assumption that "demand determines output" is a reasonable one for analyzing most short-run fluctuations of GDP from its long-run growth path.

## The Unresponsiveness of the Price Level

Firms not only adjust their production in response to changes in demand, they also adjust their prices. When an increase in demand results in a firm's producing at above-average operating levels, it usually increases its prices as well. Similarly, a decline in demand that brings a firm to below-normal operating levels will result in a price adjustment below what would have been appropriate otherwise. By adjusting its price in this way, a firm can usually both increase its profits in the short run and encourage a change in quantity demanded to a more desirable level from the firm's point of view.

There is a crucial difference, however, between the adjustment of production and the adjustment of prices in response to a change in demand: Prices appear to be very "sticky" compared with production. The adjustment of prices occurs gradually, whereas the adjustment of production and employment occurs almost instantaneously. In fact, in the very short run it is usually a good approximation to ignore price adjustment and focus on the changes in production.

We have left out one important aspect of firms' behavior in our discussion so far. Many firms maintain a stock or inventory of their finished products, so that when there is an increase in demand, the immediate response is usually to meet the demand out of the inventory. Conversely, a drop in demand can be matched by an accumulation of inventory. Clearly, changes in demand that are exactly matched by changes in inventory will not affect production or GDP. However, for the economy as a whole, increases in sales are met with increases in production. Thus, as an approximation it is possible to ignore inventory adjustments and assume that changes in demand are directly translated into changes in production. A full treatment of the process of inventory adjustment is given in Chapter 11.

## An Example: General Motors

Production in the automobile industry rises and falls by large magnitudes in response to changes in demand, and automobile purchases are a very large part of total spending, so this is an important example. During the large downturn from 1929 to 1933, for instance, annual production of automobiles in the United States fell from about 5 million to about 1 million cars. In the downturn from 1988 to 1991, production of cars at General Motors plants in the United States fell from 5.6 million to 4.3 million cars per year.

Consider what happens at GM when there is a change in the demand for automobiles. For example, suppose that there is an increase in demand for automobiles, as there typically is in a recovery period following a recession like the one that ended in 1991. In the short run this increase in demand results in more automobiles being produced; some workers are asked to work more hours, others are recalled from layoff, some new workers are hired, plants are worked an extra shift, and plants that were closed earlier are reopened. Employment and capacity utilization in the automobile industry are increased to correspond to the increase in demand.

## THE POINT OF BALANCE OF INCOME AND SPENDING

The first step in studying spending behavior is to take account of the effects of income on spending. Recall that income and spending are both measured by GDP: when we add up total spending in the economy to get GDP, we also are calculating total income. **Spending balance** occurs when the level of income used by consumers and other spenders in making their spending decisions is the same as the sum of the spending of all spenders.

It is important to distinguish spending balance from the concept of equilibrium used in the long-run growth model and in many other parts of economics. In equilibrium, supply equals demand; firms and workers cannot make changes that will make both better off. The long-run growth model portrays the economy as being in equilibrium. Spending balance is a narrower concept. Consistency of total spending and individual incomes is just one of the requirements of equilibrium. As we will see, an economy can be in spending balance yet the quantity of labor supplied can exceed the quantity of labor demanded. In other words, the situation depicted in Figure 5.6 can occur when an economy is in spending balance.[1]

To show how the principle of spending balance works, we will start with the simple case where investment, government purchases, and net exports are all fixed and do not depend on income or the interest rate.

---

[1]Some economists and some textbooks don't make this distinction. They refer to an economy in spending balance as being in equilibrium even if labor demand and labor supply are not equal.

## The Income Identity

We have already looked at the income identity in Chapter 2. It says that

$$Y = C + I + G + X, \qquad \text{The Income Identity} \qquad (6.1)$$

where $Y$ is GDP, $C$ is consumption, $I$ is investment, $G$ is government purchases, and $X$ is net exports. GDP, consumption, investment, government purchases, and net exports in this identity are all measured in real terms as discussed in Chapter 2.

We now consider the components of spending. We start with consumption.

## The Consumption Function

How do consumers make their spending decisions? The **consumption function** is a description of the total consumption demand of all families in the economy. It states that consumption depends on **disposable income.** Disposable income, as we saw in Chapter 2, is income less taxes. The consumption function is based on the simple idea that the larger a family's disposable income, the larger that family's consumption will be. Thus, total consumption for all families in the economy will be larger if disposable income in the economy is larger.

The consumption function should be viewed as a simple approximation of actual consumption. Clearly, consumption depends on other things besides current income: wealth, expected future income, and the price of goods today compared with tomorrow. We will discuss these and other factors that affect consumption in Chapter 10. The more elementary consumption function used in this chapter was first introduced to the study of macroeconomics by Keynes. Despite its simplicity, it has proved remarkably versatile as a macroeconomic tool.

The consumption function can be written algebraically as

$$C = a + bY_d. \qquad \text{The Consumption Function} \qquad (6.2)$$

Specifically, this algebraic formula says that consumption $C$ is equal to some constant $a$ plus another constant $b$ times disposable income $Y_d$. Both constants ($a$ and $b$) are positive and $b$ is less than 1. The coefficient $b$ is called the **marginal propensity to consume.** It measures how much of an additional dollar of disposable income is spent on consumption. The constant $a$ is the intercept of the consumption function. The two coefficients work together to describe the relationship between income and consumption. Remember the distinction between the constants and the variables. In this consumption function the variables are $C$ and $Y_d$. The constants, or coefficients, are $a$ and $b$.

**EXAMPLE**  If the coefficient $a = 220$ and the coefficient $b = .9$, then the consumption function looks like this:

$$C = 220 + .9Y_d.$$

If disposable income is $4,000 billion, then consumption will be $220 billion + .9 · $4,000 billion, or $3,820 billion. If disposable income rises to $5,000 billion, then consumption will rise to $220 billion + .9 · $5,000 billion, or $4,720 billion. If disposable income increases by $1,000 billion, consumption increases by $900 billion. Note how the variables, consumption and disposable income, change in this calculation but the coefficients stay fixed. The marginal propensity to consume in this example is 0.9—90 percent of each additional dollar of income is spent on consumption.

We can also represent the consumption function graphically, as in Figure 6.4. The vertical axis measures consumption. The horizontal axis mea-

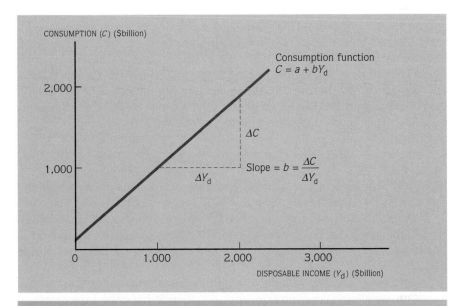

**FIGURE 6.4**  The Consumption Function

Consumption depends on income. The upward-sloping line shows that higher levels of disposable income correspond to higher levels of consumption. The slope of the line tells us how much consumption changes when disposable income changes. The slope of the line equals the marginal propensity to consume.

sures disposable income. The consumption function is shown as a straight, upward-sloping line. It indicates that as disposable income increases, so does consumption.

## THE CONSUMPTION FUNCTION

1. Disposable income is the amount of income that people have available to spend after taxes.
2. The consumption function says that there is a predictable relationship between disposable income and consumption. The higher disposable income, the higher consumption.
3. The marginal propensity to consume is the fraction of an increase in disposable income that is consumed.

We can also write the consumption function in terms of income rather than disposable income. Disposable income is obtained by subtracting income taxes from income. If the tax *rate* is given by the constant $t$, then total tax payments are $tY$. Disposable income $Y_d$ equals income $Y$ minus taxes $tY$. Thus, we can write disposable income as $Y_d = (1 - t)Y$. For example, if the tax rate $t$ is .3 and income $Y$ is \$6,000 billion, then taxes are \$1,800 billion and disposable income is \$4,200 billion. By replacing disposable income $Y_d$ with $(1 - t)Y$, the consumption function can be written

$$C = a + b(1 - t)Y. \tag{6.3}$$

This says that consumption depends positively on income. For example, if the marginal propensity to consume $b$ is .9 and the tax rate $t$ is .3, then $b(1 - t) = .63$. An increase in income of \$100 billion will increase consumption by \$63 billion. This alternative way to write the consumption function is useful because it has the same income variable $Y$ that appears in the income identity.

So far we have discussed the determinants of only one of the components of spending—consumption—but we already have the ingredients of an elementary theory of income or GDP determination. Before considering the determinants of the other components of spending—investment $I$, government $G$, and net exports $X$—we illustrate how this theory works. To do this, values for investment, government spending, and net exports must be taken from *outside* the model. Variables determined outside a model are called *exogenous variables*. Of the five variables that we discussed so far (income $Y$, consumption $C$, investment $I$, government spending $G$, and net exports $X$), this leaves two, consumption $C$ and income $Y$, to be determined *inside* the model. Variables that are determined inside a model are called *endogenous variables.*

This basic idea that the endogenous variables must simultaneously satisfy a number of relationships is central to macroeconomic analysis. In the chapters that follow we will elaborate on this simple theory by adding more endogenous variables and more relationships that they must satisfy.

The elementary model consists of two basic relationships: the income identity, summarized algebraically in Equation 6.1, and the consumption function, summarized algebraically in Equation 6.3. These two relationships can be used to determine values for the two endogenous variables of the model: consumption $C$ and income $Y$. *The values for C and Y are determined by requiring that both the consumption function and the income identity are satisfied simultaneously.*

Once we determine income and consumption in this way, we will have also determined GDP, of course, because income equals GDP. We illustrate the determination of income and consumption first using graphs and then using algebra.

## Graphical Analysis of Spending Balance

In Figure 6.5 spending is measured on the vertical axis and income on the horizontal axis. Two intersecting straight lines are shown, a **spending line** and a **45-degree line.**

The spending line (the flatter of the two) shows how total spending depends on income. Total spending is the sum of consumption, investment, government spending, and net exports. In this model only consumption depends on income, through the consumption function. Investment, government spending, and net exports are exogenous. The spending line is obtained by adding the consumption function in Equation 6.3 to investment, government spending, and net exports. The equation corresponding to the spending line is

$$\text{Spending} = \underbrace{a + b(1 - t)Y}_{\substack{\text{Consumption} \\ \text{from} \\ \text{Equation 6.3}}} + \underbrace{I}_{\substack{\text{Exogenous} \\ \text{investment}}} + \underbrace{G}_{\substack{\text{Exogenous} \\ \text{government} \\ \text{spending}}} + \underbrace{X.}_{\substack{\text{Exogenous} \\ \text{net exports}}}$$

The spending line thus incorporates the consumption function. The spending line is flatter than the 45-degree line because consumers spend only part of each added dollar of income. They save the rest.

The 45-degree line is drawn halfway between the vertical spending axis and the horizontal income axis. For any point on the 45-degree line,

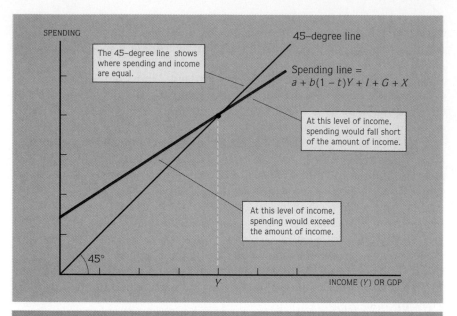

**FIGURE 6.5**  Spending Balance

The intersection of the two lines shows where consumption and income satisfy both the consumption function and the income identity. The point of intersection is the solution to the model consisting of Equations 6.1 and 6.3.

income equals spending. This line thus represents the income identity. The line makes a 45-degree angle with the horizontal axis; hence its name. Sometimes Figure 6.5 is called a **Keynesian 45-degree diagram,** or a **Keynesian cross** diagram, because of its early use to illustrate this simple model with a Keynesian consumption function.

The point of intersection of the spending line and the 45-degree line is the point where consumption and income satisfy both relationships of the model. On the 45-degree line, the income identity is satisfied. On the spending line, the consumption function is satisfied. The intersection of the two lines thus gives the value of income that we are looking for. At this point total spending in the economy equals total income, and consumption spending satisfies the consumption function. Income and spending are in balance.

The 45-degree line is steeper than the spending line. The 45-degree line has a slope of 1. The consumption function has a slope $b(1 - t)$, which is less than 1. For example, if $b = .9$ and $t = .3$, then $b(1 - t) = .63$. Because the lines have different slopes, they will always intersect.[2]

---

[2]See the box on p. 158 for a review of the concept of slope.

> ### SPENDING BALANCE
>
> 1. The simple model of income determination consists of two relationships, the consumption function and the income identity. The model determines two endogenous variables: consumption and income. Three exogenous variables—investment, government spending, and net exports—are determined outside the model.
> 2. Spending balance occurs when consumers are choosing their consumption levels, $C$, on the basis of a level of income that is the same as the level $Y = C + I + G + X$.
> 3. In terms of the equations, spending balance occurs at levels of consumption $C$ and income $Y$ that obey both the consumption function and the income identity.

## Algebraic Solution

The levels of consumption and income can also be found algebraically. Substitute the consumption function, Equation 6.3, into Equation 6.1. The result is

$$Y = \underbrace{a + b(1 - t)Y + I + G + X}_{C}. \tag{6.4}$$

The brace below Equation 6.4 shows where $C$ in the income identity has been replaced by the consumption function. Equation 6.4 has one endogenous variable: $Y$. Recall that $I$, $G$, and $X$ are exogenous variables. The variable $Y$ appears on both sides of Equation 6.4. To solve the equation for $Y$, we gather together both terms involving $Y$ on the left-hand side of the equation. Doing so, we see that the value of $Y$ that solves Equation 6.4 is given by

$$Y = \frac{a + I + G + X}{1 - b(1 - t)}. \tag{6.5}$$

This is the solution of the model and corresponds exactly to the value of $Y$, which is at the point of intersection in Figure 6.5. The solution value for consumption can then be obtained by plugging this value into the consumption function (Equation 6.3). That is,

$$C = a + b(1 - t)Y,$$

where $Y$ comes from Equation 6.5.

## Graphs, Slopes, and Intercepts versus Algebra and Coefficients

Figure 6.4 and Equation 6.2 express exactly the same idea—that consumption depends positively on disposable income—in two different ways: graphically and algebraically. A third way is *verbal* presentation and analysis, which, although sometimes less precise, is necessary if you want to explain your economic ideas to those without economic training.

In general a graph is a diagram with a line or lines showing the relationship between two variables. The lines can be straight, as with the consumption line, or they can be bending, as with the aggregate demand curve (Figure 6.1). Relationships that are shown by straight lines are called *linear* relationships to distinguish them from those represented by bending lines. Sometimes lines are called **schedules,** a term that derives from the presentation of the relationship numerically as two columns of numbers that look like a train schedule. Graphs provide a more intuitive understanding, and, because visual images are sometimes easier to recall, graphs are good memory aids.

Algebra frequently provides more accurate and direct answers, and is needed in more complex problems. Sometimes only a rough sketch is needed for a graphical analysis, but it is important to know that there is a precise connection between a graphical and an algebraic representation of an economic relationship. The variable on the vertical axis of a graph is usually the one on the left-hand side of the equal sign in the algebraic expression. For the consumption function, the variable on the left-hand side is consumption. The variable on the horizontal axis is usually the one on the right-hand

side of the equal sign in the algebraic expression. For the consumption function, the variable on the right-hand side is disposable income. The place where the vertical axis and horizontal axis cross sometimes represents the zero value for both variables, but this is not necessary. It is important to look carefully at the scale on a diagram. For diagrams that are simply rough illustrations, no numerical scale will appear.

The place where the consumption line crosses the vertical axis in Figure 6.4 is called the **intercept.** It equals the coefficient $a$ in the algebraic expression Equation 6.2. It gives the value of consumption when disposable income is zero. More generally, the intercept of any line is the place where the line crosses the vertical axis.

The steepness of the consumption line is measured by its **slope.** The slope tells us how much consumption increases when income increases by 1 unit. The slope of the line is the coefficient $b$ in the algebraic expression. Thus, if disposable income increases by an amount $\Delta Y_d$, then consumption increases by an amount $\Delta C$ given by $b$ times $\Delta Y_d$. On the graph we move to the right by $\Delta Y_d$ and up by $b$ times $\Delta Y_d$. In general, a perfectly flat horizontal line has a slope of zero, and a perfectly vertical line has a slope of infinity. If the slope is positive, then we say that the line slopes *upward* as we move from left to right; if the slope is negative, then the line slopes *downward* as we move from left to right. The slope of the consumption function is positive ($b$ is greater than zero), and clearly the consumption line slopes upward.

**EXAMPLE**    Suppose that investment equals $900 billion, government spending equals $1,200 billion, and net exports equal −$100 billion. Suppose, as in previous examples, that the marginal propensity to consume $b$ equals .9, the constant $a$ equals 220, and the tax rate $t$ equals .3. Then, according to the formula in Equation 6.5, income equals

$$\frac{220 + 900 + 1,200 - 100}{1 - .9(1 - .3)} = \frac{2,220}{.37},$$

or $6,000 billion. GDP is also equal to $6,000 billion. Using the consumption function (Equation 6.3), we get that consumption equals

$$220 + .9(1 - .3)(6,000),$$

or $4,000 billion.

## How Spending Balance Is Maintained

It is important to understand the logic of finding the values of consumption and income that satisfy both the consumption function and the income identity. When people buy more in stores, firms will produce more. As we discussed in the microeconomic example, firms will then employ more workers or have their existing workers spend more time on the job. Their added production increases the wage incomes of their existing and new workers and adds to the profits of the owners of the firms. This added income in turn stimulates more consumption. When spending is in balance, the income that consumers are receiving is the same as the income generated by their spending.

What happens if spending is not in balance? Suppose that consumers are spending too much relative to their incomes. The economy would then be in an untenable situation. Consumers would notice that they were spending too much and would contract their consumption. But then firms would produce less and workers' incomes would fall. The process of contraction would continue until consumption fell to a point of balance with income.

How do we know that the contraction of income and consumption will ultimately reach a point of balance rather than continuing to a complete collapse of the economy? When families contract their consumption because their incomes fall, the contraction in consumption is less than the fall in income. Some of the fall in income results in reduced taxes, so that disposable income does not fall as much as national income. Moreover, the marginal propensity to consume is less than 1, so that the fall in disposable income results in a smaller reduction in consumption. The smaller reduction in consumption thus generates a smaller drop in income on the second round. So the process of consumption and income contraction converges to

**TABLE 6.1**    Example of the Multiplier Process (billions of dollars)

| | Reduction in GDP | | |
| | This Round | Sum to Date | Calculation |
|---|---|---|---|
| Round 1 | 10.000 | 10.000 | Exogenous drop in investment |
| Round 2 | 6.300 | 16.300 | $b(1 - t)(10) = (.6300)(10)$ |
| Round 3 | 3.969 | 20.269 | $[b(1 - t)]^2(10) = (.3969)(10)$ |
| Round 4 | 2.500 | 22.769 | $[b(1 - t)]^3(10) = (.2500)(10)$ |
| Round 5 | 1.575 | 24.344 | $[b(1 - t)]^4(10) = (.1575)(10)$ |
| Round 6 | .992 | 25.336 | $[b(1 - t)]^5(10) = (.0992)(10)$ |

a new lower point of balance. A numerical example of this type of convergence is presented in Table 6.1.

We do not present a formal model of the detailed process by which the economy reaches spending balance. The reason is that the process seems to operate quickly—more quickly than the business cycle or price adjustment. Our model assumes that the economy has already reached spending balance over each period of observation. Balance is not achieved by magic. But it is a useful simplification to talk about the economy after it has gone through the process.[3]

## The Multiplier

In order to show how the elementary model can be used to analyze the short-run fluctuations in the economy, we consider what happens to income when there is a change in one of the exogenous variables. Suppose, for example, that there is a *decrease* in investment *I*. The exact reasons for the decrease are not important at this time, but for concreteness you may think of a sudden decline in expected profitability that reduces firms' desire to invest. What are the implications of this decline in investment demand?

We first consider the situation graphically using the spending line and the 45-degree line in Figure 6.5 reproduced in Figure 6.6. The new diagram shows the impact of a decline in exogenous investment. It *shifts* the spending line downward by the amount of the decline in investment. If investment

---

[3]Some elementary texts describe the adjustment process by focusing on inventories: If output is greater than spending, inventories begin to rise and this leads firms to cut back on output. Output and spending are thus brought into equality. We prefer not to introduce inventories at this stage of the analysis. We feel that the description in the text is a close approximation to reality. Many types of businesses—medical services, education—do not hold inventories of finished products, yet their production responds to changes in demand.

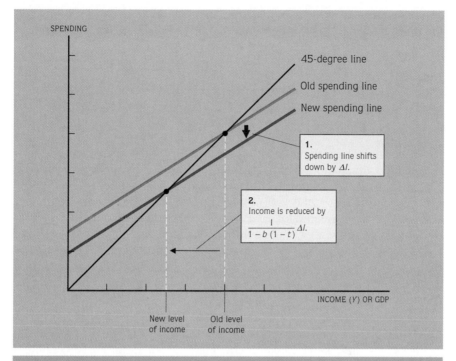

**FIGURE 6.6**  The Multiplier

A decrease in investment demand shifts the spending line down. The new point of intersection is at a lower level of GDP. The decline in GDP is larger than the decline in investment; this illustrates the multiplier mechanism. (Note that the drop in investment shown in the diagram is much larger than would be possible in the U.S. economy. The drop is exaggerated here so that it can be easily seen in the diagram.)

falls by $1 billion, then the spending line shifts down by $1 billion. To see this, note that the intercept of the spending line is $a + I + G + X$. Hence, the change in the intercept is the same as the change in investment; government spending and net exports are not changing and $a$ is constant. Figure 6.6 shows that income is lower as a result of the downward shift in the spending line.

Note that the decline in income is larger than the shift in the spending line, because the slope of the spending line is greater than zero. The economy thus "multiplies" the decline in investment into an even larger decline in income and GDP. This mechanism is called the **multiplier.** The steeper the spending line, the larger the decline in income.

The effect of the decline in investment on income can be calculated algebraically. Looking back to Equation 6.5, if we change investment by an amount $\Delta I$, then the change in income will be given by

$$\Delta Y = \underbrace{\frac{1}{1 - b(1 - t)}}_{\text{The Multiplier}} \Delta I.$$

(6.6)

This is obtained by writing Equation 6.5 in terms of the changes in the variables, and noting that neither government spending, nor net exports, nor the coefficient changes. All that is left is the change in investment.

The term $1/[1 - b(1 - t)]$, which multiplies the change in investment in Equation 6.6, is the multiplier. It is a general expression for the change in income associated with a change in investment. Since $b(1 - t)$ is less than 1, the value of the multiplier in Equation 6.6 is greater than 1. Hence, the change in GDP is greater than the change in investment, just as we found using the graphical analysis. Note that the larger the marginal propensity to consume $b$, the larger the multiplier.

**EXAMPLE**   If the marginal propensity to consume $b$ is equal to .9 and the tax rate $t$ is .3, then the multiplier is equal to $1/.37$, or about 2.7. A \$10 billion *decrease* in investment results in a \$27 billion decrease in income or GDP. Similiarly, a \$10 billion *increase* in investment results in a \$27 billion increase in income or GDP.

This example can be used to illustrate the explicit actions of consumers and firms that result in the multiplier process. Suppose that a \$10 billion decrease in investment occurs because Hertz, Avis, and several other large car-rental companies in the United States suddenly get pessimistic about future profitability and stop buying new cars from General Motors, Ford, and Chrysler. Initially, the decreased purchases of new cars decrease income and GDP by \$10 billion. But the reduced automobile production means that the incomes of workers in those companies will be reduced as they work fewer hours or are laid off. The income of shareholders of GM, Ford, and Chrysler will also be reduced, because of the decline in profits. In this example, the income of workers and shareholders falls by the full \$10 billion. If the workers and shareholders have a marginal propensity to consume of .9 and pay taxes equal to 30 percent of their income, then they will reduce their consumption by \$6.3 billion. Hence, GDP is cut by another \$6.3 billion. The total reduction in GPD is now \$16.3 billion.

But this is not the end. There is a third round. The workers and owners of the firms where the owners and employees of GM, Ford, and Chrysler cut their purchases by \$6.3 billion will have a reduction in their income of this same amount. With the same taxes and marginal propensity to consume, they will thus cut their consumption by .63 times $6.3 billion, or $3.969 billion. The total reduction in GDP is now $20.269 billion. The process will continue for a fourth and fifth round and so on, but by this time the reduction in income will be diversified across many different firms in the economy. Some of the reduced consumption demand will certainly get back to GM, Ford, and Chrysler.

If we keep summing the reduction in GDP at all these rounds, we will eventually get a $27 billion reduction in GPD—the same as the direct computation using the multiplier. As we mentioned above, the total effect of these spending reductions on GDP would usually occur in a fairly short period, certainly less than a year. The different rounds of production are summarized in Table 6.1. Note how the eventual $27 billion reduction of GDP that we calculated directly through the multiplier is almost reached after just a few rounds. Note also how convenient it is to use the multiplier rather than go through all these tedious calculations.[4]

Fluctuations in investment have always been associated with cyclical fluctuations in GDP. Such fluctuations in investment were emphasized by Keynes as an essential source of business cycle fluctuations. One of Keynes's main contributions was to show that relatively small fluctuations in investment could lead to large fluctuations in GDP. The mechanism underlying Keynes's theory was the multiplier; our example of a decline in investment leading to a large decline in GDP provides a simple illustration of Keynes's theory.

Changes in the other exogenous variables—government spending and net exports—also result in changes in income. The analysis is exactly the same as the analysis of investment. For example, an increase in government spending will raise income and GDP by a greater amount. The same multiplier process is at work. In fact, the formula for the government spending multiplier—the amount that income increases when government spending increases—is exactly the same as the investment multiplier.

The government spending multiplier can be derived in the same way that the investment multiplier was derived. To show this, we have again reproduced the 45-degree line and the spending line from Figure 6.5 in

---

[4]The formulas for the calculations in the far right column of Table 6.1 add up to the formula for the multiplier: that is,

$$\frac{1}{1 - b(1 - t)} = 1 + b(1 - t) + [b(1 - t)]^2 + [b(1 - t)]^3 + \cdots.$$

This result can be shown using the formula for a geometric series. A formal algebraic model of the adjustment process could come from putting *past* income rather than current income in the consumption function. This leads to a dynamic model—called the *dynamic multiplier*—that describes how consumption adjusts over time after a sudden change in investment.

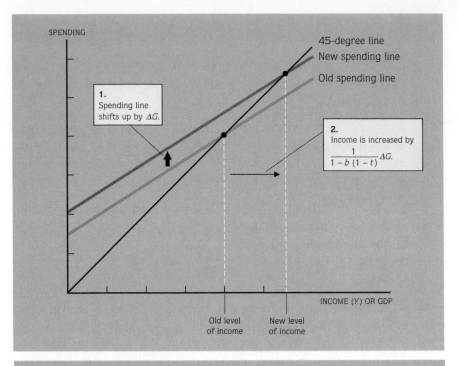

**FIGURE 6.7**    The Government Spending Multiplier

An increase in government spending shifts the spending line up. Income or GDP expands by the multiplier times the increase in government spending.

Figure 6.7. An increase in government spending will *raise* the spending line in Figure 6.7. This has an even larger effect on income, because of the multiplier process. Knowing the size of the government spending multiplier is important for assessing the impact of a change in government policy on the economy.

## THE MULTIPLIER

**1.** When investment rises, GDP rises; investment is part of total GDP.
**2.** As GDP rises, disposable income also rises, so consumption rises.
**3.** The increase in GDP is larger than the increase in investment, because of the increase in consumption. The multiplier measures the amount of GDP

stimulated by an increase in investment or other categories of spending that are not themselves sensitive to income.

4. The formula for the multiplier is $\dfrac{1}{1 - b(1 - t)}$.

5. The government spending multiplier is exactly the same as the investment multiplier. When government spending increases, GDP increases by a larger amount.

## Spending Balance When Net Exports Depend on Income

The next step is to drop the assumption that net exports are exogenous. We need to consider the influence of foreign trade and the value of the dollar on the macroeconomy. It is time to bring these crucial variables into the model—to consider the subject of **open-economy macroeconomics.**

As we saw in Chapter 2, foreign trade is divided into exports, sales of goods and services to the rest of the world, and imports, purchases of goods and services from the rest of the world. **Net exports** are simply exports less imports. When exports are greater than imports, there is a **trade surplus;** conversely, when exports are less than imports, there is a **trade deficit.**

Recall the income identity, Equation 6.1:

$$Y = \underbrace{C + I + G +}_{\substack{\text{Domestic} \\ \text{purchases}}} \underbrace{X}_{\substack{\text{Net exports} = \\ \text{Exports} - \text{Imports}}}$$

This income identity tells us two things: (1) Income and GDP are the same thing, and (2) aggregate demand—as measured by total spending—determines GDP. In thinking about how imports and exports affect the aggregate demand for goods produced in the United States, keep in mind that consumption $C$, investment $I$, and government spending $G$ by Americans all include some purchases of goods and services abroad. In order to get a measure of how much of American demand is for U.S.–produced goods, we need to subtract imports. For example, if Americans buy 1 million more cars, then consumption rises by 1 million cars. But if all these cars are imported from abroad, then imports increase by 1 million cars and aggregate demand for U.S. goods ($Y$) does not change. The reason we add exports to the identity is straightforward: When foreigners increase their purchases of U.S.–produced goods, aggregate demand increases.

For this reason, we will develop a relation between net exports and the level of U.S. income. The relation is negative. There is no reason to think that U.S. exports are much affected by U.S. income; they are affected instead by incomes in the countries purchasing the imports. But imports are affected by U.S. income. When U.S. income rises, consumers increase their spending on imported as well as domestic goods.

We can summarize the relation between income and net exports in a **net export function:**

$$X = g - mY. \tag{6.7}$$

Here $g$ is a constant and $m$ is a coefficient. For each dollar that GDP rises, imports rise by $m$ dollars. Exports remain unchanged, so net exports fall by the same $m$ dollars.

Compare the net export function with the consumption function, which we discussed earlier in this chapter. Net exports, like consumption, depend on income. But net exports *decline* by $m$ dollars for each dollar increase in income, whereas consumption *rises* by $b$ dollars for each dollar increase in income ($b$ is the marginal propensity to consume). The reason that net exports decline with income is that imports rise by $m$ dollars for each dollar increase in income. For this reason the coefficient $m$ is sometimes called the **marginal propensity to import.** The dependence of net exports on income means that we need to take account of the response of net exports to income when we calculate the effects of monetary and fiscal policy, much as we took account of the response of consumption earlier in this chapter.

Now we can proceed exactly as we did before to develop an equation for spending balance by putting the net export function and the consumption function into the income identity. We did that before to get Equation 6.4. The corresponding equation is

$$Y = a + b(1 - t)Y + I + G + g - mY. \tag{6.8}$$

Again, we can solve for the value of $Y$ at the point of spending balance. Previously, we got Equation 6.5. Now we get

$$Y = \frac{a + I + G + g}{1 - b(1 - t) + m}. \tag{6.9}$$

Note how the impact of a change in government spending on output is

$$\frac{1}{1 - b(1 - t) + m}.$$

This is the **open-economy multiplier.** Note that the multiplier is smaller when the marginal propensity to import is larger. By setting $m$ equal to zero, the multiplier is the same as the multiplier for a closed economy. For example, if the marginal propensity to consume $b$ is .9, the tax rate $t$ is .3, and the marginal propensity to import $m$ is .1, then the multiplier is $1/.47 = 2.1$, compared with a multiplier of $1/.37 = 2.7$ for the closed economy.

At this point, we can begin to analyze how policy or other economic forces affect the trade deficit. Recall from Chapter 2 that the trade deficit, as measured in the national income accounts, is just the negative of net exports. Anything that lowers net exports will raise the deficit. Looking at the net export function, Equation 6.7, we can see that net exports, in turn, respond negatively to the level of GDP. Combining the two, we can say that forces that raise GDP will also raise the trade deficit. In particular, an increase in government spending $G$ will raise GDP according to the multiplier derived in Equation 6.9. Thus, increases in $G$ raise the trade deficit. Since increases in $G$ also raise the fiscal deficit, we can see that the two deficits are related; when the government takes an action that raises its own deficit, it causes the trade deficit to rise as well.

In Chapter 2, we noted that the trade deficit is also the total amount that Americans are borrowing from overseas. An increase in the trade deficit means an increase in borrowing. Thus, we can express the relation between fiscal and trade deficits in the following way: When some force such as higher government spending raises government borrowing, part of the borrowing

## The Decline of the Multiplier

At your first exposure to the multiplier, you may be very impressed. If the marginal propensity to spend $b$ is .9 and there are no taxes, then the multiplier is 10! But then when you consider the role of taxes in reducing disposable income, you get the multiplier in Equation 6.6, which we said might be about 2.7. Then when we considered the fact that some of the purchasing power stimulated by growth in demand would go into imports rather than domestic spending, the multiplier dropped some more, to perhaps 2.1.

Other factors, which we will study in later chapters, will further reduce the multiplier. In the next chapter, we will consider the fact that higher demand raises interest rates, and these in turn discourage investment and net exports. Then the multiplier in our standard example will be only 1.1.

Some monetarists think that the multiplier is virtually zero. The real business cycle school asserts that the multiplier is low; moreover, to the extent that they believe that government spending stimulates output, it is through a different mechanism than the one we developed in this chapter. Briefly, in the real business cycle model, higher government spending raises the interest rate, and a higher interest rate stimulates more work effort. We will discuss this mechanism in Chapter 15.

is done overseas. Instead of obtaining all the resources to be devoted to government spending from the domestic economy, some of them come from foreign economies.

In the rest of the book, the models we develop will all consider net exports endogenous.

## SPENDING BALANCE IN AN OPEN ECONOMY

1. The net export function describes the negative relation between income and net exports. It arises because higher U.S. income causes higher U.S. imports from other countries.
2. The multiplier in an open economy is smaller than in a closed economy.
3. Events that raise GDP, such as higher government spending, cause net exports to fall and the trade deficit to rise. Part of an increase in the fiscal deficit is financed overseas through a higher trade deficit.

## REVIEW AND PRACTICE

### Major Points

1. In the short run, output is determined by the aggregate demand for goods and services in the economy.
2. In the short run, firms respond to an increase in demand by producing more output rather than by raising prices.
3. The consumption function expresses the positive relation between income and consumption.
4. Spending balance occurs when consumption plus investment plus government purchases plus net exports add up to the level of GDP on which the consumers made their consumption plan.
5. The investment multiplier expresses the relation between investment and GDP. When investment rises by $1 billion, GDP rises by more than $1 billion because consumption rises as GDP rises.
6. Spending balance for an open economy occurs when the sum of all spending, including net exports, equals GDP.
7. The multiplier for an open economy is less than the multiplier for a closed economy.

8. An increase in government spending increases both the fiscal deficit and the trade deficit.

## Key Terms and Concepts

spending balance
aggregate demand
income identity
consumption function
marginal propensity to consume
exogenous variable

endogenous variable
multiplier
investment multiplier
government spending
  multiplier

marginal propensity to import
net exports
net export function
trade deficit
price shocks

## Questions for Discussion and Review

1. What factors can push the economy out of equilibrium in the short run?
2. How is the level of employment determined in short-run disequilibrium situations?
3. What does the aggregate demand schedule measure?
4. How do firms typically respond to an increase in demand in the short run?
5. What happens to consumption if income rises? If taxes are cut?
6. What is true at the point of spending balance? What happens if the economy is not at a point of spending balance?
7. What happens to GDP if consumers change their behavior in such a way that the constant $a$ in the consumption function increases?
8. Why does an increase in investment or government purchases bring about a large increase in GDP?
9. Explain why the open-economy multiplier is smaller than the closed-economy multiplier.
10. How does an increase in government spending affect the trade deficit?

## Problems

### NUMERICAL

1. Suppose that the model of the economy is given by

$$Y = C + I + G + X$$

$$C = a + bY_d$$

$$Y_d = (1 - t)Y$$

$$X = g - mY$$

where $I =$ \$900 billion, $G =$ \$1,200 billion, and the constants take the following values: $a = 220$, $b = .9$, $t = .3$, $g = 500$, and $m = .1$.

a. Show that the value of GDP at the point of spending balance is $6,000 billion. Compared with the example on page 162 with exogenous net exports, is the multiplier larger or smaller?

b. What proportion of investment is private saving? Government saving? Saving by the rest of the world?

c. Now suppose that $I$ increases by $100 billion. By what proportion of the increase in investment do each of the three categories of saving increase?

2. Consider a closed-economy model given by the following equations:

$$Y = C + I + G$$

$$C = 160 + .8Y_d$$

$$Y_d = (1 - t)Y - Z$$

Investment and government spending are exogenous and each is equal to 200. The tax system has two components: a lump-sum tax denoted by $Z$ and an income tax of rate $t$.

a. Assume $Z$ is equal to 200 and $t$ is .25. Find the level of income that satisfies spending balance. How much does the government collect in taxes at that level of income? What is the level of government saving?

b. Suppose the lump-sum tax is reduced to 100. Find the new level of income that is consistent with spending balance. What is the lump-sum tax multiplier? What are the new levels of tax collections and government saving?

c. Comparing your answers in Parts a and b, does the tax cut increase or decrease tax receipts? By how much? Explain why tax receipts do not simply fall by 100 with the cut in lump-sum taxes.

d. One of the arguments of "supply-side" economists in the early 1980s was that a tax cut could actually reduce the budget deficit. Can that happen with a lump-sum tax cut in the model used in this problem? Does the spending balance model ignore factors that the "supply-siders" think are important for this problem? If so, name them.

## ANALYTICAL

1. Imagine that you operate an economic forecasting firm. Your stock-in-trade is that you know the true model of the U.S. economy. It is given by the formula

$$Y = C + I + G + X$$

$$C = a + bY_d$$

$$Y_d = (1 - t)Y$$

$$X = g - mY$$

where $I$ and $G$ are exogenous, and it is assumed that you have numerical values for all of the constants in the model.

a. Of the four spending components, which must you forecast before arriving at a forecast for the U.S. GDP? Explain.

b. Now suppose that you are trying to forecast GDP for a centrally planned economy in which the production schedules for all goods are determined a year in advance. Would forecasting $C$, $I$, $G$, and $X$ be a very good way of forecasting GDP?

2. For the model given in Problem 1, explain why private saving, government saving, and saving by the rest of the world are all endogenous variables.

3. Suppose the economy is described by the following simple model:

$$Y = C + G$$

$$C = a + bY_d$$

$$Y_d = (1 - t)Y.$$

a. Give an expression that relates private saving $S_p$ to disposable income. This is called the saving function.

b. What must the relationship be between private saving and the government budget deficit? (Hint: Refer back to the discussion in Chapter 2 concerning the relationship between saving and investment.)

c. Solve for the values of $S_p$ and the budget deficit; that is, derive an expression for each that is a function only of the exogenous variable $G$ and the constants in the model. Are your expressions consistent with your answer to Part b?

4. Balanced budget multiplier: Consider the following simple model with investment and government spending exogenous.

$$Y = C + I + G$$

$$C = a + bY_d$$

Disposable income $Y_d$ is given by $Y - T$ where $T$ is total taxes. Suppose that taxes are not directly related to income so that $T$ can be increased or decreased independently of income.

a. Derive the change in $Y$ associated with an increase in taxes $T$. Show the results graphically and algebraically. What is the tax multiplier? That is, what is $\Delta Y/\Delta T$?

b. Compare the tax multiplier with the government spending multiplier derived in the text. Aside from the difference in signs, which is larger? Why?

c. Now increase government spending $G$ and taxes $T$ by the same amount. For this change the government budget deficit $G - T$ does not change. If the budget was balanced before, it will still be balanced. What happens to income $Y$ in this case? Perhaps surprisingly it increases. Calculate by how much. That is, using algebra, calculate $\Delta Y/\Delta G$; $\Delta G = \Delta T$. The result is called the balanced budget multiplier.

5. For the model given in Problem 1, which of the following statements are true?

a. An exogenous increase in net exports (i.e., an increase in $g$) lowers the trade deficit and the government budget deficit.

b. An increase in investment lowers the government budget deficit but raises the trade deficit.

c. An increase in government spending and taxes of the same amount leaves both the government budget deficit and the trade deficit unchanged.

6. Imagine an economy in which the government spent all its tax revenues, but was prevented (by a balanced budget amendment) from spending any more; thus $G = tY$, where $t$ is the tax rate.
   a. Explain why government spending is endogenous in the model.
   b. Is the multiplier larger or smaller than the case in which government spending is exogenous?
   c. When $t$ increases, does $Y$ increase, decrease, or stay the same?

7. This question focuses on the differences in the structure of the long-run growth model of Chapter 4 and the short-run spending balance model introduced in this chapter.
   a. In the long-run model, what exogenous factors determine the level of output?
   b. In the spending balance model, what exogenous factors determine the level of output?
   c. In the spending balance model, is employment an exogenous or an endogenous variable? How is the level of employment determined in this model?
   d. Which of the two models is best described by the statement "Demand creates its own supply"? Which model is best described by "Supply creates its own demand"?

## MacroSolve Exercises

1. Plot the quarterly growth rates of real GDP and the GDP deflator ("Inflation [GDP]"). Which would you describe as being more variable? Confirm your conclusion using MacroSolve's **STATISTICS** option. Is this finding compatible with the view that prices are more sticky than output? Is the same true for the entire sample of annual data from 1930 to 1995?

2. How do your results in Problem 1 change if you split the sample period at the end of 1982 when inflation began to return to more acceptable levels? What changes in monetary policy might explain this finding?

3. Using quarterly data, graph consumption expenditure on the vertical axis against disposable income.
   a. What is the approximate slope of the consumption function (the marginal propensity to consume)?
   b. If the tax rate were zero, what would this marginal propensity to consume imply would be the value of the multiplier for a closed economy?
   c. If the tax rate were 30 percent, what would be the value of the multiplier?
   d. If, in addition, the marginal propensity to import were .1, what would be the value of the multiplier?

4. Tabulate the ratio of consumption to disposable income using quarterly data. How can the average propensity to consume be different from the marginal propensity to consume? What does this imply for the value of consumption when income is zero?

5. Plot real disposable income and real consumption expenditures and calculate their statistics. Describe the differences between the behavior of these two variables. How does the consumption function explain these differences?

# Financial Markets and Aggregate Demand

Spending balance, as we discussed in the last chapter, involves finding the level of GDP that makes the spending plans of consumers and others consistent with their actual levels of income. In this chapter, we will complete the discussion of spending balance by bringing back in another key variable, the interest rate. Spending depends on the interest rate because of the sensitivity of investment and net exports to the interest rate. In order to tell the full story of the interest rate, we have to consider the money market. We introduce the IS-LM framework to help develop the story. The IS-LM framework combines the money market and the spending process. We will use the IS-LM approach in the rest of the book to describe the determination of output and interest rates in the short run. At the end of this chapter we use the IS-LM framework to derive the aggregate demand curve.

## INVESTMENT AND THE INTEREST RATE

In the description of spending balance in Chapter 6, there were two exogenous forces that potentially could affect the level of GDP corresponding to spending balance—investment and government spending. In this section we introduce **financial variables**—interest rates and the supply of money—into the model. We show that investment depends on these financial variables. Investment is no longer determined outside the model; it now becomes an endogenous variable. The addition of financial variables to the model means that we will be concerned with the effects of changes in the money supply and interest rates, as well as with government spending.

## The Investment Demand Function

When we change investment from an exogenous variable to an endogenous variable, we need to specify a behavioral relationship to explain how investment is determined within the model. The relationship we use to describe investment is a simple but fundamental one. It states that investment depends negatively on the interest rate. This means that the demand for investment goods—the new factories, offices, and equipment used by business firms, as well as the new houses built for residential use—is low when interest rates are high, and vice versa.

The major reason for this negative relationship is that business firms and consumers finance many of their investment purchases by borrowing. When borrowing costs are high because of high interest rates, firms and consumers will tend to make fewer investment purchases. High borrowing costs effectively make investment goods more costly. Note that even if borrowing is not the source of funds for investment—such as when the funds come from selling financial securities—the interest rate still matters. If interest rates are high, then not holding those securities will represent a larger loss of income on those securities than if interest rates were low. Hence, if interest rates are high, people will be reluctant to sell those securities in order to purchase physical investment goods.

In algebraic terms the relationship for investment demand, called the **investment function,** can be represented as

$$I = e - dR. \tag{7.1}$$

As before, $I$ is investment, $R$ is the interest rate, and $e$ and $d$ are constants. Investment is measured in billions of dollars, and the interest rate is measured in percentage points. Equation 7.1 says that investment demand is equal to a constant $e$ minus another constant $d$ times the interest rate. The coefficient $d$ measures how much investment falls when the interest rate increases by 1 percentage point. Note that we have kept the convention that lowercase letters represent constant coefficients, while uppercase letters represent variables. The investment function is shown graphically in Figure 7.1. It is a downward-sloping line.

**EXAMPLE**     Suppose $e$ equals 1,000 and $d$ equals 2,000; then Equation 7.1 looks like

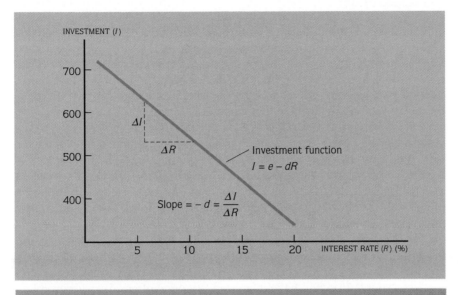

**FIGURE 7.1** The Investment Function

When the interest rate rises, the demand for investment falls. A higher interest rate means that the cost of funds required for investment is higher; only those investment projects that are particularly profitable will be undertaken.

$$I = 1{,}000 - 2{,}000\ R.$$

When the interest rate is 5 percent, investment $I$ is 1,000–2,000(.05), or $900 billion. An increase in the interest rate of 1 percent reduces investment by $20 billion. Note that we speak about the interest rate $R$ as a percent, but use decimals in algebraic formulas: "The interest rate is 5 percent" means $R$ = .05. This convention is used throughout the book.

## The Meaning and Interpretation of $R$

Note that, in changing investment from an exogenous variable to an endogenous variable, we have introduced a new endogenous variable into the model: the interest rate $R$. There are, of course, many different interest rates in a modern economy: rates on *long*-term securities, rates on *short*-term securities, rates on *risky* securities, and rates on *safe* securities. When we use the term "*the* interest rate," we are therefore simplifying the financial structure of the economy. In thinking about this simplification—that is, in trying to relate $R$ to something you can read about or look up in a newspaper—it is useful to imagine an average or representative interest rate that represents the behavior of all the different types of rates. For many purposes this abstraction is not too bad; interest rates on different types of securities—while not equal—tend to move in the same direction. That is, when interest rates on risk-free Treasury bills are abnormally high, so are interest rates on more risky corporate bonds. Of course, there are sometimes differences between short- and long-term interest-rate behavior. Long-term interest rates depend on expectations of future short-term rates. However, we will focus on the average representative interest rate $R$.

It is also important to distinguish between the real interest rate and the nominal interest rate. As we noted in Chapter 1, the nominal interest rate is simply the rate that you read about in the newspaper or that banks place in their windows to indicate what they will pay for different types of deposits. The real interest rate corrects the nominal rate for expected changes in the price level. Specifically, the real interest rate is the nominal interest rate minus the expected rate of inflation. For example, if your bank is paying 10 percent on deposits for a year and you expect inflation to be 6 percent for the year, then the real rate of interest for you is 4 percent. The real rate of interest measures how much you will earn on your deposit after taking account of the fact that inflation will have increased the price of goods that you might purchase in a year. We usually mean the real interest rate when we use the symbol $R$ in this book, but we do not generally add the adjective "real," unless the meaning is ambiguous or we want to point out a particular reason to distinguish between the real and the nominal rates. For low rates of inflation the real rate and the nominal rate are very close.

## THE INVESTMENT FUNCTION

1. Investment demand is negatively related to the interest rate. When funds are more expensive, less investment takes place. The investment function describes this negative relationship.
2. The interest rate $R$ that is in the investment function is an average of the many interest rates that we observe at banks and in the financial markets.

## NET EXPORTS AND THE INTEREST RATE

Another factor that we want to consider in building a model of aggregate demand is that net exports depend negatively on the interest rate. In Chapter 12, we will consider the reasons for this important relation in more detail.

For now, we will look at the relation in the following way: When the U.S. interest rate is higher than interest rates in other countries, it becomes attractive for people in those countries to put their funds in *dollars,* that is, to lend funds to businesses in the United States and to the U.S. government. By the same token, it is less attractive for people in the United States to put their funds in other currencies, that is, to lend overseas, where returns are lower. This means that dollars become more attractive, and this drives up the price of dollars—that is, the exchange rate rises. But a higher exchange rate makes U.S. goods more expensive to foreigners and it also makes foreign goods less expensive to U.S. residents. Less expensive foreign goods will make U.S. imports rise. Similarly, more expensive U.S. goods will make U.S. exports fall. On both accounts *net exports—exports minus imports—fall when the U.S. interest rate rises* because the exchange rate rises.

How do we incorporate this negative relationship between net exports and the interest rate into our model of aggregate demand? We must add another term to the net export function of Equation 6.7 to incorporate the negative effect of the interest rate $R$ on net exports:

$$X = g - mY - nR. \tag{7.2}$$

The new coefficient $n$ measures the decrease in net exports that occurs when the interest rate rises by 1 percentage point.

**EXAMPLE**   Suppose $g$ is 525, $m$ is .1, and $n$ is 500. Then the net export function is

$$X = 525 - .1Y - 500R.$$

## 7.3   THE IS CURVE AND THE LM CURVE

Now that we have developed all the economic relationships needed to understand short-run spending behavior, we can tackle the problem of short-run output and interest-rate determination. Recall that this is a challenging problem because output and the interest rate are determined simultaneously. The IS and LM curves are convenient ways to describe the solution to the problem.

In the short-run model, we take the price level as given or predetermined. There are five economic relationships to consider: the income identity, the consumption function, the investment demand function, the net export function, and the money demand function. The theory implies that all five relationships must hold at the same time.

## KEY MACRO RELATIONSHIPS

### Macro Variables

The *Endogenous* Variables:

| Name | Symbol |
|------|--------|
| Income | $Y$ |
| Consumption | $C$ |
| Investment | $I$ |
| Net exports | $X$ |
| Interest rates | $R$ |

The *Exogenous* Variables:

| Name | Symbol |
|------|--------|
| Government purchases | $G$ |
| Money supply | $M$ |

The *Predetermined* Variable:

| Name | Symbol |
|------|--------|
| Price level | $P$ |

### Five Relationships (how the variables interact with each other)

| Algebra | | Name | Numerical Example |
|---------|---|------|-------------------|
| $Y = C + I + G + X$ | (6.1) | Income identity | |
| $C = a + b(1 - t)Y$ | (6.3) | Consumption function | $C = 220 + .63Y$ |
| $I = e - dR$ | (7.1) | Investment function | $I = 1,000 - 2,000R$ |
| $X = g - mY - nR$ | (7.2) | Net export function | $X = 525 - .1Y - 500R$ |
| $M = (kY - hR)P$ | (5.3) | Money demand | $M = (.1583Y - 1,000R)P$ |

The analysis proceeds as follows: We take as given the values for the variables determined outside our model in any year, for example, 1995. These are the exogenous variables: the money supply $M$ and government spending $G$. They are determined by the Federal Reserve, the President, and Congress. We want to find values for income, consumption, investment, net exports, the interest rate, and the price level that are implied by the model and by the values of the money supply and government spending for that year. We also want to find out what happens if the money supply or government spending changes. Will interest rates and output rise or fall, and by how much? The economic relationships and the key macroeconomic variables are summarized in the box above.

Suppose that $P = 1$. Then the five macro relationships will determine values for the five remaining endogenous variables. The situation is analogous to that in Chapter 6 where we had to find values for two variables to satisfy two relationships. We first use graphs and then algebra.

Because graphs allow for only two variables, we need to reduce the five relationships to two relationships. A way to do this was originally proposed in 1937 by the late J. R. Hicks, the British economist who won the Nobel Prize in 1972. Hick's graphical approach, called the IS-LM approach, is still used widely today because of its great intuitive appeal.[1]

## The IS Curve

The **IS curve** is shown in Figure 7.2. *The IS curve shows all the combinations of the interest rate R and income Y that satisfy the income identity, the con-*

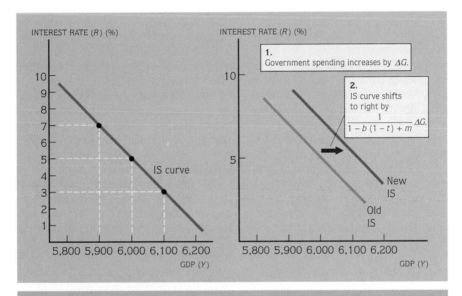

**FIGURE 7.2**   The IS Curve

The IS curve shows all the combinations of the interest rate $R$ and income $Y$ that satisfy the consumption, investment, and net export functions and the income identity. As shown in the left-hand panel, it is downward-sloping; an increase in the interest rate reduces investment and net exports. Through the multiplier, GDP falls. The right-hand panel illustrates how the IS curve shifts to the right when government spending increases.

---

[1]See J. R. Hicks, "Mr. Keynes and the Classics: A Suggested Interpretation," *Econometrica,* Vol. 6, pp. 147–159, 1937. The IS curve gets its name because, when all relationships are satisfied, investment demand, I, must equal income less consumption demand, or saving, S. The M in the LM curve stands for the money supply and the L stands for liquidity preference, which is a synonym for money demand. (Money is more liquid—easier to exchange for goods and other items—than bonds or corporate stock.)

# NEW RESEARCH IN PRACTICE
## The Stock Market

In this book, the interest rate has a fundamental role. When the interest rate is high, firms have an incentive to defer investment, households have an incentive to defer purchases, especially of cars and other durable goods, and the United States draws on the resources of other countries by importing more than it exports. For simplicity, we consider a single interest rate. In fact, not only are there many different interest rates, but the stock market is just as important as the bond market in channeling resources from sectors whose incomes exceed their purchases to sectors where resources are needed. The financial pages of the newspaper spend more space on the stock market than on the bond market. What have we left out by concentrating on the interest rate and not discussing the returns on stocks?

The Nobel Prize in economics was awarded to Harry Markowitz, Merton Miller, and William Sharpe in 1991 for their development of the theory of the relation between interest rates and returns in the stock market. Their work has not remained a theoretical abstraction. The capital asset pricing model (CAPM) they developed is used on Wall Street to make decisions about trillion-dollar portfolios. The ideas behind the CAPM help explain not only the prices of stocks, but also the prices of derivatives—securities such as options whose payoffs depend on the prices of stocks or bonds.*

The CAPM focuses on one interest rate, called the *risk-free rate*, usually measured as the interest rate on Treasury bills (short-term bonds issued by the federal government). The CAPM, along with almost all of modern finance theory, relies on the idea of *arbitrage* to explain the prices of stocks and other securities. Arbitrage occurs when an organization takes on an obligation and buys some other securities that offset the risk that it would otherwise face from the obligation. Arbitrage is profitable if the proceeds from taking on the obligation exceed the cost of the offsetting securities. Because arbitrageurs on Wall Street can deploy large

amounts of wealth and have a detailed understanding of the principles of arbitrage, no opportunities for arbitrage profits are left—the arbitrageurs have gotten rid of them. The CAPM assumes the absence of arbitrage profits to arrive at formulas for predicting the prices of stocks and other securities.

The most basic principle of the CAPM is that there is one portfolio—containing all stocks in proportion to their presence in the market—with a unique role in finance. It is called the *market portfolio*. Investors get the best combination of risk and return by holding a fraction of their wealth in Treasury bills and the rest in the market portfolio. A risk-averse investor holds mostly Treasury bills; a risk-tolerant investor holds mostly the market portfolio. The return expected from the market portfolio is 5 to 7 percentage points higher than the risk-free rate, so the investor willing to take on risk generally earns a higher return.

Arbitrage keeps the prices of individual stocks in line with the same principle. Risky stocks have higher expected returns. If the price of a stock is too high for its risk, arbitrageurs will borrow shares, sell them in the market, and hold the right combination of Treasury bills and the market portfolio to offset the risk. As they do this, they will drive the price of the stock down to where it belongs according to the CAPM.

Instead of having to think about the returns to each of thousands of different stocks and bonds, according to the CAPM, we have to think only about the risk-free rate and the expected return on the market portfolio. All other rates or returns are weighted averages of these two, with weights that depend on risk. Moreover, there are good reasons to think that the premium between the expected return on the market portfolio and the risk-free rate (the equity or risk premium) is reasonably stable over time. Then all rates move up and down along with the Treasury bill rate. In that case, the approach we take in this book, considering just one interest rate, is completely sound. One rate can stand in for all interest rates and expected returns on all stocks.

Of course, the world may be more complex than this model suggests. With the huge increase in stock prices in the 1980s and 1990s, the equity premium may have declined—it's possible that investors today are not going to earn 5 to 7 percentage points more than on Treasury bills. And

cutting-edge versions of the CAPM used on Wall Street today don't use a single market portfolio—they use models with multiple aggregate influences.

*See Richard A. Brealey and Stewart C. Meyers, *Principles of Corporate Finance*, 4th ed. (New York: McGraw-Hill, 1991).

*sumption function, the investment function, and the net export function.* In other words, it is the set of points for which spending balance occurs. The left-hand panel of Figure 7.2 shows how higher levels of the interest rate are associated with lower levels of GDP along the IS curve.

**SLOPE**   The first thing to remember about the IS curve is that it is downward-sloping. Understanding the intuitive economic reason for this downward slope is very important. *The IS curve is downward-sloping because a higher interest rate reduces investment and net exports and thereby reduces GDP through the multiplier process.* To find a specific point on the IS curve, choose an interest rate and calculate how much investment and net exports will result using the investment function and the export function. The higher the rate of interest, the lower the level of investment and net exports. Pass this level of spending through the multiplier process to find out how much GDP will result. The less of both, the less GDP. The interest rate and this level of GDP are a point on the IS curve. A self-contained explicit graphical derivation of the IS curve is shown in Figure 7.3.

**SHIFTS**   The second thing to remember about the IS curve is that *an increase in government spending shifts the IS curve to the right.* An increase in government spending increases GDP through the multiplier; as GDP increases, we move the IS curve to the right. Note that, conversely, a decrease in government spending pushes the IS curve to the left.

To find how much the IS curve shifts, pick an interest rate $R$ and calculate a corresponding level of investment and net exports. Now increase government spending. Through the multiplier process, output will increase by the multiplier times the increase in government spending. Holding the interest rate constant, the IS curve shifts to the right along the horizontal GDP axis by the amount of the multiplier times the increase in government spending. This is shown in the right-hand panel of Figure 7.2.

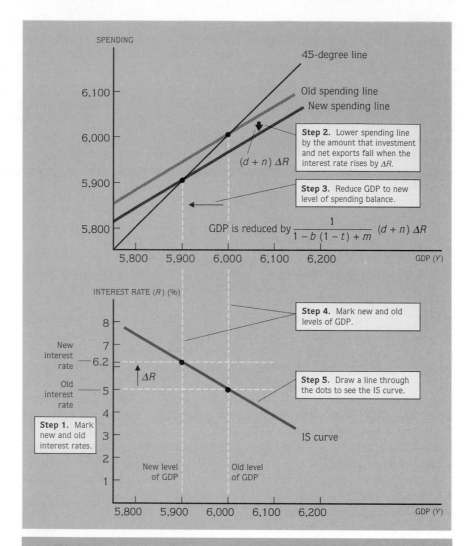

**FIGURE 7.3** Graphical Derivation of the IS Curve

The upper part of the diagram shows the 45-degree line and spending line. The lower part of the diagram is the graph where the IS curve is to be drawn. The lower diagram has the interest rate on the vertical axis, and GDP on the horizontal axis. Points on the graph are obtained as described in the instructions placed in boxes on the diagram. Start with an interest rate and find the position of the spending line for that interest rate. (Higher interest rates will lower the spending line because they reduce investment and net exports.) Then find the resulting level of GDP that satisfies the requirements of spending balance. Note how the slope of the IS curve will depend on the marginal propensity to consume $b$, the tax rate $t$, and the marginal propensity to import $m$, because these affect the multiplier. Note also that the slope depends on the sensitivity of investment and net exports to changes in the interest rate, controlled by the coefficents $d$ and $n$.

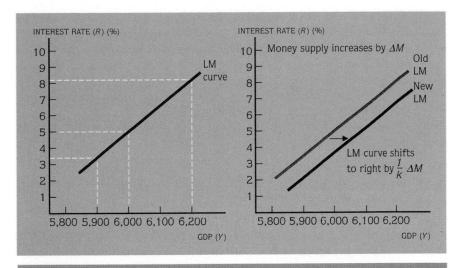

**FIGURE 7.4**   The LM Curve

The LM curve shows the values for the interest rate and income such that the supply of money is equal to the demand for money. As shown in the left-hand panel the LM curve is upward-sloping. The right-hand panel shows how an increase in the money supply shifts the LM curve to the right.

## The LM Curve

The **LM curve** is shown in Figure 7.4. *The LM curve shows all combinations of the interest rate R and income Y that satisfy the money demand relationship for a fixed level of the money supply and for a predetermined value of the price level.* The left-hand panel of Figure 7.4 shows that higher levels of the interest rate are associated with higher levels of GDP along the LM curve.

**SLOPE**   The first thing to remember about the LM curve is that it slopes upward. The reason for this is somewhat involved, but important to keep in mind. Imagine that the interest rate increases. What must happen to income if money demand is to remain equal to money supply? An increase in the interest rate $R$ reduces the demand for money. But the money supply is fixed. Hence, income must adjust to bring money demand back up. A rise in income is what is required. A rise in income will increase the demand for money and offset the decline in money demand brought about by the rise in the interest rate. In sum, the increase in the interest rate is associated with an increase in income. Thus the LM curve is upward-sloping.

To understand better the derivation of the LM curve, it is helpful to recall the concept of **real money** introduced in Chapter 1. Real money is defined as money supply $M$ divided by the price level $P$. Because the term "real money" is used so much in macroeconomics we sometimes use the term **nominal money** when we mean just plain money $M$. Real money $M/P$ is a convenient measure of money that corrects for changes in the price level. For example, if money supply increases by 10 percent and the price level increases by 10 percent, then real money does not change. The money demand function from Equation 4.4 can be written in terms of real money if we simply divide both sides by the price level. That is,

$$M/P = kY - hR. \tag{7.3}$$

This says that the demand for *real* money depends positively on real GDP and negatively on the interest rate. The real money demand equation is an attractive way to think about money demand because it depends on two rather than three variables. Looking at Equation 7.3, we see that real money demand consists of two parts: one part, $kY$, increases with income, while the other part, $-hR$, decreases with the interest rate. Of course the same economic principles apply whether we write the money demand function in terms of real money or nominal money.

Looking at Equation 7.3, we see clearly why the LM curve slopes up. If the Fed is holding nominal money constant and the price level isn't moving, then real money supply is also constant. If real money supply is constant, then an increase in the interest rate $R$, which reduces money demand by $hR$, must be offset by an increase in $Y$, which increases money demand by $kY$. Hence, when the interest rate $R$ increases, income $Y$ increases.

A self-contained graphical derivation of the LM curve, based on this line of reasoning, is shown in Figure 7.5. The left-hand panel of Figure 7.5 is a graph of the demand for real money as a function of the interest rate. Real money demand decreases with the interest rate. But note that an increase in GDP increases money demand and this shifts the money demand line to the right. If money demand is to stay equal to money supply, then the interest rate must increase, as shown in the diagram.

**SHIFTS**    The second thing to remember about the LM curve is that *an increase in the money supply shifts the LM curve to the right*. Conversely, a decrease in the money supply shifts the LM curve to the left. Looking again at Equation 7.3, we can get an economic understanding for this. An increase in the money supply increases the variable on the left-hand side, $M/P$. If money demand is to remain equal to money supply, then either output $Y$ must rise or the interest rate $R$ must fall. If we hold the interest on the LM diagram at a particular value, then output $Y$ must increase as the LM curve shifts to the right. This is shown in the right-hand panel of Figure 7.4.

Changes in the price level also shift the LM curve. Again, look at the

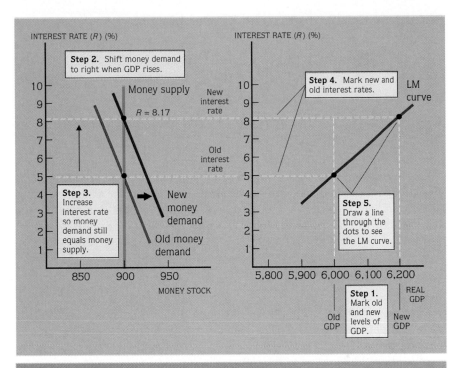

**FIGURE 7.5** Graphical Derivation of the LM Curve

The left-hand panel shows the demand for real money as a function of the interest rate. The demand schedule slopes downward because higher interest rates make the public conserve on money holdings. Money demand shifts to the right if real GDP rises. Higher GDP causes the public to hold more real money at a given interest rate. The LM curve is constructed in the right-hand panel. The instructions show how to get points on the curve. Start with a level of GDP and find the money demand suitable for that level. Then find the interest rate that equates money demand and money supply. The LM curve traces out the market-clearing interest rate for different levels of GDP.

symbols in Equation 7.3 to keep track of what is going on. An increase in the price level reduces real balances. Hence, an increase in the price level does exactly the same thing to the LM curve as a decrease in the money supply. *An increase in the price level shifts the LM curve to the left.* The rationale: An increase in the price level means that less real money is available for transactions purposes. This means that either the interest rate must rise or real income must fall to reduce money demand. Either way the LM curve shifts to the left. Conversely, a decrease in the price level shifts the LM curve to the right, just like an increase in the money supply.

## Algebraic Derivation of the IS and LM Curves

The algebraic statement that defines the IS curve is the expression of spending balance; that is, the GDP, $Y$, generated as total spending, is equal to the level of income $Y$, assumed by consumers and importers in making their spending decisions:

$$Y = a + e + g + [b(1 - t) - m] \, Y - (d + n) \, R + G. \qquad (7.4)$$

Note that the right-hand side is just the consumption function plus the investment function plus the net export function plus government spending. We want to express the IS curve as an equation giving the value of $R$ that gives spending balance at a specified level of $Y$. We solve Equation 7.4 for $R$ by moving the $R$ term to the left-hand side and dividing by $d + n$:

$$R = \frac{a + e + g}{d + n} - \frac{1 - b(1 - t) + m}{d + n} \, Y + \frac{1}{d + n} \, G. \quad \text{IS Curve} \quad (7.5)$$

Government spending $G$ increases the interest rate for a given level of income. Graphically, this looks like a shift of the IS curve to the right, a result that we saw in Figure 7.2. A higher value of $G$ raises the IS curve or, equivalently, shifts the IS curve to the right.

The coefficient

$$\frac{1 - b(1 - t) + m}{d + n}$$

that multiplies $Y$ in Equation 7.5 is the slope of the IS curve. Note that the slope of the IS curve depends on the sensitivity of investment to the interest rate, represented by the coefficient $d$. The algebraic formula shows that the slope of the IS curve is small—this means that the IS curve is fairly flat—if investment is very responsive to the interest rate. Then, small changes in the interest rate result in large changes in investment and hence large fluctuations in GDP. Similarly, the IS curve will be flat if net exports are highly sensitive to the interest rate, that is, if the coefficient $n$ is large. What matters is the sum of the two interest-rate coefficients, $d + n$. Note that the IS curve will be flat if the marginal propensity to consume $b$ is large, if the tax rate $t$ is small, or if the marginal propensity to import $m$ is small. In these cases, the multiplier is large and changes in the interest rate have large effects on GDP.

**AN EXAMPLE OF AN IS CURVE**   With the numerical values summarized in the box on page 178, the IS curve is

$$R = \frac{1,745}{2,500} - \frac{1 - .53}{2,500} Y + \frac{1}{2,500} G$$

or

$$R = .698 - .000188\,Y + .0004G. \quad \text{Numerical Example of IS Curve} \quad (7.6)$$

The slope of the IS curve is $-.000188$: Along the IS curve, when GDP rises by $100 billion, the interest rate falls by 1.88 percentage points. The IS curve that appears in Figure 7.2 is drawn accurately to scale for this numerical example. The IS curve on the left is drawn for government spending $G$ equal to $1,200 billion. The shift in the IS curve to the right in Figure 7.2 is due to an increase in government spending of $40 billion.

The algebraic expression for the LM curve is obtained simply by moving $R$ to the left-hand side of the money demand equation (7.3) and dividing by the coefficient $h$. That is,

$$R = \frac{k}{h} Y - \frac{1}{h} \frac{M}{P}. \quad \text{LM Curve} \quad (7.7)$$

Equation 7.7 says that an increase in real money balances $M/P$ lowers the interest rate for a given level of income. This means that the LM curve shifts to the right, a result that corresponds to the graph in Figure 7.4. The slope of the LM curve is $k/h$. Note that the slope of the LM curve $k/h$ is small—meaning that the LM curve is fairly flat—if the sensitivity of money demand to the interest rate is large, that is, if the coefficient $h$ is large. Then, a small decline in the interest rate raises the demand for money by a large amount and requires a large offsetting increase in income. The small change in the interest rate combined with the large change in income trace out a flat LM curve. Note also that the LM curve is flat if the sensitivity of money demand to income $k$ is small.

**AN EXAMPLE OF AN LM CURVE**   With the numerical values summarized in the box on page 178, the LM curve is

$$R = \frac{.1583}{1,000} Y - \frac{1}{1,000} \frac{M}{P}$$

or

$$R = .0001583\,Y - .001 \frac{M}{P}. \quad \text{Numerical Example of LM Curve} \quad (7.8)$$

This LM curve is drawn to scale in Figure 7.4. The shift of the LM curve for an initial money stock of 900 in the right-hand side of Figure 7.4 corresponds to an increase in the money supply of $40 billion.

## Finding Income $Y$ and the Interest Rate $R$

Finally we are ready to find the values of the interest rate and income that are predicted by the theory. We first proceed graphically. To satisfy all five relationships of the model, the values of $R$ and $Y$ must be on both the LM curve and the IS curve, that is, at the intersection of the LM curve and the IS curve. The IS curve incorporates the theory of consumption, investment, and net exports and the income identity, while the LM curve incorporates the theory of money demand and money supply. The values of the interest rate and income that we are looking for are thus at the intersection of the LM curve and the IS curve. The intersection is shown graphically in Figure 7.6.

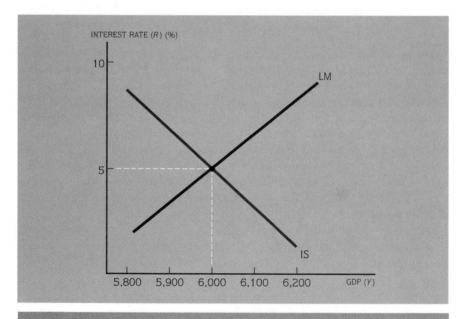

**FIGURE 7.6**   The Intersection of the IS Curve and the LM Curve

The values of the interest rate and income predicted by the macro model occur at the intersection of the IS curve and the LM curve. For these values, all five relationships of the model are satisfied. Along the IS curve consumption demand, investment demand, net export demand, and the income identity are satisfied. Along the LM curve money demand equals money supply.

Once we have determined the levels of income *Y* and the interest rate *R*, we can determine consumption *C*, investment *I*, and net exports *X*. Consumption is obtained by putting the value of income into the consumption function, investment is obtained by putting the value of the interest rate into the investment function, and net exports are obtained by putting income and the interest rate into the net export function.

Recall that all these predictions of the model are made with the price level fixed, on the "back burner." This is fine for the short run—for about a year or so—but for no longer. We look at what happens to the price level in the next chapter.

## THE IS-LM FRAMEWORK

1. The IS curve shows all combinations of the interest rate and income that satisfy spending balance.
2. The LM curve shows all combinations of the interest rate and income that satisfy money market equilibrium.
3. Given the price level, the IS-LM diagram tells the levels of GDP and the interest rate, at the intersection of the IS and LM curves. This is the only combination of *Y* and *R* that satisfies both spending balance and money market equilibrium.

## 7.4   POLICY ANALYSIS WITH IS-LM

### Monetary Policy

We are now ready to make the IS-LM approach go to work. Consider monetary policy. What happens if the Fed increases the money supply? We now know that an increase in the money supply shifts the LM curve to the right. The effect of such a change on the interest rate and income is shown in Figure 7.7. As the left-hand panel indicates, the theory predicts that *when the money supply increases, the interest rate falls and GDP rises.* This increase in GDP will probably put upward pressure on prices, but we are saving the details for the next chapter.

What is actually happening in the economy when the Fed increases the money supply? Immediately after the increase there is more money in

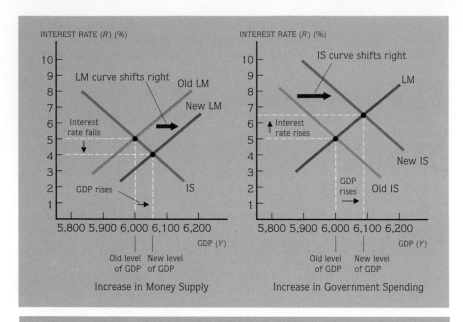

**FIGURE 7.7**   Effects of Monetary and Fiscal Policies

In the left-hand panel, an increase in the money supply shifts the LM curve to the right; this raises GDP and lowers the interest rate. In the right-hand panel, an increase in government spending shifts the IS curve to the right; this raises GDP and the interest rate. A comparison of the two panels illustrates a fundamental difference between monetary policy and fiscal policy: An expansionary monetary policy lowers interest rates, and an expansionary fiscal policy raises interest rates.

the economy than people demand. This tends to make the interest rate fall, so the demand for money increases. The lower interest rate then stimulates investment and net exports; this raises GDP through the multiplier process. In sum, GDP rises and the interest rate falls.

## Fiscal Policy

Suppose Congress passes a bill that increases defense spending. We now know that an increase in government spending pushes the IS curve to the right. Figure 7.7 shows what happens to interest rates and GDP. In the right-hand panel *an increase in government spending increases the interest rate and increases income.*

What is going on in the economy when the government purchases more goods? First, the increase in government demand increases GDP

## IS-LM in the Business Pages

Not many reporters are versed in the IS-LM model. It's not surprising to find statements like this one in the financial pages:

A new recession is feared because higher government spending for business bailouts is raising interest rates. Those higher rates are discouraging housing purchases and plant and equipment investment.

More bailout spending shifts the IS curve outward. The economy moves up and to the right along the LM curve. It is true that interest rates are higher, but this is a symptom of higher GDP, not something that will cause a decline in GDP. How about:

There is concern about declining sales and employment because of the collapse of the dollar. That collapse will be accompanied by higher interest rates,

which will lead to lower investment and total spending.

Same error. The lower dollar will lead to a diversion of demand to domestic products, which will shift the IS curve outward. GDP and the interest rate rise as the economy moves up the LM curve. And:

The only way to head off the impending recession is to bring the government's deficit under control. Otherwise, high interest rates will choke off economic activity.

It is true that an antideficit move (lower spending or higher taxes) will lower interest rates by moving the IS curve inward, but the result will be to worsen, not head off, an incipient recession.

through the multiplier. But the increase in GDP will increase the demand for money: more money is needed for transactions purposes. Since the Fed does not change the money supply, we know that interest rates must rise to offset the increase in money demand that came from the increase in GDP. This increase in the interest rate will reduce investment demand and net exports and thus offset some of the stimulus to GDP caused by government spending. The offsetting negative effect is crowding out, as discussed in Chapter 4.

**NUMERICAL EXAMPLE**   Explicit numerical values for the effect of changes in the money supply and government spending can be obtained from the numerical IS-LM curves in Equations 7.6 and 7.8. By setting the right-hand side of Equation 7.6 equal to the right-hand side of Equation 7.8 and solving for $Y$, the level of income that satisfies the IS-LM model can be written as a function of constants, the real money supply, and government purchases:

$$Y = 2,015 + 2.887 \frac{M}{P} + 1.155 \ G. \tag{7.9}$$

Suppose that the money supply $M$ is $900 billion, government spending $G$ is $1,200 billion, and the price level is 1. Then Equation 7.9 says that GDP is equal to $6,000 billion. Plugging this value for $Y$ into either the equation for the IS curve or the equation for the LM curve, we find that the interest rate is 5 percent. Figure 7.6 is drawn accurately to scale for these values. Equation 7.9 says that an increase in government spending of $1 billion increases real GDP by $1.155 billion, for a ratio of 1.155. Compare this effect with the government spending multiplier of 2.1 that we found in Chapter 6 in the model where investment is exogenous and net exports depend only on income. The effect is smaller when we take account of the financial system, because interest rates rise and crowd out investment spending. As for monetary policy, if the price level is 1, then an increase in the money supply of $1 billion increases GDP by $2.887 billion.

## The Relative Effectiveness of Monetary and Fiscal Policies

Monetary and fiscal policies differ in how effective they are in shifting aggregate demand. Two important issues must be faced in determining the relative effectiveness of monetary and fiscal policies:

1. The sensitivity of **investment demand** and **net exports** to interest rates (the magnitudes of the coefficients $d$ and $n$ in Equations 7.1 and 7.2)
2. The sensitivity of **money demand** to interest rates (the magnitude of the coefficient $h$ in Equation 7.3)

The issues can be given graphical interpretations in terms of the *slopes* of the IS curve and the LM curve. First, think about it intuitively.

**WHEN IS FISCAL POLICY RELATIVELY WEAK?**   An expansionary fiscal policy will have a relatively *weak* effect on aggregate demand if interest rates rise a lot and have a large negative effect on investment and net exports. The fall in investment and net exports will offset the positive effect that government spending has on aggregate demand. The fall in investment and net exports will be large under two circumstances, corresponding to the two issues listed above.

1. If the sensitivity of investment demand and net exports to the interest rate is *very large*, then a rise in interest rates will reduce investment and net exports by a considerable amount.
2. If the sensitivity of money demand to the interest rate is *very small*, then the increase in money demand that arises as a result of the increased government expenditures will cause a big rise in the interest rate. (The

small interest-rate sensitivity means that the interest rate has to move a lot.)

Another property of the economy that affects the strength of fiscal policy is the spending multiplier (see page 164). A high spending multiplier means more effective fiscal policy. However, if the economy has a high interest sensitivity of investment and net exports and low interest sensitivity of money demand, even a very large multiplier will not result in strong effects of fiscal policy.

**WHEN IS FISCAL POLICY RELATIVELY STRONG?** An expansionary fiscal policy will have a relatively *strong* effect on aggregate demand if interest rates don't rise by much or have a small effect on investment and net exports. This occurs under circumstances opposite to those listed under weak fiscal policy.

**WHEN IS MONETARY POLICY RELATIVELY WEAK?** An expansionary monetary policy will have a relatively *weak* effect on aggregate demand if the drop in interest rates that occurs when the money supply is increased is small or has little influence on investment and net exports. This occurs under two circumstances.

1. If the sensitivity of investment demand and net exports to interest rates is *very small*, then investment is not stimulated much by the decline in interest rates.
2. If the sensitivity of money demand to interest rates is *very large*, then the increase in the money supply doesn't cause much of a drop in interest rates. (A small drop in interest rates is sufficient to bring money demand up to the higher money supply.)

**WHEN IS MONETARY POLICY RELATIVELY STRONG?** An expansionary monetary policy will have a big effect if interest rates fall by a large amount and stimulate investment and net exports in a big way. This occurs under circumstances opposite to those listed under weak monetary policy.

## The IS-LM Interpretation

The IS curve is relatively flat if investment demand and net exports are very sensitive to interest rates, because small changes in interest rates are associated with big changes in demand. Conversely, the IS curve is relatively steep if investment and net exports are very insensitive to interest rates.

The LM curve is relatively flat if money demand is very sensitive to interest rates, because small changes in interest rates are sufficient to reduce

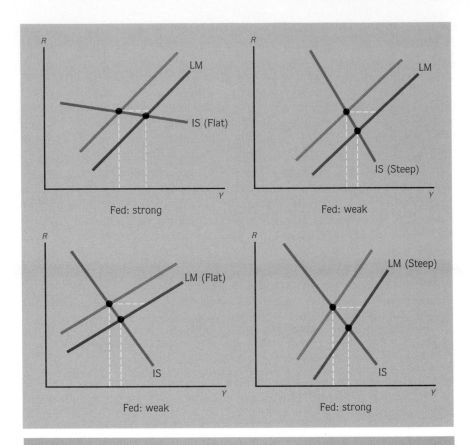

**FIGURE 7.8**   Monetary Policy: Weak or Strong?

The four IS-LM diagrams illustrate all the possibilities that have bearing on the strength of monetary policy. Each of the diagrams shows the effect of an outward shift in the LM curve under different conditions. In some cases the IS curve is flat; in other cases the LM curve is flat. In every case the LM curve is shifted outward by the same amount. At the bottom of each diagram the answer to "Weak or strong?" is given.

money demand when it increases with a change in income. Conversely, the LM curve is relatively steep if money demand is very insensitive to interest rates.

With these IS slope and LM slope interpretations of the interest-rate sensitivities, we now can review the previous discussion using the IS-LM diagrams. Eight cases exhaust the possibilities, and are shown in Figures 7.8 and 7.9.

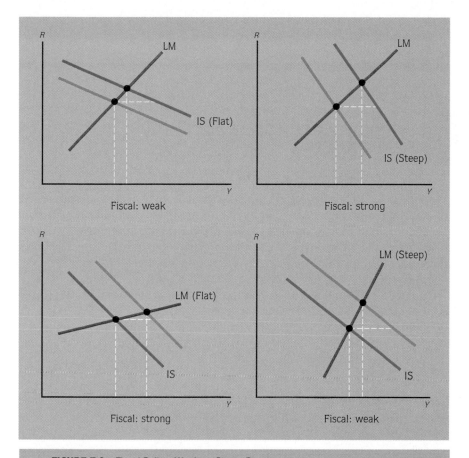

**FIGURE 7.9** Fiscal Policy: Weak or Strong?

The four IS-LM diagrams illustrate all the possibilities that have bearing on the strength of fiscal policy. In some cases the IS curve is flat; in other cases the LM curve is flat. At the bottom of each diagram the answer to "Weak or strong?" is given. In all four cases, we assume that the multiplier is the same. A higher multiplier makes fiscal policy stronger in all cases.

## WEAK AND STRONG POLICY

1. Monetary policy is strong if the IS curve is flat or the LM curve is steep. Monetary policy is weak if the IS curve is steep or the LM curve is flat.
2. Fiscal policy is strong if the IS curve is steep or the LM curve is flat. Fiscal policy is weak if the IS curve is flat or the LM curve is steep.

**3.** For given slopes of the IS and LM curves, fiscal policy is more effective if the spending multiplier is large.

# 7.5 DERIVING THE AGGREGATE DEMAND CURVE

With the IS-LM diagrams, we are in a position to derive formally the aggregate demand curve previewed in Chapter 6. The aggregate demand curve, shown in Figure 7.10, tells how much people will demand at a given level of prices. The higher the price level, the less aggregate demand. Hence, like most demand curves in microeconomics, the aggregate demand curve is downward-sloping.

Except as a mnemonic device to remember which way the aggregate demand curve is sloped, the analogy between the standard microeconomic demand curve and the aggregate demand curve of macroeconomics is a weak one, and should not be emphasized. The ideas behind the aggregate demand curve are much different from those that underlie the typical de-

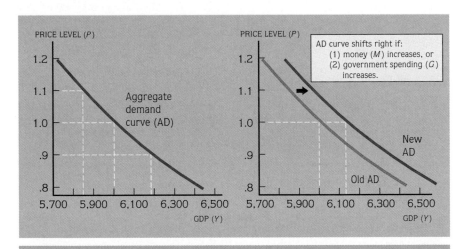

**FIGURE 7.10**   The Aggregate Demand Curve

On the left is the aggregate demand curve (AD). It shows that aggregate demand is a declining function of the price level. On the right, the aggregate demand curve shifts to the right if either monetary or fiscal policy is expansionary.

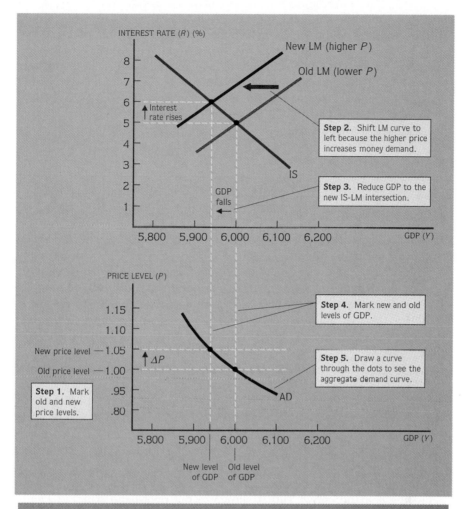

**FIGURE 7.11**   Derivation of the Aggregate Demand Curve

An increase in the price level shifts the LM curve to the left. This raises interest rates and reduces output. The resulting negative relationship between the price level and GDP is summarized in the aggregate demand curve.

mand curve of microeconomics. In particular, it is important to keep in mind that the financial system—the demand and supply for money—lies behind the aggregate demand curve.

Figure 7.11 is a graphical derivation of the aggregate demand curve. In the top part of Figure 7.11 is an IS-LM diagram. Recall that changes in the price level shift the LM curve. Higher prices shift the LM curve to the left, and lower prices shift the LM curve to the right.

Now suppose that the price level rises. The LM curve shifts to the left; this raises the interest rate, lowers investment and net exports, and ultimately lowers GDP. Thus, a higher price level reduces GDP because it increases the demand for money. The increase in demand causes interest rates to rise and causes GDP to fall. The different values for the price level and GDP constitute the aggregate demand curve.

## THE AGGREGATE DEMAND CURVE

1. The aggregate demand curve shows what level of GDP will be demanded given a particular price level.
2. The two economic principles governing the aggregate demand curve are spending balance and the equality of the demand and supply of money.
3. The aggregate demand curve slopes downward. A higher price level means that real money balances are lower and therefore that the real interest rate is higher. This means that investment, net exports, and GDP are lower.
4. An increase in government spending or an increase in the money supply shifts the aggregate demand curve to the right.

## Monetary and Fiscal Policies

Changes in the money supply and in government spending both shift the aggregate demand curve. This is shown in the right-hand panel of Figure 7.10. Suppose that the money supply increases. At a given price level, aggregate demand rises. More money means that a lower interest rate equates money demand with money supply. A lower interest rate stimulates more investment and net exports, which in turn require a higher level of GDP for spending balance. In sum, the aggregate demand curve shifts to the right when the money supply increases.

Fiscal policy also shifts the aggregate demand curve. An increase in government spending shifts the aggregate demand curve to the right. At a given price level, more government spending means more aggregate demand. Conversely, a decrease in government spending shifts the aggregate demand curve to the left.

The effects of fiscal and monetary policies are easily seen by using

Equation 7.9. Recall that this equation gives the level of income that satisfies spending balance and money market equilibrium. But that is precisely the aggregate demand curve. All combinations of $Y$ and $P$ that satisfy Equation 7.9 for given values of $G$ and $M$ represent points on the aggregate demand curve. Inspection of this equation shows clearly that increases in $M$ or $G$ will increase $Y$ for a given $P$; they shift the curve outward.

## REVIEW AND PRACTICE

### Major Points

1. Investment depends on the interest rate. A higher interest rate discourages some investment projects and lowers total investment.

2. Net exports also depend negatively on the interest rate. A higher interest rate attracts capital from other countries; this drives up the exchange rate and lowers net exports.

3. The IS-LM model determines output, the interest rate, and each of the spending components in the short run. It does not require that the economy operate at its long-run equilibrium.

4. The IS curve shows the level of GDP that brings spending balance for each interest rate. It slopes downward.

5. The LM curve shows the interest rate that brings equality of supply and demand in the money market for each level of GDP. It slopes upward.

6. The IS-LM model answers questions about the effect of policy over the period when it is reasonable to consider prices fixed. Monetary expansion raises output and lowers the interest rate. Fiscal expansion raises output and raises the interest rate.

7. Fiscal policy is most effective when money demand is sensitive to the interest rate and investment and net exports are insensitive to the interest rate.

8. Monetary policy is most effective when money demand is insensitive to the interest rate and investment and net exports are responsive to changes in the interest rate.

9. The intersection of the IS and LM curves tells the levels of GDP and the interest rate for a given price level and fiscal-monetary policies. It corresponds to a point on the aggregate demand schedule.

10. The aggregate demand schedule shows all combinations of GDP and the price level that satisfy spending balance and money market equilibrium for given fiscal and monetary policies. Fiscal and monetary expansions shift aggregate demand out.

## Key Terms and Concepts

interest rate
real interest rate
nominal interest rate
investment function

net export function
monetary policy
fiscal policy
IS curve

LM curve
aggregate demand curve

## Questions for Discussion and Review

1. What are the important determinants of aggregate demand? For each one, trace out what happens if it changes.

2. Why does a higher price level raise the interest rate? What could the Fed do to prevent the increase in the interest rate?

3. Explain why the IS curve slopes downward.

4. Explain why the LM curve slopes upward.

5. Explain why the aggregate demand curve slopes downward.

6. Why does a decrease in government spending reduce interest rates?

7. Why does an increase in the money supply reduce interest rates?

## Problems

### NUMERICAL

1. This problem pertains to the numerical example in the box on page 178. Set the price level equal to 1.
   a. Use the algebraic form of the aggregate demand curve to find the leval of GDP that occurs when the money supply is $900 billion and government spending is $1,200 billion.
   b. Use the IS curve and the LM curve to find the interest rate that occurs in this same situation. Explain why you get the same answer in each case.
   c. Use the consumption function to find the level of consumption, the investment function to find the level of investment, and the net export function to find the level of net exports for this same situation.
   d. Show that the sum of your answers for consumption, investment, government spending, and net exports equals GDP.
   e. Repeat all the previous calculations if government spending increased to $1,300 billion. How much investment is crowded out as a result of the increase in government spending? How much are net exports crowded out?

2. Savings and budget deficits: This problem pertains to the numerical example in the box on page 178 and makes use of the answers to Problem 1.
   a. Set government spending at $1,200 billion and the money supply at $900 billion. Calculate government saving (the budget surplus). Calculate the level of private saving, and show that private saving plus government saving plus rest of world saving equals investment.

b. Now repeat your calculations for a level of government spending equal to $1,300 billion. Does private saving plus government saving plus rest of the world saving still equal investment? How does each element in the identity change?

c. Explain why private saving increases as a result of government spending. In light of your calculations evaluate the statement: "Government budget deficits absorb private saving that would otherwise be used for investment purposes."

3. Compare the IS curve in the numerical example on pages 186–187 with the IS curve that you get by increasing the coefficient $d$ to 4,000.

a. What is the slope of each IS curve? Explain in words why the second IS curve is flatter.

b. For which value of $d$ does an increase in the money supply have a larger effect on output? Why?

c. Derive the aggregate demand curve in each case. Which has a larger coefficient for $M/P$? Is this consistent with your answer to Part b?

4. Compare the LM curve in the numerical example on page 187 with the LM curve you get by increasing the coefficient $h$ to 2,000.

a. What is the slope of each LM curve? Explain why the slopes are different.

b. For which value of $h$ is monetary policy more powerful? Explain.

c. Derive the aggregate demand curve in each case. Which has a larger coefficient for $M/P$? Is this consistent with your answer to Part b?

5. Using the numerical example of the chapter, calculate values for the money supply and government spending that will increase GDP from $6,000 billion to $6,100 billion *without changing the interest rate at all*.

6. The following relationships describe the imaginary economy of Nineland:

$$Y = C + I \qquad \text{(Income identity)}$$

$$C = 90 + .9Y \qquad \text{(Consumption)}$$

$$I = 900 - 900R \qquad \text{(Investment)}$$

$$M = (.9Y - 900R)P \qquad \text{(Money demand)}$$

$Y$ is output, $C$ is consumption, $I$ is investment, $R$ is the interest rate, $M$ is the money supply, and $P$ is the price level. There are no taxes, government spending, or foreign trade in Nineland.

The year is 1999 in Nineland. The price level is 1. The money supply is 900 in 1999.

a. Sketch the IS curve and the LM curve for the year 1999 on a diagram and show the point where interest rate and output are determined. Show what happens in the diagram if the money supply is *increased* above 900 in 1999.

b. Sketch the aggregate demand curve. Show what happens in the diagram if the money supply is *decreased* below 900 in 1999.

c. Derive an algebraic expression for the aggregate demand curve in which $P$ is on the left-hand side and $Y$ is on the right-hand side.

d. What are the values of output and the interest rate in 1999 when the money supply is 900?

**ANALYTICAL**

1. Higher interest rates reduce investment and increase foreign saving. What then must happen to the combination of private and government saving after a rise in interest rates? If neither private nor government saving depends directly on the interest rate, how can this change come about?

2. Graphically derive the LM curve, as in Figure 7.5, using instead a graph that relates money demand to income. (Hint: Put the stock of money on the vertical axis and income on the horizontal axis, and set this diagram above the LM diagram.)

3. Consider the following statements: (i) The IS curve is steep when investment is insensitive to the interest rate. (ii) The LM curve is flat when money demand is insensitive to income. (iii) The LM curve is flat when money demand is sensitive to the interest rate. (iv) The IS curve is flat when the marginal propensity to consume is high.
   a. Explain in words why each of these statements is true.
   b. Confirm algebraically that each statement is true. (Hint: Begin by deciding which coefficient in the model changes. Then show how a change in that coefficient affects the expression for the slope of the IS or LM curve.)

4. Suppose that money demand depended only on income and not on interest rates.
   a. What does the LM curve look like in this case?
   b. Show graphically that $G$ has no effect on the level of output $Y$. What does $G$ affect?
   c. Show the same thing algebraically. Explain why the LM equation becomes the aggregate demand equation.

5. Show how the IS curve and the LM curve can be shifted to get an increase in output without a change in interest rates. What kind of mix of monetary and fiscal policy is needed to do this? Will a reduction in interest rates while holding output constant do this?

6. Suppose that two administrations, one Democratic and the other Republican, both use fiscal and monetary policy to keep output at its potential level, but that the Democratic administration raises more in taxes and maintains a larger money supply than the Republican administration.
   a. On a single graph, show how the IS and LM curves of these two administrations differ.
   b. Indicate whether the following variables will be higher under the Democratic or Republican administration, or whether they'll be unchanged: consumption, investment, net exports, government saving, and private saving.
   c. Under which administration will foreign holdings of U.S. financial assets grow more slowly?

# MacroSolve Exercises

The model "ISLM, Closed Econ" in the **SELECT MODEL** option is described by the following equations: $Y = C + I + G$, $C = 120 + .63Y$, $I = 1,000 - 2,000R$, $M/P = (.1583 - 1,000R)$. We assume that the tax rate is .1875, so that the marginal propensity to consume out of disposable income is .77538. The equations for the IS and LM curves for this model are derived in the text as

$$\text{IS curve: } R = .560 - .000188Y + .0004G.$$

$$\text{LM curve: } R = .0001583Y - .001M/P.$$

1. *Policy Decisions 2001.* You have been hired to work for the Federal Reserve Board and your friend has been hired to work at the Council of Economic Advisers. Although you recognize the Fed's independence, you and your friend decide that is no reason for you not to agree on the current model of the U.S. economy. You both settle on MacroSolve's "ISLM, Closed Econ." First, get warmed up. Tabulate the results with no change in government spending or the money supply. Confirm that the equilibrium interest rate and the level of GDP are 5 percent and $6,000 billion, respectively.

   a. Your friend is asked by the Council to investigate fiscal policy. Of course you work together. Increase government spending by $50 billion. Display the shifts of the curves (using the **DISPLAY MODEL** option) to ensure that you understand what is being done. Tabulate the model to find the value of the government spending multiplier. Do you get the same multiplier if you increase government spending by $100 billion? Why?

   b. Convince your friend that this spending increase would be a mistake. How much is investment crowded out by a $50 billion increase in government spending? Explain why investment is crowded out by the increase in government spending. If the money supply is constant, under what conditions on the slopes on the IS and LM curves would there be no crowding out in response to an increase in government spending?

   c. Your friend argues that it would not be so bad if the Fed would just accommodate a bit. What is your opinion? By how much would the Fed have to increase the money supply to keep investment from being crowded out at all (i.e., keeping investment constant at $900 billion)? If the Fed increases the money supply to avoid any crowding out of investment, what is the value of the government spending multiplier? The size of this multiplier depends on only two parameters in the model. Which are they?

   d. Just after you finish your simulations, the Fed chair calls you in and says a major spending bill ($100 billion) has just been signed by the President. The chair asks you what the Fed should do. What do you say?

2. a. Using the "ISLM, Closed Econ" model, increase the responsiveness of investment to interest rates. Increase government spending by $50 billion (with no change in the money supply). Is the multiplier larger or smaller in this case than in Question 1? What happens to the IS curve? How is fiscal policy affected? Explain in words why the multiplier changes the way it does.

   b. Reset the interest elasticity of investment to its default value, but decrease the marginal propensity to consume. What happens to the IS curve? How is the fiscal policy affected? Explain in words why the multiplier is larger or smaller than it was in your answer to Question 1.

c. Reset the marginal propensity to consume to its default value. Increase the interest elasticity of money demand. What happens to the IS curve? How is fiscal policy affected? Explain in words how and why the multiplier changes.

3. Select the "ISLM, Closed Econ" model and reset all parameters to their default values using the **CHANGE PARAMS** option.
   a. By how much does GDP increase when the money supply is increased by $50 billion? What is the value of the money multiplier?
   b. If the interest responsiveness of money demand is increased, explain why a given change in money supply has a smaller effect on GDP than in the default case. What happens to the LM curve? How is monetary policy affected?
   c. Reset the interest responsiveness of money demand to its default value, and decrease the interest elasticity of investment. How is monetary policy affected? Explain why this reduces the effect on GDP of a $50 billion increase in the money supply.
   d. Is output more responsive to changes in the money supply when the income elasticity of money demand is increased? How is monetary policy affected? Explain why.

4. Select the "ISLM, Open Econ" model and reset all parameters to their default values using the **CHANGE PARAMS** option.
   a. By how much does GDP increase when the money supply is increased by $50 billion? What is the value of the money multiplier? How does it compare to the value of the money multiplier in the closed economy of MacroSolve Questions 1–3. Explain why monetary policy is in general more or less effective when an economy is open than when it is closed.
   b. If the interest responsiveness of net exports increases, determine whether a $50 billion change in the money supply now has a larger or smaller effect on GDP, and explain why.
   c. Reset the interest responsiveness of net exports to its default value. Supposing imports become less sensitive to changes in income, determine whether a $50 billion change in the money supply now has a larger or smaller effect on GDP, and explain why.

5. Select the model "ISLM, Open Econ" and reset all parameters to their default values using the **CHANGE PARAMS** option.
   a. By how much does GDP increase when the government spending is increased by $75 billion? What is the value of the expenditure multiplier? How does it compare to the value of the expenditure multiplier in the closed economy of MacroSolve Questions 1–3? Explain why fiscal policy is in general more or less effective when an economy is open than when it is closed.
   b. If the interest responsiveness of net exports increases, determine whether a $75 billion change in the government spending now has a larger or smaller effect on GDP, and explain why.
   c. Reset the interest responsiveness of net exports to its default value. Supposing imports become less sensitive to changes in income, determine whether a $50 billion change in the government spending now has a larger or smaller effect on GDP and explain why.

# CHAPTER
# 8

# The Adjustment Process

The long-run growth model developed in Chapters 3 and 4 is one of the basic components of our complete model. The aggregate demand schedule is the second. In this chapter, we will develop the third major component—the adjustment process that takes the economy from a position out of equilibrium (described by the aggregate demand analysis) back to potential.

## 8.1   PRICE STICKINESS AND THE DETERMINATION OF OUTPUT AND UNEMPLOYMENT IN THE SHORT RUN

Recall from Chapter 6 that prices are sticky in the sense that they are not adjusted quickly by firms in response to demand conditions. Firms wait a while before adjusting their prices. For some period of time, therefore, the price level is stuck at a predetermined level. During this time sellers are waiting to see how demand conditions change before they adjust their prices again. Prices eventually adjust, of course, but not until the next time period—a year or quarter later, for example. For the time being the price level is predetermined.

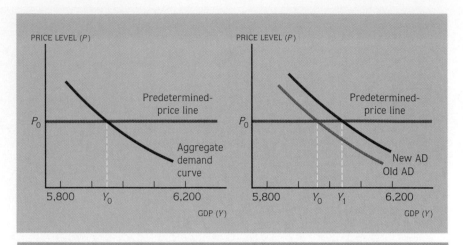

**FIGURE 8.1**   Determination of Output with a Predetermined Price

The horizontal line shows the price level predetermined for this year at level $P_0$. This year's output is at the intersection of the aggregate demand schedule and the horizontal line. In the left-hand panel the intersection occurs at the level of output marked $Y_0$. In the right-hand panel the aggregate demand curve shifts right, and output expands from $Y_0$ to $Y_1$.

## Determination of Output

Figure 8.1 shows how aggregate demand determines output at a predetermined price. The aggregate demand curve is the same one derived in the previous chapter. The predetermined price is shown by the horizontal line drawn at $P_0$. GDP is determined by the point of intersection of the aggregate demand curve and the flat predetermined-price line.

Shifts in the aggregate demand curve—caused perhaps by changes in the money supply or government spending—will result in increases or decreases in output. A rightward shift in the aggregate demand curve results in an expansion of output; a leftward shift in the aggregate demand curve results in a contraction of output.

The price level inherited from last year, when combined with the aggregate demand curve, determines the level of output this year. Output can be below potential output. Then we will observe unemployment and other unused resources. Or output can exceed potential output. These two possibilities are shown in Figure 8.2, where we have superimposed the vertical potential GDP line to indicate potential. In the left-hand panel of Figure 8.2, output is below potential. In the right-hand panel, output is above potential.

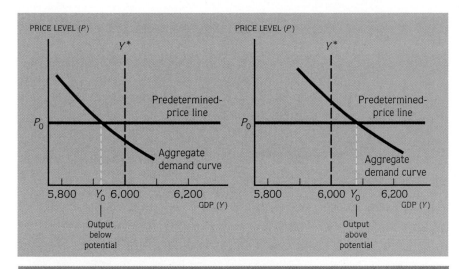

**FIGURE 8.2**   GDP Can Be above or below Potential GDP

On the left, the level of output is below potential. On the right, the level of output is above potential. Both of these positions will exert pressure on firms to change prices. On the left there is pressure to lower prices. On the right there is pressure to raise prices.

Although the price level doesn't change immediately when firms find themselves producing above or below equilibrium, there is an incentive to move back to equilibrium, as we discussed in Chapter 6. The incentive is to lower prices when output is below potential and to raise prices when it is above potential. A price cut will raise output and a price increase will lower output, so these moves will take the firm and the economy back toward equilibrium.

These adjustments lead to a changed price level for the *next year* or period—not this year. For example, if output is above potential in the year 2001, then the price level will be higher in 2002. When the aggregate demand curve is drawn to determine output for the year 2002, the predetermined price will be drawn at a higher level. If the intersection of the aggregate demand curve for the year 2002 and this new price line is still not at an output level equal to potential, then there will be a further adjustment in prices, but this will not occur until the year 2003. The process continues this way until aggregate demand equals potential output, at which point the desire for firms to adjust their prices will no longer be present. Whether or not the process converges depends on the explicit price-adjustment process, which we consider in the next section.

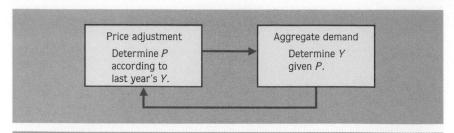

**FIGURE 8.3**  Dynamic Analysis and Predetermined Variables

The price adjustment process is shown on the left. It determines the current price level based on the recent past level of output. Then the aggregate demand schedule, shown on the right, determines the level of output given the price level.

The process by which the price level changes from one year to the next is *dynamic* in the sense that the variables are changing from one period to the next. The impact of a change in the money supply, for example, has effects on the price level that take place over a number of years. The model that we use to describe this dynamic process is an example of a **dynamic model.** The dynamic model is illustrated in Figure 8.3.

## DETERMINATION OF OUTPUT IN THE SHORT RUN

1. In the short run, the price level is predetermined. It can change over time, but in a given year, the events of that year have almost no impact on the price level.
2. The level of output is predetermined by the point on the aggregate demand schedule corresponding to the price level.
3. In the short run, output can be below or above its potential level.

## Determination of Unemployment

We noted in Chapter 3 that Okun's law establishes a close relation between real GDP and unemployment. When an adverse shock shifts the aggregate demand curve inward, real GDP falls. Figure 8.4 starts with that shift and shows how it generates an increase in unemployment as well. From the decline in real GDP, the lower left-hand diagram converts it into a change in the percentage deviation of GDP from potential, $(Y - Y^*)/Y^*$. Then the right-hand part of the diagram computes the resulting increase in unemployment by applying Okun's law.

A number of important mechanisms are at work in the process described in Figure 8.4. If GDP declines, employers need a smaller amount of labor input. They cut the length of the workweek, they reduce the intensity of work, and they cut the size of the workforce. Most of the workers who are laid off become unemployed. In addition, people who are looking for work find it harder to locate jobs. Because of the importance of hours

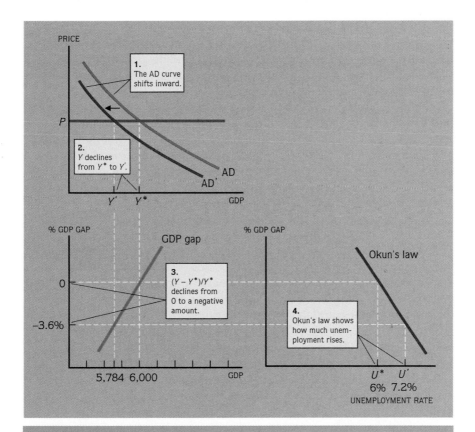

**FIGURE 8.4**   Determination of Unemployment

The upper left-hand diagram shows the aggregate demand curve in its original position and after it shifts inward. Output declines from $Y^*$ to $Y'$. The lower left-hand diagram translates the GDP decline into percentage terms. The right-hand diagram uses Okun's law to show the amount of increase in unemployment that occurs as a result of the decline in GDP.

reductions and the common pattern of retaining workers during temporary declines in demand (called *labor hoarding*), a 3 percent decline in GDP is associated with only a 1 percentage point increase in unemployment. This close negative relation is one of the most reliable generalizations that macroeconomists have found. Whenever some force causes GDP to decline, you can be confident that unemployment will rise.

## 8.2   PRICE ADJUSTMENT

Decisions about prices are made by individual firms. But moving from the level of the firm to the macro level is tricky. Finding a good way to model aggregate price adjustment has occupied much of the research time of macroeconomics during the last 30 years.

Firms adjust their prices in response to conditions in their markets. If demand has been strong and they are producing more than they think is appropriate given their current prices, they will raise their prices. If demand has been weak and they are producing less than is appropriate, they will lower their prices. When we look at the process in terms of aggregate variables—GDP and the price level—prices will tend to rise when GDP has been above potential and will tend to fall when it has been below potential. We have already mentioned this aspect of price adjustment in illustrating the dynamic analysis in the previous section.

Specifically, if demand in the previous period $Y_{-1}$ is greater than $Y^*$, then the price level $P$ in this period will be raised (the subscript $-1$ indicates the previous period). Conversely, if demand in the previous period $Y_{-1}$ is below $Y^*$, then the price level $P$ will be bid down. The percentage difference $(Y_{-1} - Y^*)/Y^*$, measures the pressure on prices to change. Note that because $P$ depends on $Y_{-1}$, it is *predetermined*, or set, according to demand conditions prevailing in the recent past.

Firms make their price decisions with the prices of their inputs in mind. The most important input is labor. Hence, the behavior of the wage rate is a major determinant of price adjustment. Wages tend to rise when conditions in the labor market are strong. Remember that when real GDP is high relative to potential, unemployment is low and employment is high. These are conditions that are likely to lead to rising wages. Wage pressure comes at the same time as the direct pressure on prices, and these two pressures combine to give a relation between the deviation of GDP from potential and inflation.

Economic intuition and historical experience both support the notion that market pressure, as measured by $(Y_{-1} - Y^*)/Y^*$, and inflation should be related. There is a different way to think about the relationship. Suppose a firm and its workers realize that it is in their mutual interest to raise the level of employment. In terms of Figure 5.6, they find themselves at a level of employment below equilibrium, where the value of the workers' time (measured by the labor supply schedule) is below the value of what they produce (measured by the labor demand schedule). The firm decides to produce more output. How can the firm get its customers to buy the additional output? By setting or accepting a lower price. Thus, even firms that do not have much control over their own prices will obey the positive relation between the output gap, $(Y_{-1} - Y^*)/Y^*$, and price change.

A second factor in the rate of change of prices is inflationary momentum. In times when prices have risen consistently in past years, they will rise this year even if there is no pressure from the market. For example, in 1989, prices rose by almost 5 percent even though the economy was not much above full employment. Inflation in 1987 and 1988 was also close to 5 percent, so it appears that the continuation of inflation at about the same level was the result of momentum. Macroeconomists usually explain the momentum in terms of expectations: When firms and workers expect a particular level of inflation, that level occurs even without any pressure from the output or labor market.

The relation between the change in the price level and its determinants is called the **Phillips curve,** after A. W. Phillips, the British economist who first studied it.[1] We let the Greek letter $\pi$ stand for the rate of inflation, $(P - P_{-1})/P_{-1}$, and let $\pi^e$ stand for the expected rate of inflation. The Phillips curve is

$$\pi = \pi^e + f\frac{Y_{-1} - Y^*}{Y^*} \qquad \text{The Phillips Curve} \qquad (8.1)$$

The coefficient $f$ controls the slope of the Phillips curve. If $f$ is large, inflation responds quickly and the economy moves back to equilibrium rapidly. If $f$ is small, a difference between output and potential persists for many years. Figure 8.5 shows the Phillips curve as a graph. When inflation becomes expected at the rate $\pi^e$, it shifts the Phillips curve upward.

The Phillips curve with the expectation term has an important property: If real GDP is above potential GDP on a permanent basis, then the rate of inflation will never stop increasing. As actual inflation rises, expected inflation $\pi^e$ will also begin to rise; as firms see actual inflation increasing, they will begin to expect higher inflation. But then actual inflation will have to

---

[1]Phillips fit this type of relationship to data for the United Kingdom from 1861 to 1957. The fit was very good. Phillips actually related percentage changes in wages to the unemployment rate. See "The Relationship between the Unemployment Rate and the Rate of Change in Money Wage Rates in the United Kingdom, 1861–1957," *Economica,* November 1957, pp. 283–299.

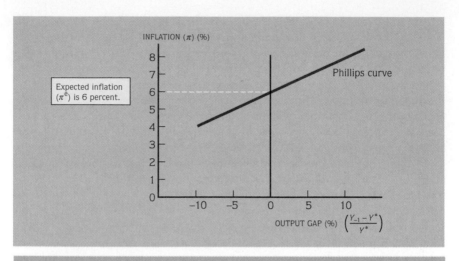

**FIGURE 8.5** The Phillips Curve

The higher GDP is relative to potential, the higher will be the rate of inflation. When GDP is below potential, the Phillips curve predicts that inflation will be below the expected rate of inflation. In booms, when GDP is above potential, actual inflation will exceed expected inflation. The higher the expected rate of inflation, the higher is actual inflation. The expectational shift is important in explaining persistent inflationary periods, like the 1970s, in the United States.

be even higher, because GDP can exceed potential only if actual inflation exceeds expected inflation. This property of the price adjustment equation is called the **natural rate property.** The terminology comes from the property that if real GDP is brought above its potential level $Y^*$, then the inflation rate will rise and the price level will accelerate. There is no way for real GDP to be held constantly above its natural level without inflation constantly rising with no limit. In an economy with reasonably stable prices, the level of real GDP will tend to be near potential on the average.

This relationship between expectations and price adjustment was developed in the late 1960s by Edmund Phelps of Columbia University and independently by Milton Friedman. At the time that they developed the relationship, most economists had not considered the role of expectations in the Phillips curve. Friedman presented his controversial theory at a large convention of economists in his presidential address to the American Economic Association in 1967.[2] At that time inflation in the United States was

---

[2]Friedman's presidential address is found in Milton Friedman, "The Role of Monetary Policy," *American Economic Review,* March 1968, pp. 1–17. Phelps first published his results in Edmund S. Phelps, "Money Wage Dynamics and Labor Market Equilibrium," *Journal of Political Economy,* July–August 1967, pp. 678–711.

pretty low and many economists were skeptical of the Friedman-Phelps theory. As it turned out, data that became available in the 1970s showed that Friedman and Phelps were right.

Figure 8.6 shows that there has been a stable Phillips curve price-adjustment relationship of the type proposed by Phelps and Friedman for the period since 1960. The vertical axis measures the amount by which inflation exceeds expectations and the horizontal axis measures the gap between actual and potential GDP. According to the theory, this relationship should be stable over time and upward-sloping. Although there are many exceptions, the general positive slope is evident. Note in particular the reduction in inflation during the 1982 slump and the increase in inflation during the 1968 boom.

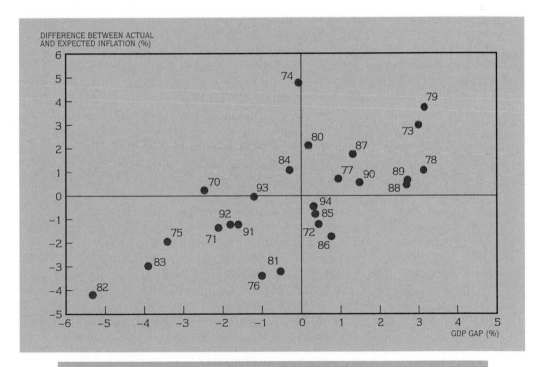

**FIGURE 8.6**   Price Adjustment in the United States Since 1960

The horizontal axis shows the percentage departure of GDP from potential. The vertical axis shows the amount of inflation relative to the expected amount. Years in the upper right are ones when output was above potential and inflation exceeded expectations. Years in the lower left are recession years when output was low and inflation subsided. Most, but not all, years fit into the general pattern predicted by the price adjustment relationship. In this diagram, the expected inflation rate is measured as the inflation rate in the year before.

## What Determines Expected Inflation?

So far we have said nothing about what determines the expected inflation term $\pi^e$ in the price adjustment equation. The simplest idea is that $\pi^e$ depends on past inflation. Suppose, for example, that GM thinks the price of Fords will increase at 60 percent of last year's inflation rate. Suppose that all firms forecast inflation in the same way. Then the expectation $\pi^e$ would be set to .6 $\pi_{-1}$. Equation 8.1 would then become

$$\pi = .6\pi_{-1} + f\frac{Y_{-1} - Y^*}{Y^*}. \tag{8.2}$$

This Phillips curve is based on a particularly simple model of expected inflation. It is a rational way for firms to forecast in an economy where abnormally high inflation does not persist year after year but eventually returns to lower inflation, so that the best guess of inflation would be simply a fraction (like .6) of past inflation. On the other hand, if high inflation tended to last a long time, then people would expect inflation to come down only a little, if at all. They might simply extrapolate from the past and set $\pi^e = \pi_{-1}$. In more complex inflationary environments, expected inflation would probably also be more complex, perhaps depending on inflation in the previous two years. Or firms might attempt to guess where inflation was heading based on what they expect the Fed to do with the money supply: if they expect the Fed to start fighting inflation, they might forecast less inflation.

But even if firms attempted to bring future policy changes into their calculations, the past rate of inflation would probably have some influence on expected inflation. Firms know that some prices will continue to rise for a while, even if they suspect that the Fed would start fighting inflation right away. Some price increases would already have been announced by other firms, and these will take place in any case. Wage setting is also a factor in price decisions, and wage increases negotiated in earlier years would continue. For unionized workers, such as the United Automobile Workers, the contractual nature of wage setting is conspicuous. Contracts frequently set wages for as much as three years in advance. The contracts of different unions are set at different times. When wage contracts are renegotiated, they are influenced by the wages currently being paid to workers under contracts settled in previous years and by what other workers are likely to get in upcoming years. The expected rate of increase in prevailing wages is thus influenced by past wage decisions, as well as by upcoming wage decisions. Overlapping contracts mean that expected inflation will be related to past inflation even if forecasters are perfectly rational and forward-looking.

We will come back to alternative ideas about expected inflation in Chapter 16. For now we will use Equation 8.2 as our Phillips curve.

Note that the larger the difference between real GDP and potential GDP, the faster will be the change in inflation. Suppose, for example, that the coefficient *f* in the price adjustment equation is equal to .2. This value implies that a 5 percent gap between real GDP and potential GDP, which lasts for one year, will reduce the rate of inflation by 1 percent. When output is 10 percent below normal for one period, the rate of inflation will be reduced by 2 percent. Of course, the price adjustment equation works the other way around as well. If real GDP is above potential GDP, then there will be an increase in inflation.

## PRICE ADJUSTMENT

1. The process of price adjustment moves the economy toward potential GDP. When the price level is too high, GDP is less than potential, prices fall, demand rises, and eventually full employment is restored.
2. If no inflation is expected, the price adjustment equation relates the rate of inflation to the deviation of GDP from potential.
3. Under conditions of expected inflation, the price adjustment relation is shifted upward by the amount of the expected inflation. When output exceeds potential, inflation will exceed expected inflation.
4. A simple model of expected inflation is that expected inflation is given by a fraction of last year's inflation.

## COMBINING AGGREGATE DEMAND AND PRICE ADJUSTMENT

The aggregate demand curve, in combination with price adjustment, governs the dynamic response of the economy to a change in economic conditions. We will look first at what happens to the economy when the money supply is increased, then at what happens with an increase in government spending.

### Response to Monetary Stimulus

We assume that the economy starts out with zero inflation and that GDP equals potential GDP. The increase in money initially pushes the aggregate

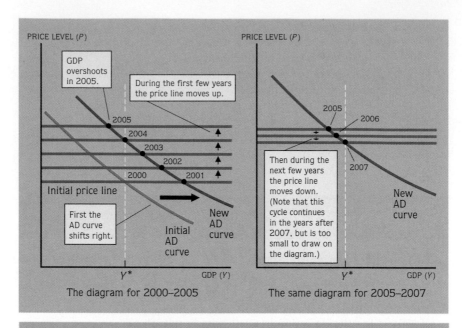

**FIGURE 8.7**   Aggregate Demand and Price Adjustment

The diagram on the left shows the aggregate demand curve intersecting the predetermined-price line at potential GDP ($Y^*$). After an increase in the money supply the aggregate demand curve shifts to the right. Then the price line begins to shift up and output declines. GDP falls below potential GDP, but then there is downward pressure on prices and the price line begins to fall. This is shown in the diagram on the right, where we see the same aggregate demand curve during the years after 2005.

demand curve to the right and increases output. Gradually prices rise to bring the economy back into equilibrium at potential GDP. We now trace out the path of GDP as it returns to potential.

On the left in Figure 8.7 we show the aggregate demand curve intersecting the predetermined-price line. The intersection occurs where output is equal to potential GDP. Suppose that this is the situation in the year 2000 but that starting in 2001 the Fed increases the money supply. The aggregate demand curve shifts to the right, and GDP expands. The economy goes into a boom during 2001, and GDP is above potential GDP. Since the stimulus to aggregate demand comes from monetary policy, we know from the IS-LM model of the last chapter that the interest rate falls, and this stimulates investment spending. Then GDP expands via the multiplier. All this occurs during the year that the money supply increased.

With firms now operating above potential, they will adjust their prices upward. The price line will shift up. We can easily calculate the exact size of the price adjustment in 2002 using the price adjustment equation (8.2): Calculate the inflation rate $(P - P_{-1})/P_{-1}$ associated with the level of GDP for 2001. Multiply this inflation rate by the previous price level $P_{-1}$ to get the absolute change in the price level, $P - P_{-1}$, and hence the price level $P$ for 2002. We shift the price line in Figure 8.7 upward by the amount of this price increase. Assuming that the Fed does not increase the money supply again, the same aggregate demand curve continues to apply in 2002. Thus, the new point of intersection of aggregate demand and the price line occurs at a lower level of output compared with 2001. The economy moves up and to the left along the aggregate demand curve.

What is happening in the economy? At a higher price level more money is demanded by people for transactions purposes. But since the Fed doesn't increase the money supply again, this puts upward pressure on the interest rate. The higher interest rate reduces investment below what it was in 2001, and this reduction has multiplier effects throughout the economy. Hence, GDP falls.

According to Figure 8.7, GDP is still above potential in 2002. Thus there will be another upward adjustment in the price level. This time the price adjustment will be the sum of two effects, which correspond to the two terms on the right-hand side of the price adjustment equation (8.2). Because there was inflation the year before, there will be expectations of continuing inflation in 2002. This factor will add to inflation. On the other hand, output is no longer so far above potential. The contribution from that term in the Phillips curve will be smaller. In the scenario in Figure 8.7, the price rises by about the same amount in 2003 as it did in 2002. Again the aggregate demand curve doesn't move, so output falls again in 2003. As before, the interest rate rises because of the increased demand for money, and this reduces investment.

If output is still above potential or if inflation is still above where it started in 2000, there will be another price adjustment. Hence, GDP will continue to fall. Note that GDP will fall below—overshoot—potential because expected inflation keeps the price line moving up.

This overshooting is shown in Figure 8.7, where GDP falls below potential GDP in the year 2005. But this overshooting creates forces that reverse the decline in GDP and bring it back to potential GDP. When actual GDP is below potential GDP, the depressed economic conditions place downward pressure on prices. As firms bid down their prices, the price line begins to shift down as shown in the right-hand panel of Figure 8.7. As the price line reverses its previous movement and begins to shift down, GDP will start to rise. The process continues period after period until GDP eventually returns to potential. In Figure 8.7 we show GDP getting very close to potential in the year 2006, though there are tiny movements (too small to see on the diagram) after that. By 2007 inflation has returned to zero, where it began in 2000, though the price level has permanently increased. The price level has increased by the same proportion that the money supply increased by.

Note how the graphical analysis in Figure 8.7 is divided into different phases. In the first phase (on the left), the price line is moving up. In the second phase (on the right), the price line is moving down. The graphs are divided into phases because it is confusing to draw in the new price lines for 2006 and 2007 on top of the previous ones for 2000 to 2005. Rather, the new diagram on the right has simply omitted the previous price lines. The important thing to imagine visually is that the price line moves up and then reverses direction and moves down. Getting out a pencil and paper and shifting the price lines yourself will convince you of the dynamic nature of this adjustment process. Alternatively, this movement can be shown very nicely with computer graphics in which you can see the price line moving gradually over time. The MacroSolve Exercises at the end of this chapter are designed to illustrate this process.

The fact that the economy returns to potential GDP, as shown in Figure 8.7, is a key result in macroeconomic theory. In the long run, an increase in money does not increase GDP. The increase in money eventually leads to an increase in the price level of the same proportion. This raises interest rates back to where they were before the monetary expansion and eventually reduces investment back to its original level. Note that all other variables—except the price level—are also back to where they were before the increase in the money supply. In the long run the increase in money had no effect on real variables. Thus, our complete model has the property of monetary neutrality in the long run. But money is not neutral in the short run. It has a powerful effect on output in the short run before prices have had a chance to adjust. The same analysis holds in reverse for a decline in the money supply. This short-run effect of money on real output distinguishes our complete model from the real business cycle model of fluctuations. Recall that in that model monetary neutrality holds even in the short run.

Figure 8.8 is a summary of how GDP and the price level move over time according to the calculations given above. The upper panel shows GDP and the lower panel shows the price level. Note how GDP returns to potential after overshooting and how the price level permanently rises to a new level.

## Response to Fiscal Stimulus

Fiscal policy works a little differently from monetary policy. Suppose that in the same circumstances government spending, rather than the money supply, is increased in 2001. Again the aggregate demand curve shifts to the right just as in Figure 8.7, and GDP rises. But now, from IS-LM results of the previous chapter, we know that interest rates rise during the first year and

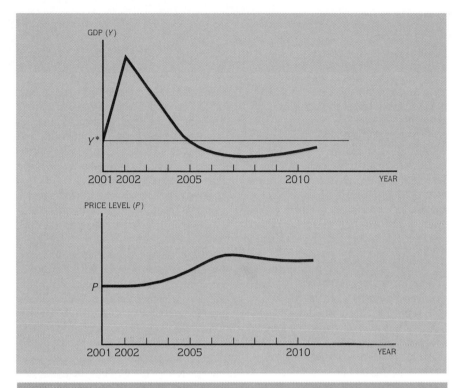

**FIGURE 8.8** GDP and the Price Level after an Increase in Money

The top panel shows GDP and the bottom panel shows the price level. Time (years) is measured on the horizontal axis of both diagrams. The money supply is increased in the year 2001, which is marked on both graphs. At first, GDP increases and the price level does not move. In 2002 the level of GDP begins to fall, and the price level begins to rise. The movements continue in 2003 and so on until GDP returns to potential GDP, and the price level rises by the full proportion that the money supply increases.

thus crowd out investment, net exports, and consumption and partly offset the stimulus to demand from government spending. As the price level begins to rise, interest rates rise further, and more investment and exports are crowded out.

In the long run, GDP returns to potential GDP even though government spending has been increased. As a result we know that in the long run, investment spending, net exports, and consumption must have been reduced by the same amount that government spending was raised. Otherwise, the income identity would be violated. In the long run, fiscal policy completely crowds out investment spending, net exports, and consumption. The rise in

## NEW RESEARCH IN PRACTICE
## The Other Complete Model

The complete model in this book is a simplified version of a model that has evolved over the sixty years since Keynes published his ideas in his *General Theory.* The model is used by the most practical macroeconomists to study the effects of policy changes and other shocks to the economy. The Federal Reserve Board uses its own version of the complete model to formulate monetary policy. Data Resources, Inc., is a private economic consulting firm with its own version of the complete model to make forecasts and perform analyses for its clients.

Research economists at universities, starting in the early 1980s, have developed a different complete model. Finn Kydland of Carnegie-Mellon University and Edward Prescott of the University of Minnesota introduced the new complete model in an influential paper published in 1982. Since then, economists such as Marianne Baxter, Martin Eichenbaum, Robert King, and Charles Plosser have pushed the new complete model to an advanced stage. Today's younger research economists are adding rapidly to the literature on the new complete model.

The new model is often called the **real business cycle model.** This name doesn't convey much about the model. How is it related to the complete model of this book?

Our complete model and the real business model have much in common. They both start from the same growth model—the economy's ability to produce goods and services depends on the labor available, on capital, and on technology. People's willingness to work depends on the real wage. The two models share the same life-cycle view of consumption, the same ideas about invest-ment, and the same analysis of the influence of the global economy. The models agree that fluctuations can be the result of changes in taxes and government spending and of spontaneous shifts in consumption. Despite its name, there are versions of the real business cycle where monetary shocks influence the economy.

There are two crucial differences between our complete model and the real business cycle model. First, in the complete model, prices are sticky. When a shock occurs, prices do not respond immediately. In the real business cycle model, prices are not sticky and do respond immediately.

The second crucial difference is that the real business cycle model does not consider unemployment. The model does not treat a recession as a time when larger numbers of people are searching for work but having trouble finding it. The model does consider recessions and explains why employment falls during them. But the explanation rests on the idea that wages and prices (and the interest rate) send signals to workers that recessions are unattractive times to work. That is, their labor supply functions are elastic with respect to wages and other market signals.

In the complete model, monetary policy can make an important contribution by offsetting spending shocks and thus stabilizing output and employment. Monetary policy also has to aim for stable prices. Solving these problems makes monetary policy prominent and challenging. In the real business cycle model, prices are flexible. Monetary policy affects only the price level; it can't change output or employment. Monetary policy can single-mindedly stabilize prices. There is nothing interesting or challenging about monetary policy.

the price level increases the demand for money; this leads to higher interest rates and less investment spending, net exports, and consumption. Again, notice that in the long run, our complete model preserves the policy implications of the long-run growth model. But since shifts in demand are capable of causing employment to diverge from its equilibrium level in the short run, both fiscal and monetary policy can influence real output in the short run.

## Algebraic Derivation

The response of the economy to a change in the money supply can also be analyzed with algebra. Suppose the aggregate demand curve is

$$Y = 3,401 + 2.887 \frac{M}{P}, \tag{8.3}$$

where we have set government spending to $1,200 billion. We combine this aggregate demand curve with the price adjustment equation (8.2) to describe the evolution of the economy. We then use Equation 8.2 along with Equation 8.3. The algebraic calculations proceed in flip-flop fashion, just like the graphical analysis: Take the price level as given, use Equation 8.3 to find output $Y$, and plug the value of output into Equation 8.2. Calculate the inflation rate $\pi$ and the price level $P$ for the next year. Then go back to Equation 8.3 with the new price level, determine a new output level, and so on. The answers you get at each stage are the same as the ones that can be read off the numerical scales in Figure 8.7.

We have now completed our first description of the complete macro-economic model. In the short run, the price level inherited from the previous year, together with the current aggregate demand schedule, determines the level of output. In the medium run, the process of price adjustment moves the economy closer to potential GDP. Eventually, the economy will reach potential GDP. Our next step is to use this complete model to examine the important issues of monetary and fiscal policy.

## THE MOVEMENT TO POTENTIAL GDP

1. The aggregate demand curve and the price adjustment line govern the movement to potential GDP. After being pushed away from potential GDP by monetary policy or fiscal policy—whether toward slack or overfull employment—the economy will eventually reach potential GDP.
2. Because expected inflation responds to past inflation, the economy overshoots potential GDP. However, it will still eventually reach potential GDP.
3. An increase in the money supply increases GDP in the short run, but eventually this effect wears off as the price level rises. In the long run an increase in the money supply has no effect on GDP.

4. An increase in government spending also increases GDP in the short run, though there is some reduction in the other components of spending: investment, net exports, and consumption. In the long run, the stimulus to GDP is completely offset by a decline in the other components as interest rates rise. In the long run fiscal policy completely crowds out the other components.

## REVIEW AND PRACTICE

### Major Points

1. In the long run, the economy moves to potential GDP.
2. In the short run, the price level is predetermined. GDP is determined by aggregate demand at the predetermined price level.
3. The process of price adjustment takes the economy to potential GDP over time. When output is above potential, prices rise; when output is below potential, prices fall.
4. If inflation becomes expected by the public, the price adjustment schedule is shifted upward by the amount of the expected inflation.
5. The economy reaches potential GDP through the repetition of price adjustment year after year. Each year, conditions in the previous year determine the price level coming into the year. Then the aggregate demand curve determines GDP.
6. Because expected inflation fluctuates according to recent actual inflation, the economy overshoots its potential on the way to its final resting point at potential.

### Key Terms and Concepts

| | | |
|---|---|---|
| predetermined price level | price adjustment | expected inflation |
| dynamic model | Phillips curve | natural rate property |

### Questions for Discussion and Review

1. Explain how the Phillips curve is derived from a model of relative price setting. What happens to the Phillips curve if firms expect inflation?
2. Explain why money is neutral in the long run but not in the short run.
3. Does government spending completely crowd out private investment and net exports in the long run? What about the short run? Why?

4. Why does the economy overshoot potential GDP when expectations of inflation depend on last year's inflation?

5. What would happen to inflation if policymakers attempted to hold unemployment below the natural rate year after year?

6. If firms expect the Fed to start fighting inflation with an aim of bringing it to zero, will their expectations of inflation suddenly drop to zero? Why?

## Problems

### NUMERICAL

1. Suppose the economy has the aggregate demand curve

$$Y = 3,401 + 2.887 \frac{M}{P},$$

and the price adjustment schedule

$$\pi = 1.2 \left( \frac{Y_{-1} - 6,000}{6,000} \right).$$

The money supply is $900 billion.

a. Plot the aggregate demand curve and the potential GDP line. Explain why the *aggregate demand curve is not a straight line.*

b. If $P_0 = .5$, what will $Y_0$ be? Will this place upward or downward pressure on prices?

c. Compute the path of the economy—that is, calculate GDP, the price level, and inflation—for each year until GDP is within 1 percent of potential.

d. Diagram the economy's path on the demand curve plotted in Part a. Then draw your own version of Figures 8.7 and 8.8. (You may assume that inflation was initially zero). From these graphs, does the economy overshoot or converge directly to equilibrium?

e. Assume now that inflation is given by $\pi = .6\pi_{-1} + 1.2 \, [(Y_{-1} - 6,000)/6,000]$. Compute the path of the economy for the first five years, and diagram the economy's path as in Part d. Now is there overshooting?

f. In Part e, what does the $.6\pi_{-1}$ term in the price adjustment equation represent? Explain the relationship between this term and overshooting.

2. Again, suppose that the model of the economy is given by

$$Y = 3,401 + 2.887 \, M/P$$

$$\pi = .6\pi_{-1} + 1.2 \, [(Y_{-1} - 6,000)/6,000]$$

a. For what value of $M$ will GDP equal potential? Assuming that $M = \$850$ billion, calculate output, inflation, and the price level for years 0 through 5.

b. Using the numerical IS-LM equations given in Chapter 7, find out what happens to the interest rate, consumption, investment, and net exports in each of these years. What is the long-run equilibrium value for each of these variables?

c.  Note that income, consumption, and investment tend to overshoot and under-shoot at the same time. Using the IS-LM diagram, explain why this is necessarily so. Why isn't the same true of net exports?

## ANALYTICAL

1.  In view of Okun's law, is it possible for both output and the unemployment rate to increase from one year to the next? Explain.

2.  According to the price adjustment equation (8.2), is inflation a predetermined variable? Explain.

3.  Using the expectations-augmented Phillips curve, explain what happens when the unemployment rate decreases for one year and then returns to the natural rate. Then describe what happens when the unemployment rate stays below the natural rate year after year.

4.  From a position of potential GDP and zero inflation, the government increases defense spending. Describe qualitatively, using words and graphs but no algebra, what happens to GDP, the price level, interest rates, consumption, investment, and net exports. Assume at first that expectations of inflation remain at zero. Then describe how your answers change if expectations of inflation depend on last year's inflation.

5.  Suppose that there is a sudden and permanent decline in potential GDP. Describe the behavior of prices, output, interest rates, consumption, investment, and net exports.

6.  Suppose that output is below potential output in year 0. Prices that year are given by $P_0$. In year 1 (with the level of potential output unchanged) the Fed stimulates the economy by shifting the aggregate demand curve until it intersects the point $(P_0, Y^*)$.

    a.  Sketch the aggregate demand curve for years 0 and 1. Describe the action taken by the Fed.

    b.  Assume that the price adjustment process is given by Equation 8.2. If inflation in year 0 was zero, how will prices behave in year 1? Sketch the price adjust-ment curve for year 1.

    c.  Explain why output in year 1 will be above potential.

    d.  In which direction should the Fed have shifted the aggregate demand curve in order to set $Y_1 = Y^*$? Is it possible to say?

    e.  Given the Fed's action, is it possible to say whether prices will increase or decrease in year 2? Why or why not?

7.  The Phillips curve originally described a relationship between inflation and un-employment. In this problem we look at some of the properties of the Phillips curve.

    a.  Use Okun's law and the price adjustment equation (8.1) to derive a relation-ship between inflation and unemployment. Is inflation related to current or past values of unemployment? Sketch a graph of this relationship with inflation on the vertical axis and unemployment on the horizontal axis.

    b.  How would a change in $Y^*$ shift the curve? How about a change in $U^*$?

c. How would a change in $\pi^e$ shift the curve?

d. In view of your answers to Parts b and c, how might the Phillips curve have actually shifted in the 1970s and again in the 1980s? Explain.

8. When thinking about the adjustment process, remember that underlying the aggregate demand curve are the IS and LM curves.

a. During the adjustment process, is it the IS or LM curve that moves? Why does it move?

b. Assume that the economy is initially in equilibrium and then the IS curve is shifted out. Using the IS and LM graphs, show the adjustment process (i) for the case when the economy returns directly to equilibrium and (ii) for the overshooting case.

c. Repeat Part b for the case where the LM curve is initially shifted out.

9. Suppose that at the end of 1997 $Y$ is equal to potential, $P = 1.2$, and $M = \$1,080$ billion. Assume that prices in 1997 have risen by 5 percent. The aggregate demand and price adjustment equations for the economy are given by:

$$Y = Y_0 + 2.887\ M/P$$

$$\pi = \pi^e + f[(Y_{-1} - Y^*)/Y^*]$$

a. What is the real money supply? What is the nominal money supply?

b. Suppose the Fed wishes to maintain output at a potential for each of the years 1998 through 2001. If $\pi^e = \pi_{-1}$, what are the required increases in the real and nominal money stocks for each of the four years? Repeat your calculations for $\pi^e = .6\pi_{-1}$.

c. Qualitatively, how would your answers to Part b differ if the Fed expected government spending to increase in each of these years?

## MacroSolve Exercises

In this chapter, we continued to use the basic model of aggregate demand. To it, we added consideration of potential output, and price adjustment when output differs from potential output. The price adjustment schedule that we added has the form

$$\pi = .8\ [(Y_{-1} - Y^*)/Y^*] + \pi^e.$$

1. Suppose first that $\pi^e = 0$ (i.e., there is no expected inflation). This model is available in the **SELECT MODEL** option as "AD/PA zero exp. $\pi$." Change government spending by $\$100$ billion and make a table of multipliers (the change in GDP per dollar change in government spending) for each time period. Explain in words why the steady-state (or long-run) multiplier differs from its value in Equation 7.9.

2. Now select the "AD/PA, Closed Econ" model, in which inflation expectations are determined in the following manner: $\pi^e = .4\pi_{-1} + .2\pi_{-2}$. Repeat the analysis of Question 1 with this model. Explain why the time taken for the multiplier to settle down to its long-run value differs from the previous case.

3. Is adjustment of the price level to a change in the money supply faster or slower when inflation expectations respond to past inflation (as in Question 2) than when they do not (as in Question 1)? Explain why.

4. *Policy Decisions 2001:* You have been hired by the Bundesbank, the central bank of Germany. You were hoping to help in the continuing transition of the former East Germany into a market economy. But the president of the Bundesbank finds out you did well in macroeconomics and that you kept your copy of MacroSolve. The last six years have seen continued trouble with the budget deficits, with constant pressure on the Bundesbank to ease policy. But the Bundesbank has remained tight trying to fight inflation.

   a. Use the dynamic model ("AD/PA, Closed Econ") to show what would be predicted to happen to interest rates, output, saving (which you can calculate as the differences between disposable income and consumption), and investment under an expansionary fiscal policy and a tight monetary policy.

   b. In order to defend the Bundesbank policies, the president of the Bundesbank asks you to prepare a comparison of the German experience with that of the United States in the years 1981 to 1986. Check the actual data for the U.S. economy during this period by plotting, tabulating, or graphing them to see if the theoretical predictions for these variables actually occurred. Were there any significant deviations from the model's predicted results? If so, give reasons to the Bundesbank president.

5. *Policy Evaluation 2001.* You have just been contacted by your old college buddy, who now serves as your counterpart in the United States Federal Reserve System. He is under pressure now because he paid less attention than you did in macroeconomics and because his MacroSolve disk caught a virus. He asks for your help in explaining to the Federal Reserve Board chair why the United States failed to perform as the model predicted with respect to interest rates, output, saving, and investment.

   a. To make his predictions he set all the parameter values to their default level, chose the "AD/PA, Open Econ" model, and then ran the same kind of expansionary fiscal and contractionary monetary policy you did using the "AD/PA, Closed Econ" model in Question 4. He is concerned with the time period 1981 through 1995, so use the **SET NUMBER OF PERIODS** option to extend your forecasts through 15 periods and show what his predictions would have been.

   b. Now compare these to the actual U.S. economic data by plotting, tabulating, or graphing them to see how they differed from the theoretical predictions for these variables. How might you explain these differences?

CHAPTER

9

# Macroeconomic Policy

Monetary and fiscal policy have powerful effects on the economy. Changes in the money supply or in government spending have an immediate impact on real GDP and a delayed impact on the price level. An increase in the money supply, for example, will stimulate output and employment in the short run, with inflation rising later, and real GDP eventually returning to normal.

In this chapter we take a systematic look at the effects of macroeconomic policy, that is, monetary and fiscal policy. The fact that monetary and fiscal policy have the potential to affect the economy suggests that these policies might be used to improve macroeconomic performance. We will want to investigate whether this is the case.

Sometimes there are economic **shocks** or **disturbances** to the economy that might call for policy response. We distinguish between two types of disturbances in this chapter: **aggregate demand disturbances** and **price disturbances.** An aggregate demand disturbance is some event other than a change in policy that shifts the aggregate demand curve. A price disturbance is some event that shifts the price adjustment relationship. The immediate effect of a price disturbance is to change the price level, unless policy acts to offset the disturbance. Another important policy problem is disinflation—getting the inflation rate down after it has been built into the economy. This chapter considers the appropriate policy responses.

# 9.1  SHOCKS AND DISTURBANCES TO THE ECONOMY

Unforeseen or unpredictable events are commonplace in the economy. At the most basic level, many of the relationships we use to describe the economy depend on human behavior, which is frequently erratic. Keynes used the term "animal spirits" to characterize the moods of businesspeople. Other economic relationships depend on technology; the money demand relationship, for example, depends on how technically advanced the financial system is. It seems that, no matter how successful we are in describing the systematic parts of economic behavior, there will always be some room for uncertainty, and thus for shocks and disturbances to our economic relationships. The model we developed in Chapters 3 through 8 would certainly be affected by such shocks.

## Shocks to Aggregate Demand

Consider two examples of shocks to the behavioral relationships of the extended model of aggregate demand:

1. Foreign demand suddenly shifts away from U.S. goods. Net export demand falls.
2. A new type of credit card makes it easier to get by with less cash. The money demand schedule shifts inward.

These two examples are illustrated graphically in Figure 9.1. The reduction in the demand for exports shifts net exports inward for each interest rate. The decline in money demand shifts the demand for money inward for each interest rate.

Disturbances can be distinguished according to whether they are temporary or permanent. This distinction is important for policymakers: A temporary disturbance might be ignored because its effects will disappear soon anyway. In practice it is difficult to distinguish between temporary and permanent shocks when they occur. In the following examples we will assume that the disturbances are permanent.

## Analyzing the Effects of Aggregate Demand Shocks

We will look at the effects of different kinds of disturbances on the aggregate demand curve. Before we start, we need to clarify one point. Monetary and

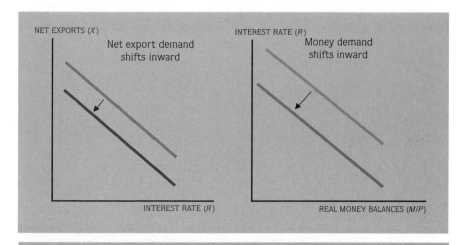

**FIGURE 9.1** Shocks: Inward Shifts in Net Exports and Money Demand

On the left, a shift in foreign demand away from U.S. goods shifts the net export schedule inward. On the right, technological change reduces money demand. The money demand function shifts inward.

fiscal policies are themselves important determinants of the shape and position of the aggregate demand curve; the curve is not just a property of the economy itself. In order to talk about the effect of a disturbance on the curve, we need to take a position on how monetary and fiscal policy will react to the disturbance. To start the discussion, we will assume that monetary policy keeps the money stock the same no matter what kind of disturbance hits the economy. We will also assume that fiscal policy—taxes and spending—does not respond at all to the disturbance. Both these assumptions are arbitrary and unrealistic, but they are a good place to start. Later (in Chapters 13 and 14) we will turn to more realistic assumptions about the Fed's response to disturbances.

Under our assumptions about monetary and fiscal policies, disturbances both to spending and to money demand, the two major components of our model of aggregate demand, shift the aggregate demand curve: the downward shift in net export demand pushes the aggregate demand curve to the left. The downward shift in money demand has the same effect as an increase in the money supply, which we know shifts the aggregate demand curve to the right.

These shifts in the aggregate demand curve have immediate impacts on real GDP, as shown in Figure 9.2.

From the analysis used in Chapter 8 we can trace out the full dynamic movement of the economy in response to the aggregate demand shocks.

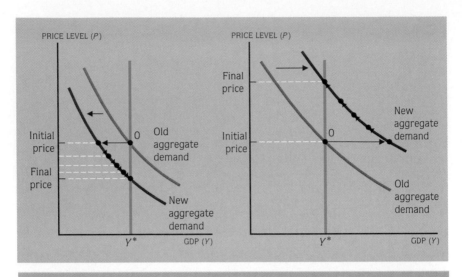

**FIGURE 9.2**   Disturbances Shift the Aggregate Demand Schedule

On the left, aggregate demand has shifted inward because of the decline in the net export schedule. On the right, aggregate demand has shifted outward because of the decline in money demand. On the left, GDP falls at first. Then the economy moves down and to the right along the AD schedule until it reaches equilibrium again at a lower price level. On the right, GDP rises at first. Then the economy moves up and to the left along the AD schedule until it reaches equilibrium again at a higher price level.

1.  With real GDP below potential GDP after the drop in net exports, the price level will begin to fall. Firms will have found that the demand for their products has fallen off and will start to cut their prices. This drop in the price level is shown in Figure 9.2 as a movement down and to the right along the aggregate demand (AD) schedule. The lower price level causes the interest rate to fall. With a lower interest rate, investment spending and net exports will increase. The increase in investment and net exports will tend to offset the original decline in next exports. This process of gradual price adjustment will continue as long as real GDP is below potential GDP. By the time that real GDP has again recovered and returned to potential GDP, investment and net exports will have increased by just the amount that net exports fell in the first place. The interest rate will be lower by enough to stimulate this much investment and net exports. In the long run, real GDP will be back to normal, but during the period of gradual price adjustment the economy will have gone through a recession with an increase in unemployment.

2. When the demand for money drops, the aggregate demand curve will shift outward. The interest rate will drop; investment, net exports, and consumption will rise. But higher GDP will cause prices to rise, and this will tend to raise the interest rate. Through this process of gradual price adjustment the economy will eventually return to normal. In the meantime, however, the economy will have experienced a period of inflation and a boom in economic activity.

To summarize the examples, in both cases there is a shock to aggregate demand that temporarily moves the economy away from potential GDP and sends the economy into either a boom or a recession. Through gradual adjustment of the price level, the economy eventually returns to normal.

## Shocks to the Price Level

The shocks considered so far had the effect of shifting the aggregate demand curve. Another type of shock occurs when the price level shifts. There are several reasons why this might occur.

1. The price of an input to the economy might suddenly rise; the best example is an increase in the price of oil, such as occurred in the 1970s and again in 1990. Suppose that there is a cutback in crude oil production and, as a result, an increase in the price of crude oil. This will tend to increase the price of all petroleum-related products. Moreover, prices in other energy industries will also tend to increase. Unless there is a fall in the price of other goods, when the price of crude oil rises there will be an increase in the overall price level.
2. A large group of workers—perhaps during a union negotiation—may get a wage increase that is abnormally high. When firms pass on the wage increase in the form of higher prices, there will be an upward shift in the price level—a price shock.
3. Firms might simply make a mistake and increase their prices, perhaps because they mistakenly expect an increase in inflation.

A price shock is shown in Figure 9.3. If monetary and fiscal policies do not change, then real GDP will fall below potential GDP. After the initial price shock the economy will be operating below its full-employment level at $Y_1$. With no increase in the money supply, this will in turn cause prices to fall as firms try to cut prices to increase sales. The fall in prices corresponds to a downward movement in the price adjustment curve, which will continue until real GDP is equal to potential GDP. Eventually, therefore, the economy will return to normal operating levels. In the meantime the price shock will have caused a recession. The period of recession will put downward pressure on prices and offset the original price shock.

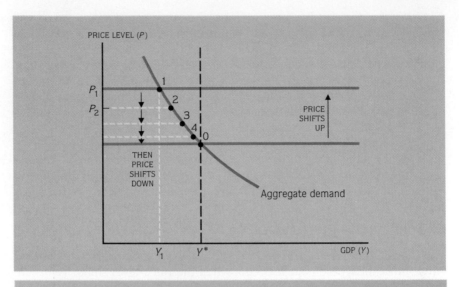

**FIGURE 9.3**   An Upward Shock in the Price Level

Real GDP is reduced when the price level jumps up; the economy moves to point 1, up and to the left along the aggregate demand curve. Then the process of price adjustment causes the economy to return gradually to its original equilibrium as the price level falls.

## ECONOMIC SHOCKS

1. There can be unexpected shifts in spending; for example, the amount of investment undertaken by businesses at any given interest rate might rise or fall.

2. There can be unexpected shifts in the money market; for example, the amount of money demanded by the public at any given interest rate might rise or fall.

3. Spending or money market shifts will in turn shift the aggregate demand curve. At first, real GDP will rise or fall. Later, as price adjustment occurs, real GDP will return to equilibrium and the price level will move to a permanently different level.

4. Prices may shift unexpectedly as well. When that occurs, real GDP will change at first. Then price adjustment will return the economy to its original equilibrium. Neither the price level nor GDP will change in the long run.

## Model Validation: Four Oil-Price Shocks

The U.S. economy was buffeted by four major oil-price shocks in the last 20 years. In 1973, the Arab oil embargo ushered in a huge increase in the price of crude oil and oil products. In 1978, the Iranian revolution and the Iran-Iraq war set off another large increase. At the beginning of 1986, the oil market collapsed. Finally, in 1990, the Iraqi invasion of Kuwait caused a near doubling of crude oil prices.

To measure the size of the shocks themselves, we can look at the retail price of gasoline, as reported in the consumer price index (CPI). The percentage changes in gasoline prices for the four episodes were:

| 1973–74 Arab Oil Embargo | 1978–79 Iranian Revolution | 1985–86 Market Collapse | 1989–90 Invasion of Kuwait |
|---|---|---|---|
| 35 | 35 | −22 | 14 |

Oil price shocks are clearly passed along into total inflation. The increases in the rate of inflation as measured by the overall CPI were:

| 1973–74 Arab Oil Embargo | 1978–79 Iranian Revolution | 1985–86 Market Collapse | 1989–90 Invasion of Kuwait |
|---|---|---|---|
| 4.8 | 3.7 | −1.7 | 0.6 |

Moreover, as the aggregate demand analysis suggests, the economy moves down along the AD schedule when a price shock occurs. The changes in GDP in the year following the shocks were:

| 1975 | 1980 | 1987 | 1991 |
|---|---|---|---|
| −.8 | −.5 | 3.1 | −.6 |

The effects are quite pronounced and confirm the predictions of the model in all four cases.

## 9.2 RESPONDING TO AGGREGATE DEMAND SHOCKS: STABILIZATION POLICY

In considering appropriate responses to aggregate demand shocks, let us first consider the case of a shift in the aggregate demand curve caused by a shift in the demand for money. A negative shock to money demand occurs because people want to hold less money at every interest rate and income level than they did before. In the early 1990s some economists at the Federal Reserve Board worried that a negative shift to money demand was occurring because people were putting less money into savings accounts at Savings

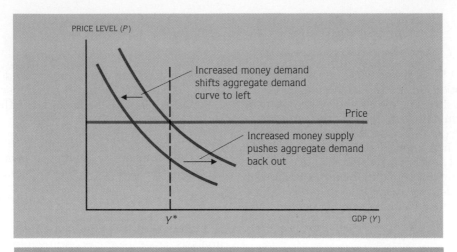

**FIGURE 9.4**   Increase in Money Demand

An increase in money demand shifts the aggregate demand schedule to the left; that is, it raises interest rates and reduces real GDP. Timely action by the Fed to increase the money supply could offset the reduction in GDP.

and Loans, as many of these institutions were being shut down. Positive shocks are also possible. For example, increased money demand could be caused by an increase in uncertainty about the future, creating the need for very liquid assets such as cash and demand deposits.

Figure 9.4 shows the effect of an *increase* in money demand. Unless the Federal Reserve takes action to offset such a change in money demand, interest rates will rise and the aggregate demand curve will shift to the left. What action would be appropriate for the Fed? An increase in the money supply to match the increase in money demand would exactly offset any leftward movement in the aggregate demand schedule shown in Figure 9.4. On the other hand, if a negative shock to money demand were occurring in 1990 and 1991, then the appropriate policy for the Fed would be to reduce money growth. In fact, money growth was below the Fed's targets in both 1990 and 1991.

Other types of aggregate demand shock raise many of the same issues for aggregate demand policy. Starting in 1990, around the time of Iraq's invasion of Kuwait, there was a sharp decline in consumer confidence, which caused a slump in consumption that pushed the aggregate demand schedule to the left. Without any policy response, we know from the discussion above that this would result in a temporary decrease in GDP followed by a period of decrease in the rate of inflation. Policymakers could avoid this instability by taking some action to increase aggregate demand: the money supply or government spending could be increased or, alternatively, taxes could be cut. Any of these actions would have the effect of bringing the aggregate demand schedule back to the right. Many economists argued that such actions were appropriate in 1991. The Fed expanded the money supply, interest rates fell, and the economy began to expand.

The type of aggregate demand policy outlined in these two examples is called **countercyclical stabilization policy,** because it attempts to counter those disturbances to the economy that otherwise would cause cyclical fluctuations in real GDP and the price level. Such a policy is also sometimes called *activist,* because the policymakers are actively manipulating the instruments of monetary and fiscal policies.

## When Do Macroeconomists Disagree about Stabilization Policy?

The underlying objective of policy in the above examples is to maintain a steady or stable level of aggregate demand. The importance of a stable aggregate demand has been recognized by most economists since the 1930s. Even economists who normally differ on other issues agree on the principle that it is desirable to maintain a stable growth of aggregate demand. Keynesians such as the late Walter Heller of the University of Minnesota and James Tobin of Yale University, who served together on President Kennedy's first Council of Economic Advisers, agree with monetarists such as Milton Friedman. As we showed in Chapter 2, the U.S. economy has been much more stable in the period following World War II—even if one includes the turbulent 1970s and early 1980s. Many economists feel that this improvement in macroeconomic performance is related to the recognition of the importance of stable aggregate demand growth.

Although macroeconomists agree on the basic goal of stable aggregate demand growth, there is disagreement about the means of achieving this goal. Monetarists argue that the most effective way to maintain a steady growth of aggregate demand is to keep the rate of money growth constant. But how does such a view make sense in light of our previous arguments that timely changes in the money supply can be used to offset disturbances to the economy?

Monetarists have no disagreement about the powerful effects that changes in the money supply can have on real GDP in the short run; for example, Milton Friedman has said, "Because prices are sticky, faster or slower monetary growth initially affects output. . . . But these effects wear off. After about two years the main effect is on inflation.[1] However, for a

---

[1]See *Newsweek,* July 12, 1982, p. 64.

number of reasons, monetarists feel that it is not possible to use monetary policy in the way that we illustrated. Their criticism of activist policy is that the impact of monetary policy occurs with a lag and the length of this lag is uncertain. Because of the lag, monetary stimulus or restraint may come too late. In an attempt to offset a decline in investment, the policy response may come after the recession is over, when the economy is recovering back to potential GDP. This might add to the expansion in economic activity and exacerbate the economic fluctuations. Figure 9.5 illustrates this possibility. Because of the practical difficulties of conducting monetary policy in an uncertain world, monetarists argue that attempts to manipulate monetary policy to offset disturbances to the economy could result in more rather than fewer fluctuations in economic activity.

A second argument of the monetarists against activist countercyclical policy is that the instruments of policy might be used to overstimulate the economy and bring about higher and higher rates of inflation. In our examples of countercyclical policy we never considered the possibility that policymakers might try to push the economy beyond its potential output, $Y^*$. But clearly this is feasible. With prices temporarily sticky, real GDP can be raised above potential output $Y^*$. The long-run consequence of such a policy will be a higher price level, but, in the short run, real GDP growth could appear quite attractive. The danger of such an inflationary policy becomes quite serious when policy decisions are made in a political environ-

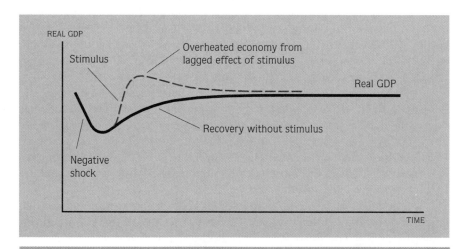

**FIGURE 9.5**   Lags in Policy

A change in the policy instrument that arrives too late might exacerbate the fluctuations in the economy.

ment, as usually happens in the United States. The long-run disadvantages of such a policy may be overlooked in favor of short-run advantages when election day nears.

A fundamentally different objection to countercyclical policy comes from economists who view GDP as being close to its potential value in recessions and booms as well as in normal times. Monetary policy mainly affects the price level in their view; it has no effect on output and employment. They think it would be frivolous to try to use monetary policy to offset a decline in employment in a recession. In the long run fiscal policy can affect employment and output in their model, but its use to offset fluctuations is probably undesirable.

## POLICY RESPONSE TO DEMAND SHOCKS

1. **When an aggregate demand shock occurs, monetary or fiscal policy can offset it. Whatever inward or outward shift of the aggregate demand curve has taken place can be reversed through a policy move in the opposite direction.**
2. **Though almost all economists agree on the desirability of stable aggregate demand, many believe that active policy might add to the instability rather than offset it. Monetarists generally oppose enacting policy that attempts to act against aggregate demand shifts.**
3. **Another argument against active policy comes from economists who believe that a systematic policy of offsetting demand disturbances won't have much effect on GDP.**

## 9.3  RESPONDING TO PRICE SHOCKS

The response to a price shock raises more difficult issues than does the response to a demand shock. Even under the best of circumstances—no lags or uncertainty in the conduct of policy—such a shock will inevitably affect either the price level or real GDP.

Suppose, for example, that there is a price shock of the type illustrated in Figure 9.6. As we discussed above, with no policy response, such a price shock tends to reduce real GDP and raise the price level. This is shown in the left-hand panel of Figure 9.6.

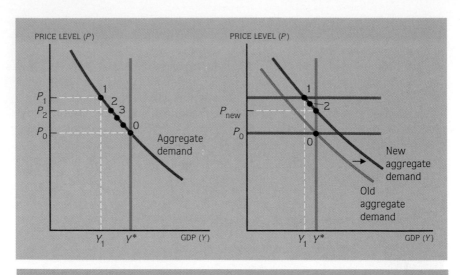

**FIGURE 9.6** Monetary Response to a Price Shock

On the left, monetary policy does not respond to the price shock. The shock raises the price level from $P_0$ to $P_1$. Output falls from $Y^*$ to $Y_1$. Then the price adjustment process starts. In the next year the price level drops to $P_2$. Eventually prices fall back to normal and output returns to potential output. On the right, monetary policy responds to the price shock. The money supply is increased and the aggregate demand curve moves outward. At the new intersection of the price line (point 1), there is less downward pressure on the price level because output at $Y_1$ is closer to potential than in the panel on the left. Assuming that the new aggregate demand curve is maintained, eventually the price level falls to the level marked $P_{new}$.

Now, suppose that the monetary authorities increase the money supply permanently in response to the price shock. As shown in the right-hand panel of Figure 9.6, this shifts the aggregate demand curve outward and tends to mitigate the downward fluctuation in real GDP. However, the increase in the money supply will accommodate the temporary increase in the price level. If output does not fall much below potential, there will be little downward pressure on the price level. The price level will stay high and never return to its previous level. As shown in the right-hand panel of Figure 9.6, the price line will remain at a higher level if the aggregate demand curve remains at its new higher position. In the sense that there is less downward pressure on the price level so that it never returns to its previous level, there is thus less long-run price stability with the policy that tries to offset the fluctuation in real GDP. In other words, with a price shock there is a trade-off between the stability of real GDP and the stability of the price level.

Policies that increase the money supply in response to positive price shocks are called **accommodative policies.** A policy that holds the money supply constant is called **nonaccommodative.** Figure 9.7 summarizes, for

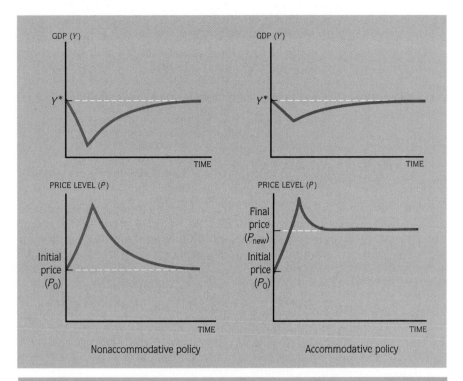

**FIGURE 9.7** The Response of the Price Level and GDP to Price Shocks for Accommodative and Nonaccommodative Policies

These charts summarize the calculations from Figure 9.6. The nonaccommodative policy is shown on the left and the accommodative policy is shown on the right. Output is more stable with the accommodative policy, but the price level is less stable.

the two policies, the behavior of GDP and the price level after a price shock. The plots show the results of the calculations of GDP and the price level from Figure 9.6. The accommodative policy is better in terms of GDP performance, but worse in terms of price level performance.

## POLICY RESPONSE TO PRICE SHOCKS

**1.** In the absence of a policy response (that is, with a nonaccommodative monetary policy), a positive price shock causes a rise in the price level and a sustained period of economic slack.

**2.** Price shocks create a serious problem for policy. If policy tries to limit the decline in GDP from a positive price shock, it will make the price level less stable. If it tries to head off the inflation, it will deepen the recession.

## Okun Gaps and Harberger Triangles

As in the microeconomic analysis of intervention in particular markets, the case for macroeconomic intervention rests on identifying some kind of market failure that can be corrected. Recessions appear to be market failures. The marginal product of labor exceeds the value of workers' time. The basic case for an expansionary intervention is that there is a social gain equal to the difference between marginal product and value of time. The most active debate in macroeconomics concerns the magnitude of that social gain. The late Arthur Okun of the Brookings Institution was a strong advocate of intervention to offset recessions; the social gain from correcting a recession is sometimes called the "Okun gap" as a result. Arnold Harberger of the University of Chicago pioneered the measurement of the social cost of market failure at the microeconomic level by measuring the area of the triangle formed between the supply curve and the demand curve when the quantity produced is below the equilibrium level. James Tobin of Yale University—another ardent proponent of aggressive policies to offset recessions—made the famous remark: "It takes a thousand Harberger triangles to fill an Okun gap." He meant that the social cost of a recession dwarfed the costs of the failures that occur in individual markets.

Other macroeconomists are less convinced of the importance of market failure. For example, Robert Lucas of the University of Chicago has calculated the welfare benefits from a policy of smoothing out the flucuations of the economy but keeping the same average level of production. He finds the benefits to be tiny.

## 9.4   MONETARY POLICY RULES

Our discussion of the appropriate response of monetary policy to shocks naturally gives rise to the question of whether the money supply is an exogenous variable, as we have been assuming all along. If the money supply responds to events in the economy, then it no longer can be exogenous, for it is determined in the model. Many different monetary policy rules have been proposed and adopted around the world. Holland runs its monetary policy to keep its exchange rate with Germany almost exactly constant. Germany, on the other hand, runs its policy to keep the German price level close to constant. The policy rule of the Federal Reserve in the United States is less clearly stated, but seems to aim to keep inflation at low rates while offsetting swings in unemployment as well.

Even if policymakers do not determine policy according to a mechanical formula, they do respond to economic events. Their behavior and its impact on the economy are therefore probably more accurately described by a systematic behavioral relationship. If so, we can think of the behavioral relationship as a policy rule. The money stock becomes an endogenous variable when we build a policy rule into the model. We will examine monetary policy rules in Chapters 13 and 14. We will also look at fiscal policy rules in those chapters.

## 9.5 SETTING MONETARY POLICY TO HIT A TARGET LEVEL OF GDP

One question sure to arise in setting monetary policy is what supply of money is needed to achieve a particular target level of real GDP. The real GDP target may be directly the goal of policy, or it may arise out of some other goal, such as a particular reduction in inflation. Recall that with the price adjustment equation, the price level is predetermined during the course of any particular year. Recall also that monetary and fiscal policies shift the aggregate demand curve to the right or left. The intersection of the aggregate demand curve with the price line gives the current value of real GDP. Hence, by changing monetary policy, the Fed can achieve just about any value of real GDP that it wants. Note that this ability of the monetary authorities to pinpoint real GDP perfectly needs to be qualified by the inherent uncertainty and lags in the effect of monetary policy that we discussed above. In addition, we know that aiming for a value of real GDP above potential GDP will soon result in an inflationary spiral.

So far we have used the aggregate demand curve to find a level of GDP for a given level of the money supply or government spending. Now we must use the curve in reverse. We want to find a level for the money supply for a given target level of GDP. The idea is illustrated in Figure 9.8. The economy is shown to be operating at potential output $Y^*$. Suppose that the Fed wants to set the money supply to push the economy to a lower target level $Y_1$. What level of the money supply should it choose? The answer, as shown in the right-hand panel of Figure 9.8, is to reduce the money supply to the level that sets the aggregate demand curve at a point of intersection with the predetermined-price line at the target level of output $Y_1$.

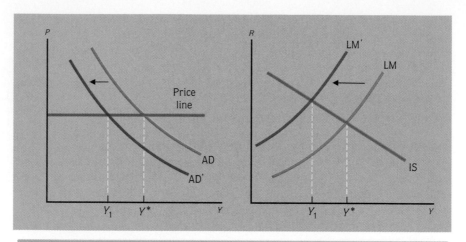

**FIGURE 9.8**   Aggregate Demand in Reverse: The Money Supply Is Set to Hit a
GDP Target

The left-hand panel shows the situation in the economy. Output is equal to potential output Y*. The
Fed wants to set the money supply so that output is reduced to the level $Y_1$. To do this it must shift
the aggregate demand curve inward from AD to AD'. As shown in the right-hand panel, the Fed
thus reduces the money supply by an amount that makes the LM curve shift in and intersect the IS
curve at a level of output equal to $Y_1$.

**NUMERICAL EXAMPLE**   Suppose that the aggregate demand curve is the
one that we studied in Chapter 7, Equation 7.9, namely,

$$Y = 2,015 + 2.887 \frac{M}{P} + 1.155G. \tag{9.1}$$

Suppose that Congress has set government spending $G$ at $1,200 billion and
that the predetermined price level $P$ equals 1. Potential GDP is $6,000 billion.
The Fed now wants to choose a money supply $M$ to bring actual GDP below
potential to $5,900. For $G = 1,200$ and $P = 1$, the aggregate demand curve
looks like this:

$$Y = 3,401 + 2.887M. \tag{9.2}$$

The level of the money supply is found by setting output $Y$ in Equation 9.3
equal to 5,900 and finding $M$. The answer is

$$M = \frac{5,900 - 3,401}{2.887} = \frac{2,499}{2.887} = 866. \tag{9.3}$$

Note how this calculation is just the reverse of setting $M$ to a value and finding $Y$, as we did in the numerical example in Chapter 7 (page 178).

 **9.6     DISINFLATION**

The problem of maintaining price stability in the face of price shocks is closely related to another type of price stabilization problem: that of bringing down the rate of inflation when it has become too high and has become incorporated into people's expectations and price-setting behavior. This is called the problem of **disinflation,** that is, reducing the rate of inflation. Though there has been little need for disinflation in the United States in the past decade, there was an important episode in the early 1980s, and there have been more recent episodes in other countries, such as Argentina in the early 1990s. Developing a disinflation policy requires close attention to the role of expectations in the Phillips curve.

The Phillips relationship, as we saw in Chapter 8, can be written

$$\pi = \pi^e + f\frac{Y_{-1} - Y^*}{Y^*}. \tag{9.4}$$

The most challenging problem of disinflation occurs in the case where the expected rate of inflation equals last period's inflation rate, $\pi^e = \pi_{-1}$. With this expectation of inflation, the only way that inflation can be reduced is by letting actual output $Y$ drop below potential output $Y^*$. Equation 9.4 states that the change in the rate of inflation over its previous level $\pi_{-1}$ depends on the percentage deviation of GDP from potential GDP.

The Phillips curve tells us that if the inflation rate is viewed by policymakers as being too high and in need of reduction, then some type of a recession is inevitable. The essential policy questions related to disinflation are how long and how deep the recession should be. In other words, how sharply should the policymakers reduce the policy instruments to bring about a path for real GDP that is consistent with the desired reduction in inflation?

## Alternative Disinflation Paths

Suppose that the rate of inflation is running at 10 percent and that the Fed wants to disinflate. Table 9.1 shows three alternative paths for the deviation of GDP from potential GDP, $(Y - Y^*)/Y^*$, and corresponding paths for the inflation rate. Year 0 shows the starting point, with inflation at 10 percent

**TABLE 9.1**   Three Paths for Inflation and the GDP Gap

|       | Path 1 | | Path 2 | | Path 3 | |
| --- | --- | --- | --- | --- | --- | --- |
| Year | GDP Gap | Inflation | GDP Gap | Inflation | GDP Gap | Inflation |
| 0 | 0 | 10 | 0 | 10 | 0 | 10 |
| 1 | 0 | 10 | −5 | 10 | −10 | 10 |
| 2 | 0 | 10 | −5 | 9 | −10 | 8 |
| 3 | 0 | 10 | −5 | 8 | −10 | 6 |
| 4 | 0 | 10 | −5 | 7 | −10 | 4 |
| 5 | 0 | 10 | −5 | 6 | 0 | 2 |
| 6 | 0 | 10 | −5 | 5 | 0 | 2 |
| 7 | 0 | 10 | −5 | 4 | 0 | 2 |
| 8 | 0 | 10 | −5 | 3 | 0 | 2 |
| 9 | 0 | 10 | 0 | 2 | 0 | 2 |
| 10 | 0 | 10 | 0 | 2 | 0 | 2 |

*Note:* The GDP gap is the deviation of GDP from potential measured in percent; that is, gap $= (Y - Y^*)/Y^*$ times 100. Inflation is the percentage change in the price level. Each path shows the GDP gap and inflation over a 10-year period. The calculations are made with the Phillips curve of Equation 9.1, with $f$ equal to .2. In the first path, policy holds real GDP at its potential level. Inflation stays at 10 percent. In the second path, real GDP is depressed below potential. Inflation drops steadily to 2 percent. When it reaches 2 percent, policy eases and GDP pulls back up to potential. In the third path, policy is even more contractionary at first; GDP is 10 percent below normal. Inflation drops to 2 percent sooner than in the second path.

and GDP equal to potential GDP. The Fed begins to take actions to reduce inflation in year 1. The values in Table 9.1 are obtained directly from the Phillips curve in Equation 9.4. For these calculations, we assume that the coefficient $f$ in Equation 9.4 is .2. Recall also that we assume the public believes inflation will persist unless the Fed contracts the economy. The simple model of expected inflation with this property that we use is $\pi^e = \pi_{-1}$. Inflation expected this year is last year's actual inflation.

The three alternatives given in Table 9.1 are all feasible for the Fed to undertake. Clearly, if the Fed can pick any value of output $Y$ it wants in the short run, it can also pick any value for the deviation of output from potential output, $(Y - Y^*)/Y^*$, since potential GDP $(Y^*)$ is exogenous. By setting the money supply so that the aggregate demand curve is in the appropriate place, the Fed can set output and hence the deviations of output from potential output to the desired level.

The three alternatives were selected to indicate the kind of choice that the monetary authorities have to make when faced with excess inflation. Perhaps the most important thing to note about the choices is that none of them is a good one. The latter two involve a recession, as the inflation rate is decreased. The first avoids a recession, but gets no reduction in inflation.

The second two paths are both successful in getting the inflation rate down from 10 to 2 percent. But there are important differences between the two paths. Path 2 involves a longer, but shallower, recession: GDP is just 5 percent below potential for the entire period of the disinflation, but it takes eight years to get the inflation rate down to 2 percent. Path 3 involves a shorter recession, but it is quite deep: GDP is 10 percent below potential. In this case the inflation rate is reduced more quickly; it reaches 2 percent in four years. Clearly, more extreme possibilities are open to policymakers. Or a compromise between Path 2 and Path 3 is another possibility. The paths we have presented in Table 9.1 are meant to be representative of the choices facing policymakers.

In comparing these paths, it is important to note their implications for unemployment. Suppose the natural rate of unemployment that corresponds to potential GDP is 6 percent. Recall from Chapter 3 that Okun's law trans-lates a GDP gap of 1 percent into .3 percentage point of unemployment. Thus, for Path 2, the unemployment rate rises to 7.5 percent for eight years, and for Path 3, the unemployment rate rises to 9 percent for four years. Of course the unemployment rate stays at 6 percent, the natural rate, for all years in Path 1.

Inflation in the United States reached about 10 percent per year in 1980. A policy of disinflation was in place from then until 1985. Figure 9.9 shows the actual rates of inflation and the GDP gap that occurred starting from 1979.

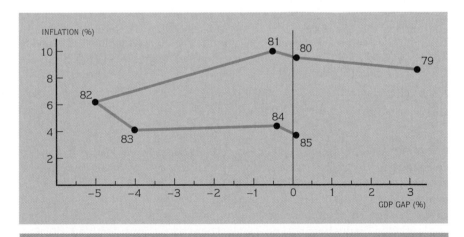

**FIGURE 9.9**   The 1979–85 Disinflation

As money growth was reduced, GDP fell below potential. For a while there was little effect on inflation. The tight monetary policy was continued and eventually inflation came down.
Source: *Economic Report of the President,* 1995, Table B-3.

## Other Schools of Thought on Disinflation

Figure 9.9 seems to give strong support to the general view we have expressed in this book: It takes time for prices to adjust, and during that time there can be large departures of GDP from potential. A negative shock to aggregate demand has the effect of sending the economy into recession.

Other schools of thought do not agree that recession is inevitably the result of a policy to bring down inflation quickly. One of the most influential critics of the view expressed in this book is Thomas Sargent of Stanford University. Sargent has written:

> . . . Inflation only *seems* to have a momentum of its own; it is actually the long-term government policy of persistently running large deficits and creating money at high rates which imparts the momentum to the inflation rate. An implication of this view is that inflation can be stopped much more quickly than advocates of the "momentum" view have indicated and that their estimates of the length of time and the costs of stopping inflation in terms of forgone output ($220 billion of GDP for 1 percentage point in

the inflation rate) are erroneous. This is not to say that it would be easy to eradicate inflation. On the contrary, it would require far more than a few temporary restrictive fiscal and monetary actions. It would require a change in the policy regime; there must be an abrupt change in the continuing government policy, or strategy, for setting deficits now and in the future that is sufficiently binding as to be widely believed [emphasis added].*

Sargent examines the experiences of four countries—Austria, Hungary, Germany, and Poland—in the aftermath of World War I to test his theory. In his view, the magnitude of the recession that accompanied huge decreases in the inflation rate in these countries was small in those instances where there was a complete change in government policy and the public believed that highly expansionary fiscal and monetary policy had ended.

*"The Ends of Four Big Inflations," in Robert E. Hall, ed., *Inflation: Causes and Effects,* a National Bureau of Economic Research Project Report (Chicago: University of Chicago Press, 1982), pp. 41–97.

---

Inflation was very high in 1979, when the GDP gap was above zero. As the Fed tightened its policy, the economy began to slow and GDP fell below potential GDP. Because of the slow reaction of prices to the depressed demand conditions, inflation did not slow for a while (in fact it increased slightly). The Fed continued with a tight policy and the GDP gap got larger, until inflation finally began to give way. There was a considerable reduction in inflation in 1982, and by 1985 inflation had come down to below 4 percent.

Comparing the actual experience from 1979 to 1985 with the two alternative paths, Paths 2 and 3, it looks as if Path 3 was chosen by the Fed. GDP fell to about 7 percent below potential in 1982 and the inflation rate came down much more quickly than in the gradual path. This disinflation was brought about by monetary policy. Fiscal policy was in fact stimulative during that period.

## DISINFLATION

1. The price adjustment equation is the key to understanding the problem of disinflation. Unemployment must rise above its natural rate to reduce inflation.
2. Monetary policy can be set to aim for a target level of GDP. Policymakers have a choice of disinflationary paths; the more unemployment they choose, the faster disinflation will occur.
3. From 1979 through 1988, rapid disinflation occurred in the United States, with GDP well below potential and high rates of unemployment.

## REVIEW AND PRACTICE

### Major Points

1. One important type of macroeconomic shock shifts the aggregate demand curve. Such a shock can originate anywhere in the spending and financial parts of the economy.

2. The other important type of shock shifts the price level.

3. In principle, monetary and fiscal policy can be used to offset shifts in aggregate demand, so that the shifts have little effect on GDP or the price level. But some economists question the feasibility or the wisdom of trying to counteract every demand shift.

4. Price shocks create a much more serious problem for policy. Without a policy response, shocks bring lower GDP and higher inflation. Policy can limit the GDP decline only by permanently increasing the price level.

5. An important policy issue is how to phase out inflation once it is established. Policy can choose between ending inflation rapidly, with high unemployment, or disinflating gradually, with unemployment closer to the natural rate.

## Key Terms and Concepts

aggregate demand disturbance
price disturbance
accommodative policy

activist policy
accommodation of price
  shock

disinflation

## Questions for Discussion and Review

1. What are some of the possible reactions of the economy in the short run to an event that causes an aggregate demand shift? To an event that causes a price shock? What about in the long run? What if both types of shocks occur at the same time?

2. Explain how the economy would respond to a negative price shock if there were no policy response.

3. What are the dangers of a vigorous response to a demand shock? What are the benefits?

4. Explain why an extended period of unemployment above the natural rate is needed to bring about disinflation. Do you find your explanation completely convincing?

## Problems

### NUMERICAL

1. Suppose the economy is initially described by the following equations:

$$Y = C + I + G$$

$$C = 220 + .63Y$$

$$I = 1,000 - 2,000R$$

$$X = 525 - .1Y - 500R$$

$$M = .1583Y - 1,000R$$

$$\pi = 1.2\ [(Y_{-1} - 6,000)/6,000]$$

The money supply is equal to $900 billion, government spending is $1,200 billion, and output is at its potential level of $6,000 billion with a price level of 1. Then there is a money demand shock. The new money demand equation is given by

$$M = .1583Y - 2,000R.$$

a. In the year of the shock, compute the value of GDP, the price level, interest rates, and the real money supply.
b. Using aggregate demand curves, illustrate the economy's path in the year of the shock and in subsequent years.

   c. Calculate the new long-run equilibrium values for income, prices, interest rates, and the real money supply.

   d. Could the Fed have done something to avert the adjustment process? If no, why not? If yes, describe exactly what it could have done.

2. Repeat Exercise 1, Parts a to c, assuming now that the shock is to investment. The new investment equation is given by

$$I = 800 - 2{,}000R.$$

What change in fiscal policy, if any, would have offset the shock?

3. Suppose the economy has the aggregate demand schedule

$$Y = 3{,}401 + 2.877 \frac{M}{P}$$

and a price adjustment schedule

$$\pi = .6\pi_{-1} + 1.2[(Y_{-1} - Y^*)/Y^*] + Z,$$

where $Z$ is an exogenous price shock; potential GDP is $Y^* = 6{,}000$.

   a. Graph the aggregate demand schedule for $M = 900$. Graph the price adjustment schedule. Find the price level for $Z = 0$.

   b. Suppose the economy starts with a price level of 1.0 and zero expected inflation. A price shock of 5 percent occurs in the first year ($Z = .05$). No further price shocks occur ($Z = 0$ in all future years). Trace the path of the economy back to potential by computing the values of the price level, GDP, unemployment, and expected inflation in each year for five years.

   c. Repeat the calculations for the following monetary accommodation: The money supply is 5 percent higher starting in the second year. Compare this new path for inflation and unemployment with the original path.

   d. Suppose, instead, that monetary policy tries to limit inflation by contracting the money stock by 5 percent starting in the second year. Repeat the calculations and compare with the original path.

   e. Now suppose that there is no price shock ($Z = 0$ in all years), but that the economy starts with expected inflation of 3 percent. Compute the path to potential. How much excess unemployment (over the natural rate of 6 percent) occurs in the process of returning to potential? Use Okun's law.

4. Consider the following closed-economy model of aggregate demand:

$$
\begin{array}{ll}
C = 835 + .56Y_{\mathrm{d}} & \text{(Consumption)} \\
I = 640 - 2{,}000R & \text{(Investment)} \\
M = 139.5P/(R + .66) & \text{(Money demand)}
\end{array}
$$

Government taxes ($T$) equal $tY$ where the tax rate $t$ is .29. Government purchases $G$ are constant at 690. Each time period represents one year. In addition prices adjust according to

$$\pi = \pi_{-1} + .3[(Y_{-1} - Y^*)/Y^*]. \qquad \text{(Price adjustment)}$$

Suppose that it is January 2001 and you have just been hired as an adviser to the chair of the Fed. Because the Fed is trying to put on a low-budget image, the chair asks you to bring a hand calculator to your new job. History has repeated itself and the rate of inflation in 2000 was 10 percent—that is, the price level increased from .909 in 1999 to 1.0 in 2000. The Fed set the money supply for 2000 at 186, and real output in the economy in 2000 was equal to potential. What was potential output in 2000?

Assume that potential output remains constant at its 2000 value until 2005. What follows pertains to your new Fed job.

a. The chair asks you what actual output will have to be in 2001, 2002, and 2003 in order for inflation to be reduced to 7 percent in 2002, to 4 percent in 2003, and then held constant at 4 percent in 2004. What is your answer based on the above model?

b. The chair decides to disinflate the economy according to the path that you calculated in Part a and asks you to give a recommendation to the Federal Open Market Committee (FOMC) about where to aim the money supply in 2001, 2002, and 2003 to achieve this path. What do you say?

c. Suppose the FOMC ignores your recommendation and increases the money supply by 20 percent to 223 in 1997. What will happen to output in 1997, and inflation in 1998?

**ANALYTICAL**

1. Suppose that the economy is initially in equilibrium and that there is a permanent increase in money demand. The following year the money supply is increased so that at the old equilibrium level of prices, income, and interest rates, money supply equals money demand.

    a. Illustrate the shock and the Fed's reaction to it with an aggregate demand graph. Using arrows, as in Figure 9.2, sketch the economy's path.

    b. What happens to prices, income, and interest rates in the year of the shock, the year immediately following the shock, and all subsequent years?

    c. Whose views of countercyclical stabilization policy does this example illustrate?

2. Evaluate the following statement: It is price changes, not higher prices, that bother people so much. Therefore, the best response to a price shock is full accommodation. This will prevent output from falling below potential, as well as avoiding any additional price changes.

3. Explain the following statement: The reason that price shocks pose a dilemma for policymakers is that they cannot directly control the price level. Contrast this situation to the case of aggregate demand shocks.

4. Suppose that the Fed fully accommodates a price shock, shifting out the aggregate demand curve until aggregate demand equals $Y^*$ at the higher price level. The behavior of income and of the price level are given by the following graphs:

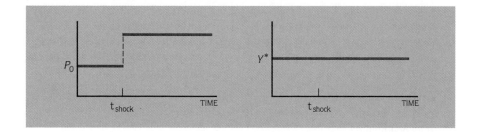

a. Assumming that aggregate demand is given by the usual relationship, which of the following equations must describe the adjustment of prices?

$$\pi = f[(Y_{-1} - Y^*)/Y^*] \qquad \pi = .6\pi_{-1} + f[(Y_{-1} - Y^*)/Y^*]$$

b. Assume now that there is the same policy response, but that prices are governed by the other equation. Describe the path followed by output and prices.

5. Suppose the Fed used monetary policy to keep the interest rate at 7 percent no matter what else happened in the economy.

a. When would such a policy be inflationary? How would the nominal money stock and output behave in this instance?

b. When would such a policy be deflationary? How would the nominal money stock and output behave in this instance?

c. What other policy is available for targeting the interest rate? What are its advantages?

6. "Stagflation" was a term coined in the 1970s to describe a sustained period of high inflation and unemployment. Using graphs, describe how stagflation may come about in the wake of a price shock.

7. The "political business cycle" is said to occur because the administration expands policy in the election year in order to get reelected. How could this be prevented?

8. One example of a monetary policy rule is $Y = Y^*$.

a. What does the aggregate demand curve look like for such a policy rule?

b. Explain why the money stock is an endogenous variable under such a rule. How is the money stock affected by price shocks? By aggregate demand shocks?

c. Explain why $P = P_0$ is not a feasible policy rule.

9. Suppose that the only source of instability in the economy is disturbances to investment demand and that the administration is considering adopting a rule for government spending that can be expressed as

$$G = G_0 + r(Y - Y^*),$$

where $G_0$ and $r$ are positive constants. Will a rule of this form reduce the fluctuations in GDP? Why or why not? If not, indicate how you would change the rule to accomplish stabilization.

10. Understanding the source of shocks to the economy is important for determining the appropriate policy response. For each of the following sources of shocks describe the correlations you would expect to observe between real GDP and real interest rates in the short run. (Assume monetary and fiscal policy are exogenous.)

   a. Shocks in investment demand.
   b. Shocks to money demand.
   c. Shocks to the price level.
   d. Shocks to net exports.

   For each of these sources of shocks, describe the combination of monetary and fiscal policy that could offset the disturbance completely and keep real output and the price level unchanged.

11. Assume that the only source of instability in the economy is price shocks. Compare a policy of fixed money supply with each of the following monetary policy rules. Indicate whether the aggregate demand schedule becomes flatter or steeper or if you are uncertain. Justify your answer. (Suppose output initially equals $Y^*$, $P = 1.0$, and $M_0$, $s$, and $r$ are positive constants.)

   a. $M = M_0 + s(P - 1.0)$.
   b. $M = M_0 + s(Y - Y^*)$.
   c. $M = M_0 + s(P - 1.0) - r(Y - Y^*)$.

## MacroSolve Exercises

In this chapter we have continued to assume that the aggregate demand side of the economy is given by the IS-LM model, and we have added to our price adjustment equation the influence of supply shocks. Our price adjustment equation becomes

$$\pi = .8[(Y_{-1} - Y^*)/Y^* + \pi^e + Z,$$

where $Z$ represents a price shock. This model is called "AD/PA, Open Econ."

1. Select a price shock of 5 percent. Assume that government spending and the money supply are kept constant.

   a. How much output is "lost" in the following five periods, where lost output is measured as the sum of the deviation of output from potential output over those years?
   b. Increase the responsiveness of investment to interest rates. Is the output loss greater or smaller than it was with less responsive investment? Explain in words why this is the case; emphasize the role of changes in the interest rate in transmitting price shocks to the real side of the economy.
   c. Reset the interest responsiveness of investment to its default, and make prices less responsive to aggregate demand. Explain why the price shock has a more prolonged depressing effect on GDP when prices are more "sticky."

2. Continue to assume that the 5 percent price shock hits the economy, and reset all parameters to their default values. Assume the Federal Reserve runs a fully accommodative monetary policy. By how much must the Fed increase the money

supply? Compare again the output loss over the first five years with that in Question 1. Why would policymakers ever choose not to accommodate a price shock in this manner (a) in the short run or (b) in the long run?

3. Suppose that instead of relying on the Federal Reserve to increase the money supply, the fiscal policymakers increase government expenditures to keep output constant in the period of the price shock.

   a. Explain how the solution differs from the previous case where the money supply was increased.

   b. What variables are significantly different in the last period of the two (monetary and fiscal policy response) simulations? What explains their differences? Why might a policymaker prefer one over the other?

4. *Policy Decisions 2001.* The day you arrive at your job with the Federal Reserve System there is another crisis in the Middle East and the price of oil skyrockets. You have to make a presentation to the Board of Governors the next day about the problem. The board wants you to find a way to keep GDP from falling if the shock raises the price level 10 percent. Select the "AD/PA, Open Econ" model from MacroSolve and use it to find a path for the money supply that meets the board's request.

5. Suppose the Fed adopts a policy to fight inflation. What should it do in response to an increase in government expenditures? Select the "AD/PA, Open Econ" model and increase government spending by $50 billion.

   a. What change in the money supply is required to maintain stability of the price level?

   b. Now suppose the economy suffers a 5 percent price shock (instead of an increase in government spending). How should you respond according to the inflation-fighting policy? What is the impact of your response on output? Are GDP fluctuations larger or smaller?

PART

4

# Micro-foundations of Macro-economics

# Consumption Demand

Consumer behavior—what, how much, and when individuals consume—
has been a lifetime study of thousands of economists. This is not surprising,
for in economics the consumer occupies center stage. A first principle of
microeconomics is that consumers choose their consumption plans in order
to maximize their satisfaction or utility. And ever since Adam Smith, the
performance of an economic system has been judged by how efficiently it
allocates scarce resources to satisfy the wants of consumers. So it is natural
to start with consumers in our examination of the micro foundations of macroeconomics.

Traditionally, macroeconomists have been concerned with consumption because consumption is such a large and important component of aggregate demand. In Part I we saw that consumption is about two-thirds of
all spending and that the response of consumption to changes in income—
the consumption function—is a crucial ingredient in macroeconomic analysis. In the first section of this chapter we look at the empirical evidence on
consumption. We show that this evidence raises questions about the simple
consumption function, and then we show how consumption theory has been
reconstructed in light of this empirical evidence. We also examine the response of consumption to interest rates.

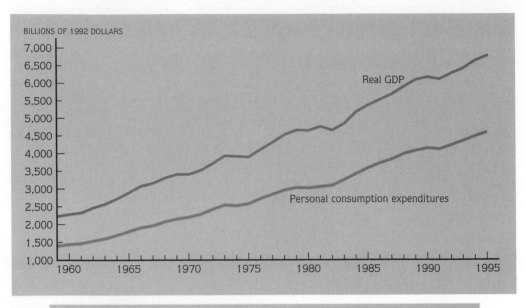

BILLIONS OF 1992 DOLLARS

**FIGURE 10.1**   Consumption Expenditures and GDP

Real GDP and real personal consumption expenditures grow at about the same rate over long periods of time so that, on average, consumption expenditures maintain roughly a two-thirds share of GDP. However, over the business cycle, consumption expenditures fluctuate much less than GDP. Consumption expenditure is less volatile than the other components of GDP.
Source: *Economic Report of the President*, 1996, Table B-2.

# 10.1 FLUCTUATIONS IN GDP, CONSUMPTION, AND INCOME

As the overall economy grows and fluctuates, so does consumption. Figure 10.1 shows how real GDP and personal consumption expenditures have grown and passed through cycles together during the period 1959 to 1995. Note that *over the long run, consumption expenditures and GDP grow at about the same rate, but over short-run business cycles, consumption expenditures fluctuate less than GDP*.[1] The smoother path for consumption ex-

---

[1]Note that the increasing gap between real GDP and real consumption in Figure 10.1 is not inconsistent with the fact that the *ratio* of real consumption to real GDP remains constant. The gap gets larger as the level of the two series increases.

penditures is particularly evident during the period 1980 to 1984 when real GDP fell and rose sharply, while consumption expenditures slowed down only slightly before returning to a more normal pace. This relatively smooth behavior of consumption expenditures compared with GDP is one of the most important facts of the business cycle.

The smoothness of consumption differs greatly by type of consumption. Figure 10.2 shows the breakdown of personal consumption expenditures into its three components: durables, nondurables, and services. Note that the relatively smooth behavior of consumption expenditures is most striking for services, which grow steadily regardless of the fluctuations in the economy. Nondurables fluctuate a bit more, but most of the business cycle fluctuations in consumption expenditures are due to durables. When recessions occur, people reduce their purchases of durable items such as furniture and automobiles much more than their purchases of nondurable items such as food; service items such as medical care hardly fluctuate at all. Note, too, that services now represent the largest and fastest-growing component of

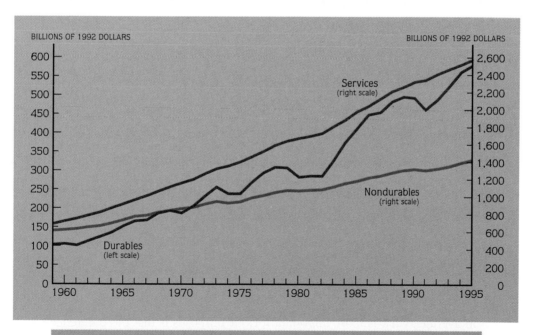

**FIGURE 10.2**   Fluctuations in the Components of Real Personal Consumption Expenditures

Expenditures on services grow smoothly with little cyclical fluctuation. Expenditures on durables are the most volatile component of consumption.
Source: *Economic Report of the President*, 1996, Table B-2.

consumption. As services become more important, we might expect overall consumption expenditures to become less volatile.

Overall consumption behavior would show even smaller fluctuations if we looked at the true economic measure of **consumption** rather than at **consumption expenditures.** The distinction between consumption and consumption expenditures is a subtle one, but takes on special importance in the case of durables. Consider a car, for example. Expenditure on a car occurs at the time that we buy the car and bring it home from the car dealer, even if we finance it by borrowing. Consumption of the car is then spread out over several years as we drive the car and it gradually deteriorates through normal wear and tear. Expenditure occurs when the car is acquired; consumption occurs as the car is used up. Consumption of durables is more spread out over time and is smoother than expenditure on them. For services and nondurable items there is no meaningful distinction between consumption and expenditure: when we purchase a haircut, we consume it at the same time. Because consumption of durables fluctuates less than expenditures on durables, it is clear that total consumption has smaller fluctuations than total consumption expenditures.

## GDP and Personal Disposable Income

Why does consumption fluctuate less than GDP? Part of the answer can be found in the behavior of disposable personal income. As we saw in Chapter 6, according to the simplest theory, consumption depends on personal disposable income: when fluctuations in disposable income are small, fluctuations in consumption will be small as well. We stressed in Chapter 2 that GDP is very different from the personal disposable income that is available to consumers for spending. GDP is about 40 percent greater than personal disposable income. Part of GDP is not really income at all because it includes the depreciation of machines, factories, and housing. An important part of GDP is unavailable to consumers because it is paid to the various levels of government in the form of taxes. Still another part is plowed back into corporations in the form of retained earnings rather than being paid out to consumers. On the other hand, some people receive transfers from the government—such as unemployment compensation or social security—that are not related to current production.

Although the difference between GDP and disposable income is large on average, what is more important for our purposes is that the difference shrinks during recessions and expands during booms. Taxes fall during recessions, and transfers increase because more people collect unemployment insurance and social security. Therefore disposable income does not fall as much as GDP. These changes in taxes and transfers are sometimes called **automatic stabilizers** because of their stabilizing effect on disposable in-

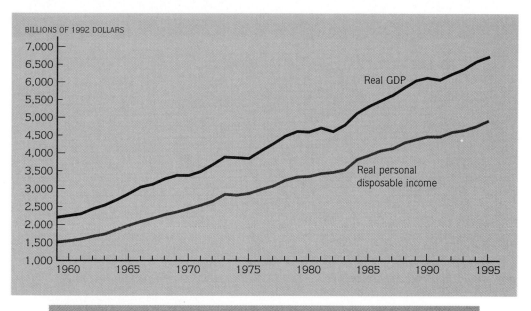

BILLIONS OF 1992 DOLLARS

**FIGURE 10.3** Real GDP and Real Personal Disposable Income

Disposable income fluctuates much less than real GDP. The automatic stabilizers—taxes and transfers—as well as the dividend policies of corporations prevent disposable income from falling as far as GDP during recessions.
Source: *Economic Report of the President*, 1996, Tables B-2 and B-27.

come; we will be studying them in more detail in Chapter 13. Retained earnings also fall during recessions, because corporations don't cut their dividends very much and thus further mitigate the effect on disposable income. The sum of these effects is shown in Figure 10.3, where real GDP and real disposable income are plotted for the years 1959 to 1995.

Figure 10.3 shows that personal disposable income fluctuates less than GDP. On average, when GDP falls during a recession, disposable income does not fall as much. There are exceptions to this general rule, but, again, on average, over this period a fall in real GDP of $10 billion reduced real disposable income by only $4 billion.[2]

[2]The relationship was estimated by comparing real disposable income and real GDP in the United States each year during the 1959–1995 period. The least-squares relation between the *change* in real disposable income and the *change* in real GDP has a slope coefficient of .4. The least-squares line is the straight line that minimizes the sum of squared vertical distances between the dots and the line.

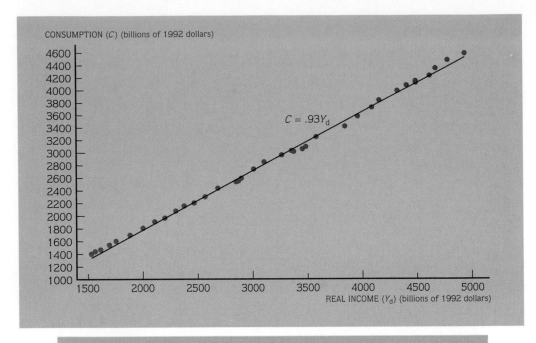

**FIGURE 10.4**   The Relation between Real Disposable Income and Real
Consumption Expenditures

The horizontal position of each dot shows real disposable income in that year and the vertical
position shows real consumption in that year. The straight line is a simple consumption function
that is fit through the scatter of dots. The vertical distances between the line and the dots measure
the error in the consumption function.
Source: *Economic Report of the President,* 1996, Table B-27.

## The Relation between Real Disposable
## Income and Consumption

As we have just seen, part of the reason why consumption fluctuates less
than real GDP is that disposable income fluctuates less than GDP. But can
all of consumption behavior be explained by current personal disposable
income, as the simplest consumption function would suggest? In Figure 10.4
we examine the relationship between personal consumption expenditures and personal disposable income for the period from 1959 through 1995.
Each dot in Figure 10.4 represents real consumption and real disposable
income in the United States for one year. We can summarize the relation-

ship by drawing a straight line through the dots.[3] The straight line gives the relationship

$$C = .93Y_\mathrm{d} \tag{10.1}$$

which is in the form of the simple consumption function; the **marginal propensity to consume (MPC)** is .93. On average, the U.S. public spends about 93 percent of its disposable income on consumption goods and saves 7 percent. Figure 10.4 indicates that consumption is sometimes less and sometimes greater than predicted by the simple consumption function. The errors are given by the equation

$$\mathrm{Error} = C - .93Y_\mathrm{d} \tag{10.2}$$

and are measured by the vertical distances between the line and the dots in Figure 10.4. The errors appear to be small. The simple consumption function seems to give a surprisingly good description of consumption.

## DEFECTS IN THE SIMPLE KEYNESIAN CONSUMPTION FUNCTION

Unfortunately, Figure 10.4 paints too rosy a picture about the reliability of the simple consumption function. Although the errors in Figure 10.4 appear small to the naked eye, for some purposes—such as forecasting or policy analysis—they are actually quite large. A more revealing picture of the errors is found in Figure 10.5, where the error in the simple consumption function (as calculated in Equation 10.2) is plotted for each year. The vertical scale in Figure 10.5 is much finer than the vertical scale in Figure 10.4. This magnifies the errors, much like a photographic enlargement, and makes them easier to analyze.

Very large negative errors occurred in 1973 through 1975. People consumed much less than normal given their disposable incomes; they acted as if they distrusted their income figures in those years. Why? Perhaps they were becoming pessimistic about their incomes in the future; the stock market had

---

[3]We estimated this relationship by finding the straight line that minimizes the sum of the squared vertical distances between the dots and the line (that is, the least-squares line) for the years 1959 through 1995. This line has a negligible intercept or constant term, which is therefore omitted from Equation 10.1.

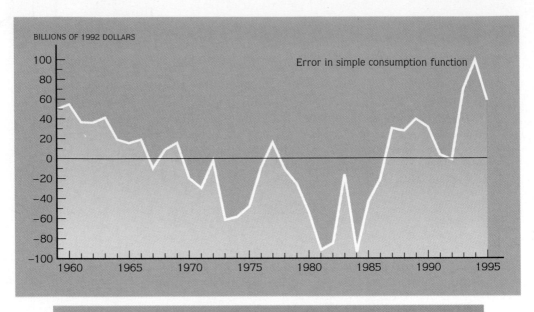

BILLIONS OF 1992 DOLLARS

Error in simple consumption function

**FIGURE 10.5**   Error Analysis in the Simple Consumption Function

This diagram gives a microscopic view of the errors in the simple consumption function that are
barely visible in Figure 10.4. It blows up the distances between the actual consumption-income dots
and the simple consumption-income line in Figure 10.4. The distances are then plotted each year
from 1959 through 1995.
Source: The errors are computed from Equation 10.2 with consumption and income data from Figure 10.4.

recently fallen and the price of oil rose dramatically starting in 1973. These
uncertainties about the future could have led to caution and increased saving.

At the other extreme, consumption rose well above its normal relationship to disposable income in the 1987-through-1990 period. The economy
was on a consumption binge. Surveys confirmed that families were more
confident about their own financial positions and the prospects for the economy than they had ever been before. A similar buying binge occurred just
after World War II, another episode of high confidence about the future. One
factor in the high confidence of 1987 to 1989 may have been the Tax Reform
Act of 1986, which lowered tax rates for many families. In 1987, consumer
confidence was matched by confidence on Wall Street; the stock market
reached record levels in relation to corporate earnings. Even the crash of the
stock market in October 1987 did not mark the end of high consumer confidence or high levels of consumption in relation to disposable income.

In 1991 and 1992, consumption was closer to its normal relation to
disposable income. Surveys of consumer confidence showed large declines

in 1991 and 1992. The fall of consumption from far above its normal relation to income to a more moderate level, still above the normal relation, was one of the factors leading to slow recovery from the recession that started in July 1990. Consumption was again high in 1993 and 1994 as the economy boomed.

Note that these informal but plausible explanations of the errors in the simple theory imply a much more sophisticated consumer than the one that simply looks at current income, as the Keynesian model postulates. Expected future income enters the decision. The main contribution of the newer theories of consumption described in the next section is to bring these expectations of the future explicitly into account.

## The Effect of Consumption Errors on Forecasting and Policy

Some perspective on the practical importance of these errors in the consumption function can be gained by looking at their effect on economic forecasting and policy. These errors can have significant effects on economic forecasts. For example, as shown in Figure 10.5, the error in the consumption function in 1994 was about $59 billion. From 1993 to 1994 real GDP increased by $208 billion, or by 4.0 percent. A forecaster who missed the error in the consumption function in 1993 would have underpredicted real GDP growth by $59 billion—predicting a GDP growth of about 2.9 percent rather than the 4.0 percent that actually occurred.

Such large forecasting errors can obviously lead to economic policy errors. More fiscal stimulus might have been called for in 1974 and 1975 if the unusually low consumption demand had been correctly forecast in advance. Moreover, if consumers don't automatically spend 93 cents of every dollar of additional disposable income—as the simple model predicts—then a reduction in taxes aimed at stimulating demand might not work as planned; it might generate too little or too much stimulus. More complicated consumer behavior makes policymaking difficult, especially if policymakers don't understand the more complicated behavior.

## Short-Run versus Long-Run Marginal Propensity to Consume

There is one systematic feature of the errors in the simple consumption function that is difficult to see in the charts with a naked eye, but that nonetheless has provided a crucial insight and stimulus to advanced research on consumption: *On average, consumption is smoothed out compared with disposable income; consumption fluctuates less than disposable income.* This phenomenon can be detected and illustrated by using the concept of the long-run and short-run marginal propensity to consume. Figure 10.6 shows

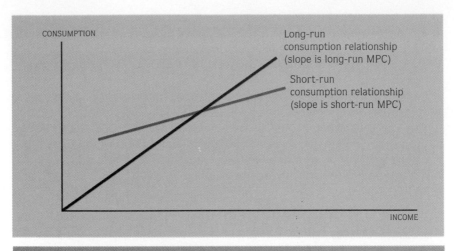

The steeper line shows how consumption rises with income in the long run. Its slope is the long-run marginal propensity to consume (MPC). The flatter line shows how consumption rises with income in the short run. Its slope is the short-run MPC.

how the long-run and the short-run marginal propensities to consume differ for total consumption. The **long-run marginal propensity to consume** tells us how much consumption will increase over the long haul when personal disposable income rises. For total consumption the long-run marginal propensity to consume is .93, as we have already seen in Equation 10.1.

The **short-run marginal propensity to consume** tells us how much consumption will rise over the short run—during one year or during one business cycle—when disposable income rises. As Figure 10.6 illustrates, the short-run marginal propensity to consume is less than the long-run marginal propensity to consume.

Table 10.1 shows the actual difference between the short-run and the long-run marginal propensity to consume in the United States from 1959 to 1994 for total consumption and two of its components. The short-run marginal propensity to consume can be calculated statistically by noting how much consumption changes from one year to the next when disposable income changes. For total consumption the short-run MPC is .72, compared with .93 for the long-run MPC. The difference is even more pronounced for consumption of nondurables plus services: for each dollar decrease in disposable income, nondurables and services consumption falls by 41 cents in the short run, but the fall is 78 cents over the long run if that dollar shortfall in income persists. Note that the difference between the long-run and the

**TABLE 10.1**   Short-Run and Long-Run Marginal Propensity to Consume 1959–94

|  | Total Consumption | Nondurables plus Services | Durables |
|---|---|---|---|
| Long-run MPC | .93 | .78 | .15 |
| Short-run MPC | .72 | .41 | .31 |

*Note:* The long-run MPCs are based on the least-squares fit of the annual *levels* of real consumption and real disposable income. The short-run MPCs are based on the fit of the year-to-year *changes* in the same two variables.

short-run MPC is reversed for durable expenditures; unlike the other components of consumption, durables are more sensitive to income in the short run than in the long run. A complete theory of consumption has to come to grips with these empirical observations.

## GDP, CONSUMPTION, AND INCOME

1. Consumption fluctuates much less than GDP. The least stable component of consumption expenditures is durables consumption. Services and nondurables consumption grow more smoothly.
2. The main reason that consumption fluctuates less than GDP is that disposable income fluctuates less than GDP. Consumption is financed out of disposable income.
3. Over the past few decades in the United States, consumption has more or less tracked income, according to a simple Keynesian consumption function, with a marginal propensity to consume of .93. Of each incremental dollar of disposable income, 93 cents has been spent on consumption goods and 7 cents has been saved.
4. There have been significant deviations from the simple consumption function. Just after World War II, consumers spent more than the simple function predicted. In the mid-1970s, they spent quite a bit less. And in 1987 to 1990 they again consumed much more than the simple function predicted.
5. A systematic feature of consumption behavior is that the short-run marginal propensity to consume is less than the long-run marginal propensity to consume. The change in consumption that results from a change in income is apparently spread over a number of years.

# THE FORWARD-LOOKING THEORY OF CONSUMPTION

A number of different theories of consumption have been developed in response to the deficiencies in the simple consumption function. The most durable and widely accepted today are the **permanent-income theory** developed in the 1950s by Milton Friedman and the **life-cycle theory** developed independently at about the same time by Franco Modigliani of the Massachusetts Institute of Technology.[4] The two theories are closely related, and together they have served as a foundation for most of the rational expectations research on consumption in macroeconomics in recent years. We will refer to them jointly as the **forward-looking theory of consumption.** The theory embodies the basic idea that individual consumers are forward-looking decision-makers. The life-cycle theory gets its name from its emphasis on a family looking ahead over its entire lifetime. The permanent-income theory is named for its distinction between permanent income, which a family expects to be long-lasting, and transitory income, which a family expects to disappear shortly. In practice the theories differ primarily in the types of equations used to express the basic idea of forward-looking consumers and to implement this idea empirically.

Like the simple consumption function, the forward-looking theory of consumption assumes that families or individuals base their consumption decisions on their disposable incomes. To simplify matters, we will begin by ignoring factors other than disposable income that might also influence consumption, such as interest rates. The forward-looking theory breaks ranks with the simple consumption function by saying that consumers do not concentrate exclusively on this year's disposable income. Instead, it also looks ahead to their likely future disposable income, which will depend on their future earnings from working, on their future income from wealth they have accumulated, and on how high taxes will be in the future. Based on their current income and expected future disposable income, they decide how much to consume this year after taking account of their likely consumption in future years as well.

---

[4]Friedman published his findings in 1957 in a famous book, *A Theory of the Consumption Function* (Princeton University Press); the findings on the life-cycle theory were published in a series of papers, the most important of which are F. Modigliani and R. E. Brumberg's, "Utility Analysis and the Consumption Function: An Interpretation of Cross-Section Data," in K. K. Kurihara, ed., *Post-Keynesian Economics* (New Brunswick, N.J.: Rutgers University Press, pp. 388–436), and A. Ando and F. Modigliani, "The 'Life-Cycle' Hypothesis of Saving: Aggregate Implication and Tests," *American Economic Review,* Vol. 53 (March 1963), pp. 55–84.

The consumption decision is thus much like a plan; this year's consumption is the first year of a plan that covers perhaps the next 50 years. Next year, the plan will have to be adjusted to take account of all the new information that has become available, but if everything works out as expected the plan will be followed. Although few consumers actually sit down and work out formal forward-looking plans in great detail, it is likely that a significant fraction do some informal planning when they borrow to buy now and plan to pay off the loan later with future anticipated earnings, or when they save for retirement. We will talk about a very self-conscious plan, of the sort that an economist might make, but we recognize that most families are much more informal in their planning.

## The Intertemporal Budget Constraint

To describe how such a planning process results in a consumption decision, we will focus on a single family. The family could be a single individual, a couple, a single-parent household, or two parents and their children. The first aspect we will look at is the budget constraint the family faces. The budget constraint applies not to one single year, but to many future years taken together. The constraint is more flexible in any one year than it is over time; in any one year a family can consume more than its disposable income by borrowing or by drawing down some of its financial assets. But a family can't go on forever consuming more than its disposable income; eventually it will run out of assets or places to borrow. The family faces an **intertemporal budget constraint** that limits its consumption over the years. In some years, a family will consume less than its income; the excess of income over consumption—saving—is then added to the family's financial assets and can be used for consumption in later years. Consumption this year is thus reduced so that consumption in later years can be increased. The budget constraint incorporates the accumulation of assets that results from savings.

The intertemporal budget constraint can be described in words as follows:

> Assets at the beginning of next year
> = Assets at the beginning of this year
> + Income on assets this year    ⎱ Disposable
> + Income from work this year    ⎰ income              ⎫
> − Taxes paid this year                                 ⎬ Saving
> − Consumption this year                                ⎭

Assets include items such as bank deposits, bonds, corporate stock, and pension funds. There are two types of income: (1) income on assets, such as interest payments from the bank where the family holds its deposits, and (2) income from work. If a family adds to its assets, then it also adds to its future income on those assets. Hence it is important to distinguish between the two types of income.

Disposable income is, of course, income on assets plus income from work minus taxes. Note that the budget constraint simply states that each year's saving—disposable income less consumption—is added to assets.

To give a clearer picture of the intertemporal budget, we introduce the following symbols:

$$A_t = \text{Assets at the beginning of year t}$$

$$R = \text{Interest rate on assets}$$

$$E_t = \text{Income from work during year t}$$

$$T_t = \text{Taxes during year t}$$

$$C_t = \text{Consumption during year t}$$

The small subscript indicates the year. The interest rate $R$ tells us how much income a given amount of assets will earn. For example, if the interest rate is 5 percent and assets $A_t$ equal \$1,000 in year t, then income on assets is \$50 in year t. (The interest rate $R$ is the *real* interest rate, that is, the nominal interest rate less the expected rate of inflation).

Using these symbols, the intertemporal budget constraint can be written as follows:

$$A_{t+1} = A_t + RA_t + E_t - T_t - C_t. \tag{10.3}$$

The six algebraic terms in Equation 10.3 correspond one for one with the six items listed in the budget constraint that we wrote in words above. The subscript t + 1 indicates assets at the beginning of year t + 1. (For example, if year t is 1995, then year t + 1 is 1996.) The budget constraint, Equation 10.3, applies to all years of the family's future—working years and retirement years. By applying this equation year after year, the family can figure out what its asset position will be many years in the future, given expectations about the interest rate, income from work, and taxes. By reducing consumption this year, the family can increase its assets in future years. The increased assets—plus the interest earned on these assets—could be used for consumption on timely items such as the children's education, for retirement, or as a bequest. (The interest rate $R$ is measured in fractions in this formula: if the interest rate is 5 percent, then set $R$ equal to .05 in Equation 10.3. Then $R$ times $A$, for example, equals \$50 if $A$ equals \$1,000.)

A consumption plan is feasible if it does not involve an impractical asset position at any time in the future. Any positive amount of assets is practical, since it means the family is lending to others, rather than borrowing. For most people, it is impractical to have their assets drop significantly below zero. Our concept of assets is *net* across all borrowing and ownership of the family; if a family buys a house with a 20 percent down payment and takes on a mortgage for the remaining 80 percent, its net asset position is positive. The value of the house as an asset exceeds the liability of the mortgage. Borrowing from a positive net asset position is perfectly practical—almost everybody does it. But it is difficult to borrow when there is a negative net asset position. An exception might be medical or business school students who borrow because their expected future incomes are so favorable.

## Preferences: Steady Rather than Erratic Consumption

Many different consumption plans are feasible. As long as the family is careful not to consume too much, it has a wide choice about when to schedule its consumption. It could consume very little in the early years and build up significant assets by middle age. Or it could consume as much as possible and keep its assets only barely positive. Which of the feasible plans will the family choose? The forward-looking theory of consumption assumes that *most people prefer to keep their consumption fairly steady from year to year.* Given the choice between consuming $10,000 this year and $10,000 next year, as against $5,000 this year and $15,000 next year, people generally choose the even split. There are exceptions, but it seems that most people prefer not to have ups and downs in their standard of living.

Figure 10.7 shows a typical path for income for a family with a steady consumption plan. Income from employment is low in the early years and gradually rises until retirement, as job experience and seniority increase. During retirement, income from work is zero. Note how consumption is relatively large compared with income in the early years of work; young families tend to borrow when they can in anticipation of greater future income in later years. During the years immediately before retirement, consumption is relatively low as the family saves more in anticipation of retirement. Finally, during retirement consumption is much greater than income as the family draws down its assets.

## Preferences: How Large an Inheritance for the Next Generation?

Figure 10.7 illustrates the important features of the typical smooth consumption path. But the assumption that families prefer a smooth consumption path is still not sufficient to pin down one consumption path among those that are feasible. The family can choose a high smooth consumption plan or a low smooth consumption plan. Different smooth paths of consumption

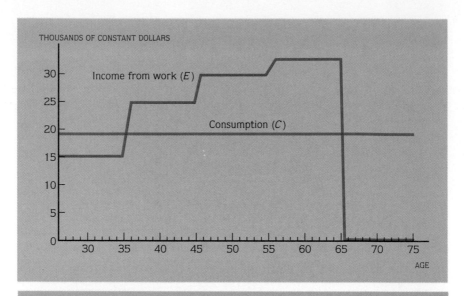

**FIGURE 10.7**   Illustration of Steady Consumption Compared with Income Growth and Decline

Income from work is assumed to grow as experience and seniority increase and then drop to zero during retirement. Thoughtful forward-looking consumers who prefer a smooth consumption path will tend to borrow during their early years, save in their middle years, and draw down their assets during retirement.

will leave the family with different levels of assets at the end of the parents' lifetimes. Figure 10.8 shows the path of assets for the smooth consumption path already shown in Figure 10.7 (Path 2) along with asset paths for higher (Path 1) and lower (Path 3) consumption paths.

A higher consumption path leaves fewer assets at the end of the lifetime. To pin down the consumption path completely, we need to make an assumption about what the parents' preferences are for assets at the end of their lifetimes. How much will they want to leave to the next generation as inheritance? If parents are convinced that their children can make it on their own, they may prefer to consume most of their assets during retirement. Or they might want to reward their children for doing well by giving a large bequest. There is little agreement among economists on what motivates bequests.[5] Fortunately, however, many of the important empirical predictions

---

[5]Douglas Bernheim, Andrei Shleifer, and Lawrence Summers argue that parents use bequests to influence their children's actions in "The Strategic Bequest Motive," *Journal of Political Economy,* Vol. 93 (December 1985), pp. 1045–1076.

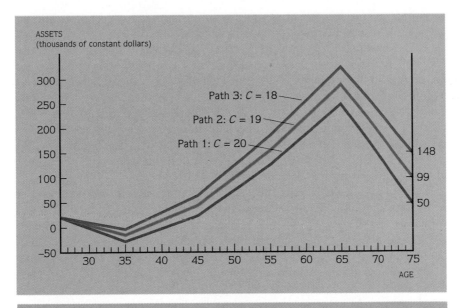

**FIGURE 10.8** Assets and Bequests under Smooth Consumption Paths, Starting with $15,000

If consumption follows Path 1 over the family's lifetime, assets will follow the path marked 1, with little left for the next generation. If consumption follows Path 2, sufficiently more assets are accumulated to leave more for the next generation. Along Path 3, consumption is even lower and assets left for inheritance are even higher.

of the life-cycle and the permanent-income hypotheses hold regardless of what assumption we make about inheritance. We will discuss the effect of alternative assumptions below, where the assumption about inheritance does matter.

## The Marginal Propensity to Consume out of Temporary versus Permanent Changes in Income

It should already be apparent from Figure 10.7 that there is a relation between the family's current assets plus its expectations about future earnings from work and its consumption decisions. If news comes along that the family is better off, either because it has higher assets today or because it expects higher earnings in the future, the family will adjust its consumption upward. Moreover, it will adjust its future consumption plans upward by about the same amount. If the family reacted to good news by changing only current consumption and not future planned consumption, it would be planning a consumption path that would not be smooth.

By how much does consumption change when disposable income changes? For forward-looking consumers the answer depends on how long the change in income will last—in particular, whether the change is viewed as *temporary* or *permanent*.

Consider first the case where income increases permanently. An interesting and important example is a permanent cut in taxes, though any other change, such as the winning of a state lottery that pays the family a yearly payment for life, would serve just as well. Suppose that the family learns that its taxes will be lower by a certain amount—say $1,000—this year, next year, and every year in the future. Disposable income increases in the first year by $1,000, and the increase is viewed as permanent. Assume that the tax cut was unexpected so that the family could not have planned for it in advance. If the family didn't change its consumption plans, future assets would pile up quickly. Next year, assets would be higher by $1,000. In later years, this would grow as interest compounded. But next year, there would be another increment to assets in the amount of $1,000, and in later years this too would earn compound interest. Moreover, if the family raised its consumption, assets would still pile up unless the increase in consumption were equal to the decrease in taxes, $1,000. The family's exact plan would depend on how much of the income improvement it wanted to pass on to the next generation. Assuming that the amount of the improvement passed on is zero, we get a simple conclusion: *The marginal propensity to consume from the increase in disposable income is 1. Consumption rises by the full amount of the increase in income when the increase is viewed as permanent.* If the family wanted to pass on some of the increased income as a bequest, then the marginal propensity to consume would be smaller.

Now consider a temporary tax cut of $1,000 that will last only one year; taxes are then expected to return to their normal level in the remaining years. Again assume that the tax cut was unexpected, so that the family could not have adjusted its plans in advance. If the family raises its consumption by $1,000 in the year of the tax cut, then it will finish the year with nothing extra saved. At the end of the year it will have to reduce its consumption to the level previously planned; this goes against the rule that consumption should be smooth. The family can achieve a better consumption plan by raising consumption less than the tax cut and accumulating some assets. Hence, the marginal propensity to consume will be less than 1. But how much less?

We can determine the amount by using the forward-looking model. If the family didn't change its consumption plans at all, the $1,000 would be added to the family's assets and would start earning interest at rate $R$. Suppose that the interest rate is 5 percent. As the years passed, the increment to assets, including compound interest, would become quite large. After 50 years, $1,000 left to compound at 5 percent interest becomes $12,000. But rather than leave this much more for the next generation, the typical family will probably raise its planned consumption. If it raises planned consumption by the amount of the interest, $50 per year, then after 50 years the family will have just the additional $1,000, not the extra $11,000 in compound interest. Thus, one option for the family is to plan to consume an extra $50 per year and leave an extra $1,000 to the next generation. Or, the family could consume just a bit more and leave nothing extra to the next generation. The intertemporal budget constraint, Equation 10.3, can be used to figure out how much more than $50 the increase in consumption would have to be to exhaust the $1,000 windfall after 50 years.

The forward-looking theory predicts the following consumption rule from this planning process: *If a family receives an unexpected temporary increment to its disposable income, it will raise its consumption by the interest earned by the increment, plus a bit more if it does not want to pass the full amount on to the next generation.* If the tax cut is $1,000, then the rise in consumption is $50, or a little more if not all of the $1,000 is passed on. The marginal propensity to consume from the one-year temporary tax cut, or any other temporary increase in income, is the same as, or a little greater than, the interest rate, or about .05 in this example. It is far, far less than the marginal propensity to consume arising from a permanent increase in income, which is closer to 1. It is also much less than that suggested by the simple consumption function we looked at earlier in the chapter. The difference between the marginal propensity to consume out of a temporary change in income and the marginal propensity to consume out of a permanent change in income is the single most important feature of the newer theories of consumption based on a forward-looking consumer.

## Anticipated versus Unanticipated Changes in Income

In each of the above examples we assumed that the change in income was unanticipated. If the change was anticipated, then the family would adjust its plans in advance. How? If the family learns about the temporary tax cut of $1,000 one year in advance, then it will increase its consumption before the tax cut actually takes place. Postponing the increase in consumption to the year of the tax cut would mean that the planned consumption path would not be smooth, and this would violate the steady consumption rule. The increase in the consumption path will be slightly less than in the case where the tax cut was unanticipated, simply because there is one more year of consumption to spread the improved income over. If the family wants to leave the full $1,000 to the next generation, then the increase in consumption will be slightly less than the interest rate times the tax cut. If the tax cut occurs with 50 years on the planning horizon, then consumption will be spread over 51 years. The increase in consumption will thus be about $48.

Note that the marginal propensity to consume in the year that the tax cut is anticipated is astronomical. The change in income is zero in that year and consumption increases by about $48. The marginal propensity to consume is literally infinite! But the important point is that with forward-looking consumers the marginal propensity to consume depends not only on whether the change in income is temporary or permanent, but also on whether it is anticipated or unanticipated.

## THE FORWARD-LOOKING MODEL

1. The forward-looking model of consumption assumes that households choose current consumption as part of a lifetime consumption plan.
2. The intertemporal budget constraint implies that total planned consumption cannot exceed total household resources (the sum of current wealth and expected future income). If the household plans to leave a bequest, total planned consumption is less than total resources.
3. Although the forward-looking model can accommodate any pattern of preferences, it is typically assumed that households prefer smooth consumption profiles.
4. The theory predicts that the marginal propensity to consume out of permanent changes in income will be close to 1. The marginal propensity to consume out of temporary changes in income will approximately equal the rate of interest.
5. Another important insight that comes from the theory is that current consumption responds not only to changes in current income, but also to changes in expected future income.

# HOW WELL DOES THE FORWARD-LOOKING THEORY WORK?

The key point of the forward-looking theory of consumption is that the marginal propensity to consume from new funds depends on whether the new funds are a onetime increment or will recur in future years. The marginal propensity to consume from temporary increases is low—only a little above the interest rate. The marginal propensity to consume from permanent increases in earnings is high—close to 1.

Consumption in the economy as a whole is the aggregation of the consumption decisions of millions of families. Some tests of the forward-looking model focus on aggregate consumption. Many of the events that matter a great deal for an individual family—births and deaths, promotions, winning big at the racetrack—don't matter at all in the aggregate. The "law of large numbers" guarantees that purely random individual experiences do not influence the total. But some of the influences affecting individual families are common across all families, as, for example, when the economy goes into recession.

## The Short-Run and Long-Run MPC: A Rough Check of the Theory

Before looking at the particular methods that Friedman, Modigliani, and other economic researchers have used to test this theory formally, let's see how well it explains the facts of aggregate consumption that we presented in Section 10.3. The most important statistical regularity that the simple consumption function misses is that the short-run marginal propensity to consume is less than the long-run marginal propensity to consume; that is, consumption does not increase as much with income over short-run business cycle periods as it does over long-run growth periods. If consumers usually expect short-run business cycle fluctuations in their income to be temporary, then the forward-looking consumption theory provides an explanation for this finding. If they expect the drop in income that they experience during a recession to be temporary, then they will not cut their consumption as much as if they thought the drop was more lasting. Similarly, they will not increase their consumption so much during the boom stage of a cycle. Is is plausible that many consumers tend to view recessions and booms as temporary? Throughout U.S. history, recessions and booms have in fact been temporary. If consumers can remember this experience, then an expectation that recessions are temporary seems reasonable. Moreover, economic forecasters usually predict a return to a steady growth path following a recession—they at least remember what happened in the last cycle—and their forecasts are covered on television, in newspapers, and in magazines.

There is even an important exception that seems to prove the rule: In the recession that followed 1973 the dramatic increase in the price of oil and other energy sources probably made many consumers feel that the drop in real income they were experiencing was unlike a typical recession and was likely to be more permanent. According to the forward-looking consumption model, consumers therefore would have cut their expenditures by more than the decreased consumption of a typical recession. This is just what happened in 1973 through 1975. (See Figure 10.5, which shows that consumption was well below normal during that period.) Overall the forward-looking theory of consumption seems to pass this rough check pretty well.

## Why Is the Saving Rate Higher in Japan Than in the United States?

Personal saving is personal disposable income less consumption and interest paid by households. The *personal saving rate* is personal saving as a percentage of personal disposable income. For example, in 1994, saving was 204 billion and the saving rate was 4.1 percent (the calculation is $[204/4,959] \times 100 = 4.1$). The 4.1 percent personal saving rate was one of the lowest in the United States since the post–World War II consumption binge of 1947. This low saving rate is just another way to think about the huge errors in the consumption function for 1994 shown in Figure 10.5 and discussed in the text (consuming an abnormally high fraction of disposable income is the same thing as saving an abnormally low fraction of disposable income).

A 4.1 percent saving rate is low even by U.S. standards, but saving rates in the United States are always low by Japanese standards. For most of the post-World War II period, the personal saving rate in Japan was almost double that in the United States. In a detailed study of saving behavior in Japan and the United States, Fumio Hayashi of Osaka University showed that Japanese saving rates are higher than U.S. saving rates, even for alternative saving definitions that include business and government saving and after adjustments for several different measurement concepts.

Why is the saving rate higher in Japan? The forward-looking theory of consumption may provide part of the answer. In countries with high growth rates, the young tend to have higher incomes than the old people did when they were young. Since young people tend to save and old people tend to dissave according to forward-looking models, the young people with higher incomes will tend to raise the overall saving rate.

Because Japan has a higher growth rate than the United States, the Japanese saving rate will be higher according to the forward-looking model. Simulations of detailed life-cycle models suggest, however, that the growth differential between Japan and the United States is not the entire explanation of the saving rate differential.

There are other possible explanations. Land and housing prices are very high in Japan. Hence, families need to save more for a down payment to buy a house. Further, there is not as extensive a social security system in Japan; families may feel they have to save more for old age. The tax system in Japan is also thought to favor saving.

There are also some noneconomic explanations. As stated by Hayashi, "If all else fails, there is a cultural explanation. The Japanese are simply different. They are more risk-averse and more patient. If this is true, the long-run implication is that Japan will absorb all the wealth in the world. I refuse to comment on this explanation."*

*Fumio Hayashi, "Why Is Japan's Saving Rate So Apparently High?" in S. Fischer, ed., *Macroeconomics Annual,* Vol. 1, National Bureau of Economic Research, 1986.

## Ando and Modigliani: Do Assets Matter for Consumption?

One of the earliest formal statistical tests of the forward-looking theory was done by Albert Ando of the University of Pennsylvania in collaboration with Modigliani. Ando and Modigliani formulated consumption as depending on two factors: (1) current income from work and (2) total assets. In their formulation a change in income, given the value of assets, is assumed to be indicative of a permanent change in income (the current level of income would be representative of all future income). Hence, the marginal propensity to consume from a change in income from work—holding constant the level of assets—would be close to 1. The equation would have to be made more complicated if current income was known to be different from likely future income. On the other hand, their formulation assumes that a change in the value of total assets, given the level of income, would tend to be a temporary change—an example would be a onetime increase in the value of corporate stock. Hence, the marginal propensity to consume from a change in the value of total assets would be close to the interest rate. Algebraically, the Ando-Modigliani consumption function takes the form

$$C = b_1 Y_d + b_2 A, \tag{10.4}$$

where $Y_d$ is disposable income, $A$ is assets, and $b_1$ and $b_2$ are coefficients. Note that Equation 10.4 is a modification of the simple Keynesian consumption function: assets have been added as a second factor to income. When Ando and Modigliani fit this simple equation to data in the United States during the period after World War II, they found that $b_1$ was close to .7 and $b_2$ was close to .06; this provided striking confirmation for their ideas about consumption. Moreover, the addition of total assets to the equation could eliminate some of the errors in the simple Keynesian consumption function that we noted earlier. For example, the bulge of consumption relative to income in the years just after World War II could be explained by the high level of consumer assets from wartime savings. The decline in consumption starting in 1973 could be explained by the drop in the stock market and other asset valuations. Fluctuations in asset values are not much help in explaining the fluctuations of consumption in recent years, however. Neither the sharp fall in the stock market in 1987 nor the large rise in 1995 and 1996 seemed to have much effect on consumption.

## Friedman: Does Past Income Matter for Consumption?

Friedman expressed the ideas about forward-looking consumers in a slightly different way. He simply defined permanent income as that constant level of annual income that has a present value equivalent to the family's assets and expected future income. All other changes in income are then viewed as transitory. Friedman argued that the marginal propensity to consume from permanent income should be close to 1, and the marginal propensity to consume from transitory income should be close to zero. Algebraically, he formulated the consumption function as

$$C = b_\mathrm{p} Y_\mathrm{p,} \tag{10.5}$$

where $Y_\mathrm{p}$ is permanent disposable income and $b_\mathrm{p}$ is a coefficient. According to Friedman's formulation $b_\mathrm{p}$ should be close to 1.

An important part of Friedman's formulation was his assumption that permanent income is an average of income over the last several years. Thus, if current income suddenly increased, there would be only a small increase in permanent income; income would have to increase for several years in a row before people would expect that permanent income had increased. To test the theory, he thus substituted an average of current income and previous income over the past several years for permanent income in Equation 10.5. Effectively, therefore, consumption should depend on past income as well as on current income. Past income should matter for consumption because it helps people to forecast future income. Although it is an admittedly simple model of people's expectations, Friedman found that his formulation of the consumption function fit the facts better than the simple Keynesian function with current income.

## Where Do We Stand Now?

The empirical work of Ando, Modigliani, and Friedman is now more than 40 years old. Economic research in recent years has led to more revealing tests of the forward-looking theory and has raised puzzling new questions. Three strands of the new research are particularly important: the use of rational expectations to measure future income prospects, the analysis of data on the histories of thousands of individual families, and case studies of particular economic policy "experiments."

**RATIONAL EXPECTATIONS**   The hypothesis of consumers as forward-looking decision-makers already postulates a considerable degree of rationality to consumers. The hypothesis of rational expectations postulates more, but not necessarily less plausible, rationality. Recall that Ando, Modigliani, and Friedman postulated rather naive assumptions about what people expected about their future income: that it would tend to stay where it was recently. The rational expectations approach attempts to look at the actual historical behavior of income and use this to describe statistically how people expect income to behave in the future.

The approach is a statistical formalization and a much finer version of the rough check on the theory that we described at the start of this section. Rather than just saying that people expect business cycles to be temporary, the approach assumes that people act as if they have a little model of the behavior of income over the business cycle in their heads and that they use this model when guessing their future income. Of course, nobody would actually use such a model in their personal family planning: The idea is that by watching television, reading the newspaper, or just talking with friends, people get a view of future economic developments that is not much different from that of the average professional economist who actually uses such a model.

The rational expectations approach is used by many economists engaged in macroeconomic research.[6] The most straightforward version of this approach is to substitute the forecasts of income from such a model into the permanent-income equation (10.5) for consumption. More technical versions substitute forecasts of future income into the intertemporal budget constraint, Equation 10.3, and calculate the optimal plan for consumption directly without the intermediate step of Friedman's permanent-income equation. Using rational expectations this way clearly requires advanced mathematical skills, and understandably the approach has attracted economists who specialize in such skills.

It is clear now from this research that the forward-looking consumption theory does not fare as well as when people are assumed to forecast rationally. One problem is that consumption is a bit too responsive to temporary changes in income, although clearly not as responsive as in the simple Keynesian consumption theory. In other words, the forward-looking theory with rational expectations suggests that the short-run marginal propensity to consume should be even smaller than is observed in the United States data summarized in Table 10.1.

**INDIVIDUAL FAMILY HISTORIES**    One of the most important improvements in our knowledge of the economy in recent years is the availability of data on the economic histories of individuals and families over a span of several years. At the University of Michigan, for example, a survey called the

---

[6]The research referred to is found in a series of papers published in the *Journal of Political Economy:* Robert Hall, "Stochastic Implications of the Life Cycle–Permanent Income Hypothesis: Theory and Evidence," *Journal of Political Economy,* Vol. 86 (December 1978), pp. 971–988; and Marjorie Flavin, "The Adjustment of Consumption to Changing Expectations about Future Income," *Journal of Political Economy,* Vol. 89 (October 1981), pp. 974–1009. Lars Peter Hansen and Kenneth Singleton have incorporated rational expectations into the budget constraint in a formal intertemporal planning process in their "Stochastic Consumption, Risk Aversion, and the Temporal Behavior of Asset Returns," *Journal of Political Economy,* Vol. 91 (April 1983), pp. 249–265. All these papers are technically demanding. They are listed here as sources; we suggest them as reading only for the more mathematically inclined students.

Panel of Study on Income Dynamics has kept tabs on the major economic and personal events of thousands of families since 1969. Such surveys that collect information on individuals over a number of years are typically called **panel** or **longitudinal surveys.** They are useful to macroeconomists because they tell how families experience recessions and booms individually. Aggregate data tell us only about all families in the economy added together. One study has looked at how well the forward-looking consumption model performs in describing the consumption behavior of about 2,000 families in the Michigan panel data set.[7] The results show an excess sensitivity of consumption to temporary changes in disposable income. The marginal propensity to consume from temporary income was about 30 percent of the marginal propensity to consume from permanent income. This is higher than the 5 to 10 percent ratio that the pure forward-looking model suggests. The results seem to say that about 80 percent of the families behaved according to the forward-looking model, while about 20 percent behaved according to a simple model in which consumption is proportional to disposable income.

**POLICY EXPERIMENTS**   In 1968 during President Johnson's administration, Congress passed a temporary surcharge on the personal income tax; the surcharge raised taxes by 10 percent. One purpose was to restrict consumption temporarily and thereby reduce aggregate demand in an economy overheated by Vietnam War expenditures. A similar temporary tax change occurred during President Ford's administration, but in the reverse direction. When the economy was in the trough of the 1974–75 recession, a tax rebate and social security bonus of $9.4 billion was paid out. The hope was to stimulate the economy by increasing aggregate demand. According to the forward-looking theory of consumption, families who realized that these tax changes were temporary would adjust their consumer expenditures by only a small amount; if so, the policy changes would not have their desired effect of restricting demand in 1968 or stimulating demand in 1975. On the other hand, according to the simple consumption function, these tax changes would be translated into large changes in consumption and thereby in aggregate demand.

Although clearly not conceived as experiments, these two changes in policy gave economists a rare opportunity to test the predictions of the forward-looking theory of consumption. It is probably as close as macroeconomics will ever get to a laboratory experiment. As it turned out, the response of consumption to the change in disposable income seemed to be small in both cases. After the increase in taxes in 1968 consumers simply saved less of their reduced income and thereby reduced their spending only slightly.

---

[7]Robert Hall and Fredric Mishkin, "The Sensitivity of Consumption to Transitory Income: Estimates from Panel Data on Households," *Econometrica,* Vol. 50 (March 1982), pp. 461–481.

In the second quarter of 1975 the rate of saving as a fraction of disposable income rose to almost 10 percent, from about 6 percent in the first quarter. Almost all the increase in disposable income was saved, evidently because people knew the temporary nature of the income changes. In addition to providing evidence in favor of the forward-looking theory of consumption, the lesson from these two policy experiments has been to make policymakers much more reluctant to use such temporary tax changes to affect aggregate demand. Economists in the Ford administration wrote in the 1977 *Economic Report of the President:* "Consumers normally adjust expenditures to their 'permanent' or long-run income." In 1977 President Carter came into office proposing another rebate to stimulate the economy out of an apparent slowdown in the recovery, but the proposal was criticized by many economists and was not passed by Congress.

In 1992 President Bush proposed to reduce the amount of taxes that were withheld from workers' paychecks in order to speed the recovery from the 1990–91 recession. However, the reduction in withholding in 1992 implied a smaller refund for taxpayers in 1993. This proposal was much like the temporary tax cuts of the 1970s. As predicted by the forward-looking consumption model, the effect on consumption was small.

Statistical research on temporary tax experiments indicates that the marginal propensity to consume from a temporary tax change is about half the marginal propensity to consume from a permanent tax change. This ratio is a bit above that found in the Michigan panel data (.3). In other words, the world is split about 50–50 between forward-looking consumers and those who consume a constant proportion of their current disposable income. Perhaps the most important lesson from these experiments is that the response of the economy to a temporary income tax change is not the sure, predictable stimulus predicted by the simple consumption function.[8]

## Defects in the Forward-Looking Model

Overall the empirical research discussed above indicates that the forward-looking model works fairly well: the marginal propensity to consume from temporary income is always less than the marginal propensity to consume from permanent income, as the theory predicts. But why doesn't it work better? Why does consumption respond as much as it does to temporary income? One reason is that the tests might be incorrectly estimating expectations of future income. In the case of temporary tax changes, for example, families may not be so aware of the machinations of the government. Perhaps

[8]Alan Blinder, "Temporary Income Taxes and Consumer Spending," *Journal of Political Economy,* Vol. 89 (February 1981), pp. 26–53. The figures on tax rebates and saving mentioned in the previous paragraph are tabulated in Blinder's paper.

they pay no attention to the news about tax changes. If they see the benefits of a tax cut in the form of reduced withholding deductions from their paychecks, they may mistakenly assume that this cut in deductions is permanent. Then they will apply their regular marginal propensity to consume from

## NEW RESEARCH IN PRACTICE
### Locked-Up Savings

The life-cycle theory of consumption says that families should gradually accumulate assets in order to finance retirement. It doesn't say how families might hold their savings—they could be in savings accounts, mutual funds, or in individual stocks and bonds. The theory says that families should treat their savings as a pool—it does not predict that families would have separate funds earmarked for retirement.

In fact, most families hold virtually all their savings in locked-up form. Even among families close to retirement, only a minority have assets in accounts where they are free to withdraw. Most families have the great bulk of their assets tied up in home equity, retirement plans, and life insurance. They follow the life-cycle principle, but keep their savings locked away. It appears that they do not trust themselves not to dip into savings if the savings are not locked away.

David Laibson of Harvard University has developed a theory of locked-up saving. He hypothesizes *hyperbolic discounting of future satisfaction*—consumption this month delivers much more satisfaction than you foresee from consumption in future months and years. As a result, you will plan to consume as much as you can this month, by drawing down all available assets.

Hyperbolic preferences are evenhanded in their weighting of the near future and the distant future—you think about spreading consumption in just the way the life-cycle model describes. In particular, you would like to plan to save for retirement. But you can see that your propensity to spend everything you can on current consumption

will defeat a saving plan. In the first place, the plan you make today won't include any saving today. You will plan to start saving next month. When next month rolls around, though, you will defer the onset of savings. You will never start your saving program.

Now suppose someone offers you a contract. After signing it today, you are obligated to pay into an account each month starting next month. You can't withdraw from the account until you are 65. You will sign the contract enthusiastically. It solves the problem of providing for retirement by locking your savings up.

The three main forms of locked-up saving are retirement programs, mortgages, and life insurance. These account for a large fraction of the saving of all but the richest families.

Financing retirement is not the only objective of locked-up savings. Some people join Christmas clubs, where their savings are locked up until the next Christmas.

Some forms of locked-up saving—life insurance and Christmas clubs—offer poor returns compared to ordinary investments, yet remain popular.

Laibson's theory of locked-up saving seems to explain some of the features of the way families save. And it may explain the political popularity of the single biggest locked-up fund, the social security system.

Although hyperbolic preferences are different from the preferences that underlie the life-cycle model, as long as families can make full use of locked-up accounts, their actual behavior will be almost the same as predicted by the life-cycle model.

income. Moreover, when they find their deductions back up to the old level, they will reduce consumption accordingly.

Or suppose the family pays close attention to the economic news and believes that a temporary tax cut will accomplish its purpose of stimulating the economy. The family will benefit in the next year or two from the more favorable performance of the economy. According to the life-cycle and permanent-income hypotheses, the family should immediately increase its consumption because of its expected increase in economic well-being. Even though such a family would spend only a little of its tax rebate, it might raise its total consumption level because of the improved national economy.

Another possibility is that consumers cannot borrow as easily as the forward-looking model suggests and that especially during recessions they cannot obtain the funds to maintain their consumption. Economists call such consumers **liquidity constrained.**[9] Such consumers might be described very well by the simple Keynesian model; they would increase their expenditures as they receive more income regardless of whether it is permanent or temporary.

In concluding our discussion of the forward-looking model of consumption, it is important not to lose sight of the central ideas by focusing too much on the particular equations or tests that express them. The basic point is that families are thoughtful about consumption decisions. The way they react to a change in economic circumstances depends on the context of the change. If the change is transitory—if it involves a windfall gain or loss—consumption is likely to respond relatively little. If the change in income will sustain itself for the foreseeable future, consumption will change almost by the full amount of the change in income.

## EMPIRICAL EVIDENCE ON THE FORWARD-LOOKING MODEL OF CONSUMPTION

1. Verification of the forward-looking model with aggregate data confirms its main implications.
2. More detailed tests with data on individual families reveal some shortcomings. Liquidity constraints may help explain the discrepancies between theoretical predictions and actual behavior.

---

[9]See Fumio Hayashi, "Tests for Liquidity Constraints: A Critical Survey and Some New Observations," in Truman Bewley, ed., *Advances in Econometrics,* Vol. 2 (Cambridge, England: Cambridge University Press, 1987), pp. 91–120.

# REAL INTEREST RATES, CONSUMPTION, AND SAVING

Thus far we have assumed that consumers want a steady consumption path. They would like to consume about the same amount this year as next year and every year thereafter. This is a reasonable assumption if the price of future consumption goods is not too low or too high relative to present consumption goods. But suppose that the price of future consumption goods is suddenly expected to fall; suppose, for example, that sales taxes will be repealed starting next year! Clearly people would postpone their consumption expenditures until next year to take advantage of the lower price. They would do this as long as they were not so impatient that they couldn't get along without the goods this year. Consumption today would fall and consumption next year would rise.

The interest rate becomes a factor in consumption because it affects the price of future consumption relative to current consumption. In fact, the *real* interest rate is the relative price between present consumption and future consumption. It thus directly affects the choice of whether to consume more today or tomorrow. Recall that the interest rate quoted in the newspaper, the *nominal* interest rate, does not correct for changes in purchasing power. The real interest rate $R$ equals the nominal interest rate minus the expected rate of inflation $\pi^e$. For example, if the nominal interest rate is 7 percent, but prices are expected to rise at 3 percent per year, then the real interest rate is 4 percent. If you postpone 1 unit of consumption this year, you can consume 1.04 units next year by investing at a 7 percent nominal rate and losing 3 percent to inflation.

If the real interest rate is positive, as it generally is, people face an incentive to defer spending: a dollar saved today will buy more than a dollar's worth of goods tomorrow. Hence people will tend to defer consumption unless they are too impatient. Economists have a measure of impatience called the **rate of time preference.** If the real interest rate is higher than the rate of time preference, then people will tend to shift their consumption a bit toward the next year. If the real rate of interest is high, today's consumption will tend to be low. This factor makes consumption negatively related to the real rate of interest. Saving, which is simply the difference between disposable income and consumption, is therefore positively related to the real rate of interest.

Changes in the interest rate do something else in addition to changing tomorrow's price of goods relative to today's. They change income. If interest rates rise, for example, a family can earn a higher real return from its accumulated assets. This makes the family better off. On this account, planned

consumption is higher. This increase in consumption might offset the reduced consumption that comes from the incentive to defer consumption
from today to tomorrow. Hence, we can't say unambiguously whether consumption in the first year falls or rises; the *income* effect makes it rise, while
the incentive to make a *substitution* of future consumption for present consumption makes it fall. Similarly, the effect of change in the real interest rate
on saving is also ambiguous.[10] Of course, this offsetting tendency of the
income effect and the substitution effect is common to many relative price
changes in economics, not only to interest-rate changes.

It is a controversial matter whether or not consumption is negatively
related to the interest rate in the U.S. economy.[11] The most difficult problem
in interpreting the data is that consumption depends on disposable income
as well as on the interest rate, and during the business cycle income and the
interest rate tend to move together. It is difficult to separate out the effect of
just the interest rate.

Another complication in examining the relation between real interest
and consumption is that the real interest rate is not observed directly. What
we observe is the nominal interest rate. To convert it to a real rate, we must
subtract the expected rate of inflation. Measuring the expected rate of inflation is difficult.

## Effect of Real Interest Rates on Work

There is one last complication in our analysis of consumption. For this whole
chapter we have assumed that individuals do not or cannot change how
much they work. Income from work was taken as exogenous. But some
people are free to vary how much they work. In particular, if real interest
rates rise, the value of income from working today relative to tomorrow rises.
People could gain from working harder and longer hours now and taking
time off to spend the earnings later. Hence, in principle, income from work
is a positive function of the real interest rate. Because saving is the difference
between disposable income and consumption, this positive effect of real
interest rates on income from working reinforces the negative effect of real
interest rates on consumption to make saving positively related to income.

Detecting the effect of real interest rates on work effort has proved
even more elusive than detecting the effect of real interest rates on consumption. It appears that most people cannot or do not adjust their work
effort very much in response to interest-rate changes. This corresponds with
casual observation.

---

[10]The income and substitution effects are shown graphically in the appendix to this chapter.

[11]One attempt to measure the substitution effect alone is Robert E. Hall, "Intertemporal Substitution in Consumption," *Journal of Political Economy,* Vol. 96 (April 1988), pp. 971–987.

## CONSUMPTION, SAVING, AND THE INTEREST RATE

1. The consumption planning process should take the interest rate into account. The real interest rate—the nominal interest rate less the expected rate of inflation—is the trade-off facing the consumer between current and future consumption. When real interest rates are high, future consumption becomes cheaper relative to consumption this year.
2. It is difficult to isolate the effect of interest rates on consumption in actual data. There is no strong empirical confirmation of the theoretical possibility that saving responds positively to real interest rates, at least for the variation in real interest rates observed in the United States.
3. In principle, interest-rate changes may cause people to reallocate labor supply over time. Higher interest rates today increase the return to current labor effort measured in units of future consumption. Evidence suggests this effect is very weak.

# 10.6    CONSUMPTION AND THE IS CURVE

In Chapter 7 we introduced the IS curve. It shows all the combinations of real GDP and interest rates where spending balance occurs. To find a point on the IS curve, we consider a particular interest rate. Then we find the level of GDP that gives spending balance at that rate. The IS curve is downward-sloping in the IS-LM diagram with the interest rate $R$ on the vertical axis and output $Y$ on the horizontal axis. The slope of the IS curve and how much it is shifted by fiscal policy are crucial for evaluating the effects of monetary and fiscal policy.

Recall that the simple Keynesian consumption function was used in the derivation of the IS curve in Chapter 7. How is the IS curve affected by the factors considered in this chapter?

## The Slope of the IS Curve

Consider first the slope of the IS curve. The smaller the marginal propensity to consume, the steeper the slope of the IS curve. A small MPC means that the multiplier is small and changes in interest rates thereby have a small effect on output. The results considered in this chapter make us scale down the

MPC. In our complete model, departures of output from potential are best thought of as temporary changes in income. Thus, the variation in income along the IS curve is a variation in temporary income, for which the marginal propensity to consume is likely to be quite small. On this account the IS curve is steeper than it seemed in Chapter 7, because output is less sensitive to the interest rate.

However, the interest-rate effects on consumption considered in the preceding section have an opposite effect on the IS curve. If consumption depends negatively on the interest rate, then a higher interest rate will shift the consumption function down, in which case the level of GDP corresponding to spending balance will be lower. On that account the IS curve is flatter than it seemed in Chapter 7, because output is more sensitive to the interest rate.

On balance it is an empirical question whether the true IS curve that incorporates the issues raised in this chapter is flatter or steeper than the IS curve derived in Chapter 7.

## Shifts in the IS Curve Due to Tax Changes

The IS curve in Chapter 7 did not distinguish between temporary and permanent changes in taxes. A cut in tax payments of any kind would shift the IS curve to the right by the same amount and thereby stimulate output by the same amount. The forward-looking theory of consumption says that the shift in the IS curve should be much larger if the tax cut is permanent rather than temporary. A purely temporary tax cut—such as the 1975 tax rebate— would have a very small effect on the IS curve.

Because it is sometimes difficult to tell whether people think a tax cut is permanent or temporary, the forward-looking theory points to an element of uncertainty in our ability to determine how much the IS curve will shift in response to tax changes.

Finally, the forward-looking theory says that the IS curve will shift to the right in response to an *expectation* of future tax cuts. Future tax cuts will stimulate consumption today because lifetime disposable income has increased.

## REVIEW AND PRACTICE

### Major Points

1. Consumers finance their consumption from their incomes, and consumption has tracked income reasonably closely in U.S. history.

2. There have been, however, significant deviations from a simple consumption function.

3. The forward-looking consumption theory relates consumption to current and expected future income rather than to just current income.

4. In this view, the marginal propensity to consume from transitory changes in income is much lower than that from permanent changes in income.

5. Tax policy does not operate in a mechanical way through disposable income. Families raise their consumption only if a tax cut makes them feel better off, which may not happen with some types of cuts.

6. The forward-looking model passes empirical tests with aggregate data quite well, but still has some defects, which have been revealed mainly by studies of individual family behavior.

7. Though higher real interest rates ought to stimulate saving by making consumers defer consumption, this hypothesis has not been firmly established by the data.

8. The marginal propensity to consume is one of the determinants of the slope of the IS curve. Because of automatic stabilizers and the low short-run marginal propensity to consume of forward-looking consumers, the IS curve may be steeper than the one derived in Chapter 7.

## Key Terms and Concepts

consumption
disposable income
Keynesian consumption function
marginal propensity to consume (MPC)
intertemporal budget constraint
smooth consumption path
Friedman permanent-income model
Ando-Modigliani life-cycle model

rational expectations tests
panel data tests
real interest rate
rate of time preference
long-run marginal propensity to consume
short-run marginal propensity to consume
forward-looking theory of consumption

marginal propensity to consume out of temporary income
marginal propensity to consume out of permanent income
substitution effect
automatic stabilizers

## Questions for Discussion and Review

1. List some of the reasons that disposable income is less than GDP. What factors tend to raise disposable income even though they are not part of GDP?

2. How can you tell if a simple consumption function governs the relation of consumption and income?

3. What is an estimate of the marginal propensity to consume from the historical relation of consumption to income? Why is this estimate probably an overstatement of the reaction of consumption to a temporary tax cut? What is an estimate of the short-run marginal propensity to consume?

4. Outline the way that a family might plan its consumption. How would it react to learning that tax rates are going to rise in the future?

5. Why is the marginal propensity to consume out of temporary income a bit above the real interest rate?

6. List some of the reasons that a tax cut has an uncertain effect on consumption.

7. Review all the steps involved in constructing the IS curve, including the possibility that consumption responds to the interest rate.

## Problems

### NUMERICAL

1. Use the intertemporal budget constraint for this problem. To make calculations easy, assume that a family lives for 5 years with 4 years of work and 1 year of retirement. (A more realistic assumption would be a 50-year horizon with 40 years of work and 10 years of retirement.) Consider a family that wishes to consume the same amount each year. Assume earnings of $25,000 per year and an interest rate of 5 percent. Assume initial assets of zero.

   a. Find the level of consumption such that the assets at the end of 5 years are roughly zero, say within $100. What is the level of assets at the beginning of retirement?

   b. Repeat the calculation of consumption, but with initial assets of $1,000. By how much does consumption rise? Compare this with the interest earnings on $1,000 at 5 percent, namely, $50 per year. Would the increase be closer to $50 if the family lived for 50 years?

   c. Repeat the calculation of consumption, with initial assets of zero, but with earnings of $26,000 per year. By how much does consumption rise? Explain why the increase in consumption is larger than in Part b.

2. Suppose that we have a consumption function of the form

$$C = 220 + .9Y_p,$$

where $Y_p$ is permanent disposable income. Suppose that consumers estimate their permanent disposable income by a simple average of disposable income in the present and previous years:

$$Y_p = .5(Y_d + Y_{d-1}),$$

where $Y_d$ is actual disposable income.

   a. Suppose that disposable income $Y_d$ is equal to $4,000 in year 1 and is also equal to $4,000 in year 2. What is consumption in year 2?

   b. Suppose that disposable income increases to $5,000 in year 3 and then remains at $5,000 in all future years. What is consumption in years 3 and 4 and all remaining years? Explain why consumption responds the way it does to an increase in income.

   c. What is the short-run marginal propensity to consume? What is the long-run marginal propensity to consume?

   d. Explain why this formulation of consumption may provide a more accurate description of consumption than the simple consumption function that depends only on current income.

3. Suppose that consumption is given by the same equation as in Problem 2, but that

consumers set their permanent income $Y_p$ equal to the average of their expected income in all future years.

   a. Suppose that, as in the previous problem, disposable income is $4,000 in years 1 and 2, but suppose also that in year 2 consumers expect that disposable income will be $4,000 in all future years. What is consumption in year 2?

   b. Suppose that in year 3 disposable income rises to $5,000 and that consumers expect the $5,000 level to remain in all future years. What is consumption in year 3?

   c. Explain why consumption in year 3 is different from that in Problem 2 even though the disposable income is the same.

4. Suppose again that consumption is given by the same equation as in Problem 2 and that permanent income is estimated in the same way as in Problem 2. Place this consumption function into a simple macro model like the one in Chapter 7. That is, disposable income $Y_d$ is equal to income $Y$ less taxes $T$, where taxes equal $.3Y$, and the income identity is $Y = C + I + G$.

   a. Suppose that in year 2 investment $I$ is $650 and government spending $G$ is $750. Suppose that disposable income $Y_d$ in year 1 was $2,800. What are consumption, income, and disposable income in year 2?

   b. Suppose that in year 3 government spending increases to $800 and then remains at $800 for all future years. What are consumption, income, and disposable income in year 3? (Make sure to use your calculation from Part a of disposable income in year 2 when you calculate consumption in year 3.)

   c. Calculate income and consumption for years 4, 5, and 6. Do you see a pattern developing?

   d. Where do you think income will end up after it stops changing? Compare your answer with the simple case where consumption depends on current disposable income only, so that the multiplier formulas of Chapter 6 apply.

5. Suppose that the consumption function is given by

$$C = 270 + .63Y - 1,000R$$

rather than by the consumption function in Chapter 7. Add this consumption function to the other four equations of the macro model:

$$Y = C + I + G + X$$

$$M = (.1583Y - 1,000R)P$$

$$I = 1,000 - 2,000R$$

$$X = 525 - .1Y - 500R.$$

Treat the price level as predetermined at 1.0, and let government spending be $1,200 and the money supply be $900.

   a. Derive an algebraic expression for the IS curve for this model and plot it to scale. Compare it with the IS curve in the examples in Chapter 7. Which is steeper? Why?

   b. Derive the aggregate demand curve and plot it to scale. How does it compare with the aggregate demand curve in the example in Chapter 7?

c. Calculate the effect of an increase in government spending on GDP. Is the effect larger or smaller than in the case where consumption does not depend on the interest rate? Describe the process of crowding out in this case.

d. Calculate the effect of an increase in the money supply on GDP. Is the impact larger or smaller than in the case where consumption does not depend on the interest rate? Explain.

6. The problem of the family choosing a consumption plan can be analyzed using utility functions from intermediate microeconomics. In fact, this is how the forward-looking theory has been tested in recent research. Consider a very simple two-year horizon for a family planning consumption. The family wants to determine how much to consume in year 1 and in year 2. Let consumption in year 1 be $C_1$, and let consumption in year 2 be $C_2$. Suppose that the family's satisfaction, or utility, from consuming $C_1$ and $C_2$ is given by the function

$$\text{Utility} = \sqrt{C_1} + \frac{1}{1 + \text{RT}} \sqrt{C_2}$$

where RT is the rate of time preference. Start with the rate of time preference equal to zero.

a. Show that this utility function means that the family prefers smooth consumption to erratic consumption. Which plan for consumption gives the family the greater utility: $3,600 in the first year and $4,900 in the next, or $4,250 in both years?

b. Show that when the rate of time preference is high, the family will prefer to consume more in the first period. Do the following comparison: First set RT equal to zero and evaluate the utility of $3,600 in the first year and $3,000 in the second year versus $3,300 in both years; then raise RT to .25 and make the comparison again.

## ANALYTICAL

1. Which of the following facts are consistent with forward-looking theories of consumption? Which are not? Justify your answer in each case. Where the facts are not consistent with the theory, can you suggest some alternative explanations?

a. The marginal propensity to consume out of current income is less for old people than for middle-aged people.

b. The marginal propensity to consume out of current income is less for farmers than for most other occupations.

c. Most European countries have both more extensive social welfare systems for older people and higher saving rates than the United States.

d. The saving rate for the United States fell in the early 1980s.

e. The marginal propensity to consume out of temporary tax cuts is around .3 to .5.

f. Across the population as a whole, people with lower incomes have lower saving rates than people with higher incomes.

g. The amount of wealth in the economy is far greater than what current wage earners will consume in their retirement.

2. Suppose that actual GDP is below potential GDP, that inflation is low, and that the President and Congress want to cut taxes in order to increase aggregate demand and bring the economy back to potential.
   a. Describe the situation using an IS-LM diagram. Show where you want the IS curve to move in order to reach potential.
   b. In light of the forward-looking theory of consumption, describe some of the problems that might arise with the tax cut plan.

3. Draw a sketch of an IS-LM diagram. Compare two cases, one where the consumption function depends on the interest rate and the other where the consumption function does not depend on the interest rate. Compare the relative effectiveness of monetary and fiscal policy in the two different situations.

4. Explain the following puzzle: Saving depends positively on the interest rate, investment depends negatively on the interest rate, and saving equals investment. How does an increase in the money supply that lowers the interest rate and thereby increases investment also increase saving? It would seem that with the lower interest rate, saving would be lower. What's going on?

5. An important implication of the permanent-income hypothesis is that fiscal policy operates with a lag.
   a. Explain why a permanent increase in government spending may cause the IS curve to shift out slowly over time, rather than shift out all at once.
   b. If permanent income is a weighted average of last period's and this period's income, what determines the speed at which the IS curve shifts out over time?

6. Suppose a family wants a smooth consumption profile and does not wish to leave a bequest. Indicate how each of the following factors would affect the magnitude of the marginal propensity to consume out of a temporary change in income.
   a. The size of the temporary income change.
   b. The length of the family's planning horizon.
   c. The rate of interest.

7. Suppose that you know the true magnitudes of the marginal propensities to consume out of temporary and permanent changes in income and that they are stable over time. Explain what can be learned about households' perceptions of the nature of changes in income from observations on the short-run marginal propensity to consume. In particular, what is implied by unusually large changes in consumption relative to income in a given year? What about unusually small changes?

## MacroSolve Exercises

1. Provide explanations consistent with the permanent-income hypothesis for the unusual behavior of the ratio of consumption to income in 1972–74, and for the reversal in trend beginning in 1982. To see this behavior, either plot or tabulate the quarterly time series of the APC (average propensity to consume) or graph consumption expenditures against disposable income.

2. Using the basic fixed-price model in MacroSolve ("ISLM, Closed Econ"), investigate the implications of changing the marginal propensity to consume. Explain how and why the slope of the IS curve changes when the marginal propensity to consume increases.

3. Given your findings in Question 2, what are the sizes of the corresponding multipliers for a change in the money supply? Is monetary policy now more or less effective in changing the level of economic activity?

4. In the basic AD/PA model, does an increased responsiveness of consumption to current income lead to faster or slower adjustment to equilibrium GDP following a cut in the money supply? Explain your answer in words.

5. Plot the saving rate ("Saving/GDP%") using quarterly data from 1980.1 to 1983.4. What major event during this time period may account for the pattern in the saving rate?

# APPENDIX: A Graphical Approach to Consumption Planning

In this appendix we show how a two-period consumption planning problem can be represented graphically. Suppose that the representative family must choose how much to consume this year and next year. Figure 10.9 shows how the family's pref-

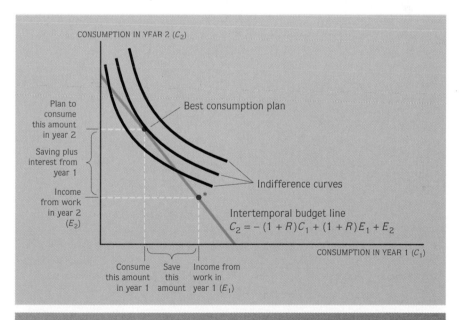

**FIGURE 10.9** Indifference Curves and the Intertemporal Budget Line for Consumption Planning

The indifference curve is the combination of consumption in the two years that gives the same level of satisfaction to the family. The straight line is the budget constraint. The family tries to get to the highest indifference curve. This occurs where the indifference curve and the budget line just meet at a point of tangency.

erences for consumption in the two periods might look; the vertical axis is consumption next year (Year 2) and the horizontal axis is consumption this year (Year 1). The curved lines are **indifference curves;** they give the alternative values for consumption in the two years between which the family is indifferent. The slope of the line measures how many dollars of consumption next year must be given up when consumption this year rises by 1 dollar for the family to maintain the same level of satisfaction, or utility. This is sometimes called the **marginal rate of substitution** between consumption this year and consumption next year. The family is better off when the indifference curves are farther out and up.

The straight line in Figure 10.9 is simply the intertemporal budget constraint for the two periods. The slope of the line is $-(1 + R)$ because the family will have an additional $(1 + R)$ dollars of consumption next year for each dollar of consumption that is reduced (and thus saved) this year. [The equation for the budget line comes directly from Equation 10.3 with no taxes, no initial assets, and no bequest, and is applied for two periods. Then Equation 10.3 is $A_2 = E_1 - C_1$ in year 1, and $0 = (1 + R)A_2 + E_2 - C_2$ in year 2. Putting $A_2$ into the equation for year 1 gives the equation for the budget line.] The point on the line marked * represents the amount of income

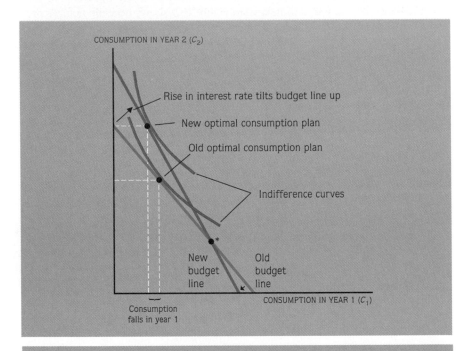

**FIGURE 10.10**  Increase in the Interest Rate

As the interest rate increases, the budget line gets steeper. This leads to a higher level of utility. As drawn, the family consumes less this period. But it is uncertain whether the family will consume less if other indifference curves are drawn.

from work this year and next year. Moving up the line from * means that the family is saving this year, because income is greater than consumption. Moving down on the line means that the family borrows this year.

The family tries to maximize utility or, in terms of the graph, to get to the highest indifference curve. This occurs at a point of tangency between the budget line and the indifference curve, as shown in the diagram. At this point the slopes are equal so we know that the marginal rate of substitution between consumption next year and consumption this year is equal to 1 plus the interest rate.

Now, suppose that the interest rate increases. This is shown in Figure 10.10. The budget line will then tilt in a steeper direction, pivoting around the point *. A higher level of utility is thereby achieved. As the graph is drawn, less is consumed this year. But note that this depends very much on how the indifference curves are drawn. (Try to draw another for which the reverse occurs). The tilting of the curve represents the substitution effect, which certainly causes consumption this year to fall. But the budget line has also moved out to the right from where it was before on the indifference curve. This is the income effect. It certainly leads to more consumption today.

# Investment Demand

Investment is the most volatile component of GDP. While smaller in magnitude than consumption, it fluctuates more. Keynes argued that investment is the primary driving force in the business cycle, that it fluctuates erratically because of capricious shifts in business expectations, whereas consumption responds passively according to the simple consumption function.

In looking at the microeconomic underpinnings of investment we will see that this distinction between investment and consumption is not so pronounced. For one thing, investment, much as consumption, responds to income and output in a systematic way. When investment rises, it may be the result, not the cause, of an increase in spending elsewhere in the economy. Moreover, while investment decisions do depend on business expectations, these expectations are based on calculated estimates of future changes in demand and prices that businesses are likely to face. In making their investment decisions, business firms are at least as forward-looking as the consumers that we described in Chapter 10.

# 11.1 FLUCTUATIONS IN INVESTMENT SPENDING

We saw in Chapter 2 that investment spending is divided into three categories:

1. Nonresidential fixed investment—business purchases of new plant and equipment
2. Residential fixed investment—construction of new houses and apartments
3. Inventory investment—increases in stocks of goods produced but not yet sold

Nonresidential fixed investment was 10.2 percent of GDP in 1995. Residential investment was 4.3 percent of GDP in the same year. But the shares of the different types of investment in GDP are not good measures of their importance in economic fluctuations. Although plant and equipment investment is the dominant component of total investment, it is the most stable over time. Since inventory investment is negative as stocks of unsold goods fall and positive when stocks of goods rise, its share of GDP is not a very meaningful statistic. Yet inventory investment is particularly volatile and has a major role in recessions. Finally, residential investment is important because housing construction drops when mortgage interest rates go up.

Figure 11.1 shows how tightly fixed investment is linked to overall economic activity. Reductions in investment frequently occur at about the same time as the economy goes into a recession. Recoveries from recessions—as in the years following the 1990–91 recession—are usually periods when investment rises rapidly. The fluctuations of investment are larger in percentage terms than the fluctuations in real GDP. Sometimes fluctuations in investment occur without fluctuations in GDP, when consumption, government spending, or net exports move in the opposite direction. Note that investment slowed down in 1986, although there was no slowdown in real GDP growth in 1986.

The behavior of the two components of fixed investment—business (nonresidential) and residential—is shown in Figure 11.2. In most recessions, residential investment turns down before business investment turns down. This was true of the downturn in 1990. We will show later that rising interest rates have large negative effects on residential investment and that the start of most recessions is accompanied by rising interest rates. Note that in 1986 business fixed investment declined even though residential investment continued to grow. As we will see, this decline may have been due to the increase in taxes on business capital that was passed into law in 1986.

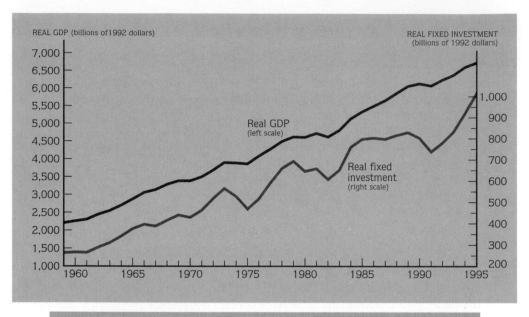

**FIGURE 11.1** Fixed Investment and GDP

Real fixed investment and real GDP fluctuate together. Investment and GDP rose together in the great expansion of the 1960s, fell together in the recession beginning in 1974, rose again in the late 1970s, fell together in the early 1980s, and fell together again in 1990–91. Investment has risen since 1991. However, as percentages, the fluctuations in fixed investment are larger than the fluctuations in total GDP.
Source: *Economic Report of the President,* 1996, Table B-2.

Real GDP and *business* fixed investment move together almost in tandem. We cannot tell from the data whether movements in GDP are inducing movements in business investment or movements in business investment are inducing movements in GDP. Another mechanism to be considered is that both GDP and business investment are responding to the same underlying stimulus, which is causing both to move together.

In the economy as a whole, the volume of investment observed is the joint outcome of three factors: (1) **investment demand,** decisions made by businesses about the amount of investment to undertake; (2) **saving supply,** decisions made by consumers about the amount to save; and (3) **investment supply,** decisions made by producers of investment goods about how much to supply.

This chapter focuses on investment demand. A complete model of the economy that combines saving behavior as described in Chapter 10 and the supply side of the economy is necessary to give a complete picture of in-

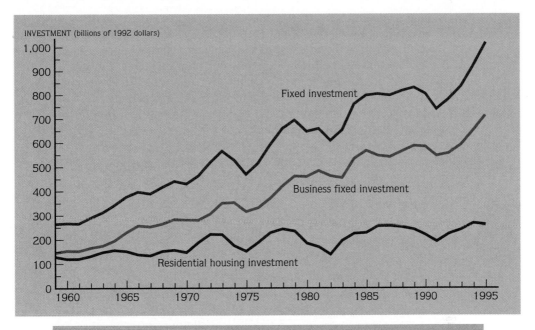

**FIGURE 11.2**   Housing versus Factories and Equipment

Separating housing investment from business investment reveals some important timing differences.
Both business investment and housing investment fluctuate widely during recessions and booms.
But housing investment leads real GDP while business investment moves together with real GDP.
Source: *Economic Report of the President*, 1996, Table B-2.

vestment. The economy reconciles the decisions of the various groups with
the interest rate and the price of capital goods. If businesses want to invest
more than consumers are willing to lend, the interest rate rises enough to
depress investment and stimulate saving to the point of equality. If businesses
want to invest more than the producers of investment goods want to produce, the price of capital goods rises. Then investment demand falls and the
supply of capital goods rises, again to the point of equality.

## INVESTMENT ANALYSIS

1. Investment is the flow of newly produced capital goods. It consists of
   plant and equipment investment, residential investment, and inventory
   investment.

2. Investment is much more volatile than consumption. Declines in business fixed investment are closely timed with declines in the overall economy. Declines in housing investment lead the declines in the overall economy.

3. The overall level of investment depends on three elements: the investment demand of firms and households, the funds available for investment, and the amount of investment goods produced. Interest rates and the prices of investment goods move to equate the three elements. In this chapter we focus on investment demand.

# HOW FIRMS MAKE INVESTMENT DECISIONS

In examining the micro foundations of investment demand, we will start with business fixed investment and look at the decision process of a typical business firm. From a firm's perspective there are really two decisions that can be distinguished. The first thing for the managers to decide is how many factories and machines they want. That is, what is the firm's desired **capital stock**? The second question is how fast to build the factories and when to order the machines that they want. That is, what is the **flow of investment**? Here we start with the question of the desired capital stock, and derive the flow demand subsequently.

It is helpful to pose the typical firm's problem in the following rather abstract way: Suppose a firm has already figured out how much output it plans to produce during the upcoming year. Further, suppose that whatever capital it will use it will *rent* from another firm in the equipment rental business. For example, a firm in the business of offering typing services to its customers would rent word-processing equipment from a computer-leasing firm. (Many firms own most of their capital, but we will look at that case a little later.) The idea of thinking about a firm's investment decision as a choice about how much capital to rent was developed through models by Dale Jorgenson of Harvard University in the early 1960s.[1] It is a useful abstraction because it makes the capital decision much like the decision to employ other factors used in production, such as labor and raw materials.

How much capital will the firm choose to rent? Microeconomics tells us the answer: the amount that equates the marginal benefit to the marginal cost. The **marginal benefit** is the amount of dollars saved by using fewer of the other factors of production when more capital is employed. A firm

---

[1]Dale Jorgenson, "Capital Theory and Investment Behavior," *American Economic Review*, Vol. 53 (May 1963), pp. 247–259.

with more capital will need fewer workers, less energy, or fewer materials to produce the same amount of output. For example, with a word processor, a firm offering typing services might require fewer hours from proofreaders and typists, and perhaps fewer correction materials (like Liquid Paper). Note that the firm must look ahead to determine the marginal benefit of employing more capital during the period that it will rent the capital. Firms are thus assumed to be *forward-looking* in this theory of investment.

The **marginal cost** of capital is just the rental cost charged by the renting firm. For example, it is the amount that the computer-leasing firm charges each year for word-processing equipment.

The firm's decision can be illustrated graphically. The most important input to production is labor, so consider the case where the input displaced by capital is labor. The production function relating labor input to output produced is shown in Figure 11.3. When there is more labor input, there is more output. For example, for the typing-services firm, when typists and proofreaders work more hours, more typed pages are produced. When there is more capital in the firm, the production function relating labor input to output produced is shifted upward, as shown in Figure 11.3. In this case fewer hours worked by typists and proofreaders result in the same number of typed pages. In Figure 11.3, $N$ is the level of employment needed to produce planned output with the existing capital stock, and $N'$ is the reduced level of employment needed to produce planned output if extra capital is

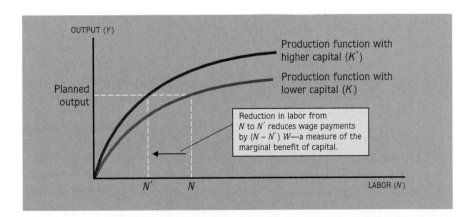

**FIGURE 11.3** The Production Function and the Marginal Benefit of Capital

The production function shows the amount of output produced from different amounts of labor. The lower production function describes the situation with the existing capital of the firm. In order to produce the planned output, the firm will have to employ $N$ workers. The upper production function applies if the firm decides to rent some extra capital. In that case, to produce the planned output, only $N'$ workers need to be employed. The marginal benefit of capital is the reduced wage payments, $(N - N')W$.

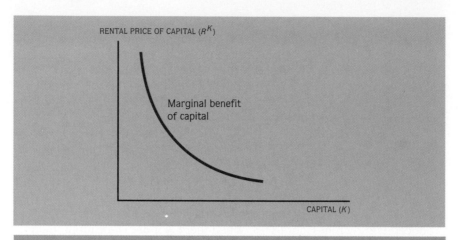

**FIGURE 11.4**    The Marginal Benefit of Capital Schedule

The marginal benefit of capital is a declining function of the amount of capital because of the diminishing marginal product of capital. The position of the schedule depends on the level of planned output and on the wage rate.

rented. If the wage per worker is $W$, the marginal benefit of the extra capital is $(N - N')W$.

We assume that capital has a **diminishing marginal product,** which means that the amount of the upward shift in the production function and the corresponding decrease in labor requirements decline as the amount of capital grows. For example, if the typing-services firm began with one full-time typist and one half-time proofreader, the first word processor would result in more labor saved than a second word processor. The third and fourth word processors would displace essentially no labor. We can describe the relationship between capital and the marginal benefit of additional capital in a **marginal benefit of capital** schedule, as shown in Figure 11.4.

The marginal benefit of capital schedule is the firm's **demand curve for rented capital** as well. To choose its level of capital, the firm simply finds the amount of capital that equates the marginal benefit of capital to the marginal cost of capital, which is the rental price. We call the rental price of capital $R^K$. The superscript $K$ is a mnemonic for capital. Figure 11.5 illustrates the process.

What happens if the firm decides to produce more output? Looking back at Figure 11.3, you can see that producing more output with the same capital stock will require more labor. That, in turn, raises the marginal benefit of capital. To equate the marginal benefit to an unchanged rental price of capital, the firm will have to rent more capital. Figure 11.6 shows how the firm responds to an increase in output.

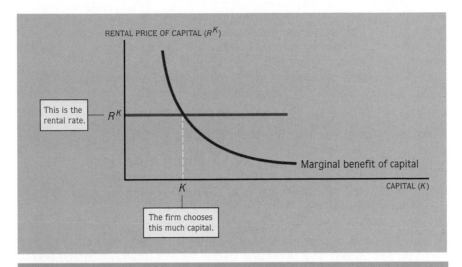

**FIGURE 11.5** Choosing the Capital Stock

The marginal benefit of capital schedule is the firm's demand function for rented capital. The firm chooses its capital stock by equating the marginal benefit of capital to its rental price. With planned output and the wage rate held constant, the firm will choose to rent more capital and employ less labor if the rental price falls.

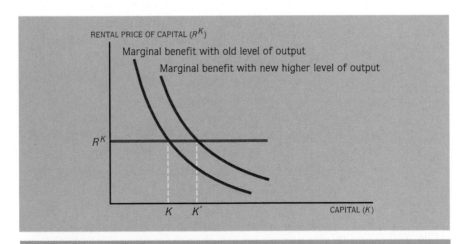

**FIGURE 11.6** Effect of Higher Output

When planned output rises and the rental price of capital and the wage remain the same, the firm's demand for capital rises. Higher planned output shifts the marginal benefit for capital schedule to the right. The firm's demand for rented capital rises from $K$ to $K'$.

We have not said anything yet about investment, only about the firm's decision to rent capital. A firm could rent more capital without bringing about any investment in the economy as a whole. The firm might just rent some existing capital that another firm had decided not to rent anymore. The relation between the decisions of individual firms and total investment in new capital goods is the subject of Section 11.3.

## Determination of the Rental Price of Capital

How would the market set the rental price of capital? We can answer this by looking at the costs faced by a rental firm—like a computer-leasing firm—that is in the business of owning machines and renting them out. We will make use of the following terms and assumptions:

$P^K$ is the price for purchasing a new machine from a producer of machines. The price is assumed to be unchanging for now. The price is measured in "real" terms, that is, relative to the price of other noncapital goods, like haircuts or typing services.

$R$ is the real interest rate.

$d$ is the rate of depreciation. At the end of each year, the rental firm has to spend an amount $d$ times the original amount spent on the machine $P^K$ in order to make up for wear and tear on the machine.

$R^K$ is the rental price of the equipment. This is the amount received by the rental firm for renting out the machine for one year.

First, consider the cost side of the rental operation. Suppose the rental firm decides to sell the machine after one year in the rental market. At the beginning of the year it borrows $P^K$ to buy the machine at an interest rate of $R$ and incurs an interest cost of $RP^K$. It has to pay $dP^K$ to make up for depreciation. Total rental costs are therefore

$$(R + d)P^K. \tag{11.1}$$

In words, Equation 11.1 states:

> The cost of renting out one machine for one year
> = (The rate of interest + The rate of depreciation)
> × The price of a new machine.

For example, if the price of a word processor is $10,000, the interest rate $R$ = .05, and the depreciation rate $d$ = .15, then the rental price is $2,000 per year.

What will be the market rental price? If the renter does not have a monopoly in the rental market, the market rental price will exactly equal the cost of renting. If it were any higher, new firms would enter the rental business and bid down the rent. If the rent were below cost, some rental firms would go out of business and rents would rise. Thus, the rental price of a machine for a year is just as spelled out above—the interest rate plus the rate of depreciation times the price of a new machine. Algebraically, we have

$$R^K = (R + d)P^K. \tag{11.2}$$

Now we can go back to Figure 11.5 and relate the demand for capital by the firm that uses capital to the underlying determinants of the rental price of capital. Remember that the firm's demand for capital is a declining function of the rental price, so that the demand for capital is a declining function of the price of new equipment and a declining function of the real interest rate.

## DEMAND FOR CAPITAL AND RENTAL PRICE

1. The demand for capital declines if the rental price of capital rises. The rental price will rise if the price of new equipment rises or if the interest rate rises.
2. The demand for capital rises if planned output rises.
3. The demand for capital rises if the wage rises.

## The Rental Price and the Decision to Buy New Capital Goods

Much of the capital equipment in U.S. industry is in fact rented, so the analysis we have just presented is more than an abstraction. But the bulk of capital is owned by the firm that uses it in production. Moreover, the one-year perspective we used to solve for the rental price of capital is not representative. Most firms purchase capital for the long run. Their concern is not just with the payoff in the first year, but with the financial success of the project over a decade or more. They must look ahead and estimate the benefits of a new capital project under the assumption that it will operate for quite a number of years.

Jorgenson's approach determines the desired capital stock in terms of the rental price of capital. He showed that the same formula for the desired capital stock applies in the more common case where a firm owns the capital instead of renting it. Firms are constantly formulating and evaluating investment projects. An investment project that consistently earns more than the rental price of capital is worth undertaking. The project is a winner because the firm earns more than it would have to pay to borrow money to finance the project plus pay to cover the depreciation of the capital required for the project. Similarly, an investment project that consistently earns less than the rental price of capital is not worth undertaking. It is a loser.

Because of the diminishing marginal product of capital, as the winning projects are put into effect, they will depress the earnings of future projects. Eventually, the last winning project will earn just the borderline revenue, namely, the rental price of the capital. On the margin, the firm taking a long-term view and purchasing its own capital will reach just the same point it would if it chose to rent capital and made a year-by-year decision about the amount of capital to use. Both the capital budgeting approach and the rental approach arrive at the same conclusion: *The firm makes use of capital up to the point where the marginal benefit of capital equals the rental price of capital.*

Not all investment decisions fit neatly into this analysis. If the firm's technology requires that investments take place in large lumps—like building blast furnaces or power plants—it may not be able to find a combination of projects with the property that the marginal benefit of investment in each year is just equal to the rental price of capital. It may have to settle for a situation where the marginal benefit is higher in some years and lower in others. The basic criterion for selecting winning investment projects remains the same for these lumpy investments. On the average, the marginal benefit of capital will be equated to the rental price even in those cases. An investment theory based on the equality of marginal benefit and rental price seems a reasonable approximation by which to deal with the aggregate economy, even when some of the thousands of firms in the aggregate are making decisions about lumpy investments.

## Expected Changes in the Future Price of Capital

So far we have assumed that the relative price of capital, $P^K$, does not change, and is therefore not expected to change. What happens if the relative price of capital goods is expected to change? The forward-looking aspects of the firm's investment decision now become important. Consider first the rental firm. Suppose that the price of capital is *expected* to *decrease* during the period that the capital equipment is rented out. On this account the rental firm stands to take a loss. It purchased the capital for $P^K$, and the capital will be worth less than that, say $P^K{}_1$, next year when the equipment is returned. The rental firm expects to lose $P^K - P^K{}_1$. Recall that a competitive firm in the rental market must break even in equilibrium. Thus, the rental rate must increase. For example, if the price is expected to fall from $P^K = \$1,000$ to $P^K{}_1 = \$950$ next year, then it would increase the rental price by $50. Conversely, if the rental firm expected an increase in the price of capital, it would stand to gain. It could cover its costs by charging a lower rental price. In general the rental price is decreased by the amount of the *expected* increase in the price of capital, $\Delta P^K$.

With capital goods prices expected to change, the formula for the rental price becomes the old formula in Equation 11.1 less the expected change in the price of capital equipment:

$$R^K = (R + d)P^K - \Delta P^K.$$

The same thing can be written a bit more compactly as

$$R^K = (R - \pi^K + d)P^K,$$

where $\pi^K$ is the expected percentage change in the relative price of capital equipment: $\pi^K = \Delta P^K / P^K$.

This modification of the earlier rental price formula becomes very important when the price of capital is expected to change by a large amount relative to the price of other goods. As we will see below, for example, changes in taxes can alter the effective price of capital. If these changes in taxes are *anticipated* by firms, then the rental price of capital will change. Since firms increase their desired capital stock when the rental rate falls, a decline in the rental rate due to an expected change in taxes will increase capital spending.

 ## THE INVESTMENT FUNCTION

To keep things simple in our derivation of the investment function, we will assume that firms purchase all their capital. As we have just seen, the rental price of capital is the central economic variable for investment decisions.

The firm's **investment demand function** tells how much capital equipment the firm will purchase given its planned level of output and the rental price of capital. If the firm has been in business for a while, it will have an existing stock of capital at the beginning of the year. After examining the planned level of output and the rental price of capital, it will decide on a level of capital to use during the year. Finally, it will purchase enough new capital to make up the difference. In a nutshell, this is the theory of investment.

Earlier we showed that the firm chooses the amount of capital it uses by equating the marginal benefit of capital to the rental price of capital. When the amount of capital is high, the marginal benefit of further capital is low. By adjusting the amount of capital, the marginal benefit can be brought into equality with the rental price. The result of this process is the firm's **desired capital stock,** which we call $K^*$.

An example of an algebraic formula describing the desired capital is

$$K^* = .5(W/R^K)Y. \tag{11.3}$$

In this formula, $W$ is the wage rate, $Y$ is the firm's level of output, and $R^K$ is the rental price of capital. The formula says that the desired capital stock equals .5 times the ratio of the wage to the rental price of capital, times the level of output. Hence, the firm will want to increase its use of capital whenever the wage to rental price ratio rises. When labor becomes more expensive relative to capital, the firm substitutes toward capital. Whenever planned output $Y$ rises, the firm will also want to use more capital.

Now consider how the **actual capital stock** changes. Suppose that the firm finishes the last year with a capital stock of $K_{-1}$ (the subscript $-1$ means last year) that is not equal to the desired capital stock for this year, $K^*$. If there is no depreciation, then the level of investment will increase the capital stock by the amount of the investment. That is, investment equals the change in the capital stock:

$$I = K - K_{-1}. \tag{11.4}$$

If the firm wants its capital stock $K$ to equal the desired capital stock $K^*$, then its investment demand $I$ during the year is obtained by substituting $K = K^*$ into Equation 11.4. That is,

$$I = K^* - K_{-1}. \tag{11.5}$$

This much investment added to its existing capital will give the firm its desired level of capital for this year. This formula is the firm's **investment function.** The investment function for the example formula for the desired capital stock $K^*$ in Equation 11.3 can be written out as

$$I = .5(W/R^K)Y - K_{-1}. \tag{11.6}$$

Then it is apparent that *investment depends positively on the wage rate, negatively on the rental price of capital, and positively on output.*

The effect of output on investment is called the **accelerator.** To simplify the notation, set $.5(W/R^K)$ equal to the simple expression $v$. Then, Equation 11.3 states that $K^* = vY$. If the firm always adjusts its capital stock each year so that it is equal to the desired stock, then

$$\underbrace{K = vY}_{\text{This year}} \text{ and } \underbrace{K_{-1} = vY_{-1}.}_{\text{Last year}} \tag{11.7}$$

Investment, which is the change in the capital stock, must therefore be given by the difference between the two expressions in Equation 11.7. That is,

$$I = vY - vY_{-1} = v\Delta Y. \tag{11.8}$$

In words, the *level* of investment $I$ depends on the *change* of output $\Delta Y$. When output accelerates, that is, when its change gets bigger, investment is stimulated. A rise in output from one level to another causes a burst of investment, but if output remains at its higher level, investment subsides. This accelerator process seems to explain a large fraction of the movements in investment.[2] It certainly is part of the reason for the close association between investment and GDP that we noted at the beginning of the chapter.

## Depreciation and Gross Investment

If the capital stock depreciates, as of course it does in reality, then the investment equations we have derived so far are only for net investment; recall that net investment is the change in the capital stock. A gross investment equation can be easily derived by adding a term to Equation 11.6 that measures the part of investment that goes for replacing worn-out capital. One assumption is that a constant fraction $d$ of the existing capital stock wears out each period.[3] Then $d$ times $K_{-1}$ is added to Equation 11.6 and to all the related forms of the investment demand function in this chapter. Depreciation accounts for a very large part of gross investment. In 1995, for example, gross private domestic investment was $1,026 billion, while depreciation was $676 billion. Net investment was therefore $350 billion.

---

### PROPERTIES OF THE INVESTMENT FUNCTION

1. When the growth of output $Y$ is high, investment is high.
2. When the rental price of capital ($R^K$) is high, investment is low. In particular:
   a. When the real interest rate is high, investment is low.
   b. When the price of new capital goods is high, investment is low.
3. When wages are high, investment is high.

---

[2]See Peter K. Clark, "Investment in the 1970s: Theory, Performance and Prediction," *Brookings Papers on Economic Activity,* Vol. 1 (1970), pp. 73–113.

[3]There has been relatively little research on replacement investment. A good but somewhat mathematical discussion is in Martin S. Feldstein and Michael Rothschild, "Towards an Economic Theory of Replacement Investment," *Econometrica,* Vol. 42 (March 1974), pp. 393–423.

4. The amount of replacement investment due to depreciation is a large fraction of investment in a typical year. This large fraction of investment is closely related to the level of the capital stock and thus to the level of output.

## Lags in the Investment Process

A somewhat unrealistic element in the investment function we just derived is that the capital stock is adjusted to its desired level immediately. The investment function in Equation 11.6 assumes that the firm puts new capital in place as soon as it becomes aware that the level of output, the rental price of capital, and the wage warrant the new capital. For some kinds of equipment, this assumption is reasonable. But for many projects, there is a **lag** of several years between the firm's realization that new capital is needed and the completion of the capital installation. To put it another way, much of the investment occurring this year is the result of decisions made last year, the year before, and even the year before that. The decisions were governed by the expectations prevailing in those years about economic conditions this year. New information about this year's conditions that became available after the launching of the projects cannot affect this year's investment in those projects. Much of this year's investment was predetermined by earlier decisions.

To set down an algebraic expression of lags in the investment process, we will assume that firms invest so that their capital stock is adjusted *slowly* toward the desired capital stock. Suppose that firms change their capital stock by a fraction $s$ of the difference between the desired capital stock and the capital stock at the end of the last year. That is,

$$I = s(K^* - K_{-1}). \tag{11.9}$$

Comparing this equation with Equation 11.5, we see how the investment function is modified to take account of lags in the investment process. The investment demand function in Equation 11.9 has all the properties of the original investment demand function plus one more: The more slowly the capital stock is adjusted (the smaller $s$ is), the weaker will be the reaction of investment demand to any of its determinants—planned output, the rental price of capital, or the wage rate.

Economic researchers have reached the conclusion that the responsiveness of investment to its determinants is very much attenuated by lags.[4] Only certain types of investment can take place in the year that economic changes make it apparent to firms that more capital is needed. Investment

[4] See Clark, "Investment in the 1970s," pp. 73–113.

in this category includes tools, trucks, office equipment, and other portable items that are not produced to order. Major investments like whole plants or new custom-made equipment take one or more years to put in place.

## The Aggregate Investment Demand Function

Our discussion has looked at investment in the firm. We need to go from the firm to the economy as a whole. We will assume that total investment in plant and equipment is governed by Equation 11.9, with the wage to rental ratio taken as an economywide average and output taken as total real GDP. Of course, going from the firm to the total economy involves an element of approximation, because the firms we are adding together do not all have the same investment functions. Still, an aggregate investment demand function is a reasonable approximation. Even if firms are diverse, the basic properties of the investment process still hold: Investment responds positively to planned output and negatively to the rental price of capital. The strength of the response depends on how quickly investment plans can be carried out.

### THE INVESTMENT FUNCTION

1. The firm's investment demand function tells how much investment it needs to make this year in order to raise its capital stock to the desired level. Investment demand depends negatively on the rental price of capital and positively on the planned increase in output and on the wage.
2. Lags in putting new investment in place limit the response of investment to changes in its determinants. Only certain types of investment are put in place in the first year.

 **11.4**    **TAXES AND INVESTMENT**

Taxation of capital tends to discourage investment by reducing the earnings the firm receives from its investment. This effect of taxation can readily be incorporated into the rental price formula.[5] We first consider the effect of permanent tax changes.

---

[5]This method of incorporating taxes into the rental price of capital is based on the work of Robert E. Hall and Dale W. Jorgenson, "Tax Policy and Investment Behavior," *American Economic Review,* Vol. 57 (June 1967), pp. 391–414.

## Permanent Tax Changes

Consider again our derivation of the rental price of capital. Suppose the rental firm has to pay a tax rate of $u$ on rental income. In addition, suppose the rental firm receives a payment of $z$ dollars as an investment incentive from the government for each dollar of capital purchased. We derived the formula for the rental price by equating the rental income of the rental firm to the costs of renting. We can modify that analysis to take account of taxes by equating the after-tax rental income to the after-tax costs of renting. After-tax rental income is $(1 - u)R^K$. The effect of the investment incentives is to make the cost of purchasing a machine equal to $(1 - z)P^K$. Equating after-tax rental income to after-tax costs gives

$$(1 - u)R^K = (R + d)(1 - z)P^K. \tag{11.10}$$

Dividing by $1 - u$ gives

$$R^K = \frac{(R + d)(1 - z)P^K}{1 - u}. \tag{11.11}$$

The net effect of taxation and investment incentives is to multiply the rental cost by $(1 - z)/(1 - u)$.

For example, suppose the marginal tax rate applied to the revenue from capital is 50 percent. That is, $u = .5$. This by itself would double the rental price of capital; if rental firms lose half their revenue to taxation, they have to double their earnings to cover the costs of holding capital.

Suppose further that there is an investment incentive of 10 percent and that tax deductions for depreciation on investment are worth 30 cents of current benefits for each dollar of investment. The combined effect of the two makes $z$ equal .4. In this example, the tax multiplier in the rental price of capital, $(1 - z)/(1 - u)$, is .6/.5, or 1.2. The tax system adds 20 percent to the rental price of capital.

For investments that are financed by issuing debt or taking on mortgages, the tax system gives further incentives to invest because firms can deduct their interest costs as well. Suppose that borrowing adds another 20 cents in current tax benefits for each dollar of investment. In that case, $z$ would be .6 and the tax multiplier would be .4/.5, or .8. Tax incentives then outweigh the direct effect of taxes, and the net effect of the tax system is to subsidize investment.

Changes in taxes and tax incentives for investment have powerful effects on investment spending. One of the largest recent tax changes affecting investment occurred in the mid-1980s. The Tax Reform Act of 1986 raised the rental price of capital by as much as 10 percent. An elimination of the investment tax credit, a lower depreciation allowance, and a reduction in the value of deductions for interest payments were the main factors raising the rental price.

Suppose the desired capital stock falls by .75 percent for each percentage point that the rental price of capital is increased (that is, the elasticity is −.75). Then the desired capital stock would fall by 7.5 percent as a result of this legislation. If the capital stock of plants and equipment in the United States is about $4,000 billion, then this reduction would amount to a fall in investment of $300 billion. Even if it were spread over 10 years, the effect on aggregate demand in each year could be substantial.

## Anticipated Tax Changes

The above calculations assume that the tax rates are always in effect and that tax changes are not anticipated by firms. If firms are forward-looking, as we have argued, then anticipations of future tax changes can also affect investment. The effects are tricky to calculate, and can go in a direction opposite from unanticipated changes.

Suppose, for example, that U.S. firms anticipated in 1985 that the 10 percent investment tax credit would be repealed starting in 1986. In fact, this is a very realistic example, because such a repeal was proposed by the Reagan administration and widely discussed in 1985. The repeal occurred as part of the Tax Reform Act of 1986 and was made effective on January 1, 1986.

Firms that anticipated such a change would realize that they would have to pay 10 percent more for capital goods starting in January 1986 than in 1985. Accordingly they would want to buy capital in 1985 before the effective price rise. If possible, they would shift their purchases of equipment from 1986 to 1985.

Rental firms would also cut their rental price in 1985 in anticipation of the repeal of the investment tax credit. With the effective price of capital goods expected to increase, rental firms could charge less for rent because of the expected capital gain on the capital that they owned. With a decrease in the rental price there would be more investment in 1985. Hence, an *anticipated* elimination of the investment tax credit would increase investment in the year that the elimination was anticipated.

The behavior of investment in the United States in 1985 and 1986 provides dramatic confirmation of this forward-looking anticipatory behavior of firms. Investment in business equipment grew by 19 percent at an annual rate in the last quarter of 1985 and then fell by about the same amount in the first quarter of 1986. Evidently firms bunched their capital purchases in the last months of 1985 right before the effective date of the repeal. Investment remained rather low throughout 1986, as we have discussed previously.

These same anticipatory effects can work in the opposite direction. If firms anticipated a reenactment of the investment tax credit, perhaps because

# NEW RESEARCH IN PRACTICE
## The Effect of Tax Policy on Investment

Investment is the key component of spending that usually falls the most in recessions. Thus recessions create the desire for tax policies to increase investment. Moreover, higher investment would lead to higher productivity in the long run. Three types of tax policies would increase investment.

## The Investment Tax Credit

The investment tax credit first came into being in 1962, just after the recession of 1960–61. The credit is essentially a percentage subsidy on investment. As it applied in the United States from 1962 through 1986, it subsidized investment in equipment only. The investment tax credit is part of the variable $z$ in Equation 11.11 for the rental price of capital; a 10 percent investment credit adds .1 to $z$. A permanent investment credit creates an incentive for a permanently higher capital stock, so it stimulates a burst of net investment as the economy makes the transition to the higher stock.

But there are pitfalls in the systematic use of changes in the investment credit to stabilize the economy. If firms anticipate that an investment tax credit will be enacted during a recession, then a forecast of a recession could lead firms to hold back on investment and help bring on the recession. These are the findings of Lawrence Christiano of Northwestern University, whose work shows that the anticipation of changes in the investment tax credit can actually increase the volatility of investment.*

## Write-Offs

A permanent feature of tax laws is write-offs (depreciation deductions) for fixed investment. The

present discounted value of these write-offs is another factor increasing the variable $z$ in Equation 11.11. When write-offs can be made faster (accelerated depreciation), their present discounted value is higher and the rental price of capital is lower. Write-offs were dramatically reduced in the 1986 tax bill, which passed during a period of strength in the economy. The recession of 1990–91 brought forth proposals for speeding up write-offs as one of the ways to get investment moving again.

## Capital Gains Taxes

It stands to reason that lower capital gains taxes should stimulate investment. Essentially, the capital gains tax rate is one of the determinants of the interest rate $R$, which appears in Equation 11.11. Many firms invest their shareholders' funds—most commonly by keeping the funds within the firm rather than paying them out as dividends. The tax rate that matters in that case is the tax that shareholders will have to pay when the investment generates added profit for the firm. Part of the tax is the personal income tax on capital gains. Thus a lower capital gains rate will stimulate investment.

## How Large is the Effect?

Recent empirical research which examines the behavior of individual firms has found the incentive effect of tax policies to be quite large. A change in tax policy which lowers the rental price of capital by 1 percent would raise investment by about 1 percent over several years, according to one recent study.[†]

*See "A Re-examination of the Theory of Automatic Stabilizers," *Carnegie-Rochester Conference Series on Public Policy*, 1984, Vol. 20. (Amsterdam: North Holland, 1984) pp. 147–206.

[†] J. Cummins, K. Hasset, and R. G. Hubbard, "Tax Reforms and Investment: A Cross-Country Comparison," *Journal of Public Economics* (1996).

of a prolonged economic slump, then the rental price of capital would increase at the time of anticipation, and investment would actually fall.[6]

## TAX INCENTIVES

1. The government can influence the level of investment through tax policy. Heavier taxation raises the rental price of capital and discourages investment.
2. Tax incentives such as investment tax credits and depreciation deductions lower the rental price of capital and stimulate investment.
3. Anticipated increases in tax incentives can reduce investment today, because firms will postpone their capital purchases until they can take advantage of the incentives.

## 11.5   RESIDENTIAL INVESTMENT

The economic theory of residential investment can be approached in much the same way as the theory of business investment. We can start again with the concept of the rental price. Because a significant amount of housing of all kinds is rented in the open market, there is nothing unfamiliar about the idea of a rental price of housing. Even though many American families own their houses rather than rent them, we can examine their decision about how large a house to own by looking at the rental price they pay implicitly when they own. Let $R^H$ represent the rental price for houses. As before, the rental price is the interest rate plus a rate of depreciation times the price of houses ($P^H$):

$$R^H = (R + d)P^H. \tag{11.12}$$

An important quantitative difference is the rate of depreciation, $d$. The equipment that makes up the bulk of business investment depreciates at around

---

[6]For rational expectations approaches to consequences of anticipated changes in investment incentives, see Lawrence H. Summers, "Taxation and Corporate Investment: A $q$-Theory Approach," *Brookings Papers on Economic Activity,* Vol. 1 (1981), pp. 67–140; and John B. Taylor, "The Swedish Investment System as a Stabilization Policy Rule," *Brookings Papers on Economic Activity,* Vol. 1 (1982), pp. 57–97.

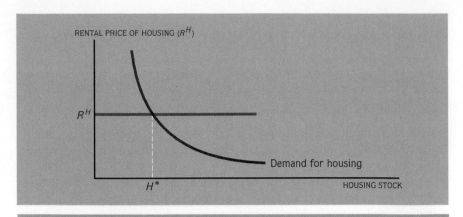

RENTAL PRICE OF HOUSING ($R^H$)

$R^H$

Demand for housing

$H^*$     HOUSING STOCK

**FIGURE 11.7**   Determination of the Desired Housing Stock

The desired stock of housing, $H^*$, is found at the point on the demand curve for housing where the rental price of housing, $R^H$, has the value determined by the real interest rate and the price of houses.

10 percent per year, so $d$ is .10 in the formula for $R^K$. Houses hardly depreciate at all. A reasonable value for $d$ in the formula for $R^H$ is .02. Consequently, the real interest rate is a much larger fraction of the rental cost of housing than it is of the rental cost of business investment. As we will see, residential investment is much more sensitive to interest rates than is business investment.

The public has a demand function for housing just as it has a demand function for any good. When the rental price of housing is high, the public demands less rental housing. We can find the public's **desired stock of housing** by finding where the rental price of housing intersects the demand curve, as in Figure 11.7.

Lags in housing construction are not nearly as long as lags in business investment. It is reasonable to suppose that the bulk of housing can be put in place within a year after a change in demand. The investment demand function for housing is just

$$I = H^* - H_{-1,}  \tag{11.13}$$

where $H_{-1}$ is the stock of houses in the previous year and $H^*$ is the desired stock of houses.

The accelerator principle operates for housing investment as well as for business investment. The stock of housing is related to the level of real income. Thus investment, which is the change in the stock, is related to the change in real income.

## Housing Investment and Monetary Policy

Of all the components of aggregate demand, housing investment is the most sensitive to real interest rates. We have already noted one reason for the sensitivity: Because housing depreciates at a low rate, the real interest rate is the dominant element in the rental price of housing. Most of what you pay your landlord is compensation for the capital tied up in your apartment. If you own a house, most of your annual cost is mortgage interest. Therefore, when a monetary contraction or other influences raise interest rates, housing investment declines the most. As the economy slowed in 1990 after interest rates rose, residential investment fell sharply. Then the Fed acted to lower interest rates, with mortgage rates falling below 9 percent for the first time since the early 1970s. Residential investment rose in the recovery, by 34 percent from 1991 to 1994.

---

### HOUSING INVESTMENT

1. Housing investment is negatively related to the interest rate $R$. A higher interest rate makes housing more expensive by raising the rental price. A higher rental price depresses investment demand.
2. Housing investment is positively related to real GDP. Higher incomes raise the demand for housing and so raise investment demand.
3. Housing is the component of investment most sensitive to monetary policy through interest rates. Because housing depreciates so slowly, its rental price is dominated by interest cost.

---

## 11.6 INVENTORY INVESTMENT

Inventories are stocks of goods in the process of production and also finished goods waiting to be sold. In 1995, total inventories were about $1251 billion. Gross domestic product was about $7300 billion, so about 17 cents' worth of inventories were held for each dollar in annual GDP. A significant amount of capital is tied up in inventories in the U.S. economy.

Inventories fit into the general framework for analyzing investment set up at the beginning of this chapter. Inventories have a rental price, equal to the real interest rate times the price of goods held in inventory.

Firms choose a desired level of inventories by equating the marginal benefit of inventories to the rental price. What benefits do inventories provide the firm? We can distinguish two basic functions. First, and quantitatively most important, inventories are an intrinsic part of the physical production process. We will call this the **pipeline function** of inventories. In the oil industry, large amounts of oil are unavoidably in transit in pipelines at any moment. The pipeline function also includes goods in process. Inside an auto plant, you will always find stocks of parts ready to be made into cars together with a large number of cars partway through the assembly process. The manufacturer has made a basic decision about the design of the production process that balances the advantages of inventories against their holding cost. About two-thirds of all inventories seem to be held because of the pipeline function.

The other third of inventories are finished goods. Auto plants have cars sitting in parking lots ready for shipment to dealers. The dealers themselves also keep quite a number of cars in their lots and showrooms. As a general matter, substantial inventories of finished goods ready for sale are held at the wholesale and retail level. One of the reasons for holding these inventories is to maintain a **buffer stock** to accommodate unexpected changes in demand. The buffer stock is the second major function of inventories. The grocery store keeps dozens of bottles of ketchup on the shelves because there is always a chance that an unusual number of people will buy ketchup on any given day.

Buffer-stock inventories are held at a certain average level that equates the marginal benefit to the rental cost. When sales surge, the inventories decline to below the desired stock. The firm then adjusts its purchases to replenish the stock. When sales fall short of expectations, inventories build up. The firm then decreases its purchases to run inventories down to their desired level.

Occasionally, unintended disinvestment and investment in buffer-stock inventories show up in the aggregate amount of inventory investment throughout the economy. For example, in 1989, aggregate final sales of goods in the U.S. economy slowed. The production of goods continued to rise despite slowing sales. As a result, inventory investment bulged. Inventory investment was 30 billion 1987 dollars in 1989.

We can get an idea of the relative importance of the pipeline and buffer-stock influences on inventory investment by looking at the relationship between the *change* in real GDP and the *level* of inventory investment in the U.S. economy. Figure 11.8 shows this relationship for the years 1959 to 1995.

We can draw two important conclusions about inventory investment from Figure 11.8. First, inventory investment tends to be closely related to changes in production. When higher levels of output are being produced, there are more goods in the pipeline. Filling up the pipeline to the higher level requires more inventory investment. Consequently, years of rapid GDP

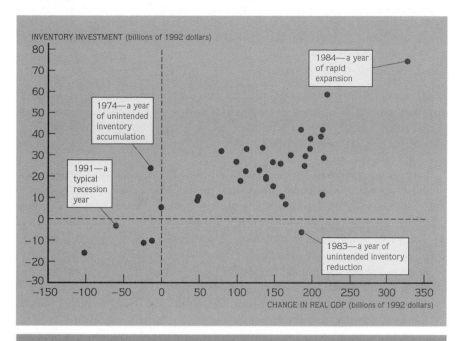

**FIGURE 11.8**   Inventory Investment and the Change in GDP

The amount of inventory investment tends to be closely related to the change in real GDP. Each dot corresponds to a year in the period from 1960 through 1991. The horizontal axis shows the change in real GDP and the vertical axis shows the real amount of inventory investment. As a rule, inventory investment is high when real GDP is growing and low when it is contracting. There are two large exceptions—1974 and 1983—that prove the rule. The dot in the upper left is for 1974, when real GDP fell but inventory investment was high. In 1974, there was probably substantial unwanted inventory accumulation. The dot to the right and below the general trend is for 1983, when real GDP grew rapidly but inventory investment was negative. In 1983, there was probably unintended reduction of buffer stocks because sales were unexpectedly high. As a general matter, intended changes in inventory stocks dominate unintended changes. Years of high GDP growth are years of high inventory investment and vice versa.

growth tend to be years of high inventory investment. This is the third important place where the accelerator principle is in operation. The accelerator effect is particularly strong for inventory investment, because lags are less important for inventories than for any other component of investment.

Second, there are occasional episodes when businesses are caught by surprise and inventories pile up or are depleted unintentionally. In these episodes, inventory investment departs from its usual relation to the change in real GDP. In Figure 11.8, the small number of dots away from the prevailing upward-sloping line are years when unintended accumulation or depletion of inventories occurred. There is no systematic tendency for buffer stocks to absorb every change in real GDP. Instead, big movements of buffer stocks are a rare surprise. Research on inventory behavior has confirmed the general proposition that relatively few important movements of inventories can be traced to surprises in sales.[7]

## INVENTORY INVESTMENT

1. Inventories provide two benefits to firms. The production process involves a pipeline of partly produced goods. When the level of output is high the stock of goods in the pipeline is high. Inventories of finished goods also function as a buffer stock against unexpected changes in sales.
2. The pipeline function of inventories dominates inventory investment in most years, but occasionally economywide surprises in sales are large enough for changes in buffer stocks to contribute an important component to inventory investment.
3. The increase in pipeline inventories when output rises is a major part of the accelerator in the short run.

# THE INVESTMENT FUNCTION AND THE IS CURVE

Total investment is the sum of investment in plant and equipment, residential housing, and inventory. We can summarize the ideas of this chapter in an overall investment function. Investment depends positively on real GDP and negatively on the interest rate $R$.

The accelerator principle is important in investment. Higher output requires firms to invest in new plant and equipment, it causes families to want to increase their stock of housing, and it calls for higher pipeline stocks of inventories. For all three reasons, an increase in GDP stimulates added investment. However, the stimulus is stronger in the short run than in the long run. If the economy moves once and for all to a higher level of GDP, there

---

[7]See Albert A. Hirsch and Michael Lovell, *Sales Anticipations and Inventory Behavior* (New York: John Wiley & Sons, 1969). For a formal treatment of the pipeline function of inventories see Valerie A. Ramey, "Inventories as Factors of Production and Economic Fluctuations," *American Economic Review,* Vol. 79 (June 1989), pp. 338–354.

will be a bulge of investment as the economy moves to the new, higher stock of plant, equipment, housing, and inventories desired at the new level of GDP. Once the new stock is reached, investment will subside to normal levels.

Investment depends negatively on the real interest rate. When the real rental cost of plant and equipment rises, firms substitute toward other inputs, especially labor. When the real rental price of housing rises, families substitute toward other forms of consumption. When the real cost of holding inventories rises, firms reduce their stocks of inventories, though this effect appears to be small. But the influence of higher real interest rates in depressing total investment is unmistakable.

Investment is central to the IS curve—in fact, as we mentioned in Chapter 7 the "I" in IS stands for investment. Recall that the IS curve can be defined as the set of combinations of real GDP and the interest rate where investment and saving are equal.

As a general matter, the IS curve slopes downward because it takes a lower interest rate to stimulate spending enough to achieve spending balance at a higher level of GDP. The investment function is a key part of that process. Lower interest rates stimulate investment—the effect is most important for housing and least important for inventories. The interest sensitivity of investment is an important determinant of the slope of the IS curve. If investment is highly responsive to the interest rate, the IS curve is flat; small changes in the interest rate cause large changes in investment and thus large changes in the level of GDP. If investment is not very responsive to interest rates, and other components are also unresponsive, the IS curve will be steep. Because investment and other categories of spending are unable to respond in the very short run (say, one month) to changes in interest rates, the IS curve is close to vertical in the short run.

## REVIEW AND PRACTICE

### Major Points

1. There are three types of investment: business purchases of new plant and equipment, construction of new housing, and addition to inventories.

2. A business determines its desired capital stock by equating the marginal benefit of capital to the rental price of capital. A household determines its desired stock of housing in the same way.

3. The desired capital stock falls if the rental price of capital rises. It also rises if output or income rises. A business's desired capital stock rises if the wage rises, because it will substitute away from labor and toward capital.

4. The rental price of capital depends on the real interest rate and the price of capital goods.

5. The investment function tells how much investment will occur in a given year depending on conditions in that year. Although firms would like to invest up to the point where actual capital equals desired capital, they generally cannot do so. Only a fraction of the move to the new level can occur in the first year.

6. Because of the lag in investment, a large fraction of the investment that occurs in one year is actually the result of investment projects initiated in earlier years. This part of investment is predetermined in the current year and does not respond to current economic conditions.

7. For plant and equipment, it is a good approximation to say that suppliers will supply whatever amount of new investment goods businesses demand.

8. Tax incentives, including depreciation deductions and interest deductions, have an important influence on investment. A higher investment credit lowers the rental price of capital and stimulates investment.

9. Inventory investment contributes an important part of the fluctuations in total investment. The stock of inventories tends to be proportional to real GDP, so an increase in GDP is accompanied by a period of inventory investment.

10. Overall, investment responds positively to both the level of and the change in real GDP. The relationship with the level of GDP is due to replacement investment. The relationship with the change in GDP, called the accelerator, is due to the need to increase the capital stock in order to maintain output at higher levels and because desired inventories will grow when output increases.

11. Investment is negatively related to the interest rate since the interest rate is an important determinant of the cost of inventories. If the relationship is strong, the IS curve will be relatively flat.

## Key Terms and Concepts

| | | |
|---|---|---|
| investment | rental price of capital | depreciation deductions |
| nonresidential fixed investment | demand for capital | desired stock of housing |
| plant and equipment investment | rate of depreciation | buffer-stock function of |
| residential investment | desired capital stock | inventories |
| inventory investment | investment demand function | pipeline function of inventories |
| investment demand | accelerator | |
| marginal benefit of capital | tax incentives | |

## Questions for Discussion and Review

1. What variables adjust so that the level of investment chosen by firms and households is equal to the amount of funds available for investment?

2. Why do investment and GDP move so closely together?

3. Suppose that a firm can reduce its energy bill by adding some capital. How does this enter the marginal benefit of capital schedule?

4. Why does the marginal benefit of capital schedule shift upward when output rises?

5. Explain the various predetermined elements in the investment function.

6. What are the effects of tax policy on investment in the long run?

7. Why is housing especially important in the economy's response to a high-interest-rate policy?

8. Explain exactly what happens to the three categories of investment as you move down the IS curve.

9. Explain how announcements of future changes in tax policy can affect current investment demand.

## Problems

### NUMERICAL

1. Suppose that the demand for investment is given by the model

$$I = s(K^* - K_{-1}),$$

where $K^*$ is the desired stock of capital given by

$$K^* = .1Y/R,$$

where $Y$ is output and $R$ is the interest rate. Assume that there is no depreciation and that $R = .05$. Let $s = .25$ to start.
   a. Calculate the desired capital stock in year 1 if output is 200. Calculate the level of investment in the first year if the capital stock was 400 at the beginning of the first year.
   b. Suppose now that output rises from 200 to 250 in year 2 and then remains at this new level forever. Calculate the level of investment and the capital stock in years 2, 3, and 4. What are the new long-run levels of investment and capital? Explain why investment reacts with a lag to the increase in output.
   c. Repeat the calculations in Parts a and b for $s = 1$ and comment on the difference between your answers.

2. Repeat Problem 1 for the case where investment is given by

$$I = s(K^* - K_{-1}) + .1K_{-1}.$$

The last term on the right is replacement investment. Explain the reason for the differences between the answers to Questions 1 and 2.

3. Suppose that the investment function is given by

$$I = 400 - 2,000R + .1Y$$

rather than by the investment function given in Chapter 7. Add this investment function to the other four equations of the IS-LM model:

$$Y = C + I + G + X$$

$$C = 220 + .63Y$$

$$X = 525 - .1Y - 500R$$

$$M = (.1583Y - 1,000R)P$$

Treat the price level as predetermined at 1.0, and let government spending be 1,200 and the money supply be 900.

a. Derive an algebraic expression for the IS curve for this model and plot it to scale. Compare it with the IS curve in the examples of Chapter 7. Which is steeper? Why?

b. Derive the aggregate demand curve and plot it to scale. How does it compare with the aggregate demand curve in the example of Chapter 7?

c. Calculate the effect of an increase in government spending on GDP. Is the effect larger or smaller than in the case where investment does not depend on output $Y$? Describe what is going on.

d. Calculate the effect of an increase in the money supply on GDP. How does the impact compare with the situation where investment does not depend on output?

4. Multiplier-accelerator interaction: Consider a macro model that has both a consumption function that depends on lagged income (like Friedman's permanent-income equation) and an investment equation that depends, with a lag, on changes in income. Ignore interest-rate effects. In particular assume that the following equations describe the economy:

$$Y = C + I + G$$

$$C = 220 + .63Y_p, \text{ with } Y_p = .5(Y + Y_{-1})$$

$$I = 900 + .2(Y_{-1} - Y_{-2})$$

$$G = 1,200$$

a. By algebraic substitution of $C$ and $I$ into the income identity, obtain a single expression for output $Y$ in terms of output in the previous years ($Y_{-1}$ and $Y_{-2}$).

b. Calculate the constant level of output $Y$ that satisfies all the relationships in the model. (Hint: Set $Y_{-1} = Y$ and $Y_{-2} = Y$ in the equation from Part a and solve for $Y$ using algebra.)

c. Suppose that $Y$ has been equal to the value that you calculated in Part b for the past two years (years 1 and 2). But now suppose that government spending increases by $50 billion (in year 3). Calculate the effect on output in year 3. Calculate the effect on output in years 4 through 10. Be sure to use the relationship that you derived in Part a, and substitute the values for $Y_{-1}$ and $Y_{-2}$ that you calculated in the previous two steps.

d. Plot the values of $Y$ on a diagram with the years on the horizontal axis. Do you notice any cyclical behavior in $Y$? Explain what is going on. (This algebraic model was originally developed by Paul Samuelson of M.I.T. while he was a student at Harvard in the 1930s.)

5. (This problem refers to the material in Appendix A.) Consider the case where the price of capital goods $P^K$ and the revenues from investment $J$ are the same each year. Work with the equation for the financial position $V$:

$$V_t = (1 + R)V_{t-1} - dP^K + J.$$

Always start with $V_0 = -P^K$. In the last period of the project the firm sells the capital good for $P^K$.

a. Show that, regardless of the length of the project, $V$ is zero if the revenues from investment $J = (R + d)P^K$.

b. Calculate the financial position for each year of a 10-year project that costs $100,000 and earns a revenue of $16,000 per year. Use an interest rate of 5 percent and a depreciation rate of 10 percent. Is the project a winner or a loser?

c. Repeat the above calculation for an interest rate of 10 percent. Is the project a winner or a loser? Explain the difference between this answer and the answer to Part b.

## ANALYTICAL

1. What theory of inventory investment predicts that inventory investment is negative when GDP suddenly rises? What theory predicts the opposite? For both theories explain what happens at firms during a sudden *decline* in GDP.

2. Consider a firm whose capital stock is initially equal to its desired capital stock, where $R = .05$, $d = .1$, $P^K = 100$, and $P^K$ is initially not expected to change in the future.

a. Suppose $P^K$ suddenly rises to 110. Ignoring taxes, what must the firm expect $P^K$ to be next year in order for its desired capital stock to remain unchanged?

b. Suppose now that $P^K$ is expected to return to 100 the following year and to remain at 100 in all future years. Assume that this is in fact what happens. Describe the behavior of investment in the year of the price increase and in all future years. Consider both the case where the capital stock adjusts immediately to its desired level and the case where it adjusts with a lag.

3. In this problem we consider an economy in which the price of *new* capital goods never changes. It is always equal to 100.

a. Assuming $R = .05$, $d = .1$, and the corporate income tax is 50 percent, what is the rental cost of capital?

b. The government is considering an investment tax credit (ITC) where 10 percent of the purchase price of a new capital good can be subtracted from a firm's taxes. Under such a proposal, what will the rental cost of capital be? Assuming that the ITC is unanticipated, describe the behavior of $I$ and $K^*$ in the year that it is implemented.

c. Assuming that the old capital goods are perfect substitutes in production for new capital goods, what will the price of old capital goods be under the ITC? If the value of a firm's capital stock changes in the year the ITC is implemented, will this change directly affect the firm's investment decision?

    d. Assume now that such a proposal is announced a year ahead of time. What will the rental cost of capital be in the year in which firms learn about the ITC? Compare your answer with the rental cost calculated in Parts a and b. Explain any differences.

    e. Compare the level of investment in the year in which the ITC is announced with what it would be without the ITC. Compare the level of investment in the following year when the ITC is implemented with what it would be if the ITC was implemented *unannounced* that year.

4. How sensitive would you expect automobile production to be to the interest rate? In answering this question, consider (i) the sensitivity of the desired stock of automobiles to the interest rate, (ii) the lags in the adjustment of the automobile stock to its desired level, and (iii) the impact of changes in final automobile sales on inventory investment in automobile manufacturing.

5. *Paradox of Thrift.* Assume a closed-economy model with $Y = C + I + G$. Suppose that investment demand depends on the level of income but not on the interest rate, according to the formula

$$I = e + dY$$

and that consumption also depends on income according to the consumption function

$$C = a + b(1 - t)Y.$$

    a. Sketch the spending line for the economy that shows how total spending increases with income $Y$. (Put spending on the vertical axis and income on the horizontal axis.) Draw a 45-degree line and indicate where spending balance is.

    b. Suppose that consumers decide to be more thrifty, to save more. They do this by reducing $a$ once and for all. Show the new point of balance in the diagram.

    c. What happens to investment as a result of consumers' attempts to save more? Explain.

    d. Explain the paradox of thrift, that the attempt to save more may result in a reduction in private saving. What happens to total saving?

    e. Explain why the paradox of thrift is a short-run phenomenon. Introduce interest rates into the investment function, and add a money demand function and price adjustment equation to the model. If the economy is operating at potential GDP before the reduction in $a$, will it eventually return to potential after the reduction in $a$? What happens to saving and investment when prices have fully adjusted?

6. Suppose the desired capital stock is given by the expression

$$K^* = vY/R^K$$

where $v$ is a constant and $R^K$ is the rental cost of capital.

    a. Assuming that output in the economy is fixed at $Y^*$, will a permanent increase in the interest rate have a permanent or a temporary effect on the level of investment?

   b. Is your answer to Part a consistent with the investment function incorporated in the IS curve?
   c. Suppose now that output in the economy is growing each period so that $\Delta Y = g$. Assuming that the actual capital stock adjusts immediately to its desired level, answer Part a.

7. Sketch an IS-LM diagram. Compare two cases: one in which the investment demand function depends on income and the other in which it is independent of income. In which case are both monetary and fiscal policy more effective? Explain.

8. Suppose that GDP is below potential GDP, and that inflation is low. The President and Congress are talking about reducing taxes on investment in order to get the economy back to potential.
   a. Sketch the situation on an IS-LM diagram. Show where you want to move the IS curve to get back to potential.
   b. In light of lags in the investment process and the forward-looking nature of firms' investment decisions, describe some of the problems that the policymakers need to worry about in enacting the tax legislation.

9. The 1986 Tax Reform Act called for an increase in taxes on businesses and a decrease in taxes on consumers, with total revenue remaining about the same. Describe the effects the tax had on *investment demand*. Be explicit: Did these effects occur immediately, or did they occur with a lag? Distinguish between the effects that work through the rental rate on capital and the effects that work through the accelerator. Which of these two effects was likely to have been larger in the long run?

10. Countercyclical policy in recent recessions has typically involved increases in incentives for investment, often through increases in the investment tax credit. How might firms' behavior at the beginning of future recessions be affected by beliefs that government may take actions to reduce the cost of investment? What effect would this have on the behavior of real GDP?

## MacroSolve Exercises

1. Graph the real long-term interest rate on the vertical axis and the level of real investment expenditures on the horizontal axis for both annual and quarterly data.
   a. Describe the relationship that you see. Is it compatible with the theoretical model in the chapter?
   b. Why might the relationship between investment and the real interest rate be obscured in the graph?
   c. How might you be able to distinguish whether the movements in the real interest rate caused by other factors are causing the changes in investment, or shocks to investment are shifting the IS curve and causing interest rates to change?

2. Graph the real long-term interest rate on the vertical axis and the level of real investment expenditures on the horizontal axis for both annual (1948–95) and quarterly (1967–95) data.

a. Calculate the statistics for both the annual and the quarterly data. Do the correlation coefficients and your visual observations from drawing the graphs support the theoretical model developed in the chapter?

b. Subdivide the data into two sample periods: annual 1948–80 and 1981–95, and quarterly 1967–80 and 1981–95. Redraw the graphs for each of these sample periods and recalculate the statistics. How do your findings compare to those in Part a?

c. What violation of a critical assumption regarding the relationship between investment and real interest rates might explain the difference between your findings in Parts a and b?

d. What political or economic events can you point to as possible explanations for this change at the beginning of the eighties?

3. Compare the behavior of the ratio of investment to GDP and the growth rate of GDP for both annual and quarterly data. (Hint: Try graphing one series against the other and plotting both of the time series on the same screen.) Is this relationship consistent with the theoretical model in the chapter? Would you expect to see a closer relation between investment and the GDP gap or between investment and the growth of GDP?

4. How does the interest elasticity of investment affect the size of the government spending multiplier in the fixed-price IS-LM model? Use the model "ISLM, Open Econ" to illustrate your answer.

5. a. How does the interest elasticity of investment affect the size and time pattern of the government spending multiplier in the dynamic AD/PA model? Explain why.

b. Why does the interest elasticity of investment have no effect on the long-run government spending multiplier?

c. Is the output cost of reducing the price level by cutting the money supply higher or lower the more responsive investment is to the interest rate? Explain why.

 # APPENDIX A:   Capital Budgeting and the Rental Price of Capital

In this appendix we show that Jorgenson's rental price approach gives the correct answer to the question of what the desired capital stock should be for a firm that *buys* capital. As discussed in the text, the key result is that investment projects that earn more than the rental price will be undertaken and those that earn less than the rental price will not be undertaken. We use a capital budgeting formulation to describe the firm's investment decision.

Suppose that a firm is considering buying some capital equipment that will contribute an amount $J_t$ to revenue in each future year t. The year of the decision is t = 0. The equipment costs $P^K$.

The firm keeps track of its financial position—benefits less costs—for this capital project using an intertemporal budgeting process in the following way. Let $V_t$ be the financial position in year t. The firm starts in the hole by the cost of the capital equipment $P^K$. That is, the financial position in year 0 is

$$V_0 = -\text{The price of the capital equipment} = -P^K. \tag{11.14}$$

For example, if the capital equipment cost \$1,000, then $V_0 = -\$1,000$. In the next year, the firm may be even deeper in the hole because it pays interest at rate $R$ on the funds it used to pay for the project last year plus the additional spending it made at the end of last year to make up for wear and tear, or depreciation. For example, for the \$1,000 equipment, if the interest rate was 5 percent ($R = .05$) and 10 percent of the equipment needed to be replaced because of wear and tear ($d = .10$), then the financial position would be reduced by another \$50 + \$100 = \$150. On the other hand, the project contributed an amount $J_0$ to revenue in its first year. For example, if the revenue is \$200, the position in the project at the beginning of the second year is

$$V_1 = -\$1,000 - \$50 - \$100 + \$200 = -\$950. \tag{11.15}$$

The same process repeats each year. In words:

> Position at the beginning of next year
>
> = Position at the beginning of this year
>
> + Interest owed this year
>
> − Depreciation this year
>
> + Revenue from the project this year.

The general algebraic form is

$$V_t = V_{t-1} + RV_{t-1} - dP^K + J_{t-1}. \tag{11.16}$$

Note that this equation is like the intertemporal budget constraint from the forward-looking consumers in Chapter 10. It is essentially the firm's intertemporal budget for the project in question. At the end of the project, the firm will be able to sell the capital equipment. If the firm has been paying for all the wear and tear each year, so that the equipment is like new, then the firm will be able to sell the equipment for what it paid for it. The firm will sell the equipment for $P^K$, and the firm's financial position will be increased by $P^K$ at the end of the project. (Recall that we assume that the price of new equipment is unchanging.)

With the repeated application of Equation 11.16, the firm can figure out its financial position in the project as long as the project is still in existence. The firm's projects will fall into two categories: **winners,** for whom the position becomes positive (the initial investment pays itself back) and then becomes more and more positive, and **losers,** for whom the position is always negative and the project never pays for itself. A reasonable theory of investment is that the firm goes with the winners and rejects the losers. This is equivalent to the capital budgeting recommendation, which says that projects that have a positive present discounted value should be undertaken and those with a negative present discounted value should be rejected. The present discounted value of a project is simply the financial position $V_t$ as we have defined it divided by $(1 + R)^t$. When the financial position is positive, so is the present discounted value. When the financial position is negative, so is the present discounted value.

Now, to prove that the rental approach gives the same answer as the capital budgeting approach, we need to show that *an investment project that consistently earns more than the rental price is a winner and a project that consistently earns less than the rental price is a loser.*

Suppose a project earns exactly the rental price each year; that is,

$$J_t = (R + d)P^K. \tag{11.17}$$

As we noted, the financial position in year 0 is

$$V_0 = -P^K. \tag{11.18}$$

In the next period the financial position is

$$V_1 = -(1 + R)P^K - dP^K + J_0, \tag{11.19}$$

where we have used the budget equation (11.16). Substituting $J_0 = (R + d)P^K$ into Equation 11.19, we get

$$V_1 = -(1 + R)P^K - dP^K + (R + d)P^K, \tag{11.20}$$

which, after canceling out terms on the right-hand side, simply equals $-P^K$. If you repeat this procedure to obtain the financial position after two years $V_2$, three years $V_3$, and so forth, you will find that the firm's financial position is always equal to *minus the current price of a machine*. At the end of the project the firm sells the machine. Because the firm receives the current price of the machine $P^K$, the financial position at the end of the project is exactly zero. That is, the investment is just on the borderline between being a loser and being a winner.

If the investment earned a little more than the rental price each year, the firm's financial position would end up positive. The investment would be a clear winner. If the investment earned a little less than the rental price each year, the financial position would turn out negative. The firm would reject it. Hence, the rental price is the key factor in the investment decision, even though the firm is buying the capital.

# APPENDIX B: Tobin's $q$ and the Rental Price of Capital

We saw in Section 11.3 that investment takes place with a lag. This lag has implications for the observed relationship between investment, the rental price of capital, and a related variable called Tobin's $q$. To understand this relationship, suppose that the

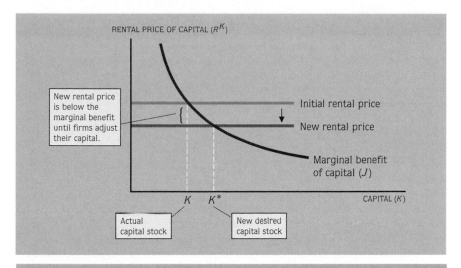

RENTAL PRICE OF CAPITAL ($R^K$)

New rental price is below the marginal benefit until firms adjust their capital.

Initial rental price

New rental price

Marginal benefit of capital ($J$)

$K$    $K^*$            CAPITAL ($K$)

Actual capital stock

New desired capital stock

**FIGURE 11.9**   Desired Capital Greater than Actual Capital

When the rental rate on capital falls, firms do not immediately adjust their capital to the new desired level. The adjustment takes place with a lag. Until the capital stock is adjusted, the rental price of capital $R^K$ is below the marginal benefit of capital $J$.

rental price $R^K$ suddenly falls below the marginal benefit $J$ of capital. The situation is illustrated in Figure 11.9, which is a replica of Figure 11.5. The firm will want to raise its capital stock until the marginal benefit of new capital is reduced to the new rental price. But if the firm must adjust its capital slowly, the marginal benefit of capital will remain above the rental price during the adjustment period when the firm is investing in new capital. Only when the adjustment is complete and the actual capital stock equals the new desired level will the marginal benefit of capital equal the rental price. In the meantime, the greater the difference between the desired capital stock and the actual capital stock, the greater the difference between the rental price and the marginal revenue of capital. Investment is positively related to this difference between $J$ and $R^K$.

Alternatively stated, investment will be a positive function of the ratio of the marginal benefit of new capital $J$ to the rental price of capital $R^K$. When this ratio ($J/R^K$) is greater than 1, the rental price is below the marginal benefit of capital and the firm is investing in new capital. When the ratio is less than 1, the firm wants to reduce its capital stock and thus does not invest at all.

The ratio $J/R^K$ of the marginal benefit of capital to the rental price of capital has an interesting interpretation. Suppose that the firm issues shares that can be bought or sold on a stock market, such as the New York Stock Exchange. If the interest rate on bonds is $R$, then the market value (MV) of the firm's shares should be such that the return on the shares $J/\text{MV}$—the ratio of the marginal benefit of capital $J$ to the value of the shares (MV) that represent ownership of that capital—is equal to the interest rate $R$. Then the return on holding the firm's shares is the same as the return on bonds. In other words, the market value MV of the firm's shares is directly related to the marginal benefit $J$ of capital by the formula $MV \times R = J$. For example, if $J = \$10$ per share and $R = .05$, then the market value MV of shares should equal \$200.

There is a similar relation between the price of capital at the firm $P^K$ and the rental rate $R^K$. Ignoring depreciation, the formula for the rental price of capital says that $P^K \times R = R^K$. Combining these two formulas, we get

$$\frac{J}{R^K} = \frac{MV \times R}{P \times R} = \frac{MV}{P^K} = q.$$

The ratio on the far right ($MV/P^K$), the market value of the firm divided by the price of the firm's capital, is called Tobin's $q$, after James Tobin of Yale University, who emphasized the importance of the ratio for investment.[8] It is clear from our discussion thus far that investment should be positively related to $q$.

Tobin's $q$ provides a very useful way to formulate investment functions because it is relatively easy to measure. Data on a firm's share price can usually be obtained from a stock exchange, and the price indexes for capital are tabulated as part of the national income and product accounts (NIPA). For this reason, Tobin's $q$ is a useful gauge of the climate for investment. For example, in 1983 when investment was booming in the United States, Tobin's $q$ was quite large, even though the measured real interest rate and the rental price of capital suggested an unfavorable climate for investment. The microeconomics of investment that underlie Tobin's $q$ approach to investment are really no different from the rental price approach that we focus on in this chapter.

[8]See James Tobin and William Brainard, "Asset Markets and the Cost of Capital," in Bela Balassa and Richard Nelson, eds., *Economic Progress, Private Values and Public Policy: Essays in Honor of William Fellner* (New York: North-Holland, 1977), for more details about $q$.

# Foreign Trade and the Exchange Rate

Foreign trade is a central issue in U.S. economic policy. International trade contributes to long-term economic growth. Equally, trade is a factor in economic fluctuations. In the recession of 1990–91, for example, strong exports moderated the downturn. But when consumers decide to purchase foreign rather than American cars, the demand for U.S.-made goods declines. The immediate effect is a decline in GDP and employment in the United States.

The international value of the dollar affects foreign trade and thereby influences aggregate demand, GDP, and employment. Fluctuations in the dollar have been common since the 1970s. Against other major currencies, the dollar rose to extreme heights in the first half of the 1980s and then fell almost continuously to reach new lows in the mid-1990s.

Many commentators have called for policies to reduce the U.S. trade deficit. Some think that restrictions on imports from Japan and other countries with trade surpluses would be appropriate. Others call for a correction of the fiscal budget deficit in order to reduce borrowing from foreigners. Some economists feel that the volatility of the value of the dollar in relation to other currencies needs to be controlled by intervention in the foreign exchange market or even by pegging exchange rates at fixed levels. Proposals for policy intervention are founded on the belief that there is something wrong with a trade deficit or a volatile currency. A contrary view, held by many economists, is that the trade deficit and the value of the dollar

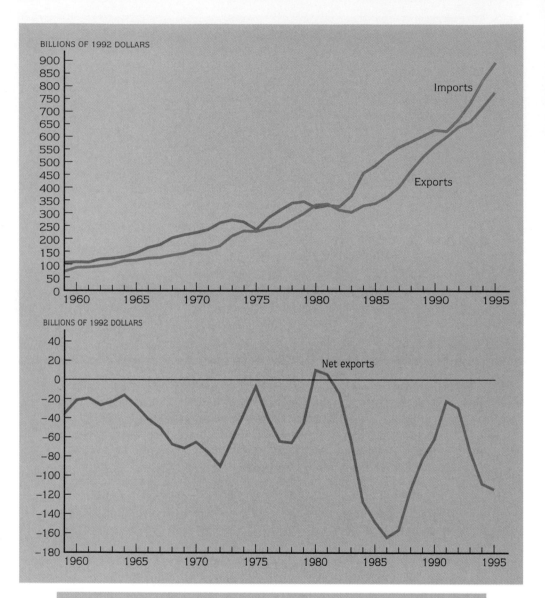

**FIGURE 12.1**   Exports, Imports, and Net Exports in 1987 Dollars

The top panel shows the quantities of goods exported out of and imported into the United States in constant 1987 dollars. The difference between the two is net exports, shown separately in the bottom panel. Imports grew very rapidly in the early and mid-1980s while exports were roughly constant. Net exports turned sharply negative.
Source: *Economic Report of the President*, 1996, Table B-2.

should be set in international markets, free from intervention by the United States or other governments. In this chapter, we will study the determinants of net exports and exchange rates. We will look at the ways that changes in trade affect the domestic economy and how policy can respond. We will also look at policies aimed at influencing the trade deficit and the international value of the dollar.

# FOREIGN TRADE AND AGGREGATE DEMAND

Figure 12.1 shows what happened to the flows of goods and services into and out of the United States between 1959 and 1995. Generally, imports and exports have been about equal, but since the mid-1980s, there has been a huge excess of imports over exports.

The quantity of goods and services flowing into and out of the United States is not the only important dimension of trade. It matters how much we have to pay for imports and how much we can get for our exports. In this respect, nominal or dollar flows are important in foreign trade, whereas it is real flows that concern us in considering domestic production. If imports become more expensive, it is costly to the United States even if net exports in real terms do not change. The **terms of trade** is the ratio of the price of exports to the price of imports. When the prices of imports rise, we say there has been an adverse shift in the terms of trade.

When the value of American imports exceeds the value of exports, either because of a high quantity of imports or because of the high price of imports, the United States must borrow enough from foreigners to pay for the difference. As we saw in Chapter 2, U.S. borrowing from abroad is called a capital inflow. For example, in 1995 net exports were −$110 billion; the United States had to borrow in order to finance the excess of imports over exports. Actually, total borrowing was even larger because the United States also paid transfers to people outside the country of about $30 billion.

The capital inflows since the mid-1980s have been large by historical standards. They brought the United States from a net creditor position with the rest of the world to a net debtor position. In other words, Americans now owe more to foreigners than foreigners owe to Americans.

## FOREIGN TRADE AND AGGREGATE DEMAND

**1.** Foreign trade influences U.S. aggregate demand in two ways. First, Americans can purchase their goods from abroad instead of from U.S. producers. When they do, their imports contribute to aggregate demand in the rest of the world instead of to U.S. aggregate demand. Second, foreigners can purchase goods produced in the United States. These exports enter U.S. aggregate demand.

2. When exports are less than imports, Americans must finance the difference plus any other expenditures abroad by borrowing. This borrowing— or, equivalently, investment by foreigners in the United States—is called **capital inflow from abroad.**

 ## 12.2   THE EXCHANGE RATE

The **exchange rate** is the amount of foreign currency that can be bought with 1 U.S. dollar. For example, on February 28, 1985, the exchange rate between the German mark and the dollar was 3.1 marks per dollar. If you went to a bank with $100 on that day you could have obtained 310 marks. Like other prices, the exchange rate can change: on April 30, 1996, the exchange rate between the mark and the dollar was 1.5 marks per dollar. The exchange rates between the dollar and foreign currencies are listed in the financial pages of most newspapers.

The exchange rate is determined in the **foreign exchange market,** where dollars and other currencies are traded freely. The foreign exchange market is not in one location; it is a global market. Banks all over the world actively buy and sell dollars and other foreign currencies for their customers. The banks are linked by a network of telecommunications that allows instantaneous contact around the globe. Because of different time zones, the foreign exchange market is open 24 hours a day.

In today's monetary system the dollar exchange rate is allowed to **float** against the currencies of other large countries. For this reason the system is called a floating or **flexible exchange-rate system.** The United States and other major Western countries permit a free market in foreign exchange. Neither the United States nor other major countries try to fix the exchange rate with the dollar within narrow bands as they did prior to the early 1970s. This does not mean that the United States is powerless to affect the exchange rate or must ignore the exchange rate when it sets macro policy. As we will see, changes in monetary and fiscal policy have strong influences on the exchange rate, and these influences must be considered when setting macro policy.

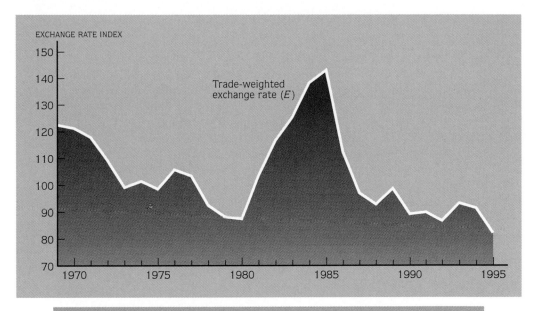

**FIGURE 12.2** The Trade-Weighted Exchange Rate

The trade-weighted exchange rate is the best overall measure of the dollar exchange rate. It is an average of exchange rates with many different currencies, including the Canadian dollar, the French franc, the German mark, the Japanese yen, and the British pound. The exchange rate fluctuates by large amounts. It was very high in the early 1970s and in the early 1980s. The dollar was low in the late 1970s.
Source: *Economic Report of the President*, 1996, Table B-106.

Since there are many countries in the world, there are many exchange rates for the dollar. A convenient single measure of the dollar exchange rate is the **trade-weighted exchange rate,** which we will denote by the symbol $E$. This is an average of several different exchange rates, each one weighted according to the amount of trade with the United States. Figure 12.2 shows the trade-weighted exchange rate $E$ for the United States for the years 1969 to 1994. The dollar fluctuated widely during this period. **Depreciation** of the dollar occurs when the exchange rate $E$ falls. **Appreciation** of the dollar occurs when the exchange rate $E$ rises. The dollar depreciated steadily by 17 percent from 1976 to 1980. The dollar then turned around and appreciated by over 60 percent through 1985. From 1985 to 1987 it fell by over 30 percent and thus reversed the appreciation. The dollar has fallen about 13 percent more since 1987 in a relatively tranquil period for foreign exchange markets.

## The Exchange Rate and Relative Prices

In our discussion of the role of the exchange rate in foreign trade, we will speak of the rest of the world (ROW) as if it were a single country with a single monetary unit, a single price level $P_w$, and a single level of GDP. Then, the trade-weighted exchange rate $E$ is simply the exchange rate between the U.S. dollar and the foreign monetary unit. Like the exchange rate, the price level in the rest of the world $P_w$ is measured by taking an average of the price levels in the countries that trade with the United States.

The **real exchange rate** is a measure of the exchange rate that is adjusted for differences in price levels between the United States and the ROW. It is a measure of the relative price of goods produced in the United States compared with goods produced in the ROW. If $P$ is the U.S. price level, the real exchange rate can be written in symbols as

$$\text{Real exchange rate} = \frac{\text{Foreign price of U.S. goods}}{\text{Foreign price of ROW goods}} = \frac{E \times P}{P_w}.$$

When the real exchange rate is high, foreigners have to pay more for goods produced in the United States compared with the price of goods produced in the rest of the world. For example, when the mark-dollar exchange rate rises from 1.8 to 2.0 marks per dollar, the price of a $2,000 computer produced in the United States rises from 3,600 marks to 4,000 marks in Germany. Note that the exchange rate for the individual item is multiplied by its price in the United States to get the price outside the United States; similarly, we multiply $E$ times $P$ in the numerator of the real exchange rate to get a measure of the average price of U.S. goods in the ROW.

Recall our basic assumption that prices set by U.S. producers are fixed in the short run. Aggregate demand in this period, domestic or foreign, will not influence the dollar price level $P$ in this period. We make the same assumption about the ROW. The price level $P_w$ set by ROW producers is fixed in the short run.

The exchange rate $E$, on the other hand, varies minute by minute. Thus the real exchange rate ($EP/P_w$) varies minute by minute. The price of U.S. products in the ROW is flexible in the short run because the exchange rate is flexible. By the same token, the dollar price of ROW products is flexible in the short run.

When the dollar appreciates, ROW products become cheaper to Americans. At the same time, U.S. products become more expensive in the ROW. If the United States and the ROW produced identical, readily transportable products, the exchange rate would not fluctuate in the short run. We would always buy from the cheapest producer. The exchange rate would always have the single value that equated the dollar prices of U.S. and ROW products. The real exchange rate would never change. If the United States and the ROW produced all the same products, the exchange rate could not fluctuate in the short run and would change in the longer run only by as much as prices in the ROW rose by more than prices in the United States. This theory of exchange-rate fluctuations is called **purchasing power parity.** The theory does not work for short-run fluctuations. Exchange rates fluctuate far more than the theory predicts. We can see this easily. According to the theory, the *real* exchange rate ought to be constant over time. The real exchange rate between the U.S. dollar and the currencies of the rest of the world is shown in Figure 12.3. The real exchange rate is not at all constant.

Clearly, purchasing power parity is not a good theory of the determination of the exchange rate in the short run. On the other hand, the theory has a powerful economic logic. How can we reconcile the fact of wide variations in the real exchange rate with the principle that people buy at the lowest possible price?

One answer is that different countries produce different products. Japanese cars are not identical to American cars, for example. When the dollar

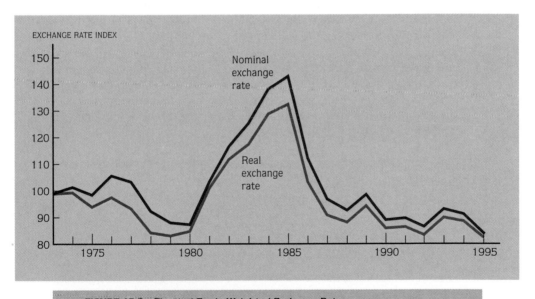

**FIGURE 12.3** The Real Trade-Weighted Exchange Rate

The real exchange rate between the United States and the ROW is the nominal exchange rate adjusted for changes in the domestic purchasing power of the dollar and the currencies of the ROW. When the real exchange rate falls, it means that Americans find foreign goods more expensive. Through much of the 1970s, the real exchange rate fell. The price of American goods relative to foreign goods fell from .99 in 1974 to .83 in 1979. In the early 1980s, the relative price of American goods rose dramatically; then it fell sharply in 1986.
Source: *Economic Report on the President,* 1996, Table B-106.

appreciates, Japanese cars become cheaper, but the U.S. public does not stop buying American cars altogether. Instead, the new price advantage of Japanese cars raises Japanese sales in the United States somewhat and depresses sales of American cars somewhat. The same thing occurs in hundreds of other markets. Appreciation of the dollar makes it more difficult for U.S. producers to sell their output, but it does not wipe them out. The exchange rate has room to vary. It is not locked in place by purchasing power parity.

## THE EXCHANGE RATE AND PURCHASING POWER PARITY

1. The exchange rate is the number of units of foreign currency that a dollar is worth. An increase in the exchange rate is an appreciation of the dollar.
2. The real exchange rate measures the relative purchasing power of the dollar by adjusting the nominal exchange rate by the price levels in the respective countries. When the real exchange rate is high, U.S. goods are expensive for foreigners and foreign goods are inexpensive for U.S. buyers.
3. Purchasing power parity asserts that the nominal exchange rate must equate the prices of tradable goods across countries. This implies a constant real exchange rate, which is inconsistent with the empirical evidence. Nonetheless, purchasing power parity exerts some influence on the exchange rate.

# THE DETERMINANTS OF NET EXPORTS

## The Effect of the Exchange Rate

As we have just seen, fluctuations in the exchange rate change the relative price of U.S. and ROW goods and thereby affect the demand for imports and exports. Imports depend positively on the exchange rate. If the dollar is strong, it buys a lot of foreign currency, and the goods sold by the ROW are correspondingly cheaper. Exports, too, are sensitive to the exchange rate. A strong dollar—that is, a high exchange rate—makes U.S. goods more expensive in the ROW. In the period of the strong dollar in the early 1980s,

U.S. export industries like construction equipment suffered from the increase in their prices as perceived by the ROW, even though dollar price increases were moderate.

## The Effect of Income

In Chapter 6, we noted that net exports depend on U.S. income. Higher incomes make consumers spend more on imported products; this relation is particularly sensitive because many types of products that consumers spend extra income on, such as electronics and cars, are frequently imported. In addition, some investment goods are imported, such as machine tools from Germany. When GDP rises and investment strengthens, part of the increase in investment goods comes from overseas. Thus, in general, imports respond positively to GDP. On the other hand, there is little connection between U.S. exports and U.S. GDP. Hence net exports depend negatively on GDP.

## The Net Export Function

As we have seen, we can combine imports and exports into a single measure, net exports $X$, defined as exports less imports. Our conclusions about the determinants of net exports are as follows:

1. Net exports depend negatively on the real exchange rate. When the dollar is strong, exports are lower and imports are higher. Net exports are lower on both counts.
2. Net exports depend negatively on real income in the United States. This dependence comes from subtracting imports, which depend positively on real income.

We can summarize these ideas in a simple algebraic formula:

$$X = g - mY - n\frac{EP}{P_{\mathrm{w}}}. \quad \text{The Net Export Function} \quad (12.1)$$

Equation 12.1 is the net export function. It says that net exports equal a constant $g$ minus a coefficient $m$ times income $Y$, minus a coefficient $n$ times the real exchange rate. The net export function summarizes how net exports depend negatively on both income $Y$ and the real exchange rate ($EP/P_{\mathrm{w}}$).

How well does the net export function work? Figure 12.4 shows the relation between net exports and the exchange rate since 1973. The negative relation is quite evident; note especially that the increase in the dollar exchange rate in the mid-1980s was accompanied by a decline in net exports. The effect of the other determinant of net exports—real income in the United States—is not so evident in Figure 12.4 because exports rose as income in

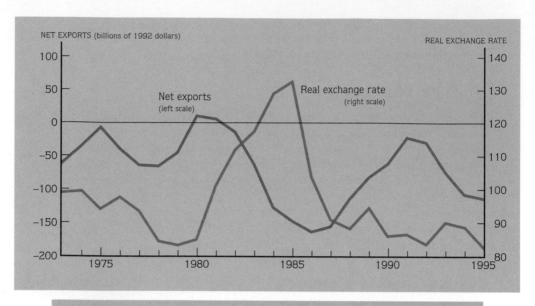

**FIGURE 12.4**   Net Exports and the Real Exchange Rate

The real exchange rate and net exports move at the same time, but in opposite directions. When the real exchange rate rises, net exports fall; conversely, when the real exchange rate falls, net exports rise.
Source: *Economic Report of the President,* 1996, Tables B-2 and B-106.

the ROW increased in this period. However, in the early 1980s the economy of the United States grew more rapidly than the economies of many European countries and this added to the trade deficit. The weakening of the dollar in the late 1980s was the dominant factor in the increase in net exports.

**EXAMPLE**   A numerical example of the net export function can be written

$$X = 600 - .1Y - 100\,\frac{EP}{P_\mathrm{w}}. \qquad \begin{array}{l}\text{Numerical Example of the}\\\text{Net Export Function}\end{array} \qquad (12.2)$$

Suppose that the price level in the United States and the price level in the ROW are both predetermined at the value of 1.0. If output $Y$ is $5,000 billion and the exchange rate $E$ is 1.0, then net exports $X$ equal zero. If output $Y$ rises by $100 billion, then net exports fall by $10 billion because imports rise by this amount. If the exchange rate falls from 1.0 to 0.6, about as much as it did from 1985 to 1992, then net exports would rise by $40 billion.

Net exports is an endogenous variable that depends on the exchange rate. To complete our theory, we therefore need to explain what determines the exchange rate. As we have just seen, purchasing power parity doesn't work very well. We now develop a theory that relates the exchange rate to the interest rate.

# 12.4 A MODEL OF THE REAL EXCHANGE RATE

Fluctuations in the exchange rate are closely related to interest rates in the United States and the ROW. In particular, policies in the United States that raise interest rates tend to cause the dollar to appreciate. The appreciation of the dollar in the early 1980s, for example, was related to the monetary and fiscal policies that brought extraordinarily high interest rates. Why are interest rates and the exchange rate positively related?

The financial markets of the major developed countries are closely linked. Investors are constantly comparing the returns they make by investing in Germany (in stocks and bonds that pay in marks), in Japan, in Britain, and in many other countries. There are billions of dollars and marks and trillions of yen of "hot money" that will migrate almost instantly to the place where it will earn the highest return.

As we stressed in Chapter 2, when the dust settles, trade flows and capital flows have to equal each other, except for measurement error. The net exports of the United States must be equal to the amount of U.S. capital flowing to the rest of the world less the amount of foreign capital coming into the United States. It is not possible for there to be a large U.S. trade deficit at the same time that large amounts of capital are flowing out of the United States to seek a higher return in other countries. The exchange rate and interest rates fluctuate minute by minute to keep trade flows and capital flows equal to each other.

When the U.S. interest rate is high in comparison with foreign interest rates, capital will be attracted to the United States.[1] Even a fraction of a percentage point of extra return could bring hundreds of billions of dollars of wealth to be invested in the United States. In order to prevent such a large flow, something else must happen at the same time that the U.S. interest rate rises. What happens is an appreciation of the dollar. When foreign investors

---

[1] Just as in the case of consumption and investment, the interest rate that matters for the foreign exchange market is the real interest rate. If the U.S. nominal interest rate is high only because expected U.S. inflation is high, foreigners will not be attracted to U.S. investments. They will anticipate that the value of the dollar and so the value of dollar-denominated bonds will decline in the future at the expected rate of inflation.

see the combination of attractive U.S. interest rates and a strong dollar, they reason in the following way: On the one hand, I like the high return I can earn in dollars. But on the other hand, I am not so sure that the return I will earn in my own currency is any better than at home. The dollar is strong today, but it is likely to come back to normal over the next year or two, as it always has in the past. As the dollar depreciates, I will lose some of my capital when I convert it back to my own currency.

The more the dollar rises when the U.S. interest rate rises, the more powerful will be the second part of that logic. Hence, there is some degree of appreciation of the dollar that will block the huge capital inflow that would otherwise accompany a higher U.S. interest rate. Figure 12.5 shows the relation between the U.S. interest rate and the exchange rate that is needed to stave off the capital inflow.

In algebra, we can express the positive relation between the real exchange rate and the U.S. interest rate as

$$\frac{EP}{P_{w}} = q + vR, \tag{12.3}$$

where $R$ is the U.S. interest rate and $q$ and $v$ are constants. Recall that it is the rise in the U.S. interest rate relative to foreign interest rates that brings

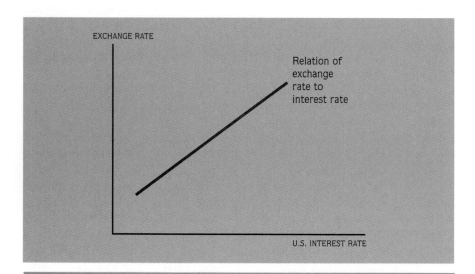

**FIGURE 12.5**   Relation between the U.S. Interest Rate and the Exchange Rate

A higher U.S. interest rate requires a stronger dollar. If not, huge capital inflows would occur, which would be inconsistent with trade flows. The stronger dollar discourages the capital inflow that would otherwise occur by creating expectations of a subsequent depreciation of the dollar, which would offset the advantage of the higher U.S. interest rate.

about the rise in the exchange rate. In Equation 12.3 we suppress the foreign interest rate under the assumption that it does not move as much as the U.S. interest rate.

**EXAMPLE**   If prices are measured in such a way that the real exchange rate $EP/P_w$ is equal to 1 when purchasing power parity holds, then the relation between the U.S. interest rate and the real exchange rate might be

$$\frac{EP}{P_w} = .75 + 5R. \quad \text{Numerical Example of the} \atop \text{Exchange Rate–Interest Rate Relation} \qquad (12.4)$$

When the net export function, Equation 12.2, is combined with this relation, we get the numerical example of the net export relation used in Chapter 7:

$$X = 525 - .1Y - 500R.$$

## THE INTEREST RATE AND THE EXCHANGE RATE

1. The exchange rate and the interest rate are positively related. When the real interest rate rises, say because of an increase in government spending, the exchange rate also rises.
2. The relationship between the interest rate and the exchange rate comes about as investors shift their funds between different countries to obtain the best return. When the interest rate rises in the United States, investors buy dollar-denominated bonds and this drives up the exchange rate.
3. When U.S. interest rates are high relative to the rest of the world, it must be the case that investors expect the dollar to depreciate at an annual rate equal to the interest-rate differential. Expectations of future depreciation require a strong dollar today. Thus, there is a positive relation between the interest rate and the exchange rate.

## 12.5  THE IS CURVE AND ECONOMIC POLICY IN AN OPEN ECONOMY

Recall that the IS curve describes the combinations of interest rates $R$ and incomes $Y$ that satisfy the income identity and the equations for spending: consumption, investment, and net exports. *Without* net exports in the income identity, the IS curve is downward-sloping because higher interest rates reduce investment and, through the multiplier, reduce GDP. *With* net exports, more things happen to spending when the interest rate rises. An increase in the interest rate raises the exchange rate and thereby reduces net exports; this tends to augment the effect of the interest rate on investment and makes the IS curve flatter than it would be in a closed economy. Not only do high interest rates cause firms to invest less, they also cause Americans to meet their needs with imported goods and foreigners to divert their demand away from U.S. products.

But the presence of net exports also reduces the size of the multiplier, and this tends to make the IS curve steeper. Net exports depend negatively on GDP. As GDP rises, part of the increase in spending goes overseas and does not enter domestic aggregate demand. This spillover abroad is sometimes called **leakage** and it reduces the size of the multiplier.

In Chapter 7, we derived the open-economy IS curve graphically and algebraically. The next section adds some more details in the process of deriving it algebraically.

## Algebraic Derivation of the Open-Economy IS Curve

The IS curve is derived algebraically by substituting the functions for consumption $C$, investment $I$, and net exports $X$ into the income identity. That is,

$$Y = \underbrace{a + b(1 - t)Y}_{C} + \underbrace{e - dR}_{I} + G + \underbrace{g - mY - n(EP/P_w)}_{X}.$$ (12.5)

Putting the interest rate on the left-hand side gives

$$R = \frac{a + e + g}{d} - \frac{1 - b(1 - t) + m}{d} Y - \frac{n}{d}\frac{EP}{P_w} + \frac{1}{d} G.$$ (12.6)

This equation relates the interest rate $R$ to output $Y$, the real exchange rate $EP/P_w$, and government spending $G$. It shows that the interest rate is negatively related to the real exchange rate. Appreciation of the dollar shifts the IS curve downward; depreciation raises the curve. To get the IS curve, substitute Equation 12.3 into Equation 12.6 in order to eliminate the real exchange rate:

$$R = \frac{a + e + g - nq}{d + nv} - \frac{1 - b(1 - t) + m}{d + nv} Y + \frac{1}{d + nv} G.$$ (12.7)

The coefficient on $Y$ shows that the IS curve slopes downward for two reasons: the negative response of investment to the interest rate, described by $d$, and the negative response of net exports, described by $nv$.

The IS curve of Equation 12.7 is the one we discussed in Chapter 7.

## Effects of Monetary and Fiscal Policy on Trade in the Short Run

Monetary and fiscal policy have important effects on trade and the exchange rate. Suppose that the Fed increases the money supply. This shifts the LM curve to the right; that is, it lowers interest rates and stimulates investment. The decline in interest rates depreciates the exchange rate; net exports rise. Because of the rise in investment and net exports, GDP rises. However, the increase in GDP tends to decrease net exports because imports rise. There are thus two offsetting effects of an increase in the money supply on net exports. Exports definitely rise, but imports may rise by a greater amount. In any case, interest rates fall, the dollar depreciates, and GDP rises. Conversely, when the money supply is decreased, interest rates rise, the dollar appreciates, and GDP falls.

Now suppose that government spending is increased. The IS curve is pushed to the right, and interest rates rise. The rise in interest rates reduces investment spending, but also causes the exchange rate to appreciate. The higher exchange rate reduces exports as U.S. goods become relatively expensive compared with foreign goods. Hence, the increase in government spending crowds out export industries as well as investment. Imports also rise because of the increase in the dollar and because GDP has increased. Thus an increase in government spending increases the trade deficit or reduces the trade surplus, as it stimulates the economy.

## Price Adjustment

What happens in these alternative policy scenarios when firms begin to adjust their prices? In the case of the increase in the money supply, if output is equal to potential output, the price level will begin to rise because output increases above potential. The increase in prices will lower real money balances and the interest rate will begin to rise. As it does, the real exchange rate will begin to rise. These adjustments will continue until the economy has returned to potential. Eventually the price level will have increased by the amount of the original increase in the money supply. The real exchange rate will have returned to normal so that the nominal exchange rate $E$ will have depreciated by the amount of the increase in the price level. In the long run money is neutral.

An increase in government spending will also eventually bring about an upward adjustment in prices. The reduction in real balances will raise interest rates and further reduce investment and net exports. Eventually, output will return to potential output, and the sum of investment and net exports will have declined by exactly the amount of the increase in government spending. The real exchange rate and the interest rate will be permanently higher after the process is complete.

## OPEN-ECONOMY IS CURVE AND POLICY

1. **The downward slope of the IS curve in an open economy comes in part from the positive relation between the interest rates and the exchange rate. Net exports decline when the interest rate rises.**
2. **The offset to fiscal expansion through crowding out is stronger in an open economy. Fiscal expansion raises the interest rate and depresses net exports.**
3. **Monetary policy has an enhanced effect through the interest rate in an open economy. A monetary expansion lowers the interest rate and stimulates net exports as well as investment in the short run.**
4. **In the long run, money remains neutral with respect to all real variables. The price level increases and the nominal exchange rate depreciates in proportion to the increase in the money supply.**

# 12.6   THE EXCHANGE RATE AND THE PRICE LEVEL

One of the macroeconomic principles we have stressed in this book is that the price level is very unresponsive to most economic events in the short run. For example, a sudden contraction in monetary policy does not seem to have any measurable impact on the price level within the first year, even though its eventual effect is to lower prices considerably. One important exception is that prices respond quickly to changes in costs of imports such as oil. The dramatic price rises of 1974–75, 1979–80, and 1990 and the sudden slowing of inflation in 1986 can be linked directly to events in the world oil market. To a certain extent, fluctuations in the exchange rate can influence the price level in a similar way. A rise in the dollar is like a decline in world oil prices; it makes imports cheaper. A collapse of the dollar, as in 1986–87, is an adverse price shock.

In a small economy, the domestic price level is closely tied to the exchange rate. Many consumption and investment goods are imported; those that are not compete with imports. A small country's exports trade in large world markets and are usually constrained to sell at home for essentially the world price. Hence, changes in a small country's exchange rate bring immediate and important changes in that country's price level.

In the large U.S. economy, the situation is quite the reverse. For Japanese cars, for example, the U.S. market is over half the total market worldwide. The setting of the U.S. dollar price for foreign products is a major business decision for the makers of those products. Frequently, the outcome of that decision is to keep the dollar price of foreign products unchanged in the United States, even though the exchange rate has risen or fallen sharply. For example, when the dollar rose dramatically against the German mark in 1983, German auto companies raised the mark price of cars in order to stabilize their dollar prices in the United States. They might have chosen to let the dollar price fall in order to sell more cars. Similarly, when the dollar fell sharply relative to the mark after 1985, the mark price of cars shipped to the United States fell. Again, the dollar price was stable. German car makers maintained a stable share of the U.S. market and kept their cars at stable prices relative to other cars in the market. Many other foreign sellers of products with well-known brands in the United States behaved in the same way.

From its peak in early 1985 until late 1986, the real exchange rate declined by over 15 percent. The real price of imports to the United States rose by only about 1 percent over the same period. All the rest of the change in the exchange rate was absorbed by a decline in profit margins by importers. For Japan, the numbers are particularly striking: stated in yen, the cost of producing products in Japan rose by about 6 percent from the beginning of 1985 to the middle of 1986. But the number of yen received by the Japanese for their typical exported product declined by 23 percent over the same period.[2] Costs and profit margins of U.S. exporters appear to be much less sensitive to exchange-rate fluctuations. Dollar prices of U.S. exports are largely unaffected by exchange-rate changes; this implies that foreign-currency prices of U.S. goods change roughly in proportion to the exchange rate.[3]

Because importers tend not to adjust their U.S. prices quickly in response to changes in the exchange rate, large movements in the exchange rate do not create price shocks in the U.S. economy. The price adjustment process we described in Chapter 8 applies reasonably well to the prices of imported goods as well as those made in the United States. We will not stress

[2]The data are from Paul Krugman and Richard Baldwin, "The Persistence of the U.S. Trade Deficit," *Brookings Papers on Economic Activity*, Vol. 1 (1987), pp. 1–43.

[3]See the comparative study by Michael Knetter, "Price Discrimination by U.S. and German Exporters," *American Economic Review*, Vol. 79 (March 1989), pp. 198–210.

the immediate impact of the exchange rate on the U.S. price level. That impact would be large in a small, highly open economy, but appears to be quite small in the U.S. economy.

# 12.7  PROTECTIONISM VERSUS FREE TRADE

All industries in the United States that produce products that can be shipped from one country to another face foreign competition. These industries make up the tradables sector. Only industries like services, communications, and utilities are insulated from that competition. If foreign competition could be eliminated or discouraged, domestic producers would enjoy increased profits. The losers would be U.S. consumers, who would pay higher prices as a result of lessened competition.

Industries in the tradables sector push constantly in favor of protectionist measures. These measures include:

1. Tariffs, which are a tax on imports
2. Quotas, which limit the quantity of imports
3. Outright bans of certain imports

The incentive to seek protection exists all the time. However, the likelihood of convincing Congress to enact protectionist legislation rises dramatically when imports are high and domestic industries are suffering from diminished sales and high unemployment.

The history of protection in the United States can be characterized in the following way. In normal times, under the leadership of the President, trade barriers are gradually reduced. Consumer interests predominate in the long run; purchasers in the United States are generally free to take advantage of bargains that foreigners make available. But in times of recession or large trade deficits, strong pressures develop for protectionist legislation. Tariffs and quotas are tightened in those times. When the emergency is over, protectionism lingers for some years, but eventually is reduced.

## Macroeconomic Effects of Protectionism

A tariff or quota has the effect of shifting the net exports schedule in the direction of higher net exports given the exchange rate. That shift enters the spending process just like any other shift in a spending schedule or an increase in government purchases. The IS curve shifts to the right. The interest rate and GDP increase along the LM curve, which remains unchanged. All the usual accompaniments to a spending stimulus occur. In particular, the higher interest rate makes the dollar appreciate.

Because protectionism makes the dollar appreciate, the actual effect on prices and trade is smaller than it might appear at first. Although a tariff makes imports more expensive, a stronger dollar offsets this to some extent. In other words, the exporting country pays part of the tariff, rather than the U.S. consumer. Moreover, to the extent that the exporter tends to stabilize its dollar price in the United States, as we discussed in the previous section, it is even more true that the exporter, not the consumer, pays the tariff. At the same time, the macroeconomic stimulus becomes smaller, because if U.S. consumers see no price change, they will not cut their imports. Note that this effect cannot apply to quotas. If a quota forces the quantity of imports to decline, it must cause an increase in the prices paid by U.S. purchasers.

Our analysis assumes foreign countries do not respond to trade restrictions with similar sanctions against U.S. products. Retaliation would certainly undo whatever short-run benefits protection might bring. In fact, the infamous Smoot-Hawley tariff touched off a trade war in the 1930s that contributed to the Great Depression.

## PROTECTIONISM

1. Protectionist policies lessen foreign competition faced by domestic producers. They generally help domestic producers and hurt domestic consumers. They include tariffs on imports, quotas on the quantities of imports, and bans on some imports.
2. Protectionist measures stimulate net exports. They shift the IS curve outward, raise the interest rate, and raise GDP.
3. Protectionism raises the exchange rate; this discourages net exports and offsets some of the effects of protection.
4. Protection runs the risk of retaliation by our trading partners. A trade war would certainly undo any temporary benefits protectionism might bring and would reduce the welfare of the nations involved.

**12.8**

# STABILIZING THE EXCHANGE RATE

The wild swings in the exchange rate shown in Figure 12.2 have been of concern to both Americans and foreigners. When the dollar was strong, U.S. producers of tradables suffered, while U.S. purchasers of imports had the advantage of bargains. The collapse of the dollar in the mid-1980s reversed the situation. Many observers have suggested that the world would have been better off with more stable exchange rates, though there is no detailed analysis that has tried to add up the benefits and costs of both consumers and producers. Most discussions consider only the interests of producers and fail to give weight to the benefits that consumers receive when the rest of the world is making bargains available to the United States.

How might U.S. policy be changed to stabilize the exchange rate? Recall that there is a simple relation between the exchange rate and the U.S. interest rate, holding constant economic conditions in the rest of the world. When the rest of the world is quiescent, the United States would have to hold its own interest rate constant in order to keep the exchange rate constant. Figure 12.6A illustrates the necessary policy in terms of the LM curve. A commitment on the part of the Fed to keep the interest rate constant means that the LM curve is perfectly flat. A shock in spending—say, unexpectedly strong investment—would shift the IS curve to the right, as shown in the figure. GDP would rise by the full amount of the spending shift together with the resulting multiplier effects. The normal offset from higher interest rates would not occur. Thus GDP would be highly vulnerable to spending disturbances under a policy that kept the exchange rate constant.

Note that the flat LM curve also indicates that fiscal policy is more powerful when the central bank stabilizes the exchange rate. An increase in government spending pushes the IS curve to the right. With floating exchange rates, we saw that the increase in government spending partially crowds out private investment *and* net exports because interest rates rise and the exchange rate appreciates. With the exchange rate stabilized there is no appreciation of the currency and the interest rate does not rise. Hence, there is no crowding out. Production increases by the full amount of the shift in the IS curve. This is illustrated in Figure 12.6A.

Figure 12.6B shows what would happen if there were a shock in the rest of the world that would normally have made the dollar depreciate (such as an increase in interest rates in other countries). The Fed would have to shift the LM curve upward by enough to prevent the depreciation. As a result of the higher interest rate, the level of GDP would fall, as the economy moved up and to the left along the IS curve. When the Fed takes an action like this— deliberately contracting the economy to raise the dollar—it is called "defending the dollar." It sacrifices stability of employment and output in the United States in order to stabilize the exchange rate.

The important point is that making monetary policy responsible for stabilizing the exchange rate prevents monetary policy from achieving other goals, such as stability of employment or prices. We cannot ask the Fed to prevent fluctuations in the purchasing power of the dollar without recognizing that it must sacrifice the stability of other variables, which may be more important.

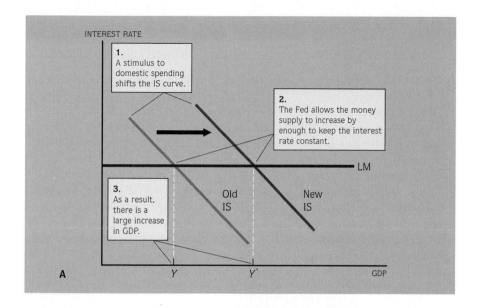

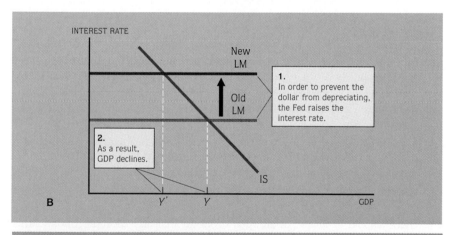

**FIGURE 12.6** Effect of a Spending Shock and a Foreign Shock under Exchange-Rate Stabilization

(A) When the Fed is operating monetary policy under the principle of keeping the exchange rate stable, it must keep the interest rate constant. That is, the LM curve is a horizontal line. When the IS curve shifts, it causes large changes in output. (B) When a change occurs in the rest of the world, such as a monetary contraction in a major foreign country, the Fed must raise the interest rate to prevent depreciation of the dollar if it has a policy of stabilizing the exchange rate. Such a move contracts output in the United States.

## STABILIZING THE EXCHANGE RATE

1. To stabilize the exchange rate, the Fed would have to set a horizontal LM curve.
2. With a stable exchange rate, a domestic spending shock would have a large effect on GDP. The normal cushioning through interest-rate fluctuations would not occur, because it would cause exchange-rate fluctuations.
3. With a stable exchange rate, the Fed would have to change the U.S. interest rate in response to each foreign shock. It could not insulate GDP and employment from those shocks as it could with a floating rate.

## REVIEW AND PRACTICE

### Major Points

1. The long-run value of the exchange rate is determined by purchasing power parity. In the short run, expectations and conditions in financial markets create large deviations from purchasing power parity.
2. The interest-rate differential between two countries is equal to the expected rate of depreciation.
3. When the U.S. interest rate is relatively high, the exchange rate must be high also so that interest-rate parity holds in the short run and purchasing power parity holds in the long run.
4. The net export function depends negatively on income and on the real exchange rate.
5. The multiplier is smaller in an open economy than in a closed economy. This makes the IS curve steeper.
6. In an open economy, an increase in the interest rate has a larger first-round effect on spending because it reduces net exports as well as investment. This makes the IS curve flatter.
7. An expansionary monetary policy lowers the interest rate and the exchange rate. Investment and exports are stimulated in the short run. In the long run, money is neutral.
8. An expansionary fiscal policy raises the interest rate and the exchange rate. The policy crowds out the investment industries and export industries.
9. Changes in the exchange rate do not have large immediate effects on the price level. The U.S. price of imported products is sticky.

10. Protectionist policies such as tariffs and quotas will reduce the trade deficit and stimulate GDP in the short run. They also tend to make the dollar appreciate, which offsets some of their effects. Protectionism is harmful to consumers because it raises prices of foreign products and is likely to lead to retaliation by foreign governments.

11. If the Fed sets a policy of stabilizing the exchange rate, it must give up other goals, such as employment stability. When the exchange rate is being held constant, domestic spending shocks have large effects on GDP. In addition, the policy makes GDP vulnerable to shocks occurring in foreign countries.

## Key Terms and Concepts

| | | |
|---|---|---|
| purchasing power parity | real exchange rate | quotas |
| interest-rate parity | net export function | protectionism |
| interest-rate differential | flexible exchange rate | exchange-rate stabilization |
| exchange rate | tariffs | |

## Questions for Discussion and Review

1. Explain how you would compare the return on a Japanese bond with the return on a U.S. bond.

2. What happens to the exchange rate between the U.S. dollar and the Italian lira when chronic inflation in Italy is well above inflation in the United States?

3. Why is it rational for investors to expect that the exchange rate will depreciate when it is above normal? Under what circumstances would it not be rational to expect this?

4. Summarize the steps and assumptions that link the exchange rate and the interest rate. What would happen to the relationship if the ROW decided to use a more expansionary policy?

5. Describe what happens to consumption, investment, and net exports when you move down the IS curve.

6. What happens to net exports, investment, and consumption when government spending is decreased? Distinguish the long run from the short run.

7. What happens to net exports, investment, and consumption when the money supply is decreased? Why is monetary policy neutral in the long run, but not in the short run?

8. Describe the changes to the U.S. price of Japanese cars when the yen appreciates, in the short and medium runs.

9. What would happen to the interest rate, GDP, exchange rate, and trade deficit if a uniform 10 percent tariff were placed on all imports? What would happen to these variables if foreign countries retaliated with an equal tariff on U.S. goods?

10. What must the Fed do to keep the exchange rate constant if interest rates in Europe rise because of monetary contraction there?

## Problems

**NUMERICAL**

1. Consider a macro model consisting of the following relationships:

$$Y = C + I + G + X$$

$$C = 220 + .63Y$$

$$I = 400 - 2,000R + .1Y$$

$$M = (.1583Y - 1,000R)P$$

$$X = 600 - .1Y - 100\ EP/P_w$$

$$EP/P_w = .75 + 5R$$

where government spending $G$ equals 1,200 and the money supply $M$ equals 900. Suppose that the ROW price level $P_w$ is always equal to 1.0 and that the U.S. price level is predetermined at 1.0.

   a. Which are the endogenous variables and which are the exogenous variables in this relationship?

   b. Find the values of $Y, R, C, I, X,$ and $E$ that are predicted by the model.

   c. Derive an algebraic expression for the aggregate demand curve in which the money supply $M$, government spending $G$, and price level $P$ explicitly appear. For $M = 900$ and $G = 1,200$ draw the aggregate demand curve accurately to scale.

   d. Keeping the price level $P$ at 1.0, calculate the effect a decrease in government spending of \$10 billion will have on output, the interest rate, consumption, investment, net exports, and the exchange rate. Do the same thing for an increase in the money supply of \$20 billion.

2. Using the same numerical example as in Problem 1, calculate private saving, the government budget surplus, and the capital inflow from abroad for the case where $G = 1,200$ and $M = 900$. Show that the sum of these three equals investment. Repeat your calculation for $G = 1,190$ and $M = 920$. Comment on what happens to the three components of saving.

3. For the same numerical example as in Problem 1, calculate a change in the mix of monetary and fiscal policy that will leave output equal to the level it is when $M = 900$ and $G = 1,200$, but in which the interest rate is 3 percent rather than 5 percent. Describe what happens to the value of the dollar, net exports, the government budget deficit, and investment for this change in policy.

4. Now assume that prices adjust according to the price adjustment equation

$$\pi = 1.2(Y_{-1} - Y^*)/Y^*,$$

where $\pi$ is the rate of inflation and potential output $Y^*$ is equal to \$6,000 billion. Continuing where you left off in Problem 1d, calculate the effect on the endogenous variables in the second, third, and fourth years after the increase in the money supply of \$20 billion. Do the same for the decline in government spending of \$10 billion. Describe the economy after prices have fully adjusted.

5. Consider a small economy that is much more open than the one in the previous examples. Its net export function is

$$X = 900 - .1Y - 400\ EP/P_\mathrm{w}$$

and the relationship between the interest rate and the exchange rate is

$$EP/P_\mathrm{w} = 10R + .5.$$

The other equations are the same.
a. Explain why this economy is more open.
b. Calculate what happens in the first year and in the long run when the money supply increases by $10 billion. Calculate what happens when government spending increases by $10 billion.

## ANALYTICAL

1. Suppose it was agreed that the United States would spend less on defense and that Japan would spend more.
   a. How would a reduction in defense spending affect the U.S. trade balance?
   b. How would an increase in Japan's defense spending affect the U.S. trade balance?
   c. To the extent that the United States and Japan purchase defense goods from each other, how will this affect your answer?
2. Purchasing power parity (PPP) is a theory of exchange-rate behavior as described in Section 12.2.
   a. Explain why the real exchange rate never changes under the theory of purchasing power parity.
   b. What governs the behavior of nominal exchange rates under PPP? Under what conditions are nominal exchange rates sticky?
   c. Suppose that inflation in the United States is 4 percent while in the rest of the world it is 7 percent. Under PPP, how does $E$ change over time? Does the dollar appreciate or depreciate?
   d. PPP clearly doesn't hold up in the short run; see Figure 12.3, where the real exchange rate is calculated using the GDP deflators for the United States and the ROW. If the real exchange rate were instead calculated using price indexes for manufactured goods, would you expect it to vary by more or less than it does in Figure 12.3?
3. On any given day, interest rates will differ from country to country. For example, U.S. government securities may pay 10 percent interest while comparable Japanese securities are paying 5 percent interest.
   a. Assume Japanese investors have access to U.S. securities. Why would any of them invest in Japanese securities when they could earn a higher interest rate on U.S. securities? Be specific.
   b. Is it likely that any American investors would want to hold the Japanese securities?
   c. Suppose that PPP (see Question 2) holds exactly, that interest rates in the United States and Japan are 10 percent and 5 percent respectively, and that

the U.S. inflation rate is 5 percent. If international investors are to be indifferent between holding U.S. and Japanese securities, what must the Japanese inflation rate be?

4. Given the net export function developed in this chapter, explain why the effect of fiscal policy on the trade balance is unambiguous, whereas the effect of monetary policy is ambiguous.

5. The topic box in Section 12.5 summarizes the relationship between trade deficits and budget deficits.
   a. Are *increases* in the trade deficit an inevitable result of *increases* in the budget deficit?
   b. Consider the cases where investment is very sensitive to the interest rate and where it is very insensitive. Compare the effect that an increase in the budget deficit will have on the interest rate, the exchange rate, investment, and the trade deficit for each case.

6. In Chapter 7 we developed a model in which net exports were a function of the interest rate. In this chapter we have described in more detail why net exports depend on the interest rate.
   a. What factors determine the sensitivity of net exports to the interest rate?
   b. Consider the cases where net exports are very sensitive to the interest rate and where they are very insensitive. Compare the effect that an increase in the money supply will have on output, the interest rate, investment, and the trade balance for each case.
   c. Suppose foreign manufacturers maintain a fixed dollar price for their goods regardless of the exchange rate. Will this result in net exports' being more or less sensitive to the interest rate?
   d. Given this behavior, explain why the only way the monetary authorities could act to reduce the trade deficit is by inducing a recession.

7. Suppose that the economy is at potential, but that the trade deficit is thought to be too large and the dollar is overvalued. Describe a change in monetary and fiscal policy that will keep the economy at potential, but will lower both the dollar and the trade deficit. Explain intuitively how the change in policy will bring about the desired results. Illustrate your answer using an IS-LM diagram.

8. Suppose that the economy is operating at potential but that inflation is thought to be too high. Macro policy will therefore have to turn contractionary, in order to reduce inflation. Describe the pros and cons of using monetary policy or fiscal policy to bring about the contraction, paying attention to the international factors.

## MacroSolve Exercises

1. Graph the exchange rate on the vertical axis and real net exports on the horizontal axis using quarterly data. Why would it not be valid to conclude from recent experience that a high exchange rate necessarily leads to low net exports?

2. *Policy Decisions 2001.* It is early 2001 and you have been hired by the Federal Reserve Board. After the 2000 election, the new administration and Congress are planning to pass a massive government spending package to build more roads, bridges, telecommunications channels, and so on. The program involves com-

mitting $100 billion a year for the indefinite future. You bring your MacroSolve computer program to work. Using the flexible-rate IS-LM model, analyze the effects of these policies.

a. Describe what happens to interest rates, exchange rates, net exports, and output under two Fed policies: a fixed money growth and an increase in money growth.

b. Repeat the analysis for the comparable dynamic models. (Hint: You may find it helpful to increase the number of periods using the **SET NUM OF PERIODS** option and use the **CONTINUE DISPLAY** option to show the time paths of these variables on the screen.)

c. The Fed is being pressured to keep the dollar and interest rates from rising. What do you recommend?

d. How would your recommendation change if this increase in government spending were thought to also increase potential GDP by $100 billion?

3. a. Select the closed-economy dynamic model and increase government spending by $100 billion. Calculate for the first two years of policy the increase in the budget deficit, the change in investment, and the change in savings. Is the budget deficit primarily financed by a reduction in investment or an increase in saving? Increase the number of periods and do the same again once GDP remains at potential. Is the financing of the deficit generally the same as in the previous periods?

b. Repeat for the open-economy dynamic model with a flexible exchange rate. Calculate the changes in the government deficit, investment, saving, and net exports in the first two periods and again once GDP remains at potential. Explain why the pattern of financing changes in this model. What variables account for this change?

4. Suppose as Fed chair you want to keep the exchange rate within a 1 percent band. What must you stabilize in order to keep the exchange rate constant? Select the "ISLM, Open, Flexible Nominal Exchange Rate" model and increase government spending by $50 billion. Next, increase the money supply by $10 billion, $15 billion, and $20 billion. What happens to the exchange rate? Which is the correct policy choice to meet your 1 percent goal? How are output, consumption, investment, and net exports affected? What happens to the relative strength of fiscal policy?

5. Suppose that instead of targeting exchange rates your goal as Fed chair was to maintain a stable level of employment, i.e., you were determined to keep unemployment within a 1 percent band. Select the "ISLM, Open, Flexible Nominal Exchange Rate" model and increase government spending by $50 billion. Next, determine by how much the money supply must be decreased or increased in order to keep unemployment at its natural rate. What happens to the exchange rate? How are output, consumption investment, and net exports affected? What happens to the relative strength of fiscal policy?

# CHAPTER

# 13

# Spending, Taxes, and the Budget Deficit

The budget of the U.S. federal government has been in deficit every year since 1969 and is expected to remain in deficit at least through the end of the twentieth century. How does the budget deficit affect the economy? First, government purchases contribute directly to demand. Second, transfer payments such as social security and unemployment compensation augment income. Third, interest paid on the national debt also augments income. Fourth, personal and business income taxes reduce income. In the last three cases demand is indirectly influenced because incomes change. The effect of the budget deficit is best analyzed in terms of these components of the deficit: purchases plus transfers plus interest on the national debt less taxes. In this chapter we will examine in detail the effects of these components on the economy.

Traditionally in macroeconomics government purchases have been considered exogenous—not explained in the model. This was so, for example, in the long-run growth model of Part I, where government purchases $G$ were taken as an exogenous variable. Empirically speaking, however, the government sector reacts to the state of the economy—partly because of conscious attempts to affect the economy. Transfers and taxes react to the state of the economy even more than purchases do. The equation describing government behavior is typically called a **reaction function.** Sometimes it is called a **policy rule** because, as we saw in Chapter 9, government actions are policy in one way or another, and if the behavior is systematic, it is like a rule. For example, generally, taxes decline in recessions.

There are two ways to look at economic policy—from the **normative** perspective and from the **positive** perspective. Normative policy analysis asks what the best policy is and how one policy is better than another. For instance, normative analysis might study what policy can give the lowest rate of unemployment consistent with a prescribed rate of inflation. Positive analysis tries to describe policy actions without inquiring whether or not they are good for the country. We took the normative perspective in Chapter 9 and will do the same in Chapter 18. In this chapter, on the other hand, most of our discussion will be positive and descriptive.

## 13.1 GOVERNMENT BUDGETS

Because the United States has a federal system of government, we need to distinguish between the different types of government: federal, state, and local. In 1995 federal government purchases were 38 percent of total purchases, and state and local purchases were 62 percent.

### The Federal Government Budget and Deficit

The best place to start looking at the budget deficit's effect on the economy is with the federal **budget.** The federal government budget summarizes all three of the types of effects on aggregate demand: purchases, transfers, and taxes. The overall budget totals do not distinguish between purchases and transfers. Rather, purchases of goods and services and transfers are lumped together as government **outlays.** The federal government's budget for 1995 is shown in Table 13.1.

Government outlays consist of purchases and transfers. Purchases involve the use of goods and services by the government, whereas transfers move funds to people outside the government. Less than a third of federal outlays take the form of purchases of goods and services. National defense accounts for about two-thirds of federal purchases. Federal purchases in 1995 were $454 billion, out of which $302 billion went for defense. Clearly, a major direct contribution of the government to aggregate demand is military spending. In 1995 total federal purchases of goods and services were about 7.1 percent of GDP.

Note that a substantial part of the government's expenditures is interest on the debt. As the debt has risen with high deficits in recent years, these

**TABLE 13.1**   The 1995 Budget of the United States
Government (billions of dollars during the calendar year)

| | |
|---|---:|
| RECEIPTS | 1490 |
|    Individual income taxes | 620 |
|    Corporate income taxes | 189 |
|    Social security taxes | 592 |
|    Other taxes and receipts | 89 |
| OUTLAYS | 1648 |
|    Purchases | |
|       National defense | 302 |
|       Other purchases | 152 |
|    Transfer payments | 727 |
|    Grants to local governments | 204 |
|    Interest on the debt | 233 |
|    Subsidies less enterprise profits | 31 |
| DEFICIT | 158 |

Source: *Economic Report of the President*, 1996, Table B-8.

interest payments have also risen. In 1995 interest payments on the debt represented about $1,800 for each person in the labor force on average. There is little that the government can do to change interest payments in a given year. The payments depend on past deficits and on the interest rate on past borrowing.

Aside from national defense, the major role of the federal government is to take in funds through taxes and pay them out as transfers. Most of the transfer takes the form of taxing families through the personal income tax and the social security tax and then paying out the proceeds as family benefits. The great bulk of these benefits are social security payments for retirement, disability, and medical needs.

The $158 billion deficit at the bottom of Table 13.1 is simply expenditures less receipts. The federal government has spent more than it received in every recent year, but the deficit has declined in recent years in relation to GDP.

## State and Local Government Budgets

One of the major developments in the 1980s and 1990s has been to shift responsibility away from the federal government to the local level, especially state governments. If this decentralization process continues, the state and local governments will play an increasingly important role in the economy in the future.

Table 13.2 shows the receipts and outlay figures in 1995 for all state and local governments combined in the United States. Compared with the federal government, a much larger percentage of state and local government outlays are purchases of goods and services that add directly to demand. The largest single purchase item for state and local governments is education—about one-third of total purchases. Much as defense dominates federal government purchases, education dominates state and local government purchases.

In marked contrast to the federal government, the state and local government ran a combined budget surplus in 1995. A combined budget surplus at the state and local level has been typical in recent years. This state and local surplus tends to offset the federal government deficit. Many municipal governments have laws that prevent their operating budgets from going into large deficits. In recent years balanced budget laws have been enacted in many states. Of course, some local governments do run serious deficits even though there is a general surplus.

A large percentage of state and local government receipts—about 51 percent—comes from property taxes and sales taxes. The federal government raises only a negligible part of its revenues from these sources. This means that the economy will have different effects on state and local governments' budgets than it has on the federal government's budget.

---

**TABLE 13.2**   The 1993 Combined Budgets of State and Local Governments (billions of dollars)

| | |
|---|---:|
| RECEIPTS | 1000 |
|   Personal tax | 181 |
|   Corporate tax | 35 |
|   Sales and property taxes | 508 |
|   Payroll tax | 72 |
|   Grants from federal government | 204 |
| OUTLAYS | 908 |
|   Purchases (goods and services) | 687 |
|   Transfer payments | 294 |
|   Net interest paid | −60 |
|   Subsidies less enterprise profits | −13 |
| SURPLUS | 93 |

*Source: Economic Report of the President*, 1996, Table B-8.

# FLUCTUATIONS IN THE DEFICIT: PURCHASES, TRANSFERS, AND TAXES

**13.2**

From the point of view of macroeconomic *fluctuations*, what matters most about the government budget deficit is not its average level, but the way the budget responds to conditions in the economy. How large is this response? How do the fluctuations in the government deficit compare with the fluctuations in the economy as a whole? We will try to answer these questions separately for purchases, transfers, and taxes. We do not consider changes in the fourth component of the deficit, interest on the national debt, because the federal government has no separate control over that component. The amount of debt was determined by past deficits, and the interest rate is determined by monetary and fiscal policy and by nonpolicy factors.

First, federal purchases of goods and services do not seem to change much as real activity in the private economy fluctuates. This is shown in Figure 13.1. During the post–World War II period, federal spending has fluc-

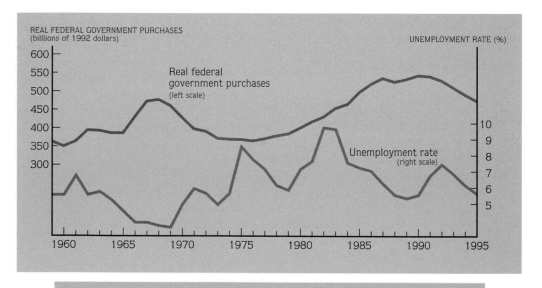

**FIGURE 13.1** Real Federal Government Purchases and Unemployment

Federal purchases of goods and services have not responded in any systematic way to the state of the economy, as measured by the unemployment rate. There was a big increase in federal spending in the late 1960s and again in the early 1980s. Except possibly for the 1980s, spending has not cranked up the economy during recessions by increasing relative to aggregate demand.
Source: *Economic Report of the President*, 1996, Tables B-2 and B-38.

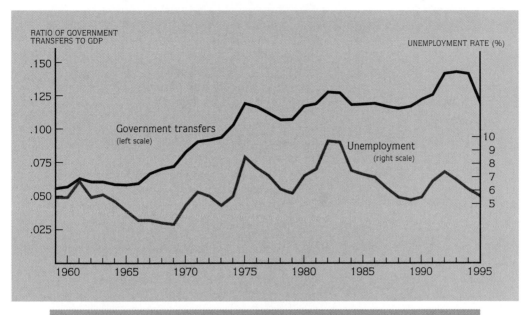

RATIO OF GOVERNMENT
TRANSFERS TO GDP

UNEMPLOYMENT RATE (%)

Government transfers
(left scale)

Unemployment
(right scale)

**FIGURE 13.2** Government Transfers and Unemployment

Government transfer payments tend to rise in years of high unemployment and fall in years of low unemployment. This has been especially true in recent years. The synchronization has been achieved mainly through unemployment insurance and other programs that make the rise in transfers during recessions automatic.
Source: *Economic Report of the President*, 1996, Tables B 1, B-38, and B-84.

tuated mostly because of defense spending. Federal spending rose during the Vietnam War, when unemployment was low, and during the defense buildup of the early 1980s. Except possibly for the early 1980s, when defense spending increased as the Fed tightened monetary policy and there was a recession, federal spending has not increased during recessions. Federal purchases were flat during the recession starting in 1990.

Every recession brings programs to raise spending and provide added government employment. In fact, however, spending programs have been small and have taken several years to get into gear. Programs launched in the depths of a recession frequently do not generate a significant contribution to aggregate demand until several years later. By then, the economy might be approaching boom conditions. This is another example of the lags in the effect of policy that we mentioned in Chapter 9.

On the other hand, the federal government's transfers usually do fluctuate in the right direction and offset other movements in the economy. Government transfers rise when unemployment rises, as can be seen clearly in Figure 13.2.

**TABLE 13.3**   Automatic Stabilizers: Government Transfer Programs That Respond to the State of the Economy

| Program | Description |
| --- | --- |
| Unemployment insurance | A combined federal-state program that pays benefits to workers who have lost their jobs. |
| Food stamps | A federal program that pays benefits to any family with an income below a certain threshold; in recessions, additional families become eligible. |
| Welfare programs | A combined federal-state program that pays benefits to poor families with dependent children; as incomes fall during recessions, payments increase. |
| Medicaid | A combined federal-state program that assists poor families with medical benefits; the number drawing these benefits rises during recessions. |
| Social security | A federal program that supports people in retirement; some people who are eligible for benefits choose to work instead, but their number declines in a recession and the volume of benefits rises. |

Government transfers rise in recessions and fall in booms largely through the normal operation of benefit programs. No discretionary intervention on the part of government officials is required. As we discussed in Chapter 10, when unemployment rises and incomes fall, a number of government programs automatically increase their income transfers to families. For this reason they sometimes are called *automatic stabilizers*. These programs are listed in Table 13.3.

Taxes also rise and fall with the level of economic activity. The data are summarized in Figure 13.3. In each recession since 1959 federal government tax receipts dropped sharply. This behavior was particularly dramatic in the 1969–70, the 1974–75, and the 1981–82 recessions. On the other hand, the decline in the 1990–91 recession was small. The drop in tax receipts in these periods was larger in percentage terms than the drop in real GDP. The **elasticity** of year-to-year changes in real tax receipts with respect to changes in real GDP was above 1 (an elasticity is the percentage change in one variable induced by a 1 percent change in another variable). This can be seen directly in Figure 13.3 as a decline in the tax receipts–GDP ratio in each recession.

One reason that tax receipts fall by more than real GDP—why the elasticity is greater than 1—is that the items that are not taxed do not fluctuate much compared with the items that are taxed. Depreciation, which is not taxed, hardly fluctuates at all. Corporate profits, on the other hand, fluctuate widely. Another reason that the elasticity is greater than 1 is that average tax

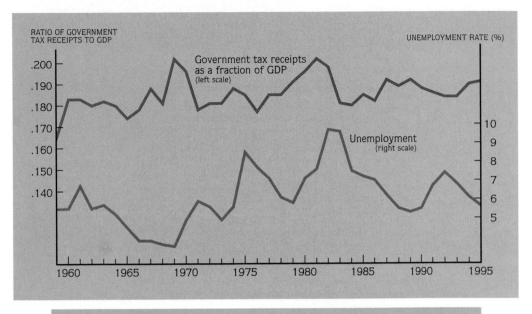

**FIGURE 13.3** Government Tax Receipts and Unemployment

As the economy fluctuates in and out of recessions and booms, government tax receipts also fluctuate. Tax receipts tend to fall in years of high unemployment and rise in years of low unemployment. The decline in tax receipts mitigates the drop in demand and helps stabilize the economy.

Source: *Economic Report of the President*, 1996, Tables B-38 and B-78.

*rates* rise and fall with income. Some of the fluctuations in tax rates occur automatically because of the progressive tax system in the United States. As incomes fall in a recession some people fall into lower tax brackets, or even fall into the region in which no taxes are paid. Hence, the proportion of their income that is paid in taxes goes down as income falls. Conversely, the proportion goes up as income rises.

Some of the reductions in tax rates in recessions have occurred because the tax law was changed by Congress in order to mitigate the drop in aggregate demand. These are **discretionary changes** rather than automatic changes, but they have been fairly regular and should be included as part of our behavioral description of the reaction of government to the economy. Proposals to cut taxes to stimulate the economy out of a recession in the early 1960s were made by President Kennedy, and most of these changes were enacted into law by Congress. Proposals to cut taxes were made by President Reagan during the depressed economic conditions of the early 1980s. Although the rationale for these tax cuts was not the conventional

**TABLE 13.4**   Discretionary Stabilization Measures: Ways the Federal Government Can Affect Demand through Fiscal Policy

| Measure | Description |
|---|---|
| Temporary income tax change | A temporary cut in personal income taxes will stimulate consumption and offset a recession; a temporary surcharge will discourage consumption and cool off a boom. |
| Investment tax credit | A subsidy to investment through the tax system will stimulate investment for the period when the credit is in effect and discourage investment before it takes effect and after it is removed. |
| Home purchase credit | A subsidy for home purchases by individuals has the same effect as an investment credit, but on residential investment. |
| Public works | An increase or speedup in highway construction and other government purchases adds directly to demand. |

countercyclical one—some in the Reagan administration argued that the tax cuts would greatly increase supply, others argued that they were necessary to offset the effect that inflation had on tax rates—in retrospect they fit right into the general story that tax rates are usually cut during periods of high unemployment. Other examples are the temporary tax surcharge of 1968 and the tax rebate of 1975. Discretionary policies are summarized in Table 13.4. Although there were proposals for tax cuts to offset the 1990–91 recession, none were enacted.

In Chapter 6 we wrote tax receipts $T$ as a constant proportion of income $Y$:

$$T = tY \tag{13.1}$$

where $t$ is the constant tax rate. The discussion of the previous two paragraphs means that it is incorrect to treat the tax rate $t$ as a constant. The tax rate $t$ actually falls when income $Y$ falls, and rises when income rises.

Much of the overall impact of the government's influence through taxes and transfers eventually shows up in personal disposable income. Recall that in Chapter 10 we looked at the relation between disposable income and GDP and found that the fluctuations in disposable income were much smaller (look back to Figure 10.3 for a review). Disposable income changes by only about 40 percent as much as total income. Consumers see only about 40 percent of the total loss in the economy's income when a recession hits. Automatic stabilizers and discretionary changes in taxes and transfers soak up much of the other 60 percent. (Recall that a bit of the 60 percent is due to the fact that corporations try to maintain their dividend payouts when corporate profits fall during recessions.)

Note that the effect of such countercyclical movements in taxes and transfers is to reduce the multiplier of the IS-LM model. When there is an increase in investment spending, for example, the increase in GDP leads to a smaller increase in disposable income and hence a smaller effect on consumption. The multiplier effect is smaller due to the automatic stabilizers.

# THE EFFECTS OF
# THE GOVERNMENT DEFICIT

13.3

Why is the government deficit so controversial and mysterious? Part of the reason is that the deficit is just a summary statistic that reflects the behavior of many other variables. It is really just the tip of an iceberg. We emphasized that the budget deficit is simply the difference between government *expenditures* (purchases and transfers) and *receipts*. Moreover, from the government accounting identity discussed in Chapter 2, we know that deficits must be financed by issuing *bonds* or *money* to the pubic. The overall impact of the budget on the economy can thus be pieced together by looking at the effects of receipts, expenditures, bonds, and money.

In this section we address some of the questions raised about the deficit in the 1980s by examining the cyclical behavior of the deficit, the empirical relation between deficits and interest rates, and the implications of the simple fact that the government must borrow to finance its deficits.

## Cyclical versus Structural Deficits

The government budget deficit always goes deep in the red during recessions. We know the reasons for this from the last section: Expenditures rise and receipts fall during recessions. The automatic stabilizers exacerbate the swing of the deficit during a recession.

Figure 13.4 shows the relationship between the deficit and the cyclical fluctuations in unemployment for the years 1959 to 1995. When the economy is below potential, the budget deficit is large. When the economy is above potential, the budget is in surplus, or at least less in the red. Economists have developed the concept of the **full-employment deficit** to adjust for cyclical effects.[1] The full-employment deficit is the deficit that would occur if the

[1]The idea of the full-employment deficit was used by E. Cary Brown in "Fiscal Policy in the Thirties: A Reappraisal," *American Economic Review,* Vol. 46 (December 1956), pp. 857–879. He showed that the actual deficits observed in the early 1930s were large surpluses in the full-employment deficit.

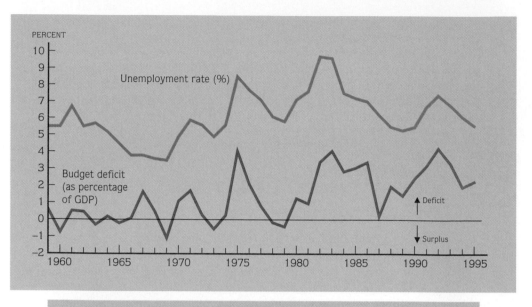

**FIGURE 13.4**    The Cyclical Behavior of the Deficit

The chart shows the budget deficit, as a percentage of GDP, and the unemployment rate. The latter is a measure of the state of the economic cycle. The deficit is strongly cyclical.
Source: *Economic Report of the President*, 1996, Tables B-1, B-38, and B-83.

economy were at full employment. The full-employment deficit takes out the cyclical effects on the deficit. This is done by estimating reaction functions for expenditures and receipts and calculating what expenditures and receipts would occur at potential GDP and full employment.

In more recent years the concept of the full-employment deficit has usually been discussed by distinguishing between the structural and cyclical parts of the deficit. The **structural deficit** is the same thing as the full-employment deficit, and the **cyclical deficit** is the difference between the actual deficit and the structural deficit.

## Have Deficits Been Related to Interest Rates in Recent U.S. History?

The relation between the deficit and interest rates is one of the most important issues with respect to the government's role in aggregate demand. In Chapters 6 and 7 we showed that an increase in the government's budget deficit, brought about by either an increase in expenditures or a cut in taxes, would raise interest rates and expand output by shifting the IS curve to the right. How does that theory fit the facts? Here we look at some of the relevant

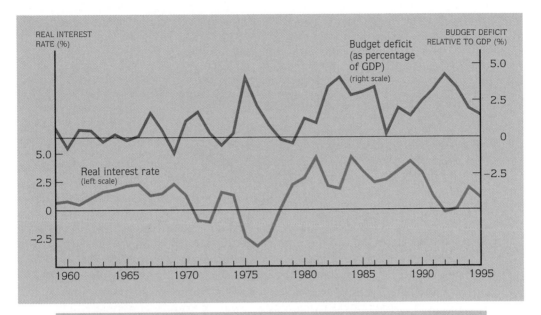

**FIGURE 13.5**  Budget Deficits and Real Interest Rates

During much of the past 35 years interest rates have fallen during periods when the federal government was running a deficit. However, this does not mean that deficits cause lower interest rates. Falling interest rates and deficits are both largely the result of recessions. The 1980s was one of the few periods when high budget deficits and high interest rates occurred at the same time. Note: The real interest rate is the three-month Treasury bill less the average of the rate of change in the GDP deflator during the previous three years. Source: *Economic Report of the President,* 1996, Tables B-1, B-3, B-72, and B-83.

facts. Figure 13.5 shows the historical relation between a measure of the real interest rate and the budget deficit. Two things are important from the chart.

First, over short-run periods and for much of the last 35 years, it appears that the real interest rate falls when the government budget goes into the red. Deficits do not appear to cause high real interest rates. Before you jump to any conclusions, recall the previous discussion, which pointed to the cyclical behavior of the deficit. Deficits occur when the economy is in a slump. Now, there are many reasons for interest rates to be low during a slump: the demand for money is low and investment demand is low. It is thus likely that much of the relation between interest rates and the deficit during the last 35 years is due to other factors in the economy.

Second, what evidence there is indicates a positive relation between the budget deficit and interest rates during the 1982–90 period. Real interest rates were higher than normal rates during this period and the budget deficit reached a high-water mark as well. Perhaps the very large deficits—and prospects for future deficits—raised interest rates. This would be the prediction of both the long-run and short-run models we have developed. But real interest rates fell in 1991 and 1992 even though massive deficits continued.

## The Deficit and the Explosion of Government Debt

When the government runs a deficit, it must borrow from the public. The top panel of Figure 13.6 shows how budget deficits have led to an explosion of outstanding national debt. Most of the debt consists of interest-bearing bonds, but part is non-interest-bearing money. As we will see in the next chapter, the Federal Reserve System **monetizes** part of the government debt when it purchases it and issues currency and non-interest-bearing deposits. In the United States the Fed has monetized only a small amount of the debt. It monetizes the debt primarily to provide sufficient money for the economy to work efficiently, rather than to raise revenues.

During World War II the government also ran a large deficit, as is typical of most wars. Government expenditures were, of course, abnormally high in the war years; rather than raise taxes temporarily to pay for the war, the government borrowed the money. This shifted some of the burden of the war to future generations who would have to pay the interest on the borrowings. After the war years until the 1960s the federal government ran a surplus in its budget, with some exceptions during recessions. The debt fell slightly during the surplus years, but was relatively unchanged compared with the increase during World War II.

Scaling the debt by nominal GDP gives a better perspective of the importance of the debt for the whole economy, as shown in the lower panel of Figure 13.6. At the end of World War II the government debt relative to GDP reached an all-time high of a bit over 100 percent. Since World War II the public debt divided by GDP fell steadily until the mid-1970s. Then the stock of outstanding debt began to grow relative to GDP as we had a big deficit in the recession of 1974–75 and even bigger deficits in the 1980s and early 1990s. The ratio of the debt to GDP is below the levels reached at the end of World War II. Recent growth of the ratio has been low.

We can express the relation between the deficit and the accumulation of debt formally as

Debt at the start of next year

    = Debt at the start of this year

    + Purchases this year

    + Transfers this year          } Deficit

    + Interest on the debt this year

    − Receipts this year.

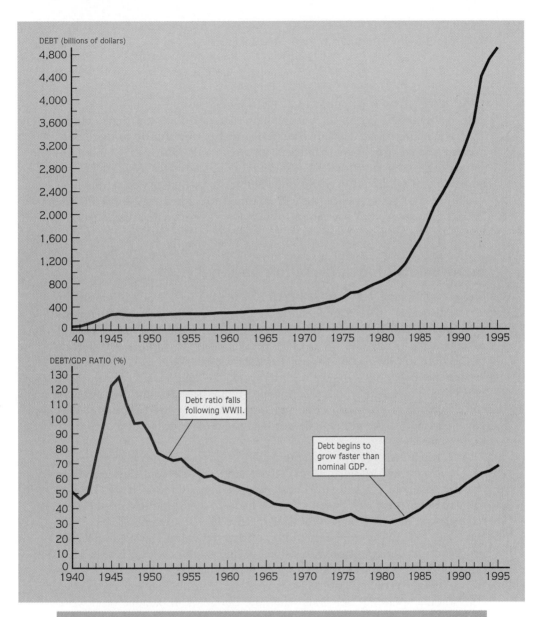

**FIGURE 13.6** The National Debt

The national debt has had two big periods of rapid growth: during the war years in the 1940s and from 1981 onward. In between, the debt dropped as a ratio of GDP.
Source: *Economic Report of the President*, 1996, Tables B-1 and B-74.

Using the notation $D$ for debt, $G$ for purchases, $F$ for transfers, $T$ for receipts, and $R$ for the interest rate, we can write this as

$$D_{t+1} = D_t + G_t + F_t + RD_t - T_t. \tag{13.2}$$

Each of the terms in Equation 13.2 corresponds with the verbal description of the relation between the deficit and debt accumulation. Note that Equation 13.2 is nothing more than an **intertemporal government budget constraint** faced by government officials. It corresponds exactly to the intertemporal budget constraint for the households in our analysis of forward-looking consumption (Chapter 10). The only difference is that the government is usually a net debtor; hence we call its outstanding financial stock $D$. The household's asset stock was simply called $A$; we assumed that the household was usually a net lender.

## Economic Significance of the National Debt

The growth of the U.S. national debt has attracted a lot of attention from economists and other commentators. The debt exists because the federal government sold bonds in order to finance spending in excess of current revenue. Historically, the U.S. debt has grown mainly in wartime. The decline in the debt to GDP ratio through 1974 shown in Figure 13.6 is typical of earlier U.S. experience except during major wars and is also typical of the peacetime experience of other countries. The massive accumulation of debt since 1981 is an unusual event. Similar buildups occurred in many other advanced industrial countries (Canada and Belgium, for example) during the same period.

During the 1990s, federal purchases of goods and services have declined as a fraction of GDP, from 7.4 percent to 6.2 percent. But growth in transfer payments made up the difference. The ratio of transfers to GDP was 8.9 percent in 1990 and rose to 10.0 percent in 1995. Interest on the debt rose slightly, from 3.1 percent of GDP in 1990 to 3.2 percent in 1995.

The federal debt appears to be an important element in the political process for making spending decisions. When there is relatively little debt outstanding, spending on goods and services and income maintenance tends to rise above revenue. Those in Congress have trouble saying no to their constituents' spending demands when the budget is in balance or close to it. A deficit develops and debt builds up. Rising interest on the debt adds to spending growth. As the deficit grows, political opposition to spending rises. The economy reaches a sustainable path where spending growth is held down to the rate of growth of the economy. Debt also grows at the rate of growth of the economy, so the path can be sustained year after year. The economy may have reached this equilibrium in 1990.

Economists are divided on the question of the purely economic significance of the national debt. A good way to think about the issue is to ask how the 1980s and early 1990s would have been different if the government had spent the same amount but had not financed any of the spending by borrowing. There are two differences between what actually happened and the hypothetical zero-deficit case. First, consumers had more disposable income because they paid lower taxes. Borrowing made up for the taxes that would have been levied in the zero-deficit case. Families felt better off and consumed more than they would have in the hypothetical case. Second, taxpayers are worse off because they now have to pay higher future taxes to finance the interest on the debt. Their consumption is lower than in the zero-deficit case because of this factor.

Which effect is larger? Economists have usually emphasized the first effect. The increase in current disposable income is immediate and concrete; the increase in future taxes is distant and theoretical. Deficit spending makes families think they are better off than they really are. They consume too much and the economy has fewer resources for investment. There is a *burden of the national debt*. Debt displaces productive capital in portfolios.[2] But one analysis reaches the conclusion that the two effects offset each other precisely; it asserts that there is no burden of the debt. This analysis—called **Ricardian equivalence**—was put forward in its modern form by Robert Barro, currently at Harvard University.[3] (David Ricardo, a 19th-century British economist, was the originator of the analysis.)

Ricardian equivalence holds if consumption is independent of the timing of taxation. When the government defers taxation by building up debt, as it did in the 1980s and 1990s, consumption is just the same as it would have been with the same amount of government spending financed by current taxes. Moreover, it is through consumption that income taxes affect other macro variables. Looking at the IS-LM model of Chapter 7 or the underlying long-run growth model of Chapter 3, we can see that a change in income taxes that has no effect on consumption will have no effect on interest rates, investment, trade, GDP, or inflation. On the other hand, if there is a burden of the debt—if deficit spending encourages consumption—all variables will be affected. Higher consumption will mean a higher real interest rate, less investment, a larger trade deficit, and lower potential GDP in the longer run. Figure 13.5 shows the evidence on the real interest rate. There is little overall relation between deficits and real interest rates.

Two assumptions are critical to Ricardian equivalence. First is that families think about the future when they make consumption plans. The forward-looking theory of consumption, based on the idea of rational

[2]See Peter Diamond, "National Debt in a Neoclassical Growth Model," *American Economic Review,* Vol. 32 (June 1965), pp. 161–168.

[3]See Robert Barro, "Are Government Bonds Net Wealth?" *Journal of Political Economy,* Vol. 82 (November–December 1974), pp. 1095–1117.

expectations and rational behavior, supports this assumption. Second is that families look as far into the future as the taxes will be levied. If the government never pays off the debt from the 1980s, but simply continues paying interest on it forever, then strict Ricardian equivalence would require that families look into the indefinite future. One of Barro's important contributions to the theory of Ricardian equivalence was to point out that families may look into the indefinite future even though individual lifetimes are limited. Families may be linked across generations through gifts and bequests. When the government defers taxes to future generations, the current generation may respond by saving more in order to make gifts to future generations. These gifts would spread the burden of taxation evenly across generations.

Ricardian equivalence takes the path of government spending as exogenous. If, on the contrary, spending responds to the conditions of the budget, the analysis becomes more complex. Some of the supporters of tax cuts see lower revenue as a way to force down government spending. They consider most government spending as wasteful. To them, the buildup of debt following a tax cut is just part of the process of scaling back government. On the other hand, lower revenue may cut into government investment. Then the burden of the debt includes the displacement of public as well as private capital.

Although the business press accepts the burden of the debt as absolute economic truth, with the support of many prominent economists (such as Martin Feldstein of Harvard University), the burden has been hard to quantify. The bulge of consumption during the 1980s may have been a response to artificially high disposable income, or it may have been the result of great consumer optimism. High real interest rates in the 1980s may have been the result of huge amounts of federal borrowing, or they may just have reflected the combined effect of optimistic consumers, strong government purchases of goods and services, and favorable investment opportunities in the United States in comparison with the rest of the world. There is no strong consensus among macroeconomists that the federal debt is either a large or a small burden on the economy.

# THE GOVERNMENT AND THE IS CURVE

## 13.4

Fiscal policy can shift the IS curve in two ways. First, government purchases of goods and services $G$ enters spending directly. In Chapters 6 and 7 we looked at how changes in $G$ shift the IS curve through the multiplier process. We noted in this chapter that the federal government rarely offsets fluctuations in aggregate demand by altering its purchases of goods and services. Historically, government purchases do not appear to be an effective instrument to control aggregate demand but rather another shock or disturbance to aggregate demand. Recent experience with large deficits does not indicate that this situation is likely to change soon.

Second, policies on taxes and transfers can influence consumption. A tax cut increases income and stimulates consumption and so shifts the IS curve to the right. However, the magnitude of this shift is highly uncertain because of people's uncertainty about how permanent the tax cut will be. Moreover, there is a possibility that some people may increase their saving because they figure that taxes will rise in the future in order to pay the interest on the increased government debt.

Fiscal policy also influences the *slope* of the IS curve. We noted in this chapter that the automatic stabilizers operating through taxes and transfers reduce the multiplier. Because of the automatic stabilizers an increase in interest rates along the IS curve brings about a smaller decline in consumption and GDP. Therefore the IS curve is steeper as a result of the automatic stabilizers.

## REVIEW AND PRACTICE

### Major Points

1. Government purchases, transfers, and receipts are not exogenous. They respond to the state of the economy.

2. Expenditures rise and receipts fall in recessions. Real tax receipts fall by a greater percentage than real GDP during recessions. This is mainly because of the progressive tax system.

3. The deficit fluctuates countercyclically with GDP.

4. The structural or full-employment deficit has had these cyclical effects removed.

5. Public debt is the cumulation of past deficits.

6. The debt has declined relative to GDP for most of the period since World War II. It has increased since the early 1980s, however.

7. Higher government purchases of goods and services shift the IS curve to the right, though the federal government has not used this policy instrument to try to stabilize the economy in the past few decades.

8. Taxes influence both the position and the slope of the IS curve. A tax cut shifts the IS curve to the right, though the magnitude of the shift is uncertain. Automatic stabilizers make the IS curve steeper.

## Key Terms and Concepts

outlays
purchases
policy rule
reaction function
full-employment deficit

elasticity of tax revenues
automatic stabilizers
government budget
  constraint

government debt
defense expenditures
Ricardian equivalence

## Questions for Discussion and Review

1. Explain the difference between government purchases and government transfers. Which is larger for the federal government? For state and local governments? Which fluctuates more with the business cycle? In which direction?

2. What are the major automatic stabilizers? What is their significance for economic fluctuations?

3. Why is the budget typically in deficit during periods when the unemployment rate is high? What is the full-employment budget deficit? Does the full-employment deficit fluctuate with the state of the economy?

4. Explain why a progressive tax structure leads to an increase in the tax revenue–GDP ratio when the economy is growing rapidly in a boom.

5. Why has the deficit usually been large when interest rates have been low? Does this mean that the deficit does not cause interest rates to rise as predicted by the IS-LM model?

6. Describe the behavior of the government debt since World War II. Why did the debt decline as a fraction of GDP until 1981?

## Problems

**NUMERICAL**

1. Use the following example of a progressive tax schedule to compute what happens to average tax rates in the economy during a typical recession.

| Income Bracket | Marginal Tax Rate |
|---|---|
| 0–9,999 | 0 |
| 10,000–29,999 | .2 |
| 30,000–49,999 | .4 |
| 50,000 and above | .6 |

To make it easy, suppose that there are just three income groups of taxpayers. Just before the recession there are 200,000 taxpayers making $20,000, 700,000 making $40,000, and 100,000 making $60,000.

a. Compute the average tax rate for the whole economy before and just after the recession if everybody's income drops by $10,000 during the recession. Has anyone moved to a different tax bracket?

b. What happens to the average tax rate if everybody's income is reduced by $20,000?

c. Suppose that the government introduces a flat tax whereby everyone making equal to or more than $10,000 pays the same proportional tax of 25 percent. For this new tax system recalculate your answers to Parts a and b.

d. Comment on the effect on stabilization policy of a move from a progressive tax-rate system to a flat tax-rate system.

2. Suppose that federal tax receipts, transfers, and purchases are given by $T = .25\,YP$, $F = .15\,YP$, and $G = 400$, all in billions of current dollars. Suppose that at the start of 1984 the federal debt $D$ was $800 billion, the interest rate $R$ was 9.5 percent, real GDP was $3,500 billion, and the price level $P$ was 1.08.

a. Calculate the actual and full-employment budget deficit for 1984 in current dollars assuming that real potential output is $3,700 billion. Include interest payments in your calculation of the deficit using Equation 13.2.

b. Two forecasts made in early 1985 (the Reagan administration's and an average of three private forecasters: Data Resources, Chase Econometrics, and Wharton) for real GDP growth, the rate of inflation $(P - P_{-1})/P_{-1}$, and the interest rate for 1985 through 1988 are given below.

| | Real GDP Growth | | Inflation | | Interest Rate | |
|---|---|---|---|---|---|---|
| | Admin. | Priv. | Admin. | Priv. | Admin. | Priv. |
| 1985 | 3.9 | 3.6 | 3.8 | 3.6 | 8.1 | 8.2 |
| 1986 | 4.0 | 2.8 | 4.4 | 3.9 | 7.9 | 8.9 |
| 1987 | 4.0 | 3.4 | 4.2 | 4.4 | 7.2 | 9.4 |
| 1988 | 4.0 | 3.6 | 3.9 | 4.8 | 5.9 | 8.4 |

Assuming that $G$ increases at 5 percent per year, calculate the deficit for 1985 through 1988 for the two sets of forecasts. Start with the 1984 figures in Part a. Be sure to use Equation 13.2 to calculate the change in federal debt.

3. Assume that government outlays and taxes are initially zero, as is the stock of government debt. In year 1 the government begins to spend $50 billion per year, in real terms, on environmental protection. Each year the government issues enough debt to finance this program, as well as to repay the interest on the previous stock of debt. The stock of government debt and the deficit, measured in current dollars, obeys the equations

$$D_t = (D_{t-1} + G_{t-1})(1 + R)$$

$$DEF_{t-1} = D_t - D_{t-1}$$

where $G$ is measured in current dollars. The initial price level is 1.

a. For an interest rate of 5 percent and an inflation rate of zero, calculate the real and nominal values of government debt and the deficit for each of the first five years.

b. Now suppose prices rise at an annual rate of 5 percent. Assuming that the interest rate remains at 5 percent, repeat your calculations for Part a.

c. Finally, assume an inflation rate of 5 percent and an interest rate of 10.25 percent. Again, repeat your calculations for Part a.

d. Compare the path of real debt under Parts a, b, and c. Explain any differences.

    e. Comparing Parts a and c, you should find that the real debt stock is the same for Part c, but that the real deficit each year is higher. Why doesn't a higher deficit lead to a higher stock of debt?

    f. In which case was inflation anticipated by financial markets? Explain your answer.

4. Suppose that instead of *G* being exogenous, it is given by the formula

$$G = 1{,}200 - .1(Y - Y^*),$$

where $Y^*$ is potential GDP and is equal to \$6,000 billion. Suppose that the other relationships in the economy are given by the example considered in Chapter 7:

$$C = 220 + .63Y$$

$$I = 1{,}000 - 2{,}000R$$

$$M = (.1583Y - 1{,}000R)P$$

$$X = 525 - .1Y - 500R$$

where the price level is predetermined at $P = 1$ and the money supply is 900.

    a. Derive an algebraic expression for the IS curve for this model. Plot it to scale. Compare it with the IS curve of Chapter 7, in which government purchases are exogenous. Which is steeper? Why?

    b. Derive the aggregate demand curve and plot it to scale. How does it compare with the aggregate demand curve when government spending is exogenous?

    c. Calculate the effect on GDP of an increase in the money supply of \$10 billion. Is the effect larger or smaller than the case where government spending is exogenous? Explain in words what is going on.

    d. Is this equation an accurate description of government purchases in the United States? If not, what other components of the government budget act as automatic stabilizers? How is the impact of aggregate demand and price shocks affected by such stabilizers?

5. (Simple proof of the Ricardian equivalence.) Consider the intertemporal budget constraint for families that we introduced in Chapter 10 and the intertemporal budget constraint for the government that we introduced in this chapter. Suppose that taxes are cut by \$1,000 in year 1 and the government debt increases.

    a. If the interest rate is 5 percent, by how much will taxes have to increase next year if the government debt is to come back to normal by the end of next year?

    b. What is the effect of this decrease and subsequent increase in taxes on the intertemporal budget constraint for consumers? How would you expect this change to affect consumption?

## ANALYTICAL

1. The President is required by law to submit each year projections of budget deficits for the next five years. In discussing this law about budget projections, President Reagan said in 1985, "Frankly, I pay no attention to [the budget projections]. . . .

There isn't any economist in the world who can do that and accurately tell you what you're going to need down the road." He then proposed that the law be abolished (*New York Times,* January 12, 1985).

    a. Obtain a copy of a recent *Economic Report of the President* and evaluate whose forecasts in Numerical Problem 2 have proven more accurate: those of the Reagan administration or those of the private forecasters.

    b. In light of the relation between economy and the budget (again, see Numerical Problem 2), comment on the proposal made by Reagan.

2. Suppose our model of the economy is the simple spending balance model of Chapter 6. The equations of the model are

$$Y = C + I + G + X$$

$$C = 100 + .9Y_d$$

$$Y_d = Y + F$$

where $I = 750$, $X = 0$, and $F$ stands for government transfer payments.

    a. You are told that government outlays equal 500, and there are no taxes. With this information can you calculate the point of spending balance?

    b. What is the maximum value of income for which there could be spending balance? What is the minimum value?

    c. Explain why government transfers and spending affect aggregate demand differently. Be specific.

3. Explain why imports act as automatic stabilizers. Compare the case in which imports consist mainly of necessities with the case in which they consist mainly of luxury goods.

4. Suppose it is 2001, and the newly elected President, in order to win, promised not to raise taxes and not to tamper with social security and other transfer programs. At 6 percent unemployment, output is very close to potential. There still, however, are the two nagging problems of the government budget deficit and the trade deficit.

    a. In the short run, how can the administration reduce the budget deficit without breaking any of its campaign promises? Be specific about the policy. What effect will the policy have on output and interest rates? How will this policy reduce the budget deficit? Describe the effect of this policy on the trade deficit. Is it unambiguous?

    b. Will this policy reduce the budget deficit in the long run? Again, be specific. What are its long-run effects on the trade deficit?

    c. What will the effects of such a policy be, in the short run and in the long run, on the real value of government debt outstanding?

    d. Recall the relationship between nominal interest rates and expected inflation discussed in Chapter 7. How might the expectations of such a policy affect long-term nominal interest rates?

5. Suppose that government spending is increased when the economy is below potential GDP. Why doesn't the decrease in government saving lead to an equal decline in total saving and investment?

6. Sketch an IS-LM diagram. Compare two cases, one in which government spending is exogenous, and the other in which government spending declines when

the economy rises above potential GDP and increases when the economy is below potential GDP. Which curve is steeper? For which curve is monetary policy more powerful?

7. Suppose that the President and the Congress agreed to raise personal income taxes by $100 billion per year starting in 1998 in an attempt to reduce the budget deficit by 2000. However, the legislation actually increased taxes only until 2000; starting in 2001, taxes would automatically be lowered back down by $100 billion. What would be the effect of this tax increase on *consumption demand*? Use the forward-looking theory of consumption to explain what the impact of the tax increase would be.

8. Consider once again the simple spending balance model of Chapter 6. Suppose now that the model is

$$Y = C + I + G + X$$

$$C = 100 + .9Y_d$$

$$Y_d = Y + F - T$$

where $I = 750$, $X = 0$, and $G$, $T$, and $F$ are initially zero.
   a. Calculate the initial point of spending balance.
   b. Suppose that the country goes to war for a year—requiring government expenditures of 100—and that taxes are temporarily raised to 100 in that same year. Calculate consumption and the point of spending balance in the war year and all future years.
   c. Now suppose that the government issues war bonds instead of raising taxes. The war bonds are 5 percent consoles. Consoles are bonds on which interest is paid forever and the principal is never repaid. Again, calculate consumption and the point of spending balance in the war year and in all future years.
   d. What is the net effect of the government's running a deficit in the war year instead of raising taxes? Is your result consistent with the idea of Ricardian equivalence? If not, how can you explain the difference?

9. In deriving the aggregate demand curve, we have implicitly assumed that the government announces a budget in real terms. In practice, the budget is announced in nominal terms for the coming fiscal year before the price level is known with certainty. This practice of not indexing public-expenditure plans to the price level has implications for the shape of the aggregate demand schedule. Relative to an aggregate demand schedule with constant real government expenditures, will a schedule with constant nominal government expenditures be flatter or steeper? Is the policy rule of nominal budgeting stabilizing or destabilizing with respect to GDP in the presence of unanticipated price shocks?

10. In an attempt to stimulate the economy, the government announces that it will drastically reduce taxes for one year with no change in government spending. Describe the effect of the temporary tax cut on output, consumption, investment, and net exports for each of the following assumptions about household consumption behavior.
   a. Households obey the simple Keynesian consumption function.
   b. Households are forward-looking but do not anticipate future tax increases to offset the current reduction.

c. Households are forward-looking and anticipate future tax increases to offset the current reduction.

## MacroSolve Exercises

1. Plot the government deficit as a percentage of GDP, and both short- and long-term real interest rates against time using annual data. On two additional graphs, one for each interest rate, graph the short- and long-term real interest rates against the government deficit since 1960. On the basis of this, could you agree with the current public sentiment that high deficits cause high interest rates? Why might the statement not make any sense? (Hint: Consider what is exogenous and what is endogenous in macroeconomic models.)

2. Plot the quarterly values of the ratios of net exports and the government deficit to GDP for the period 1981.1 to 1983.4. Do you see a positive or negative relationship between the two? (You may also want to graph one series against the other and calculate the statistics for the same period to help you answer the question). Does your finding suggest that high government deficits cause high trade deficits? Repeat the analysis for the period 1967.1 to 1980.4. Why do your findings change in this period?

3. Select the "ISLM, Closed Econ" model.
   a. Increase government spending by $100 billion. What happens to the interest rate and the government deficit?
   b. Reset the change in government spending to zero. Decrease the money supply by $50 billion. What happens to the interest rate and to the government deficit?
   c. Do your answers to Parts a and b imply that "deficits cause high interest rates"? Explain your answer.

4. Select the "ISLM, Open Econ, Flexible Exchange Rate" model. Tabulate the model and decrease government expenditures by enough to balance the budget.
   a. Retabulate the model and explain why the budget still is not balanced.
   b. Explain how the algebraic model could be used to determine the exact level of government expenditures that would balance the budget.

5. Select the "AD/PA, Closed Econ" model. Increase government expenditure by $100 billion.
   a. Explain why the government deficit increased by less than $100 billion in the second period.
   b. Explain why the government deficit tends toward a $100 billion increase in subsequent periods (becoming exactly $100 billion at the end of the simulation period). How is this consistent with your answer to Part a?
   c. Compute the change in investment and saving to show "how the deficit is financed" in the second and last periods. Explain why the pattern of financing changes between the periods.

6. *Policy Decisions 2001.* The Congressional Budget Office has hired you to help give economic advice to the new Congress. A bill to slash defense spending, which would lower government spending by $100 billion in 2001, is pending. Analyze the macroeconomic impact of the legislation.

# CHAPTER 14

# The Monetary System and the Fed's Policy Rule

A monetary system is an arrangement through which people express economic values and carry out transactions with each other. A well-developed monetary system is essential to a smoothly operating economy. History has shown that poorly developed monetary systems have been responsible for severe recessions and inflations. But even normal, everyday economic life is greatly facilitated by an efficient monetary system.

The monetary system is just one of many social arrangements that exist in any civilization. Language is another. Weights and measures are a third. Some of these arrangements have evolved without formal or conscious social agreements; others have been the result of organized planning and formal agreement. Although monetary systems originally evolved informally in primitive cultures, in modern times most countries have enacted laws and institutions that define their monetary systems. One of the concerns of macroeconomics is whether certain revisions to these laws and institutions might improve macroeconomic performance.

In Chapter 9 we saw how changes in the money supply affect real GDP in the short run and prices in the long run. The central bank carries out monetary policy through actions that change the money supply. A country's monetary institutions—its central bank and the powers of the central bank over the rest of banking—together with its monetary policy make up the country's monetary system.

Because changes in the money supply have such powerful effects on the economy, monetary policy is often in the news. When the chair of the Federal Reserve testifies before a congressional committee, hoards of reporters crowd the room. Each sentence uttered by the Fed chair is dissected for clues about whether the Fed might increase or decrease interest rates. News about changes in the Fed's policies influences financial markets instantaneously around the world. Guessing right about the Fed's next move means big profits for those involved in financial markets.

In this chapter we first look at the microeconomic foundations of money supply and money demand. We then examine how the Fed makes decisions about monetary policy. We go beyond our preliminary policy analysis of Chapter 9 by making the money supply an endogenous variable—determined according to the principles of the **monetary policy rule.**

## 14.1    ELEMENTS OF A MONETARY SYSTEM

A monetary system must specify two things: first, the way that payments are to be made; second, the meaning of the numbers that merchants put on goods and the numbers that appear in contracts. The first is called the **means of payment,** and the second the **unit of account.**

In most monetary systems one item is designated as a universally acceptable means of payment. Traditionally, it was a precious metal, gold or silver. With gold or silver serving as the means of payment, it was natural for merchants to price their goods with numbers that corresponded to units of these precious metals; horse traders would find it natural to charge a certain number of gold pieces for a horse. Hence, designated amounts of precious metals became units of account as well as means of payment. For example, in England at the time of William the Conqueror, silver was the universally accepted means of payment and the pound of silver became the unit of account. Ever since, the English unit of account has been called the pound, though its purchasing power has become much less than the value of a pound of silver.

As financial systems developed, means of payment came into use that were different from the underlying unit of account. For example, in the United States before the Civil War, the unit of account was .04838 of an ounce of gold, but the most common means of payment was paper money issued by private banks. A dollar bill from a bank carried a promise that it could be redeemed for gold at any time.

In the twentieth century, governments became more involved in the monetary system. In the United States, banks are not allowed to issue dollar bills; only the Federal Reserve has that power. Moreover, the unit of account no longer has anything to do with gold. Instead, the unit is the government's dollar bill. Though dollar bills are widely used as means of payment, other means of payment are even more important, such as checks and credit cards.

Although there is no law in the United States that requires prices to be quoted in dollars, nobody would choose to quote prices in another unit, such as French francs. The public is familiar with dollar prices and reluctant to think in any other terms. Even if you are good at doing arithmetic in your head, it is a lot more convenient to do all your financial thinking in one set of units.

Together, the government's paper money and coins are called **currency.** Until the nineteenth century, currency was virtually the only means of payment. As monetary systems evolved during the nineteenth and twentieth centuries, currency began to be replaced by other means of payment in the great majority of transactions. Nevertheless, all transactions continue to be denominated in the units of the government's currency. By law, if you owe somebody a dollar debt, that person can require you to pay in currency. For larger debts, this right is rarely exercised. Instead, the person's right to receive currency sets up a situation where the two of you agree on some alternative, more convenient way to settle the debt. The other person may agree to accept a personal check from you. A check is an instruction to the banking system to make accounting entries to transfer wealth from you to the other person.

A great many customs exist about what means of payment are acceptable besides currency. In prisoner-of-war camps during the Second World War, prisoners used cigarettes as a means of payment. In modern times, credit cards are frequently an acceptable means of payment. Credit cards are another way to issue instructions to the banking system to transfer funds from one person to another. Like accepting checks, the acceptance of a credit card in place of currency is voluntary. When you buy a house, neither a personal check nor a credit card is likely to be accepted. You will be expected to present a bank check, which is a promise by the bank itself to pay from its own funds and a guarantee that the funds actually exist. Customs differ by country as well. In Japan, for example, currency rather than a personal check is a much more common means of payment than it is in the United States.

As discussed in Chapter 5, we use the term *money* to mean currency plus the deposits in checking accounts. Checking accounts are held usually at banks, but sometimes at other financial institutions, such as savings and loan associations. Some checking accounts pay interest, but usually at rates below market interest rates. The Federal Reserve monitors the sum of currency and checking accounts in the United States, which they call $M_1$. In

February 1996, $M_1$ was $1,117 billion, of which $373 billion was currency. Another measure of money is $M_2$. Savings deposits or small time deposits against which checks cannot be directly written are included in $M_2$ ($M_2$ includes everything that is in $M_1$ as well). Money market mutual funds and money market deposit accounts at banks that can be used for checking are also included in $M_2$. In February 1996, $M_2$ was $3,690 billion.

## THE MONETARY SYSTEM

1. A monetary system includes a unit of account and various means of payment. Usually, one of the means of payment (in the United States, the dollar bill) defines the unit of account.
2. Various means of payment make up the money supply. The money supply includes the means that are close substitutes for currency. These are primarily balances in checking accounts.

# HOW THE FED CONTROLS THE MONEY SUPPLY

We now consider how the Fed controls the money supply. The money supply consists of currency (CU) and checking deposits (D) that individuals and firms hold at banks. We will not distinguish at this point between $M_1$ and $M_2$ by distinguishing between different types of deposits. Rather, we let the symbol $D$ represent all deposits at banks (or private financial institutions more generally) and let $M$ be the resulting money supply. The money supply $M$ is thus defined as

$$M = \text{CU} + D. \tag{14.1}$$

Because deposits at banks are part of the money supply, we must consider how the Fed's actions affect these deposits. Table 14.1 shows a set of balance sheets for four sectors of the economy: the private nonfinancial sector (consumers and businesses), the banks, the Federal Reserve, and the government. This balance sheet shows how the sectors are related financially.

**TABLE 14.1**  Financial Relationships (Balance Sheets) between the Banks, the Fed, the Government, and the Private Sector

| Private Nonfinancial | | Banks | | Fed | | Government | |
|---|---|---|---|---|---|---|---|
| **Assets** | **Liabilities** | **Assets** | **Liabilities** | **Assets** | **Liabilities** | **Assets** | **Liabilities** |
| Currency (CU) | | | | | Currency (CU) | | |
| Deposits (D) | | | Deposits (D) | | | | |
| Bonds (B) | | Bonds (B) | | Bonds (B) | | | Bonds (B) |
| | | Reserves (RE) | | | Reserves (RE) | | |
| | Loans | Loans | | | | | |

In the balance sheet assets are shown on the left and liabilities on the right. Assets are the things owned by the individual or organization, and liabilities are the amounts owed to others. For example, loans are assets for banks and liabilities for borrowers. Note that all the things listed in these accounts appear at least twice; once in somebody's assets and again in somebody else's liabilities.

The "Banks" column of the balance sheet includes all depository institutions that accept checking deposits and that hold reserves at the Fed. Thus "banks" include not only commercial banks, but also those savings and loan associations and mutual savings banks that provide checking services to their customers. The "Fed" column of the balance sheet includes the assets and liabilities of all 12 district banks of the Federal Reserve System.[1]

Note where the major assets and liabilities appear on the balance sheets of each sector:

**CURRENCY (CU) AND DEPOSITS (D)**   The private sector holds currency that is issued by the Fed.[2] As we discuss below, it is the Fed's job to supply the currency that the private sector demands. The private sector also holds

---

[1]The 12 District Federal Reserve Banks are in Atlanta, Boston, Chicago, Cleveland, Dallas, Kansas City, Minneapolis, New York, Philadelphia, Richmond, St. Louis, and San Francisco. The San Francisco Fed has the largest amount of reserve assets. Open-market operations take place at the New York Fed.

[2]Part of the reserves held by the banks is in the form of paper money in the vaults of the bank. The term "currency" in the text always means paper money and coin *outside* banks. Vault cash is essentially equivalent to bank reserves held on deposit at the Fed.

deposits at the banks. These are assets of the account holders and liabilities of the banks.

**GOVERNMENT BONDS (B)**   Government bonds are shown as a liability of the government. The private sector, the banks, and the Fed hold bonds as assets.

**RESERVES (RE)**   These are what the banks hold on deposit at the Fed. The Fed acts as a banker's bank by accepting deposits from banks. By law, these reserves must be held at a fixed fraction of the checking deposits that the banks have as liabilities.

**LOANS(L)**   The last line in the balance sheet shows the loans of the banks to the private sector. One of the main reasons that banks are in business is to issue loans to their customers. They take deposits from some individuals and make loans to others. This is the **intermediation role** of the banks. They intermediate between individuals.

The Fed controls the money supply by selling bonds to, or by purchasing bonds from, the banks and the public. These purchases or sales of government bonds by the Fed are called **open-market operations.** To see how these open-market operations affect the money supply, we first define the **monetary base** ($M_B$). The monetary base is defined as currency plus reserves.[3] That is,

$$M_B = CU + RE. \tag{14.2}$$

The Fed does not try to exercise separate control of reserves and currency. Instead, it controls only the total of the two. The Fed lets the banks and the private sector decide how much of the monetary base is currency and how much is reserves. Any bank can withdraw currency from its reserve account whenever it wants, and any bank can put currency into its reserve account and receive credit dollar for dollar.

Using open-market operations, the Fed can add to or subtract from the total amount of bank reserves plus currency whenever it chooses. An open-market operation to expand the monetary base involves a purchase by the Fed of government bonds from the banks. Look again at the balance sheet in Table 14.1. When a bank sells a bond to the Fed, the bank receives a credit in its reserve account that adds to the total amount of reserves. The simple fact that assets must equal liabilities in the Fed's balance sheet indicates that any purchase of bonds must lead to an increase in the sum of currency and reserves, that is, an increase in the monetary base. Whenever a bank transfers funds to another bank, nothing happens to total reserves; one bank's reserves

---

[3]The monetary base is also called *high-powered money.*

| **TABLE 14.2**  Currency, Reserves, and the Monetary Base (billions of dollars) | | | | |
|---|---|---|---|---|
| | | **December** | | |
| | **1974** | **1984** | **1995** | 2000    2005 |
| Currency | 67 | 156 | 373 | 520 |
| Reserves | 18 | 27 | 56 | 110 |
| Monetary base | 88 | 187 | 434 | 630 |

*Source: Economic Report of the President,* 1995, Tables B-66 and B-67.

rise by the exact amount that the other bank's fall. But a purchase of bonds by the Fed must raise the monetary base. Similarly, a sale of bonds by the Fed must reduce the monetary base.

The effects of the Fed's open-market operation on the monetary base over the last 20 years are shown in Table 14.2. Note that the amount of currency is much larger than the amount of reserves. About three-quarters of the monetary base is currency.

There is a direct relationship between the monetary base and the money supply, and this is how the Fed achieves its control of the money supply. The relationship between the monetary base and the money supply is due to two factors.

1. *Reserve requirements.* Banks are required to hold a certain ratio of their checking deposits on reserve at the Fed. This ratio is called the **reserve ratio** ($r$). For example, $r$ might equal .1 (or 10 percent). Reserves (RE) are then given by the formula

$$RE = rD. \tag{14.3}$$

2. *Currency demand.* Most people want to hold some of their money in the form of currency. We will discuss the determinants of currency demand in Section 14.3. For now we can describe this demand in terms of a simple ratio. The **currency deposit ratio** ($c$) measures how much currency people want to hold as a ratio of their deposits. For example, the currency deposit ratio $c$ might equal .2. Currency demand is thus given by

$$CU = cD. \tag{14.4}$$

Now we can derive the relationship between the monetary base and the money supply. From the definition of the money supply,

$$M = CU + D = cD + D = (1 + c)D,$$

$$M_B = CU + RE = cD + rD = (c + r)D.$$

Dividing $M$ by $M_B$, we get

$$M = \frac{1 + c}{r + c} M_B. \qquad (14.5)$$

The coefficient that multiplies $M_B$ is called **money multiplier,** which we will call $m$. If $r = .1$ and $c = .2$, then the money multiplier is 4. Open-market operations that increase the monetary base by \$1 billion would then increase $M$ by \$4 billion. Here the reserve ratio and the currency ratio are assumed to be fixed, so the Fed can control the money supply as accurately as it wants by controlling the monetary base.

## Excess Reserves and Borrowed Reserves

In the United States, the reserve requirement for banks is 10 percent. Since banks are penalized if their reserves fall below their reserve requirements, they always keep some **excess reserves.** The amount of excess reserves is small because banks do not receive any interest on their reserve balances at the Fed. They prefer to keep reserves close to the minimum required amount and invest the rest of their funds in loans or bonds.

Banks can also increase their reserves by borrowing reserves from the Fed. The part of bank reserves that is borrowed from the Fed is called **borrowed reserves.** One of the traditional functions of the Fed has been to provide loans to troubled banks. This tradition developed because of the frequent bank failures and bank panics in the late nineteenth and early twentieth centuries. The Fed was created to serve as "lender of last resort" to the banks.

The Fed usually makes loans to banks at the borrowing "window" of one of the 12 District Federal Reserve Banks. The interest rate on the borrowings is called the **discount rate.** In the past, changes in the discount rate have signaled movements in the Fed's monetary policy. In recent years the discount rate has been adjusted to follow market interest rates, though usually with a time lag. When market interest rates are above the discount rate, the banks prefer to borrow at the discount window and make profits by lending out at a higher rate. Hence borrowings increase with market interest rates. There is a limit on this, however, because the Fed refuses to lend very much to banks without good reason.

What happens to the monetary base when a bank borrows reserves from the Fed? Because bank reserves increase, the monetary base increases, just as with an open-market operation. However, if the Fed wants to insulate the monetary base from changes due to an increase in borrowings, then all it needs to do is make an offsetting open-market sale. Even when banks are borrowing heavily at the discount window, the Fed can set the monetary base at any level it chooses. Hence, the existence of borrowed reserves does not change the basic principle of money-supply analysis that the Fed can control the monetary base.

## Distinguishing between Monetary and Fiscal Policies

Our analysis of the money supply and the monetary base raises some definitional questions about monetary and fiscal policy. The government budget identity implies a relationship between the monetary base, government bonds, and government expenditures that must be kept in mind when distinguishing between monetary and fiscal policies. The monetary base, gov-

## Financing Government through the Printing Press

How much does the United States resort to the printing press to raise revenues to pay for government expenditures? The monetary base gives a good measure of this. Suppose, for example, that Congress passes a bill authorizing highway construction for an amount of $2 billion. But Congress does not raise taxes to pay for the highways. In order to pay for the construction, the government issues bonds. But rather than selling the bonds to the public, it sells the bonds to the Fed in exchange for currency, which it then pays out to the construction workers and firms that build the highways. In effect, the increase in government expenditures was financed by the printing of more currency. Note that the monetary base increased by $2 billion.

Just as in this example, the increase in the monetary base is a measure of the amount of government revenue that is raised each year through the printing press rather than through taxes or borrowing. In 1995 the monetary base in-

creased by $17 billion. Compared with the $1,519 billion of government expenditures during 1995, this is a trivial amount: only about 1 percent of government expenditures were financed by the printing press in 1995. This small percentage is typical in recent U.S. history. Hence, the printing presses are not a very important source of revenue for the United States in modern times. But this was not always true. About 80 percent of American Revolutionary War expenditures were financed by printing paper money called "continentals." So much money was printed that a serious inflation occurred: prices rose by over 300 percent from 1776 to 1778 and by 1,000 percent from 1778 to 1780; hence the phrase "not worth a continental." The printing press set off even worse inflations in Germany and several other European countries in the 1920s and in Argentina, Brazil, and other South American countries in the 1970s and 1980s.

ernment bonds, and the deficit are related to each other by the following government budget identity:

$$G + F + N - T = \Delta M_{\mathrm{B}} + \Delta B, \tag{14.6}$$

where $\Delta M_{\mathrm{B}}$ is the change in the monetary base and $\Delta B$ is the change in government bonds. As defined in Chapter 2, $G$ is government purchases, $F$ is transfers, $N$ is interest payments, and $T$ is taxes. Equation 14.6 says that the government budget deficit is financed by increasing either the monetary base or government bonds. Note that the base as well as government expenditures and taxes appear in this equation, so that there is a link between monetary policy and fiscal policy.

To separate monetary policy changes from fiscal policy changes, we therefore need to specify what is happening to budget financing.

Fiscal policy is defined as bond-financed changes in government expenditures and taxes. That is, the monetary base and the money supply remain unchanged, and bonds are issued if government spending increases or taxes are reduced.

Monetary policy is defined as a change in the monetary base matched by a change in government bonds in the opposite direction. This exchange of money for bonds is an *open-market operation*. Note that open-market operations do not affect government purchases ($G$), transfers ($F$), interest payments ($N$), or taxes ($T$). Thus open-market operations do not affect fiscal policy.

## THE MONETARY SYSTEM AND THE FED

1. The monetary system in the United States is based on the dollar, which is the unit of account. The Fed and other institutions provide means of payment denominated in dollars.
2. The institutions most prominent in providing the means of payment are the Federal Reserve System and banks. The liabilities of the Fed—currency and reserves—make up the monetary base.
3. The money supply consists of currency and deposits at banks and other financial intermediaries. The supply of money is directly related to the monetary base.
4. The Fed controls the monetary base by buying and selling bonds. In doing so it controls the supply of money. The control over the supply of base money is the fundamental source of the Fed's leverage over the economy.

# THE DEMAND FOR MONEY: CURRENCY AND CHECKING DEPOSITS

Having considered the determination of the supply of money, we now explore the demand for money. John Maynard Keynes distinguished three motives in people's demand for money: a **transactions motive,** a **precautionary motive,** and a **speculative motive.** More recent research has refined these categories, and Keynes's classification scheme has been revised somewhat. However, our discussion of money demand will touch on all three of these elements.

## What Are the Opportunity Costs of Holding Funds as Money?

Before discussing the different motives for holding money, we need to consider the costs of holding money. When you put funds in a checking account, you are giving the bank the use of the funds. The bank earns the interest you would have earned if you had invested the funds. In exchange, the bank may pay you some interest, but less than what the bank is earning. In addition, if you have a sufficiently high balance, the bank may excuse you from service charges you would otherwise have to pay. Your opportunity cost per dollar in your checking account is the interest you forgo (the rate you might have received elsewhere less the amount you receive from the bank) less the avoided service charges. As usual in economics, what matters precisely is the *marginal* opportunity cost—the interest forgone on the last amount added to your balance less the reduction in service charges if you took it out. For example, suppose you would earn 7 percent elsewhere and your bank pays 3 percent interest on checking accounts. Suppose that, over the year, it will excuse you from $2 in service charges if you raise your average balance by $100, so you earn 2 percent on the $100. Then your opportunity cost for the $100 of funds placed in your checking account is

$$7\% - 3\% - 2\% = 2\%.$$

We call the opportunity cost of holding money $R_o$, the subscript o standing for "opportunity." When you think about the added convenience of having another $100 in your account on the average over the year, you will keep in mind that you are sacrificing 2 percentage points of annual return on the funds.

Whatever complicated system the bank has for paying you interest on the one hand and charging you for services on the other, you can boil it down to an annual net opportunity cost of the account. This is the price we have in mind for checking deposits as one of the many financial services available to you.

For currency, the computation of the opportunity cost is easy. There are no service changes at all. Currency pays no interest. Therefore, the cost of holding currency is just the forgone interest. If you are contemplating meeting your needs by holding an average amount of currency of $500 and you could earn 7 percent on the funds elsewhere, then the cost is just 7 percent of $500, or $35 per year.

Another hypothetical way of handling your finances might be to avoid money altogether. You could open a special savings account and obtain a credit card. The savings account would allow you to write three checks a month, one of which could pay for your credit card charges. You would pay for everything with the credit card. Suppose the special savings account pays you 6 percent interest (1 percent less than the 7 percent that you could get outside the bank) and the credit card has no finance charges if you pay the bill on time. If you keep an average balance of $2,500 in the account, your only cost would be the opportunity cost of 1 percent of $2,500, or $25 per year.

By now it should be clear that each type of financial service has its own opportunity cost. But consumers do not simply pick the cheapest service on the market. Different services have different characteristics. Choosing among them is like choosing laundry detergent at the grocery store.

## The Transactions Demand for Money: An Inventory Theory

One of the reasons that families and businesses hold currency and keep funds in their checking accounts is the same as the reason stores keep inventories of goods for sale. Because income is received periodically and expenditures occur every day, it is necessary to hold a stock of currency and checking deposits. This inventory theory of the demand for money falls into Keynes's category of **transactions motive.**[4]

We first illustrate the inventory theory of money demand with a simple case. Suppose a family earns an amount $W$ every month. The family consumes $W$ over the month, in equal amounts each day. If the family draws down its money to zero just before being paid, then its money balance starts at $W$ and declines smoothly to zero over the month. Figure 14.1A illustrates how the family's money holdings decline smoothly each day during the

---

[4]The inventory theory of the demand for money was first worked out by William Baumol in "The Transactions Demand for Cash: An Inventory Theoretic Approach," *Quarterly Journal of Economics,* Vol. 56 (November 1952), pp. 545–556; and James Tobin, "The Interest Rate Elasticity of the Transactions Demand for Cash," *Review of Economics and Statistics,* Vol. 38 (September 1956), pp. 241–247.

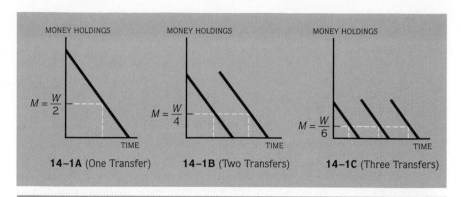

**FIGURE 14.1A, B, and C**   Three Alternative Money Management Strategies

In A, the family puts all its money into its checking account at the start of the month. Average money holdings are large. In B, the family leaves half its income in a savings account at the start of the month and withdraws the rest at the middle of the month. Average money holdings are less than in A. In C, the family makes three withdrawals and money holdings are even lower. Hence, when there are more withdrawals, the family's average money balance is lower.

month. Its average level of money balances $M$ is $W/2$. This family has a demand for money ($W/2$) that is proportional to its income $W$ and does not respond to the prices of financial services. For one reason or another, the family has rejected ways other than money to hold its funds.

Next, take the same family with one additional financial option. It can have its paychecks deposited for free in a savings account. It can transfer any amount of funds to its checking account. The cost of each transfer is $k$. The cost $k$ includes the value of the time of the family members who make the transfer—it might involve a trip to the bank. The checking account has an opportunity cost $R_o$. The family chooses an average balance to hold in its checking account. The higher the average balance, the fewer transfers have to be made from the savings account. But the higher the average balance, the larger is the opportunity cost. The family wants to balance one cost against the other. For example, if the family makes one transfer at the beginning of the month, its money balance is the same as in Figure 14.1A. If the family makes two transfers to checking, one at the start of the month and one halfway through, as in Figure 14.1B, the average money balance is half as much as when it makes one transfer. If three transfers are made, as in Figure 14.1C, the average money holdings are lower still.

In general, the average money balance $M$ is half the amount transferred from savings to checking on each transfer. The total number of transfers is the size of each transfer, 2 times $M$, divided into the total amount of consumption planned over the month, $W$. That is, the family will make $W/2M$

transfers during the month. The total cost of the transfers is $k$ times $W/2M$ (remember that $k$ is the cost of one transfer). The opportunity cost over the month is just $R_o$ times the average balance, that is, $R_oM$. The family wants to choose its average balance to minimize the sum of the two costs. Algebraically it wants to find $M$ to minimize total cost:

$$\frac{kW}{2M} + R_oM. \tag{14.7}$$

A famous theorem from management theory is the **square-root rule** for inventories. The square-root rule says that stores should hold inventories proportional to the square root of sales. The same square-root rule applies to the demand for money. Specifically, the theorem says that the value of the average checking balance $M$ that minimizes total cost is given by[5]

$$M = \sqrt{\frac{kW}{2R_o}}. \tag{14.8}$$

The square-root rule gives the family's transactions demand for cash. Note that the formula would be the same if they chose to keep their transactions balance in the form of currency instead of in a checking account. In that case, because currency earns no interest, the opportunity cost of currency would be the interest rate paid on their savings account.

According to the square-root rule, the family holds less money if the opportunity cost $R_o$ of holding money increases. The services of money are just like anything else the family consumes; they make do with less when the price rises. The square-root rule also says something about the relation

---

[5]Calculus is not necessary to derive the square-root rule. Rather, one can use a "complete the square" approach as follows. The total cost is

$$\begin{aligned} kW/2M + R_oM &= \sqrt{(kW/2M + R_oM)^2} \\ &= \sqrt{(kW/2M)^2 + kWR_o + (R_oM)^2} \\ &= \sqrt{(kW/2M)^2 - kWR_o + (R_oM)^2 + 2kWR_o} \\ &= \sqrt{(kW/2M - R_oM)^2 + 2kWR_o}. \end{aligned}$$

The second term under the last square-root sign does not depend on $M$. Thus costs are minimized when the first term under the square-root sign is at its smallest value, which is zero. This term is equal to zero when

$$M = \sqrt{kW/2R_o},$$

which is the square-root rule. Alternatively, if you have had calculus you can differentiate Equation 14.7 with respect to $M$.

between total spending and income $W$ and the family's demand for money: Demand depends on the square root of total income. In comparing two families, one with double the income of the other, we should find that the second family has a transactions balance only 41 percent higher (the square root of 2 is 1.41).

## The Demand for Money as a Store of Wealth

Some families hold their wealth in the form of money; if they completely distrust all financial institutions, they might accumulate dollar bills under a mattress. Criminal activities generate wealth that is held as currency to avoid detection. People who are not thinking very hard about their affairs sometimes leave large amounts idle in their checking accounts at zero or low interest rates.

Keynes's notions of precautionary and speculative demand for money fit into this store-of-wealth category. Under the precautionary motive individuals save some wealth in the form of money in case of an emergency need for funds. Since currency and checking deposits are the easiest funds to obtain, it might seem natural to hold money in this form. However, in the United States, other interest-bearing assets serve the precautionary demand perfectly well. In politically unstable countries or in countries without a well-developed financial system, this motive for holding money would be more important.

Keynes's speculative motive captures the idea that changes in market interest rates will change the value of bonds. For individuals, bonds paying fixed interest rates are one of the main alternatives to holding the money in financial institutions. But when interest rates rise, the price of these bonds falls.[6] Keynes argued that when interest rates were high, more people would expect them to fall or, equivalently, would expect bond prices to rise and would therefore want to hold bonds and less money. Thus, the demand for money declines as interest rates rise. Changes in bond prices also add risk to holding bonds. People are assumed to be averse to risk; hence, they do not put all their wealth in a risky asset. Some of their wealth will be held as relatively riskless money. Unless they are unwilling to take on any risk, they will balance their wealth between money and bonds. This balancing gives rise to a demand for money as an aversion to risk.

## Recent Trends in Currency and Deposits

Currency holdings have increased slightly relative to GDP in recent years after many previous years of gradual decline. This is shown in Figure 14.2.

---

[6]Interest rates and prices of existing bonds have an inverse relation. When the interest rate falls, the market price of a bond issued earlier rises. The bond continues to pay its interest payments, but new bonds have smaller payments. Hence, the old bond has a higher market price.

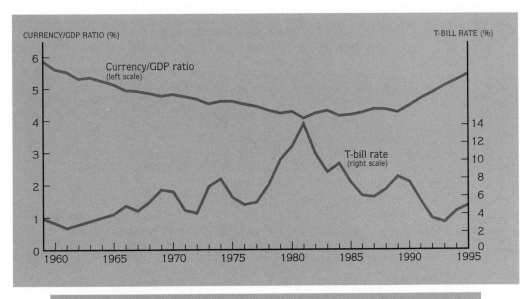

**FIGURE 14.2** Currency Divided by GDP

Holdings of currency have increased slightly in recent years. The upper line is the total amount of currency in circulation, divided by nominal GDP. The interest rate on T-bills is also shown in the diagram. Higher interest rates are associated with less currency as a percentage of GDP.
Source: *Economic Report of the President*, 1996, Tables B-1, B-66, and B-69.

Even though credit cards are much more widely used today and checking accounts have more favorable terms than they used to, the public has increased slightly the amount of currency it holds per dollar of production. The sustained level of demand for currency may be due to an "underground economy"—activities not reported to the Internal Revenue Service and not part of GDP, such as "under-the-table" wages or illicit drug sales. There appear to be substantial holdings of U.S. currency in some foreign countries, as well.

We would expect that periods of low income and high interest rates would be periods of low holdings of currency. Currency holdings do drop a little during recessions, and seem to be inversely related to interest-rate trends. With the extremely high interest rates of the late 1970s and early 1980s, currency fell quite a bit, but it has increased with low interest rates more recently.

The behavior of checking deposits, as shown in Figure 14.3, is similar to the behavior of currency. There was a downward trend in checking deposits until the early 1980s. After interest rates reached a peak around 1980, the decline in demand deposits in relation to GDP ended.

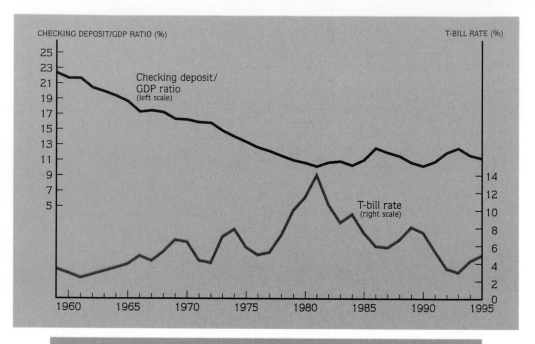

**FIGURE 14.3**   Checking Deposits Divided by GDP

Checking deposits declined steadily in the 1960s and 1970s when divided by nominal GDP, but the decline ended in the early 1980s. The interest rate on T-bills is also shown in the diagram. Higher interest rates are associated with lower checking deposits.
Source: *Economic Report of the President*, 1996, Tables B-1, B-66, and B-69.

## The Demand Function for Money

We can summarize the previous discussion about the demand for currency and checking deposits in two demand functions,

$$CU = CU(R, \, PY) \tag{14.9}$$

$$D = D(R, \, PY), \tag{14.10}$$

where CU is currency and $D$ is checking deposits. The equations show that the demand for currency and the demand for checking deposits are functions of the market interest rate $R$ and nominal income $PY$ (the price level $P$ times real income $Y$). Total **money demand** is the sum of these two demands, that is,

$$\text{Money demand} = CU(R,\ PY) + D(R,\ PY). \qquad (14.11)$$

Our discussion implies the following characteristics for total money demand:

1. Money demand depends negatively on the costs of holding currency and checking balances. These costs depend on the interest rate $R$.
2. Demand is positively related to the price level $P$.
3. Demand is positively related to real income or output $Y$.

Why does the opportunity cost of checking balances depend on the interest rate $R$? Banks pay some interest on checking deposits. When interest rates rise, banks pay somewhat higher interest on checking accounts. However, the account holder does not get the full benefit of an increase in interest rates. For one thing, the bank has to hold 10 percent of the account holder's funds as reserves at the Fed, and these reserves do not pay any interest. The bank therefore cannot be expected to pass along any more than 90 percent of any increase in interest rates. Another reason why the opportunity cost of checking balances rises with interest rates is that the rate banks pay on checking accounts has proven to be quite sticky. The rate may stay at 2 percent per year as the market rate rises from 5 to 7 percent. In that case, the opportunity cost rises by the full 2 percentage points of the increase in the market rate.

Knowing that the opportunity cost of checking balances depends on the market interest rate, we can write the demand function for checking balances using $R$ rather than $R_o$. When the interest rate $R$ rises, it raises the opportunity cost of checking balances and so depresses the demand for checking balances. The strength of this effect is greater if checking-account interest rates are sticky and if account holders conserve aggressively on balances when the opportunity cost rises.

## THE DEMAND FOR MONEY

1. The demand for currency depends negatively on the interest rate and positively on income and the price level.
2. The demand for checking deposits depends negatively on the difference between the interest rate and the rate that banks pay on checking deposits and positively on income and the price level.
3. The demand for money is the sum of the demand for currency and the demand for checking deposits.

# 14.4  THE MONETARY POLICY RULE

We saw in Section 14.2 how the Fed can use open-market operations to change the monetary base and the money supply by any amount that it wants to. And we know from the IS-LM price adjustment analysis of Chapters 8 and 9 that changes in the money supply have effects on real GDP in the short run and on prices in the long run. Thus, by undertaking open-market operations the Fed has great power to affect the economy. The central question for monetary policy is: How should the Fed use this power to achieve its objectives of keeping inflation low and economic fluctuations small?

Decisions about monetary policy in the United States are made by the *Federal Open Market Committee (FOMC)*. The FOMC consists of the seven members of the Board of Governors of the Federal Reserve System plus the presidents of the district Federal Reserve Banks around the country. The FOMC meets about eight times each year in Washington, D.C. At any one meeting there are 12 voting members of the FOMC, including the chair of the Fed, the other 6 members of the Board, and 5 of the 12 presidents of the district banks. The chair of the Fed serves as chair of the FOMC and the president of the New York district Federal Reserve Bank serves as vice-chair. The New York district is particularly important for monetary policy because the open-market operations of the Fed are conducted in Wall Street financial markets by bond traders who work at the New York Fed. The other presidents rotate their voting responsibilities on the FOMC.

## Setting Interest Rates or Money Growth

How does the FOMC make its decisions? What are the issues which the FOMC votes on? FOMC decisions are usually specified in one of the following two alternative ways.

1. *Set the growth rate of the money supply.*

With this approach, the FOMC votes on what the growth rate of the money supply should be. For example, the FOMC might vote to set money supply growth at 5 percent per year for the next year. Milton Friedman and other monetarist economists have long recommended that the FOMC should set the growth rate of the money supply, and the Fed did make use of such a procedure in the late 1970s and early 1980s, though it does not do so now. Under a money-supply procedure, the FOMC communicates its decision to the bond traders at the New York Fed and they make the appropriate open-market purchases or sales to bring about the FOMC's money-supply growth setting. To determine the correct amount of open-market purchases or sales, the bond traders use the equation $M = mM_B$ relating the monetary base ($M_B$) to the money supply ($M$) through the money multiplier ($m$); see Equation 14.5. For example, if the money multiplier $m$ is 4 and the FOMC instructions call for an increase in the money supply $M$ by \$8 billion, then the traders make open-market purchases to increase the monetary base $M_B$ by \$2 billion. Then the money supply increases by $2 \times 4 = 8$ billion dollars as instructed by the FOMC.

### 2. *Set the short-term interest rate.*

With this alternative approach, the FOMC decides at its meetings whether to raise or lower the short-term interest rate. The short-term interest rate the FOMC looks at is the federal funds rate, which is the one-day interest rate on loans between banks. For example, the members of the FOMC might vote to lower the federal funds rate from 5½ percent to 5¼ percent as they did at their January 31, 1996, meeting. The FOMC has been using this approach to monetary policy since the mid-1980s and now explicitly announces its decision about interest rates after each FOMC meeting. Once a decision is made, the FOMC instructs the bond traders at the New York Fed to make open-market purchases or sales to bring about the desired change in the interest rate. If the FOMC calls for a reduction in the interest rate, then bond traders buy bonds, which increases the money supply and reduces interest rates. If the FOMC calls for an increase in the interest rate, then the bond traders sell bonds, which decreases the money supply and raises the interest rate. The bond traders then keep the interest rate at the new level until they are given a new set of instructions from the FOMC to change the interest rate. For example, suppose the instruction from the FOMC is to set the interest rate at 5 percent. Then, if the interest rate starts to rise above 5 percent, the bond traders buy bonds; if the interest rate starts to fall below 5 percent, the bond traders sell bonds.

Which of these two approaches—setting the money supply or setting the interest rate—is better? In either case the Fed must decide what levels to set and what factors to consider when setting them. For example, if the FOMC is setting interest rates, it might decide to raise the short-term interest rate if inflation or GDP starts to rise. Alternatively if the FOMC is setting money growth, it may decide to lower money growth if inflation or GDP starts to rise.

The choice between interest-rate setting and money-supply setting usually boils down to practical questions about which variable is easier to measure and interpret. As discussed earlier in this chapter, the money supply is difficult to measure—for example, should it be $M_1$ or $M_2$?—and there appeared to be changes in the behavior of $M_1$ in the early 1980s. If we do not know how to measure money, then the money-demand function and the LM curve, which are the bases for our assessment of the effects of money on the economy, are not reliable. A situation where money demand is difficult to

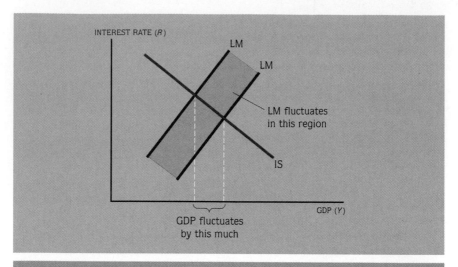

INTEREST RATE (*R*)

LM

LM

LM fluctuates
in this region

IS

GDP (*Y*)

GDP fluctuates
by this much

**FIGURE 14.4**   Shifts in the LM Curve

If there are large shifts in the LM curve, it is better for the Fed to set interest rates. Then GDP
would not fluctuate as much.

measure or interpret is illustrated in Figure 14.4; the location of the LM curve
is shown to be uncertain and shifting around in Figure 14.4 because of uncertainty about how to measure money. For example, if the Fed's demand
for money function shifts down because the Fed is mismeasuring the money
supply, then the LM curve will shift to the right (recall from Chapter 9 that a
downward shift in money demand has the same effects as an increase in the
money supply). Or if the demand for money increases, the LM curve will
shift to the left. As shown in Figure 14.4, such shifts in the LM curve will
cause interest rates to fluctuate and cause undesirable fluctuations in real
GDP; the fluctuations in real GDP will also cause fluctuations in inflation and
are therefore doubly harmful to the economy. With such uncertainty about
money and the LM curve, interest-rate setting is a more appropriate policy
for the Fed because it reduces these fluctuations. The difficulty with measuring money is the main reason why the FOMC is now concentrating on
interest-rate setting rather than money-supply setting.

However, interest rates have their own measurement problems. Recall
that it is the *real* interest rate that affects spending in the economy. Measuring
the real interest rate requires a good measure of the expected rate of inflation
(recall that the real interest rate is the nominal interest rate, which the Fed
sets, minus the expected rate of inflation). It is especially difficult to measure

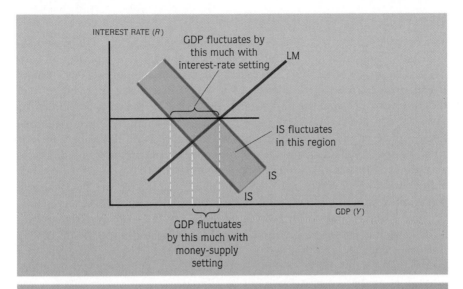

INTEREST RATE ($R$)

GDP fluctuates by this much with interest-rate setting

LM

IS fluctuates in this region

IS

IS

GDP ($Y$)

GDP fluctuates by this much with money-supply setting

**FIGURE 14.5** Shifts in the IS Curve

The band around the IS curve illustrates the shifts perhaps due to unobserved changes in the real interest rate. If such shifts are large, money-supply setting results in smaller GDP fluctuations than interest-rate setting.

people's expectation of inflation during periods when inflation is very high and fluctuating. Unobserved fluctuations in the real interest rate affect investment spending and thereby cause the IS curve to fluctuate as shown in Figure 14.5. To emphasize a situation where the Fed sets the nominal interest rate, the vertical axis in Figure 14.5 is the nominal interest rate. If the real interest rate shifts in such a situation, the IS curve in Figure 14.5 will shift; thus uncertainty about the real interest rate will cause real GDP (and thus inflation) to be volatile. More generally, if the IS curve is fluctuating as in Figure 14.5, then interest-rate setting is a poor policy. With such uncertainty about the IS curve, money-supply setting is a more appropriate policy for the Fed.[7] This explains why in the late 1970s, when the inflation rate was high and the real interest rate was uncertain, the FOMC shifted away from interest-rate setting toward money-supply setting in its policy deliberations. By 1982, when inflation declined and the real interest-rate fluctuations apparently became less uncertain, the FOMC moved back to the interest rate.

[7]See William Poole, "The Optimal Choice of Monetary Policy in a Simple Stochastic Macro Model," *Quarterly Journal of Economics,* Vol. 84, pp. 197–216.

## Reacting to Events in the Economy

Whether setting the money supply or the interest rate, the FOMC's ultimate goal is to keep inflation low and stable and the fluctuations of real GDP small. Like many other central bankers, the FOMC members have a **target inflation rate,** a level of inflation they would like to see on average over the long term. Let $\pi$ be the inflation rate and let $\pi^*$ be the target rate inflation rate. Then, if the central bank is successful in its inflation goals, the actual inflation rate $\pi$ will fluctuate around the target $\pi^*$, with the fluctuations as small as possible. The idea of an inflation target is becoming more and more accepted among central bankers. Some central banks have been very explicit about their target inflation rate. The German central bank, the Bundesbank, sets money growth with a 2 percent target inflation rate. The Reserve Bank of New Zealand seeks a range of 0 to 2 percent inflation, with an implicit target inflation rate of 1 percent. The Bank of England also has an explicit inflation target. The Fed is less explicit about its target inflation rate, but statements of many FOMC members indicate that they have a low inflation-rate target, perhaps about 2 percent on average.

Central banks are also concerned with the fluctuations of real GDP and unemployment. Most central bankers recognize that monetary policy has no impact on the level of real GDP or unemployment in the long run; in other words, they recognize that potential GDP ($Y^*$) or the natural unemployment rate ($u^*$) do not depend on monetary policy. But they know that monetary policy affects real GDP and unemployment in the short run. Thus, central banks try to keep business cycle fluctuations small; in other words, they endeavor to keep the gap between real GDP and potential GDP as small as possible. To derive the implications of these endeavors for monetary policy, let $\hat{Y} = 100$ times $(Y - Y^*)/Y^*$, or simply the percentage deviation of real GDP from potential GDP. Then central bankers try to keep $\hat{Y}$ as close to zero as possible; alternatively stated, they try to keep the fluctuations in $\hat{Y}$ small.

How do the Fed and other central banks set the money supply or the interest rate to achieve their long-run inflation and output-stability goals? A convenient way to describe the actions of a central bank is through a **monetary policy rule,** or reaction function. As described briefly in Chapter 9, a policy rule is simply a function which describes how the Fed, or any other central bank, sets the money supply or the interest rate in response to variables in the economy. Just as a consumption function describes how aggregate consumption reacts to economic variables such as income or wealth, a policy rule describes how the money supply, or the interest rate, reacts to economic variables, such as real GDP or inflation. The consumption function describes the behavior of consumers, while the monetary policy rule describes the behavior of Fed policymakers. The idea of describing the behavior of central bank policymakers through a policy rule is increasingly common among macroeconomists.

A monetary policy rule which describes interest-rate settings for the Fed is given by the equation

$$R = \pi + \beta\hat{Y} + \delta(\pi - \pi^*) + R^f \qquad (14.12)$$

where $R$ is the short-term interest rate set by the Fed (the federal funds rate). The coefficients $\beta$ and $\delta$ are both greater than zero and indicate how much the Fed changes its setting for the interest rate $R$ when real GDP or inflation change. The variables $\hat{Y}$ and $\pi$ have been previously defined as the percentage deviation of real GDP from potential GDP and the rate of inflation, respectively. Finally, $R^f$ is a coefficient.

**EXAMPLE.** Suppose that $\beta = .5$, $\delta = .5$, $\pi^* = .02$, and $R^f = .02$. Then the policy rule in Equation 14.12 becomes

$$R = \pi + .5\hat{Y} + .5(\pi - \pi^*) + .02.$$

Thus, if real GDP rises above potential GDP by 1 percentage point, the policy rule says the Fed will raise the short-term interest rate by .5 percent. On the other hand, if real GDP falls below potential GDP, as it would in a recession, the Fed will cut the interest rate according to the example policy rule. Changes in inflation also cause the Fed to change interest rates. If the inflation rate rises by 1 percentage point, then the Fed raises the interest rate by 1.5 percentage points. The reason why the Fed raises the interest rate by more than the inflation rate in the example is that the Fed tries to raise the real interest rate when inflation rises in order to slow down the economy and reduce inflationary pressures. When real GDP equals potential GDP ($\hat{Y} = 0$) and inflation equals its target ($\pi = .02$), the interest rate $R$ equals 4 percent, which implies that the real interest rate ($R - \pi$) equals 2 percent.

How accurate a description of the Fed policy is the policy rule in Equation 14.12? Figure 14.6 compares the actual value of the short-term interest rate with that predicted from the example policy rule. While the policy rule is not a perfect predictor, it gives a very accurate description, as accurate as other macroeconomic relationships, such as the consumption function (the errors in the consumption function are shown in Figure 10.5).

While the example policy rule explains Fed behavior in recent years, it does not explain the behavior during the 1970s, when the inflation rate was very high. It is implausible that the Fed had a target inflation rate as low as 2 percent during that period, when inflation rose above 10 percent. It appears that since the 1970s the Fed policy rule has shifted to one with a lower target rate of inflation; that is, the term $\pi^*$ in the policy rule Equation 14.12 changed. In the next section we consider a shift in the policy rule due to a change in another coefficient in Equation 14.12, namely $R^f$.

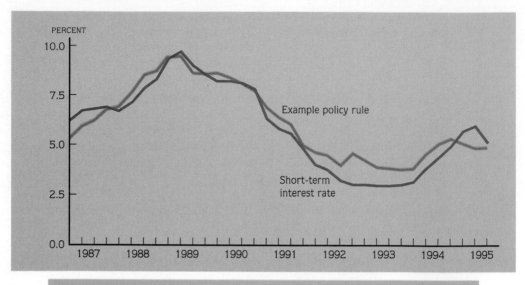

**FIGURE 14.6**   The Monetary Policy Rule

The example in the text describes the setting of the short-term interest rate by the Fed. Although there are differences between the two, the rule is as accurate as many other macroeconomic relationships.

# 14.5   INTERACTION BETWEEN MONETARY AND FISCAL POLICY

As we have already discussed, one of the difficulties with interest-rate setting is that the real interest rate can change. If the Fed does not adjust its interest-rate setting to correspond to this change, there could be adverse effects on inflation and real GDP. One important reason why the real interest rate might change is because of a change in fiscal policy. As we saw in Chapter 4, a reduction in the government budget deficit, perhaps due to a reduction in government purchases as a share of GDP, would reduce the real interest rate. If there is such a reduction in the real interest rate, then the Fed—using an interest-rate-setting procedure—should change its policy. If the central bank does not change its policy rule, then it will set an interest rate which is too high; this will have the effect of lowering the inflation rate below the target inflation rate.

The relationship between the interest rate and the inflation rate is illustrated in Figure 14.7. The nominal interest rate is on the vertical axis

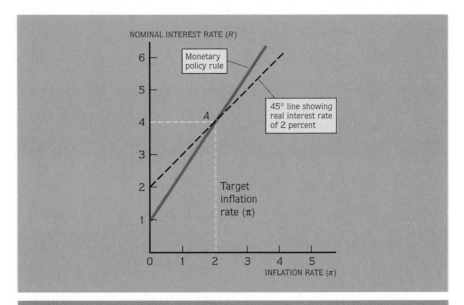

**FIGURE 14.7**  Graph of Monetary Policy Rule

The policy rule of Equation 14.12 shown for the situation where GDP equals potential GDP ($\hat{Y} = 0$). Higher inflation causes the Fed to raise interest rates by more than the increase in inflation, because the slope of the policy rule is greater than 45°.

and the inflation rate is on the horizontal axis. The relatively steep up-ward-sloping lines show the monetary policy rule: when inflation rises above the target inflation rate the Fed takes action to increase the interest rate. The flatter dashed line shows the relationship between the *nominal* interest rate and the inflation rate corresponding to a given *real* interest rate. The real interest rate is assumed to be 2 percent for the dashed line.

An equilibrium occurs where the dashed and solid lines in Figure 14.7 intersect. At the intersection point *A* the real interest rate is equal to its long-run equilibrium value of 2 percent and the central bank is following its monetary policy rule. The inflation rate is also on target at 2 percent.

Now suppose that the equilibrium real interest rate falls by 1 percentage point because of a change in fiscal policy. This is represented as a downward shift in the dashed line from 2 percent to 1 percent, as shown in Figure 14.8 (the decline in the real interest rate is 1 percent, so we shift the line down by 1 percent). If the monetary policy rule does not change, then a downward shift in the real interest rate will bring about a decline in the inflation rate to point *B* in Figure 14.8. Observe that the decline in the inflation rate is larger than the decline in the real interest rate. This multiplier effect occurs because

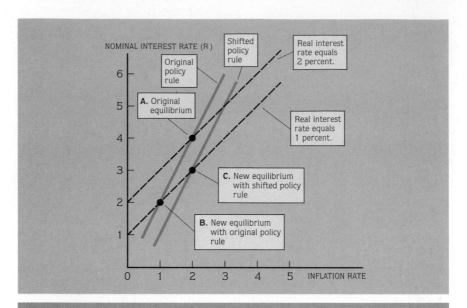

**FIGURE 14.8**   Effect of Fiscal Policy Change on Inflation

The fiscal policy change is assumed to reduce the real interest rate by 1 percentage point. If the monetary policy rule does not shift, the inflation rate falls to 1 percent, below the assumed target, at point *B*. If the monetary policy rule shifts down, the inflation rate remains unchanged at 2 percent (point *C*).

of the responsiveness of the interest rate to the inflation rate—as seen by the upward, but not vertical, slope of the monetary policy rule.

Figure 14.8 also shows how a change in the monetary-policy rule can prevent a change in the inflation rate: if the policy rule is shifted down by 1 percentage point, then the inflation rate does not change despite the decline in the real interest rate. In this case the equilibrium would be at point *C* and the inflation rate would be 2 percent. Hence, even if the central bank is concerned only with inflation, it should reduce the interest rate by the amount that the long-run real interest rate declines.

This example illustrates one important way in which monetary policy influences the impact of fiscal policy on the economy. As we saw in Chapters 7, 8, and 9, the interaction between fiscal policy and monetary policy needs to be considered in many other situations. For example, in Chapter 7 we showed that a reduction in the budget deficit has short-run effects on real GDP; if the Fed lowers the interest rate it can mitigate these effects.

# LAGS IN THE EFFECT
# OF MONETARY POLICY

**14.6**

Monetary policy affects real GDP and prices with a lag. In Chapter 11, we stressed the lags in the investment process. Businesses take months to get almost any investment plan into effect; those involving the construction of new plants or the ordering of special equipment can take years. Housing investment takes six months or a year to respond strongly to a change in the interest rate.

Less is known about the lags in the response of net exports to dollar depreciation. Exchange rates respond immediately to changes in the interest rate. But buyers in the United States and overseas do not switch their purchases immediately when U.S. goods become cheaper. Americans who have learned that Japanese cars offer good value do not immediately reconsider U.S.–produced alternatives when the value of the dollar declines and causes the dollar price of Japanese cars to rise. It takes time for foreigners to discover the advantage of American products as well.

Although there are many uncertainties about the lag in the effect of monetary policy, the peak effect on GDP probably occurs between one and two years after the expansion. The effect on prices takes much longer. At first, a monetary expansion drives down the interest rate without much effect on GDP. After a year or so, the response of spending to the interest rate is stronger and GDP expands.

The lag in the economy's response to monetary expansion greatly complicates the conduct of monetary policy. The Fed can step on the gas to try to head off a recession, but the peak effect of the stimulus will occur well after the worst part of the recession is over. In fact, if the recession is brief and is followed by a brisk recovery, the monetary stimulus may hit hardest when it is least needed; in the worst case, it can worsen the boom that follows the recession and cause inflation to rise.

Because the main effect of monetary expansion occurs in the year after the expansion is launched, when formulating monetary policy the Fed must always think about the likely conditions in the economy a year in the future. Even if the economy is in bad shape this year, the Fed will not expand if it anticipates that the economy will recover on its own by next year. There is little the Fed can do to help the economy this year; any stimulus it adds now will only create problems next year, if a recovery is impending.

The Fed never knows with any confidence what will happen in the future. As a general matter, the more uncertain the Fed is about conditions next year, the more cautious it will be about policy actions this year. The response of the Fed to developments in the economy as described by the

## NEW RESEARCH IN PRACTICE
## The Depression of the 1990s in Japan

For most of the 1970s and 1980s, real economic growth in Japan was stronger and steadier than in the United States and most European countries. This amazing strength of the Japanese economy led to fears that the Japanese would "win the economic war" with the United States; calls for the United States to adopt policies like those used in Japan were common.

Then suddenly, at the start of 1990s, the Japanese economy began to deteriorate. Real economic growth fell sharply; there was virtually no economic growth for the first half of the decade with an upturn only becoming visible in 1996. Assuming that potential GDP growth remained at 4 percent per year, real GDP was 20 percent below potential GDP by 1995, a shortfall nearly as large as the Great Depression of the 1930s in the United States!

What caused this prolonged downturn? One explanation is monetary policy. The growth rate of the money supply in Japan declined sharply in 1990 about the same time that real GDP growth declined sharply (see chart). The theory of economic fluctuations would imply that such a large decline in money growth would bring about a decline in real GDP: the LM curve would shift to the left, causing real GDP to decline. This explanation is reminiscent of the explanation now favored by many economists for the prolonged depression of the 1930s in the United States. But why did the central bank of Japan—the Bank of Japan—permit such a large and persistent decline in money growth? There are several possible reasons.

First, in the late 1980s the Japanese economy was overheating in what was referred to as "the bubble." Inflation was picking up and asset prices were rising rapidly. To counteract this bubble the Bank of Japan reduced money growth and was unwilling to let it rise again for several years for fear of causing another bubble.

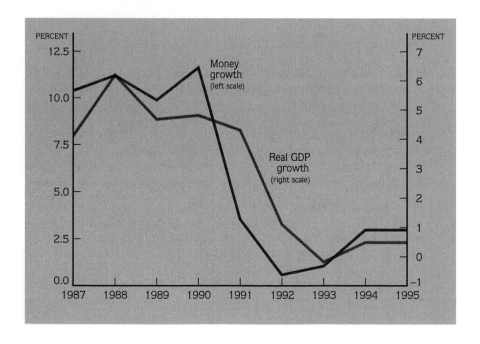

Second, during the period of the Japanese depression interest rates were very low and some monetary policy officials felt that lowering them further would not do any good. But in fact, interest rates were not so low in real terms, because there was a deflation: the real interest rate—the market interest rate minus the inflation rate—was greater than the market interest rate.

Third, some argued that the money growth slowdown was not the cause of the depression; they argued that nonmonetary factors—such as a need to restructure businesses—caused real GDP to decline, and that money growth slowed because real GDP declined. Hence, according to this view, increasing money growth would not increase real economic growth.

It is useful to note that all three of these reasons were given by monetary policy officials in the United States in the 1930s as a rationale for not worrying about the decline in money growth at that time.

---

policy rule must take account of the lags and uncertainty. After examining the effects of monetary policy on prices more closely in the next chapter, we will consider how different monetary policies deal with the lags and uncertainties.

## LAGS IN MONETARY POLICY

1. Monetary policy operates through interest rates. Consequently, there is a lag before the policy influences GDP.
2. The evidence suggests that the peak effect of monetary policy on GDP occurs after a lag of between one and two years.
3. Today's monetary policy has to be formulated with the state of the economy a year from now in mind. Even if GDP is well below potential, it may not be desirable to launch a monetary expansion.
4. Uncertainty about the future state of the economy adds to the caution of monetary policymakers.

## REVIEW AND PRACTICE

### Major Points

1. A monetary system is an agreement on the way to quote prices and convey purchasing power.
2. In the United States, the Fed issues currency and also reserves. Reserves are accounts at the Fed equivalent to currency. The sum of currency and reserves is the monetary base.

3. The Fed's policy rule determines the LM curve. A policy of targeting $M_1$ gives a steep but not vertical LM curve. A policy of targeting the interest rate gives a horizontal LM curve. A policy of targeting GDP gives a vertical LM curve.

4. The effects of a fiscal stimulus depend on the Fed's policy rule. If the Fed chooses a horizontal LM curve by targeting the interest rate, fiscal stimulus raises GDP strongly. If the Fed chooses a vertical or near-vertical LM curve by targeting GDP, then fiscal stimulus raises interest rates but has little or no effect on GDP.

5. An interest-rate target for monetary policy cushions the economy against the effects of shifts in money demand, while a money-supply target provides greater stability against shifts in spending.

6. Monetary policy influences GDP with a lag. The immediate effect of monetary stimulus is to lower interest rates. After the lags in investment and foreign trade work themselves out, the stimulus raises GDP. Because of the lag and because of the Fed's uncertainty about the future, monetary policy needs to be used with caution.

7. Fiscal and monetary policy can be used in tandem to achieve any desired combination of GDP and the interest rate. Fiscal and monetary expansion together can raise GDP without changing the interest rate. Fiscal expansion and monetary contraction can raise the interest rate without chainging GDP. Monetary expansion and fiscal contraction can lower the interest rate without changing GDP.

8. Monetary policy influences the exchange rate and net exports. Monetary expansion makes the dollar depreciate but has an ambiguous effect on the trade deficit.

## Key Terms and Concepts

| | | |
|---|---|---|
| means of payment | financial intermediaries | store of wealth |
| unit of account | monetary base | open-market operation |
| currency | reserve requirements | discount rate |
| reserves | transactions motive | money multiplier |
| checking deposits | precautionary motive | monetary policy rule |
| money supply | speculative motive | |

## Questions for Discussion and Review

1. Why is the dollar the unit of account and the medium of exchange in the United States?

2. In what sense do commercial banks play a role as financial intermediaries? What other role do they play in determining the nation's money supply?

3. Why doesn't the Fed have separate control over the quantities of both reserves and currency?

4. Why do some banks borrow reserves from the Fed? How does the Fed decide on the discount rate on these borrowings?

5. How does the Fed control the monetary base? What types of open-market operations increase the monetary base?

6. Does the demand for currency depend on the real rate of interest or on the nominal rate of interest?

7. How does the Fed set interest rates?

8. Why might the Fed want to set interest rates?

9. What happens to short-term interest rates if the Fed's actions are described by a policy rule and real GDP falls? What if inflation falls?

## Problems

### NUMERICAL

1. Suppose that money demand is given by an expression similar to Equation 14.8,

$$M = \sqrt{\frac{kY}{2R_o}}$$

where $Y$ is income, the opportunity cost of holding money is given by

$$R_o = q_1 R - q_o,$$

and the transaction cost $k$ is equal to 2.

a. Assuming $q_1 = 1$ and $q_o = .06$, what is the level of money demand at $Y = 2,500$ and $R = .08$? Suppose the money supply is set equal to this value. Find the interest rate at which money supply equals money demand for $Y = 1,000$ and for $Y = 4,000$. Plot the points to scale on a graph.

b. Now let $q_1 = .25$ and $q_o = 0$. Find the level of money demand at $Y = 2,500$ and $R = .08$. Again, supposing that the money supply is set equal to this value, find the interest rate at which money supply equals money demand for the values of $Y$ given in Part a. Plot these points on the same graph.

c. Suppose the Fed's policy rule is to target $M$. For which values of $q_o$ and $q_1$ given above will the LM curve be steeper? Give a brief economic interpretation of your result.

2. In this problem we consider the relationship between monetary policy and the financing of the deficit.

a. Suppose that the reserve ratio $r$ is equal to .1, and the currency ratio $c$ is equal to .2. Assume that $G - T + F = \$200$ billion. By how much would the money supply, the monetary base, currency, and bank reserves have to change if the Fed were to finance the entire budget deficit?

b. Suppose now that the money supply is initially equal to $600 billion, with output equal to potential. Suppose further that potential output is increasing by 2 percent per year, prices are expected to grow by 3 percent, and monetary velocity ($V = PY/M$) is expected to remain constant. If the Fed wishes to keep output at potential, what percentage of the deficit will it have to finance?

3. Suppose that the required reserve ratio is .12 for deposits and that there are no excess reserves. Suppose also that the total demand for currency is equal to .3 times deposits.

a. If total reserves are $40 billion, what is the level of the money supply?

b. By how much does the money supply change if the Fed increases the required reserve ratio to .20? Assume that total reserves are unchanged at $40 billion.

   c. By how much does the money supply change if the Fed buys $1 billion of government bonds in the open market? (Keep the required reserve ratio at .12.)

## ANALYTICAL

1. Suppose that as a result of recent tax cuts, the amount of activity in the underground economy is significantly reduced.
   a. What effect would this have on the demand for currency?
   b. Explain why such a change would have an expansionary effect on the economy (holding the Fed's open-market operations fixed).
   c. Describe the Fed's response to such a change under each of the three policy rules discussed in Section 14.4.

2. Use Equation 14.8 to write an expression for real money demand as a function of real income and real transactions costs. Assuming that nominal income and nominal transactions costs increase proportionately with changes in the price level, describe how real money demand is affected by a change in prices. How is the nominal demand for money affected?

3. Consider the following cash management problem. A college student earns $400 a month which she uses to meet personal expenses. All expenses are paid for in cash. She maintains a savings account at a local bank which pays 1 percent per month (12 percent annually) in interest. At the beginning of each month she deposits her $400 paycheck in her savings account and makes periodic cash withdrawals throughout the month. Cash withdrawals are made through an automatic teller at a service charge of 25 cents each.
   a. Calculate the student's average currency holdings and the number of withdrawals made each month.
   b. Suppose it's observed that the student always withdraws $40. There are several possible explanations. Perhaps she doesn't wish to risk losing larger amounts of cash. Protection against such loss is one of the benefits of a savings account. In addition, she may wish to avoid the temptation of spending more money than she can really afford. Call this the "piggy bank" value of savings accounts. What must the value of such benefits be, expressed as a rate of return, in order for her withdrawals of $40 to be optimal?

4. Suppose that competition in the credit card industry drives down the cost of using credit cards.
   a. How is that likely to affect money demand? Illustrate the macroeconomic impact using an IS-LM diagram.
   b. If the Fed is aware of such a trend, but cannot be certain of its timing, what kind of policy rule should it use?

5. Explain the effect that a lowering of the discount rate has on the money supply. In particular, consider the effect of such a change on the money multiplier and the monetary base.

6. Suppose that banks began both to pay market rates of interest on all checking accounts and to charge the full costs of providing such accounts. These costs would not be waived, regardless of one's average balance. Describe the possible effects of such a change on money demand.

7. The velocity of money $V$ is defined by the expression

$$V = PY/M.$$

One way the Fed can set the money supply is described as follows. First, it is assumed that the velocity of money remains roughly constant from year to year. Next, the Fed forecasts this year's rate of inflation (which is viewed as being predetermined and thus beyond its control). Finally, the Fed chooses its target rate of growth for real output. This results in a target rate of growth for the money stock.

a. Suppose that inflation for the current year is forecasted to be 5 percent and that the Fed's target rate of growth for output is 2 percent. By how much should it increase the money stock this year?

b. Suppose now that money demand is given by the expression

$$M/P = kY - hR.$$

Derive an expression for the velocity of money $V$. On what does $V$ depend?

c. What kinds of changes in the economy could affect $V$? Consider both the cases where $h > 0$ and $h = 0$.

8. Suppose the U.S. government budget deficit is reduced through a cut in government purchases. Assume that the Fed sets the *interest rate* according to the policy rule in Equation 14.12. What happens to the inflation rate in the long run?

9. Monetary policy is one of the most hotly debated issues in macroeconomics. Yet the policy implications of the IS-LM model would seem to be rather clear: Assuming that the Fed wishes to maintain output at potential, simply set the LM curve to intersect the IS curve at $Y^*$. Provide a brief explanation of why monetary policy isn't so simple a matter.

10. There is reason to believe that money demand may be more closely related to consumption than to total output. Suppose this is indeed the case. The money-demand function takes the form

$$M = (sC - hR)P \quad s > 0$$

where the rest of the economy is described by the usual spending equations:

$$C = a + b(Y - T)$$
$$I = e - dR$$
$$X = g - mY - nR.$$

a. What is the slope of the LM curve for this model?

b. Suppose taxes $T$ are lump-sum rather than proportional to income. Show the short-run effect of a tax cut in this modified model using an IS-LM diagram. Comment on the qualitative effect on interest rates and income in relation to the model in which money demand depends on income rather than on consumption.

11. A 1995 proposal by Senator Connie Mack called for a zero-inflation goal for the Fed as being favorable for long-run economic growth. Describe how zero inflation might promote growth in potential GDP relative to a policy regime in which there is no commitment to any particular inflation rate. Could a policy that commits to 4 percent inflation accomplish the same thing as one that commits to 0 percent inflation?

## MacroSolve Exercises

1. Velocity is the ratio of nominal GDP to the money supply. Plot the behavior of the velocity of $M_1$ using quarterly data. Is velocity procyclical or countercyclical? Why do you think this is? Do you find the same result using annual data?

2. Velocity used to be thought of as a constant. If nominal GDP increases, the money supply would increase, keeping velocity relatively stable. Plot velocity, nominal growth in GDP, and the money growth rate against time using annual data from 1930 to 1995 to confirm this theory. Now plot the same variable using quarterly data from 1979.1 to 1987.4. What happened to the relationship? What other variable might be affecting velocity? (Hint: Graph velocity against the short-term interest rate.)

3. Graph velocity against the short-term interest rate using quarterly data. What relation do you see between them?
   a. Is this relationship consistent with the money demand theory that you have learned?
   b. Do you see the same relationship in the annual data?
   c. Will this type of velocity movement make the effects of monetary policy on GDP greater or smaller than they would be if velocity were constant? Explain why.
   d. Will this type of velocity movement make the effects of fiscal policy on GDP greater or smaller than if velocity were constant? Explain why.

4. *Policy Decisions 2001.* Suppose you have just been appointed as one of the seven members of the Federal Reserve Board of Governors. Based on your own research prior to joining the Fed, you discover that in determining the next open-market trade of U.S. Treasury bonds the Fed has underestimated the sensitivity of investment expenditures to changes in the interest rate. Assuming you are correct, use the "ISLM, Open Econ" model to show whether the Fed will have to increase or decrease the money supply, and by how much more or less than first anticipated in order to eliminate a negative GDP gap of $200 billion.

5. *Policy Decisions 2001.* Suppose you have been hired to be an economic analyst for the new treasury secretary. After the first meeting with finance ministers from several other large countries, the treasury secretary wonders whether pegging the exchange rate to that in the other countries by targeting U.S. interest rates would work. In particular, you are asked about the effects of such a policy of maintaining a constant real interest rate of 5 percent. Using the "ISLM, Open Econ" model, show how this policy affects the potency of fiscal policy, compared with a policy of fixing the money supply.

# The Microeconomic Foundations of Price Rigidity

Why does an increase in the money supply have a positive effect on real GDP in the short run? The most common reason given by economists—from the first monetary economist, David Hume, in the 18th century, to John Maynard Keynes, Milton Friedman, and Robert Lucas in the 20th—is that, in the short run, the price level does not increase as much as the money supply. Thus, real money—the money supply divided by the price level—increases, causing the interest rate to decline and directly stimulating spending and production. The short run is different from the long run: in the long run the price level does fully increase by the same percentage as the money supply, real money does not change, and real GDP is therefore unaffected.

This chapter delves into the reasons why the price level does not increase by as much as the money supply—a phenomenon we refer to as **price rigidity.** We will review several different microeconomic explanations for price rigidity. The explanations can be classified into two broad groups—those based on *imperfect information* and those based on *sticky prices* or *nominal wage contracts*. Both kinds of explanation are necessary for a complete understanding of price rigidity in the real world, as the 1995 Nobel price winner Robert Lucas emphasized in his Nobel address ("The Neutrality of Money"). Moreover, understanding the microeconomic foundations of price rigidity clarifies how macroeconomists view the effects of monetary policy. While macroeconomists disagree about the size and timing of the effects, they agree that the efficacy of monetary policy depends on price rigidity.

# 15.1 THE IMPERFECT INFORMATION THEORY

We first consider explanations of price rigidity that are based on imperfect information. Explanations based on imperfect information start from the premise that prices at individual firms are perfectly flexible, just as in the long-run neoclassical growth model. But because of imperfect information about whether a change in the money supply or some other factor is the source of the shift to a firm's demand curve, prices change by less than they would if the firms were fully informed. Robert Lucas did the original research on this imperfect information theory.[1]

The role of information is very important in Lucas's theory. According to basic microeconomics, a firm produces up to the point where its *price equals marginal cost.* Marginal cost depends on the price of the firm's inputs to production. If the price of the firm's output rises *relative* to the price of other goods in the economy, including its inputs, then the firm will produce more. However, if all other prices rise by the same amount that the firm's output price rises, there will be no incentive for the firm to produce more. In other words, the firm will produce more only if the price of its output rises relative to some other prices in the economy—in particular, its input prices.

Firms are assumed to have difficulty getting information about prices in the economy other than their own output price. There are temporary information barriers through which firms cannot see what is going on in other markets. Put another way, firms specialize in monitoring conditions in their own market. They know very quickly when demand drops off and prices begin to fall. On the other hand, they are relatively uninformed about developments in other markets and learn relatively slowly what is happening in them.

---

[1]The two main references for the work of Lucas on this topic are Robert Lucas, "Expectations and the Neutrality of Money," *Journal of Economic Theory,* Vol 4. (April 1972), pp. 103–124, and "Some International Evidence on Output-Inflation Tradeoffs," *American Economic Review,* Vol. 63 (June 1973), pp. 326–334. These papers, especially the first, had a major impact on macroeconomics because of the use of rational expectations and microeconomic principles to deal with key macroeconomic problems for the first time. The second paper is less technical and our discussion follows that paper.

## Derivation of the Lucas Supply Curve

To explain how this works, we start with the supply curves of individual firms and show how we can derive a supply curve for the whole economy from these individual curves. We will use the subscript i to represent an individual firm. The representative firm's supply curve is given by

$$Y_i = h(P_i - P) + Y_i^*, \tag{15.1}$$

where $Y_i$ is the firm's production, $P_i$ is the firm's price, $P$ is the aggregate price, and $Y_i^*$ is the firm's potential or normal production. In words the equation says that the firm's output $Y_i$ is greater than the normal $Y_i^*$ by an amount equal to a constant $h$ times the difference between the firm's price $P_i$ and the general price level $P$. We enter the general price level into the supply curve as an indicator of the prices in all other markets. As we described above, the firm will supply more output only if its price rises relative to these other prices. The supply curve is upward-sloping ($h > 0$) in terms of the difference between $P_i$ and $P$, and is shown graphically in Figure 15.1.

Note that if the price of the firm's product rises by the same amount as the overall price level, there will be no change in the firm's supply, according

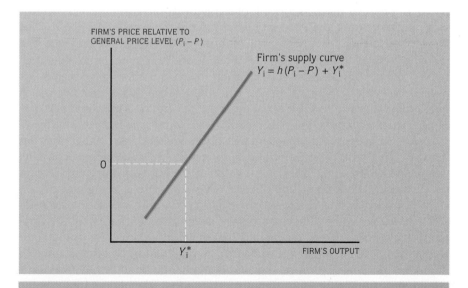

**FIGURE 15.1**   The Firm's Supply Curve

The firm's supply decision depends on its own price relative to the general level of prices in the economy. If $P_i$ and $P$ rise in the same proportion, then $Y_i$ does not change.

to the supply equation. The firm will see that although it can receive more for its output, the prices of all other items in the economy have increased by the same amount. Hence, in relative terms there has been no change.

Suppose, however, that the firm does not know what is going on in other markets in the economy. The information about the rest of the economy may arrive late, or the firm's managers may not have the time to monitor economic conditions throughout the economy. When information is restricted in this way, firms will not know the prices of other commodities in the economy. Hence, they will not know the aggregate price level; they will have to guess it. We therefore rewrite Equation 15.1 to reflect this fact:

$$Y_i = b(P_i - P^e) + Y_i^*. \qquad (15.2)$$

The superscript e on the $P$ indicates the firm's *estimate* of the overall price level.

Now consider again the case where all prices in the economy rise by the same amount. Each firm will observe only the increase in price of its own product, and will have to make a guess about all the other prices as summarized in the index $P$. If the firm does not adjust its guess of $P$, then it will clearly produce more. The firm thinks that its own relative price has increased. If the other firms in the economy behave the same way, then they could all produce more as a result of the general increase in prices. In this way, all the firms in the economy would mistake the general price rise for an increase in their own price. With all firms producing more than their potential $Y_i^*$, output in the economy as a whole will surely be above potential.

In an economic environment where there is a close relationship between economic activity in different industries, a firm would be naive not to guess that other firms in the economy were having the same type of experience. In other words, the observation that the price is high in one firm's market is an indication to that firm that prices are likely to be high in other markets. This would be especially true in a highly inflationary economy, where an increase in the price of one commodity is usually only an indication that inflation is continuing: the price of everything else is going up, too.

Consider, first, an extreme case where economic conditions are such that relative prices of different products never change; that is, all the fluctuations in prices are due to general inflation where all prices move together. If relative prices never change, then firms would realize that any change in their own price simply represents an equal change in all prices. The firms would instantaneously adjust their expectations of other prices by the same amount that their own price increased. In Equation 15.2, $P^e$ would increase by exactly the amount that $P_i$ increased. Hence, the firm's production would not change. In this example, the information-based explanation for the departure of real GDP from potential disappears. Although this example is extreme, even in a less extreme situation we would expect firms to make use of information available in their own market when guessing economic conditions elsewhere. More specifically, when a firm observes the price of its own product it will adjust its expectation of prices elsewhere. This adjustment will be based on the relationship between the firm's price and the general price level that the firm has experienced over time.

A simple way to describe the adjustment of the firm's expectation is through the equation

$$P^e = \hat{P} + b(P_i - \hat{P}). \tag{15.3}$$

In words this means that the firm's guess $P^e$ of the general price is greater than what was forecast $\hat{P}$ at the start of the year by an amount equal to a constant $b$ times the difference between the firm's own price $P_i$ and the forecast of the general price $\hat{P}$. For example, if the coefficient $b$ is .3, the forecast of the general price $\hat{P}$ is 1.0, and the firm observes a price $P_i$ in its own market equal to 1.1, then the best guess of the general price is 1.0 + .3(1.1 − 1.0) = 1.03. In the example, the firm observes a price 10 percent higher in its own market, and its guess is that the general price is 3 percent higher than originally forecast.

Note that if $b = 0$, the firm's own price does not influence its estimate of the general price level. At the other extreme is the case where $b = 1$. Then the firm increases its estimate of the general price level by exactly the amount that its own price increases. This case corresponds to the extreme example we considered earlier, where there are never any changes in relative prices.

In general, however, the coefficient $b$ is less than 1 and greater than zero. The size of $b$ depends on whether the relative price variability is large compared with the general price variability. The larger the general price variability, the more the firm changes its estimate of the general price level when it sees its own price increase. For example, in a typical high-inflation economy, the general price variability is high. Firms usually guess that their own price increase is a signal for another increase in inflation.

If we substitute the firm's best guess (Equation 15.3) into the firm's supply equation (15.1), we get

$$Y_i = h[P_i - \hat{P} - b(P_i - \hat{P})] + Y_i^* \tag{15.4}$$

or,

$$Y_i = h(1 - b)(P_i - \hat{P}) + Y_i^* \tag{15.5}$$

Equation 15.5 shows how the representative firm produces more when its own price is greater than the forecast of the general price level. It has the same form as the firm's supply function except for the fact that the supply coefficient is related to the coefficient $b$. If $b$ is near 1, then $b(1 - b)$ is near zero and the firm does not supply much additional output. At the other extreme, when $b$ is near zero the supply coefficient is larger.

The supply curve for the entire economy is obtained by adding up all the representative firms' supply curves. Real GDP, or $Y$, is the sum of all the individual firms' $Y_i$. The aggregate price level $P$ is simply the sum of the individual firms' prices $P_i$ divided by $n$, the number of firms.

If we add up Equation 15.5 for all the firms in the economy, we get

$$Y = nb(1 - b)(P - \hat{P}) + Y^*, \qquad (15.6)$$

which is called the **Lucas supply curve.** It shows that if the price level $P$ rises above the forecast of $P$, then real GDP will rise above potential GDP. In order to graph the Lucas supply curve with $P$ on the vertical axis, we must rewrite it with the price level $P$ on the right-hand side. The Lucas supply curve then looks like:

$$P = \hat{P} + c(Y - Y^*), \qquad (15.7)$$

where $c = 1/(nb(1 - b))$. Equation 15.7 is plotted in Figure 15.2.

## The Appearance of Price Rigidity

How does the Lucas supply curve generate price rigidity? Suppose that the aggregate demand curve is given by

$$Y = k_0 + k_1 (M - P), \qquad (15.8)$$

where $M$ is the money supply. We plot the aggregate demand curve in Figure 15.2 along with the Lucas supply curve. If the Fed increases the money supply, then the aggregate demand curve will shift up by the amount of the money-supply increase, as shown in Figure 15.2. This leads to a new intersection with the Lucas supply curve. However, note that as long as the Lucas supply curve is not perfectly vertical, the price level rises by less than the increase in the money supply. This explains why real GDP rises when the money supply increases.

Thus, we have shown that price rigidity can occur as a result of the limited information firms have about what is going on in other markets. If they were fully informed (that is, if $b = 1$) then the Lucas supply curve would be perfectly vertical and the price would increase by the same amount as the increase in money. Price rigidity would not appear.

In the long run, of course, firms will become informed about what is happening in other markets and their *estimate* of the price level $\hat{P}$ will rise

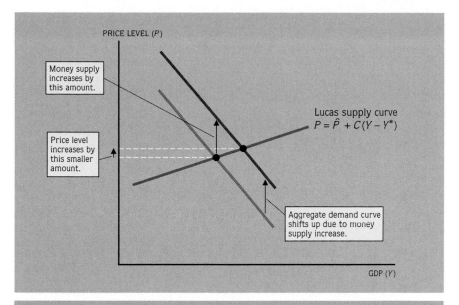

**FIGURE 15.2** The Lucas Supply Curve

The upward-sloping line is a plot of Equation 15.8, or the Lucas supply curve. Price rigidity is revealed when the aggregate demand curve shifts up by the amount that the money supply increases but the price level rises by a smaller amount. If firms were fully informed, the price level would rise by the same amount as the price increase, because the Lucas supply curve would be vertical.

as much as the *actual* price level $P$. Then the Lucas supply curve will shift up by the amount that prices have risen and the actual price rise will be the same amount as the money supply increase. In the long run there is no impact on real GDP.

## Policy Ineffectiveness Theorem

The Lucas supply curve has an interesting implication which has fascinated macroeconomists since it was first pointed out in a paper by Thomas Sargent and Neil Wallace.[2] Suppose that the Fed announces that it is increasing the money supply. Suppose also that people believe the Fed's announcement

---

[2]Thomas Sargent and Neil Wallace, "Rational Expectations, the Optimal Monetary Instrument, and the Optimal Money Supply Rule," *Journal of Political Economy,* Vol. 83 (1975), pp. 241–254.

and that they have rational expectations about the future—in other words, they act as if they understand the implications of the theory in Equations 15.7 and 15.8 or Figure 15.2. Looking closely at Equation 15.7, we can see that the price level $P$, or output $Y$, must increase. Since people are rational in forming their expectations of $P$, they also are looking at Equations 15.7 and 15.8 trying to figure out what is going to happen to $Y$ and $P$ when the money supply goes up. They also anticipate the money-supply increase and therefore *expect* that the price level will rise. That is, their rational expectation of the price level $\hat{P}$ increases. But note from the Lucas supply function shown in Equation 15.8 that this means that $Y$ does not rise at all: $P$ and $\hat{P}$ rise in the same proportion when an increase in $M$ is anticipated. Now looking back at Equation 15.7 it is clear that if $Y$ does not change then $P$ must rise by the same amount that $M$ increases. Graphically, the Lucas supply curve in Figure 15.2 shifts up immediately and real GDP does not change.

In summary, with rational expectations an *anticipated* increase in the money supply will result in no increase in real output. It will result only in an increase in the price level that matches the increase in money. *Anticipated monetary policy is ineffective.* This result is called the **policy ineffectiveness theorem.**

Sargent and Wallace's starting point was the premise that the central bank has essentially the same information about the economy as people have. If the Fed uses information—say, about real GDP—to make monetary policy, then people will use the same information to take account of the Fed's policy when forming their expectation $P_t^e$. The Fed can affect employment only by surprising people. But it can't surprise people by expanding the money stock every time real GDP rises, because people know the real GDP data. Put differently, people with rational expectations cannot be surprised by systematic policy. According to this theory, surprise monetary expansions have an important influence on employment, but unanticipated expansions based on observed conditions affect only the price level. The policy ineffectiveness theorem has profoundly influenced economists since the 1970s and has had an impact on thinking in the government and the Federal Reserve.

## Critique of Imperfect Information Theory

Although the idea that surprises about monetary policy are an important driving force in fluctuations had a profound impact on macroeconomists, the policy ineffectiveness theorem receives less attention today than in past decades. First, early evidence supporting the theory[3] is now seen as showing

---

[3]Robert Barro, "Unanticipated Money Growth and Unemployment in the U.S.," *American Economic Review*, Vol. 67 (March 1977), pp. 101–115.

only that monetary changes precede employment and output fluctuations. It does not show that imperfect information, rather than some other channel of influence, is at work. Second, recent evidence shows the importance of other types of shocks in macro fluctuations. Monetary variables explain only part of the total variability of real GDP. The economics profession has moved to the more general view that a variety of forces—technological shocks and changes in preferences—are at least as important as monetary developments. The diminishing importance of monetary shocks is partly a reflection of the stability of monetary policy in the United States and other major economies from 1982 to the present.

## THE LUCAS SUPPLY CURVE

1. An important explanation of the effects of changes in money on real GDP is the imperfect information theory developed by Robert Lucas. According to this theory people are not perfectly informed about what is going on in other parts of the economy.
2. Thus, when firms see an increase in prices—whether due to a shift in their demand curve or to changes in other parts of the economy—they respond by producing more. This response is the Lucas supply curve.
3. Price rigidity is an implication of the Lucas imperfect information theory: when the money supply increases, the aggregate price level increases by a relatively small amount. Hence, real money balances rise and real GDP rises above potential GDP.

## STICKY PRICES AND NOMINAL WAGE CONTRACTS

In Lucas's theory, imperfect information produces a type of price rigidity. Now we will consider another explanation of price rigidity. We will find that firms and workers have incentives to keep prices and wages from changing too much or too rapidly. Price change may be costly, giving rise to sticky prices. Or firms and workers may have agreed in a contract not to change wages by more or less than a certain prespecified amount.

## Sticky Prices

Firms' prices are set in dollars. Studies show that the dollar amount appears "stuck" at one value for long periods; in other words, prices are sticky. We could imagine a world where prices were sticky but not in dollar terms. For example, firms could set their prices relative to the price of some standard commodity. Instead of setting the price of a six-pack of Coke at $2.50, Coca-Cola bottlers could set the price at the level of six pounds of sugar. Someone buying a six-pack would have to find out how much a pound of sugar currently cost in order to know how much they would have to pay. Under the hypothetical sugar reference point for prices, there would be stickiness in the relative prices of goods compared with sugar, but not in their dollar prices. Sugar policy would be an important determinant of overall economic activity, whereas monetary policy would have little impact on output and employment. It is important for macroeconomists to explain why price stickiness takes the particular form of setting prices in dollars rather than in sugar or some other relative price.

Not every economy follows the price-setting conventions that are familiar in the United States. In countries with histories of extreme inflation, prices are sometimes set in terms other than those countries' monetary units. For example, in Chile, there is a unit called the Unidad de Fomento or UF. Chile also has a standard monetary unit called the peso. The peso has suffered a great deal of inflation in the past and still continues to have declining purchasing power. The UF has a constant purchasing power, as defined by the cost-of-living index. The number of pesos making up a UF gradually rises in order to keep the UF's purchasing power constant. For example, if the UF is 200 pesos in one month, and the peso price level rises by 1 percent the next month, the new UF is worth 202 pesos. Many prices and values are quoted in UFs rather than in pesos, including rents for apartments and balances in savings accounts. Macroeconomic analysis for Chile cannot make the same type of sticky-price assumptions that are appropriate for the United States. Other countries have found other alternatives to their own monetary units for quoting prices. One of the most common is to use the U.S. dollar. In countries where this "dollarization" has reached an advanced stage, domestic monetary policy has less impact and U.S. monetary policy is correspondingly more important.

In the United States and other countries that have avoided extreme inflation, prices are almost invariably set in terms of the country's own currency unit, not in commodity units, units like the UF, or another country's currency unit. For this reason, the assumption that prices are sticky in terms of the nominal currency unit makes sense in the U.S. economy and in similar economies.

Studies of nominal stickiness have found enormous variations in the length of time over which prices remain the same in nominal terms. Stickiness tends to be most extreme in cases where there are significant hardware costs for change in the price: pay telephone calls cost a dime for decades before jumping to 25 cents. Magazine prices remain the same for several years and then jump up by 25 cents.[4] A study by Dennis Carlton of the University of Chicago showed that businesses tend to keep the same price for a given customer for a year or more even when they have set new prices for new customers.[5]

Prices printed in catalogs, on price sheets, and on menus can be sticky simply because it is costly to print new versions with new prices. These **menu costs** are a possible contributor to overall price stickiness, though it is not known what fraction of total transactions occur under this type of pricing.[6]

Not every price is sticky. Many agricultural and industrial commodities trade in open markets where prices change every few seconds. In addition, many prices paid in transactions between businesses are linked to these open-market prices. Among businesses, and, to a lesser extent, between businesses and consumers, many prices are set on the spot by negotiations. There is no reason to expect stickiness of negotiated prices. However, if the retailer pays a sticky price at wholesale, stickiness will be passed on at retail. Even though you negotiate a price for a car from a dealer, the result of that negotiation will be sticky if the car manufacturer sets a dollar price in advance that the dealer pays at wholesale.

## Sticky Nominal Wages

In the next section we show that an important reason why prices are sticky is that wages are sticky. But we first need to show why wages are sticky. One of the most important principles of macroeconomics, dating back to Keynes, is that *the wage bargain is made in money terms.* Wages are not set in pounds of sugar, UFs, or foreign currency units. Even though the importance of the fact that wages are set in dollars has been evident to macroeconomists for over 50 years, the reasons for nominal wage stickiness are still imperfectly understood and controversial. Many economists feel that we should simply accept the fact that wages are predetermined in money terms and build it into our macro models. In the next section we will discuss more of the institutional detail about how wages are set in the U.S. labor market. All the details support the basic idea of nominal wage stickiness.

[4]Stephen G. Cechetti, "The Frequency of Price Adjustment," *Journal of Econometrics,* Vol. 20 (April 1986), pp. 255–274.

[5]Dennis Carlton, "The Rigidity of Prices," *American Economic Review,* Vol. 76 (September 1986), pp. 637–658.

[6]N. Gregory Mankiw, "Small Menu Costs and Large Business Cycles: A Macroeconomic Model of Monopoly," *Quarterly Journal of Economics,* Vol. 100 (May 1985), pp. 529–539.

As we will see in the next section, many wage-setting institutions link wages at one firm to the general level of wages. But it is difficult to measure wages in general and complicated to update wages at one firm based on whatever measures are available. Keeping wages on a predetermined nominal track between occasional rebargaining seems to be a workable approximation of the goal of setting wages at one firm in line with wages elsewhere in the economy. And the reason we discussed earlier for the use of the currency unit rather than other units of purchasing power in the case of price setting applies equally to wage setting.

## The Relation of Wage Stickiness to Price Stickiness

For a competitive firm, price equals marginal cost. For a firm with market power, price is a fixed markup over marginal cost where the market depends on the elasticity of demand. In either case price moves directly with marginal cost. Marginal cost depends on the wage and on the prices of inputs the firm buys. If the wage and input prices are sticky in nominal terms, then the firm's price will be sticky in nominal terms as well. This conclusion holds even if the firm carefully sets its price and output at exactly the optimum. And this leads to an important conclusion: *Prices can be sticky in nominal terms because firms have limited incentives to set their prices at the exact optimum and they find it convenient to stay with existing prices. A second, independent cause of sticky nominal prices is that wages are sticky in nominal terms, and this makes prices sticky even if firms price at the exact optimum.*

Research has not succeeded in determining which source of nominal price stickiness is the more important. For pay telephone calls, magazines, and many other goods and services, straight price stickiness is probably the most important factor. For basic industrial goods sold by businesses to one another, price rigidity probably derives mainly from wage stickiness. And, of course, for some products (such as precious metals or commodities) price stickiness is not a significant factor at all.

### NOMINAL PRICE AND WAGE STICKINESS

1. In the United States and in other countries with relatively low inflation, prices tend to be sticky in terms of the domestic currency unit. In inflation-prone economies, prices are set in terms of some other unit that has stable purchasing power.

2. Nominal price stickiness can arise in a number of ways. Because of menu costs, firms may have little incentive to change their prices when conditions change. If wages are sticky in nominal terms, prices will be sticky because costs are sticky.

## Wage Determination in the United States

Most workers in large labor unions change their contracts about once every three years. Contracts are unsynchronized; not all workers sign contracts at the same time. Wage negotiations are staggered over the 36 months of the basic contract cycle. At any one time, only a small fraction of the workers are signing contracts; the remaining workers either have recently signed their contracts or will sign their contracts in the future. The period in which one contract is in force overlaps the period in which other contracts are in force.

What are the factors that determine the size of the wage adjustment when it does occur? Wage and salary decisions are made in collective-bargaining meetings for which both management and labor leaders spend extensive time preparing. While the outcome of any one bargaining situation cannot be predicted with much certainty, a number of factors clearly influence the outcome in particular directions.

The first and perhaps most important is the state of the labor market. If unemployment is high, labor will be in a relatively weak bargaining position. Conversely, if unemployment is low, workers will be able to bargain for larger wage increases. The threat of a strike is more credible in good times than in bad. Moreover, firms are likely to settle for larger wage increases in tight market conditions, because they will be better able to pass on their costs in the form of higher prices.

A second factor influencing wage bargaining is the wage paid to comparable workers in other industries. Because not all contract negotiations are synchronized, there are two components of this comparison wage: the wage settlements of workers who have recently signed contracts, and the expected wage settlements of workers who will be signing their contracts in the near future. Looking back at the wage settlements in recently signed contracts makes sense in a current negotiation because those settlements will be in force during part of the contract period under consideration. This backward-looking behavior tends to give some built-in inertia to the wage-determination process. If one union group gets a big increase, then the next group of workers in the wage-determination cycle will also tend to get a big increase. But looking forward to future settlements also makes sense, because the current contract will be in force when these changes take place.

In other words, wage determination generally combines elements of forward-looking and backward-looking behavior.

A third factor that will influence wage decisions is the expected rate of inflation. If inflation is expected to be high, workers will ask for larger wage increases and management will be willing to pay them because their own prices are expected to rise. As with the effect of comparable wage increases, the effect of expected inflation will have both a backward-looking element and a forward-looking element.

It is very common for workers who are not in unions to receive wage and salary adjustments once each year. Although there is no formal contract involved, it is unlikely that this wage decision will be changed before the next scheduled adjustment period. Hence, the nominal wage stickiness is very similar to that in the union contracts.

For example, our university adjusts our salaries once each year. We get a letter from the dean in July giving our salary for the 12-month period beginning September 1. This nominal wage rate is rarely changed before the next salary adjustment period the following year. This type of annual wage-setting is common in many sectors of the economy.

In preparation for a wage adjustment, the management of nonunion firms must obtain information very similar to that obtained by the management of unionized firms preparing for a collective-bargaining meeting. In a large nonunion firm there are usually specialists called wage and salary administrators who must make a wage decision. They obtain information about the current labor-market situation. They conduct wage surveys or subscribe to a wage survey performed by an outside group. They also attempt to forecast the rate of inflation.

Although the wage decision will usually be made under more competitive conditions than exist in a collective-bargaining situation, the same factors—the state of the labor market and wage and price inflation—will influence the final outcome in similar directions. If unemployment is very low and is expected to remain low for the next year, management will try to pay a relatively high wage compared with other firms employing similarly skilled workers. An attractive wage will prevent workers from quitting and help to lure workers from other firms if necessary for expansion. On the other hand, if unemployment is high, there will be less of a worry that workers will quit to look for jobs elsewhere. Moreover, if the year is expected to be bad for sales, an expansion of production requiring more workers would be unlikely.

Although there is little direct evidence on when most nonunion firms have their scheduled wage increases, it is unlikely that they all occur at the same time. Hence, there is a type of nonsynchronization that we observe also for the union sector. Figure 15.3 illustrates the simple situation where there are four wage adjustment periods through the year: January 1, April 1,

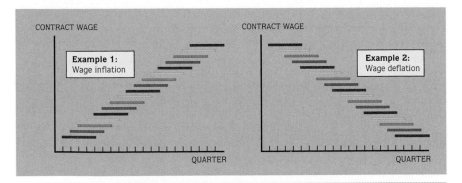

**FIGURE 15.3**   Staggered Annual Wage-Setting with Four Wage-Adjustment Periods throughout the Year

There are four groups of workers in each example. The contract wage of each worker group is denoted by a different color shade, from very dark to very light. Because wages are not all set at the same time (that is, they are not synchronized), the contract wage of one group overlaps that of all the other groups. This is shown in the diagram as flat contract wage lines on top or below each other. In the left panel, there is a general inflation: each group attempts to get above the previous group. In the right panel, there is a general deflation: each group tries to get below the previous group.

July 1, and October 1. It is clear from this illustration that staggered wage-setting gives rise to an overlapping of wage decisions.

## Why Are Wages Set for Long Periods with Few Contingencies?

We have just seen that workers generally have their wages predetermined in contracts. Only a fraction of these contracts are contingent on the cost of living, and none, to our knowledge, is contingent on any other economic variable.

**ADJUSTMENT COSTS**   The costs of adjusting wages and salaries may be high. Consider the situation where wage rates are determined in collective-bargaining negotiations between large corporations and labor unions. In preparation for these negotiations management spends months surveying wages in other industries, estimating changes in labor productivity, forecasting changes in the firm's own profits, and obtaining estimates of the general inflation during the upcoming contract period. To be adequately informed during the collective-bargaining sessions, labor leaders must be equally and independently prepared; hence, they must also spend months preparing for negotiations. Moreover, there is a threat of a strike in almost every collective-bargaining situation. An actual strike obviously is costly for both sides, but the mere preparation for a possible strike is also costly. The firm must accumulate and finance additional inventories to be used if a strike occurs. Hence, production will be abnormally high before negotiations and abnormally low after negotiations as firms draw down inventories when a strike does not occur. These swings in production raise average costs to the firm.

**INDEXING**    Why aren't the contracts that are negotiated contingent on events that that may occur before the next renewal? We have noted that some of the contracts include cost-of-living adjustments, whereby the wage is indexed to the consumer price level. However, these clauses rarely involve 100 percent protection from cost-of-living changes, and many contracts do not have any such clauses. Moreover, cost-of-living clauses represent only one of many possible contingency clauses. For example, the contracts could be directly linked to the unemployment rate, GDP, or more local measures of the performance of the economy and the value of workers' time.

The primary reason why more contracts are not indexed to the cost of living is that such indexing can be harmful if there are import price or technology shocks. Suppose that the marginal productivity of labor is reduced because of a shift in the production function. Recalling the flexible-price model of Chapter 3, we know that such a shift will eventually require a reduction of the real wage; that is, $W/P$ must decline so that it is equal to the marginal productivity of labor. But a 100 percent indexed contract will prevent such a decline. The escalator clause will call for an increase in $W$ in the same proportion as the increase in $P$. Hence, $W/P$ remains constant and too high. It is understandable that many firms and workers are reluctant to institute an arrangement that rules out any adjustments in the real wage if prices should rise suddenly during the contract period. Of course, if the reason for the increase in prices is a general monetary-induced inflation, then there will be no need for a reduction in the real wage. Unfortunately there is usually no way to tell in advance whether the price rise is due to monetary effects or to shifts in the production process.

Why not index wages to unemployment, GDP, or other indexes that might indicate whether the shocks are to money or to productivity? Part of an answer is similar to the reason we gave for caution in indexing to the cost of living. For instance, some of the shifts in overall unemployment are not relevant for the productivity of a particular group of workers. When a special event, not a recession, makes unemployment zoom for autoworkers, the unemployment rate may not reveal much about the jobs available to computer workers.

A final reason why contracts do not have many indexing clauses is that they add complexity. There are good reasons to have a straightforward contract that the rank and file can easily understand and vote on. Similarly, contingency clauses appear to add uncertainty about the wage that the workers will actually get. Many workers would object to this added uncertainty, even though the economic theorist might argue that the uncertainty would make the worker better off.

## Why Is Wage Setting Staggered?

In a decentralized economy like that of the United States, firms and workers decide by themselves when their wages and salaries are adjusted. The fact that these decisions are not synchronized therefore seems natural; one would be surprised to see a coordinated wage (or price) adjustment without some centralized orchestration of such a move. Historical accident would be enough to explain why the autoworkers always negotiate just before the machinists.

Imagine what would happen if all wages and prices were set *at the same time* and without a central planner to tell workers and firms what to do. A firm which thought that a relative wage increase was appropriate for its workers would not know what other wages were; hence it could not achieve that relative increase.

Staggered wage-setting provides information to firms and workers about wages and prices elsewhere. Even though other wages will be adjusted before the current contract expires, there will be a period of time when the desired relative wage is in force. Nonsynchronized wage and price setting thus seems desirable in a decentralized economy.[7]

Moreover, staggered wage-setting adds some stability to wages. Without staggering, all wages and prices would be up for grabs each period; there would be no base for setting each wage. Tremendous variability would be introduced into the price system.

### WAGE CONTRACTS

1. Workers typically have wage adjustments infrequently, about once per year or less often. These adjustments are staggered over time. Since the wage is rarely changed within the year, this wage-setting process creates wage stickiness.

---

[7]See Gary Fethke and Andrew Policano, "Will Wage Setters Ever Stagger Decisions?" *Quarterly Journal of Economics*, Vol. 101 (November 1986), for further discussion of the rationale for nonsynchronized wage-setting.

2. Wages are set for long periods because collective bargaining, threats of strikes, or simply careful reviews of worker performance make adjusting the wage costly. Wages are rarely indexed in the United States because supply shocks as well as demand shocks occur. With indexing, the real wage does not adjust enough after supply shocks. Moreover, extensive contingency clauses add complexity and apparent uncertainty to wage contracts.

# 15.3  A MODEL WITH STAGGERED WAGE-SETTING

In this section we present a simple stylized model of staggered wage-setting to illustrate the ideas about wage and price stickiness discussed in the previous section. In the model, wage setting is nonsynchronized, prices are given by a markup over costs, and expectations are rational.

Suppose that all wage contracts last two years, that all wage adjustments occur at the beginning of each year, and that there is no indexing.

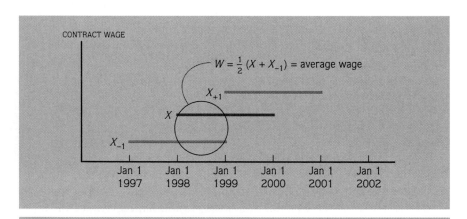

**FIGURE 15.4**   Configuration of Wage Setting in the Simple Model

There are two groups of workers in the economy. One group has a wage adjustment January 1 of the even years and the other group has a wage adjustment January 1 of the odd years. The average wage $W$ is shown to be equal to the average of this period's contract wage $X$ and last period's contract wage $X_{-1}$. In the figure the average wage for 1998 is shown. It is the average of the contract wage set in 1997 and the contract wage set in 1998.

Half the workers sign contracts at the start of even-numbered years and half at the start of odd-numbered years. This configuration of assumptions is shown in Figure 15.4, where $X$ represents the contract wage and $W$ the average wage. Since we need to distinguish between past and future variables, we let the subscript $-1$ represent the *previous* year and the subscript $+1$ represent the *next* year. Of course, events in the next year are not known; people must form expectations of them. The average is given by

$$W = \frac{1}{2}(X + X_{-1}).$$  (15.9)

In words, the wage $W$ *this year* is the simple average of the contract wage signed *last year* $X_{-1}$, which is still outstanding, and the contract wage signed *this year* $X$. For example, suppose that the contract wage is 10 in 1991 and 8 in 1992. Then the average wage is 9 in 1992.

An algebraic relationship that describes how the contract wage is set each period might be given by

$$X = \underbrace{\frac{1}{2}(W + W_{+1})}_{\substack{\text{Effect of} \\ \text{expected} \\ \text{average wage}}} - \underbrace{\frac{d}{2}[(U - U^*) + (U_{+1} - U^*)]}_{\substack{\text{Effect of} \\ \text{current and} \\ \text{future unemployment}}},$$  (15.10)

where $U$ is the unemployment rate, $U^*$ is the natural rate of unemployment, and $d$ is a coefficient describing the response of wages to unemployment.

Equation 15.10 leads to an interesting observation. Rewrite Equation 15.10 with $W$ and $W_{+1}$ replaced by the expressions in Equation 15.9. That is,

$$X = \frac{1}{2}\left[\underbrace{\frac{1}{2}(X + X_{-1})}_{\substack{W \text{ from} \\ \text{Equation 15.9}}} + \underbrace{\frac{1}{2}(X_{+1} + X)}_{\substack{W_{+1} \text{ from} \\ \text{Equation 15.9}}}\right] - \frac{d}{2}[(U - U^*) + (U_{+1} - U^*)].$$  (15.11)

Now gather together the $X$ terms (without the subscripts) and put them on the left-hand side of the equation. After some cancellation (you can work it out in the margin), we get the simpler expression:

$$X = \frac{1}{2}(\underbrace{X_{-1}}_{\substack{\text{Backward-} \\ \text{looking} \\ \text{component}}} + \underbrace{X_{+1}}_{\substack{\text{Forward-} \\ \text{looking} \\ \text{component}}}) - d[(U - U^*) + \underbrace{(U_{+1} - U^*)}_{\substack{\text{Expected future} \\ \text{unemployment} \\ \text{is also a factor}}}].$$  (15.12)

Equation 15.12 shows how wage determination has a backward-looking component $X_{-1}$ and a forward-looking component $X_{+1}$. The backward-looking component is what makes inflation persist from year to year. Workers base their wage decisions partly on what previous wage decisions were. The forward-looking component, also discussed previously in words, is what makes expectations of the future so important. Expectations of moderate wage settlements next year will tend to moderate wage settlements this year. For example, if wage settlements next year are expected to be 10 percent lower, then, according to Equation 15.12, actual settlements this year will be 5 percent lower. The coefficient on $X_{+1}$ is 1/2.

Equation 15.12 also shows how expected future unemployment conditions next year can affect wage settlements this year. If the unemployment rate is expected to rise next year by 2 percent, then wage settlements this year will be 2 times $d$ percent lower. For example, if $d$ equals .5, then wage settlements this year will be 1 percent lower. The expectation of a slump in the future with its accompanying increase in unemployment has a simple effect: It decreases wage inflation today.

With prices given by a constant markup over costs, all these effects on wages will be passed through to prices. The policy implications are therefore clear. Expectations of a monetary policy that is noninflationary in the future and that will let unemployment rise if necessary in the future, should inflation rise, will have favorable effects on inflation today. These favorable effects on inflation can actually work with little or no adverse effects on unemployment. The expectation of a credible stance against inflation in the future should therefore have a favorable effect on the trade-off between inflation and unemployment.

Consider, finally, the operations of the model in a steady inflation. Say the contract wage $X$ increases by the same amount each year. For example, let the amount of increase be 10. In a steady inflation the *change* in the contract wage this year, $X - X_{-1}$, and the change in the contract wage next year, $X_{+1} - X$, will be the same, namely 10. Equation 15.12 can then be written as

$$\underbrace{\frac{1}{2}(X - X_{-1})}_{5} = \underbrace{\frac{1}{2}(X_{+1} - X)}_{5} - \underbrace{d[(U - U^*) + (U_{+1} - U^*)]}_{0}. \tag{15.13}$$

Notice that there is a $10/2 = 5$ on the left-hand side and a $10/2 = 5$ on the right-hand side. The two cancel out. The term involving unemployment must equal zero. This implies that $U = U^*$ and that $U_{+1} = U^*$. In other words, the unemployment rate is always equal to the natural rate. The same result holds, of course, for any steady change in prices, not just 10. Regardless of the rate of inflation, as long as it is steady and anticipated, there is no trade-off between inflation and unemployment in the long run.

The simple model consisting of Equations 15.9, 15.10, 15.11 can be viewed as an alternative, more microeconomic-based representation of the price adjustment equation that we introduced in Chapter 8, Equation 8.2. As such, it can be combined with a model of aggregate demand that tells how the money supply and government spending shift demand when prices are predetermined. Simulating such a model requires a large computer and sophisticated computer programs. Fortunately, most of the results can be conveyed in a more intuitive and less complex way by introducing some simple approximations to capture the essence of forward-looking and rational expectations behavior. We turn to this in the next chapter.

## STAGGERED WAGE CONTRACTS

1. Wage determination will have backward-looking and forward-looking elements when contract negotiations are staggered over time.
2. The backward-looking component reflects the influence of last year's contracts on this year's prices. This influence of the past on the present gives inflation persistence.
3. The forward-looking component reflects the impact of next year's contracts on this year's prices. This influence of the future on the present makes expectations about policy important. The more accommodative policy has been to price shocks in the past, the more inflation may be expected in the future.

## REVIEW AND PRACTICE

### Major Points

1. The imperfect information model assumes that people are unaware of the nature of changes in demand, which may represent relative price increases or pure inflation. If some probability is attached to each possibility, firms will alter supply when the price level changes.

2. In the imperfect information model, unobserved changes in the money supply can affect real output. If workers can rationally anticipate the behavior of the Fed and thus the money supply, then money has no effect on output. This is known as the policy ineffectiveness theorem.

3. The situation in which prices are infrequently adjusted is known as nominal price stickiness. In inflation-prone countries, price stickiness may exist with respect to a unit with stable purchasing power.

4. Sticky prices may result from sticky wages. Much empirical evidence suggests that price-cost margins are quite stable over time.

5. Workers typically have their wages adjusted about once each year. The size of the wage adjustment is influenced by expectations of inflation, expectations of the wages paid to other workers, and the level of unemployment.

6. Wage setting is staggered. Not all workers obtain wage adjustments at the same time. This staggering adds to the inertia of wage movements.

7. A specific model of wage adjustment with overlapping contracts confirms that an unvarying unemployment rate is consistent with any chronic rate of inflation.

## Key Terms and Concepts

imperfect information
Lucas supply curve
markup pricing
price rigidity

Unidad de Fomento
menu costs
sticky prices
sticky wages

indexation
staggered contracts
relative wage-setting
policy ineffectiveness theorem

## Questions for Discussion and Review

1. Which assumption of the imperfect information model is essential to generate a Lucas supply curve?

2. Suppose the money supply evolves according to a policy rule that is known by all firms and households. Would you expect movements in the money supply to have any correlation with output?

3. What factors contribute to price rigidity?

4. What is staggered wage-setting? Why does it occur?

5. Describe the typical wage adjustment for workers. Are these wage-setting dates staggered? Why aren't wages adjusted more frequently?

6. Is monetary policy effective when expectations are rational? Why? Do any wages adjust when expectations of future monetary policy change?

7. What are the forward-looking and the backward-looking components of wage determination? What is their significance?

8. Why is there no long-run trade-off between inflation and unemployment, even though there is a short-run trade-off?

## Problems

### NUMERICAL

1. Suppose that the Lucas supply curve is

$$Y = nb(1 - b)(P - \hat{P}) + Y^*,$$

with $nb(1 - b) = 20{,}000$ and $Y^* = 4{,}000$ (billions of dollars). For example, when the price level $P$ is 1.01 and the expected price $\hat{P}$ is 1.0, output $Y$ is 4,200, or 5 percent above potential output $Y^* = 4{,}000$. Suppose that the aggregate demand curve is

$$Y = 1{,}101 + 1.288\ G + 3.221M/P.$$

a. Suppose that the economy has been at rest for some period with output at potential, and that no changes in policy are expected for the near future. The money supply $M$ is 600 and government spending $G$ is 750. What is the price level? (Hint: If there are no surprises, actual and expected price levels will be the same.)

b. Now suppose that the Fed announces that it will increase the money supply from 600 to 620. What are the new levels of output and price level?

c. Now suppose that the Fed announces that it will increase the money supply from 600 to 620 but actually increases it to 670. What are the new levels of output and price level?

2. Suppose that automatic stabilizers cause government purchases to rise when GDP is below potential and to fall when GDP is above potential. Algebraically we might represent this as

$$G = 750 - g(Y - Y^*),$$

where potential output $Y^*$ is 4,000. The coefficient $g$ measures the strength of the automatic stabilizer.

a. Substitute this expression for $G$ in the aggregate demand function in Problem 1, and solve for output $Y$ in terms of $P$ ($M$ is held fixed at 600). This is the aggregate demand curve incorporating the automatic stabilizer. Describe how the slope of the aggregate demand curve depends on the coefficient $g$.

b. For three different values of $g$ (0, .01, and .1) describe the effect on output of an unanticipated increase in money like the one in Problem 1c. Assume that people know the value of $g$ in each case. Do the effects on output depend on the value of the coefficient $g$? If they do, then does it appear that even well-understood automatic stabilizers are effective in that they influence output? Explain your results intuitively. Why might automatic government-spending stabilizers affect output while anticipated changes in money do not? (See B. T. McCallum and J. K. Whitaker, "The Effectiveness of Fiscal Feedback Rules and Automatic Stabilizers under Rational Expectations," *Journal of Monetary Economics,* Vol. 5 [1979], pp. 171–186, for a further discussion of this type of policy problem.)

3. Using tight monetary policy, the Fed is able to bring about a deceleration of prices, so that inflation falls from 10 percent to zero. The time path of the price level is as follows:

| Year | Price Level |
|------|-------------|
| 1 | 1.000 |
| 2 | 1.100 |
| 3 | 1.188 |
| 4 | 1.259 |
| 5 | 1.310 |
| 6 and later | 1.336 |

There are two groups of workers, those whose wages are set in odd years and those whose wages are set in even years. When the wage is set, it is equal to 10 times the price level in the preceding year, raised by the amount of inflation that occurred in that year relative to the year before; that is, $W = 10P_{-1}(1 + \pi_{-1})$ and $\pi = (P - P_{-1})/P_{-1}$. In the second year of the contract, the wage is increased in proportion to the inflation that occurred in the first year relative to the year before; that is, $W_{+1} = W(1 + \pi)$. Compute the wages paid to the two groups and the average wage across the two groups starting in year 2. Compute the rate of wage inflation and the real wage. Comment on the problems that disinflation creates when there are lags in wage setting, using the numbers from this example.

4. A firm enjoys a monopoly; its average revenue schedule is $15 - .25Y$ and its marginal revenue schedule is $15 - .5Y$ ($Y$ is its amount of output). Its marginal cost schedule is $(Z + W)(.3 + .01Y)$. $Z$ and $W$ are the price of materials and the wage rate, respectively. For $Z = 2$ and $W = 8$, find the price and amount of output that maximize the monopolist's profit. Now suppose that the intercept in marginal and average revenues rises from 15 to 21 because demand rises. Find the price and level of output. Compare these with the case of markup pricing, where $P = (Z + W)m$ and the markup $m$ exceeds 1 and does not change when demand rises. Now go back to the original average revenue and marginal revenue schedules and compute price and output when $Z$ rises to 3. Again, compare these with the case of markup pricing. Conclude by comparing the general nature of markup and monopoly pricing, using your calculations as examples.

## ANALYTICAL

1. If the Lucas supply curve is written with output on the right and price surprises on the left, it looks like a Phillips curve. Explain what happens to this Phillips curve when (i) price changes are mostly due to changes in the local conditions and relative prices, and (ii) when price changes are mostly due to changes in the supply of money.

2. Discuss the relationship between Lucas's imperfect information model and the overlapping contracts model in terms of correlation between output and the price level.

3. Suppose our model of the economy is given by

$$Y = k_0 + k_1(M/P) \quad \text{(Aggregate demand)}$$
$$Y = h(P - P^e) + Y^* \quad \text{(Lucas supply)}$$

Assume further that workers have complete information about the model of the economy, including the value of the money supply. Potential output is equal to 4,000. The aggregate demand curve goes through the point (4,000, 1.5).
   a. Consider three possible Lucas supply curves going through the points (4,000, 1), (4,000, 1.5), and (4,000, 2). What is the value of $P^e$ for each of these curves?
   b. Which of the three curves in Part a is the rational expectations Lucas supply curve? In what sense would the other two curves not satisfy rational expectations?

4. In what way does an economy in which prices are determined by the condition that marginal revenue equal marginal cost respond differently to an aggregate demand shock than an economy in which prices are set as a markup over cost? Does it matter how wages are set in the latter case? How does each type of economy respond to a price shock?

5. Suppose that wage contracts last for three years. Each year, one-third of the economy's wage contracts are renegotiated. Contract wages are set according to

$$X = \frac{1}{3}(W + W_{+1} + W_{+2}) - \frac{d}{3}[(U - U^*) + (U_{+1} - U^*) + (U_{+2} - U^*)].$$

   a. Provide an expression for the average wage rate $W$.
   b. Derive an expression analogous to Equation 15.12. How far backward- and forward-looking is the wage-determination process? What determines the responsiveness of contract wages to *current* labor market conditions?

6. "If expectations are rational, monetary policy has no effect on output." Is this statement true or false? Explain your answer calling on both models with the Lucas supply function and models with wage contracts and sticky prices.

7. On a graph (three to four inches square) sketch an aggregate demand curve and a Lucas supply curve. Label their intersection point as $Y^*$ and $P^*$. Now draw two aggregate demand curves, each one 1/4 inch to either side of your initial curve. Label the intersection points with the Lucas supply curve $Y+$, $P+$ and $Y-$, $P-$. Finally, draw two more aggregate demand curves, 3/4 inch or so to either side of the original curve, and label the intersection points as $Ys$ and $Ps$ with $++$ and $--$.
   a. What kinds of shocks can cause the aggregate demand curve to vary in the way shown on your graph? What is the relationship between the magnitude of those shocks and the variability in $Y$ and $P$?
   b. Suppose initially that shocks to the money supply cause the aggregate demand curve to vary within the narrow region. Assume that the Lucas supply curve shown in your graph is the appropriate curve given the magnitude of these shocks. In what sense is the curve "appropriate"?

c. Now suppose that shocks to the money supply cause the aggregate demand curve to vary within the wider region. How will the new Lucas supply curve appropriate to these shocks compare with your initial Lucas supply curve? Sketch the new curve. How do the swings in output and price level compare with $P--$, $P++$ and $Y--$, $Y++$?

d. Use these results to explain why output may not deviate much from potential in periods of either highly stable or highly variable prices, but may deviate considerably from potential in the transition period from stable to variable prices. Relate your analysis to the experience of the U.S. economy in the late 1960s.

## MacroSolve Exercises

Use MacroSolve's **"PLOT, GRAPH, AND STATISTICS"** options and compare the differences between quarterly and annual data to complete Questions 1 through 4 below. Also, try splitting the sample on the year 1980, when conditions in the financial sector led to the passage of the Depository Institutions Deregulation and Monetary Control Act of 1980.

1. Compare inflation and the GDP gap. Do the two series move closely together? Does one appear to lead the other?

2. Compare inflation and money growth. Do the two series move closely together? Does one appear to lead the other?

3. Compare money growth and GDP growth. Do the two series move closely together? Does one appear to lead the other?

4. Compare real money balances and the GDP gap. Do the two series move closely together? Does one appear to lead the other?

5. Considering this chapter's presentation of imperfect information theory and wage and price rigidities, do your answers to Questions 1 through 4 provide any basis for choosing a sticky-price model over a flexible-price model?

PART

5

# Macroeconomic Policy

# CHAPTER 16

# Inflation and Output Fluctuations

In Chapter 9 we examined macroeconomic policy, focusing on the impact of onetime changes in government spending and the money supply on the economy. Our detailed study of consumption, investment, international trade, government, the monetary system, and the behavior of prices in the ensuing six chapters has paved the way for a more thorough examination of economic policy. In this chapter we expand the framework for policy analysis of Chapter 9 to include more realistic descriptions of price adjustment, lags, and expectations. We also incorporate the modern idea of policy rules explicitly into the framework. In the final two chapters we use this expanded framework for an assessment and evaluation of macroeconomic policy in the United States and other countries.

 **16.1** **PRICE ADJUSTMENT**

Our basic theory of price adjustment indicates that inflation rises when demand conditions are tight, when expectations of inflation rise, or when there are price shocks. A simple algebraic summary of this theory can be written as follows:

$$\pi = f\hat{Y}_{-1} \quad + \quad \pi^e \quad + \quad Z.$$

Market          Expecta-      Price
conditions      tions of      shocks                    (16.1)
(slack or       inflation
tight)

Here $\hat{Y}_{-1} = (Y_{-1} - Y^*)/Y^*$, the percentage deviation of real GDP from potential GDP. The subscript $-1$ indicates that current inflation is related to market pressure in the previous period, reflecting the lags in price and wage adjustment. The last term, $Z$, representing price shocks, describes the upward or downward effect of a change in world oil prices or other factors that affect inflation through channels other than market conditions or expectations. In most years $Z$ is close to zero, but occasionally sharp movements in oil, grain, or other markets create noticeable shocks in the process of inflation.

One of the most important properties of Equation 16.1 is that there is no long-run trade-off between inflation and the level of GDP. A country with a high average inflation rate will not have any higher output than a country with a low inflation rate that is generally expected to continue. That there is no trade-off follows from Equation 16.1: on average, the effect of price shocks will be zero ($Z = 0$), and expected inflation $\pi^e$ will equal actual inflation $\pi$ in the long run regardless of the level of actual inflation. Hence, according to Equation 16.1, the market conditions term $\hat{Y}_{-1}$ equals zero, or, equivalently, actual output equals potential output. The proposition that there is no long-run trade-off between output and inflation is sometimes called the *natural-rate property* because the unemployment rate is equal to the natural rate regardless of the rate of inflation; it is also sometimes called the **accelerationist property** because attempts to keep output above normal result in accelerating prices.

The theories of price rigidity discussed in Chapter 15 indicate that there are several alternative interpretations of Equation 16.1. For example, both the imperfect information theory (Section 15.1) and the staggered-wage-setting model (Section 15.3) can explain the positive relationship between the rate of change in prices and real GDP in Equation 16.1. This equation is an approximation which explains the basic facts of inflation and which is consistent with these theories, but in using it for policy we must be careful how we interpret the coefficients. In particular, the sensitivity of inflation to recent market conditions ($f$) is likely to change when the economic environment changes. Here we consider three important examples of changes in the economic environment: an increase in the amount of indexing, a reduction in the average size and length of business cycles, and changes in the average rate of inflation.

## The Effect of Wage Indexing

As we saw in Chapter 15, there is some indexing in the United States of union labor contracts (cost-of-living adjustment provisions). Indexing is more prevalent in other countries; a good example is Italy. With indexing, each time the price level rises by 1 percent, wages rise by a fraction of a percent $a$, automatically. The indexing coefficient is greater than zero and can be as high as 1. How would indexing affect the price adjustment relationship? Indexing means that the wage will respond to the current rate of inflation as well as to the lagged rate of inflation. The effect of this is to speed up the overall response $f$ of inflation to changes in unemployment. To see this, suppose there is an increase in output that initially increases wage inflation by 1 percent. This will quickly have an upward influence of 1 percent on prices. But if wages are indexed, the upward adjustment of price inflation will mean a further upward adjustment of wage inflation of the amount $a$. This in turn will increase price inflation by $a$, through the markup process. Again indexing will raise wage inflation, now by an amount $a$ times $a$, or $a^2$. And the process will continue for a third round, where inflation will increase by another multiple of $a$ ($a^3$). The whole process is called a **wage-price spiral.** As long as indexing is less than 100 percent (that is, as long as $a <$ 1), the process will eventually settle down, but the end result has been to make wages adjust more to the increase in output than if there had not been any indexing. The total effect is

$$1 + a + a^2 + a^3 + \cdots = \frac{1}{1 - a}$$

using the formula for the geometric series. Note that the total effect is much like the formula for the multiplier. For example, if $a$ equals .5, then the effect of market conditions on inflation is doubled: $1/(1 - .5) = 2$. In general, indexing makes inflation more responsive to market conditions, as represented by a higher value for the coefficient $f$ in Equation 16.1.

For the same reasons, indexing also increases the response of inflation to price shocks $Z$. When the cost of materials rises, firms increase their prices. But because of indexing, this price increase will raise wages. In turn, the increase in wages increases prices again. The wage-price spiral thus multiplies the effect of a raw materials price on inflation. If there is no indexing, so that the wage does not respond at all to prices, other costs will go directly into prices with a coefficient of 1. But because wages rise when prices rise, there is a feedback effect—the wage-price spiral. The feedback effect can more than double the impact of a price shock.

## Length and Severity of Business Cycles

In Chapter 15 we looked at the implications of forward-looking behavior: Workers and firms look ahead to future labor market conditions and to price and wage inflation. If workers expect a recession to be short, then they will be more reluctant to accept lower wages than if they expect the recession to last for a number of years. In the price adjustment equation, the market conditions term $\hat{Y}_{-1}$ not only represents current conditions but also stands in for future excess supply or demand. Usually business cycles last for a number of years, so if output is below potential this year, that is an indication that output will probably be below normal for a few more years.

But suppose that departures of output from potential become less persistent; for example, suppose that the average length of business cycles is reduced from four to two years. Then if GDP is below potential today, there is no implication that GDP will be below potential two years from now. The best guess is that GDP will be back to potential two years from now. As a result inflation will be less responsive to recessions. Algebraically, the coefficient $f$ in Equation 16.1 will be smaller when recessions are expected to be less prolonged.

## Models of the Expected Inflation Term

One of the most difficult issues in the price adjustment equation is how to determine the measure of expected inflation $\pi^e$. There are two important factors to consider.

1. *Forward-looking forecasts*

The expectation that prices and other wages will rise in the future influences the process of wage setting between the worker and the employer and the wage that emerges from it. The amount of inflation that is forecast to occur in the future is therefore part of the expected inflation term. If workers and unions are informed about the economy, these forward-looking forecasts will match rational expectations theory.

2. *Staggered contracts and backward-looking wage behavior.*

The influence of today's expectations on the expected inflation term is only part of the story, however. Because of wage contracts and staggered wage-setting, the expectations term involves inertia that cannot be changed overnight. Workers and firms take account of the wages that will be paid to other workers in the economy. Since wage setting is staggered over time, some wages are set by looking back at the previous wage decisions of other workers; once these wages are set, they are not changed during the contract period unless economic conditions change drastically. Wage inflation has a momentum due to contracts and relative wage-setting. The expectations term must take account of this momentum as well as of the pure expectational influence.

Our description of expected inflation must be consistent with the actual behavior of inflation as observed over a number of years. If inflation typically tends to have momentum, then the public's model of expected inflation will also have momentum. But if inflation tends to be temporary, because of a policy to stabilize prices, for example, then people's view of expected inflation will incorporate the belief that a burst of inflation will probably not be followed by continued inflation.

For the above reasons, any model of expected inflation is itself endogenous to the type of economy or type of policy that is in operation. If policy changes, the model of expected inflation should change.[1] For example, if the Fed announces that it is switching to a new policy that puts more weight on controlling inflation and the public believes it, the model of expected inflation will change. If, on the other hand, people are highly skeptical about promised changes in government programs, then it may take an actual change in inflation to convince them that expected inflation has changed. In that case, a simple backward-looking model of the expected inflation term is closer to the truth—at least for the period of time that it takes the government to convince people that it means business.

The simplest model says that this year's expected inflation depends on actual inflation last year:

$$\pi^e = \pi_{-1}. \qquad (16.2)$$

This description of expected inflation is far from satisfactory, however. Suppose monetary policy tried to keep GDP above potential GDP ($Y > Y^*$) year after year. Because of the lag in forming expected inflation, it appears that this policy would be feasible, although it would mean that inflation would rise each year. In reality, a policy that increased inflation each year would not keep output above potential indefinitely. Eventually the public would catch on and build the steady increase in inflation into its expectations of inflation. Then actual and expected inflation would be equal, and, from Equation 16.1, output would be at potential, not above.

We could look at more complicated models of expected inflation that try to keep up with the rate of change of inflation as well as its level, but the

---

[1]Robert Lucas made this point forcefully in his critique of macroeconomic models as they existed in the early 1970s. He pointed out that these models failed to consider that rational individuals would change their behavior when policy rules change. Fixed models of expected inflation in the Phillips curves were a particular target of his criticism. See Robert Lucas, "Econometric Policy Evaluation: A Critique," in Karl Brunner and Allan Meltzer, eds., *The Phillips Curve and Labor Markets,* Carnegie-Rochester Conference Series on Public Policy, Vol. 1 (Amsterdam: North-Holland, 1976), pp. 19–46.

main ideas should already be clear. There is a very general point at work here: *No mechanical model of expected inflation is universally applicable.* If the public has a particular way of arriving at expected inflation, the government can design a policy that fools the public and makes actual inflation continually exceed expected inflation. But then the public will revise its method of calculating expected inflation so that it will no longer be fooled.

If the government uses a policy that does not attempt to fool the public by making actual inflation exceed expected inflation, then there can be a stable way that the public arrives at expected inflation. In particular, if the government aims at a steady inflation rate and acts to offset occasional bursts of inflation from materials prices and elsewhere, then our simple model of expected inflation is a reasonable description of the process.

A policy that attempts to keep output above normal permanently will fail. Eventually the public will catch on to the policy and revise expected inflation by a method that makes it keep up with actual inflation.

## A Graphical Representation of Price Adjustment

Our discussion of the pitfalls in using the price adjustment equation (16.1) does not imply that the equation is useless. In fact, such an equation is an integral part of the tool kit of practical economists and policymakers.

The graph shown in Figure 16.1 depicts the price adjustment process in a way useful for policy analysis. The inflation rate is on the vertical axis and real GDP measured as the deviation from potential GDP is on the horizontal axis. Because *lagged* real GDP ($Y_{-1}$) rather than current real GDP is on the right-hand side of Equation 16.1, the inflation rate does not depend on the current level of real GDP, which is on the horizontal axis. Hence, we represent Equation 16.1 as a flat line, labeled PA for price adjustment. According to Equation 16.1, the PA line will

1. shift up, indicating higher inflation, if real GDP was above potential GDP last year and shift down if real GDP was below potential GDP;
2. shift up if the expected rate of inflation $\pi^e$ rises and shift down if the expected rate of inflation falls; and
3. shift up if there is a positive price shock (positive value of $Z$) and shift down if there is a negative price shock.

Note that Figure 16.1 has the inflation rate on the vertical axis, while the diagram we used in our earlier study of policy in Chapter 9 had the price level on the vertical axis. We now put the inflation rate on the vertical axis in order to consider monetary policies that focus on inflation rather than on the price level. These policies typically result in low but positive rates of

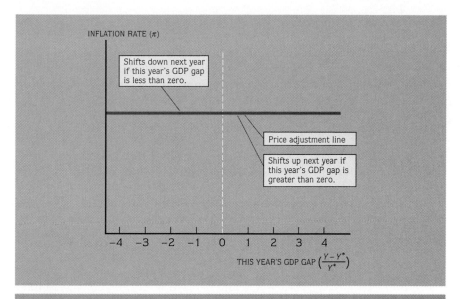

**FIGURE 16.1**   Price Adjustment Line Determining the Inflation Rate

In the price adjustment equation (16.1), the inflation rate is predetermined because it depends on the lagged GDP gap rather than on the current GDP gap. Hence, the price adjustment line is flat in a graph with inflation on the vertical axis and the current GDP gap on the horizontal axis. Because expected inflation responds to lagged inflation, the line shifts up (or down) gradually over time when the GDP gap is positive (or negative).

inflation, such as the 2 to 3 percent inflation in the United States in the first half of the 1990s.

## 16.2   SUMMARIZING THE IS CURVE

In Chapter 7, we discussed and derived the IS curve. It is a downward-sloping curve showing all the combinations of GDP and the interest rate that correspond to spending balance. The economy always operates at a point on its IS curve, because the economy is always in spending balance. Monetary policy determines where the economy is on its IS curve. In this chapter, we need to state the IS curve in a somewhat different way than we did in earlier chapters.

Take a look at the algebraic IS curve in Equation 7.5, page 186, and also at the elaboration we introduced in Chapter 12, Equation 12.7, page 348, which brings the exchange rate into the picture. One of the factors we stressed in Chapters 10 through 13 is that spending depends on the real interest rate, $R - \pi$, rather than on the nominal interest rate, $R$. To capture this factor, and to use a simpler notation, we now write the IS curve as

$$R - \pi = s_0 - s_1 Y + s_2 G. \tag{16.3}$$

Here $s_0$ is the intercept of the IS curve, $s_1$ is the slope coefficient showing that the IS curve slopes downward, and $s_2$ shows the amount of the upward shift of the IS curve when government purchases rise. Now think about the economy at the point on the IS curve corresponding to full employment, where $Y = Y^*$. We define $R^*$ as the real interest rate at the full-employment point and we call it the **equilibrium real interest rate.** It is

$$R^* = s_0 - s_1 Y^* + s_2 G. \tag{16.4}$$

Now we can subtract Equation 16.4 from Equation 16.3 to get a relationship between the difference between the actual real interest rate and the equilibrium real interest rate, on the one hand, and the gap between actual and potential output, on the other hand:

$$R - \pi - R^* = - s_1(Y - Y^*). \tag{16.5}$$

Notice how government purchases dropped out. Fiscal policy affects the real interest rate, but does not affect the difference between the actual real interest rate and the equilibrium real interest rate.

One last step: In our discussion of price adjustment, we have always measured the gap between actual and potential output in percentage terms, using the variable $(Y - Y^*)/Y^*$. We want our new version of the IS curve to use this variable too, so we rewrite equation 16.5 as

$$R - \pi - R^* = - (s_1 Y^*)\left(\frac{Y - Y^*}{Y^*}\right) \tag{16.6}$$

We let $\sigma = s_1 Y^*$; it is the slope of the IS curve, and we use the variable we defined earlier, $\hat{Y} = (Y - Y^*)/Y^*$, the percentage output gap. Then the IS curve is:

$$R - \pi - R^* = - \sigma \hat{Y}. \tag{16.7}$$

In words, there is a simple relation between the gap between the actual and equilibrium real interest rates and the gap between actual and potential output. The relation has a negative slope—if output is below potential, the real interest rate is above its equilibrium level. Thus, if the Fed wants to contract the economy and lower output, it needs to raise the real interest rate.

# 16.3    COMBINING PRICE ADJUSTMENT WITH AGGREGATE DEMAND

We now integrate the price adjustment equation into a model that describes monetary policy and traces its effect on aggregate demand. Because our analysis now focuses on the inflation rate rather than on the price level, we do not use the aggregate demand curve. Instead, we derive a new curve that relates aggregate demand to inflation. The starting point is the IS curve we just developed in the last section.

To incorporate monetary policy, we consider the case where the Fed sets the interest rate $R$. We assume that the Fed's monetary policy rule is the one we discussed in Chapter 14 (Equation 14.12):

$$R = \pi + \beta\hat{Y} + \delta(\pi - \pi^*) + R^f. \tag{16.8}$$

Here $\pi^*$ is the Fed's target rate of inflation, and $R^f$ is a coefficient.

Equations 16.1, 16.2, 16.7, and 16.8 form a model of economic fluctuations. The model is an extended version of the model we used for policy analysis in Chapter 9. In the new version, we can study the role of the monetary policy rule rather than focusing on onetime changes in the money supply. Because the policy rule has the Fed targeting inflation, we carry out the analysis in terms of the inflation rate rather than the price level.

Figure 16.1 showed Equations 16.1 and 16.2 as a price adjustment line. Figure 16.2 combines Equations 16.7 and 16.8. We call it the **aggregate demand–inflation curve.** It is a downward-sloping relation between inflation and the GDP gap, and it has the same role as the aggregate demand curve did when we were considering policies that focus on the price level, in Chapter 9. The curve shows that when inflation rises above target the Fed raises interest rates (according to the monetary policy rule, Equation 16.8) and this reduces the GDP gap (according to the IS curve, Equation 16.7). To derive the aggregate demand–inflation curve, we substitute Equation 16.8 into Equation 16.7. That is, we substitute

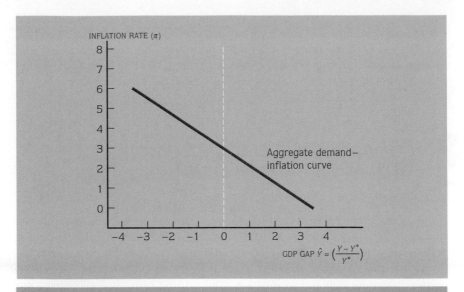

**FIGURE 16.2**  The Aggregate Demand–Inflation Curve

The curve shows a negative relationship between inflation and the GDP gap. When inflation increases, the Fed raises interest rates and this causes real GDP to fall; when inflation declines, the Fed lowers interest rates and this causes real GDP to rise; these are movements along the curve. Changes in the Fed's target rate of inflation or shocks to the IS curve cause the aggregate demand–inflation curve to shift. (See Equation 16.5.)

$$R - \pi - R^f = \beta \hat{Y} + \delta(\pi - \pi^*)$$

into

$$R - \pi - R^* = -\sigma \hat{Y}$$

to get

$$-\sigma \hat{Y} = \beta \hat{Y} + \delta(\pi - \pi^*) + (R^f - R^*)$$

or

$$\hat{Y} = -\frac{\delta}{\beta + \sigma}(\pi - \pi^*) - \frac{R^f - R^*}{\beta + \sigma} \tag{16.9}$$

Equation 16.9 is the aggregate demand–inflation curve in algebraic form; it is a negative relation between the output gap, $\hat{Y}$, and the amount of inflation above target, $\pi - \pi^*$, as shown in Figure 16.2. On the upper left part of the curve, inflation is high and the Fed has contracted the economy; on the lower right, the situation is the opposite. From Equation 16.9, we see that the aggregate demand–inflation curve shifts to the right when the Fed changes its policy rule to a higher target rate of inflation, $\pi^*$.

Now we combine the price adjustment line of Figure 16.1 and the aggregate demand–inflation curve from Figure 16.2 in the same diagram, Figure 16.3. The intersection of the two curves gives the values of the GDP gap and inflation, $\hat{Y}$ and $\pi$. Figure 16.3 describes the operation of the model in a single picture. If there is a shift in either the price adjustment line or the aggregate demand–inflation curve, then the economy will move to a new combination of output and inflation, $\hat{Y}$ and $\pi$.

We use this approach to look at two examples, a boom and an oil price shock. In the examples we start the economy at full employment, with inflation equal to a target of 2 percent and then push the economy away from full employment with a shock.

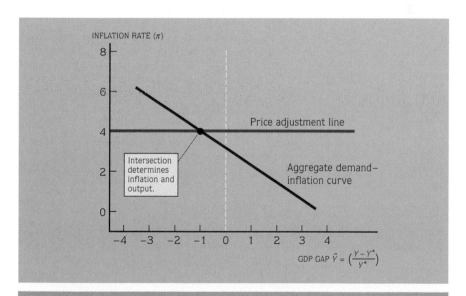

**FIGURE 16.3** Simultaneously Determining Inflation and Output

The four-equation macro model (Equations 16.1 through 16.4) can be represented by these two curves. The solution of the model is found at the combination of inflation and output that is at the intersection of the two curves. When either of the curves shifts, the intersection changes and traces out patterns of inflation and the GDP gap.

## Example 1: A Boom

What happens in the short, medium, and long runs when an outward shift in the aggregate demand–inflation curve sets off a boom? The outward shift could occur because the Fed adopted a higher inflation target or because of a shift in the IS curve, such as permanently higher government spending (note that equation 16.4 shows that a higher $G$ raises $R^*$). At first, higher aggregate demand raises output. But higher output means inflation. In response to the higher inflation, the Fed raises interest rates and GDP falls. Eventually, the economy gets back to equilibrium, with output equal to potential and inflation at a higher level. In the new equilibrium, the only effect of the increase in aggregate demand is to raise the inflation rate. The path of the economy in response to an increase in aggregate demand is shown in Figure 16.4.

The path starts at equilibrium in year 1. There is 2 percent inflation and output is at potential. In year 2, the outward shift in aggregate demand raises output sharply. Because the inflation rate does not respond immediately,

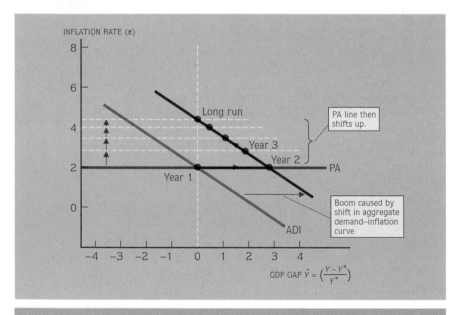

**FIGURE 16.4**  A Boom (Example 1)

The economy starts in equilibrium in year 1, with output equal to potential (zero GDP gap) and 2 percent inflation. In year 2 the aggregate demand–inflation curve shifts outward. Real GDP rises immediately. Inflation then worsens. As inflation rises, aggregate demand falls and output begins to recede toward equilibrium. The GDP gap returns to zero, but the inflation rate is permanently higher.

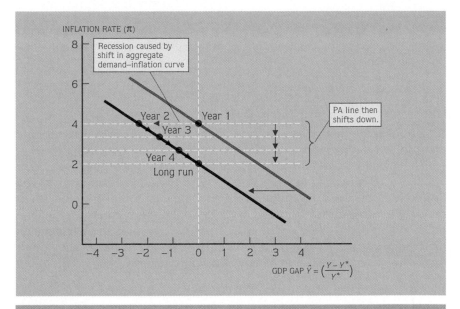

INFLATION RATE ($\pi$)

Recession caused by
shift in aggregate
demand–inflation curve

PA line then
shifts down.

Year 2       Year 1
Year 3
Year 4
Long run

GDP GAP $\hat{Y} = \left(\frac{Y - Y^*}{Y^*}\right)$

**FIGURE 16.5**   Disinflation (Example 2)

Here the Fed reduces the target rate of inflation from 4 percent to 2 percent. In the short run, real
GDP declines below potential GDP and inflation does not change. Eventually inflation declines
toward the new target of 2 percent and the economy returns to potential, with zero GDP gap.

output increases by the full amount of the shift in aggregate demand. For the
next few years, a series of increases in inflation depresses aggregate demand
as the Fed acts to resist the inflation. Inflation gradually stops rising because
output is less and less above potential. In the long run, output returns to its
potential level and inflation settles at its new level.

 If the original source of the boom was an outward shift of the IS curve—
for example, from permanently higher government spending—the Fed will
need to raise the constant $R^f$ in its policy rule, Equation 16.8, in order to
prevent the inflationary boom.

## Example 2: Disinflation

Suppose now that the inflation rate is 4 percent, and the Fed decides that
this is too high. Suppose that the Fed decides to reduce the target rate of
inflation from 4 percent to 2 percent. In this case the aggregate demand–
inflation curve shifts to the left, as shown in Figure 16.5.

 At first, real GDP falls below potential GDP as the Fed raises the interest
rate, but there is little change in inflation. Eventually, however, the rate of

inflation falls, and as it does the Fed reduces the interest rate and the economy recovers gradually back to potential. Observe that this disinflation example has a path for inflation and output that is the mirror image of the
boom in Example 1.

## Examples 1 and 2 Combined: A Boom Followed by a Disinflation

It is useful to combine Examples 1 and 2 into a single scenario. First, suppose
that the Fed starts on an expansionary monetary policy, as in Example 1,
which shifts the aggregate demand–inflation curve to the right, starting a
boom, but then leading to a higher inflation rate. Second, suppose the Fed
decides that this new, higher inflation is too high and reverses itself by shifting back to a lower inflation target, as in Example 2; the aggregate demand–
inflation curve now shifts to the left, starting a recession and eventually a
lower inflation rate.

 This combined scenario is shown in Figure 16.6, where we see a boom

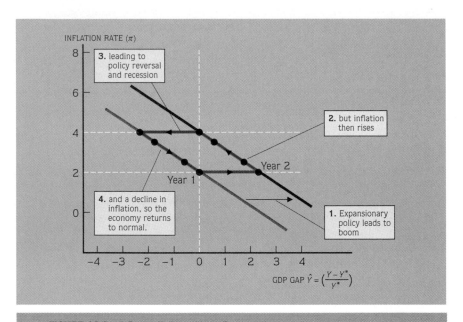

**FIGURE 16.6**   A Boom Followed by a Recession

First the aggregate demand–inflation curve shifts to the right, causing a boom and an eventual rise
in inflation. Then the Fed decides it has let the inflation rate rise too much and engages in a
disinflation; real GDP falls below potential in a recession, but eventually the inflation rate returns to
the 2 percent target.

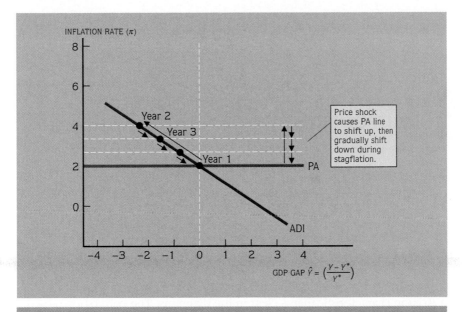

**FIGURE 16.7** An Oil Price Shock (Example 3)

The economy starts at equilibrium in year 1. In year 2, inflation rises because of the higher oil price. In year 3, the GDP gap is negative because inflation is higher. Eventually a recovery takes place because inflation begins to fall. Output returns to potential, with zero GDP gap.

(real GDP above potential GDP) in the economy followed by a period of slack (real GDP below potential GDP). During the boom, inflation is rising, while during the slack period, inflation is falling.

## Example 3: An Oil Price Shock

In the 1970s and in 1990, the U.S. economy was battered by large and sudden increases in oil prices that sent the economy into periods of stagflation. We can trace out the reaction to a onetime price shock $Z$. Suppose $Z$ increases in year 2 and then returns to zero for the indefinite future. The path of inflation and output is shown in Figure 16.7.

In year 2, inflation jumps as a result of the oil price shock. Higher inflation causes the Fed to tighten, and this depresses output; the economy is in a state of stagflation. The recovery from stagflation proceeds as in Figure 16.5. As inflation subsides, aggregate demand begins to recover. The economy gradually returns to potential GDP and to the original 2 percent inflation.

The only effect of the price shock in the long run is a higher price level—there is no effect on real GDP or the rate of inflation.

# 16.4   EXPERIENCE WITH INFLATION AND OUTPUT IN THE UNITED STATES

How well does this model work as an explanation of the record of inflation and output fluctuations in modern economies? Before proceeding with policy analysis in the next chapter, it is important to check whether the theory is consistent with experience.

The inflation-output diagrams of the previous section (such as Figures 16.4, 16.5, and 16.6) provide a way for us to confront the theory with the facts. In the examples we considered, the model economy was displaced from its long-run potential. In each case the return path to potential displays a striking characteristic that is clear in the diagrams: The path (shown by the arrows in the figures) is counterclockwise because the economy tends to return to potential in a counterclockwise fashion. Note in particular how Figure 16.6 shows a complete counterclockwise loop.

Do inflation and output actually behave this way? Since real-world economies are constantly being shocked by many events, it is difficult to separate out isolated episodes like the special shocks in the model economy. Nevertheless, inflation and output fluctuations do display such counterclockwise loops. They are not so smooth as in the model economy, but they are there nonetheless.

In Figure 16.8 we show inflation and GDP gap pairs in the United States for each of the years from 1971 through 1995. Three loops are evident: one from 1971 through 1976, another from 1976 through 1986, and a third from 1987 to 1995. The first loop starts with the monetary-induced boom of 1971–73 and continues with the recession of 1975. The second loop occurred under very similar circumstances: a boom in 1977–78, followed by a subsequent large recession in the early 1980s. Note that the second loop started at a higher rate of inflation because expected inflation was high during that period. The third loop started from the lowest level of inflation in the boom of 1987–88 and had the smallest movement of GDP around potential, as the 1990–91 recession was relatively mild.

Overall, the model is consistent with the dynamic movements of inflation and output. While these graphical tests focusing on loops may appear overly simplistic, they are confirmed by more accurate statistical techniques, and we believe they capture the essence of the theory and the facts.

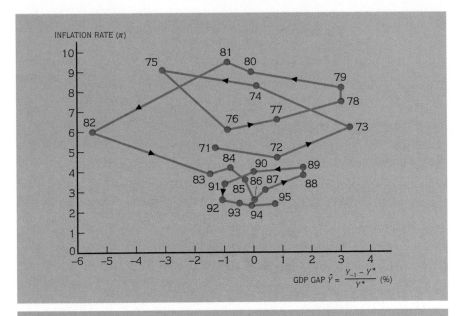

**FIGURE 16.8** Inflation–GDP Gap Loops in the United States, 1971–95

During the 1971–95 period there were three big loops in the United States. The second loop started from a higher rate of inflation than the first and was the largest of the three.
Source: *Economic Report of the President*, 1996, Tables B-2 and B-3.

## REVIEW AND PRACTICE

### Major Points

1. A model of price adjustment must incorporate the response of inflation to excess demand and to expected inflation.

2. Expected inflation has forward-looking features and backward-looking features. Expectations and contracts are both part of the micro underpinnings of the expected inflation term.

3. The model of price adjustment in this chapter is the same as in the model of Chapter 9 except that the coefficients of the model can change.

4. No simple mechanical formula is satisfactory as a model of expected inflation. Any such model would be inconsistent with actual inflation behavior if policy or the economic environment changed.

5. In the long run, unemployment will equal the natural rate regardless of how high inflation is, as long as inflation is steady; this proposition is called the natural-rate property or the accelerationist property.

6. A model that combines aggregate demand with price adjustment implies that inflation and output will fluctuate or spiral as the economy returns to potential after a shock.

7. From the 1970s to the present the United States went through economic fluctuations that displayed such spirals of counterclockwise loops.

## Key Terms and Concepts

| | | |
|---|---|---|
| accelerationist property | indexing | natural-rate property |
| aggregate demand–inflation curve | stagflation | oil price shock |
| | inflation–GDP gap loops | wage-price spiral |
| expected inflation | | |

## Questions for Discussion and Review

1. What are the three elements included in the price adjustment equation?

2. How is expected inflation related to forward-looking behavior? To staggered wage-setting?

3. How can you determine potential output from the price adjustment equation?

4. Why does a one-year stimulus cause inflation to remain higher for many years?

5. Trace out the effects over time of an increase in materials prices, assuming that output is held constant.

6. What happens if policy tries to hold output above the natural rate for an extended period?

7. What are the four relationships that make up a model that shows how the economy fluctuates over time?

8. Explain why the economy approaches equilibrium in a loop in the inflation–real GDP diagram.

## Problems

### NUMERICAL

1. Example 1 of Section 16.3 looked at the inflation effects of a stimulus to output. In this problem we show how such effects vary with different models of inflationary expectations. Consider the following alternatives to Equation 16.2: (i) $\pi^e = .4\pi_{-1} + .2\pi_{-2}$; (ii) $\pi^e = .9\pi_{-1}$; (iii) $\pi^e = .5\pi_{-1} + .5\pi_{-2}$; (iv) $\pi^e = .33\pi_{-1} + .33\pi_{-2} + .33\pi_{-3}$. Assume $f = .25$ and $Z = 0$.
   a. For each of these expressions find the inflation effects of a permanent 3 percent stimulus to output ($\hat{Y} = .03$). Calculate the inflation rate for years 1 through 10.
   b. Estimate the long-run rate of inflation in each case.

c. Do any of the expressions for inflationary expectations given above lead to systematic errors in forecasting inflation? If so, which ones? If not, explain the relationship between expected and actual inflation when fiscal and monetary policy are used to keep output at potential. Is one expression for expected inflation more likely to prevail than another?

2. In this problem we consider the behavior of the economy following a recession. We look at how the recovery is influenced by the model used for inflationary expectations. Suppose the economy starts off with output at potential ($Y = Y^*$) and $\pi = .02$. Aggregate demand is given by Equations 16.7 and 16.8 with $\sigma = .1$, $\beta = .5$, $\delta = .5$, $\pi^* = .02$ and $R^f = .02$; price adjustment is given by Equation 16.2 with $f = .25$. In year 1 the Fed lowers its target inflation rate to zero; this creates a recession.

   a. Calculate the path of inflation and output in years 1 through 6, assuming (i) $\pi^e = .4\pi_{-1} + .2\pi_{-2}$ and (ii) $\pi^e = \pi_{-1}$.

   b. For which model of expectations does the return to potential output take longer?

   c. We assumed here that the value taken by $f$ in the price adjustment equation was the same for both models of inflationary expectations. Explain why in reality the value of $f$ might differ from one model to the other.

3. In this problem we look at how the recovery from an oil price shock is affected by the model used for inflationary expectations. Let the model of the economy and its initial conditions be the same as in Problem 2. In year 1 let $Z = .025$.

   a. Calculate the path of inflation, the price level, and output in years 1 through 6 under each of the models for $\pi^e$ given in Part a of Problem 2.

   b. In each case, how long does it take inflation to first return to its target level ($\pi^*$)? Analyze the factors that cause inflation to fall in each case.

   c. In which case is the fall in output greater? How do you explain this result?

## ANALYTICAL

1. Describe the behavior of investment and interest rates during the boom described in Example 1 of Section 16.3 assuming that the boom was created by an exogenous increase in investment. How do interest rates and investment behave during and following an oil price shock?

2. What is the correlation between output and interest rates implied by the inflation-output loops of Section 16.3? What assumption is made about monetary policy in constructing these loops? Are the predictions of the model consistent with the data presented in Chapter 1?

3. Suppose that the public uses all available information to make unbiased, but not error-free, forecasts of inflation. In that case, we can say that

$$\pi_1 = \pi_t^e + e_t,$$

where $e_t$ is a forecast error whose average value is zero.

   a. What does this relationship between $\pi$ and $\pi^e$ imply about the average value of the output gap? (Hint: Use the price adjustment equation.)

b. Suppose now that $\pi^e$ was formed so that $\pi^e$ always differed from $\pi$ by a constant, $e$. Using the price adjustment equation, show that the accelerationist hypothesis doesn't hold.

## MacroSolve Exercises

1. Using annual data, graph the GDP gap on the horizontal axis against the inflation rate on the vertical axis. You will get inflation-output loops such as those shown in the text. The loop between 1930 and 1935 is clockwise, while most of the postwar loops observed in the data are counterclockwise. (It will be easier to see this if you slow down the display: remember that you can then stop the display by pressing any key.) What might explain the difference in the directions of the loops in the different periods?

2. If prices were very flexible, would you expect to see flatter or steeper inflation-output loops following an increase in demand? Would the same be true for the loops following a price shock?

3. Simulate the "AD/PA, Open Econ, Flexible Exchange Rate" model in response to a 3 percent price shock.

   a. Does output overshoot in its return to potential? In which period does output first return to potential?
   b. Now increase the responsiveness of inflation expectations and repeat the price shock. Are output fluctuations now more or less severe?
   c. Explain both why this change occurs and its policy implications.

4. Using the ADI/PA model, assume that government spending were to be reduced by 50.

   a. Would this action result in inflationary or deflationary pressures? And by how much would inflation change?
   b. Would the resulting inflation output loop circle clockwise or counter-clockwise?

5. Using the ADI/PA model, assume that the Fed changes monetary policy such that it now targets the inflation rate at zero percent.

   a. Compared to the fiscal policy change in Question 4, how does the behavior of the ADI curve and the resulting adjustment process change?
   b. How do the effects of monetary policy change if the Fed were to raise the target real rate of interest rather than lower the target inflation rate?

CHAPTER

17

# Designing and Maintaining a Good Macro Policy

The previous chapter presented a positive theory of economic fluctuations in output and inflation. What are the normative policy implications of this theory? This chapter begins with a review of the principal features. After examining the problem of matching policy instruments to targets and the problem of uncertainty in implementing policy, we go on to apply these principles to macroeconomic policy problems in the United States. In Chapter 18 we extend this analysis to the world economy.

 ## 17.1 GENERAL PRINCIPLES OF MACRO POLICY ANALYSIS

Much of our discussion of the recent developments in macroeconomics—rational expectations, policy rules, theories of wage and price rigidities, the nature of economic fluctuations—has been technical. It is important not to lose sight of the central ideas by focusing too much on the technical details. The central ideas are summarized in the following five propositions.

1. ***When making decisions, people think about the future, and their expectations of the future can be modeled by assuming that they have a sense of economic fluctuations and use their information to make unbiased (but not error-free) forecasts.***

The notion that people make the most of the information available to them when forecasting the future was originally proposed by John Muth in 1960 for use in microeconomic applications, such as the demand and supply for agricultural commodities.[1] Farmers need to predict future prices in order to know how much to grow. Muth suggested that we model a farmer's expectations by simply assuming that the supply-and-demand model is known to the farmer. Robert Lucas applied rational expectations to macroeconomics, which eventually led to his receiving the Nobel Prize.

The idea has proved useful in macroeconomic applications. Many features of economic fluctuations are recurrent from one business cycle to another; there are established statistical regularities. We have documented many of these regularities. Since business cycles have been observed for hundreds of years, it makes sense to assume that people have become familiar with them. Of course, in the face of new, unprecedented events, people will make significant errors in trying to look forward.

2. ***Macroeconomic policy can be usefully described and evaluated as a policy rule, rather than by treating the instruments as exogenous and looking only at onetime changes in them.***

Because people are forward-looking, their expectations of future policy actions affect their current behavior and the state of the economy. Hence, in order to evaluate the effect of policy on the economy, we need to specify not only current policy changes but also future ones. In other words, we need to specify a contingency plan that describes how policy will react to future events. Such a contingency is nothing more than a rule for policy. The contingency plan could be as specific as a constant growth rate rule for the money supply, but more generally it establishes a range of reactions depending on the state of the economy.

The rational expectations approach almost forces a macroeconomic analyst to think about policy as a rule or a strategy. We will see in our policy evaluation study in the latter part of this chapter that it is natural and convenient to specify policy as a rule. Note that the focus on rules does not mean that the effect of one-shot changes in policy should never be calculated; such a calculation can be a useful exercise to help understand the

---

[1]John Muth, "Rational Expectations and the Theory of Price Movements," *Econometrica,* Vol. 29 (1960), pp. 315–335.

workings of the model. We did this in Chapter 9 in our first look at macro policy.

In his famous critique of traditional policy evaluation, Robert Lucas argued in the early 1970s that traditional macro models, like the model of Chapter 8, could give incorrect answers to policy evaluation questions if expectations were forward-looking and there was a change in the policy rule.[2] Since these traditional models were based on adaptive backward-looking expectations, their parameters would change when the policy rule changed. This was the negative part of the critique, and it has clearly made policy analysts wary of using the traditional models. But there was also a positive side. The critique provided a general framework for modifying the traditional models; stipulating policy as a rule, it is possible to calculate by how much the parameters of the traditional models would change. An example of this was discussed in Chapter 16, where we showed how the sensitivity of inflation to recessions would diminish if business cycles became less prolonged—due, perhaps, to a change in policy. Similarly, the model of the expected inflation term in the price adjustment equation (Equation 16.1) would change if monetary policy changed.

Some macroeconomists, such as Christopher Sims of Yale University, have argued that the focus on policy rules is irrelevant.[3] Sims argues that we rarely get big changes in rules anyway, so we might as well use conventional models for policy. Indeed, there is a utopian flavor to the policy rules approach. The search is for big policy reforms that would improve economic welfare over a long period of time. The reforms would probably require changes in the policymaking institutions or the creation of new institutions. Such reforms are by their very nature rare. But they do occur. The creation of the Federal Reserve System in 1913 and the departure from the gold standard and the shift to floating exchange rates in 1971 are examples. These reforms seem to have had substantial effects on the economy. A careful analysis of the effects of future policy reforms therefore seems quite relevant.

3. *In order for a particular policy rule to work well, it is necessary to establish a commitment to that rule.*

The possibility that policymakers will find it tempting to change their plans in the future is a reason for maintaining a commitment to a stated rule. The value of commitment was first pointed out in macroeconomics by Finn

---

[2]Robert E. Lucas, "Econometric Policy Evaluation: A Critique," in Karl Brunner and Allan Meltzer, eds., *The Phillips Curve and Labor Markets,* Carnegie-Rochester Conference Series, Vol. 1 (Amsterdam: North-Holland, 1976), pp. 19–46.

[3]Christopher Sims, "Policy Analysis with Econometric Models," *Brookings Papers on Economic Activity,* Vol. 1 (1982), pp. 107–164.

Kydland of Carnegie-Mellon University and Edward Prescott of the University of Minnesota and by Guillermo Calvo of the University of Maryland.[4]

In attempting to find optimal policies for economies where people are forward-looking, these researchers found that once policymakers began an optimal policy, there was incentive in future periods for them to change the plan—to be inconsistent. Policymakers could make things better by being inconsistent. This was true even if the policymakers had the interests of the public in mind. One example close at hand is that of a teacher giving an examination. It is tempting to call off an examination after the students have studied and learned the material in a course in anticipation of the exam. Then they do not have to sweat through the exam, and the teacher does not have to grade the exam papers. The government's patent laws provide a similar problem of inconsistency. Patent laws confer a temporary monopoly as a reward for inventions. Hence, they spur inventiveness. But the monopoly is undesirable: it would be tempting to remove patents when an invention is completed, so that the new product would be produced and marketed competitively. Another example from the government sphere is the construction of dams for flood plains. The government tells people not to build houses on a dangerous flood plain, because there will be no dams for flood control built. But when people move in anyway, the government finds it desirable to build the flood-control project in order to protect them.

However, by being inconsistent, policymakers are likely to lose credibility; people begin to assume that the policymakers will change the rules and this leads to a new policy plan that is generally inferior to the original policy plan. For example, if the students knew for sure that the exam would be called off, they probably would not study for it. The implication is that, to prevent this inferior outcome, it is better to maintain a firm commitment to a policy rule.

Returning to the patent example, a policymaker who had the discretion to award patents each year would indeed be tempted not to do so. By holding back the patent, the economic inefficiencies of a monopoly would be avoided. Fortunately, reneging on patent promises does not occur in practice because it is so clear that future inventive activity would suffer. Instead, we have patent laws that limit such discretion. The time inconsistency research suggests that discretion should be limited for similar reasons in macroeconomic policy.

---

[4]Finn Kydland and Edward Prescott, "Rules Rather than Discretion: The Inconsistency of Optimal Plans," *Journal of Political Economy,* Vol. 85 (1977), pp. 473–491; and Guillermo Calvo, "On the Time Inconsistency of Optimal Policy in a Monetary Economy," *Econometrica,* Vol. 46 (1979), pp. 1411–1428. Also see Stanley Fischer, "Dynamic Inconsistency, Cooperation, and the Benevolent Dissembling Government," *Journal of Economic Dynamics and Control,* Vol. 2 (1980), pp. 93–107.

It is important to distinguish between **activist policy rules** and **discretionary policy.** Activist policy rules involve *feedback* from the state of the economy to the policy instruments, but the feedback is part of the rule. Sometimes the term **passive policy rule** is used to refer to special rules without feedback, like the fixed growth rate rule for the money supply. An example of an activist policy rule is the monetary policy rule discussed in Chapter 14. Discretionary policy is formulated on a case-by-case and year-by-year basis, with no attempt to commit to or even talk about future policy decisions in advance. Those in favor of discretionary policy disagree with the whole concept of a rules-of-the-game approach, whether the rule is a feedback rule or a fixed setting for the policy instruments. Activist and constant-growth-rate policy rules have much more in common with each other than do activist policy rules and discretionary policy. Both types of policy rules involve commitments and lead to the type of policy analysis suggested by the rational expectations approach.

4. *The economy is basically stable; after a shock it will eventually return to its normal trend paths of output and employment. However, because of rigidities in the economy, this return could be slow.*

The macro models we have looked at are *dynamic* systems continually disturbed by *shocks*. After each shock the economy has a tendency to return to the normal or natural growing level of output and employment, although there may be overshooting or a temporary cumulative movement away from normal. A smooth return is never observed in practice, however, because new shocks are always hitting the system. Since the economy is viewed as always being buffeted by shocks, the equilibrium is really a random or stochastic equilibrium. The combination of the shocks and the dynamics of the model is capable of mimicking the actual behavior of business cycles surprisingly well, as we saw in the previous chapter; the properties of the random equilibrium are much like the actual behavior of business cycles.

The shocks can be due to many factors, but usually have been money shocks, demand shocks, or price shocks. The dynamics are due to many possible rigidities in the economy, but price-wage rigidities and slow adjustment of capital (including inventories) have been the most important empirically.

Combined with these structural rigidities is the supposition that expectations are not restrained by similar rigidities. A shock can change expectations of inflation, exchange rates, and other variables overnight even though there are rigidities that cause the economy to take additional time to adjust fully to the shock. The expectations take account of the structural rigidities since these are part of the model. The combination of rigidities in the economy with perfectly flexible expectations is an essential feature of most rational expectations models.

There has been a tendency to get expectations assumptions mixed up with assumptions about how markets work. Hence, the comment that expectations might be rational in flexible auction markets but not in sticky wage-labor markets is frequently heard. But there is no reason why expectations are not rational in both areas. Labor union staffs may spend more time predicting future wage and price inflation than the staffs of brokerage firms. When workers and firms set wages and prices, they look ahead to the period during which the prices or wages will be in effect—to demand conditions, to the wages of other workers, and so on. This means that expectations of future policy actions affect wage and price decisions, a property that is quite unlike models of wage and price rigidities with purely backward-looking expectations. The view that the economy will eventually return to normal—however slowly—after a shock is also inconsistent with the view that the economy stagnates permanently below potential.

5. *The objective of macroeconomic policy is to keep inflation low and to reduce the size (or the duration) of fluctuations in output, employment, and inflation after shocks hit the economy. The objective is to be achieved over a long period of time, which will in general include a larger number of business cycle experiences. Future business cycle fluctuations are not viewed as less important than the current one.*

By responding to economic shocks in a systematic fashion, economic policy can offset their impact or influence the speed at which the economy returns to normal. It thus can change the size of the fluctuations. How this should be done is a main area of disagreement among proponents of different policy rules.

From a technical standpoint the disagreement can be addressed by inserting alternative policy rules into a rational expectations model and calculating how each rule affects the variability of output, employment, and inflation in the moving equilibrium that describes the business cycle fluctuations. We want to choose a policy that provides the best economic performance. One simple criterion is the minimization of the size of the fluctuations in output and inflation. Since in many models with price and wage rigidities there will be a trade-off between the reduction of output and inflation variability, it will usually be necessary to stipulate a welfare or loss function that reflects certain value judgments. Frequently one policy will so dominate another that the particular welfare weights do not matter much, however. This approach to policy will be used later in this chapter.

The average rate of inflation can obviously be influenced by monetary policy, and it is important to choose a target rate that maximizes economic welfare. The objective of macroeconomic policy is then to keep the inflation rate close to this target rate, that is, to minimize fluctuations around the target, regardless of what the actual value of the target is. Alternatively, if a zero inflation target is appropriate, the objective of policy is to keep inflation near zero.

## 17.2  INSTRUMENTS, TARGETS, AND UNCERTAINTY

Generally stated, the macro policy problem is one of choosing policy rules that describe how the *instruments* of policy should respond to economic conditions in order to improve the performance of the *target* variables. The instruments of macro policy are things like the monetary base and interest rates. The targets of policy are the endogenous economic variables that we care about: inflation, unemployment, capital formation, and economic growth.

To describe our objectives for the target variables, it is useful to define a **social welfare function** that summarizes the costs of having the target variables deviate from their desired levels. Such a social welfare function should reflect the values of individuals in society. If people do not like inflation, then deviations of inflation from zero should register as a loss of welfare in the social welfare function.

We can view the macro policy problem much as any other economic problem: we want to choose policy rules for the instruments to maximize the social welfare function. Analogously, in a consumption problem the consumer chooses a contingency plan for consumption—a decision rule—to maximize utility.

In most macro problems we are faced with the typical economic problem of scarcity. Whenever there is scarcity in economics we are faced with a *trade-off* between competing goals. In fact, scarcity is the most fundamental problem in economics. An important principle of optimal macro policy is that whenever there is a scarcity of instruments—that is, the number of instruments is less than the number of target variables—there is a trade-off between the different target variables. Jan Tinbergen, the Dutch economist who won the Nobel Prize for his work on macro modeling and on techniques for macro policy evaluation, established this important principle relating the number of instruments to the number of targets.[5] As long as the number of instruments is less than the number of targets, society is faced with a cruel choice between meeting one goal or another. The choice between inflation and unemployment is the best example of this type of cruel choice in macroeconomics, and we will consider it in detail later in this chapter. Another

---

[5]Jan Tinbergen, *On the Theory of Economic Policy* (Amsterdam: North-Holland, 1952).

example that we will consider is the trade-off between money-supply instability and interest-rate instability.

It is very important to note that equality between the number of instruments and the number of targets is not sufficient for avoiding a cruel choice. In many cases the different instruments are not independent enough in their effects on the target variables. Again, the best example of this is the inflation-unemployment trade-off. A simple counting of instruments and targets could lead to the following type of incorrect reasoning: "We have two instruments, monetary policy and fiscal policy, and two target variables, inflation and unemployment. Thus there is no cruel trade-off. We can use monetary policy to control inflation and fiscal policy to control unemployment." This reasoning is wrong because it assumes that monetary and fiscal policies affect inflation and output in different and independent ways. In fact, we already know from our macro model that monetary and fiscal policies affect output and inflation in the same way—by shifting the aggregate demand curve. Unless one instrument can directly affect inflation without going through aggregate demand, we are left with a trade-off. For example, if monetary policy had a separate effect on expected inflation or if tax policy could affect price setting, then there would be a separate channel by which one or the other policy could affect inflation.

## Uncertainty and Timing Considerations

In practice, the target-instrument approach described above is too simple. It ignores the inherent uncertainty that exists in our understanding of the economy. If there is uncertainty about the effect of an instrument of policy on the economy, then we must be careful not to exploit that relationship too much. Very active use of an uncertain instrument can be risky. This is one of the central reasons for using less active policies in practice.

When there are many instruments and uncertainty, the theory of economic policy tells us to use a mix of the instruments in a way that minimizes the risk. William Brainard of Yale University showed how the choice of instruments under uncertainty is much like the problem of choosing an optimal portfolio of common stocks.[6] Just as an individual should attempt to diversify a portfolio of stocks—"Don't put all of your eggs in one basket"—policy-makers should diversify their instruments in order to reduce risk.

Another reason why macroeconomic policymaking is difficult is that its benefits do not occur at the same time as its costs. An expansionary monetary or fiscal policy, for example, involves balancing the short-term benefits of a stimulative move against the long-term costs of inflation the move will

---

[6]William Brainard, "Uncertainty and the Effectiveness of Policy," *American Economic Review, Papers and Proceedings,* Vol. 57 (1967), pp. 411–425.

bring. Conversely, the costs of a contractionary policy occur in the short run and the benefits occur later and are perhaps drawn out over many years. We will start with a look at the benefits and costs. Then we will set up a framework within which policymakers can make an intelligent choice between expansion and contraction.

# THE BENEFITS OF FULL EMPLOYMENT AND PRICE STABILITY

Economic analysis deals with trade-offs of many types. For example, consider a consumer who cannot afford an expensive car and an expensive home; to buy a better car, the consumer will have to settle for a more modest home, and vice versa. Micro theory describes the consumer's preferences in terms of indifference curves. The consumer chooses the combination of car and house on the best indifference curve within the consumer's budget. The combination is at a point of tangency of an indifference curve and the line showing all the different combinations of car and house the consumer can afford.

We can look at the nation's choice between employment and price stability in the same way. Preferences give a set of indifference curves. The behavior of the economy, as described by the model of Chapter 16, gives the set of different combinations of employment and price stability that can be achieved. We call the curve showing those combinations the **policy frontier.** The optimal policy is at the point of tangency of an indifference curve and the policy frontier.

The starting point for the analysis is to choose the two axes for the indifference curves and for the policy frontier. One axis has something to do with price stability and the other has something to do with output and employment stability. For inflation, it seems clear that the desirable level is near zero. Large departures above zero have been the big problem in recent decades. Departures below zero were the problem in the depression of the 1930s and in some earlier contractions. There is no good reason to think that the cost of a positive error is any different from the cost of a negative error. In addition, it seems reasonable to suppose that *the marginal cost of an inflation or deflation error rises with the magnitude of the error.* A simple measure of the loss associated with these properties is the **squared error.**

This suggests that a good general summary of the economic loss caused by inflation is the average of the squared deviation of the inflation rate from its target, near zero. We will call this the **inflation loss.** If everything else is held the same, the ideal macro policy will keep the inflation loss at zero. In real life, the inflation rate cannot be kept exactly at zero, and the average inflation loss will be positive.

For the output-employment-unemployment side of the economy, the situation is a little different. For a number of reasons, the *natural* unemployment rate is probably not the *optimal* unemployment rate. Because of factors including taxes and unemployment compensation that make the social cost of unemployment exceed the private cost and because of monopoly power, it is likely that social welfare rises whenever unemployment drops below the natural rate. Thus, if it were feasible, policy should keep the average unemployment rate below the natural rate. But, in Chapter 16, we stressed that macro policy cannot influence the average rate of unemployment or the average GDP gap; it can only influence the fluctuations of unemployment around the natural rate and the GDP gap around zero. Consequently, macro policymakers should do what they can do: limit the fluctuations of output and employment. Based on this logic, we define the **output loss** as the average squared GDP gap.

Social preferences about inflation and output stability can be displayed in a family of indifference curves as shown in Figure 17.1. Note that the indifference curves bend in the opposite direction from the usual ones for the theory of the consumer. Consumer theory deals with things people like. Inflation and output losses are things the public does not like, so the indif-

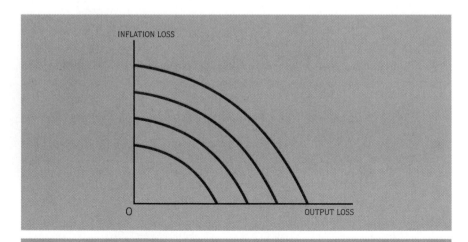

**FIGURE 17.1** Social Preferences about Inflation and Output Losses

Each indifference curve shows the locus of combinations of average inflation loss and average output loss that the public finds equally acceptable. The curve that is farthest from the origin is the worst one. The public prefers curves that are closer to the origin.

ference curves have the opposite curvature. At the upper left end of each curve, the public is willing to trade quite a bit of added output loss to reduce their inflation loss a little from its high level. At the lower end, they will accept only a small added amount of output loss to reduce their inflation loss quite a bit. Curves closer to the origin are socially preferred because they involve lower amounts of both output loss and inflation loss.

## Why Is Inflation Undesirable?

The American public has made it abundantly clear that inflation is unpopular. In 1976 and 1980, two Presidents—Ford and Carter—were denied reelection soon after large bursts of inflation. Stringent anti-inflation policies in the early 1980s seem to have been politically acceptable, even though they brought on a pair of recessions. Whenever inflation rises above 10 percent per year, public opinion polls show that inflation is the number-one economic problem, even when unemployment is high.

Though some specific economic costs of inflation have been identified, it is hard to quantify and assess them. The areas of economic costs include the following:

1. *"Shoe-Leather Costs" of Holding Money.* When inflation is high, currency and non-interest-bearing checking accounts are undesirable because they are constantly declining in purchasing power. People will wear out their shoes making extra trips to the bank to avoid holding much money. These trips involve genuine economic costs, and these costs would be avoided with stable prices. One response to inflation was the development of checking accounts that pay interest closer to market interest rates. This change in banking has reduced the cost of inflation because people do not have to spend so much time and effort transferring money between accounts.

2. *Tax Distortions.* The brackets for the personal income tax are indexed, as we discussed in Chapter 13, and they rise with the consumer price index. But many other parts of the tax system are not indexed; the presumption is that the purchasing power of the dollar is stable from one year to the next. For example, businesses take depreciation deductions that are based on the original dollar cost of plant and equipment investments. When inflation rages, the actual value of these deductions is much less than it should be, thanks to the declining purchasing power of the dollar. But this problem has been offset by speeding up the deductions. Even better, the tax law could be changed so that the deductions automatically rise along with the cost of living.

3. *Unfair Gains and Losses.* When inflation hits, some people gain and some lose. Retired people whose pensions are fixed in dollar terms lose. Home-

owners gain because they can pay off their mortgages in less valuable dollars. In total, losses equal gains. In each transaction set in dollars, when inflation is high, there is somebody who wins and somebody who loses exactly the same amount. The social loss occurs because inflation makes long-term transactions more unreliable. There seems to be no clear tendency for inflation to favor the rich over the poor or the poor over the rich. Gains and losses from inflation are more or less randomly distributed in this respect.

4. *Nonadapting Economic Institutions.* Certain standard economic practices have not adapted readily to inflation, and the public has suffered as a result. The most important is private retirement arrangements. The typical private pension plan pays its retirees a certain number of dollars per month when they retire. The number of dollars is based on their earnings in the last few years of work. In this respect, the pension keeps up with inflation. But once retirement starts, the amount of the pension is fixed in dollars. A pension that starts out at a generous level may dwindle to inadequacy as a result of inflation. One way retirement plans could adapt would be to build in an allowance for, say, 5 percent inflation. Payments would rise by 5 percent every year. They would start at a lower level than they do now, but keep up better with inflation.

Many of these costs are avoidable by apparently simple means. Shoe-leather costs have been cut by permitting banks to pay market interest rates on checking accounts. Changing the tax system to avoid distortions from inflation is not too difficult and would be even easier if some other highly desirable tax reforms were instituted, such as immediate tax write-off for investment instead of depreciation deductions. Gains and losses could be avoided completely by linking payments and receipts to government price indexes, as many businesses do today in their transactions with other businesses. Better pension plans with cost-of-living indexation have been designed and put forward by a number of economists.

The public's negative view of inflation seems to come from sources other than these identifiable economic costs. One is the notion that the dollar is supposed to be a unit of purchasing power just as the yard is a unit of length. If the government decreased the length of the yard randomly by 5 or 10 percent each year, the public would be upset in a way that would also be out of proportion to the technical costs a changing unit of length would impose on us. It is a sign that the government is doing its job when its units of weights, measures, or purchasing power are reliable. Inflation is historically associated with the breakdown of government.

Perhaps another reason some people may be upset about inflation is that they do not take the same broad view as an economist, who sees inflation as a general rise in all prices and dollar incomes. Recall that in a general inflation, wages and prices increase by the same amount. If wages increase less rapidly than prices, then something else in addition to inflation—like a drop in productivity—is affecting the economy. Someone who does not think about the economy in that way will not associate an increase in income with the increase in prices that goes with it. Such a person may imagine that the increase in income would have occurred even without the inflation. In that case, the inflation appears to diminish the purchasing power of the income and so to be a loss. To put it another way, some people may not realize that both their incomes and the prices they pay will not rise as fast under an anti-inflation policy.

## COSTS OF INFLATION

1. There are some specific economic costs of inflation, but they are hard to quantify. These include:
   - Shoe-leather costs of conserving money holdings
   - Distortions because much of the tax system is not indexed
   - Capricious losses suffered by holders of dollar claims, though offset by surprise gains enjoyed by those paying fixed-dollar debts
   - Problems caused by the failure of retirement plans and other institutions to adapt to declining purchasing power
2. People see inflation as a breakdown of the basic government responsibility to provide a stable unit of purchasing power.
3. Some people may not understand the relation between their own incomes and rising prices. To them, higher prices represent diminished real income.

## Costs of Output Loss and Unemployment

There is less mystery about output and unemployment losses, especially on the downside. As we noted in Chapter 10, Section 1, when real GDP falls by a billion dollars, people lose about $400 million immediately in the form of reduced disposable income. Reduced corporate retained earnings account for part of the reduction. The remainder, hundreds of millions of dollars, takes the form of reduced tax revenues for federal, state, and local governments. The public suffers from this reduction as well, in the form of either cuts in government services or future higher taxes.

In addition to the obvious economic costs of lost output, there are other serious costs of a period of low output and high unemployment. Young workers are particularly likely to become unemployed. Many of them are working in low-wage jobs where part of the benefit is the training they are receiving. When they stop work, the loss includes not just what they were producing, which is included in GDP, but also the value of the training, which is not included in GDP. The experience of unemployment itself may have social costs beyond reduced GDP. Unemployed people are more likely to turn to crime or to become physically or mentally ill.

The direct costs of lost GDP are overwhelming. In a typical recession, GDP falls below potential by around 5 percent for about two years. Total lost GDP is about 10 percent of one year's GDP, or almost $800 billion at 1996 levels. There are about 100 million families in the United States, so the loss is about $8,000 per family. Some recessions are much deeper and involve even larger losses.

In order to get a full picture of the net social impact of a recession, however, we have to look at the benefits as well. If workers are able to engage in useful activities other than work in the market, or if they can store up memories of the leisure they enjoy during a recession, then there is an offset to the lost output during a recession. Data do show that people make some good uses of their extra time during recessions. For example, school and college attendance rises in recessions.

Taxes are one important reason to think that the offset is far from complete. Because work in the market is taxed but leisure and most other non-market uses of time are not taxed, there is a bias in the economy against market work. The social value of market work exceeds the worker's private earnings by the amount of payroll and income taxes. Any perturbation in the economy, such as a recession, that moves people from market work to non-market activities has a social cost even if it does not have a private cost.

The other important reason for less than full offset from the value of nonmarket activities is wage rigidity. If employers face a flat labor-supply schedule because contracts and customs require it, but workers actually have steep labor-supply schedules, then workers gain little from the extra time that becomes available during a recession. The marginal value of their time drops sharply in a recession because they quickly use up the backlog of valuable uses of time other than work in the market. With wage rigidity, there is a gap between the social value of work and the value of time to workers. As a result, recessions are socially costly.

Economists have thought less about the costs of episodes when GDP is above potential. The microeconomic argument supporting the idea that the costs are important is the following: The extra work effort needed to push GDP above potential is worth more than the extra GDP. Instead of working as many hours as they do during a boom and consuming and investing the extra output, the public would be better off with less output and more time to spend with their children, on their houses, and in recreation. Again, because of high taxes, the private value of time is well below the social value of work, so there is at least a range where a boom is socially beneficial even though it is privately costly to workers to be working longer hours.

In terms of unemployment, there is little disagreement that the marginal social costs of unemployment are higher at higher rates of unemployment. Remember that it is not the overall level of the marginal social cost that matters, but the extent to which the marginal social cost of unemployment is higher in recessions than in booms. The value of the extra time at home that becomes available with higher unemployment is much lower for people who are already partly idle because of a recession than it is for people who are busy because of a boom. Consequently, keeping the variability of unemployment low is an important social goal.

## COSTS OF OUTPUT FLUCTUATIONS AND UNEMPLOYMENT

1. The marginal social cost of unemployment is higher when unemployment is high.
2. If labor supply is inelastic, the marginal value of time in other uses falls if employment falls, and rises if employment rises above normal.
3. Because of these considerations, the economy is better off with stable output at its full-employment level, as against fluctuating output and employment.

## THE POLICY TRADE-OFF BETWEEN INFLATION AND OUTPUT FLUCTUATIONS

In Chapter 9 we saw that when aggregate demand shifts for some reason not related to macro policy, the shift can be offset through a policy that moves aggregate demand back to its original position. Then output and inflation will be back at their original levels as well. There is no need for aggregate demand shifts to cause either inflation losses or output-unemployment losses. Both can be avoided by a simple reversal of an aggregate demand shift.

Recall the price adjustment equation from Chapter 16 (combine Equations 16.1 and 16.2):

$$\pi = f\hat{Y}_{-1} + \pi_{-1} + Z. \tag{17.1}$$

Here we again use the assumption that the expectations term is simply the lagged value of inflation, $\pi^e = \pi_{-1}$. But recall that alternative models of the expectations term may be more appropriate depending on the type of policy that is used. The last term in Equation 17.1, $Z$, represents price shocks, like increases in the price of oil.

We can characterize the policy alternatives in terms of the slope of the aggregate demand–inflation curve introduced in Chapter 16, which we now write as:

$$\hat{Y} = -g(\pi - \pi^*). \tag{17.2}$$

Compare Equation 17.2 to 16.9 (for simplicity, assume $R^* = R^f$) and note that $g = \delta/(\beta + \sigma)$, so it depends on the policy rule through the response coefficient for output, $\beta$, and for inflation, $\delta$. In words, the output gap is reduced below zero by $g$ percentage points if inflation rises above target by one percentage point. If $g$ is zero, the policy rule keeps output at potential (and unemployment at the natural rate). With $g$ equal to zero, there is no attempt to control inflation. If $g$ is greater than zero, the policy response lowers output and raises unemployment in order to stabilize inflation. The larger $g$ is, the larger is the reduction in output when an inflation shock occurs, as shown in Figure 17.2. The coefficient $g$ measures how accommodative policy is to inflation. For $g = 0$, policy is fully accommodative to inflation. Larger values of $g$ represent less accommodative policies.

We can use the price adjustment equation to find out how much inflation will be reduced by different choices of the response coefficient $g$. If we substitute the ADI curve, Equation 17.2, into the price adjustment equation, we get

$$\pi - \pi^* = (1 - fg)(\pi_{-1} - \pi^*) + Z. \tag{17.3}$$

When $g$ is large, past inflation affects future inflation less, and the effects of a single price shock disappear more quickly. Define $k$ as $1 - fg$. The coefficient $k$ measures how long and how much a price shock affects inflation. If $g$ is zero (a fully accommodative policy), so that $k = 1$, then the price shock permanently raises the inflation rate by $Z$. In this situation the effects of the price shock are never withdrawn from inflation. If inflation was zero before the price shock, it will be permanently above zero after the price shock. If, at the other extreme, $k = 0$, then the effect of the price shock disappears after only one year. If $k$ is in the intermediate range, between 0 and 1, then

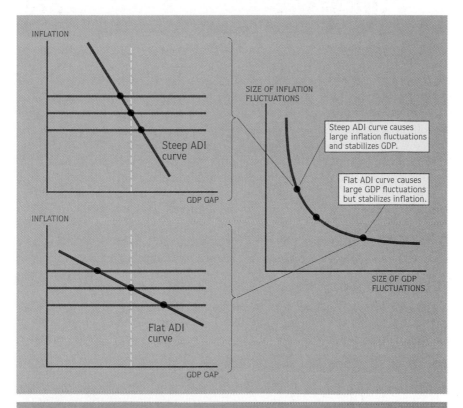

**FIGURE 17.2** Slope of Aggregate Demand–Inflation Curve Represents Different Policies

The slope of the aggregate demand–inflation curve (Equation 17.2) depends on the monetary policy rule. If the Fed raises interest rates sharply when inflation rises above target, for example, then the curve is flatter. A flatter curve results in smaller fluctuations in inflation but larger fluctuations in real GDP and employment as shown in the diagram. A steeper curve due to a more accommodative monetary policy rule would result in larger fluctuations in inflation.

the effect of the price shock *gradually* disappears: excess inflation, $\pi - \pi^*$, is $k$ times the price shock in the year after the shock, $k^2$ times the price shock in the second year, $k^3$ in the third year, and so on, eventually back to zero inflation. For example, if $k$ is .8, target inflation $\pi^*$ is zero, and inflation is initially raised from zero to 10 percent because of the price shock, then inflation is 8 percent in the next year, 6.4 percent in the third year, 5.1 percent in the fourth year, 4.1 percent in the fifth year, and so on, eventually getting to zero inflation.

A policy that aggressively counters price shocks (with $g$ large and $k$ near zero) will result in large fluctuations in output and unemployment. This is clear from Equation 17.2. Suppose that the sensitivity of inflation $f$ to output is .2. Then, to achieve a value of $k$ equal to .8, we set $g$ equal to 1. With these coefficients, suppose that a positive shock initially raises inflation by 10 percent above target. With $g = 1$, according to the ADI curve in Equation 17.2, this will reduce output below potential by 10 percent in the period right after the shock. Eventually output will come back to potential as inflation declines. When $g$ is large, the drop in output is large and, because of Okun's law, the rise in unemployment is large. On the other side, a negative shock that lowers inflation by 10 percent will require output to rise by 10 percentage points above potential if $g$ is 1. According to Okun's law, unemployment falls in this case. A policy that rolls completely with price shocks ($g$ equal to zero) will have a completely stable level of output and employment.

The implications of the choice of the coefficient $k$ for inflation and output losses are shown in Figure 17.3. Because the inflation loss and output loss are related to the squared deviations from normal, the two curves sag as $k$ is raised from zero.

There is another way we can depict the same trade-off. In Figure 17.4, we draw a curve representing the policy frontier in a diagram where average

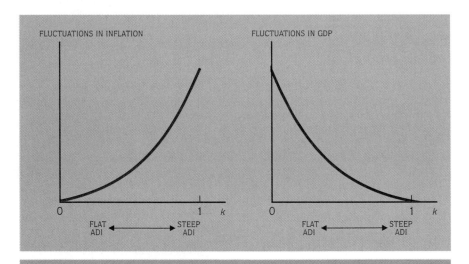

**FIGURE 17.3**   Inflation and Output Losses for Alternative Policies

For $k = 0$, policy changes output enough to make price shocks disappear from inflation after only one year. The average inflation loss is small, but the output loss is substantial. At $k = 1$, policy keeps real GDP equal to potential GDP and lets the price shock influence actual inflation fully.

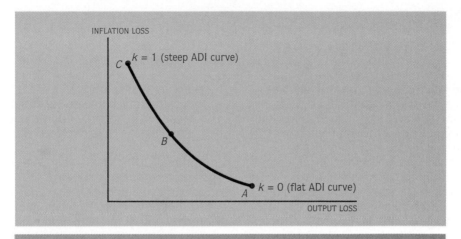

**FIGURE 17.4**  The Policy Frontier for Output and Inflation Losses

Every point on the frontier can be achieved by a policy that lets output respond to inflation. At the upper left is the point of minimal output loss and maximal inflation loss ($k = 1$). At the lower right is the point of low inflation loss and high output loss, corresponding to the other extreme ($k = 0$).

GDP fluctuations are on the horizontal axis and average inflation fluctuations are on the vertical axis. Note how Figure 17.2 demonstrates that the policy rule determines a point on this trade-off.

## THE INFLATION-OUTPUT POLICY FRONTIER

1. The optimal policy response to a shift in aggregate demand is to reverse the shift through a change in aggregate demand policy. In that case, the shift does not cause either an inflation loss or an output loss.
2. A general policy for dealing with price adjustment shocks is to let the actual amount of inflation be a fraction $k$ of the amount of the shock. The rest of the shock is canceled through aggregate demand policy.
3. An aggressive anti-inflation policy has a value of $k$ close to 0.
4. There is a policy frontier defined by different values of $k$ from 0 to 1. The frontier shows the available combinations of average inflation loss and average output loss. The frontier curves toward the origin.

## What Would an Optimal Policy Have Been in 1979 to 1995?

In the late 1970s inflation was high. A large price shock had hit the U.S. economy in 1978 and 1979, when a revolution in Iran overthrew the Shah early in 1979 and Iraq invaded Iran. The result was a substantial fall in world oil production and a dramatic increase in oil prices. The inflation shock was several percentage points and actual inflation rose about 2 percentage points. Then, in 1982, an adverse aggregate demand shock occurred.

With the policy actually pursued, the response of the economy to these two shocks is shown in the diagram. Nominal growth remained at high levels through 1981 and then fell drastically in 1982. A vigorous recovery then followed in 1983 and 1984, with more modest growth in 1985 and 1986. Growth was higher in 1987 to 1990, but fell to a very low level in 1991. Starting in 1992, nominal GDP growth became stable at about 5 percent per year.

What would an optimal policy have looked like? A reasonable set of targets

for nominal GDP starting in 1979 is shown by the black line in the diagram. The decline is in accord with the optimal policy rule of $k = .9$, with underlying real growth.

Nominal GDP growth was 1.6 percentage points above this target in 1979; an error of this magnitude is reasonable and would not have represented a failure of monetary policy. In 1980, nominal growth was almost exactly on target. In 1981, nominal growth was 2.9 percentage points above target. Such an error is outside the bounds of normal variation. In 1982, nominal GDP growth was 4.0 percent below target. Such an excessive contraction is clearly below the targets of the nominal GDP-based policy. Growth in 1983 was close to target, but growth in 1984 again exceeded the target. Some of this later fast growth was appropriate because of the mistake in 1982 which dropped real output too far below potential. The recession in 1991 was the only important departure from target after

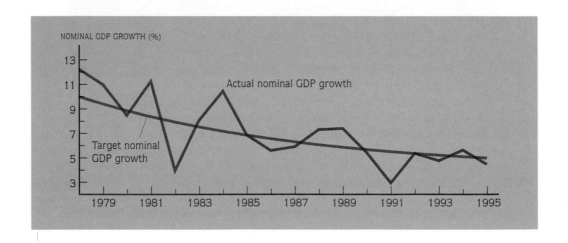

1984—nominal growth was 2.6 percent below target.

Judged by the nominal GDP targets, the policy for handling inflation and the oil price shock in 1979–80 was appropriate. This meant that unemployment jumped and real GDP slumped. But any macro policy to reduce inflation would require some extra unemployment.

On the other hand, nominal GDP growth fell too much in 1982 and 1991. Real output fell, unemployment rose, and

inflation dropped faster than a smooth decline in nominal GDP growth would have implied. Keeping nominal GDP growth at 8 percent for 1982 and 5.5 percent in 1991 would have offset the demand shocks. Except for these departures, policy has followed the path recommended in this box reasonably closely.

Source: *Economic Report of the President,* 1992, Table B-1.

## Finding an Optimal Policy

The policy frontier of Figure 17.4 shows the alternative combinations of inflation and output loss that are available using different policies. The best policy will achieve a compromise between the two types of losses. Remember that the best policy is the one closest to the origin, that is, the one that achieves low values of both output loss and inflation loss. Uncompromising policies are unattractive for two reasons:

1. A policy of strict price stability (a flat ADI curve, with $k = 0$, the point at the lower right-hand end of the policy frontier) involves a large amount of output loss. It takes large movements of output to keep inflation exactly at zero in the face of oil price shocks and other shifts in the process.

2. A policy of strict output stability (a vertical ADI curve, with $k = 1$, the point at the upper left-hand end of the policy frontier) involves a large amount of inflation loss. When an inflationary shock occurs, the policy does nothing to offset the shock. Not only does inflation jump upward in the year of the shock, but inflation is higher in future years as well, because the shock raises expected inflation.

Uncompromising policies are unsuitable because, in both cases, the trade-off set by the policy frontier strongly favors making at least a small compromise. From strict inflation stability, a small move toward the middle of the frontier gives a large payoff in reduced output loss with only a small sacrifice of inflation loss. From strict output stability, a small move to the middle gives a large payoff in reduced inflation loss with only a small sacrifice of output loss.

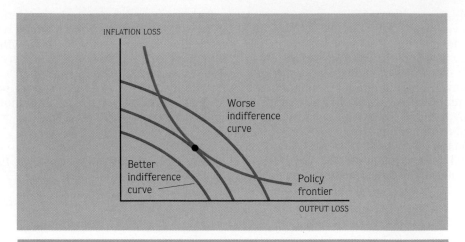

**FIGURE 17.5**    The Optimal Policy for Responding to Price Shocks

The colored line shows the policy frontier. At the upper left are policies that stabilize output at the cost of higher average inflation loss. At the lower right are policies that stabilize inflation at the cost of higher average output loss. The optimal policy is in the middle, where the frontier is tangent to the indifference curve that is closest to the origin of all the indifference curves that touch the policy frontier.

     To find the optimal compromise, we superimpose the policy frontier of Figure 17.4 on the family of social indifference curves from Figure 17.1. The best point on the frontier is the one tangent to the indifference curve closest to the origin, as shown in Figure 17.5.

     In Chapter 16 we looked at the macro performance of the United States from the 1970s to the present in terms of output-inflation loops. In these diagrams inflation is on the vertical axis and output is on the horizontal axis. Recall that the flat loops represented large output fluctuations and small inflation fluctuations, performance corresponding to values of $k$ near zero. The steep (standing-up) loops represented the reverse—large inflation fluctuations and small output fluctuations, performance corresponding to values of $k$ near 1.

## The Message for Policymakers

It is not an easy matter to conduct macro policy in an optimal way. Our analysis has reached two conclusions about the appropriate response to shocks in the economy:

1. If the shock affects only aggregate demand, then a compensating change in aggregate demand policy (monetary or fiscal) will eliminate both the inflation loss and the output loss.

2. If the shock affects the price adjustment schedule, then the best policy divides its effects between reducing inflation and unemployment according to the rule that the amount of inflation in excess of the target declines by a fraction $k$ each year.

In general, to develop policy within our model, the policymaker needs to be able to separate shocks into their aggregate demand and price adjustment components and then figure out the magnitude of the response needed to fully offset the aggregate demand shock and to partially offset the price adjustment shock. Clearly some technical analysis is necessary to do this.

## Nominal GDP Targeting: A Reasonable Way to Express Policy?

There is another, less technical, way to express the optimal policy. The alternative begins with the observation that the optimal policy tends to stabilize nominal GDP. Suppose that in some year a positive aggregate demand shock raises real GDP without much effect on prices. It shows up as above-normal growth of nominal GDP. A rule that calls for steady GDP would automatically offset aggregate demand shocks, just as our optimal policy recommends.

When a positive price-adjustment shock strikes, the optimal policy is to let part of the shock raise prices and part of the shock reduce output and raise unemployment. Keeping nominal GDP on a prescribed growth track does exactly that. Nominal GDP is the product of the price level and real GDP. If the price level jumps, real GDP must fall to keep nominal GDP growth at a prescribed rate. Keeping nominal GDP growth at a prescribed rate is a compromise policy of the type we just derived as optimal.

The degree of compromise in a policy that stabilizes nominal GDP seems to favor unemployment stability over price stability. The value of the coefficient of response $g$ for a nominal GDP policy is 1. As we showed above, when $g = 1$, the value of $k$ is .8 for the numerical example of price adjustment used here. Eighty percent of a price adjustment shock is tolerated as a continued increase in inflation the year after it occurs. Twenty percent is extinguished by permitting output to fall. Thereafter, 20 percent of inflation is offset each year, by keeping output below normal. Stabilizing nominal GDP corresponds to a fairly steep ADI curve.

Suppose the initial inflation impact from a shock is 10 percent. Under the fixed nominal GDP policy, real GDP falls by 10 percent, and inflation in the following year is reduced to 8 percent. From Okun's law, this means that unemployment rises by 3 percent in the first year.

In 1996, President Clinton reappointed Alan Greenspan to a four-year term as chair of the Fed. Greenspan, a Republican, was first appointed by President Reagan. He has a reputation and a track record as an inflation fighter. Did President Clinton bow to Wall Street pressure to make the reappointment, or is there a deeper logic to putting monetary policy into the hands of a proven inflation fighter?

Kenneth Rogoff of the University of California, Berkeley, has shown why rational citizens would want a central banker who was a single-minded enemy of inflation, even when the citizens themselves would try to balance inflation against other evils, such as unemployment.

In many arenas of life, we would benefit today if we could commit to taking some future action. For example, parents want their teenage children to believe that the children will lose their driving privileges if they get into an accident. But after an accident occurs, the parents may decide on a less serious punishment, because they will find it inconvenient if the kids can't drive themselves. The children can figure this out in advance, so the announced policy will not make them more careful drivers. In this situation, the parents would rationally choose an arrangement that took the punishment decision out of their hands—they might buy insurance that required teenagers to stop driving after an accident. The parents would turn the punishment decision over to someone tougher than themselves.

Rogoff says that the citizens choosing a central banker are in the same situation. We would like everyone to know that we have a strong anti-inflation policy. The benefits of having that policy exceed the costs of giving up a more flexible policy

in the future. But if we keep monetary policy in our own hands, nobody will believe it will be a strong anti-inflation policy. Our adoption of an anti-inflation policy will not be credible, and the public will not respond to the policy. The answer is to put monetary policy into the hands of a central banker with a strong willingness to fight inflation.

Notice what it takes to make this argument valid. First, there must be some benefit to the announcement of a tough policy—teenagers drive more carefully, or wage and price increases are moderated. Second, there must be some reason why a simple policy is not credible—parents won't actually follow through, or monetary policy will fail to counter inflation because of concerns about high unemployment. Third, the outsider must be credible. The insurance company must enforce its rule and the tough central banker must stick to the anti-inflation policy—and the relevant actors (teenage drivers or wage-price setters) must believe that this will happen.

Appointing a tough individual to be central banker is not the only answer to the problem of credibility. Another would be to put monetary policy on autopilot. Milton Friedman's proposal that the money supply should grow 3 percent per year no matter what happens is one example. Other, more sophisticated autopilot rules that respond directly to inflation might apply the principle more effectively.

The Rogoff principle explains why countries choose central bankers who are tough on inflation. The United States and many other countries have achieved low rates of inflation. President Clinton's reappointment of Greenspan is completely consistent with the principle.

---

If the public is so opposed to inflation that the optimal value of $k$ is well below .8, then nominal GDP targeting is inappropriate; it gives excessive inflation losses that will not be made up, in the public's view, by the lower unemployment losses it will bring. Or, if the public cares less about inflation, nominal GDP targeting will bring excessive unemployment losses that will not be made up by its favorable influence on inflation losses. In either case it would be possible to change the policy goal and let nominal GDP respond to the price shock. If $k = .8$ is too large, then nominal GDP should be reduced when price shocks occur. If $k = .8$ is too small, then nominal GDP could be allowed to grow a bit when a price shock occurs. But the simplicity of a fixed nominal GDP may outweigh the benefits of modifying the path of nominal GDP in this way.[7]

If nominal GDP targeting were used explicitly in practice, the process might work in the following way: Each year the Fed and the administration would announce a target rate of growth of nominal GDP for the next two or three years. Then each month, as new information became available about the growth of nominal GDP, the Fed and the administration could adjust monetary and fiscal policy to eliminate errors. If growth were above target, for example, the Fed would contract the monetary base. The FOMC would instruct the Fed's traders to sell government securities; this would reduce the monetary base and raise interest rates. If growth were below target, the Fed would expand the monetary base by buying bonds, thus lowering interest rates.

Nominal GDP targeting should not be viewed as an alternative to the optimal policies described above. Rather, it is an easy and convenient way to talk about policy procedures and goals. For example, if there is a policy mistake that brings about a very high unemployment rate, then the optimal policy is to bring the economy back to normal quickly. There is no reason to hold output $Y$ below potential $Y^*$ if inflation is low. Holding nominal GDP growth to a fixed level might not allow the economy to catch up and bring $Y$ back to $Y^*$. But even in this case the policymakers should announce their intentions for nominal GDP growth.

## 17.5   CHANGING THE POLICY FRONTIER

The policy we described in the previous section is optimal in the sense that it tells policymakers how to make the best of a bad situation. But the policy does not make the situation good. We should spend at least as much effort thinking about how to move the policy frontier toward the origin as we spend

---

[7]See Robert E. Hall, "Macroeconomic Policy under Structural Change," in *Industrial Change and Public Policy* (Federal Reserve Bank of Kansas City, 1983), pp. 85–111; and James Tobin, "Commentary," in *Industrial Change and Public Policy,* pp. 113–122. A review of the alternative proposals is found in John B. Taylor, "What Would Nominal GNP Targeting Do to the Business Cycle?" *Carnegie-Rochester Conference Series on Public Policy,* Vol. 22 (1985), pp. 61–84.

thinking about choosing the best point on the frontier. If the frontier were closer to the origin, both inflation loss and unemployment loss would be lower.

## Streamline the Labor Market

The policy frontier lies far from the origin because wages do not respond quickly and vigorously to the situation in the labor market. When an inflation shock strikes, policy has to raise unemployment to get inflation back down. When wages are less responsive, a larger rise in unemployment is necessary. If wages could be made to adjust rapidly to surpluses and shortages of labor, then the average unemployment loss needed to keep inflation loss at a given level would be lower. The policy frontier would be closer to the origin.

Because the reasons for sluggish adjustment of wages are not well understood, it is not obvious what types of new policies would speed up the process. Some proposals include the following.

1. *Facilitate Job Matching.* In the highly decentralized labor market of the United States, employers have trouble getting in touch with potential workers. There may be a large number of qualified people ready to work at a particular job at a low wage. If the employer cannot let them know about the job, it may be necessary to hire a nearby worker at a higher wage. Electronic job listing might make it possible to draw from a larger number of potential workers. Or, if better information was available about the number of qualified job seekers, firms would be in a better position to tailor wage offers to the state of the market. Federal and state employment agencies have tried to perform this service for many years, however, and have found that employers are reluctant to list most types of jobs. Employers fear having to deal with thousands of unqualified applicants if they list jobs publicly. Instead, they seem to prefer to look at smaller numbers of candidates located privately. There seems to be no basis for hoping that the labor market could be significantly improved by expansion of public job listings.

2. *Eliminate Government Price and Wage Fixing.* Hundreds of government regulations have the effect of either fixing prices and wages directly or limiting the flexibility of businesses in setting prices and wages. The Davis-Bacon Act, for example, prevents contractors from cutting construction costs by taking advantage of slack conditions in markets for construction workers. Local governments regulate bus and taxi fares, so they cannot fall to accommodate the increased supply of drivers in times of higher unemployment. Many government regulations that limited price and wage flexibility have been abolished, however. Airlines are now free to adjust fares whenever market conditions change. Most restrictions on profes-

sionals' publicizing their prices have been lifted. Still, the scope for further reform in this area is limited.

3. *Reform Unemployment Compensation.* Unemployed workers receive unemployment benefits for up to six months after a job loss. Consequently, their incentives to look for new work and to accept new jobs at lower wages are reduced. Unemployment compensation serves a vital purpose and should not be abolished, but certain types of reforms could improve incentives without making the unemployed suffer. The most important would be to make employers pay more for benefits whenever possible. If an employer had to pay for benefits during a layoff, the employer might prefer to keep an employee at work and cut prices as necessary to sell output. Publicly financed benefits create incentives to lay off a worker, produce less, and maintain a higher price when demand falls.

## Improve Indexation

In Chapter 16 we saw that when wages are linked directly to prices through cost-of-living indexation, the impact of outside price shocks is amplified; a price shock goes immediately into wages, then into costs, and finally into prices again, all within the same year. Although indexation prevents workers from being left behind by general inflation, it is harmful to the economy when wages rise in response to oil or other outside price shocks.

The ideal method of cost-of-living escalation would omit price increases that arise from imports and other materials costs. Though economists have suggested price indexes that would perform better than the CPI for wage indexation, nobody has started to use them for actual wage-setting. It is not easy to persuade a skeptical employer or labor union that a new price index is superior to the tried and true consumer price index. Proposals to make much smaller changes in the indexes used for wage indexation have encountered stiff resistance. There are no grounds for optimism that wage setters will voluntarily adopt new indexation methods. Nor is it clear that the government can or should try to force changes in this area.

## Avoid Government Price Shocks

Sometimes the government itself creates a shock in the price adjustment process. An important example occurred in Britain in 1979. The government cut income taxes and substituted a value-added tax to raise the same revenue. Because the value-added tax is imposed on firms, it adds to costs just like an increase in the price of a material input. The VAT is much like a sales tax. In terms of the price adjustment model of Chapter 16, the value-added tax adds an inflationary impetus $Z$ in the year that it goes into effect.

## NEW RESEARCH IN PRACTICE
## International Evidence on Inflation and Economic Growth

Is one of the costs of high inflation a lower long-term economic growth rate? If so, then a monetary policy which leads to high inflation could be enormously harmful to the economy, lowering living standards of future generations by huge amounts.

New research in the 1990s has examined the behavior of inflation and economic growth in many countries during the 30-year period from the 1960s through the 1980s. These research studies demonstrate that there is a strong *negative correlation* between inflation and economic growth. That is, countries which have higher inflation rates tend to have lower economic growth rates, and, conversely, countries with lower inflation rates tend to have higher economic growth rates. For example, as the following table shows, Asian countries have had lower inflation rates than countries in Latin America and they have also had higher growth rates. Moreover, as inflation fell in Asia, economic growth rose in the last 30 years. On the other hand, in Latin America there was a rise in inflation from the 1960s to the 1980s which was matched by lower economic growth.

Note that the levels of inflation in this table are quite high, double or even triple digits in most cases. Research has shown that the correlation does not appear to be nearly as strong for countries with low inflation rates; in other words we do not have comparable statistical evidence that an average inflation rate of 2 percent is associated with lower economic growth than an average inflation rate of 0 percent, for example. Nonetheless, the empirical research on inflation and economic growth has had a big impact on policy in practice. In particular, it has shown policymakers in developing countries that if they are interested in raising economic growth, they should develop monetary institutions which prevent high inflation rates such as those in Latin America in the 1970s and 1980s. In fact, in the early 1990s we saw large reductions in inflation in Argentina and Brazil; these decisions were, at least in part, motivated by a desire to improve long-term economic growth.

Of course, the correlation between economic growth and inflation does not necessarily imply that there is a causation between inflation and economic growth. Perhaps both are correlated with a third variable, or perhaps the causation is reversed: lower growth may put pressure on central banks to inflate. Thus it is important to have a theory to help explain the correlation.

Why might higher inflation be associated with lower long-term economic growth? Higher inflation may reduce economic growth by raising uncertainty and thereby reducing incentives to invest in plant and equipment. Higher average inflation usually means a higher *volatility* of inflation, and thus more uncertainty in financial markets (larger fluctuations in interest rates). With larger fluctuations in interest rates, risk premiums are higher and this could discourage investment. If higher inflation does reduce investment, then it could reduce economic growth: lower investment would lead to a lower capital stock and thereby lower productivity.

| | Latin America | | | Asia | | |
|---|---|---|---|---|---|---|
| | 1965–73 | 1973–80 | 1980–90 | 1965–73 | 1973–80 | 1980–90 |
| Inflation rate (% per year) | 10 | 80 | 250 | 12 | 9 | 8 |
| Economic growth (% per year) | 3 | 2 | −1 | 3 | 3½ | 5 |

In Britain, the value-added tax shock and the oil price shock occurred simultaneously. The British economy suffered from more inflation and a larger reduction in output than did the U.S. economy, which suffered only from the oil price shock. If self-inflicted government price shocks can be kept to a minimum, the policy frontier will be closer to the origin.

Avoiding government price shocks need not prevent tax reform or other useful changes in the government's influence on the economy. For example, a value-added tax can be changed in a simple way that does not change its favorable properties as a tax; it could be instituted so that the cost fell on workers rather than on businesses. Then the switch to the tax would not create a price shock. Changes in all types of economic policies need to be designed with the harmful effects of macro price shocks in mind.

## Use Trade Policy

One of the ways the government affects the variability of inflation is through trade policy. Generally, policies that restrict imports will raise inflation when they are imposed and lower inflation when they are removed. As we noted in Chapter 12, different protectionist policies can have very different effects on U.S. prices. Quotas have a strong and immediate effect on prices. Tariffs have a strong effect if they are not absorbed by foreign sellers. For example, an oil tariff would immediately raise the U.S. price of oil, because it is unlikely that the world oil price would fall by much in response to the tariff. On the other hand, a tariff on Japanese cars might well be absorbed by Japanese automakers, just as they absorbed most of the impact of the appreciating yen in 1995.

Each time a protectionist measure is imposed or tightened, it gives a onetime shock to inflation. If a tariff is on a single important product, such as oil, it can cause a perceptible shock to total inflation. An equal but negative shock will occur if the tariff is taken off. Stabilization policy is significantly more difficult and less successful when protectionist measures are imposed and removed in order to satisfy other goals, such as protecting ailing domestic industries, fostering energy conservation, or reducing the trade deficit.

## IMPROVING THE POLICY FRONTIER

1. Policies designed to streamline the labor market could push the inflation-output frontier toward the origin. The same amount of inflation loss would be achieved with less output loss if inflation responded more vigorously to unemployment.

2. Public job placement has not been very successful. Reduced government price and wage fixing might be a small help. Reform in unemployment compensation would also improve the frontier a little.

3. The government should be careful not to create unnecessary price shocks.

## REVIEW AND PRACTICE

### Major Points

1. The general policy implication of recent research in macroeconomics is that policy should be formulated as a rule or contingency plan.

2. Macroeconomic policy can be logically formulated and evaluated using the target and instrument framework. A social welfare function describes the goals of policy.

3. As in other areas of economics, trade-offs are widespread in macroeconomics.

4. Uncertainty in the models leads to less active use of the policy instruments.

5. High inflation is bad because it causes people to hold too little money. It is also difficult to adjust the tax system to be neutral to inflation. Inflation also sometimes brings higher uncertainty, which can interfere with efficient resource allocation. Deflation is undesirable for similar reasons.

6. Variations in unemployment are undesirable because the social costs of periods of high unemployment outweigh the benefits of periods of low unemployment.

7. Indifference curves between inflation loss and unemployment loss curve away from the origin. Higher indifference curves represent poorer macroeconomic performance.

8. Policy rules describe how accommodative the monetary policymakers are to inflation. More accommodative policy results in better output performance, but worse inflation performance.

9. A rule of keeping nominal GDP constant is a good way to characterize an optimal macroeconomic policy.

10. The only type of policy move that could improve both inflation and unemployment performance would be an inward shift of the policy frontier, but unfortunately the prospects seem limited for this type of policy.

### Key Terms and Concepts

| | | |
|---|---|---|
| social welfare function | discretionary policy | social indifference curve |
| model uncertainty | shoe-leather cost of inflation | policy frontier |

| commitment to a policy | marginal social cost of | policy rule |
|---|---|---|
| scarcity of instruments | unemployment | accommodation of inflation |
| policy trade-offs | inflation loss | shock |
| activist policy | output loss | nominal GDP target |

## Questions for Discussion and Review

1. If the purpose of the final exam is to motivate students to study, why will the instructor not cancel the final at the last minute, after all studying has occurred, in order to save everybody's time and effort?

2. What is the basic argument against discretionary policy?

3. If the effect of a policy instrument is uncertain, will policymakers be more or less aggressive in the use of the instrument than they would be under certainty?

4. Give some of the reasons why both inflation and deflation are undesirable.

5. Explain why both high and variable unemployment are undesirable. Why does the policy frontier deal just with the variability and not with the level of unemployment?

6. Explain the consequences for unemployment and inflation if policymakers fully accommodate a price shock. Repeat for zero accommodation and for 50 percent accommodation.

7. Describe the axes of the policy frontier diagram and how to find points on the frontier.

8. How should policymakers choose the best point on the frontier?

9. How much accommodation of price shocks occurs if nominal GDP targets are followed?

10. List some of the proposals that have been made to shift the policy frontier inward.

11. Trace out the effects of a restrictive quota on auto imports.

## Problems

### NUMERICAL

1. Calculate the value of $k$ that corresponds to the policy of keeping nominal GDP at a given level in the year that a price shock occurs. Assume that $f$ equals 1. Assume that the economy starts in equilibrium, with $Y = Y^*$, $\pi^* = 0$, and $\pi = 0$. Then an inflationary shock of 10 percent, $Z = .1$, occurs. Compute the change in inflation, using Equation 17.1. Compute the change in output from Equation 17.2. Show that the percentage change in real GDP plus the percentage change in the price level equals zero, the percentage change in nominal GDP.

2. The economy of Problem 2, Chapter 16, starts at potential ($\hat{Y} = 0$) with the Fed following a policy rule which implies that ($\pi = k\pi_{-1} + Z$). Then it is hit by an inflation shock of $Z = .1$. Policy uses a value of $k$ of .9. Compute the change in the interest rate necessary to achieve the policy. Also compute the changes in $\pi$ and $\hat{Y}$. Repeat the calculations for $k = .1$. Explain the differences.

3. The purpose of this exercise is to illustrate the trade-off between inflation and unemployment. However, we focus on the output gap rather than on unemployment because the two are so closely related due to Okun's law. Assume $\pi^* = 0$. Suppose that the ADI curve

$$\hat{Y} = -g\pi$$

is substituted into the price adjustment equation to get

$$\pi = (1 - .2g)\pi_{-1} + Z.$$

a. Starting from $Y = Y^*$ and $\pi = 0$ (zero percent inflation), use the second equation to calculate the effect on inflation for years 1 through 10 of a price shock $Z = .1$ (a 10 percent shock to the price level). Set $g = .5$.

b. Using the values of inflation that you calculated in Part a, calculate the value of the GDP gap, $\hat{Y}$, for all 10 years using the policy rule.

c. Plot the values of inflation and the output gap for all 10 years on two time series diagrams (put the variable on the vertical axis and the year on the horizontal axis).

d. Plot the values of the output gap and inflation on a diagram with inflation on the vertical axis and the output gap on the horizontal axis (like Figure 17.5).

e. Calculate the average squared loss for inflation. That is, square each value of inflation ($\pi^2$) for all 10 years, sum up the squares, and divide by 10. Calculate the average squared loss for the output gap in the same way. Now repeat the calculations in Parts a through d and the inflation loss and output loss for $g = .1$ and $g = .9$. You should now have three pairs of inflation loss and output loss, one for each of the three values of the policy rule $g$. Plot the three pairs on a diagram with average inflation loss on the vertical axis and average output loss (output gap) on the horizontal axis. Comment on the position of the three points. Is a trade-off between inflation loss and output loss evident? Compare your diagram with that of Figure 17.4. (Note that the output gap loss and the unemployment loss will occupy similar relative positions because of Okun's law.)

4. This exercise shows how a stochastic dynamic model with shocks can lead to business cycle fluctuations. Suppose that the income identity is

$$Y = C + I + G,$$

where $G = 750$. Consumption is equal to

$$C = 80 + .63Y_{-1},$$

and investment is a random variable given by

$$I = 650 + (7 - \text{number from a roll of a pair of dice}) \times 10.$$

   a. Roll a pair of dice 20 times, and record the number for each roll. Use the investment function to calculate investment for each roll. This gives 20 years of stochastic investment. Investment in year 1 is the first roll and investment in year 20 is the last roll. Plot the values of investment on a time series chart with investment on the vertical axis and the year on the horizontal axis. The values should look random, with investment fluctuating around 650.

   b. Now use the values of investment for the 20 years to calculate income $Y$. Substitute the consumption function into the income identity. Start with $Y_{-1}$ equal to 4,000 and with investment equal to the value that you calculated for year 1. Then calculate the second year's income by substituting in income for the first year for $Y_{-1}$ and investment in the second year. Do the same thing for the third year and so on through year 20.

   c. Plot the resulting values of income $Y$ for the 20 years, with the year on the horizontal axis. The average value should be near 4,000, but you should see some prolonged fluctuations around this average value that look like business cycles. Compare the prolonged fluctuations of $Y$ with the random but less prolonged fluctuations of investment $I$. Calculate the average time between peaks for each series. Unless your dice are loaded, the average time between peaks for income will be longer than that for investment. Try to explain why.

5. Suppose that price adjustment and inflationary expectations are given by Equations 16.1 and 16.2, respectively. Policy is given by Equation 17.2 with $g = 0$. Initially there is an oil price shock of 2.5 percent ($Z = .025$).

   a. Calculate inflation and expected inflation over time. Are expectations rational?

   b. Is the monetary authority using a policy rule? Explain your answer.

## ANALYTICAL

1. Derive the aggregate demand–inflation schedule for the case where the Fed uses the example policy rule of Chapter 16.

2. Given the discussion of optimal policy in this chapter, comment on the validity of the criticism that the Fed was too tight in 1979 and 1990.

3. In Chapter 14 we showed how monetary policy affects the economy with a lag. What are the implications of these lags for our suggestions about optimal policy in this chapter? What do lags in the effect of money imply for nominal GDP targeting?

4. Compare a policy of fixing the money stock (as described in Chapter 14) to a policy of fixing the interest rate. Prepare a brief argument in favor of each type of targeting; list advantages and disadvantages.

5. Using the IS-LM method, show what the Fed must do to the money supply to reduce output by a certain percentage when there is a price shock. Could the same actions be undertaken by fiscal policy? Why might a mix of monetary and fiscal policies be used to reduce output after a price shock?

6. Suppose that in response to a large and unexpected oil price shock the Fed acts to keep output at potential. Inflationary expectations are given by the expression $\pi^e = .9\pi_{-1}$. Prices are sticky and price adjustment is given by an equation like

Equation 16.1. The changes in the money stock, prices, and output for the first four years are given below.

| Year | %ΔM | %ΔP | %ΔY |
|------|-----|-----|-----|
| 1 | 10 | 10 | 0 |
| 2 | 9 | 9 | 0 |
| 3 | 8.1 | 8.1 | 0 |
| 4 | 7.3 | 7.3 | 0 |

a. How large was the oil price shock?

b. An economist writing for a popular newsweekly comments: "The Fed is up to its old tricks again, fueling inflation with money-stock growth." The economist goes on to note that every time the Fed increases the money supply by $x$ percent it leads to an increase in prices of $x$ percent, just as predicted by the classical model. Is this economist right; that is, has inflation over the last four years been caused by increases in the money stock?

c. The economist finishes with an admonition to the Fed to stick to a constant money stock rule. This, the economist asserts, will give us noninflationary full employment. If the Fed had held the money stock constant over the last four years, would output have remained constant? Diagram the path the economy would have followed using an output-inflation loop.

7. Suppose that as a result of the Fed's policy rule, inflation is given by Equation 17.3, where the parameter $k$ lies between 0 and 1. Sketch the output-inflation loop for the case of an oil price shock. Is there overshooting?

## MacroSolve Exercises

1. *Policy Decisions 2001.* You have been hired to work for the President's Council of Economic Advisers. After two days on the job there is a major increase in the price of oil because of a crisis in the Middle East. You are asked to provide answers to a series of questions. Suppose you feel that a reasonable welfare function is the sum over five years of the square of the inflation rate and the square of the GDP gap (the percentage deviation of real GDP from potential GDP). Use the "ADI/PA, Open Econ" model. Assume that there is a price shock of 10 percent.

a. What happens if neither the monetary policy rule nor government spending is changed? What is the value of your welfare function?

b. What happens if the inflation response coefficient ($\delta$) in the policy rule is cut in half? What is the value of the welfare function now? By this criterion, is the economy better or worse off after this policy of accommodation?

c. What happens if, instead, the government follows an extinguishing policy of doubling the size of $\delta$ in the policy rule? Is this policy preferred by the welfare criterion to the policy of accommodation?

2. An alternative index of welfare that is often discussed during presidential elections is the so-called misery index, the sum of the inflation rate and the unem-

ployment rate. Recall that the unemployment rate is related to the GDP gap by Okun's law (Chapter 3). If the natural unemployment rate is 6 percent, then the unemployment rate is generated by the following equation:

$$U = 6 - (\text{GDP gap} \div 3).$$

Use this equation to calculate the misery index corresponding to the situations in Parts a, b, and c of Question 1. Comment on the differences between the relative desirability of the alternative policies between the two welfare functions.

3. Balancing the federal budget has received significant attention. Using both methods of measuring welfare losses as defined in Questions 1 and 2, and the "ADI/ PA, Open, Nom. Flex. Ex. Rate" model, evaluate the following two budget balancing choices:

   i. Cut government spending by the amount of the deficit in period 0.
   ii. Raise taxes enough to balance the budget in the same number of fiscal periods. Comment on the preferability of the two policies both based on each welfare measure and overall.

4. Suppose monetary authorities were sympathetic to having a balanced budget and chose to "ease the pain" as much as possible. Using the "ADI/PA, Open, Nom. Flex. Ex. Rate" model once again, determine to what extent monetary authorities can offset the effects of balancing the budget as described in Question 3. (Hint: Using multiplier analysis will greatly speed this process.)

5. Using the MacroSolve models and scenarios developed in Questions 1 and 3, comment on the qualitative effects of negative disturbances to both the supply and demand sides of the economy when the economy simultaneously, whether naturally or as a result of policy, experiences high potential GDP growth. Begin your analysis by letting potential GDP grow by 10 percent and then resimulating the disturbances.

CHAPTER

18

# The World Economy

We saw in Chapter 12 that changes in U.S. macroeconomic policy can have significant effects on foreign trade and on the exchange rate. An expansionary fiscal policy, for example, increases demand for imports from abroad and thereby increases aggregate demand in other countries as well as in the United States. An expansionary fiscal policy also raises interest rates in the United States, and this causes the dollar to appreciate. An appreciated dollar reduces demand for U.S. exports and induces U.S. consumers and firms to import goods from abroad, rather than purchase goods produced at home. This further stimulates aggregate demand in other countries, while it reduces the stimulus to the U.S. economy. Hence, an expansionary fiscal policy crowds out spending not only in interest-sensitive capital goods industries, but also in export industries and in import-competing industries.

This chapter extends our analysis of international macroeconomic issues in a number of ways. First, we look at the international monetary and financial system from a world perspective rather than just considering the role of the United States in the system. In addition to describing the system as it exists in the 1990s, we describe the history of the system. Then we examine how national macroeconomic policy operates within the modern world economy and especially how concern about exchange rates affects policy. Next we consider the worldwide credit market and international capital-trade flows. We consider policies that try to influence these flows by changing saving and investment, on the one hand, or imports and exports on the other hand. Finally, we study the idea of monetary union, the ultimate stopping point of moves toward fixed exchange rates. Monetary union is a major issue in Europe today, just as it was among the 13 colonies after the American Revolution.

# THE INTERNATIONAL FINANCIAL AND MONETARY SYSTEM

Within the United States, the financial and monetary system has a seamless quality. It is almost as easy to make a payment or borrow three thousand miles away, over many state borders, as it is in your own state or city. The world economy is not as seamless. With relatively minor exceptions, U.S. currency cannot be spent directly in other countries. Borrowing in another country is possible only for larger corporations and then only in a few countries with advanced, open capital markets. In some countries, such as the People's Republic of China, there are detailed controls on the movement of currency and securities across the border in both directions. In many countries, the government tries to push up the price at which foreigners can trade dollars and other currencies for the domestic currency. The result is a black market or a curb market where the traveler gets a better deal but may run into trouble with the law. Currency black markets flourished in the former Soviet Union as law enforcement weakened, but artificially high exchange rates were maintained for the ruble.

There is a strong trend toward making the world economy more integrated. For example, the nations of western Europe are almost completely integrating their financial markets, so that it is as easy for a European business to borrow or lend in another European country as it is for an American business to borrow or lend in another state. Some of the nations are planning to use a single monetary unit, which will put them close to the United States in monetary integration as well. At the same time, there will be a continuing trend toward free movement of currency and financial securities across the borders of countries that have previously controlled those flows.

In the 1990s, the world financial and monetary system can be summarized in the following way: There are economies with sophisticated, integrated financial markets—such as the United States, Japan, Germany, and Britain. These countries have large, active markets in stocks, bonds, options, and other financial instruments. They permit foreigners to trade in their markets on essentially an equal footing with their own citizens, and they do not interfere with their citizens' transactions in foreign markets. There are no inhibitions to completely free markets in their currencies and central bank reserves. Holders of checking accounts in any of the four countries can move central bank reserves from one country to another by writing checks, just as account holders in the United States can move them from one bank to another. The four currencies (dollar, yen, deutsche mark, and pound) exchange for each other at rates set in extremely fluid, free markets.

Although the four major governments do not control the financial markets directly, the governments influence the behavior of the markets by trading. The four central banks (the Federal Reserve, the Bank of Japan, the Bundesbank, and the Bank of England) hold large portfolios of short-term government securities. Each bank usually has large holdings of securities issued by each of the four major governments. There are two basic dimensions of central bank policy. One is standard monetary policy, as we discussed in Chapter 14. If the Bundesbank buys more German government securities and expands its reserves correspondingly, that is an expansionary move that lowers the German interest rate and stimulates the German economy. The second dimension is the split of the central bank's portfolio between domestic and foreign securities. The Bank of Japan could sell Japanese government securities and use the proceeds to buy U.S. Treasury bills, for example. This move is called a **foreign exchange market intervention** and is often called "selling yen and buying dollars." However, a more detailed description is "selling yen-denominated securities and buying dollar-denominated securities." The effect of the intervention is to raise the exchange rate of the dollar relative to the yen. The magnitude of the exchange-rate effect per billion dollars of intervention may be very small because the securities markets where the intervention occurs are enormous.

Some of these countries with sophisticated financial markets have chosen to run their central bank policies with the single-minded effect of keeping their exchange rate at a constant level. Most European countries keep their currencies at fixed values relative to the deutsche mark. Other countries—such as Canada—let their exchange rates fluctuate over time.

A number of nations still maintain some degree of insulation from the world financial and monetary system. The most common form of separation is controls on the movement of capital. The governments of these countries require permits for financial transactions across their borders. Often the intention is to trap economic activity within the country's borders. Other times it is to limit foreign entrepreneurs from undertaking profitable activities that might otherwise go to citizens. The People's Republic of China, for example, limits outsiders to less than a 50 percent interest in most investments. Controls on the movement of goods are also common. Many countries require permits for some or all types of imports. Finally, some countries try to suppress free-market transactions in their currencies. These currencies are **inconvertible,** meaning that they cannot be bought and sold in open markets.

All around the world there is a powerful trend toward reducing restrictions on financial markets. The specific steps that a country needs to take to free up its financial markets and thereby join the world financial and monetary system are as follows:

1. *Open up currency transactions.* Permit anyone inside or outside the country to exchange the country's currency for any other currency at a market-determined price.
2. *Open up capital movements.* Permit anyone in the country to purchase stocks, bonds, or other financial instruments from other countries or to raise funds by selling instruments in other markets. Permit foreigners to buy or sell securities in the country's markets and to borrow or lend to businesses or individuals.
3. *Open up movements of goods.* Permit anyone in the country to buy goods and services anywhere else in the world and permit foreigners to buy and sell goods and services in the country.

It is worth noting that the list requires new freedoms, not new government institutions. It is not important that a country have a central bank operating on the same principles as the Federal Reserve Bank. A country need not accumulate foreign reserves (foreign securities owned by the central bank) in order to function within the world system. But all the major players in the current world system have conventional central banks.

## How a Central Bank Carries Out Its Exchange-Rate Policy

Central banks buy and sell government securities in order to affect exchange rates, interest rates, and ultimately the domestic price level. In Chapter 14 we studied the way that the Fed sets the monetary base in the United States. Central banks in other countries operate in almost exactly the same way. The only important difference across countries in central banking is that not all countries have reserve requirements. But all central banks issue reserves as well as currency. Here we will extend the discussion of the central bank to consider foreign reserves as well as domestic assets.

Table 18.1 shows the balance sheet of a central bank. On the asset side of the balance sheet are securities that the central bank has purchased. A similar balance sheet for the Fed was presented in Chapter 14. Here, there are two types of securities: domestic and foreign. Domestic securities are denominated in domestic currency; these may be government bonds or even loans to private firms. The value of domestic securities held by a central bank is frequently called **domestic credit.** Domestic credit is the total credit that the central bank has extended to the home economy, whether to the gov-

**TABLE 18.1**    Balance Sheet of a Central Bank
with Foreign Reserves

| Assets | Liabilities |
| --- | --- |
| Domestic credit | Currency |
| Foreign reserves | Bank reserves |

ernment or to the private sector. Foreign securities are denominated in foreign currency. Most frequently these are bonds issued by foreign governments. Foreign securities are **foreign reserves.**

Recall that the monetary base is defined as currency plus bank reserves. Because assets must equal liabilities, we know that domestic credit plus foreign credit equals the monetary base. That is,

$$\text{Monetary base} = \text{Domestic credit} + \text{Foreign reserves}. \quad (18.1)$$

Suppose that the central bank wants to increase the money supply in order to stimulate the economy. It purchases government bonds in the open market—an open-market purchase; this causes domestic credit to rise. This means that the monetary base and the money supply will tend to increase. The increase in the money supply will lower the interest rate. Capital will flow out of the country, and the currency will start to depreciate as soon as the interest rate begins to fall below the world interest rate.

What if the central bank wants to prevent depreciation? As foreign-denominated bonds begin to look more attractive relative to domestic bonds, the central bank must provide the increased demand for foreign exchange by selling foreign reserves in order to prevent the exchange rate from depreciating. It does this by entering the foreign exchange market and selling its foreign reserves for domestic currency. Foreign reserves decrease. The decrease in foreign reserves lowers the monetary base and offsets the previous effect of the open-market operation. In fact, since the interest rate does not fall, we know that the decrease in foreign reserves must be exactly equal to the increase in domestic credit. This keeps the money supply from increasing.

In the case of an open-market sale, the same channels keep the money supply from falling. The upward pressure on interest rates leads the central bank to buy foreign reserves; this increases the money supply. If the bank wants to maintain the exchange rate at parity, it cannot change the money supply. Monetary policy cannot be used both for domestic purposes and to stabilize the exchange rate.

Now suppose that there is an expansionary fiscal policy—an increase in government spending. This increase in government spending does not increase the interest rate if the central bank is fixing the exchange rate, because the money supply automatically increases.

## Sterilized Intervention

A central bank can offset a potential depreciation of its currency by selling foreign reserves. Then the money supply contracts, the interest rate rises, and the potential depreciation is offset. However, it is possible for the central bank to sell foreign reserves and buy domestic credit at the same time in the same amount. Such a move is called a **sterilized foreign exchange intervention.** From Table 18.1, it is apparent that a sterilized intervention has no effect on the assets of the central bank. Thus it has no effect on the monetary base and no effect on the domestic economy.

Under modern conditions with highly integrated capital markets, a sterilized intervention is unlikely to have much effect. A central bank would have to sell a huge volume of foreign reserves to defend its currency against a threatened depreciation. Its ability to make such a move is limited by its stock of foreign reserves. After exhausting its stock, the bank would have to revert to normal monetary contraction.

## Capital or Exchange Controls

Capital controls, such as restrictions on the amount of foreign currency that domestic residents can purchase, would permit the domestic interest rate to be different from the world rate. In fact, capital controls are still being used in many small countries for exactly this reason. Although they enable monetary policy to be more effective, capital controls have the disadvantage that they reduce the efficiency of international capital markets. Economic efficiency requires that different types of capital be allocated according to their after-tax rate of return. There are already many taxes in the world that distort the allocation of capital, so more taxes would distort the allocation even further.

### EXCHANGE-RATE POLICY

1. With high capital mobility and no expected change in the exchange rate, the domestic interest rate will be the same as the world interest rate.
2. Under fixed rates, the central bank must act to keep the domestic interest rate equal to the world rate.

**3.** Fixed exchange rates can also be achieved with capital controls, but capital controls interfere with the efficient allocation of capital.

# 18.2   HISTORY OF THE WORLD FINANCIAL AND MONETARY SYSTEM

Until early in the 20th century, almost all countries defined their monetary units in terms of gold or silver. Among all the countries on the gold standard, there was no room for variation in exchange rates. The dollar and the pound had a relative value of about $5 per pound because the pound was defined as five times as much gold as the dollar. Under the gold standard, convertibility was not an issue. Further, the prevailing notions of the role of government in the 19th century limited government restrictions on flows of capital and goods. In particular, very large flows of capital from Britain to the United States and other rapidly growing countries helped speed the process of economic development.

After World War I and the Great Depression in the 1930s, currencies began to lose their connection with gold. Even though the United States did not formally leave the gold standard until 1971, the Federal Reserve stopped redeeming dollar bills for gold in 1933. Similar changes occurred in other countries. Ever since the 1930s, each country's monetary unit has been defined as its paper currency or reserves, not gold or silver. The type of monetary system we described in Chapter 14 has been almost universal. As a result, there has been no automatic determination of exchange rates as there was under the gold standard.

Near the end of World War II, in 1944, representatives of major economies (including John Maynard Keynes for Britain) met in Bretton Woods, New Hampshire, to design a new world financial and monetary system to replace the gold standard. Because large fluctuations in exchange rates in the 1920s and 1930s seemed to be undesirable in contrast to the fixed rates guaranteed under the gold standard, the Bretton Woods System proposed to keep exchange rates almost constant. The dollar was to be the reference point of the system. Other countries adopted dollar values for their currencies (called **par values**), such as $2.80 per British pound. Each central bank agreed to keep its own currency within plus or minus 1 percent of the par value.

Under the Bretton Woods System, central banks held substantial amounts of dollar securities, mostly U.S. Treasury bills. When a country's currency rose a little above par, its central bank would purchase dollar securities and sell securities denominated in its own currency and thus depress the value of its own currency. When the currency dropped a little below par, the bank would sell dollar securities and buy securities in its own currency. In addition, the central bank might tighten its overall monetary policy by reducing its total holdings of securities (an open-market operation, as we described in detail in Chapter 14).

The dollar securities of foreign central banks under the Bretton Woods System constituted their foreign *reserves*. When a central bank was preventing an appreciation of its currency by purchasing dollar securities, there was a *reserve inflow*. This was generally considered a favorable sign for that economy. When the central bank was defending its currency by selling dollar securities, there was a *reserve outflow*. A reserve outflow could last only as long as the central bank had a stock of reserves of dollar securities. After the stock ran out, the bank would have to turn to other restrictive measures, or cease its policy of stabilizing the exchange rate. Reserve outflows were a matter of great publicity and concern under the Bretton Woods System.

The Bretton Woods System had a built-in instability that ultimately led to its collapse. Its architects did not completely eliminate the possibility of changes in par values. Once a central bank ran out of dollar securities, it would defend its own currency through monetary contraction or it could **devalue**—reduce the par value of its currency. Monetary contraction is a painful process with adverse political consequences most of the time. But if traders in the exchange market perceive that a devaluation is likely, they push down the market rate immediately. The result is an exchange-rate crisis. The British pound went through a crisis in 1967. The market perceived that British monetary policy was letting the purchasing power of the pound drop below its earlier relation to the dollar and that a reversal of policy was politically unlikely under a Labour government. The Bank of England sold all its dollar securities and borrowed extensively in order to sell even more. But the market saw that the par value of the pound of $2.80 exceeded the value that monetary policy would achieve. Traders started selling pound securities and buying dollar and other securities. The Bank of England lacked the power to keep the exchange rate at par. Finally, in November 1967, the British government validated the traders' judgment by lowering the par value to $2.40.

A second problem with the Bretton Woods System was its vulnerability to mistakes in U.S. monetary policy. In order to maintain fixed exchange rates, other countries had to keep their inflation rates in line with the U.S. inflation rate. High U.S. inflation in the late 1960s made it difficult for most other countries in the system to keep their currencies from rising above par. They bought huge volumes of U.S. government securities to keep their currencies down, but, as in the pound sterling crisis, this type of intervention was not enough. Either the other countries had to expand their monetary policies and match U.S. inflation, or they had to revalue their currencies.

## The Devaluation of the Dollar and the Collapse of Bretton Woods

The Bretton Woods System finally broke down in the early 1970s. On August 15, 1971, the Nixon administration launched a series of moves that effectively ended the system. First, the United States ended its commitment to sell gold to other governments for $35 per ounce. Though few governments had used their right to buy gold at this price, the U.S. move made it clear that the United States was not prepared to make a permanent commitment to a fixed purchasing power for the dollar. Second, the United States used the club of a special tariff to force other countries to revalue their currencies against the dollar. The general revaluation of other currencies was equivalent to a dollar devaluation.

The system continued to evolve after 1971. In 1973–74 the price of oil increased fourfold and inflation accelerated. The acceleration was worse for some countries than for others, as shown in Figure 18.1. With widely different

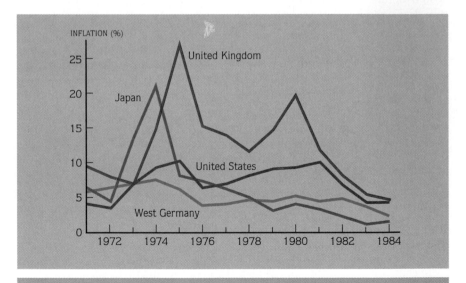

**FIGURE 18.1**   The Great Inflation of the 1970s

The inflation rate increased in most countries in the 1970s. The increase was larger in Japan and the United Kingdom than in the United States and West Germany. The timing of the increase was also different in different countries.
Source: *International Financial Statistics Yearbook*, International Monetary Fund, 1991, various tables.

inflation rates in different countries, the 1971 parities were soon abandoned as countries found it increasingly difficult to maintain them. The 1974–75 recession, which hit all countries, put additional pressure on existing parities.

The desire of different countries to choose their own macroeconomic policies in response to the 1974–75 recession meant that exchange rates would have to shift further. Eventually most currencies began to float with no set parities, although there were considerable interventions aimed at preventing large movements. The world had emerged from the 1973–74 inflation and the 1974–75 recession with an essentially floating exchange-rate system.

## Exchange-Rate Policies Today

The United States does not completely refrain from exchange market intervention. The Federal Reserve Board and the U.S. Treasury are jointly responsible for U.S. exchange-rate policy. The Fed has complete control over the size of its portfolio and therefore the size of the monetary base, but the Treasury can order the Fed to exchange dollar-denominated securities for securities of other governments. Though concerns about the value of the dollar in relation to other currencies have been an influence on both dimensions of central bank policy, the United States has not had a systematic exchange rate policy. It has permitted the dollar to float in relation to other currencies, with occasional interventions when the dollar has reached extreme highs or lows. In 1985, when the dollar was extraordinarily high, the United States, Germany, Japan, Britain, and France agreed to intervene to bring the dollar down. Subsequently, the dollar fell by a great deal, more than 50 percent relative to the yen. There have been sporadic interventions to counteract large movements in the value of the dollar in both directions since 1985, but the United States has had far from stable exchange rates.

Japan is the other major economy that has not made any specific policy commitment with respect to exchange rates. It permits substantial fluctuations in the value of its currency relative to the dollar and other major currencies, but it considers exchange rates when making central bank policy.

Some of the European countries have tried to limit exchange-rate fluctuations among themselves by maintaining stable exchange rates with the deutsche mark. The Bundesbank has followed policies that keep the purchasing power of the DM stable.

Some smaller countries, such as Canada, the Philippines, and Uruguay, have independent monetary policies and floating exchange rates. Again, exchange rates influence policy, but there is no commitment to keeping exchange-rate fluctuations within a particular band around any other currency. Many smaller countries subordinate monetary policy by using it to achieve a fixed or gradually changing exchange rate relative to the dollar or the French franc or to a package of currencies.

## THE INTERNATIONAL MONETARY SYSTEM

1. From the late 1940s to the early 1970s, the major economies operated under the Bretton Woods System, with fixed exchange rates. Each central bank aimed to keep the value of its currency within a narrow band around its dollar exchange rate.
2. When inflation rates vary across countries, a system of fixed exchange rates ultimately breaks down. The Bretton Woods System was abandoned in 1971 after inflation worsened in the United States.
3. Under the current system, the dollar floats freely; U.S. policy does little to control its movements.

# 18.3    MACROECONOMIC POLICY, EXCHANGE RATES, AND INFLATION

In this section, we will consider international economic policy issues, extending our analyses from the previous chapter.

## Policy with Floating Rates

Even though a country that has chosen not to stabilize its exchange rate is free to conduct monetary and fiscal policy with domestic goals in mind, exchange and trade issues figure prominently in policy discussions. The situation of Britain at the end of 1989 is a good illustration of the dilemma that can arise from considerations of the exchange rate. Coming into 1989, the British economy seemed to be in good shape. Output was close to potential. Inflation was less than 5 percent. Forecasts called for continued moderate growth and low inflation. The pound, at $1.80, was about normal in real terms. British interest rates were slightly above U.S. interest rates. But during the year, the situation deteriorated. The Conservative government lost several important midterm parliamentary elections. The pound dropped to about $1.60; commentators blamed anticipation of the election of a Labour government for the depreciation of the pound. The foreign exchange market may have anticipated that a Labour government would follow a more inflationary policy.

The Conservative government faced an unusually adverse choice. The decline in the pound was immediately inflationary; a lower exchange rate meant higher prices for imported products. Because the British economy is smaller and more open than the U.S. economy, the transmission of exchange rates to prices is more complete and widespread in Britain. The Bank of England chose to offset some of the forces depreciating the pound by tightening monetary policy and raising interest rates. However, monetary tightening slowed the economy. Growth of output slowed by the end of 1989, and the British economy stalled in the early 1990s.

The Bank of England compromised during 1989. It could have been even more contractionary and raised interest rates high enough to keep the pound at $1.80 and avoid a worsening of inflation. Then the economy would probably have been in recession by the end of the year. Or, the Bank could have kept unemployment and real growth at their earlier levels and allowed a greater depreciation of the pound. Then inflation would have risen even more. The change that gave rise to this adverse policy choice was the original downward force on the value of the pound in relation to other currencies, which had a political origin.

Exchange-rate shocks are less important in the United States than in economies that are smaller and more open. Because the United States is such a large part of the world market for many goods, foreign suppliers often absorb exchange-rate changes in their own prices rather than keeping the prices in their own currencies constant and letting the dollar prices change. The U.S. price of Japanese cars did not come close to doubling between 1985 and 1987, even though the purchasing power of the dollar in terms of the yen fell by half. Even so, changes in exchange rates are a source of shocks in the United States. Some economists feel that the unusually good performance of the U.S. economy from 1983 to 1985 was the result of a favorable foreign exchange movement. The sharp appreciation of the dollar over the period may have come in part from perceptions about political developments. By helping inflation fall, the appreciation of the dollar made it possible for the Fed to expand so that output grew rapidly and unemployment fell. The story of the United States from 1983 to 1985 may be exactly the story of Britain in 1989 in reverse.

## Policy with a Fixed Exchange Rate

Numerous countries around the world have chosen to commit policy to maintain one particular exchange rate at close to a constant level. For example, the Netherlands keeps a close watch on its exchange rate with the deutsche mark. When the rate dips slightly, the central bank has two options. It can sell securities to lower the money supply and raise the domestic interest rate to halt the incipient depreciation. Alternatively, it can sell DMs or other foreign securities and buy domestic securities at the same time. This will leave the money supply unchanged but will add to the supply of foreign securities and reduce the supply of domestic securities in the world market. The result will be an upward force on the domestic currency to offset the incipient depreciation. And, of course, the bank sometimes uses a combination of monetary contraction and portfolio shift. Then the bank's currency appreciates and the domestic interest rate rises. The economy cools off a little. If the original depreciation was the result of expectations of inflation above the German rate, the slacker economy helps drive the expected rate of inflation back down and removes the original impetus for depreciation.

Such fixed-rate regimes eliminate discretionary monetary policy. A fixed exchange rate is one of the ways of putting monetary policy on autopilot. For the Netherlands, monetary policy is made, in effect, by the Bundesbank. In turn, the Bundesbank must conduct a smooth, noninflationary policy in order to continue to play the role of the central bank.

What about fiscal policy? Changes in taxes and spending remain important open choices for an economy that has chosen to fix its exchange rate with monetary policy. Tax cuts or spending increases can stimulate employment and output. In fact, fiscal policy has bigger effects in an economy where the central bank is fixing the exchange rate than it would in the same economy with a floating rate. However, like the United States, the countries in the EMS tend not to rely on fiscal policy for stabilization.

## Analysis of Fixed- and Floating-Rate Policies

The exchange rate, price level, and monetary policy for an economy in the long run are related by

$$PE = P_w. \tag{18.2}$$

That is, the domestic price level $P$ times the exchange rate $E$ equals the foreign or world price $P_w$. Equation 18.2 says that *purchasing power parity* holds in the longer run. Purchasing power parity is not a reliable principle in the short run, but there are good reasons for it to hold in the long run.

Recall from Chapter 5 that the price level $P$ is simply proportional to the money supply in the long-run model. Given an exchange-rate target $E$, we can solve Equation 18.2 for the price level needed to achieve that exchange rate:

$$P = P_w/E. \tag{18.3}$$

Thus, to fix the exchange rate $E$, the money supply has to be held proportional to the level $P_w/E$. If the world price rises by 50 percent over a decade, the money stock must also rise by 50 percent. A fixed exchange rate locks monetary policy to the price level in the country whose currency is the basis for the fixed rate. For example, the German price level, as determined by the Bundesbank's monetary policy, dictates monetary policies in the Netherlands.

With a floating exchange rate, Equation 18.2 has a different interpretation. We can solve it for the exchange rate:

$$E = P_{\text{w}}/P. \tag{18.4}$$

Monetary policy uses whatever principles it wants to set the money supply and thus set the domestic price level $P$. If the central bank chooses to raise the price level by expanding the money supply, it will lower the exchange rate in the same proportion.

## World Inflation with Floating Exchange Rates

Yet another use of Equation 18.2 is to study rates of change in prices and exchange rates over time periods of a decade or longer. Stated in terms of rates of change, Equation 18.2 says

$$\pi + \frac{\Delta E}{E} = \pi_{\text{w}}. \tag{18.5}$$

The domestic rate of inflation $\pi$ plus the rate of appreciation $\Delta E/E$ equals the foreign rate of inflation $\pi_{\text{w}}$. Another way to express the same relationship is to observe that the excess of the foreign rate of inflation over the domestic rate of inflation is equal to the rate of appreciation of the domestic currency:

$$\pi_{\text{w}} - \pi = \frac{\Delta E}{E}. \tag{18.6}$$

How accurate is this equation as a description of the long-run behavior? In Figure 18.2 the inflation differentials and exchange-rate appreciations between six economies and the United States are shown. The difference between inflation in each country ($\pi_{\text{w}}$) and inflation in the United States ($\pi$) is shown on the vertical axis. The rate of appreciation ($\Delta E/E$) of the dollar against each of the corresponding currencies is on the horizontal axis. The 45-degree line is then the relation between inflation differentials and exchange-rate depreciation implied by Equation 18.6. The actual inflation rates and exchange-rate behavior come very close to the theoretical prediction. Germany has had the strongest currency and the lowest inflation rate compared with the United States. Italy is at the other extreme, with a comparatively weak currency and a high inflation rate compared with the United States. This relation between inflation and exchange-rate behavior is even more striking for countries with very high inflation rates. For example, during

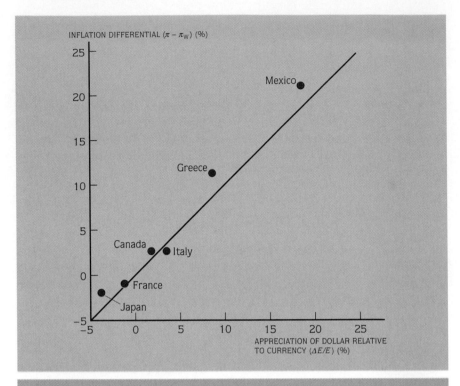

**FIGURE 18.2**  Inflation Differentials and Appreciation of the Dollar Relative to Six Countries, 1988–95

The inflation rates are measured by the consumer price index in each country. The rates of inflation and appreciation are annual averages for the eight-year period. When the inflation differential is high, appreciation of the dollar against that country's currency is high.
Source: *Economic Report of the President*, 1996, Tables B-104 and B-106.

the period from 1973 to 1989, the difference between the inflation rate in Argentina and that in the United States was about 50 percent per year. The Argentine peso depreciated by nearly 50 percent per year against the dollar during that period.

The freedom that a floating exchange rate gives to countries in determining their own inflation rates is a mixed blessing according to some economists. They feel that discipline rather than freedom is needed because of the tendency for many countries' political systems to generate too much inflation. For a small country it might be better to peg its currency to one of its trading partners that has a relatively low inflation rate. As long as the exchange rate is maintained, the small country will then eventually also have a low inflation rate.

## MACRO POLICY AND EXCHANGE RATES

1. Under a fixed-rate regime, the central bank must keep the domestic price level in step with the price level of the country whose currency forms the base of the system. The center country thus establishes monetary policy for the group.
2. Under floating rates, each country is free to choose its own inflation rate. Inflation differentials then determine the long-run behavior of exchange rates.

# 18.4 INTERNATIONAL MACRO POLICY COORDINATION

We have examined the effects of macroeconomic policy in a number of circumstances relevant to the conditions of the international monetary system today. Monetary policy cannot be used for domestic stabilization purposes in an economy with a fixed exchange rate. If capital is mobile, as it is in advanced countries without exchange controls, the central bank will forgo control over the money supply if it must support a fixed exchange rate. Moreover, a small country with a fixed exchange rate automatically adopts price stability goals that are identical to the country that it pegs its currency to.

Floating exchange rates offer much more freedom to use monetary policy for domestic stabilization purposes. That freedom can be a mixed blessing if the country's political system requires external discipline when it comes to monetary policy.

Floating exchange rates, however, do not insulate one economy from the effects of macroeconomic policies in other countries. In principle, therefore, international coordination of macro policies might be useful. The optimal macro policy that we discussed for the United States in Chapter 17 might be different if the effects of U.S. policy on other countries were taken into account or if the effects of other countries' policies on the United States were taken into account.

Macro policymaking in the world economy can be thought of as a game. Each country is a player in the game. The objective of policymakers in each country might be the same as those we discussed in Chapter 17. Each country has a social welfare function that includes output stability and price stability. Policymakers choose their instruments to minimize a combination of each type of loss. But if there is an interaction among countries, then the choice of a policy rule in one country will affect the social welfare function in the other country. Country 1 might improve its macroeconomic performance by worsening Country 2's macroeconomic performance. But if Country 1 does so, Country 2 might retaliate, or at least watch out for itself, with harmful side effects for Country 1. This would be a **noncooperative policy choice.** A **cooperative policy choice,** on the other hand, is one in which each country agrees to use a policy rule that doesn't have an adverse effect on the other country, in exchange for getting the same treatment from the other country. Some international coordination or discussion about policies, like that at Bretton Woods after World War II, would probably be necessary for this cooperative outcome.

The second effect cannot be offset so easily, however. *The depreciation of the foreign currency will raise the price of imported products in the rest of the world.* Recall that the price shock term $Z$ in the inflation equation (17.1) was due to changes in the price of inputs to production, such as oil. If the exchange rate depreciates, then the price that firms pay for these products rises. For example, Japan Airlines will have to pay 2.5 billion more yen for a $50 million Boeing 747 jet made in Seattle if the yen depreciates from 100 yen per dollar to 200 yen per dollar. The second effect of the U.S. monetary policy is thus to create a price shock in the rest of the world.

As we already know, a price shock presents a cruel choice to policymakers: Inflation must rise, unemployment must rise, or both must rise. The magnitude of the increase in inflation or unemployment depends on how much accommodation is built into policy in the rest of the world. Some loss, however, is inevitable. This effect of the U.S. policy, therefore, does result in a loss in welfare in the rest of the world and opens the possibility of cooperation. A cooperative policy would be one in which both the United States and other countries are more accommodative to inflation than they otherwise would be. This would make monetary policy less contractionary in the face of a price shock at home and would therefore have smaller harmful effects abroad. Although it is clear that optimal cooperative policies should be more accommodative than noncooperative policies, the difference could be small. Since our historical experience with flexible exchange rates is still fairly short, there is unfortunately little empirical evidence about the size of the difference between the policies.

 ## 18.5  MONETARY UNION

Several of the nations of continental Europe have already achieved a substantial amount of cooperation. Based on the historical record of the Bundesbank in setting a stable, noninflationary monetary policy, France and several other countries have committed themselves to monetary policies that will keep their own currencies at fixed parities with the deutsche mark. However, the commitment is not irrevocable. On the one hand, the ability to adopt a different policy in the future gives protection against the possibility of significant error by the Bundesbank. On the other hand, because politicians have the power to revoke fixed rates, there remains the danger of an exchange-rate crisis. If the market guesses, rightly or wrongly, that a devaluation relative to the DM is about to occur, it presents a country with a fixed parity against the DM with the unpleasant choice of sharp increases in interest rates to head off the speculative attack or capitulation to the attack by devaluing even if that was never planned before the attack.

Are the gains from such coordination large? How different would optimal policies look if countries cooperated, rather than acting independently? For example, should countries be less or more accommodative to inflation than calculations like those in Chapter 17 indicated?[1] Or perhaps countries should use their monetary policies to reduce the size of the fluctuations in the exchange rate as well as in the inflation rate and the unemployment rate.

We saw in Chapter 12 that changes in the U.S. money supply have effects on the exchange rate. A monetary contraction raises the exchange rate and a monetary expansion lowers the exchange rate. What are the effects of these changes abroad? What might foreign macro policymakers do about these changes? Consider the case of a dollar appreciation associated with a tight U.S. monetary policy or a loose U.S. fiscal policy. Obviously, an appreciation of the dollar is a depreciation of other currencies. A depreciation in the rest of the world has two effects that must be considered by policymakers.

First, the depreciation increases aggregate demand in the rest of the world. The depreciation is like an aggregate demand shock that increases net exports in the rest of the world; the aggregate demand curve shifts to the right. According to our optimal policy analysis, the appropriate response of policymakers in the rest of the world is to offset this shift by effecting tighter fiscal or monetary policy. Policies should be coordinated to get this result, but since the effect of the U.S. policy can be offset by the appropriate choice of policies abroad, there is no loss in world welfare on this account.

The cost of the market's belief that devaluation may occur at some time in the future is not just a political headache. Countries with histories of inflation well above German levels have had to pay substantially higher interest rates than does Germany. For example, even if Italy is committed to keeping the lira at a fixed parity relative to the DM, the bond market may be sufficiently convinced that a devaluation will occur in the future that it requires a higher interest rate for lira bonds.

---

[1]See Gilles, Oudiz and Jeffrey Sachs, "Macroeconomic Policy Coordination among the Industrialized Countries," *Brookings Papers on Economic Activity,* Number 1 (1984), pp. 1–64; and John B. Taylor, "International Coordination in the Design of Macroeconomic Policy Rules," *European Economic Review,* Vol. 26 (1985), pp. 53–81.

## NEW RESEARCH IN PRACTICE
## Does Western Europe Need a Central Bank?

Europe is in the process of creating a new central bank with a single currency. A group of economists and political scientists at the European Monetary Institute in Frankfurt are responsible for the overall design.

### Alternative 1. No Government Involvement

The government does not have to sponsor a monetary unit or a currency. One answer, proposed by Friedrich Hayek and actively advocated by some economists today, is to let the available nongovernment alternatives compete. Here it is important to distinguish between the unit of value and medium of exchange roles. If there are competing units of value, there will be no national consensus on how to interpret the numbers that merchants put on goods. The confusion and inefficiency would be comparable to what would happen if there were no agreement on how to measure fluid volume. If some gas stations sold gas by the U.S. gallon, some by the imperial gallon, some by the liter, and some by their own measure, motorists would be at a disadvantage relative to a system where all stations quoted in the same unit. It appears that setting uniform standards of weight, measure, and value is one of the most useful things a government can do and that zero government involvement in the monetary system is undesirable.

### Alternative 2. Government Sponsors Use of Existing Foreign Unit

Europe could announce that the monetary unit was the U.S. dollar (or the yen or any other foreign unit). The purchasing power of the unit would be stable if the Federal Reserve kept it stable. There would be complete agreement about the unit of value and the interpretation of the numbers that

merchants put on goods. No European government would have to be involved in the monetary system beyond the determination of the unit of value. There would not be a central bank and the government would not issue currency. U.S. dollars might circulate, or bank notes repayable in dollars might be issued by local banks. Bank accounts, bonds, mortgages, and other financial instruments would be denominated in dollars. This system would achieve the minimum sensible degree of government involvement. However, it would be politically unacceptable, for it would permanently forgo monetary independence as well as a source of government revenue that is still of some importance in Europe—government revenue from the issuance of currency and reserves. A conventional central bank borrows interest-free from the public; this saves the government from paying the corresponding interest on part of the national debt. Governments are reluctant to part with the central bank as a profit center.

### Alternative 3. Government Sponsors Foreign Unit but Captures Central Bank Profit

Either of two minor variants of Alternative 2 solves the problem of forgone profit. The government could prohibit private currency and be the sole issuer of currency, denominated in dollars. This currency board system was widely used by British colonies earlier in this century. Until 1972, Hong Kong had a monetary unit that was defined to be 1 British pound sterling. A currency board issued currency and held British government securities equal to its issue of currency. The profit earned by the board was simply the interest earnings from the securities.

Another, even easier way to accomplish the same purpose would be for the government to write a contract with the Federal Reserve in which

| | Plotting Points (inflation differential) | Appreciation of Dollar (percent) |
|---|---|---|
| Japan | −2.0 | −3.8 |
| France | −1.0 | −1.2 |
| Canada | 2.6 | 1.8 |
| Italy | 2.6 | 3.5 |
| Greece | 11.2 | 8.6 |
| Mexico | 21.0 | 18.5 |

the government would permit only dollar bills to circulate as currency in exchange for a remission of the Fed's profit from the added currency to the government. The Fed discussed an arrangement like this with the government of Israel a number of years ago, though it never came into being.

## Alternative 4. Government Issues Self-Stabilizing Money

Because Europe is very unlikely to make the dollar its monetary unit, it might want to consider a system that creates a purely domestic unit with constant purchasing power, without the cost of having a central bank. The idea is to issue a particular type of debt, called a *reserve,* which is defined to be the monetary unit. The reserve pays interest. Its interest rate is indexed to the price level. If prices are above target, the reserve pays higher interest than other types of government debt, so demand is strong. This puts downward pressure on the price level. Similarly, if prices are below target, the interest rate falls and there is upward pressure on the price level. To capture the profit from currency, the government would issue currency denominated in the reserve. This is an example of a monetary policy rule under which the interest rate is automatically raised when the price level indicator rises above its target.

The European Union is now considering a further step in the evolution of the monetary system: the creation of a monetary union with a single currency. Members of a monetary union make a permanent, irrevocable commitment not to change the value of their own monetary unit relative to the unit prescribed by the union. The best way to express that commitment is to abolish the existing domestic unit and use the union's monetary unit internally. If Italy eliminates the lira and uses a European unit internally, it is much more credible that Italy will not devalue its monetary unit.

Europe has already created a monetary unit of its own, the euro. The euro is defined as a basket of European currencies. The euro is seeing increasing use; a growing fraction of bonds are denominated in euros, some families hold savings accounts in euros, and some accounting statements of multinational companies are reckoned in euros.

With the European commitment to virtually full financial union, the goal of complete monetary union has been adopted in principle. The idea is to replace the existing monetary units with a single unit. The new unit would be issued by a European central bank. All countries that join the monetary union would use the new paper currency and all banks would hold reserves at the new central bank. The Bundesbank and all the other central banks would go out of business. Although Germany would probably dominate decision making at the European central bank, the other countries generally support the idea. It would relieve them of the burden of higher interest payments and eliminate political squabbles over monetary and exchange-rate policy. Most commentators see monetary union as helping to seal the true economic unification of the European countries. With exchange rates off the political agenda, there would be less likelihood of future government interference with trade and capital flows.

Europeans are conscious of the advantages of the greatest monetary union in the world, the United States. The process of replacing a dozen monetary units with a single European unit, the euro, is the same as the process of replacing the 13 monetary units of the American colonies with the U.S. dollar. When it was created in 1792, the dollar was a brand-new unit, just as the euro may be sometime around 2000. The fact that the states of the United States do not have monetary policies and exchange rates has supported the growth of the country as a unified economy. Europeans have concluded that a "United States of Europe" would have some substantial advantages, even though it would require a transfer of political power to a supranational European government from existing national governments.

## MONETARY UNION

1. Monetary union is the last step of financial integration. The countries in a union use a common monetary unit and do not have domestic currency units.
2. Monetary union is a stronger commitment than fixed exchange rates, because it eliminates the possibility of devaluation.

## REVIEW AND PRACTICE

### Major Points

1. Free trade in goods and assets is a characteristic of an integrated global economy.
2. In an open economy, central bank policy takes two forms: monetary policy and foreign exchange market intervention. Monetary policy refers to measures that

change the total liabilities of the central bank. Exchange-rate policy refers to measures that alter the mix of foreign and domestic assets in the central bank's portfolio.

3. Under a fixed exchange-rate system the central bank must use monetary policy to keep the domestic interest rate equal to the world rate. Other goals cannot be pursued.

4. Fixed exchange-rate systems require the nations involved to have similar rates of domestic inflation. The Bretton Woods System failed in the early 1970s when U.S. inflation increased above the rate other members of the system considered acceptable.

5. Under floating exchange rates each country is free to determine its own rate of inflation. Inflation differentials then determine the long-run behavior of nominal exchange rates.

6. The European countries are considering the formation of a monetary union with a single currency.

7. Monetary union is a stronger commitment than fixed exchange rates because it rules out periodic devaluations of currencies that occur under fixed rates. This may help to lower interest rates for European countries that frequently devalued their currency in the past.

## Key Terms and Concepts

| | | |
|---|---|---|
| open economy | devaluation and revaluation | capital and exchange controls |
| floating exchange rate | inconvertible currency | sterilized intervention |
| fixed exchange rate | foreign exchange | policy coordination |
| Bretton Woods System | intervention | monetary union |

## Questions for Discussion and Review

1. Compare the Bretton Woods System with a European monetary union.

2. How has Japanese monetary policy changed since the collapse of the Bretton Woods System?

3. Why is it important to distinguish between large and small economies in discussing the international aspects of economic policy?

4. Why does high capital mobility cause equalization of interest rates under fixed exchange rates?

5. Explain why monetary policy cannot be used for domestic goals when the exchange rate is fixed. Consider fixed, fully flexible, and gradually adjusting prices.

6. Why is the response of GDP to government purchases higher under a policy of a fixed rather than a floating exchange rate?

7. What determines the price level in a small country with completely flexible prices and a fixed exchange rate?

8. What determines the price level in a country with completely flexible prices and a floating exchange rate?

## Problems

### NUMERICAL

1. Consider a macro model of a small open economy consisting of the following equations:

$$Y = C + I + G + X$$

$$C = 80 + .63Y$$

$$I = 750 - 2.000R$$

$$M = (.1625Y - 1,000R)P$$

$$X = 500 - .1Y - 100EP/P_w,$$

   where government spending $G$ equals 750. Suppose that the exchange rate is *fixed* at $E = 1$, that the world interest rate $R_w = .05$, and that both price levels $P$ and $P_w$ are predetermined at 1.0. (Note that the domestic interest rate $R$ must equal .05.)
   a. Explain why $M$ rather than $R$ is an endogenous variable in this model in con-trast to the macro model in Chapters 7 and 12.
   b. Find the values of $Y$, $C$, $I$, $X$, and $M$ that are predicted by the model.
   c. Suppose that government spending $G$ increases by $50 billion. Calculate what happens to the endogenous variables $Y$, $C$, $I$, $X$, and $M$. What mechanism brings about the change in the money supply? Is there any crowding out of investment or net exports by the fiscal policy expansion? Why or why not?

2. Suppose that prices in the small open economy in Problem 1 are determined by

$$\pi = 2\left(\frac{Y_{-1} - Y^*}{Y^*}\right)$$

   where $Y^* = \$4,000$ billion is potential GDP and $\pi = (P - P_{-1})/P_{-1}$ is the rate of inflation. Suppose that $G = 750$, $E = 1$, $R = R_w = .05$, and $P_w = 1.0$. As in Problem 1, start out with a price level $P = 1.0$, but now let prices adjust after the first period.
   a. Calculate the responses of $Y$, $C$, $I$, $X$, $M$, and $P$ to a permanent increase in $G$ of $10 billion. Give the numerical values in the first four years. Plot accurately the values for each variable against time for the first four years and then sketch what happens after the fourth year.
   b. Is there any crowding out of investment or net exports after the first year? Why or why not?

3. Suppose now that the equations in Problem 1 refer to a small classical open economy in which the price level $P$ is perfectly flexible, $Y$ is always equal to potential output, and $Y^* = \$4,000$ billion. Calculate what happens when govern-ment spending $G$ increases by $10 billion. How do your results compare with the long-run results in Problem 2?

4. Consider a model of a world economy consisting of only two countries:

$$Y = C + I + G + X \qquad\qquad\qquad Y_w = C_w + I_w + G_w + X_w$$

$$C = 80 + .63Y \qquad\qquad\qquad C_w = 80 + .63Y_w$$

$$I = 750 - 2{,}000R \qquad\qquad\qquad I_w = 750 - 2{,}000R_w$$

$$M = (.1625Y - 1{,}000R)P \qquad\qquad M_w = (.1625Y_w - 1{,}000R_w)P_w$$

$$R = R_w$$

$$X = -X_w = 100 - .1(Y - Y_w) - 100EP/P_w$$

The notation is the same as that used in the text except that the subscript w means the other country (the world). (Note that net exports from one country must equal the negative of net exports of the other country.) Suppose that the price levels $P$ and $P_w$ are both predetermined at 1.0 and that the exchange rate $E$ is fixed at 1.0.

a. Calculate the values of output, investment, consumption, net exports, and the money supply $M_w$ if $G = 750$, $G_w = 750$, and $M = 600$.

b. Calculate what happens to these same variables if $M$ increases by $50 billion, to $650 billion. Explain why the money supply $M_w$ in the other country changes.

c. Calculate what happens to these same variables if $G$ increases by $50 billion but $M$ and $G_w$ do not change.

d. Find a policy for the home country to follow to keep $Y$ unchanged when $G_w$ increases by $10 billion.

**ANALYTICAL**

1. Consider a small open economy with sticky prices under a fixed exchange rate. Explain why the aggregate demand curve is vertical. What determines the level of output at which the curve is vertical?

2. Consider again the economy described in Question 1. Explain why an increase in government spending will increase output by the same amount as in the simple spending balance model of Chapter 6.

3. In a small open economy with a fixed exchange rate, suppose that actual GDP is below potential GDP. Inflation is low, and the objective is to bring the economy back to potential.
   a. Illustrate this situation with an IS-LM diagram.
   b. Describe a policy that can bring about the desired objectives. Would the policy be any different if investment were very sensitive to the interest rate?

4. Describe what happens in a small classical open economy with a fixed exchange rate when the price level abroad falls. Illustrate your answer with an IS-LM diagram.

5. Explain why aggregate demand shocks need not lead to a policy conflict between countries while a price shock might. (Hint: Take account of the effect of the exchange rate on prices.)

6. Explain why a depreciation of the exchange rate could have an inflationary impact in one country and a deflationary impact in other countries.

7. It is often argued that zero, or at least constant, inflation should be an objective of monetary policy since it makes long-term contracts necessary for capital formation much less risky. If one accepts this line of reasoning, is there any similar case that could be made for fixed exchange rates? Explain.

## MacroSolve Exercises

1. Using MacroSolve's **GRAPH AND STATISTICS** options for both annual and quarterly data series from 1967 through 1995, examine the relationship between exchange rates and both short- and long-term, nominal and real, interest rates. With which do exchange rates have a stronger relationship, nominal or real interest rates?

2. Using MacroSolve's **GRAPH AND STATISTICS** options for both annual and quarterly data series from 1967 through 1995, examine the relationship between inflation and exchange rates and net exports. Which has the strongest relationship, even when splitting the sample period after 1980?

3. Given your findings in Questions 1 and 2, what can you conclude about the influence that inflation and interest rates have on our nation's trade balance with the rest of the world? Which appears to have a stronger influence?

4. *Policy Decisions 2001.* Suppose you are the central banker of a large open economy with a government intent on stimulating the economy through larger budget deficits. Using the "ADI/PA, Open, Nom. Fixed Ex. Rate" and "ADI/PA, Open, Nom. Flex. Ex. Rate" models, evaluate the desirability of pursuing an exchange-rate sterilization policy.

5. *Policy Decisions 2001.* As chair of the Federal Reserve Board, would your task of manipulating the level of economic activity in the United States be made more or less difficult were the United States to become an even more open economy than it already is? Select MacroSolve model "ADI/PA, Open, Nom. Flex. Ex. Rate" and adjust the model parameters accordingly to reflect the economy's becoming more open. Recall that a more open economy is more sensitive to its terms of trade with other countries.

# Glossary

**accelerator**   The principle that investment is higher when GDP is growing, because businesses must enlarge their capital stocks to meet higher demand.   (11)

**accommodative policy**   A policy that expands the money supply in response to a price shock, so that employment and output change relatively little but the price level changes quite a bit.   (9, 17)

**activist policy**   A fiscal or monetary policy that responds strongly to current developments in the economy.   (9, 17)

**aggregate demand**   Total demand for goods and services.   (6)

**aggregate demand curve**   Downward-sloping relation between GDP and the price level such that spending balance occurs and the money market is in equilibrium.   (7)

**aggregate demand disturbance**   A shift of the aggregate demand schedule caused by a change in fiscal policy or a shift in the investment, consumption, net exports, or money demand function.   (9)

**aggregate demand–inflation curve**   Downward-sloping relation between GDP and the inflation rate such that spending balance occurs and monetary policy is following a prescribed rule.   (17)

**Ando-Modigliani life-cycle model**   A theory that consumption depends on a family's present and future resources, not just on current income.   (10)

**automatic stabilizers**   Tax and transfer programs whose effect is to shield consumers from the full amount of changes in GDP—for example, transfers rise in recessions, so that disposable income does not fall as much as GDP.   (10, 13)

**balance of payments accounts**   Record transactions between the United States and foreign countries.   (2)

Numbers in parentheses indicate the chapters in which terms are explained.

**balanced growth** Growth where capital and labor grow at the same percentage rate. (3)

**Bretton Woods system** Exchange-rate system put in place after World War II in which many countries fixed their exchange rates to the dollar. (18)

**buffer-stock function of inventories** Firms hold stocks of products as inventories in order to be able to supply their customers immediately, instead of making them wait for the goods to be produced. (11)

**capital account** Records borrowing and lending between the United States and foreign countries. (2)

**capital and exchange controls** Government limits on borrowing from or lending to foreigners or trading domestic for foreign currency. (18)

**checking deposits** Accounts where money can be withdrawn by writing a check. (14)

**classical dichotomy** Describes an economy where monetary policy affects only prices and where employment and output are determined purely by nonmonetary factors. (4)

**commitment to a policy** Where the effect of a policy depends on expectations, as in monetary policy, the extent of commitment to the policy—the credibility of the policy—will determine its effectiveness. (17)

**complete model** Model of the economy that considers both growth and short-run fluctuations. (1)

**consumer price index** A measure of the cost of living obtained by averaging the prices of many goods and services purchased by families. (2)

**consumption** Purchases of goods and services by families for their immediate use and enjoyment. (2)

**consumption function** Relation between total consumption and income. (6)

**crowding out**   Reduction in investment and net exports as a result of higher interest rates caused by higher government purchases of goods and services.   (4)

**currency**   Coins and dollar bills.   (14)

**current account**   Records purchases and sales of goods and services between the United States and foreign countries.   (2)

**defense expenditures**   Government spending for military purposes.   (13)

**demand for capital**   The amount of capital input chosen by firms given the demand for their products and the rental price of capital.   (11)

**demand for money**   Amount of money the public wants to hold given their income and the interest rate.   (4)

**depreciation**   Reduction in the stock of capital as a result of aging.   (2)

**depreciation deductions**   Tax deductions granted to firms who have purchased machines and other capital goods.   (11)

**depreciation rate**   Percentage decline per year in the market value of a machine or other capital good as it ages.   (11)

**desired capital stock**   The amount of capital input chosen by firms given the demand for their products and the rental price of capital.   (11)

**desired stock of housing**   The amount of housing capital chosen by households given their incomes and the rental price of capital.   (11)

**devaluation and revaluation**   Deliberate decreases and increases in fixed exchange rates.   (18)

**discount rate**   Interest rate charged by the Fed for loans to banks.   (14)

**discretionary policy**   An approach to policy based on full consideration of all factors each year, as opposed to the use of a committed policy rule.   (17)

**disinflation**   The process of restoring low inflation rates after a period of high inflation.   (9)

**disposable income**   Income available to families for spending, net of taxes and including transfers.   (9)

**dynamic model**   Model where events occurring this year affect the economy next year—for example, high GDP this year causes the price level to rise next year, and thus GDP is lower than it would have been otherwise.   (8)

**economic fluctuations model**   Model that explains recessions and other temporary disturbances in the economy.   (1)

**economic growth**   Increase in production per person that occurs as capital accumulates and technology improves.   (3)

**efficiency wage theory**   Theory of the natural rate of unemployment, stressing the importance of job loss as a disciplinary device for employers.   (5)

**elasticity of tax revenues**   Percentage increase in tax revenue per percent increase in GDP.   (13)

**endogenous growth theory**   Theory where the growth rate of the economy in the longer run depends on the rate of saving and other factors and not just on the growth rate of the labor force, as in the neoclassical growth theory.   (3)

**endogeneous variable**   A variable, such as GDP, that is determined by its interaction with other variables.   (6)

**exchange rate**   The number of units of foreign currency that a dollar will buy.   (2, 12)

**exchange rate, fixed**   Policy to hold the price of a foreign currency constant.   (18)

**exchange rate, flexible**   Market price for one currency in terms of another, where no central bank is preventing the market price from fluctuating.   (12)

**exchange rate, floating**   Policy that lets the market determine the price for one currency in terms of another—central bank does not prevent the market price from fluctuating.   (18)

**exchange rate, real**   Price of a foreign currency with adjustment for both U.S. and foreign inflation.   (12)

**exchange rate, trade-weighted** Average of exchange rates of other countries with weights that depend on the amount of trade between the United States and the country. (2)

**exchange-rate stabilization** Purchases and sales of domestic and foreign government bonds by a central bank in order to limit movements in an exchange rate. (12)

**exogenous variable** A variable, such as government purchases, that does not respond to the current state of the economy but can be considered fixed for purposes of analysis. (6)

**exports** Goods and services produced in the United States and shipped to foreign countries. (2)

**factor incomes** Incomes received by workers, owners of capital, and other productive factors. (2)

**final sales** Goods and services purchased by all customers, equal to GDP less inventory investment. (2)

**financial intermediaries** Organizations such as banks and mutual funds that issue deposits or shares and hold financial assets themselves. (14)

**fiscal policy** Use of tax rates and government spending to influence the economy. (4)

**flexible prices** Prices that move quickly to bring supply and demand into balance. (1)

**fluctuations** Upward and downward movements of the total amount of output and level of employment in the economy. (1)

**foreign exchange intervention** Policy move by a central bank to buy or sell government securities to raise or lower an exchange rate. (18)

**forward-looking theory of consumption** Theory where consumers consider their likely future incomes in making current consumption decisions. (10)

**Friedman permanent-income model** Theory that consumption depends on a family's perception of its permanent income, or present and future resources, not just on current income. (10)

**full employment**   Situation where labor demand equals labor supply and unemployment is at its natural level.   (3)

**full-employment deficit**   Size of the gap between government spending and revenue adjusted to the size it would have if the economy were at full employment.   (13)

**GDP (gross domestic product)**   Total volume of goods and services produced in the economy measured in dollars.   (1)

**GDP, nominal**   Total volume of goods and services produced in the economy measured in current dollars.   (2)

**GDP, potential**   Level of GDP in normal times absent temporary influences such as booms or recessions.   (1)

**GDP, real**   Total volume of goods and services produced in the economy measured in physical units.   (1)

**GDP gap**   Difference between the actual level of real GDP and potential GDP, a measure of short-run fluctuations.   (5)

**GDP target, nominal**   Policy that considers both inflation and output by stabilizing nominal income.   (17)

**GNP (gross national product)**   Value of goods and services produced by U.S. factors; differs from GDP because it includes production outside the country.   (2)

**government budget constraint**   The government's outlays must equal its revenue in the long run, in the sense of present values.   (13)

**government debt**   Bonds representing promises by the government to pay investors interest and principal in future years.   (13)

**government purchases**   Purchases of goods and services by federal, state, or local governments.   (2, 13)

**government saving**   Saving by federal, state, and local governments, equal to revenue less spending (the negative of the budget deficit).   (2)

**government spending multiplier**   The amount by which GDP is higher in an economy with a higher level of government purchases in comparison to an otherwise identical economy with lower government purchases.   (6)

**growth accounting formula**   Formula that shows how much of growth is the result of more inputs and how much is the result of improved technology.   (3)

**imperfect information**   Hypothesis that the public is not fully informed about influences on the economy such as current monetary policy. (15)

**imports**   Goods and services purchased from foreign countries and brought into the United States.   (2)

**income identity**   Total income, $Y$, is the sum of spending components, $C+I+G+X$.   (6)

**inconvertible currency**   Currency for which there is no market where the currency can be traded for other currencies.   (18)

**indexation**   Linking of wages or particular product prices to the cost of living or other price indexes.   (15)

**inflation**   Increase in the price level over time.   (4)

**inflation, expected**   Increase in the price level expected by the public at the beginning of the year—feeds into price adjustment and makes up the difference between the nominal and real interest rates.   (8, 16)

**inflation–GDP gap loops**   When monetary policy switches occasionally from higher to lower inflation targets, a plot of inflation and the GDP gap shows loops.   (16)

**inflation loss**   Social loss, including shoe-leather cost, from higher inflation that is above or below target.   (17)

**inflation rate**   Percentage increase in the price level during a year.   (1)

**interest rate**   Amount received by lender to compensate for time value of money, in percent per year.   (1)

**interest rate, nominal**   The standard interest rate, not adjusted for inflation.   (7)

**interest rate, real**   The interest rate adjusted for expectations of inflation—the difference between the nominal rate and the expected rate of inflation.   (7, 10)

**interest-rate differential** Difference between the dollar interest rate and a foreign rate that arises because the foreign currency is expected to appreciate or depreciate. (12)

**interest-rate parity** Situation where the dollar interest rate is the same as the interest rate in another country, after adjusting for the amount of likely future change in the exchange rate. (12)

**interest-rate sensitivity** Decline in investment and exports as a result of higher interest rates. (4)

**intermediate goods** Goods produced by businesses and used as inputs by other businesses, such as steel. (2)

**intertemporal budget constraint** The total amount of consumption must equal total resources, now and in the future, in terms of present discounted value. (10)

**investment** Purchases of newly produced plant, equipment, inventories, and houses. (2, 11)

**investment, fixed** Purchases of plant and equipment by businesses. (2, 11)

**investment, inventory** Increase in stocks of unsold goods held by businesses. (2, 11)

**investment, net** Increase over time in the capital stock, equal to total investment less depreciation. (2, 11)

**investment demand** Level of purchases of new capital chosen by firms given the demand for their products and the rental price of capital. (11)

**investment function** Relation between investment and the interest rate. (7)

**investment multiplier** The amount of which GDP is higher in an economy with a higher level of investment in comparison to an otherwise identical economy with lower investment. (6)

**IS curve** Downward-sloping relation between GDP and the interest rate such that spending balance is preserved—at a higher interest rate, investment and net exports are lower, so spending balance occurs at a lower level of GDP. (7)

**job creation**   Opening of new jobs at individual plants or offices.   (5)

**job destruction**   Elimination of jobs at individual plants or offices.   (5)

**job-finding rate**   Percentage of the unemployed who find new jobs each month.   (5)

**job-losing rate**   Percentage of workers who lose their jobs each month. (5)

**Keynes, John Maynard**   British economist who founded modern macro-economics by seeking explanations for depressions and recessions. (1)

**Keynesian consumption function**   Relation between current disposable income and current income.   (10)

**labor demand**   Amount of labor input needed by businesses to produce a given amount of output.   (3)

**labor force**   The number of people working or available for work, equal to the sum of employment and unemployment.   (2)

**labor force participation rate**   Fraction of adults who are in the labor force, either working or unemployed.   (5)

**labor-market equilibrium**   Situation where labor demand equals labor supply and unemployment is at its natural level.   (3)

**labor supply**   Amount of effort workers will perform given the real wage. (3)

**LM curve**   Upward-sloping relation between GDP and the interest rate such that the money market is in equilibrium—at a higher interest rate, money demand is lower, so the level of income where the money market is in equilibrium is higher.   (7)

**long run**   A period of five years or more, sufficiently long that economic fluctuations are not an important factor in the economy's performance. (3)

**long-run growth model**   Model that concentrates on growth and does not try to explain short-run fluctuations.   (1)

**Lucas supply curve**  Upward-sloping relation between GDP and the price level arising from imperfect information about monetary policy.  (15)

**marginal benefit of capital**  Profit contributed by another unit of capital—the avoided cost of labor and other factors saved by the use of more capital.  (11)

**marginal propensity to consume**  Increase in consumption per unit of additional income; the slope of the consumption function.  (6)

**marginal propensity to consume, long-run**  Amount by which consumption rises in the long run when there is a permanent increase in income.  (10)

**marginal propensity to consume, short-run**  Amount by which consumption rises this year when income rises this year.  (10)

**marginal propensity to consume out of permanent income**  Increase in consumption per unit of additional permanent income—the amount spent by consumers from an increase in lifetime resources.  (10)

**marginal propensity to consume out of temporary income**  Increase in consumption per unit of additional income, when the additional income is unexpected and will not continue in future years.  (10)

**marginal propensity to import**  Increase in imports per unit of additional GDP, the negative of the slope of the net exports function.  (6)

**marginal social cost of unemployment**  Loss to the nation from an additional percentage point of unemployment, higher when there is more unemployment.  (17)

**markup pricing**  When a firm believes that the elasticity of demand is approximately fixed, it will set a price for its product that is a given markup ratio times marginal cost.  (15)

**means of payment**  A method that people use to pay for goods—money is one means of payment, credit cards are another.  (14)

**menu costs**  Costs a firm incurs to change the price of a product.  (15)

**model uncertainty**  Uncertainty about how the economy responds to deliberate changes in policy instruments.  (17)

**monetary base**   Total amount of currency and reserves.   (14)

**monetary policy**   Use of changes in the money supply to influence the economy and stabilize prices.   (4)

**monetary policy rule**   Established procedure for using open-market purchases to respond to developments in the economy, such as a rule to keep the interest rate at a prescribed level.   (14)

**monetary union**   Adoption of a common monetary unit by several countries.   (18)

**money growth**   Increase in the money stock over time.   (4)

**money market**   Market for currency and checking deposits.   (4)

**money-market equilibrium**   Situation where the demand for money equals the supply of money.   (4)

**money multiplier**   Relation between the monetary base and the money stock—there can be several dollars in money for each dollar of the monetary base because reserve requirements are around 10 percent.   (14)

**money supply**   Amount of money available to the public, as determined by the Fed. The money supply consists of the the total amount of currency and checking deposits.   (4)

**multiplier**   The amount by which GDP is higher in an economy with a higher level of government purchases in comparison to an otherwise identical economy with lower government purchases.   (6)

**national income**   Total income of all residents of the United States.   (2)

**natural rate property**   The economy eventually returns to the natural unemployment rate after a shock; monetary shocks affect the price level only in the longer run.   (8)

**natural rate of unemployment**   Amount of unemployment in normal times.   (3)

**neoclassical growth model**   Model of growth that focuses on the production function to show how capital accumulation leads to growth.   (3)

**net exports**   Difference between total exports and imports, denoted $X$.   (6)

**net exports function**   Relation between net exports and its determinants, GDP and the interest rate.   (6, 12)

**neutrality of money**   Occurs when an increase in the amount of money raises the price level but does not affect output or employment.   (4)

**nonresidential fixed investment**   Purchases of newly produced plant and equipment.   (11)

**oil shock to price setting**   Sudden increase or decreases in world oil prices cause upward and downward jumps in prices not explained by other factors in the price adjustment process.   (16)

**Okun's law**   Relation between the GDP gap and the rate of unemployment—for each percent of GDP gap, there is about a third of a percentage point extra unemployment.   (5)

**open economy**   Economy that trades with other countries and has common capital markets with them as well.   (18)

**open-market operation**   Purchases or sales of government securities by the Fed—a purchase increases the monetary base because the Fed pays for the purchase with reserves.   (14)

**outlays**   Government purchases of goods and services plus government transfers for social security and other purposes.   (13)

**output loss**   Social loss from unstable output.   (17)

**peak**   Time when the economy reaches its highest level of output and employment following an expansion.   (1)

**personal disposable income**   Income available to families for spending, net of taxes and including transfers.   (2)

**Phillips curve**   Relation between GDP and price change; describes the process of price adjustment.   (8)

**pipeline function of inventories**   Firms hold stocks of products as inventories as a normal part of the production process—for example, partly built cars moving through an auto plant are in the pipeline and counted as inventories.   (11)

**plant and equipment investment**   Purchases of newly produced plant and equipment.   (11)

**policy coordination**   Central banks acting in concert to achieve joint goals.   (18)

**policy frontier**   Curve showing all the combinations of output loss and inflation loss that are consistent with the price adjustment process; different points on the frontier correspond to different choices of the slope of the ADI curve.   (17)

**policy ineffectiveness theorem**   With a Lucas supply function, a policy rule based on the same information available to the public cannot affect output and employment.   (15)

**policy rule**   Established procedure for using a policy instrument such as taxes or open-market purchases to respond to developments in the economy.   (13, 17)

**policy trade-off**   A policy that stabilizes inflation must accept high volatility of output, and vice versa.   (17)

**precautionary motive**   People hold money because they are concerned that other forms of holding wealth may not be immediately available to buy what they need.   (14)

**predetermined price level**   Because of price stickiness, this year's price level is predetermined—it does not respond to changing conditions this year, though it will respond next year.   (8)

**price adjustment**   Process by which the price level changes to bring the economy back to full employment.   (1)

**price deflator**   A price index obtained by dividing nominal GDP by real GDP.   (2)

**price index**   A measure of the cost of living or general price level obtained by averaging over the prices of many goods and services.   (2)

**price rigidity**   Firms wait to change prices after new conditions develop; prices are rigid during this period.   (15)

**price shock**   An increase in the price level caused by a force other than the GDP gap or expectations of inflation—oil price shocks are an example of such a force.   (6)

**procyclical**  Moving parallel with output and employment over the business cycle.  (1)

**producer price index**  A measure of the general price level obtained by averaging over the prices charged by producers for many goods and services.  (2)

**production function**  Relation between the amount of output produced and the amounts of labor, capital, and other inputs used in production. (3)

**production function for technology**  Relation between improved technology and the inputs devoted to research and development.  (3)

**protectionism**  Policy of using tariffs, quotas, or other measures to limit imports to a country.  (12)

**purchasing power parity**  Situation where a dollar spent in the United States buys the same amount of goods as converting the dollar into a foreign currency and spending the proceeds in that country.  (12)

**quotas**  Restrictions on the right to import foreign goods into a country. (12)

**rational expectations**  Making use of all available information about the future to form expectations about inflation, income, and other variables.  (10)

**reaction function**  Mathematical function describing an established procedure for using a policy instrument such as taxes or open-market purchases to respond to developments in the economy.  (13)

**real business cycle model**  Model that explains recessions and other temporary disturbances in the economy in terms of flexible prices.  (1)

**recession**  Contraction in the total amount of output and level of unemployment in the economy.  (1)

**recovery**  Period when output and employment are rising following a contraction or recession.  (1)

**rental price of capital**  Cost per year for the use of a machine or other piece of capital—depends on the interest rate, the rate of depreciation, the cost of new capital goods, and tax factors.  (11)

**reserve requirements**   Rules requiring banks to keep deposits at the Fed in the form of reserves in proportion to their checking deposits.   (14)

**reserves**   Accounts maintained by banks at the Federal Reserve—a form of money used within the banking system.   (14)

**Ricardian equivalence**   A proposition holding that it makes little difference if the government earns tax revenue this year or in future years; all that matters is the total amount of spending.   (13)

**saving, private**   Saving by households and other private entities, equal to total saving less government saving.   (2)

**scarcity of instruments**   Monetary policy is the only generally accepted policy instrument for influencing the overall economy—since there is only one instrument, it cannot be expected to achieve multiple goals, such as zero inflation and full employment in all years.   (17)

**shoe-leather cost of inflation**   When inflation is high, people have an incentive to keep their money balances low and to make more trips to the bank to obtain more currency.   (17)

**smooth consumption path**   Consumption is roughly the same in all years, as generally preferred by consumers.   (10)

**social indifference curve**   Curve showing combinations of output loss and inflation loss that are equally acceptable to the public.   (17)

**social welfare function**   Expression of the public's preferences about inflation and output loss.   (17)

**speculative motive**   People hold money because they believe that other forms of holding wealth, such as the stock market, will fall in value. (14)

**spending balance**   Situation where the public's planned level of spending is sufficient to generate the level of income they assumed when they made their spending plans.   (6)

**stagflation**   Combination of low levels of output and employment and continuing high rates of inflation; occurs after a price shock or when monetary policy adopts a lower inflation target following a period of high inflation.   (16)

**staggered contracts**   The overlapping of contracts lasting several years so that one comes up for renewal while another is still in effect.   (15)

**sterilized intervention**   Central bank buys or sells foreign government securities and sells or buys an equal amount of domestic government securities, in an effort to influence the exchange rate without changing the monetary base.   (18)

**sticky prices**   Prices that do not respond immediately to changing conditions in the economy.   (1, 15)

**sticky wages**   Wages that do not respond immediately to new conditions. (15)

**store of wealth**   Holding money as a way to make resources available in future years.   (14)

**substitution effect**   Change in consumption or work effort that is the result of a change in a relative price, such as the price of future consumption relative to current consumption or the real wage.   (10)

**tariffs**   Prices paid to import foreign goods into a country.   (12)

**tax incentives**   Depreciation deductions and investment credits available from the IRS as a result of buying new machines or other capital.   (11)

**time preference rate**   Tendency to choose current against future consumption—with a rate of time preference of 5 percent, the marginal utility of consumption is 5 percent higher this year than next year, when the levels of consumption are the same in both years.   (10)

**trade deficit**   Amount by which imports exceed exports—the negative of net exports.   (6)

**transactions motive**   People hold money because they expect to need it soon to purchase goods or make other transactions.   (14)

**trough**   Time when the economy reaches its lowest level of output and employment following a contraction or recession.   (1)

**unemployment rate**   Percent of labor force looking for work.   (1)

**Unidad de Fomento**   Chilean monetary unit with stable purchasing power. (15)

**unit of account**   The nationally agreed upon unit for measuring value, keeping accounts, and quoting prices; in the United States, the dollar. (14)

**value added**   Difference between the value of the output of a firm or industry and purchases from other firms or industries.   (2)

**wage-price spiral**   With substantial indexation, a price shock will drive up wages, which will then drive up prices, and so on, for many grounds. (16)

**wage-setting, relative**   The influence on wages of other wages nearby for similar work.   (15)

# Index

accelerationist property, 450
accelerator:
   defined, 310
   for housing, 318
   investment and, 310–11
accommodative policies, 238–39
accounting identity, 26
accumulation of debt, 374–76
activist economic policy, 235
   constant growth policy rules and, 473
   discretionary vs., 473
adjustment process, 205–26
aggregate demand:
   balance of income and spending in, 151–68
   defined, 149
   financial markets and, 173–204
   foreign trade and, 335, 337–38
   IS-LM approach and, *see* IS-LM approach
   output determined by, 147, 148, 206–8
   price adjustment and, 215–22, 457–64
   price level and, 196, 197–98
   in reverse, 241–42
   in short-run model, 146–51
   spending balance and, 149–51
aggregate demand curve, 146–47
   derivation of, 196–98
   fiscal policy and, 196, 198–99, 241–43
   GDP and, 241–43
   monetary policy and, 198–99, 241–43
   money demand and, 233–35
   price adjustment and, 215
   price disturbances and, 238
   real GDP and, 208–9, 229–31
   shifts in, 228–31, 233–35
   slope of, 196
aggregate demand disturbances, 227–41
   analyzing effects of, 228–33
   offsetting of, 483–89
   price adjustment and, 230–33
   recession and, 230–31
   responding to, 228–31, 233–37
   stabilization policy and, 233–37
aggregate demand-inflation curve, 457–59
aggregate investment demand function, 313
Akerlof, George, 127$n$
American Economic Association, 212
Anderson, Patricia, 124$n$
Ando, Albert, 268$n$, 279, 280
Ando-Modigliani consumption function, 279
animal spirits, 228

anti-inflation policies, 479–81
appreciation of U.S. dollar, 339, 504, 517–18, 521
arbitrage, 180
Argentina, 496, 518
Ashenfelter, Orley, 68$n$
Asia, 496
assets:
   in balance sheet, 390
   consumption and, 279
   liquid, 234
   negative, 271
auction markets, 474
automatic stabilizers:
   defined, 260–61, 368
   government transfers as, 368
   IS curve and, 379
automobile industry, 150–51

baby boom, 5, 62
backward-looking wage behavior, 433–34
   expected inflation and, 452–53
bailout spending, 191
balanced growth:
   conditions for, 72–74
   saving and, 71–75
balanced growth path, 71–75
   defined, 71
balance of payments, 43
balance sheets, 389–91, 507–8
Balassa, Bela, 334$n$
Baldwin, Richard, 85, 351$n$
Bank of England, 408, 506, 511, 515
Bank of Japan, 506, 514
banks:
   as financial intermediaries, 391
   in foreign exchange market, 338
   intermediation role of, 391
   reserve ratio of, 392
Barro, Robert, 76, 377, 428$n$
Baumol, William, 397$n$
Baxter, Marianne, 220
BEA (Bureau of Economic Analysis), 26
Bernheim, Douglas, 272$n$
Blanchard, Olivier, 124$n$
Blinder, Alan, 283$n$
BLS (Bureau of Labor Statistics), 46–47, 49, 70, 90
bond-financed changes, defined, 395

bonds:
  government, 391, 508
  interest rate and, 180, 400
  money supply and, 404–5
booms:
  consumption in, 277
  price adjustment and aggregate demand in,
    460–61, 462–63
  unemployment in, 120, 130–34
borrowed reserves:
  discount rate and, 393–94
  monetary base and, 393–94
borrowing:
  capital inflow, 41, 337–38
  from positive vs. negative asset positions, 271
Brainard, William, 334n, 476
Brazil, 496
Brealey, Richard, 181n
Bretton Woods System, 510–11, 514, 520
  collapse of, 511–13
  devaluation in, 511
Brown, E. Cary, 371n
Brumberg, R. E., 268n
Brunner, Karl, 453n
budget constraint, intertemporal, 269–71, 276,
    376
budget deficit, 362–85
  components of, 362, 371
  defined, 40
  trade deficit and, 104, 108
  see also deficits
budget surplus, defined, 40
buffer stock inventories, 320
Bundesbank, 408, 506, 513, 516, 517, 520–21,
    524
Bureau of Economic Analysis (BEA), 26
Bureau of Labor Statistics (BLS), 46–47, 49, 70, 90
Bureau of the Census, 49
Bush, George, 283
business investment, see nonresidential fixed
    investment

Caballero, Ricardo, 136n
Calvo, Guillermo, 472
Canada, 513
capital:
  changes in price of, 308–9
  controlled movement of, 506–7
  defined, 62
  diminishing marginal product of, 304
  growth of, 87–88
  marginal cost of, 303–4
  relative price of, 308–9
  renting of, see rented capital
  stimulating formation of, 87–88
  see also money
capital account, 43–44
capital asset pricing model (CAPM), 180–81

capital budgeting:
  rented capital and, 307–8, 330–32
  winner vs. loser positions in, 331–32
capital controls, 509
capital gains taxes, 316
capital inflow, 41, 337–38
capital stock, 302
  actual, 310, 333
  choosing of, 304–5
  desired, 309–10, 333
  fixed investment and, 27–28
  investment demand and, 312–13
  net investment and, 63
  slow adjustment of, 312–13
Carlton, Dennis, 431
Carter, Jimmy, 283, 479
Cechetti, Stephen G., 431n
central banks, 408, 410–12, 506–9, 522–23, 524
  anti-inflation policies and, 492
  balance sheets of, 507–8
  domestic credit in, 508
  exchange-rate policies of, 507–10
  foreign reserves of, 508, 511
  sterilized intervention by, 509, 513
  T-bills in, 510–11
checking accounts, 388
  opportunity cost for funds in, 396–97
Chevron, 32
Chile, 430
China, People's Republic of, 505
Christiano, Lawrence, 316
Clark, Peter K., 311n, 312n
classical dichotomy, 113–14, 115–16
classical macroeconomics, 17
Clinton, Bill, 492
coefficients, 110, 152–53
  defined, 110
COLA (cost-of-living adjustment), 47, 436, 451
collective bargaining, 47, 433, 435–36
complete model, 15, 20–21, 205–26
  aggregate demand in, 215–22
  long-run growth model vs., 62
  price adjustment and, 210–21
  real business cycle model and, 220
Congress, U.S., 16, 99, 190, 282, 352, 369
constant growth rate policy rules, 473
consumer behavior, 257
  backward-looking, 433–34, 452–53
  forward-looking, see forward-looking theory
    of consumption
  liquidity-constrained, 285
  rate of time preference in, 286
  see also rational expectations
consumer price index (CPI), 46–49
consumption:
  assets and, 279
  in booms vs. recessions, 279
  consumption expenditures vs., 260
  defined, 27

disposable income compared to, 265–66
of durable goods, 259–60
fluctuations in, 258–63
forward-looking theory of, *see* forward-
  looking theory of consumption
as function of income, 152–55
interest-rate sensitivity of, 102–3, 286–88
IS curve and, 288–89
life-cycle theory of, 268
in 1995, 31
past income and, 279–80
permanent-income theory of, 268
real disposable income and, 262–63
in recessions, 265, 279
retirement and, 271–72
smoothness of, 265
steady vs. erratic, 271
consumption deflator, 48
consumption demand, 257–97
consumption expenditure:
  consumption vs., 260
  durables and, 259–60
  nondurables and, 259–60
  services and, 259–60
consumption function, 152–55, 408, 409
  Ando-Modigliani, 279
  disposable income and, 152–54
  error analysis in, 263–65
  forward-looking theory of consumption vs.,
    268
  Keynesian, 263–67, 279, 281
  MPC in, 263, 265–67
  simple, 262–63
consumption planning, graphical approach to,
  295–97
consumption substitution, 287
contingency clauses, union contract, 435–37
contractionary monetary policy, 520
contracts:
  indexing of, 434, 436–37, 451, 495
  labor, 431, 433–34
  union, *see* union contracts
contributions for social insurance, 37–38
cooperative policy choice, defined, 520
cost-of-living adjustment (COLA), 47, 436, 451
counterclockwise loop, 464
countercyclical stabilization policy, 235–37
  effects of, 371
  inflation and, 236–37
CPI (consumer price index), 46–49
CPI basket, 46–47
credit cards, 388
crowding out, 105
  defined, 191
  expansionary fiscal policy and, 504
Cummins, J., 316
currency, 399, 400
  on balance sheet, 390–91
  defined, 388

depreciation of, *see* depreciation
inconvertible, 506
intervention, 511
recent trends in, 400–402
vault cash vs., 390$n$
currency deposit ratio, 392
current account, 43–44
Current Population Survey, 49–50, 121
curves:
  aggregate demand, *see* aggregate demand
    curve
  expectations-augmented Phillips, *see*
    expectations-augmented Phillips curve
  IS, *see* IS curves
  labor supply, 89
  LM, *see* LM curve
  Phillips, *see* Phillips curve
cyclical deficits, structural deficits vs., 371–72


Data Resources, Inc., 220
Davis, Steven, 123$n$
Davis-Bacon Act, 494
debt, government:
  deficit and, 374–76
  economic significance of, 376–78
deficits:
  accumulation of debt and, 374–76
  current account, 44
  cyclical vs. structural, 371–72
  fluctuation in, 366–71
  full-employment, 371–72
  government, effects of, 371–78
  interest rate and, 372–74
  monetization of, 374
  in World War II, 374–75
  *see also* budget deficit; trade deficit
deflators, 46, 48–49
demand:
  aggregate, *see* aggregate demand
  consumption, 257–97
  firm and, 205
  for housing, 318
  for imports, 504
  for labor, 66
  money, *see* money demand
  price adjustment and, 150
demand curve, macroeconomic, *see* aggregate
    demand curve
demand curve, microeconomic, for rented
    capital, 304
deposits, 390–91
  recent trends in, 400–402
depreciation:
  defined, 28
  devaluation vs., 511
  investment and, 311
  of U.S. dollar, 339
  write-offs of, 316

Depression, Great, 8, 9, 17, 19, 353, 414, 415, 510
desired capital stock:
  actual capital stock and, 310, 333
  defined, 309–10
desired stock of housing, defined, 318
devaluation, 511–13
  depreciation vs., 511
Diamond, Peter, 124$n$, 377$n$
diminishing marginal product, 304
discount rate:
  borrowed reserves and, 393–94
  defined, 393
discretionary changes in tax rates, 369–70
discretionary policy rules, 473
disinflation, 243–47
  alternative paths for, 243–47
  avoiding of, 243–47
  defined, 243
  GDP and, 243–47
  monetary policy and, 243–47
  Phillips curve and, 243
  price adjustment and aggregate demand in, 461–63
  unemployment and, 245
disposable income, 37, 152, 154
  consumption compared to, 265–66
  consumption fluctuation and, 260–63
  consumption function and, 152–54
  GDP and, 260–61
  government taxes and transfers and, 370
  intertemporal budget constraint on, 270
  real, 261–63
District Federal Reserve Banks, 390$n$, 393, 395, 404
  New York, 404, 405
disturbances, 227–41
  aggregate demand, see aggregate demand disturbances
  to money demand, 228, 233–34
  price, see price disturbances
  temporary vs. permanent, 228
dollar, U.S.:
  appreciation of, 339, 504, 517–18, 521
  Bretton Woods System and, 510–13
  creation of, 524
  depreciation of, 339, 521
  devaluation of, 512, 513
  fluctuations in, 335, 337
  international value of, 335, 337
  price of, 44–45
  for quoting prices, 430
  yen vs., 44–46
domestic credit, 507–8
durable goods, 27
  consumption expenditures and, 259–60
  consumption of, 259–60
  long-run MPC and, 267
  short-run MPC and, 267

Durlauf, Steven, 76
dynamic model:
  defined, 208
  see also price adjustment
dynamic multiplier, 163$n$

economic fluctuations, see fluctuations
economic growth, see growth
Economic Report of the President (1977), 283
Eichenbaum, Martin, 220
elasticity, defined, 368
employment, 9–10, 18
  full, see full employment
  measuring of, 49–51
  production and, 9–10
  productivity and, 90–93
  real GDP and, 9–10
  recession and, 10, 49–51 see also labor supply; unemployment
endogenous growth theory, 80–84, 85
endogenous policy, see policy rule
endogenous variables, 155
  expected inflation as, 453
  money supply as, 241
  net exports as, 345
  predetermined vs., 178–79
equilibrium, 146–48
  labor market and, 68–69, 137–38
  in money market, 112–14, 411–12
  price adjustment and, 210–15
  spending balance vs., 151
  stochastic, 473
  unemployment and, 63, 68–69
equilibrium real interest rate, 456–57
euro (European currency unit), 523–24
Europe:
  central bank for, 522–23
  financial union in, 505, 520–24
excess reserves, defined, 393
exchange rate, 44–46, 335–61, 509–10, 513–19
  appreciation of, inflation differentials and, 517–18
  balance of payments accounts and, 44–46
  central banks and, 507–10
  defined, 44, 338
  devaluation vs. revaluation of, 510
  fixed, see fixed exchange rate
  floating, see floating exchange rate
  fluctuations in, 340–42, 510, 521
  foreign exchange market and, 338
  foreign trade and, 338–47
  interest rate and, 345–47
  IS curve and, 354–55
  LM curves and, 354–56
  net exports and, 342–45
  price adjustment and, 349–50
  price level and, 350–52

purchasing power parity and, 341–42
real, 340, 345–47
relative price and, 340–42
stabilization of, 353–56
trade-weighted, 45–46, 339
between yen and U.S. dollar, 44–46, 513
exogenous variables, 154–55, 178
money supply as, 240–41
expansionary fiscal policy:
 appreciated U.S. dollar and, 504
 central banks and, 509
 crowding out and, 504
 and demand for imports, 504
 interest rate and, 504
 short-term benefits vs. long-term costs in,
  476–77
expansionary monetary policy, short-term
  benefits vs. long-term costs in, 476–77
expectations, see rational expectations
expectations-augmented Phillips curve,
  disinflation and, 243
expected inflation:
 actual behavior and, 453–54
 backward-looking wage behavior and,
  452–53
 and changes in monetary policy, 453–54
 determination of, 214–15
 as endogenous variable, 453
 forward-looking forecasts and, 452
 rate of, 406–7
 term of, 452–54
 wage determination and, 214–15, 434,
  452–53, 474
exports, 29–30, 165–68
 defined, 29
 GDP and, 29–30, 343
 net, see net exports
 see also foreign trade

factor income, 36
family histories, 281–82
Fed, see Federal Reserve System
Federal Open Market Committee (FOMC),
  404–10
 composition of, 404
Federal Reserve Board, 12, 16, 220, 233–34, 235,
  241, 246, 393–94, 404
Federal Reserve System (Fed), 99, 109, 111, 113,
  114, 387, 404, 428, 453, 457, 459, 492,
  506, 513, 522–23
 bond market and, 404–5
 functions of, 388–89
 inflation rate target, 408–9, 411
 interest rate and, 20, 404–12
 in IS-LM approach, 178
 loans to banks from, 393
 monetary policy controlled by, 241, 244,
  404–12

in monetizing government debt, 374
money supply controlled by, 18, 389–95,
  404–10; see also Fed policy rule
open-market operations by, 391, 404–5
policy rule of, see Fed policy rule
reaction of economy to, 408–10
real GDP and, 244, 406–9
reserve balances in, 393
Fed policy rule, 386–420
 establishing, 404–10
 lags in, 413, 415
 LM curve and, 405–7
 objectives of, 404, 408
Feldstein, Martin S., 311$n$, 378
Fethke, Gary, 437$n$
final goods, 32
final sales, 29
financial markets, aggregate demand and,
  173–204
financial variables, 173–204
firms:
 capital budgeting by, see capital budgeting
 and changes in demand, 205
 as forward-looking, 302–3
 information and behavior of, 422–29
 inventory investment by, see inventory
  investment
 investment decisions by, 302–9
 investment function of, see investment
  function
 nonresidential investment by, see
  nonresidential fixed investment
 price adjustments by, 210–21
 residential investment by, see residential fixed
  investment
 sticky prices of, 430
 wage setting by, see wage determination
 see also price adjustment
fiscal expansion, see expansionary fiscal policy
fiscal policy:
 aggregate demand curves and, 196, 198–99,
  241–43
 changes in, 104–5, 107
 defined, 99
 expansionary, see expansionary fiscal policy
 Fed policy rule and and effect of, 410–12
 foreign policy and, 521
 IS curve and, 456
 IS-LM approach and, 190–93, 195–96
 long-term growth and, 98–119
 monetary policy coordination with, 349
 monetary policy vs., 394–95, 410–12
 output and, 101–9
 as stimulus, 218–21
 strong, 193
 weak, 192–93, 521
 see also Federal Reserve System; Fed policy
  rule; policy rule
Fischer, Stanley, 472$n$

fixed exchange rate, 515–16
  and floating rate, 516–17
  *see also* fiscal policy
fixed investment, 299–302
  capital stock and, 27–28
  defined, 27
  write-offs for, 316
  *see also* nonresidential fixed investment;
    residential fixed investment
flat tax system, 90
Flavin, Marjorie, 281$n$
floating (flexible) exchange rate, 338, 513
  and fixed rate, 516–17
  in international macro policy coordination,
    519–20
  in macroeconomic policy, 514–15, 517–18
  world, 513–15
  world inflation with, 517–18
flow of investment, 302
fluctuations, 3–24
  in deficits, 366–71
  in exchange rate, 340–42, 510, 521
  in GDP, *see* GDP fluctuation
  government spending and, 366–67
  growth and, 3–4
  in income, 260–63
  inflation and, 10–11
  in investments, 163
  in investment spending, 299–302
  policy recommendations for, 238
  policy rules and, 408
  in short-run model, 145–72
  short-term, 4
  theory of, 17–18
  in U.S. dollar, 335, 337
  *see also* disturbances
fluctuations model, 16, 17, 20
FOMC (Federal Open Market Committee),
    404–10
  composition of, 404
Ford, Henry, 64
45-degree line, spending balance and, 155–56
Ford, Gerald R., 479
Ford administration, 282–83
forecasting, consumption function error and,
    265
foreign exchange market:
  banks in, 338
  exchange rate and, 338
foreign exchange market intervention, 506
foreign investment, by U.S., 41
foreign reserves, 511
  defined, 508
  sterilized intervention and, 509
foreign trade, 4, 5, 335–61
  aggregate demand and, 335, 337–38
  exchange rate and, 338–47
  monetary and fiscal policy in, 349

open-economy macro model and, *see* open-
  economy macroeconomics
  price adjustment and, 349–50
  spending balance and, 165–68
  *see also* exports; imports; net exports
forward-looking theory of consumption,
    268–85, 470, 472
  analysis of, 276–77
  anticipated vs. unanticipated changes in
    income and, 275–76
  consumption function vs., 268
  defects in, 283–85
  expected inflation in, 452
  intertemporal budget constraint in, 269–71
  preferences in, 271–73
  rational expectations in, 280–81
  in short vs. long run, 277
  temporary vs. permanent changes in income
    and, 273–75
  testing predictions of, 283–85
  *see also* rational expectations
France, 513
free-market economies, 506–7
free trade, protectionism vs., 352–53
Friedman, Milton, 212–13, 235, 268, 277,
    279–80, 404, 421, 492
full employment, 68–69
  benefits of, 477–83
  defined, 69
  potential GDP and, 65–70
full-employment deficit, 371–72
full-employment level of output, 69–70
functions:
  consumption, *see* consumption function
  housing demand, 318
  investment, *see* investment function
  money demand, *see* money demand function
  pipeline, 320
  production, *see* production function
  social welfare, 475


G–7, 108
GATT (General Agreement on Trade and
    Tariffs), 85
GDP (gross domestic product), 25–39
  aggregate demand curve and, 241–43
  calculation of, 33–34
  chain-weighted, 33–34
  defined, 25
  disinflation and, 243–47
  disposable income and, 260–61
  exports and, 29–30, 343
  fluctuations in, *see* GDP fluctuation
  GNP and, 36
  government spending and, 163–65, 376
  imports and, 29–30
  income and, 36–40, 155, 260–63

inflation and, 215–21
investment and, 160, 163, 164–65, 299–300, 319–22
IS curve and, 455
in long run, 107
monetary policy and, 189–90, 241–43, 413, 415
national income vs., 36–37
1995 breakdown of, 30–31
nominal, *see* nominal GDP
per capita, 31
potential, *see* potential GDP
price disturbances and, 237–40
production and, 150
real, *see* real GDP
savings and investment in, 39–43
shares of, 106–7
spending and, 26–34
spending balance and, 151–68
training and, 482
unemployment and, 481–82
value added and, 34–35
GDP fluctuation, 6–9
consumption and income fluctuation and, 258–63
investment fluctuations and, 299–300
GDP gap, 134, 243–47
GDP implicit price deflator, 48
General Agreement on Trade and Tariffs (GATT), 85
General Motors, 150–51
*General Theory of Employment, Interest and Money, The* (Keynes), 220
Germany, 505–6, 513, 524
monetary policy and, 241
monetary union and, 520–21
GNP (gross national product), 36
gold standard, 510
departure from, 510
goods:
durable, *see* durable goods
final, 32
intermediate, 32, 34
investment, 174
nondurable, 27, 259–60, 266
nonexcludable, 82
*Governing the $5 Trillion Economy* (Stein), 106
government bonds, 391, 508
government budget:
federal, 363–65
state and local, 364–65
government debt:
deficit and, 374–76
economic significance of, 376–78
government deficit, effects of, 371–78
government outlays, defined, 29, 363
government purchases, 29, 101–2, 103, 104, 366–67

government saving, 40
government spending:
accumulation of debt and, 374, 376
and changes in income, 163–64
economic fluctuations and, 18, 20, 366–67
GDP and, 163–65, 227
interest rate and, 190–92
IS curve and, 378–79
in 1995, 31
price adjustment and, 349–50
printing press in, 394
reaction function and, 362–63
and shifts in IS curve, 181
government transfers, 367–68
taxes and, 364, 370
unemployment and, 367–68
Great Depression, 8, 9, 17, 19, 414, 415, 510
Greenspan, Alan, 492
gross domestic product, *see* GDP
gross national product (GNP), 36
gross saving, 42
growth, 3–24, 62–65, 70–90
balanced, *see* balanced growth
endogenous theory of, 80–84, 85
fluctuations and, 3–4
inflation and, 496
long-run economic, 4, 13–17, 18, 76, 78, 80–84, 85
negative, 3
of potential GDP, 17
stimulation of, 84–90
growth accounting formula, 75, 77–80
growth formula:
derivation of, 75, 77–78, 96–97
historical, 78
growth path:
balanced, 71–75
stability proof of, 73–74
technological change and, 78–80
transition period and, 74–75, 76
*see also* equilibrium
growth rate policy rules, activist vs. constant, 473
growth rates, 15
increasing long-run, 82–84
neoclassical model and, 76, 82–84
policy rules on, 473
transition period and, 74–75, 76
Gulf Oil, 32

Hall, Robert E., 132$n$, 136$n$, 246$n$, 281$n$, 282$n$, 287$n$, 313$n$, 493$n$
Haltiwanger, John, 123$n$, 125$n$
Hammour, Mohamad, 136$n$
Hansen, Lars Peter, 281$n$
Harberger, Arnold, 240
Hasset, K., 316

Hayashi, Fumio, 278, 285$n$
Hayek, Friedrich, 522
Heller, Walter, 235
Heston, Alan, 76
Hicks, J. R., 179
high-powered money, 391$n$
Hirsch, Albert A., 322$n$
Holland, 241
Hong Kong, 522
hours worked per week, 50–51
housing, 317–19
   accelerator principle for, 318
   demand function for, 318
   desired stock of, 318
   monetary policy and investment in, 319
Hubbard, Glenn, 316
Hume, David, 421
hyperbolic discounting of future satisfaction,
   284

identity, 26
IMF (International Monetary Fund), 108
imperfect information, 421
imperfect information theory, 422–29, 450
   critique of, 428–29
   Lucas supply curve in, 422–28, 429
import, marginal propensity to, 166
imports, 29–30
   defined, 29
   demand for, 504
   GDP and, 29–30
   *see also* foreign trade
incentives, tax, 314–17
income, 25, 36–40
   anticipated vs. unanticipated changes in,
      275–76
   consumption as function of, 152–55
   disposable, *see* disposable income
   fluctuations in, 260–63
   GDP and, 36–40, 155, 260–63
   government spending and changes in,
      163–64
   growth rates and, 76
   interest rate and, 189
   IS-LM approach to computation of, 188–89
   national, 36–37
   net exports and, 343
   permanent vs. transitory, 268
   personal, 37
   real interest rate and, 286–88
   temporary vs. permanent changes in, 273–75
   value added and, 36
   wage, *see* wages
income effect, 67–68, 287
income identity, 152, 155, 156, 157
   IS curve and, 179, 181
   net exports in, 108, 165
income tax, 282–83

income tax brackets, 479
inconvertible currency, 506
indexing of contracts, 434, 436–37, 451, 495
indexing of tax system, 479
indexing to inflation, 434
   improvements in, 495
   in price adjustment, 451
   in union contracts, 434, 436, 451
indifference curves, 295–97
   defined, 296
inflation, 4, 5, 449–68, 514–19
   in Argentina vs. U.S., 518
   central banks and, 492
   contracts indexed to, 434, 436, 451, 495
   countercyclical stabilization policy and,
      236–37
   current vs. lagged rates of, 451
   defined, 109, 114
   economic growth and, 496
   expected, *see* expected inflation
   fluctuations and, 10–11
   gains and losses due to, 479–81
   GDP and, 215–21
   high, 496
   indexing to, *see* indexing to inflation
   interest rate and, 410–12
   measuring of, 46–49
   monetary policy and, 18, 474–75, 496
   money market and, 109–15
   nonadapting economic institutions and, 480
   output and, 213–15
   pensions and, 479–80
   policy trade-off between output and, 483–93
   potential GDP and, 215–21
   PPI as warning indicator of, 47–48
   in price adjustment, 211–15, 449–50, 454–55,
      464–65
   price disturbances and, 520–21
   public view of, 479–81
   rate of, defined, 46
   real GDP and, 10–11, 46
   recession and, 11, 243, 244–46
   target rate, 408–9, 411
   tax distortions and, 479, 480
   world, with floating exchange rates, 517–18
   zero, 477–78
   *see also* disinflation; expectations-augmented
      Phillips curve
inflation differentials, exchange rate
      appreciation and, 517–18
inflation loss, defined, 477
inflation-output loops, 464–65, 490
informational problems, 422–29
inheritance, for next generation, 271–73
instruments, targets and, 475–77
intercept, defined, 158
interest rates, 4, 11–13
   bonds and, 400
   consumption and, 102–3, 286–88

deficits and, 372–74
exchange rate and, 345–47
expansionary fiscal policy and, 504
Fed and, 20, 404–12
government spending and, 190–92
income and, 189
inflation rate and, 410–12
investment and, 102–3, 173–76
investment demand and, 192
IS-LM approach and, 189
money demand and, 109–11, 183, 192
money demand function and, 111$n$, 192
money market and, 109–11
money supply and, 12–13, 112, 191
net exports and, 102–3, 176–77, 192
nominal, 176, 286, 406–7, 411
as procyclical, 12
real, *see* real interest rate
risk-free, 180
short-term, 405, 409
short-term vs. long-term, 176
stock market and, 178–79
interest-rate sensitivity, 102–3, 286–88
intermediate goods, 32, 34
intermediate products, defined, 35
intermediation role of banks, 391
international financial and monetary system,
    505–14
  Bretton Woods, *see* Bretton Woods System
  capital controls and, 509
  current system in, 513
  exchange-rate policy of, 509–10
  free-market principles in, 506–7
  history of, 510–14
  inflation differentials and parity adjustments
    in, 517–18
  joining of, 507
  movement of capital controlled in, 506–7
international macro policy coordination, 519–20
International Monetary Fund (IMF), 108
intertemporal budget constraint, 269–71, 276,
    376
inventory investment, 28–29, 299–300, 319–22
  buffer stock and, 320
  defined, 27
  GDP and, 319–22
  pipeline function of, 320
  square-root rule and, 399
inventory theory, 397–400
investment:
  accelerator and, 310–11
  business vs. residential, 299
  crowding out and, *see* crowding out
  decisions by firms, 302–9
  defined, 27
  depreciation and, 311
  factors in volume of, 299–300, 301–2
  financial variables and, 174
  fixed, 27–28, 299–302, 316

flow of, 302
fluctuations in, 163
GDP and, 160, 163, 164–65, 299–300, 319–22
in housing, 317–19
interest rate and, 102–3, 173–76
interest-rate sensitivity of, 102–3
inventory, *see* inventory investment
lag in, 312–13
net, 28, 63
nonresidential, *see* nonresidential fixed
    investment
output and, 310–12
as primary force in economy, 298
real interest rate and, 323
recessions and, 316
residential, *see* residential fixed investment
saving and, 39–43
taxes and, 313–17
wage rate and, 311
investment demand, 298–334
  defined, 300
  interest rates and, 192
  Tobin's $q$ in, 332–34
investment demand function, 174–75
  defined, 309
investment function, 174–76, 309–13
  defined, 310
  IS curve and, 181, 322–23
investment goods, 174
investment spending:
  fluctuations in, 299–302
  interest rate and, 102–3
  *see also* inventory investment; non-residential
      fixed investment; residential fixed
      investment
investment supply, defined, 300
investment tax credits, 314–17
  for research and development, 87, 88
Iran, 488
Iraq, 488
IS curves, 177–79, 181–82, 350
  algebraic derivation of, 186–87, 348–49, 456
  automatic stabilizers and, 379
  consumption and, 288–89
  exchange rate and, 354–55
  GDP and, 455
  government and, 378–79
  graphical derivation of, 182
  investment function and, 181, 322–23
  open-economy, 347–50
  output and, 456–57
  price adjustment and, 455–57
  real interest rate and, 455–57
  shifts in, 181
  slope of, 180–81, 193–95, 288–89, 378–79
  spending balance and, 455–56
  summarizing, 455–57
  tariffs and, 352
  tax cuts and, 289

IS-LM approach, 177–79, 181–96, 216, 218–19
    Fed in, 178, 407
    fiscal policy and, 190–93, 195–96
    framework of, 189
    interest rates and, 189
    monetary policy and, 189–90, 192–94, 195, 349
    open-economy macro model in, *see* open-
        economy macroeconomics
    tariffs and, 352

Japan, 335, 351, 388, 505–6
    depression of the 1990s in, 414–15
    exchange rate in, 44–46, 513
    interest rates in, 414–15
    money supply in, 414–15
    real GDP in, 414–15
    saving rate in, 278
    SII and, 108
    trade surplus of, 108
jobs:
    creation and destruction, 120–42
    destruction of, 123–24, 132–34
    finding rate, 122–23, 124–25, 126, 127, 133
    losing rate, 122–23, 127
    loss without destruction, 124
    personal transitions, 124
    search theory and, 125–26
Johnson administration, 282
Jones, Charles, 76
Jorgenson, Dale, 302, 307, 313*n*

Kennedy, John F., 88, 235, 369
Keynes, John Maynard, 17, 18, 20, 152, 163,
        220, 227, 298, 396, 397, 400, 421, 431,
        510
Keynesian consumption function, 263–67, 279,
        281
Keynesian cross diagram, 156
Keynesian school, 19, 20
    new vs. traditional, 17
King, Robert, 220
Klamer, Arjo, 19
Knetter, Michael, 351*n*
Krugman, Paul, 351*n*
Kurihara, K. K., 268*n*
Kuznets, Simon, 26
Kydland, Finn, 18*n*, 220, 471–72

labor, 62–63
    contracts for, 431, 433–34
    defined, 62
    demand for, 66
    income effect in, 67–68
    increasing supply of, 88–90
    input, 63
    marginal product of, 65, 66, 436

    natural rate of unemployment and, 63
    real interest rate and, 287
    substitution effect in, 67
    supply of, *see* labor supply
    *see also* employment; unemployment; unions;
        wages
labor demand function, 66–67
labor force, defined, 121
labor force participation rate, 62, 121
labor markets, 134–38
    equilibrium and, 68–69, 137–38
    recessions and, 136
    sticky-wage, 431–32, 474
    streamlining of, 494–95
    unemployment and, 127–30
labor productivity, 90–93
labor supply, 66–68
    increasing of, 88–90
    real interest rate and, 287
    tax cuts and, 88–90
labor supply curves, 89
lags:
    investment, 312–13
    in monetary policy effect, 413, 415
Laibson, David, 284
Latin America, 496
leakage, defined, 348
life-cycle theory of consumption, 268, 284
line, spending, 155–57
liquid assets, 234
liquidity-constrained consumers, 285
LM curve, 177–79, 183–89
    algebraic derivation of, 186–88
    exchange rate and, 354–56
    Fed policy rule and, 405–7
    graphical derivation of, 185
    money supply and, 183
    price level and, 183, 184–85
    shifts in, 184–85
    slope of, 183–84, 193–95
    tariffs and, 352
loans, 391
longitudinal surveys, 282
long run:
    economic growth in, 4, 13–17, 18, 76, 78,
        80–84, 95
    GDP in, 107
long-run assumption, importance of, 107
long-run growth model, 14–16, 20, 61–97
    classical dichotomy and, 115–16
    complete model vs., 62
    convergence hypothesis of, 76
    defined, 61
    derivation of formula for, 96–97
    and determinants of economic growth, 62–65
    endogenous growth theory vs., 80–84, 85
    exogenous factors, 80
    monetary and fiscal policies in, 98–119
    neoclassical growth model and, 70–75

long-run marginal propensity to consume
(MPC), 265–66, 277
defined, 266
durables and, 267
nondurables and, 266
services and, 266
Lovell, Michael, 322*n*
Lucas, Robert, 19, 20, 240, 421, 422–29, 453*n*,
471
Lucas supply curve, 422–29
derivation of, 423–26
and policy ineffectiveness theorem, 427–28
price rigidity and, 426–27

$M_1$, 388–89, 405
$M_2$, 389, 405
macroeconomic model, *see* complete model
macroeconomic policy, 227–53, 447–528
activist, 235, 473
capital controls in, 509
changing policy frontier in, 493–98
consumption function error and, 265
cooperative policy choice in, 520
countercyclical stabilization policy in, 235–37
demand for currency and checking deposits
in, 396–403
design and maintenance of, 469–503
disinflation and, *see* disinflation
disturbances in, *see* disturbances
exchange rates and, 514–19
experiments in, 280, 282–83
floating exchange rate in, 514–15, 517–18
general principles in analysis of, 469–75
inflation and, 483–93, 514–19
instruments of, 470–71
international coordination of, 519–20
monetary union in, 520–24
noncooperative policy choice in, 520
output and unemployment loss in, 482–83
as policy rule, *see* Fed policy rule; policy rule
real GDP and, 99–100
social welfare function in, 475
targeting in, 241–43, 475–77, 493
uncertainty and timing in, 476–77
unemployment and, 481–83
world economy and, 504–28
*see also specific policies*
macroeconomics:
classical, 17
currents of thought in, 17–20
defined, 4–5
economic fluctuations, 143–253
introduction to, 1–58
long-run fundamentals, 59–142
microeconomics vs., 4
microfoundations of, 255–466
open-economy, *see* open-economy
macroeconomics

policy, 447–528
recent advances in, 17–18, 20
study of economics and, 19
supply side of, *see* output; potential GDP
uses of, 4–5
Mankiw, N. Gregory, 18*n*, 431*n*
marginal benefit:
of capital, 304
defined, 302
rental price of capital and, 306–7
marginal cost, 303–4
defined, 303
marginal opportunity costs, 396
marginal product, diminishing, 304
marginal product of labor, 65, 436
wages and, 66
marginal propensity to consume (MPC), 153,
154
in consumption function, 263, 265–67
decreased taxes and, 274–75
in long run, 265–66, 277
in short run, 266–67, 277
temporary vs. permanent changes in income
and, 273–75
marginal propensity to import, 166
marginal rate of substitution, 296
marginal social costs of unemployment, 482,
483
marginal tax rate, 89–90
market conditions, price adjustment and, 210
market failures, 84, 240
market portfolio, 180–81
Markowitz, Harry, 180
mass production, 64
maximum profit, point of, 66
means of payment, 387, 389
Meltzer, Allan, 453*n*
menu costs, 431
Meyer, Bruce, 124*n*
Meyers, Stewart, 181*n*
Michigan, University of, 281–82, 283
microeconomic demand curves, for rented
capital, 304
microeconomics, 4
first principle of, 257
foundations of macroeconomics, 255–446
foundations of price rigidity, 421–26
macroeconomics vs., 4, 20
Miller, Merton, 180
Mishkin, Fredric, 282*n*
models:
complete, *see* complete model
defined, 14
fluctuations, *see* fluctuations model
long-run growth, *see* long-run growth model
price adjustment, *see* price adjustment
rational expectation, *see* rational expectations
real business cycle, *see* real business cycle
model

models: (*continued*)
  real exchange rate, *see* real exchange rate
  short-run, *see* short-run model
  staggered wage setting, 438–41, 450, 452–53
  with sticky prices, *see* sticky-price model
Modigliani, Franco, 19, 268, 277, 279, 280
Mohammed Reza Shah Pahlavi, 488
monetarists, on stabilization policy, 235–37
monetary base:
  borrowed reserves and, 393–94
  defined, 391
  Fed control of, 389–95
  Fed policy rule for, *see* Fed policy rule
  foreign reserves and, 508
monetary expansion, 413, 415
monetary policy, 18, 20
  aggregate demand curve and, 198–99, 241–43
  central question of, 404
  contractionary, 520
  defined, 99
  disinflation and, 243–47
  expansionary, *see* expansionary monetary
    policy
  expected inflation and, 453–54
  Fed control of, 241, 244, 404–12
  fiscal policy coordination with, 349
  fiscal policy vs., 394–95, 410–12
  fixed exchange rate and, 515–16
  foreign policy and, 521
  GDP and, 189–90, 241–43, 413, 415
  housing investment and, 319
  inflation and, 18, 474–75, 496
  IS curve and, 455
  IS-LM approach and, 189–90, 192–94, 195, 349
  lags in effect of, 413, 415
  long-run growth and, 98–119
  sterilization in, 509
  strong, 193, 521
  targeting in, 241–43, 475–77, 493
  trade-offs in, 475–76
  weak, 193
  *see also* Federal Reserve System; Fed policy
    rule; policy rule
monetary system, 386–420
  defined, 386
  elements of, 387–89
  establishment of, 522
  international, *see* international financial and
    monetary system
  means of payment in, 387, 389
  unit of account in, 387, 389
monetary union, 520–24
monetary unit, 522–23
monetization of deficit, 374
money:
  defined, 109, 388
  demand functions for, 402–3
  high-powered, 391$n$
  $M_1$, *see* $M_1$

neutrality of, 113
  nominal, 184
  opportunity costs of holding funds as, 396–97
  real, 13, 183–84
  as store of wealth, 400, 522
  as unit of value, 522
  *see also* capital
money demand, 396–403
  aggregate demand curve and, 233–35
  currency and checking deposits in, 396–403
  disturbances to, 228, 233–34
  interest rates and, 109–11, 183–84, 192
  inventory theory of, 397–400
  precautionary motive in, 396, 400
  speculative motive in, 396, 400
  total, 402–3
  transaction motive in, 396, 397
money demand function, 111, 402–3
  interest rate for, 111$n$, 192
money market:
  equilibrium in, 112–14
  inflation and, 109–15
money multiplier, 393, 405
money supply, 18, 111
  accommodative policy and rule and, 238–39
  adjustment of, price disturbances and, 238–39
  algebraic derivation of response to, 221
  for central banks, 508–9
  defined, 12–13
  as endogenous variable, 241
  as exogenous variable, 240–41
  Fed control of, 389–95, 404–10; *see also* Fed
    policy rule
  growth rate of, 404–5
  interest rate and, 12–13, 112, 191
  LM curve and, 183
  nonaccommodative policies and, 238–39
  recession and, 13
  and shifts in LM curve, 184–85
  as stimulus, 215–18
MPC, *see* marginal propensity to consume
multiplier, 160–65
  decline of, 167
  leakage and, 348
  money, 393, 405
  open economy, 166–68
Muth, John, 470


national debt, 376–78
national income, 36–37
  GDP vs., 36–37
national income and product accounts (NIPA),
    26, 37, 39, 334
national saving, 41–42
natural rate of unemployment, 63, 122–23,
    127–30, 450
  changes in, 130
  defined, 120, 127

natural rate property of price adjustment, 212, 450
negative assets, 271
negative growth, 3
Nelson, Richard, 334$n$
neoclassical growth model, *see* long-run growth model
net export function, 166, 168, 343–45
net exports, 30, 31, 165–68
   defined, 165
   determinants of, 342–45
   as endogenous variable, 345
   exchange rate and, 342–45
   income and, 343
   in income identity, 108, 165
   interest rate and, 102–3, 176–77, 192
   interest-rate sensitivity of, 102–3
   trade deficit and, 108
   *see also* foreign trade
net foreign investment of U.S., 41
net investment:
   capital stock and, 63
   defined, 28
neutrality of money, 113
new empirical growth literature, 76
*Newsweek,* 235$n$
NIPA (national income and product accounts), 26, 37, 39, 334
Nixon administration, 512
nominal GDP, 32, 488–89, 491
   government debt and, 374–75
   targeting of, 491, 493
nominal interest rate, 176, 286, 406–7, 411
nominal money, defined, 184
nominal wage:
   contracts, 421
   sticky, 431–32
nonaccommodative policies, 238–39
noncooperative policy choice, 520
nondurable goods, 27, 259–60
   long-run MPC and, 266
   short-run MPC and, 266
nonresidential fixed investment, 27, 299–302
   residential investment vs., 299
nonunion sector, 434–35
normative perspective on policy, defined, 363
North American Free Trade Area, 85

OECD (Organization for Economic Cooperation and Development), 108
oil prices, 497
   disturbances to, 231, 233, 463–64, 497
Okun, Arthur, 134, 240
Okun's law, 134, 135, 208–9, 245, 486
open-economy IS curve, 347–50
   algebraic derivation of, 348–49
open-economy macroeconomics, 165
   fixed exchange rate in, 515–16

   floating exchange rate in, 514–15, 517–18
   IS curve in, 350
   macro policy in, 514–19
   net exports and, 165–68
   spending balance in, 168
open-economy multiplier, 166–68
open-market operations, 391–93
   by Fed, 391, 404–10
opportunity costs:
   of checking balances, 403
   of holding funds as money, 396–97
   marginal, 396
   "shoe-leather," 479, 480
Organization for Economic Cooperation and Development (OECD), 108
outlays, government, 29, 363
output, 18
   aggregate demand as determinant of, 147, 148, 206–8
   fiscal policy and, 101–9
   fluctuations in, 449–68
   full-employment level of, 69–70
   inflation and, 213–15
   investment and, 310–12
   policy trade-off between inflation and, 483–93
   potential, 244, 456–57
   price adjustment, 464–65
   real, 243
   short-run fluctuations in, 208
   in sticky-price model, 205–8
output-inflation loops, 464–65, 490
output losses:
   cost of, 481–83
   defined, 478

panel data sets, 282
par value, 510–11
passive policy rule, 473
payment, means of, 387, 389
peaks, 7
   prices and, 10
Pencavel, John, 68$n$
pensions, 479–80
permanent-income theory of consumption, 268
personal income:
   defined, 37
   disposable, *see* disposable income
personal income tax, 282–83
Phelps, Edmund S., 212–13
Philippines, 513
Phillips, A. W., 211
Phillips curve, 211–12, 214
   disinflation, and, 243
   expectations-augmented, *see* expectations-augmented Phillips curve
   price adjustment and, 211–12
pipeline function, 320

Pissarides, Christopher, 125*n*
Plosser, Charles, 220
Policano, Andrew, 437*n*
policy experiments, 280, 282–83
policy ineffectiveness theorem, 427–28
policy-makers, credibility of, 472
policy rule, 240–41, 387, 408–9
    activist, 235, 473
    as behavioral relationship, 241
    constant, 473
    defined, 241
    discretionary, 473
    of Fed, *see* Fed policy rule
    feedback and, 473
    normative vs. positive perspectives on, 363
    passive, 473
    reaction function as, 363
policy trade-off, 477
    changing of, 493–98
    between inflation and unemployment loss,
        483–93
Poole, William, 407*n*
positive perspective on policy, defined, 363
post-World War II period, high consumption
    levels in, 267, 279
potential GDP, 16, 17
    defined, 16, 17, 65, 70
    full employment and, 65–70
    growth of, 17
    inflation and, 215–21
    movement to, 221–22
    real GDP and, 16, 17, 127, 130–31, 134, 135,
        244, 245
potential output, 244
PPI (producer price index), 47–48, 49
precautionary motive, in money demand, 396,
    400
predetermined variables:
    endogenous vs., 178–79
    price level as, 178, 210
Prescott, Edward, 18*n,* 220, 472
price:
    peaks and, 10
    troughs and, 11
    *see also* sticky-price model
price adjustment, 215, 449–55, 484
    aggregate demand and, 215–22, 457–64
    aggregate demand curve and, 215
    aggregate demand disturbances and, 230–33
    algebraic statement of theory of, 449–50
    and booms, 460–61, 462–63
    changes in coefficients of, 450
    and changes in demand, 150
    complete model and, 210–21
    and disinflation, 461–63
    equilibrium adjustment process and, 210–15
    exchange rate and, 349–50
    foreign trade and, 349–50

government spending and, 349–50
graphical representation of, 454–55
indexing to inflation in, 450
inflation and, 211–15, 449–50, 454–55,
    464–65
IS curve and, 455–57
length and severity of business cycles in, 452
market conditions and, 210
and oil price shocks, 463–64
output and, 464–65
Phillips curve and, 211–12
real GDP and, 454–55
wage-price spiral in, 451
price disturbances, 227–41
    adjustment of money supply in response to,
        238–39
    aggregate demand curve and, 238
    economic forecasting and, 232
    GDP and, 237–40
    government creation of, 495, 497
    inflation and, 520
    optimal policy for, 489–93
    in petroleum-related industries, 231
    recession and, 230–31
    responding to, 237–40, 489–93
    unemployment and, 520
    from wage increases, 231
price fixing, 494–95
price indexes, 46–48, 49
price level:
    aggregate demand and, 196, 197–98
    disturbances to, 231–33
    exchange rate and, 350–52
    LM curve and, 183, 184–85
    in money market, 109–14
    natural rate property of, 450
    as predetermined variable, 178, 210
    shifts in, 231
    unresponsiveness of, 150
price level indicators, 523
price rigidities, 421–46, 450, 473
    appearance of, 426–27
    definition of, 421
    trade-off between unemployment and,
        477–83
    wage stickiness and, 18, 20
    *see also* wage rigidities
price shocks, *see* price disturbances
price stickiness, *see* sticky-price model
printing press, in raising revenues, 394
private saving, 40
procyclical interest rates, 12
producer price index (PPI), 47–48, 49
production, 5, 25
    employment and, 9–10
    GDP and, 150
    technology and, 63–64, 80–84, 86–87
    wage bargaining and, 435–36

production function:
    defined, 64–65
    for technology, 80–84
productivity, 90–93
    defined, 91
    employment and, 90–93
    improvement of, 86–87
    labor, 90–93
    marginal, of labor, *see* marginal product of
        labor
    total factor, 64, 91–92
    wages as components of, 90–93
profits, maximization of, 66
protectionism:
    free trade vs., 352–53
    macroeconomic effects of, 352–53
    stabilization policy and, 497
purchasing power parity, 516
    defined, 341
    exchange rate and, 341–42


Ramey, Valerie A., 322$n$
R&D (research and development), 86–87, 88
rate of time preference, 286
rational expectations, 20
    in forward-looking theory of consumption,
        280–81
    monetary policy and, 428
    *see also* consumer behavior
reaction function, 408
    defined, 362
Reagan, Ronald, 369–70, 492
Reagan administration, 315
real business cycle model, 20, 220
    fluctuations in, 18
real business cycle school, 18
real disposable income, consumption and,
        262–63
real exchange rate:
    defined, 340
    model of, 345–47
real GDP, 6–14, 25, 32–34, 227
    aggregate demand curve and, 208–9, 229–31
    employment and, 9–10
    Fed and, 244, 406–9
    inflation and, 10–11, 46
    macroeconomic policy and, 99–100
    percentage deviations of, 7
    potential GDP and, 16, 17, 127, 130–31, 134,
        135, 244, 245
    price adjustment and, 454–55
    and shifts in aggregate demand curve, 229–31
    target level of, 241–43
    unemployment and, 134, 408, 481–82
real interest rate, 12, 176, 406–7, 411–12
    consumption and, 286–88
    defined, 286, 406

investment and, 323
    IS curve and, 455–57
    labor and, 287
    rate of time preference and, 286
    saving and, 286–88
    work and, 287
real money, defined, 13, 183
real output, monetary and fiscal policies and,
        243
real wage, 90–91, 93
    profit maximization and, 66
recessions, 5, 7, 18, 282
    aggregate demand disturbances and, 230–31
    automatic stabilizers and deficit in, 371
    benefits of, 136
    consumption in, 265, 277
    currency holdings in, 401
    defined, 7
    employment and, 10, 49–51
    inflation and, 11, 243, 244–46
    investment and, 316
    as market failures, 240
    money supply and, 13
    price disturbances and, 230–31
    residential investment in, 299
    taxes in, 369–71
    unemployment and, 49–51, 120, 130–38
relative price setting, exchange rate and, 340–42
    *see also* price adjustment
rental price:
    residential investment and, 317–19
    taxes and, 315
rented capital:
    capital budgeting and, 307–8, 330–32
    demand curve for, 304–5
    determining price of, 302–3, 306–7
    marginal benefit vs. price of, 306–7
    Tax Reform Act and, 314, 315
    Tobin's $q$ and, 332–34
required reserves, defined, 393
research and development (R&D), 86–87, 88
Research and Experimentation Tax Credit, 87
Reserve Bank of New Zealand, 408
reserve inflow, 511
reserve outflow, 511
reserve ratio, 392
reserves:
    on balance sheet, 391
    borrowed, 393–94
    excess, 393
    in Fed, 393
    as monetary unit, 523
    required, 393
residential fixed investment, 27, 299–302,
        317–19
    nonresidential fixed investment vs., 299
    in recession, 299
    rental price and, 317–19

rest of world saving, 41–43
  defined, 41
rest of world (ROW) sector, 43–46, 340–41
retained earnings, defined, 37
retirement, 479–80
  consumption and, 271–72
Ricardian equivalence, 377
Rogoff, Kenneth, 492
Romer, Paul, 80, 81
Rothschild, Michael, 311$n$

salary administrators, 434
Sargent, Thomas, 19, 246, 427–28
saving:
  balanced growth and, 71–75
  consumption vs., real interest rate and,
    286–88
  defined, 39
  family, 284
  GDP and, 39–43
  government, 40
  gross, 42
  investment and, 39–43
  Japanese, 278
  locked-up, 284
  national, 41–42
  private, 40
  by rest of world sector, 41–43
saving rate, defined, 72
saving supply, defined, 300
scarcity, 475
schedules, defined, 158
Schuh, Scott, 123$n$, 125$n$
search theory, 125–26
services, 27
  consumption expenditures and, 259–60
  long-run MPC and, 266
  short-run MPC and, 266
Sharpe, William, 180
Shleifer, Andrei, 272$n$
shocks, see aggregate demand disturbances;
    disturbances
"shoe leather costs," 479, 480
short-run marginal propensity to consume
    (MPC), 266–67, 277
  defined, 266
  durables and, 267
  nondurables and, 266
  services and, 266
short-run model:
  aggregate demand in, 146–51
  and economy out of equilibrium, 146–48
  fluctuations in, 145–72
  money supply and, 18
  spending balance in, see spending balance
SII (Structural Impediments Initiative), 108
Sims, Christopher, 471

Singleton, Kenneth, 281$n$
slope:
  of aggregate demand curve, 196
  defined, 158
  of 45-degree line, 156
  of IS curve, 180–81, 193–95, 288–89, 378–79
  of LM curve, 183–84, 193–95
Smith, Adam, 257
Smoot-Hawley tariff, 353
social insurance, contributions for, 37–38
social security, COLA and, 47
social security tax, 37–38
social welfare function, 475
Solow, Robert M., 71–75
Solow growth model, 75, 85
speculative motive, in money demand, 396, 400
spending, 25
  budget deficit and, 362–85
  GDP and, 26–34
spending balance, 149–68
  aggregate demand and, 149–51
  algebraic solution of, 157, 159
  equilibrium vs., 151
  GDP and, 151–68
  graphical analysis of, 155–57
  IS curve and, 455–56
  maintenance of, 159–60
  net exports and, 165–68
  in open economy, 168
spending line, 155–56
squared error, 477
stabilization policy, 233–37
  countercyclical, 235–37, 371
  disagreements on, 235–37
  exchange rate and, 353–56
  in international macro policy coordination,
    519
  protectionism and, 497
  underlying objective of, 235
stabilizers, automatic, see automatic stabilizers
staggered wage setting, 437–41
  algebraic model of, 438–41
  expected inflation and, 452–53
statistical discrepancy, defined, 35
steady-state point, 73–74
Stein, Herbert, 106
sterilized intervention, 509, 513
sticky nominal wages, 429, 431–33
sticky-price model, 205–26, 430
  flexible-price model, 17–18
  output in, 205–8
  unemployment in, 208–10
sticky prices, 421, 429–31, 432–33
sticky-wage labor markets, 431–32, 474
stochastic equilibrium, 473
stock market, interest rates and, 178–79
structural deficits, cyclical deficits vs., 371–72
Structural Impediments Initiative (SII), 108

substitution:
    consumption, 287
    marginal rate of, 296
substitution effect, 67
Summers, Lawrence H., 272n, 317n
Summers, Robert, 76
supply:
    investment, 300
    of labor, see labor supply
    saving, 300
    tax cuts and, 88–90
supply-and-demand analysis, 17
    unemployment and, 134–38
supply curves:
    labor, 89
    Lucas, 422–29
surplus, trade, 30, 165
surveys, wage, 434

targeting, 241–43, 493
    instruments and, 475–77
tariffs, 352–53
    IS curve and, 352
    LM curve and, 352
tax brackets, 479
tax credits, investment, 314–17
    for research and development, 87, 88
tax cuts, 274–75, 369–70
    expectation of, 289
    IS curve and, 289
    labor supply and, 88–90
    permanent vs. temporary, 289
    of Reagan administration, 315
tax deductions, 479
taxes:
    anticipated changes in, 315, 317
    budget deficit and, 362–85
    capital gains, 316
    discretionary changes in, 369–70
    distortions in, 479, 480
    economic activity and, 369–71
    government transfers and, 364, 370
    income, 282–83
    investment and, 313–17
    marginal rate of, 89–90
    permanent changes in, 314–15
    in recession, 369–71
    rental price and, 315
    social security, 37–38
    unemployment and, 369, 370
    value-added, 495, 497
tax incentives, 314–17
tax law, discretionary vs. automatic changes in, 369–70
Tax Reform Act (1986), 264, 314, 315
tax system:
    flat, 90

    indexing of, 479
    modifications to, 479, 480
Taylor, John B., 317n, 493n
T-bills (U.S. Treasury bills), 180–81, 510–11
technological change, growth path and, 78–80
technological growth, improvement of, 86–87
technology:
    defined, 62
    production and, 63–64, 80–84, 86–87
terms of trade, 337
time preference, rate of, 286
Tinbergen, Jan, 475
Tobin, James, 19, 235, 240, 334n, 397n, 493n
Tobin's q, 332–34
total factor productivity, 64, 91–92
trade:
    barriers to, 352–53
    foreign, see foreign trade
    policy for, 497
    quotas in, 497
    terms of, 337
trade balance, 30
trade deficit, 4, 5
    budget deficit and, 104, 108
    defined, 30, 165
    foreign saving and, 42–43
    net exports and, 108
trade-offs, 475–76
trade surplus, defined, 30, 165
trade-weighted exchange rate, 45–46, 339
training, GDP and, 482
transaction motive, in money demand, 396, 397
transfers, government, see government transfers
transition period, growth rate and, 74–75, 76
Treasury Bills (T-bills), U.S., 180–81, 510–11
Treasury Department, U.S., 513
troughs, 7
    prices and, 11

UAW (United Automobile Workers), 214
UF (Unidad de Fomento), 430
underground economy, 401
unemployment, 120–42, 477–83
    analysis of, in framework of supply and demand, 134–38
    in booms, 120, 130–34
    disinflation and, 245
    equilibrium and, 63, 68–69
    flows into, 121–24, 131, 132–34
    flows out of, 121–23, 124–26, 131, 133
    government purchases and, 367
    government transfers and, 367–68
    insurance, 128–29
    marginal social costs of, 482, 483
    measuring of, 49, 121
    natural rate of, 63, 122–23, 127–30, 450
    price disturbances and, 520

unemployment (*continued*)
  price rigidity and, 477–83
  real GDP and, 134, 408, 481–82
  recessions and, 49–51, 130–38
  in sticky-price model, 208–10
  taxes and, 369, 370
  wage bargaining and, 436
  *see also* employment; full employment
unemployment compensation, reformation of, 495
unemployment loss, 481–83
unemployment rate, 130–31
  defined, 10, 121
  natural, 63, 122–23, 127–30, 450
*Unidad de Fomento* (UF), 430
union contracts, 433–34
  COLA and, 47
  complexity of, 435–37
  contingency clauses in, 435–37
  indexing to inflation in, 434, 436, 451
unions:
  in collective bargaining, 47, 433–34, 435–36
  wage and price inflation forecasts by, 474
  wage setting and, 128, 214–15, 433–34
United Automobile Workers (UAW), 214
United Kingdom, 505–6, 513
  in 1989, 514–15
  value-added tax in, 495, 497
unit of account, 387, 389
Uruguay, 513
Uruguay Round, 85


value, money as unit of, 522
value added:
  defined, 34
  GDP and, 34–35
value-added tax, 495, 497
variables, 4
  endogenous, *see* endogenous variables
  exogenous, *see* exogenous variables
  financial, 173–204
  predetermined, *see* predetermined variables
vault cash, 390$n$
Vietnam War, 282


wage administrators, 434
wage behavior, backward-looking, 433–34
  expected inflation and, 452–53
wage determination, 433–41
  contingencies in, 435–37

expected inflation and, 214–15, 434, 452–53, 474
  in nonunion sector, 434–35
  staggered, *see* staggered wage setting
  synchronization in, 437
  in union sector, 128, 214–15, 433–34
wage-price spiral, defined, 451
wage rigidities, 473
  temporary, 437
  trade-off between inflation and output and, 483–93
  wage determination and, *see* wage determination
  *see also* price rigidities
wages, 90–93
  adjustment costs of, 435–36
  bargaining and, 433–34, 435–36
  determination of, *see* wage determination
  efficiency, 127–28, 129
  fixing of, 494–95
  indexing of, *see* indexing to inflation
  investment and, 311
  marginal product of labor and, 66
  measuring of, 49–51
  minimum, 128
  nominal, 429, 431–33
  price disturbance from increases in, 231
  productivity and, 90–93
  real, *see* real wage
  "under-the-table," 401
  *see also* labor
wage surveys, 434
Wallace, Neil, 427–28
wealth, money as store of, 400, 522
Weiss, Andrew, 127$n$
work, *see* employment; labor supply
world economy, 504–28
  floating rates policies in, 513–15
  *see also* Bretton Woods System; international financial and monetary system
World War II:
  government deficit in, 374–75
  prisoner-of-war camps in, 388
write-offs for fixed investments, 316


Yellen, Janet L., 127$n$
yen, Japanese, 513, 520
Young, Alwyn, 76


zero-deficit case, 377
zero inflation, 477–78